SKILLS For SUCCESS

with Microsoft®
Office 2010

VOLUME 1

TOWNSEND | FERRETT | HAIN | VARGAS

Prentice Hall

Boston Columbus Indianapolis New York San Francisco Upper Saddle River
Amsterdam Cape Town Dubai London Madrid Milan Munich Paris Montréal Toronto
Delhi Mexico City São Paulo Sydney Hong Kong Seoul Singapore Taipei Tokyo

Library of Congress Cataloging-in-Publication Data

Townsend, Kris.
  Skills for success with Office 2010 / by Kris Townsend.
    p. cm.
  ISBN 978-0-13-703257-0 (alk. paper)
  1. Microsoft Office.   2. Business—Computer programs.   I. Title.
HF5548.4.M525T692 2011
005.5—dc22   2010016531

Editor in Chief: *Michael Payne*
AVP/Executive Acquisitions Editor: *Stephanie Wall*
Product Development Manager: *Eileen Bien Calabro*
Editorial Project Manager: *Virginia Guariglia*
Development Editor: *Nancy Lamm*
Editorial Assistant: *Nicole Sam*
AVP/Director of Online Programs, Media: *Richard Keaveny*
AVP/Director of Product Development, Media: *Lisa Strite*
Editor—Digital Learning & Assessment: *Paul Gentile*
Product Development Manager, Media: *Cathi Profitko*
Media Project Manager, Editorial: *Alana Coles*
Media Project Manager, Production: *John Cassar*
Director of Marketing: *Kate Valentine*
Senior Marketing Manager: *Tori Olsen Alves*
Marketing Coordinator: *Susan Osterlitz*

Marketing Assistant: *Darshika Vyas*
Senior Managing Editor: *Cynthia Zonneveld*
Associate Managing Editor: *Camille Trentacoste*
Production Project Manager: *Camille Trentacoste*
Senior Operations Supervisor: *Natacha Moore*
Senior Art Director: *Jonathan Boylan*
Art Director: *Anthony Gemmellaro*
Text and Cover Designer: *Anthony Gemmellaro*
Manager, Rights and Permissions: *Hessa Albader*
Supplements Development Editor: *Vonda Keator*
Full-Service Project Management: *MPS Content Services, a Macmillan Company*
Composition: *MPS Content Services, a Macmillan Company*
Printer/Binder: *WorldColor/Kendallville*
Cover Printer: *Lehigh/Phoenix*
Typeface: *Minion 10.5/12.5*

Credits and acknowledgments borrowed from other sources and reproduced, with permission, in this textbook appear on appropriate page within text.

Microsoft® and Windows® are registered trademarks of the Microsoft Corporation in the U.S.A. and other countries. Screen shots and icons reprinted with permission from the Microsoft Corporation. This book is not sponsored or endorsed by or affiliated with the Microsoft Corporation.

Many of the designations by manufacturers and seller to distinguish their products are claimed as trademarks. Where those designations appear in this book, and the publisher was aware of a trademark claim, the designations have been printed in initial caps or all caps.

Prentice Hall
is an imprint of

www.pearsonhighered.com

10 9 8 7 6 5 4 3 2 1
ISBN-10: 0-13-703257-9
ISBN-13: 978-0-13-703257-0

Contents in Brief

Table of Contents

PowerPoint

About the Authors

Kris Townsend is an Information Systems instructor at Spokane Falls Community College in Spokane, Washington. Kris earned a bachelor's degree in both Education and Business, and a master's degree in Education. He has also worked as a public school teacher and as a systems analyst. Kris enjoys working with wood, snowboarding, and camping. He commutes to work by bike and enjoys long road rides in the Palouse country south of Spokane.

Robert L. Ferrett recently retired as the Director of the Center for Instructional Computing at Eastern Michigan University, where he provided computer training and support to faculty. He has authored or co-authored more than 70 books on Access, PowerPoint, Excel, Publisher, WordPerfect, Windows, and Word. He has been designing, developing, and delivering computer workshops for more than two decades.

Catherine Hain is an instructor at Central New Mexico Community College in Albuquerque, New Mexico. She teaches computer applications classes in the Business and Information Technology School, both in the classroom and through the distance learning office. Catherine holds a bachelor's degree in Management and Marketing and a master's degree in Business Administration.

Alicia Vargas is an Associate Professor of Business Information Technology at Pasadena City College in California. She holds a bachelor's and a master's degree in Business Education from California State University, Los Angeles and has authored numerous textbooks and training materials on Microsoft Word, Microsoft Excel, and Microsoft PowerPoint.

A Special Thank You

Pearson Prentice Hall gratefully acknowledges the contribution made by Shelley Gaskin to the first edition publication of this series—*Skills for Success with Office 2007*. The series has truly benefited from her dedication toward developing a textbook that aims to help students and instructors. We thank her for her continued support of this series.

Contributors

We'd like to thank the following people for their work on Skills for Success:

Instructor Resource Authors

Erich Adickes	*Parkland College*
Sharon Behrens	*Northeast Wisconsin Technical College*
Julie Boyles	*Portland Community College*
Barbara Edington	*St. Francis College*
Ranida Harris	*Indiana University Southeast*
Beth Hendrick	*Lake Sumter Community College*
Susan Holland	*Southeast Community College—Nebraska*
Andrea Leinbach	*Harrisburg Area Community College*
Yvonne Leonard	*Coastal Carolina Community College*
Trina Maurer	*Georgia Virtual Technical College*
Anthony Nowakowski	*Buffalo State College*
Ernest Gines	*Tarrant County College—Southeast*
Stacey Gee Hollins	*St. Louis Community College—Meramec*
John Purcell	*Castleton State College*
Ann Rowlette	*Liberty University*
Amanda Shelton	*J. Sargeant Reynolds*
Steve St. John	*Tulsa Community College*
Joyce Thompson	*Lehigh Carbon Community College*
Karen Wisniewski	*County College of Morris*

Technical Editors

Lisa Bucki	
Kelly Carling	
Hilda Wirth Federico	*Jacksonville University*
Tom Lightner	*Missouri State University*
Elizabeth Lockley	
Joyce Nielsen	
Janet Pickard	*Chattanooga State Tech Community College*
Linda Pogue	*Northwest Arkansas Community College*
Steve Rubin	*California State University—Monterey Bay*
Eric Sabbah	
Jan Snyder	
Mara Zebest	

Reviewers

Darrell Abbey	*Cascadia Community College*
Bridget I. Archer	*Oakton Community College*
Laura Aagard	*Sierra College*
John Alcorcha	*MTI College*
Barry Andrews	*Miami Dade College*
Natalie Andrews	*Miami Dade College*
Wilma Andrews	*Virginia Commonwealth University School of Business*
Bridget Archer	*Oakton Community College*
Tahir Aziz	*J. Sargeant Reynolds*
Greg Balinger	*Miami Dade College*
Terry Bass	*University of Massachusetts, Lowell*
Lisa Beach	*Santa Rosa Junior College*
Rocky Belcher	*Sinclair Community College*
Nannette Biby	*Miami Dade College*
David Billings	*Guilford Technical Community College*
Brenda K. Britt	*Fayetteville Technical Community College*
Alisa Brown	*Pulaski Technical College*
Eric Cameron	*Passaic Community College*
Gene Carbonaro	*Long Beach City College*
Trey Cherry	*Edgecombe Community College*
Kim Childs	*Bethany University*
Pualine Chohonis	*Miami Dade College*
Lennie Coper	*Miami Dade College*
Tara Cipriano	*Gateway Technical College*
Paulette Comet	*Community College of Baltimore County—Catonsville*
Gail W. Cope	*Sinclair Community College*
Susana Contreras de Finch	*College of Southern Nevada*
Chris Corbin	*Miami Dade College*
Janis Cox	*Tri-County Technical College*
Tomi Crawford	*Miami Dade College*
Martin Cronlund	*Anne Arundel Community College*
Jennifer Day	*Sinclair Community College*
Ralph DeArazoza	*Miami Dade College*
Carol Decker	*Montgomery College*
Loorna DeDuluc	*Miami Dade College*
Caroline Delcourt	*Black Hawk College*

Michael Discello	*Pittsburgh Technical Institute*
Kevin Duggan	*Midlands Technical Community College*
Barbara Edington	*St. Francis College*
Donna Ehrhart	*Genesee Community College*
Hilda Wirth Federico	*Jacksonville University*
Tushnelda Fernandez	*Miami Dade College*
Arlene Flerchinger	*Chattanooga State Tech Community College*
Hedy Fossenkemper	*Paradise Valley Community College*
Kent Foster	*Withrop University*
Penny Foster-Shiver	*Anne Arundel Community College*
Arlene Franklin	*Bucks County Community College*
George Gabb	*Miami Dade College*
Barbara Garrell	*Delaware County Community College*
Deb Geoghan	*Bucks County Community College*
Jessica Gilmore	*Highline Community College*
Victor Giol	*Miami Dade College*
Melinda Glander	*Northmetro Technical College*
Linda Glassburn	*Cuyahoga Community College, West*
Deb Gross	*Ohio State University*
Rachelle Hall	*Glendale Community College*
Marie Hartlein	*Montgomery County Community College*
Diane Hartman	*Utah Valley State College*
Betsy Headrick	*Chattanooga State*
Patrick Healy	*Northern Virginia Community College—Woodbridge*
Lindsay Henning	*Yavapai College*
Kermelle Hensley	*Columbus Technical College*
Diana Hill	*Chesapeake College*
Rachel Hinton	*Broome Community College*
Mary Carole Hollingsworth	*GA Perimeter*
Stacey Gee Hollins	*St. Louis Community College—Meramec*
Bill Holmes	*Chandler-Gilbert Community College*
Steve Holtz	*University of Minnesota Duluth*
Margaret M. Hvatum	*St. Louis Community College*
Joan Ivey	*Lanier Technical College*
Dr. Dianna D. Johnson	*North Metro Technical College*
Kay Johnston	*Columbia Basin College*
Warren T. Jones, Sr.	*University of Alabama at Birmingham*
Sally Kaskocsak	*Sinclair Community College*
Renuka Kumar	*Community College of Baltimore County*
Kathy McKee	*North Metro Technical College*
Hazel Kates	*Miami Dade College*
Gerald Kearns	*Forsyth Technical Community College*
Charles Kellermann	*Northern Virginia Community College—Woodbridge*
John Kidd	*Tarrant County Community College*
Chris Kinnard	*Miami Dade College*
Kelli Kleindorfer	*American Institute of Business*
Kurt Kominek	*NE State Tech Community College*
Dianne Kotokoff	*Lanier Technical College*
Cynthia Krebs	*Utah Valley University*
Jean Lacoste	*Virginia Tech*
Gene Laughrey	*Northern Oklahoma College*
David LeBron	*Miami Dade College*
Kaiyang Liang	*Miami Dade College*
Linda Lindaman	*Black Hawk College*
Felix Lopez	*Miami Dade College*
Nicki Maines	*Mesa Community College*
Cindy Manning	*Big Sandy Community and Technical College*
Patri Mays	*Paradise Valley Community College*
Norma McKenzie	*El Paso Community College*
Lee McKinley	*GA Perimeter*
Sandy McCormack	*Monroe Community College*
Eric Meyer	*Miami Dade College*
Kathryn Miller	*Big Sandy Community and Technical College, Pike Ville Campus*
Gloria A. Morgan	*Monroe Community College*
Kathy Morris	*University of Alabama, Tuscaloosa*
Linda Moulton	*Montgomery County Community College*
Ryan Murphy	*Sinclair Community College*
Stephanie Murre Wolf	*Moraine Park Technical College*
Jackie Myers	*Sinclair Community College*
Dell Najera	*El Paso Community College, Valle Verde Campus*
Scott Nason	*Rowan Cabarrus Community College*
Paula Neal	*Sinclair Community College*
Bethanne Newman	*Paradise Valley Community College*
Eloise Newsome	*Northern Virginia Community College—Woodbridge*
Karen Nunan	*Northeast State Technical Community College*
Ellen Orr	*Seminole Community College*
Carol Ottaway	*Chemeketa Community College*
Denise Passero	*Fulton-Montgomery Community College*
Americus Pavese	*Community College of Baltimore County*
James Gordon Patterson	*Paradise Valley Community College*
Cindra Phillips	*Clark State CC*

Contributors continued

Janet Pickard	*Chattanooga State Tech Community College*	Diane Stark	*Phoenix College*
Floyd Pittman	*Miami Dade College*	Neil Stenlund	*Northern Virginia Community College*
Melissa Prinzing	*Sierra College*	Linda Stoudemayer	*Lamar Institute of Technology*
Pat Rahmlow	*Montgomery County Community College*	Pamela Stovall	*Forsyth Technical Community College*
Mary Rasley	*Lehigh Carbon Community College*	Linda Switzer	*Highline Community College*
Scott Rosen	*Santa Rosa Junior College*	Margaret Taylor	*College of Southern Nevada*
Ann Rowlette	*Liberty University*	Martha Taylor	*Sinclair Community College*
Kamaljeet Sanghera	*George Mason University*	Michael M. Taylor	*Seattle Central Community College*
June Scott	*County College of Morris*	Roseann Thomas	*Fayetteville Tech Community College*
Janet Sebesy	*Cuyahoga Community College*	Ingrid Thompson-Sellers	*GA Perimeter*
Jennifer Sedelmeyer	*Broome Community College*	Daniel Thomson	*Keiser University*
Kelly SellAnne	*Arundel Community College*	Astrid Hoy Todd	*Guilford Technical Community College*
Teresa Sept	*College of Southern Idaho*	Barb Tollinger	*Sinclair Community College*
Pat Serrano	*Scottsdale Community College*	Cathy Urbanski	*Chandler Gilbert Community College*
Amanda Shelton	*J. Sargeant Reynolds*	Sue Van Boven	*Paradise Valley Community College*
Gary Sibbits	*St. Louis Community College—Meramec*	Philip Vavalides	*Guildford Technical Community College*
Janet Siert	*Ellsworth Community College*	Pete Vetere	*Montgomery County Community College— West Campus*
Robert Sindt	*Johnson County Community College*		
Karen Smith	*Technical College of the Lowcountry*	Asteria Villegas	*Monroe College*
Robert Smolenski	*Delaware County Community College*	Michael Walton	*Miami Dade College*
Robert Sindt	*Johnson County Community College*	Teri Weston	*Harford Community College*
Gary R. Smith	*Paradise Valley Community College*	Julie Wheeler	*Sinclair Community College*
Patricia Snyder	*Midlands Technical College*	Debbie Wood	*Western Piedmont Community College*
Pamela Sorensen	*Santa Rosa Junior College*	Thomas Yip	*Passaic Community College*
Eric Stadnik	*Santa Rosa Junior College*	Lindy Young	*Sierra Community College*
Mark Stanchfield	*Rochester Community and Technical College*	Matt Zullo	*Wake Technical Community College*

A Microsoft® Office textbook that recognizes how students learn today-

Skills for Success

with Microsoft® Office 2010 Volume 1

- **10 x 8.5 Format –** Easy for students to read and type at the same time by simply propping the book up on the desk in front of their monitor

- **Clearly Outlined Skills –** Each skill is presented in a single two-page spread so that students can easily follow along

- **Numbered Steps and Bulleted Text –** Students don't read long paragraphs or text, but they will read information presented concisely

- **Easy-to-Find Student Data Files –** Visual key shows students how to locate and interact with their data files

Start Here – Students know exactly where to start and what their starting file will look like

Outcome – Shows students up front what their completed project will look like

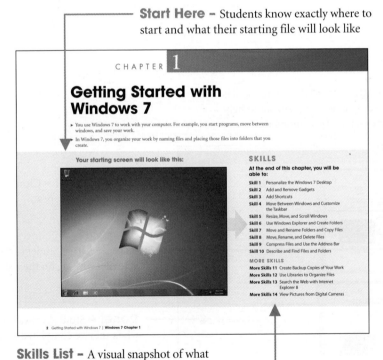

Skills List – A visual snapshot of what skills they will complete in the chapter

Sequential Pagination – Saves you and your students time in locating topics and assignments

Skills for Success

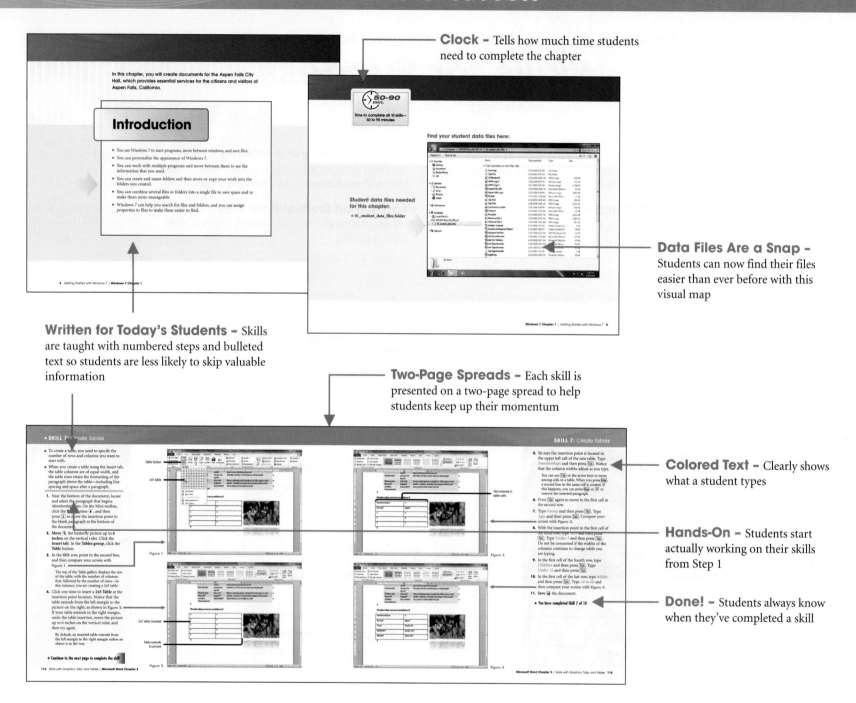

Clock – Tells how much time students need to complete the chapter

Data Files Are a Snap – Students can now find their files easier than ever before with this visual map

Written for Today's Students – Skills are taught with numbered steps and bulleted text so students are less likely to skip valuable information

Two-Page Spreads – Each skill is presented on a two-page spread to help students keep up their momentum

Colored Text – Clearly shows what a student types

Hands-On – Students start actually working on their skills from Step 1

Done! – Students always know when they've completed a skill

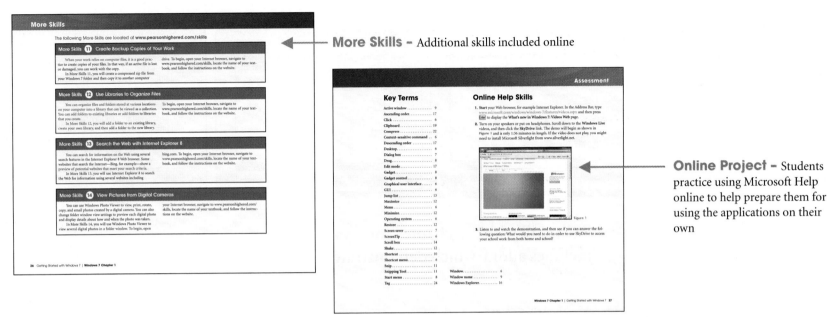

More Skills – Additional skills included online

Online Project – Students practice using Microsoft Help online to help prepare them for using the applications on their own

End-of-Chapter Material – Several levels of assessment so you can assign the material that best fits your students' needs

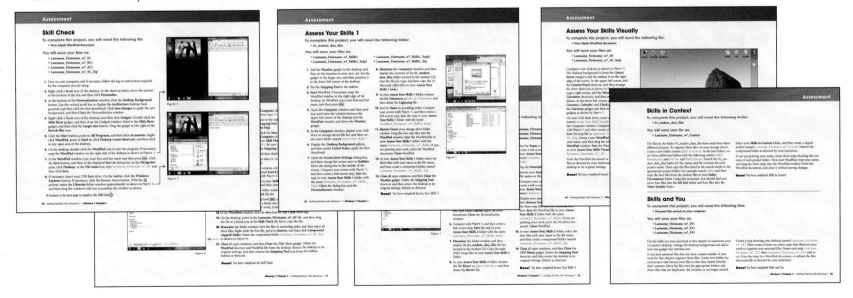

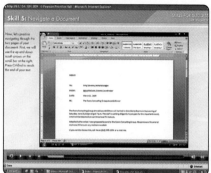
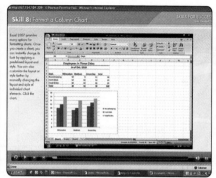

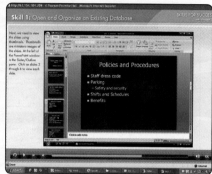

Videos! – Each skill within a chapter comes with a video that includes audio, which demonstrates the skill

All Videos and Instructor materials available on the IRCD

Instructor Materials

Instructor's Manual – Teaching tips and additional resources for each chapter

Assignment Sheets – Lists all the assignments for the chapter, you just add in the course information, due dates and points. Providing these to students ensures they will know what is due and when

Scripted Lectures – Classroom lectures prepared for you

Annotated Solution Files – Coupled with the scoring rubrics, these create a grading and scoring system that makes grading so much easier for you

Power Point Lectures – PowerPoint presentations for each chapter

Prepared Exams – Exams for each chapter and for each application

Scoring Rubrics – Can be used either by students to check their work or by you as a quick check-off for the items that need to be corrected

Syllabus Templates – for 8-week, 12-week, and 16-week courses

Test Bank – Includes a variety of test questions for each chapter

Companion Website – Online content such as the More Skills Projects, Online Study Guide, Glossary, and Student Data Files are all at www.pearsonhighered.com/skills

SKILLS
For SUCCESS
with Microsoft®
Office 2010

VOLUME 1

Common Features of Office 2010

▶ The programs in Microsoft Office 2010—Word, Excel, PowerPoint, and Access—share common tools that you use in a consistent, easy-to-learn manner.

▶ Common tasks include opening and saving files, entering and formatting text, and printing your work.

Your starting screen will look like this:

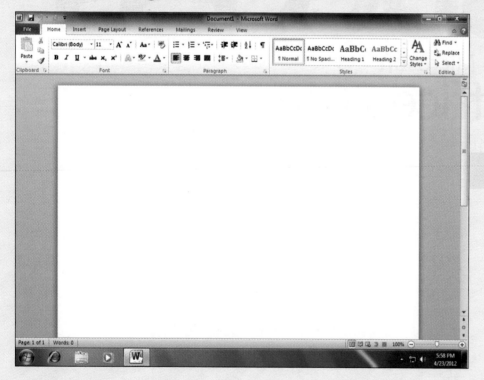

SKILLS

Skills 1–10 Training

At the end of this chapter, you will be able to:

Skill 1 Start Word and Navigate the Word Window

Skill 2 Start Excel and PowerPoint and Work with Multiple Windows

Skill 3 Save Files in New Folders

Skill 4 Print and Save Documents

Skill 5 Open Student Data Files and Save Copies Using Save As

Skill 6 Type and Edit Text

Skill 7 Cut, Copy, and Paste Text

Skill 8 Format Text and Paragraphs

Skill 9 Use the Ribbon

Skill 10 Use Shortcut Menus and Dialog Boxes

MORE SKILLS

More Skills 11 Capture Screens with the Snipping Tool

More Skills 12 Use Microsoft Office Help

More Skills 13 Organize Files

More Skills 14 Save Documents to Windows Live

Outcome

Using the skills listed to the left will enable you to create documents similar to this:

Visit Aspen Falls!

Aspen Falls overlooks the Pacific Ocean and is surrounded by many vineyards and wineries. Ocean recreation is accessed primarily at Durango County Park. The Aspen Lake Recreation Area provides year round fresh water recreation and is the city's largest park.

Local Attractions
- Wine Country
  - Wine Tasting Tours
  - Wineries
- Wordsworth Fellowship Museum of Art
- Durango County Museum of History
- Convention Center
- Art Galleries
- Glider Tours

Aspen Falls Annual Events
- Annual Starving Artists Sidewalk Sale
- Annual Wine Festival
- Cinco de Mayo
- Vintage Car Show
- Heritage Day Parade
- Harvest Days
- Amateur Bike Races
- Farmer's Market
- Aspen Lake Nature Cruises
- Aspen Falls Triathlon
- Taste of Aspen Falls
- Winter Blues Festival

Contact Your Name for more information.

You will save your files as:

Lastname_Firstname_cf01_Visit1
Lastname_Firstname_cf01_Visit2
Lastname_Firstname_cf01_Visit3

In this chapter, you will create documents for the Aspen Falls City Hall, which provides essential services for the citizens and visitors of Aspen Falls, California.

Common Features of Office 2010

► Microsoft Office is the most common software used to create and share personal and business documents.

► Microsoft Office is a suite of several programs—Word, PowerPoint, Excel, Access, and others—that each have a special purpose.

► Because of the consistent design and layout of Microsoft Office, when you learn to use one Microsoft Office program, you can use most of those skills when working with the other Microsoft Office programs.

► The files you create with Microsoft Office need to be named and saved in locations where they can be easily found when you need them.

Time to complete all
10 skills – 50 to 90 minutes

Find your student data files here:

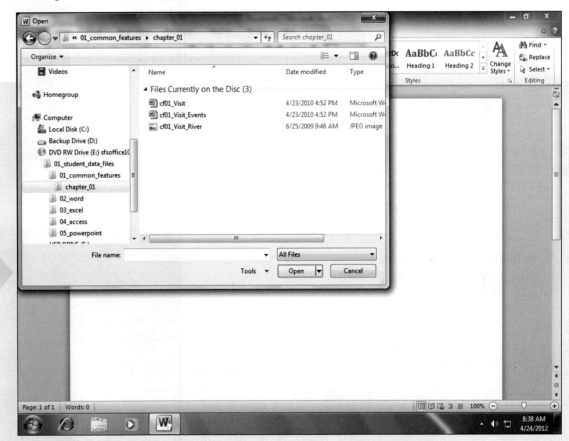

Student data files needed for this chapter:

- cf01_Visit
- cf01_Visit_Events
- cf01_Visit_River

► The Word 2010 program can be launched by clicking the Start button, and then locating and clicking the *Microsoft Word 2010* command.

► When you start Word, a new blank document displays in which you can type text.

1. In the lower left corner of the desktop, click the **Start** button 🌐.

2. In the lower left corner of the **Start** menu, click the **All Programs** command, and then compare your screen with **Figure 1**.

   The Microsoft Office folder is located in the All Programs folder. If you have several programs installed on your computer, you may need to scroll to see the Microsoft Office folder.

3. Click the **Microsoft Office** folder, and then compare your screen with **Figure 2**.

   Below the Microsoft Office folder, commands that open various Office 2010 programs display.

4. From the **Start** menu, under the **Microsoft Office** folder, click **Microsoft Word 2010**, and then wait a few moments for the Microsoft Word window to display.

5. If necessary, in the upper right corner of the Microsoft Word window, click the Maximize button ▣.

■ **Continue to the next page to complete the skill**

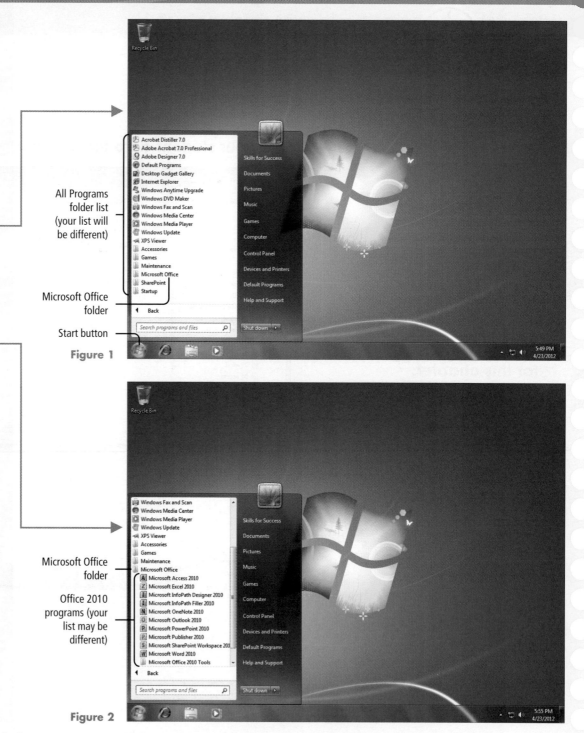

All Programs folder list (your list will be different)

Microsoft Office folder

Start button

Figure 1

Microsoft Office folder

Office 2010 programs (your list may be different)

Figure 2

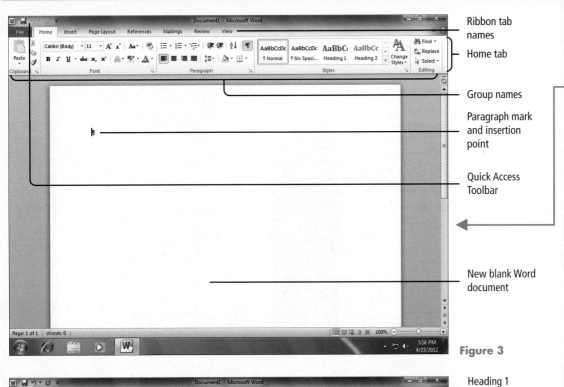

Ribbon tab names

Home tab

Group names

Paragraph mark and insertion point

Quick Access Toolbar

New blank Word document

Figure 3

6. On the Ribbon's **Home tab**, in the **Paragraph group**, click the **Show/Hide** button ¶ until it displays in gold indicating that it is active. Compare your screen with **Figure 3**.

Above the blank Word document, the Quick Access Toolbar and Ribbon display. At the top of the Ribbon, a row of tab names display. Each Ribbon tab has buttons that you click to perform actions. The buttons are organized into groups that display their names along the bottom of the Ribbon.

In the document, the *insertion point*— a vertical line that indicates where text will be inserted when you start typing—flashes near the top left corner.

The Show/Hide button is a *toggle button*— a button used to turn a feature both on and off. The paragraph mark (¶) indicates the end of a paragraph and will not print.

7. In the document, type your first and last names. As you type, notice that the insertion point and paragraph mark move to the right.

8. On the **Home tab**, in the **Styles group**, point to—but do not click—the **Heading 1** thumbnail to show the *Live Preview*—a feature that displays the result of a formatting change if you select it.

9. Click the **Heading 1** thumbnail to apply the formatting change as shown in **Figure 4**. If the Word Navigation Pane displays on the left side of the Word window, click its Close ✕ button.

■ **You have completed Skill 1 of 10**

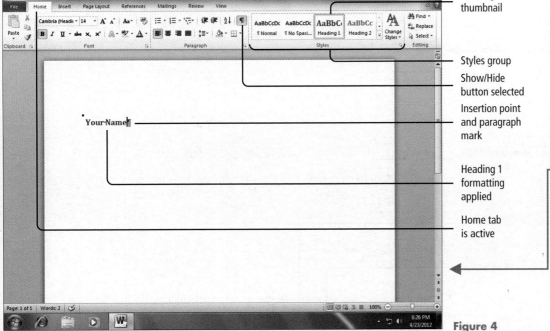

Heading 1 thumbnail

Styles group

Show/Hide button selected

Insertion point and paragraph mark

Heading 1 formatting applied

Home tab is active

Figure 4

▶ When you open more than one Office program, each program displays in its own window.

▶ When you want to work with a program in a different window, you need to make it the active window.

1. Click the **Start** button 🌐, and then compare your screen with **Figure 1.**

Your computer may be configured in such a way that you can open Office programs without opening the All Programs folder. The Office 2010 program commands may display as shortcuts in the Start menu's pinned programs area or the recently used programs area. Your computer's taskbar or desktop may also display icons that start each program.

2. From the **Start** menu, locate and then click **Microsoft Excel 2010**. Depending on your computer, you may need to double-click—not single click—to launch Excel. Compare your screen with **Figure 2.** If necessary, click the Maximize button 🔲.

A new blank worksheet displays in a new window. The first *cell*—the box formed by the intersection of a row and column—is active as indicated by the thick, black border surrounding the cell. When you type in Excel, the text is entered into the active cell.

The Quick Access Toolbar displays above the spreadsheet. The Excel Ribbon has its own tabs and groups that you use to work with an Excel spreadsheet. Many of these tabs, groups, and buttons are similar to those found in Word.

On the taskbar, two buttons display—one for Word and one for Excel.

■ **Continue to the next page to complete the skill** ▶

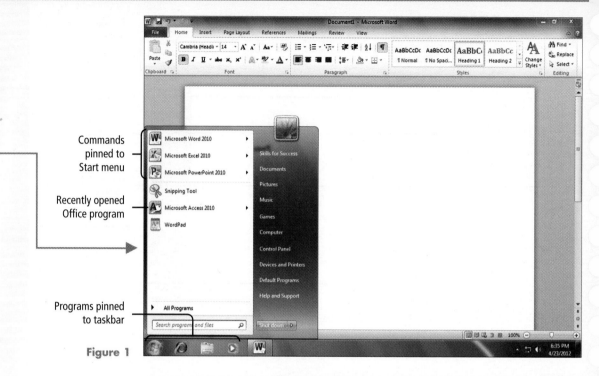

Commands pinned to Start menu

Recently opened Office program

Programs pinned to taskbar

Figure 1

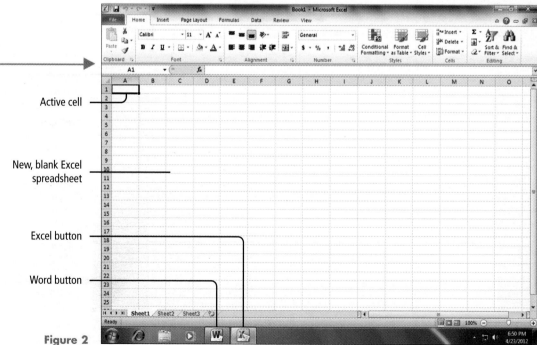

Active cell

New, blank Excel spreadsheet

Excel button

Word button

Figure 2

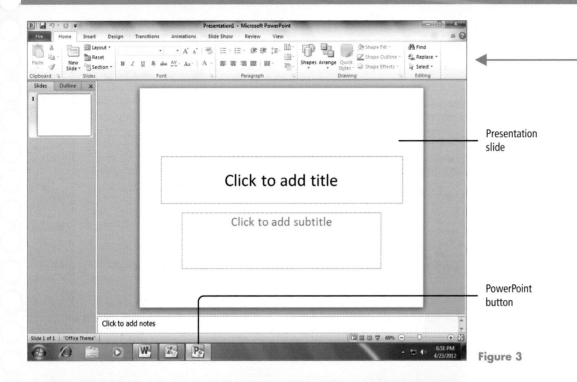

Presentation slide

PowerPoint button

Figure 3

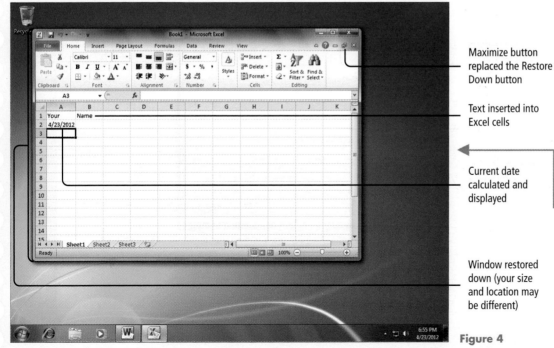

Maximize button replaced the Restore Down button

Text inserted into Excel cells

Current date calculated and displayed

Window restored down (your size and location may be different)

Figure 4

3. From the **Start** menu 🔵, locate and then click **Microsoft PowerPoint 2010.** Compare your screen with **Figure 3.** If necessary, Maximize 🔲 the Presentation1 - Microsoft PowerPoint window.

> A new, blank presentation opens in a new window. The PowerPoint window contains a slide in which you can type text. PowerPoint slides are designed to be displayed as you talk in front of a group of people.

4. In the upper right corner of the **PowerPoint** window, click the **Close** button 🔳.

5. On the taskbar, click the **Word** button to make it the active window. With the insertion point flashing to the right of your name, press Enter, and then type Skills for Success Common Features Chapter

6. In the upper right corner of the **Document1 - Microsoft Word** window, click the **Minimize** button 🔳.

> The Word window no longer displays, but its button is still available on the taskbar.

7. With the Excel window active, in the first cell—cell **A1**—type your first name. Press Tab, and then type your last name.

8. Press Enter, type =TODAY() and then press Enter to calculate the current date and to display it in the cell.

9. In the **Excel** window, click the **Restore Down** button 🔲 and then compare your screen with **Figure 4.**

> The window remains open, but it no longer fills the entire screen. The Maximize button replaced the Restore Down button.

■ **You have completed Skill 2 of 10**

▶ A new document or spreadsheet is stored in the computer's temporary memory (*RAM*) until you save it to your hard drive or USB flash drive.

1. If you are saving your work on a USB flash drive, insert the USB flash drive into the computer now. If the Windows Explorer button ▦ flashes on the taskbar, right-click the button, and then on the Jump List, click Close window.

2. On the taskbar, click the **Word** button to make it the active window. On the **Quick Access Toolbar**, click the **Save** button ▦.

   For new documents, the first time you click the Save button, the Save As dialog box opens so that you can name the file.

3. If you are to save your work on a USB drive, in the Navigation pane scroll down to display the list of drives, and then click your USB flash drive as shown in **Figure 1**. If you are saving your work to another location, in the Navigation pane, locate and then click that folder or drive.

4. On the **Save As** dialog box toolbar, click the **New folder** button, and then immediately type Common Features Chapter 1

5. Press ⎆Enter to accept the folder name, and then press ⎆Enter again to open the new folder as shown in **Figure 2**.

   The new folder is created and then opened in the Save As dialog box file list.

■ **Continue to the next page to complete the skill** ➡

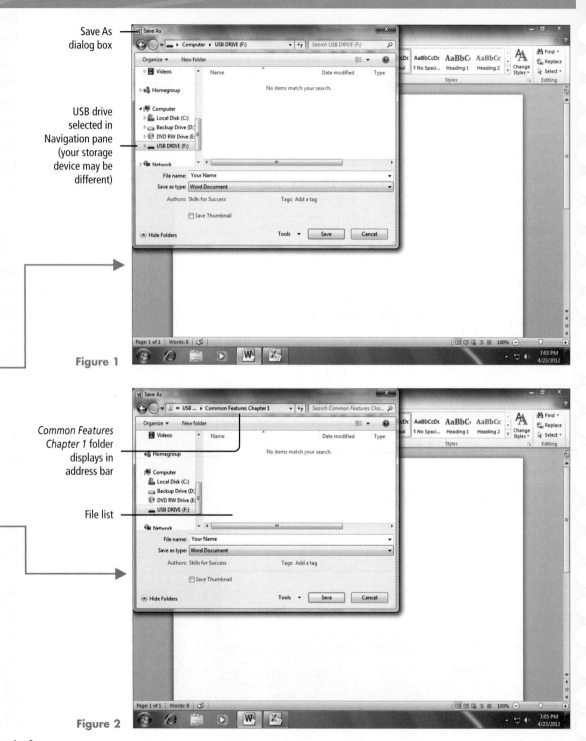

Save As dialog box

USB drive selected in Navigation pane (your storage device may be different)

Figure 1

Common Features Chapter 1 folder displays in address bar

File list

Figure 2

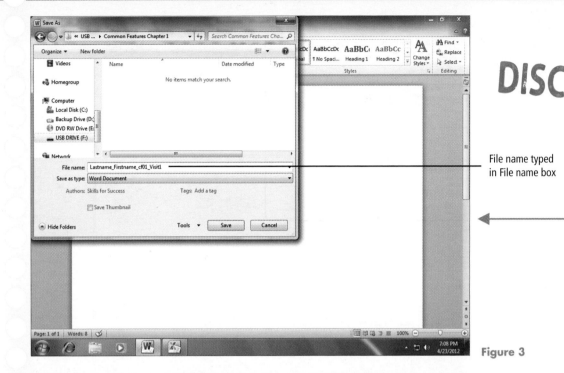

File name typed
in File name box

Figure 3

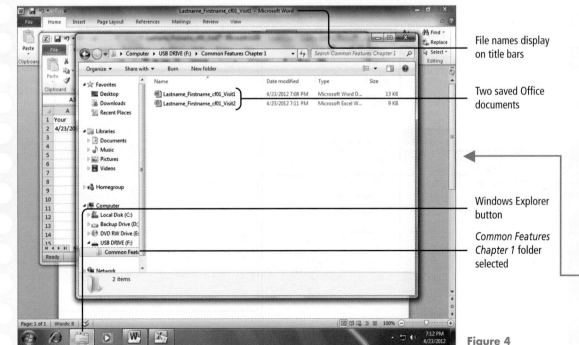

File names display
on title bars

Two saved Office
documents

Windows Explorer
button

*Common Features
Chapter 1* folder
selected

Figure 4

6. In the **Save As** dialog box, click in the **File name** box one time to highlight all of the existing text.

7. With the text in the **File name** box still highlighted, type Lastname_Firstname_ cf01_Visit1

8. Compare your screen with **Figure 3**, and then click **Save**.

After the document is saved, the name of the file displays on the title bar at the top of the window.

9. On the taskbar, click the **Windows Explorer** button 🔲. In the folder window **Navigation** pane, open ▷ the drive on which you are saving your work, and then click the **Common Features Chapter 1** folder. Verify that *Lastname_Firstname_ cf01_Visit1* displays in file list.

10. On the taskbar, click the **Excel** button to make it the active window. On the Excel **Quick Access Toolbar**, click the **Save** button 🔲.

11. In the **Save As** dialog box **Navigation** pane, open ▷ the drive where you are saving your work, and then click the **Common Features Chapter 1** folder to display its file list.

The Word file may not display because the Save As box typically displays only files created by the program you are using. Here, only Excel files will typically display.

12. Click in the **File name** box, replace the existing value with Lastname_Firstname_ cf01_Visit2 and then click the **Save** button.

13. On the taskbar, click the **Windows Explorer** button, and then compare your screen with **Figure 4**.

■ **You have completed Skill 3 of 10**

► Before printing, it is a good idea to work in *Page Layout view*—a view where you prepare your document or spreadsheet for printing.

1. On the taskbar, click the **Excel** button, and then click the **Maximize** button.

2. On the Ribbon, click the **View tab**, and then in the **Workbook Views group**, click the **Page Layout** button. Compare your screen with **Figure 1**.

   The worksheet displays the cells, the margins, and the edges of the paper as they will be positioned when you print. The *cell references*—the numbers on the left side and the letters across the top of a spreadsheet that address each cell—will not print.

3. On the Ribbon, click the **Page Layout tab**. In the **Page Setup group**, click the **Margins** button, and then in the **Margins** gallery, click **Wide**.

4. Click the **File tab**, and then on the left side of the Backstage, click **Print**. Compare your screen with **Figure 2**.

   The Print tab has commands that affect your print job and a preview of the printed page. Here, the cell references and *grid lines*—lines between the cells in a table or spreadsheet—do not display because they will not be printed.

5. In the **Print Settings**, under **Printer**, notice the name of the printer. You will need to retrieve your printout from this printer. If your instructor has directed you to print to a different printer, click the Printer arrow, and choose the assigned printer.

■ **Continue to the next page to complete the skill**

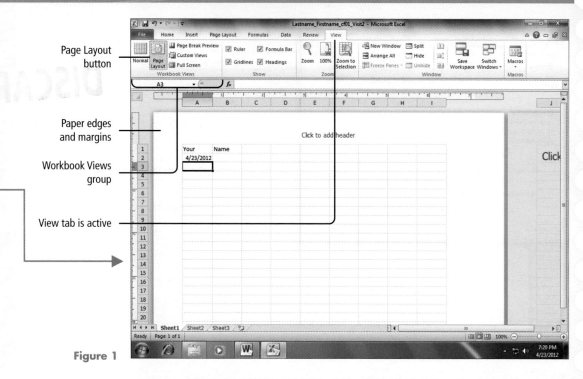

Page Layout button

Paper edges and margins

Workbook Views group

View tab is active

Figure 1

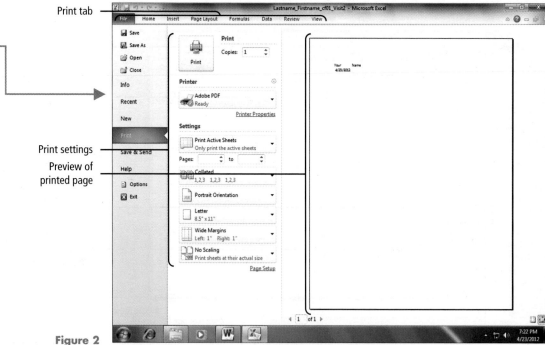

Print tab

Print settings

Preview of printed page

Figure 2

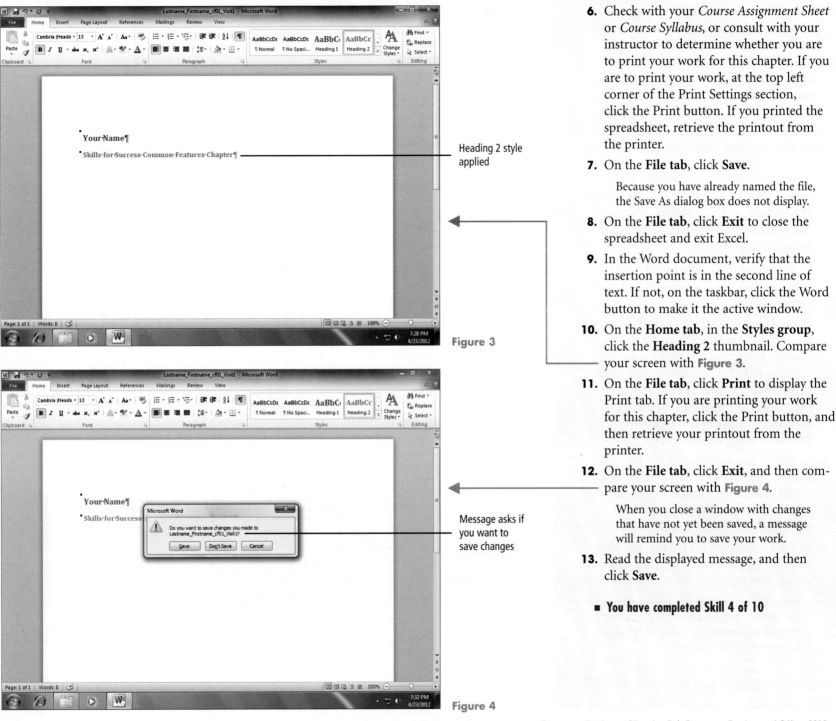

Heading 2 style applied

Figure 3

Message asks if you want to save changes

Figure 4

6. Check with your *Course Assignment Sheet* or *Course Syllabus,* or consult with your instructor to determine whether you are to print your work for this chapter. If you are to print your work, at the top left corner of the Print Settings section, click the Print button. If you printed the spreadsheet, retrieve the printout from the printer.

7. On the **File tab**, click **Save**.

> Because you have already named the file, the Save As dialog box does not display.

8. On the **File tab**, click **Exit** to close the spreadsheet and exit Excel.

9. In the Word document, verify that the insertion point is in the second line of text. If not, on the taskbar, click the Word button to make it the active window.

10. On the **Home tab**, in the **Styles group**, click the **Heading 2** thumbnail. Compare your screen with **Figure 3**.

11. On the **File tab**, click **Print** to display the Print tab. If you are printing your work for this chapter, click the Print button, and then retrieve your printout from the printer.

12. On the **File tab**, click **Exit**, and then compare your screen with **Figure 4**.

> When you close a window with changes that have not yet been saved, a message will remind you to save your work.

13. Read the displayed message, and then click **Save**.

■ **You have completed Skill 4 of 10**

► This book often instructs you to open a student data file so that you do not need to start the project with a blank document.

► The student data files are located on the student CD that came with this book. Your instructor may have provided an alternate location.

► You use Save As to create a copy of the student data file onto your own storage device.

1. If necessary, insert the student CD that came with this text. If the AutoPlay dialog box displays, click Close ⊠.

2. Using the skills practiced earlier, start **Microsoft Word 2010**.

3. In the **Document1 - Microsoft Word** window, click the **File tab**, and then click **Open**.

4. In the **Open** dialog box **Navigation** pane, scroll down and then, if necessary, open ▷ Computer. In the list of drives, click the CD/DVD drive to display the contents of the student CD. If your instructor has provided a different location, navigate to that location instead of using the student CD.

5. In the file list, double-click the **01_student_data_files** folder, double-click the **01_common_features** folder, and then double-click the **chapter_01** folder. Compare your screen with **Figure 1**.

6. In the file list, click **cf01_Visit**, and then click the **Open** button. Compare your screen with **Figure 2**.

   If you opened the file from the student CD, the title bar indicates that the document is in *read-only mode*—a mode where you cannot save your changes.

■ Continue to the next page to complete the skill

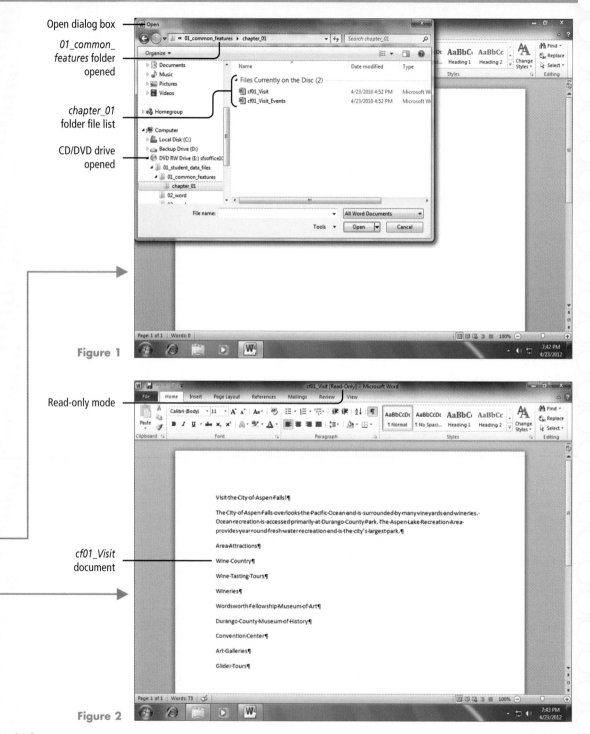

Open dialog box

01_common_features folder opened

chapter_01 folder file list

CD/DVD drive opened

Figure 1

Read-only mode

cf01_Visit document

Figure 2

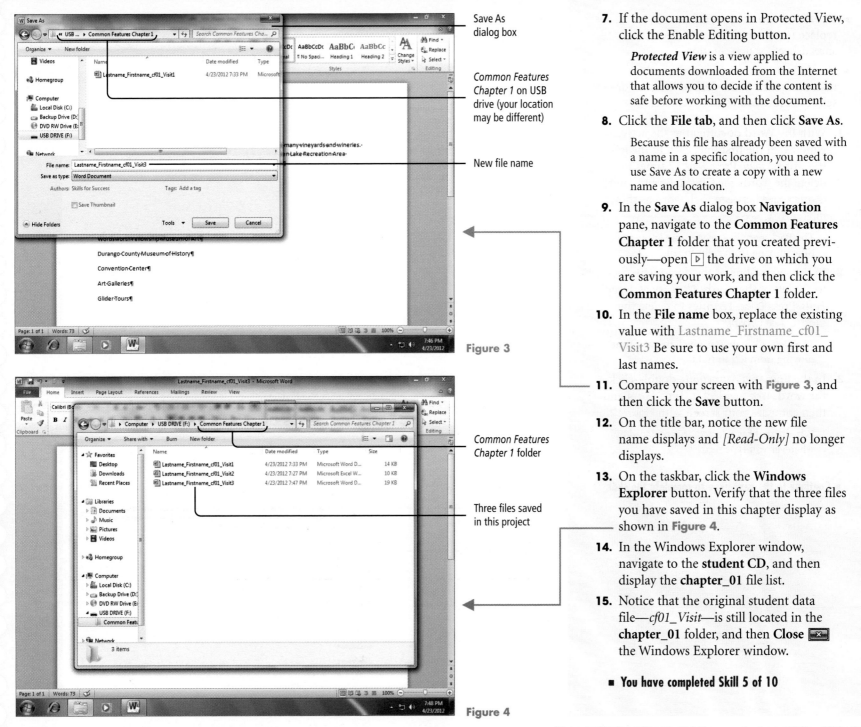

Figure 3

Figure 4

7. If the document opens in Protected View, click the Enable Editing button.

   Protected View is a view applied to documents downloaded from the Internet that allows you to decide if the content is safe before working with the document.

8. Click the **File tab**, and then click **Save As**.

   Because this file has already been saved with a name in a specific location, you need to use Save As to create a copy with a new name and location.

9. In the **Save As** dialog box **Navigation** pane, navigate to the **Common Features Chapter 1** folder that you created previously—open ▷ the drive on which you are saving your work, and then click the **Common Features Chapter 1** folder.

10. In the **File name** box, replace the existing value with Lastname_Firstname_cf01_ Visit3 Be sure to use your own first and last names.

11. Compare your screen with **Figure 3**, and then click the **Save** button.

12. On the title bar, notice the new file name displays and *[Read-Only]* no longer displays.

13. On the taskbar, click the **Windows Explorer** button. Verify that the three files you have saved in this chapter display as shown in **Figure 4**.

14. In the Windows Explorer window, navigate to the **student CD**, and then display the **chapter_01** file list.

15. Notice that the original student data file—*cf01_Visit*—is still located in the **chapter_01** folder, and then **Close** the Windows Explorer window.

■ **You have completed Skill 5 of 10**

► To *edit* is to insert text, delete text, or replace text in an Office document, spreadsheet, or presentation.

► To edit text, you need to position the insertion point at the desired location or select the text you want to replace.

1. With the **Word** document as the active window, in the first line, click to the left of the word *Aspen*. Press Bksp 12 times to delete the words *the City of*. Be sure there is one space between each word as shown in **Figure 1**.

   The Backspace key deletes one letter at a time moving from right to left.

2. In the second line of the document, click to the left of the words *The City of Aspen Falls*. Press Delete 12 times to delete the phrase *The City of*.

   The Delete key deletes one letter at a time moving from left to right.

3. In the line *Area Attractions*, double-click the word *Area* to select it. Type Local and then compare your screen with **Figure 2**.

   When a word is selected, it is replaced by whatever you type next.

■ **Continue to the next page to complete the skill**

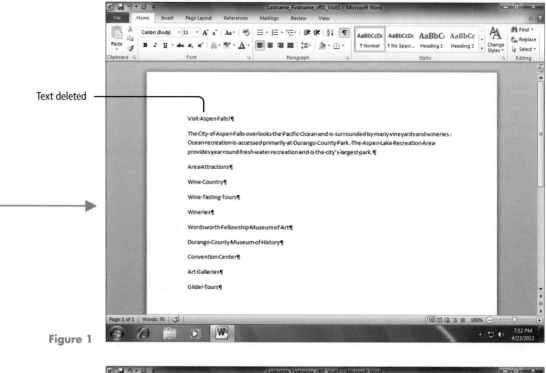

Text deleted

Figure 1

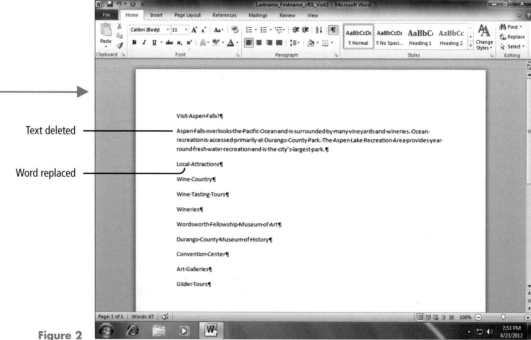

Text deleted

Word replaced

Figure 2

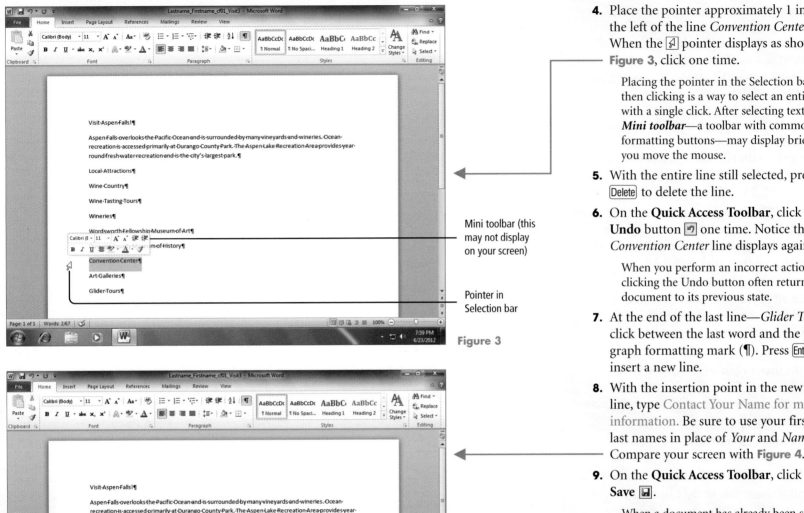

Mini toolbar (this
may not display
on your screen)

Pointer in
Selection bar

Figure 3

New line inserted

Figure 4

4. Place the pointer approximately 1 inch to the left of the line *Convention Center*. When the pointer displays as shown in **Figure 3**, click one time.

Placing the pointer in the Selection bar and then clicking is a way to select an entire line with a single click. After selecting text, the **Mini toolbar**—a toolbar with common formatting buttons—may display briefly as you move the mouse.

5. With the entire line still selected, press Delete to delete the line.

6. On the **Quick Access Toolbar**, click the **Undo** button one time. Notice the *Convention Center* line displays again.

When you perform an incorrect action, clicking the Undo button often returns your document to its previous state.

7. At the end of the last line—*Glider Tours*— click between the last word and the paragraph formatting mark (¶). Press Enter to insert a new line.

8. With the insertion point in the new line, type Contact Your Name for more information. Be sure to use your first and last names in place of *Your* and *Name*. Compare your screen with **Figure 4**.

9. On the **Quick Access Toolbar**, click **Save** .

When a document has already been saved with the desired name, click the Save button—the Save As dialog box is not needed.

- **You have completed Skill 6 of 10**

► The *copy* command places a copy of the selected text or object in the *Clipboard*—a temporary storage area that holds text or an object that has been cut or copied.

► You can move text by moving it to and from the Clipboard or by dragging the text.

1. Click the **File tab**, and then click **Open**. In the **Open** dialog box, if necessary, navigate to the student files and display the contents of the chapter_01 folder. Click **cf01_Visit_Events**, and then click **Open**.

2. On the right side of the Ribbon's **Home tab**, in the **Editing group**, click the **Select** button, and then click **Select All**. Compare your screen with **Figure 1**.

3. With all of the document text selected, on the left side of the **Home tab**, in the **Clipboard group**, click the **Copy** button 🔳.

4. In the upper right corner of the Word window, click **Close** ✖. You do not need to save changes—you will not turn in this student data file.

5. In **Lastname_Firstname_cf01_Visit3**, click to place the insertion point to the left of the line that starts *Contact Your Name*.

6. On the **Home tab**, in the **Clipboard group**, point to—but do not click—the **Paste** button. Compare your screen with **Figure 2**.

The Paste button has two parts—the upper half is the Paste button, and the lower half is the Paste button arrow. When you click the Paste button arrow, a list of paste options display.

■ **Continue to the next page to complete the skill**

cf01_Visit_Events document

Editing group

All text selected

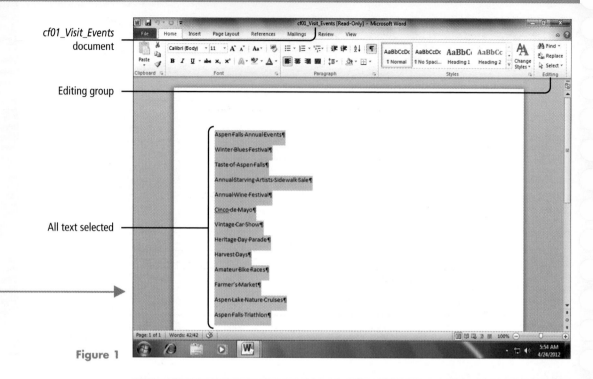

Figure 1

Paste button

Paste button arrow

Insertion point

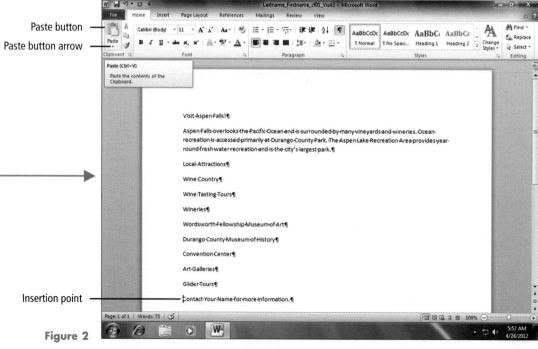

Figure 2

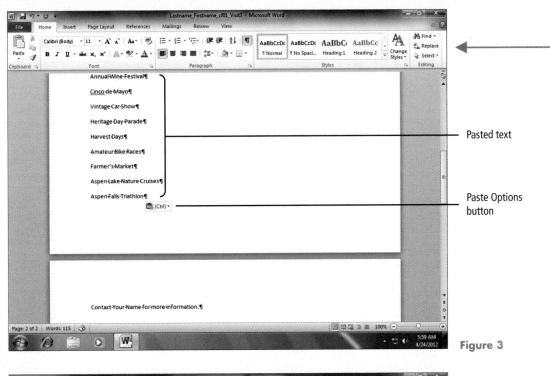

Pasted text

Paste Options
button

Figure 3

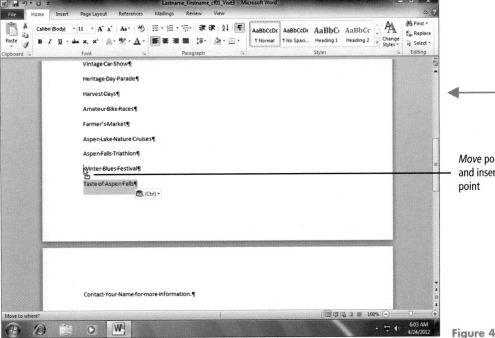

Move pointer
and insertion
point

Figure 4

7. Click the upper half of the **Paste** button to paste the selected text. Compare your screen with **Figure 3**.

> When you *paste*, you insert a copy of the text or object stored in the Clipboard and the Paste Options button displays near the pasted text.

8. Press Esc to hide the Paste Options button.

9. Scroll up to display the line *Winter Blues Festival*. Place the I pointer to the left of the W, and then drag down and to the right to select two lines—*Winter Blues Festival* and *Taste of Aspen Falls*.

> To *drag* is to move the mouse while holding down the left mouse button and then to release it at the appropriate time.

10. On the **Home tab**, in the **Clipboard group**, click the **Cut** button.

> The *cut* command removes the selected text or object and stores it in the Clipboard.

11. Click to place the insertion point to the left of *Contact Your Name*, and then in the **Clipboard group**, click the **Paste** button to insert the text.

12. Drag to select the text *Taste of Aspen Falls*, including the paragraph mark.

13. With the pointer, drag the selected text to the left of *Winter Blues Festival*. When the pointer displays to the left of *Winter* as shown in **Figure 4**, release the mouse button.

14. On the **Quick Access Toolbar**, click **Save**.

> ■ **You have completed Skill 7 of 10**

► To *format* is to change the appearance of the text—for example, changing the text color to red.

► Before formatting text, you first need to select the text that will be formatted.

► Once text is selected, you can apply formatting using the Ribbon or the Mini toolbar.

1. Scroll to the top of the document, and then click anywhere in the first line, *Visit Aspen Falls.*

2. On the **Home tab**, in the **Styles group**, click the **Heading 1** thumbnail.

When no text is selected, the Heading 1 style is applied to the entire paragraph.

3. Click in the paragraph, *Local Attractions,* and then in the **Styles group**, click the **Heading 2** thumbnail. Click in the paragraph, *Aspen Falls Annual Events,* and then apply the **Heading 2** style. Compare your screen with **Figure 1.**

4. Drag to select the text *Visit Aspen Falls!* Immediately point to—but do not click— the Mini toolbar to display it as shown in **Figure 2.** If necessary, right-click the selected text to display the Mini toolbar.

■ **Continue to the next page to complete the skill**

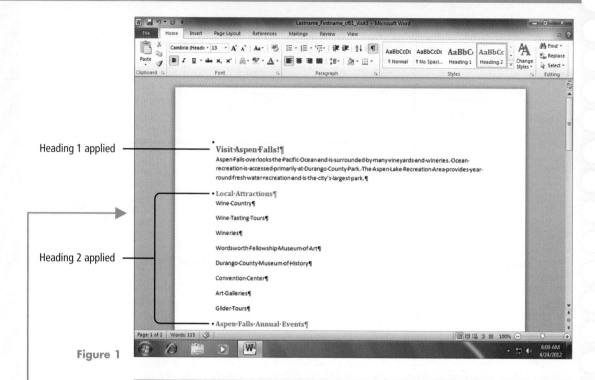

Heading 1 applied

Heading 2 applied

Figure 1

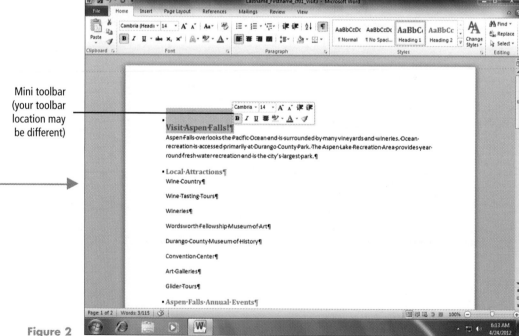

Mini toolbar (your toolbar location may be different)

Figure 2

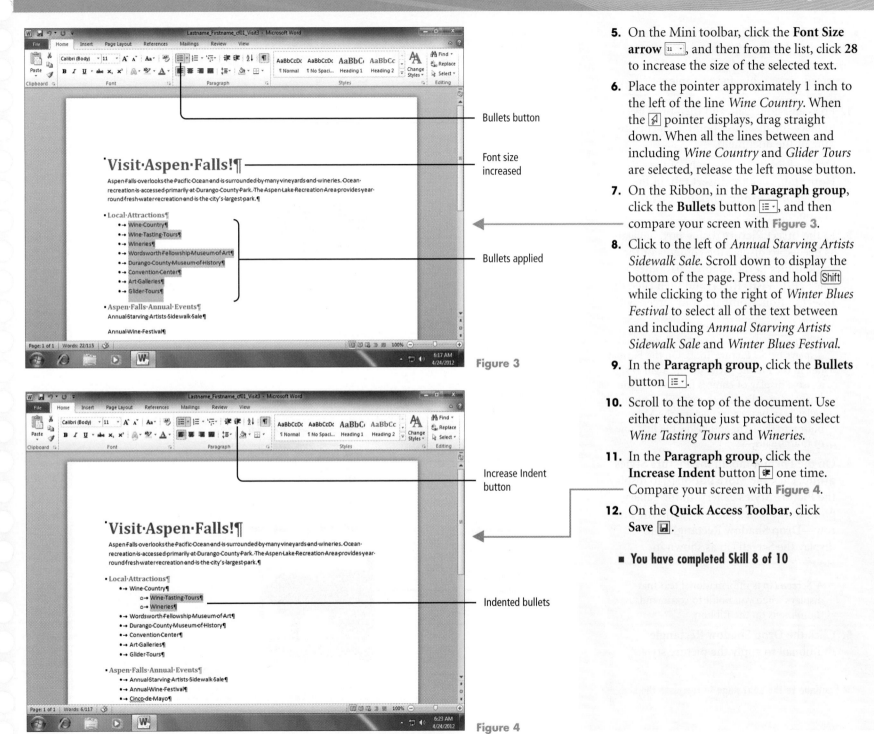

Figure 3

Figure 4

5. On the Mini toolbar, click the **Font Size arrow** ⌴, and then from the list, click **28** to increase the size of the selected text.

6. Place the pointer approximately 1 inch to the left of the line *Wine Country*. When the ⌴ pointer displays, drag straight down. When all the lines between and including *Wine Country* and *Glider Tours* are selected, release the left mouse button.

7. On the Ribbon, in the **Paragraph group**, click the **Bullets** button ⌴, and then compare your screen with **Figure 3**.

8. Click to the left of *Annual Starving Artists Sidewalk Sale*. Scroll down to display the bottom of the page. Press and hold Shift while clicking to the right of *Winter Blues Festival* to select all of the text between and including *Annual Starving Artists Sidewalk Sale* and *Winter Blues Festival*.

9. In the **Paragraph group**, click the **Bullets** button ⌴.

10. Scroll to the top of the document. Use either technique just practiced to select *Wine Tasting Tours* and *Wineries*.

11. In the **Paragraph group**, click the **Increase Indent** button ⌴ one time. Compare your screen with **Figure 4**.

12. On the **Quick Access Toolbar**, click **Save** ⌴.

■ **You have completed Skill 8 of 10**

► Each Ribbon tab contains commands organized into groups. Some tabs display only when a certain type of object is selected—a graphic, for example.

1. Press and hold [Ctrl], and then press [Home] to place the insertion point at the beginning of the document.

2. On the **Ribbon,** to the right of the **Home tab,** click the **Insert tab.** In the **Illustrations group,** click the **Picture** button.

3. In the **Insert Picture** dialog box, navigate as needed to display the contents of the student files in the **chapter_01** folder. Click **cf01_Visit_River,** and then click the **Insert** button. Compare your screen with **Figure 1.**

   When a picture is selected, the Format tab displays below Picture Tools. On the Format tab, in the Picture Styles group, a *gallery*—a visual display of choices from which you can choose—displays thumbnails. The entire gallery can be seen by clicking the More button to the right and below the first row of thumbnails.

4. On the **Format tab,** in the **Picture Styles group,** click the **More** button ⬇ to display the **Picture Styles** gallery. In the gallery, point to the fourth thumbnail in the first row—**Drop Shadow Rectangle**—to display the ScreenTip as shown in **Figure 2.**

   A *ScreenTip* is informational text that displays when you point to commands or thumbnails on the Ribbon.

5. Click the **Drop Shadow Rectangle** thumbnail to apply the picture style.

■ **Continue to the next page to complete the skill**

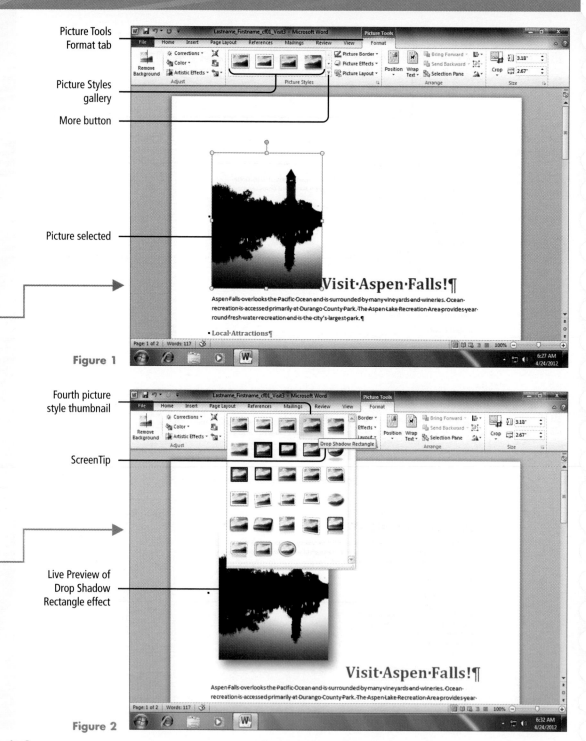

Picture Tools
Format tab

Picture Styles
gallery

More button

Picture selected

Figure 1

Fourth picture
style thumbnail

ScreenTip

Live Preview of
Drop Shadow
Rectangle effect

Figure 2

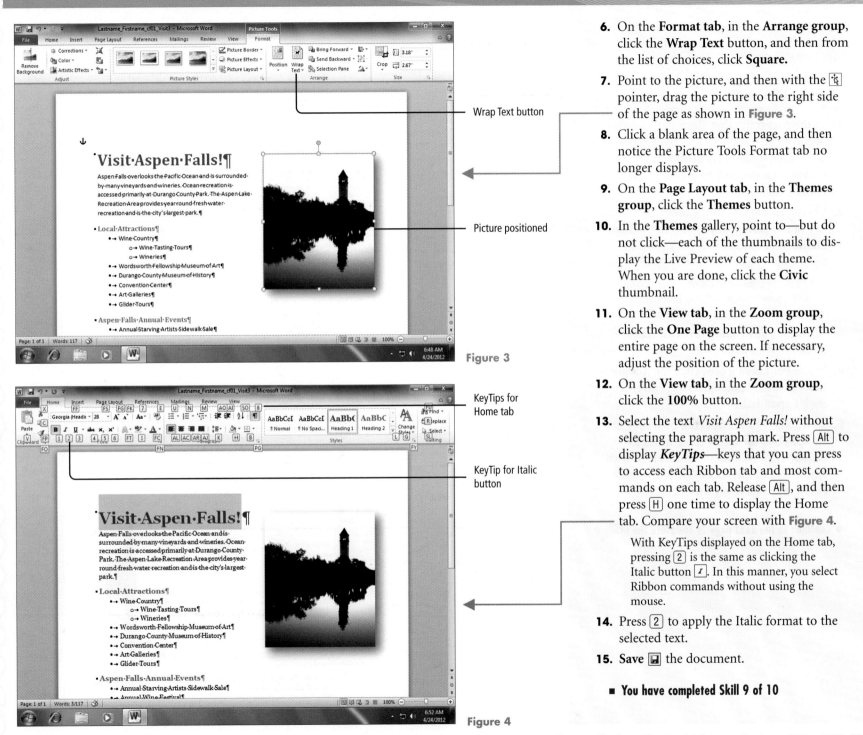

Wrap Text button

Picture positioned

Figure 3

KeyTips for Home tab

KeyTip for Italic button

Figure 4

6. On the **Format tab**, in the **Arrange group**, click the **Wrap Text** button, and then from the list of choices, click **Square.**

7. Point to the picture, and then with the pointer, drag the picture to the right side of the page as shown in **Figure 3.**

8. Click a blank area of the page, and then notice the Picture Tools Format tab no longer displays.

9. On the **Page Layout tab**, in the **Themes group**, click the **Themes** button.

10. In the **Themes** gallery, point to—but do not click—each of the thumbnails to display the Live Preview of each theme. When you are done, click the **Civic** thumbnail.

11. On the **View tab**, in the **Zoom group**, click the **One Page** button to display the entire page on the screen. If necessary, adjust the position of the picture.

12. On the **View tab**, in the **Zoom group**, click the **100%** button.

13. Select the text *Visit Aspen Falls!* without selecting the paragraph mark. Press [Alt] to display *KeyTips*—keys that you can press to access each Ribbon tab and most commands on each tab. Release [Alt], and then press [H] one time to display the Home tab. Compare your screen with **Figure 4.**

    With KeyTips displayed on the Home tab, pressing [2] is the same as clicking the Italic button [*I*]. In this manner, you select Ribbon commands without using the mouse.

14. Press [2] to apply the Italic format to the selected text.

15. **Save** [💾] the document.

■ **You have completed Skill 9 of 10**

► Commands can be accessed in *dialog boxes*—boxes where you can select multiple settings.

► You can also access commands by right-clicking objects in a document.

1. In the paragraph that starts *Aspen Falls overlooks the Pacific Ocean*, **triple-click**—click three times fairly quickly without moving the mouse—to highlight the entire paragraph.

2. On the **Home tab**, in the lower right corner of the **Font group**, point to the **Font Dialog Box Launcher** as shown in **Figure 1**.

   The buttons at the lower right corner of most groups open a dialog box with choices that may not be available on the Ribbon.

3. Click the **Font Dialog Box Launcher** to open the Font dialog box.

4. In the **Font** dialog box, click the **Advanced tab**. Click the **Spacing arrow**, and then click **Expanded**.

5. To the right of the **Spacing** box, click the **By spin box up arrow** three times to display *1.3 pt*. Compare your screen with **Figure 2**, and then click **OK** to close the dialog box and apply the changes.

■ **Continue to the next page to complete the skill**

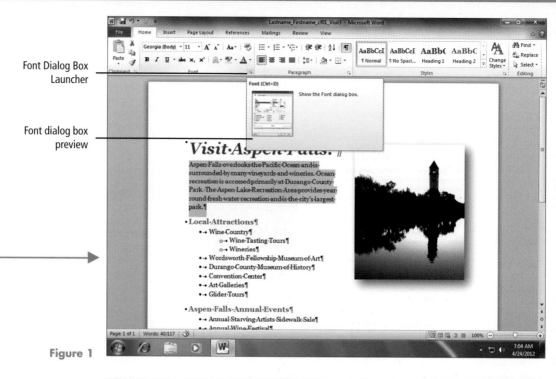

Font Dialog Box Launcher

Font dialog box preview

Figure 1

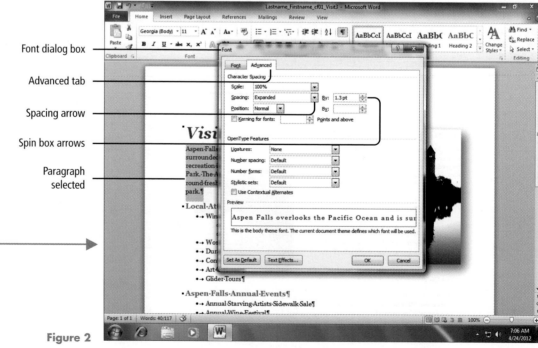

Font dialog box

Advanced tab

Spacing arrow

Spin box arrows

Paragraph selected

Figure 2

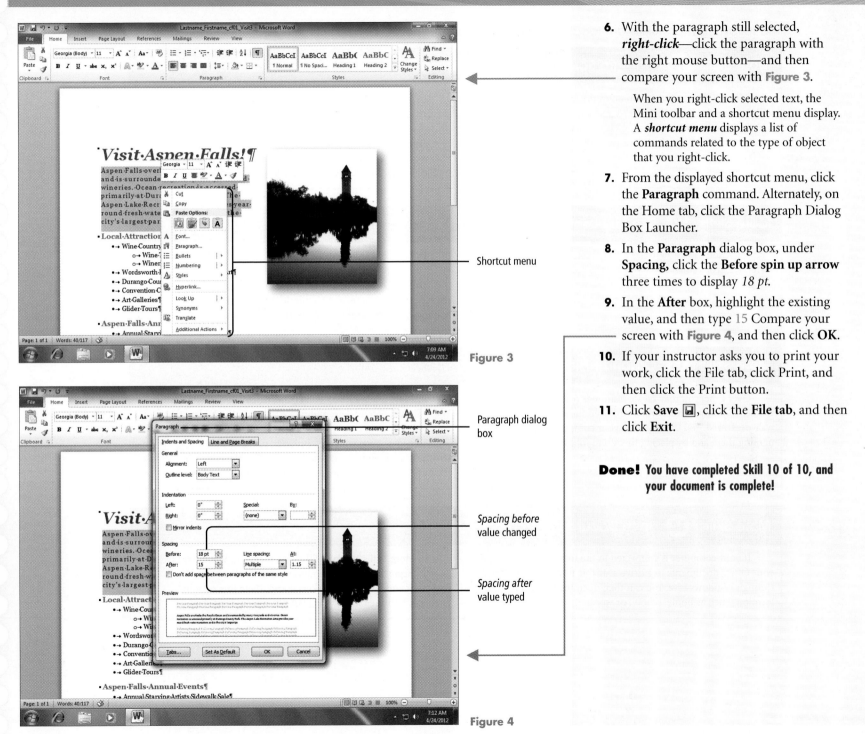

6. With the paragraph still selected, *right-click*—click the paragraph with the right mouse button—and then compare your screen with **Figure 3**.

> When you right-click selected text, the Mini toolbar and a shortcut menu display. A *shortcut menu* displays a list of commands related to the type of object that you right-click.

7. From the displayed shortcut menu, click the **Paragraph** command. Alternately, on the Home tab, click the Paragraph Dialog Box Launcher.

8. In the **Paragraph** dialog box, under **Spacing,** click the **Before spin up arrow** three times to display *18 pt.*

9. In the **After** box, highlight the existing value, and then type *15* Compare your screen with **Figure 4**, and then click **OK.**

10. If your instructor asks you to print your work, click the File tab, click Print, and then click the Print button.

11. Click **Save** 🖫, click the **File tab**, and then click **Exit.**

Shortcut menu

Figure 3

Paragraph dialog box

Spacing before value changed

Spacing after value typed

Done! You have completed Skill 10 of 10, and your document is complete!

Figure 4

The following More Skills are located at **www.pearsonhighered.com/skills**

More Skills Capture Screens with the Snipping Tool

Some of the work that you do in this book cannot be graded without showing your computer screens to the grader. You can use the Snipping Tool to create pictures of your screens. Snip files can be printed or submitted electronically.

In More Skills 11, you will use the Snipping Tool to create a picture of your screen and then copy the picture into a Word document.

To begin, open your web browser, navigate to www.pearsonhighered.com/skills, locate the name of your textbook, and then follow the instructions on the website.

More Skills Use Microsoft Office Help

Microsoft Office 2010 has a Help system in which you can search for articles that show you how to accomplish tasks.

In More Skills 12, you will use the Office 2010 Help system to view an article on how to customize the Help window.

To begin, open your web browser, navigate to www.pearson highered.com/skills, locate the name of your textbook, and then follow the instructions on the website.

More Skills Organize Files

Over time, you may create hundreds of files using Microsoft Office. To find your files when you need them, they need to be well-organized. You can organize your computer files by carefully naming them and by placing them into folders.

In More Skills 13, you will create, delete, and rename folders. You will then copy, delete, and move files into the folders that you created.

To begin, open your web browser, navigate to www.pearsonhighered.com/skills, locate the name of your textbook, and then follow the instructions on the website.

More Skills Save Documents to Windows Live

If your computer is connected to the Internet, you can save your Office documents to a drive available to you free of charge through Windows Live. You can then open the files from other locations such as home, school, or work.

In More Skills 14, you will save a memo to Windows Live.

To begin, open your web browser, navigate to www.pearsonhighered.com/skills, locate the name of your textbook, and then follow the instructions on the website.

Key Terms

Online Help Skills

1. **Start** 🕐 Word. In the upper right corner of the Word window, click the **Help** button 🔘. In the **Help** window, click the **Maximize** 🔲 button.

2. Click in the search box, type Create a document and then click the **Search** button. In the search results, click **Create a document**.

3. Read the article's introduction, and then below **What do you want to do**, click **Start a document from a template**. Compare your screen with Figure 1.

Figure 1

4. Read the Start a document from a template section to see if you can answer the following: What types of documents are available as templates? On the New tab, under Available Templates, what are the two general locations that you can find templates?

Matching

Match each term in the second column with its correct definition in the first column by writing the letter of the term on the blank line in front of the correct definition.

____ **1.** A feature that displays the result of a formatting change if you select it.

____ **2.** A line between the cells in a table or spreadsheet.

____ **3.** A mode where you can open and view a file, but you cannot save your changes.

____ **4.** A view where you prepare your document or spreadsheet for printing.

____ **5.** Quickly click the left mouse button two times without moving the mouse.

____ **6.** To insert text, delete text, or replace text in an Office document, spreadsheet, or presentation.

____ **7.** A command that moves a copy of the selected text or object to the Clipboard.

____ **8.** A command that removes the selected text or object and stores it in the Clipboard.

____ **9.** To change the appearance of the text.

____ **10.** A menu that displays a list of commands related to the type of object that you right-clicked on.

A Copy

B Cut

C Double-click

D Edit

E Format

F Grid line

G Live Preview

H Page Layout

I Read-only

J Shortcut

Multiple Choice

Choose the correct answer.

1. The flashing vertical line that indicates where text will be inserted when you start typing.
   A. Cell reference
   B. Insertion point
   C. KeyTip

2. A button used to turn a feature both on and off.
   A. Contextual button
   B. On/Off button
   C. Toggle button

3. The box formed by the intersection of a row and column.
   A. Cell
   B. Cell reference
   C. Insertion point

4. Until you save a document, it is stored only here.
   A. Clipboard
   B. Live Preview
   C. RAM

5. The combination of a number on the left side and a letter on the top of a spreadsheet that addresses a cell.
   A. Coordinates
   B. Cell reference
   C. Insertion point

6. A temporary storage area that holds text or an object that has been cut or copied.
   A. Clipboard
   B. Dialog box
   C. Live Preview

7. A toolbar with common formatting buttons that displays after you select text.
   A. Gallery toolbar
   B. Mini toolbar
   C. Taskbar toolbar

8. Informational text that displays when you point to commands or thumbnails on the Ribbon.
   A. Live Preview
   B. ScreenTip
   C. Shortcut menu

9. A visual display of choices from which you can choose.
   A. Gallery
   B. Options menu
   C. Shortcut menu

10. An icon that displays on the Ribbon to indicate the key that you can press to access Ribbon commands.
    A. KeyTip
    B. ScreenTip
    C. ToolTip

Topics for Discussion

1. You have briefly worked with three Microsoft Office programs: Word, Excel, and PowerPoint. Based on your experience, describe the overall purpose of each of these programs.

2. Many believe that computers enable offices to go paperless—that is, to share files electronically instead of printing and then distributing them. What are the advantages of sharing files electronically, and in what situations would it be best to print documents?

Create Documents with Word 2010

▶ Microsoft Office Word is one of the most common programs that individuals use on a computer.

▶ Use Word to create simple documents such as memos, reports, or letters and to create sophisticated documents that include tables and graphics.

Your starting screen will look similar to this:

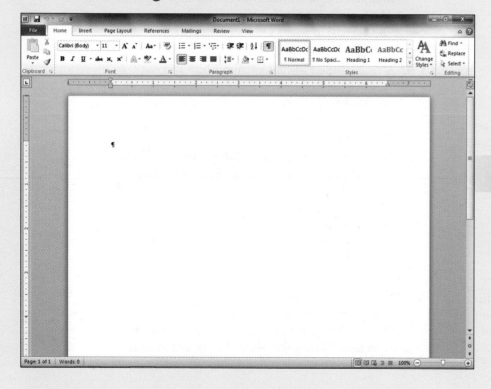

SKILLS

Skills 1-10 Training

At the end of this chapter, you will be able to:

Skill 1 Create New Documents and Enter Text
Skill 2 Edit Text and Use Keyboard Shortcuts
Skill 3 Select Text
Skill 4 Insert Text from Other Documents
Skill 5 Change Fonts, Font Sizes, and Font Styles
Skill 6 Insert and Work with Graphics
Skill 7 Check Spelling and Grammar
Skill 8 Use the Thesaurus and Set Proofing Options
Skill 9 Create Document Footers
Skill 10 Work with the Print Page and Save Documents in Other Formats

MORE SKILLS

More Skills 11 Split and Arrange Windows
More Skills 12 Insert Symbols
More Skills 13 Use Collect and Paste to Create Documents
More Skills 14 Insert Screen Shots into Documents

Outcome

Using the skills listed to the left will enable you to create documents like these:

ASPEN FALLS PUBLIC LIBRARY

255 Elm Street
Aspen Falls, CA 93463

May 5, 2012

Dr. Janis Imlay
Aspen Falls Community College
1 College Drive
Aspen Falls, CA 93464

Dear Dr. Imlay:

Subject: New Logo for Library

Thank you so much for your letter offering the services of your graphic design students for library-related projects. We currently have a project in mind that might benefit both the library and your students.

We want to update our logo to more accurately reflect the wide variety of services offered in a modern library. A logo contest would be a great idea. Call me at (805) 555-1011 to discuss this further.

I have attached a list of library activities to give the students an idea of some of the things we do.

Sincerely,

Douglas Hopkins, Director

Lastname_Firstname_w01_Library

Book Discussion Groups

There are several different book discussion groups, all led by volunteer moderators from the community. Some discussion groups focus on different types of books, such as biographies, history, fiction, classics, science and technology, and Spanish language literature.

Computer Training

Computer training is offered in the computer lab of the main branch only. The following classes are offered once a month and others are offered intermittently:

- Introduction to Computers
- Microsoft Word
- Microsoft Excel
- Adobe Photoshop
- Windows XP and Vista
- Using the Internet

Speakers and Entertainers

The library brings in noted authors once a month for an ongoing lecture series. Folk singers, small jazz ensembles, and other musical groups perform in the Hawken Community Room as they can be booked.

Bookmobile

A second bookmobile has been added, and routes are displayed on the library website. Bookmobiles visit each school in the district at least once a week.

Story Time

Story times are available in the Hawken Community Room on Saturday morning for toddlers, Saturday afternoon for early elementary students, and Sunday afternoon for kids interested in chapter books.

Game Night

Games are played in the Hawken Community Room on Friday evenings after the library closes at 6 p.m. Among the more popular games are chess, bridge, and backgammon. Experts are available to help patrons learn the games or improve their skills.

Electronic Book Downloads

More than 1,000 eBooks are available for download to an MP3 player. Library patrons can check these books out for three weeks, and can renew them one time. The books range from today's popular fiction to the classics.

Lastname_Firstname_w01_Library

You will save these documents as:

Lastname_Firstname_w01_Library
Lastname_Firstname_w01_Library_2003

In this chapter, you will create documents for the Aspen Falls City Hall, which provides essential services for the citizens and visitors of Aspen Falls, California.

Introduction

- ▶ Entering text, formatting text, and navigating within a Word document are the first basic skills you need to work efficiently with Word.

- ▶ You can change the font and font size, and add emphasis to text, but use caution not to apply too many different formats to your text. This can be distracting to the reader.

- ▶ It is easy to insert a picture into a Word document, and doing so increases the visual appeal and the reader's interest. Pictures should be clearly associated with the surrounding text and should not be inserted just to have a picture in the document.

- ▶ It is never acceptable to have errors in spelling, grammar, or word usage in your documents; you can use Word to prevent this from happening.

Time to complete all
10 skills – 50 minutes

Find your student data files here:

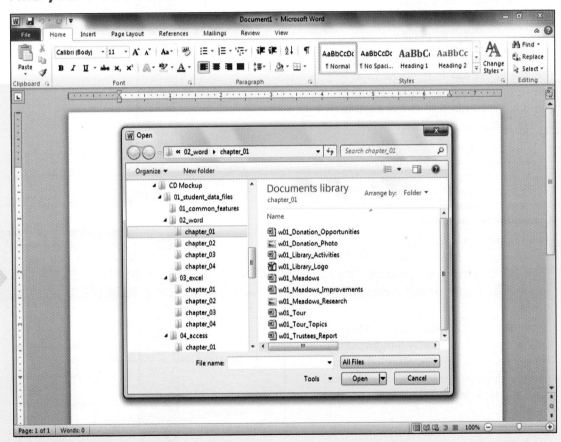

Student data files needed for this chapter:

- New blank Word document
- w01_Library_Activities

► When you start Microsoft Office Word 2010, a blank document displays.

► The first time you save the document, give it a name and choose a storage location. Then, save your changes frequently.

1. On the taskbar, click the **Start** button 🍥. From the **Start** menu, locate and then start **Microsoft Word 2010**.

2. In the lower right corner of your screen, if necessary, click the **Print Layout** button 🔲.

3. On the **Home tab**, in the **Paragraph group**, click the **Show/Hide** button ¶ until it displays in gold indicating it is active, as shown in **Figure 1**.

> When you press [Enter], [Spacebar], or [Tab] on your keyboard, characters display in your document to represent these keystrokes. These characters do not print and are referred to as *formatting marks* or *nonprinting characters*.

4. In all uppercase letters, type ASPEN FALLS PUBLIC LIBRARY and press [Enter]. Type 255 Elm Street and press [Enter]. Type Aspen Falls, CA 93463 and press [Enter] two times.

5. Type May 5, 2012 and press [Enter] three times; type Dr. Janis Imlay and press [Enter]; type Aspen Falls Community College and press [Enter]; type 1 College Drive and press [Enter]; and type Aspen Falls, CA 93464 and press [Enter].

6. Type Dear Dr. Imlay: and press [Enter]. Type Subject: New Logo for Library and press [Enter]. Compare your screen with **Figure 2**.

■ **Continue to the next page to complete the skill**

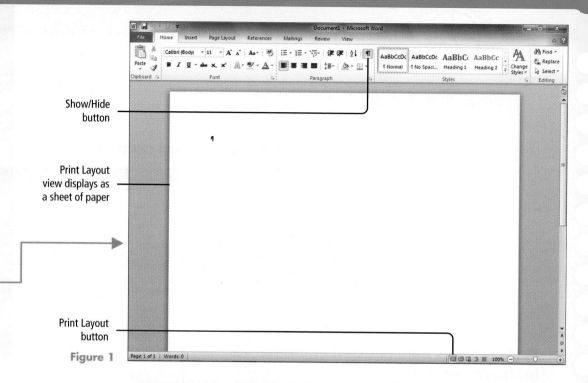

Show/Hide button

Print Layout view displays as a sheet of paper

Print Layout button

Figure 1

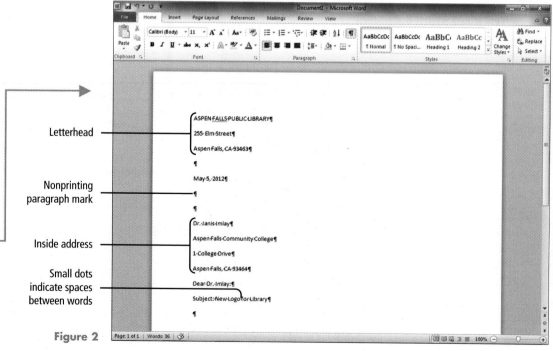

Letterhead

Nonprinting paragraph mark

Inside address

Small dots indicate spaces between words

Figure 2

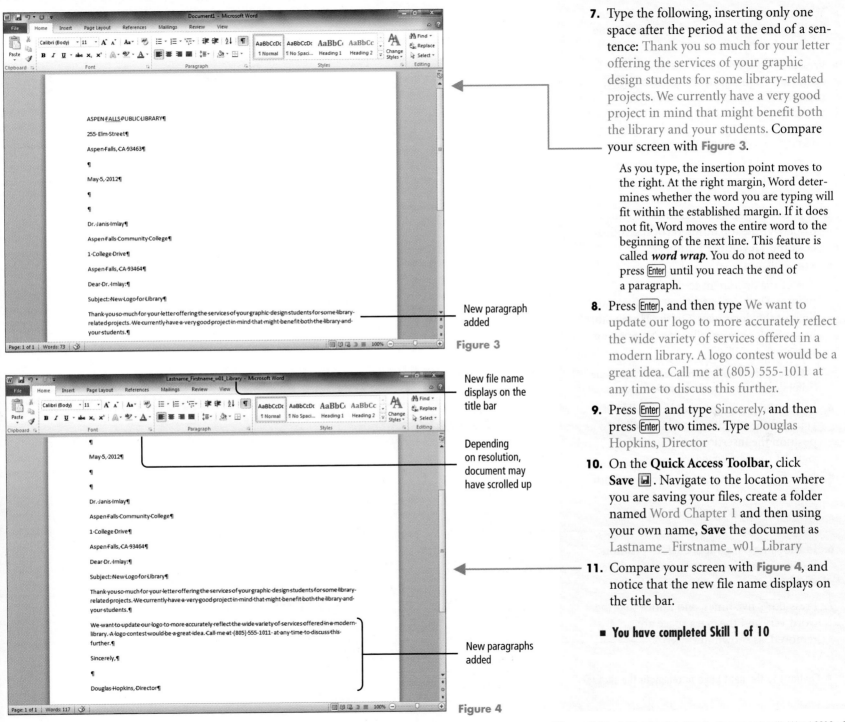

Figure 3

New paragraph added

New file name displays on the title bar

Depending on resolution, document may have scrolled up

New paragraphs added

Figure 4

7. Type the following, inserting only one space after the period at the end of a sentence: Thank you so much for your letter offering the services of your graphic design students for some library-related projects. We currently have a very good project in mind that might benefit both the library and your students. Compare your screen with **Figure 3**.

As you type, the insertion point moves to the right. At the right margin, Word determines whether the word you are typing will fit within the established margin. If it does not fit, Word moves the entire word to the beginning of the next line. This feature is called *word wrap*. You do not need to press Enter until you reach the end of a paragraph.

8. Press Enter, and then type We want to update our logo to more accurately reflect the wide variety of services offered in a modern library. A logo contest would be a great idea. Call me at (805) 555-1011 at any time to discuss this further.

9. Press Enter and type Sincerely, and then press Enter two times. Type Douglas Hopkins, Director

10. On the **Quick Access Toolbar**, click **Save** . Navigate to the location where you are saving your files, create a folder named Word Chapter 1 and then using your own name, **Save** the document as Lastname_ Firstname_w01_Library

11. Compare your screen with **Figure 4**, and notice that the new file name displays on the title bar.

■ **You have completed Skill 1 of 10**

► You can use a combination of keys on the keyboard to move quickly to the beginning or end of a document.

► Pressing Bksp removes characters to the left of the insertion point, and pressing Delete removes characters to the right of the insertion point.

1. Hold down Ctrl, and then press Home.

   This combination of keys—a *keyboard shortcut*—moves the insertion point to the beginning of the document.

2. If horizontal and vertical rulers do not display, at the top of the vertical scrollbar, click the **View Ruler** button.

3. Move the pointer to the left of the first line of the document to display the pointer. Drag down to select the first two lines of the document. On the **Home tab**, in the **Styles group**, click the **No Spacing** button.

   Extra space should be removed between the lines of the letterhead and inside address.

4. Locate the paragraph that begins *Thank you*, and then in the second line, click to position the insertion point just to the right of the word *good*.

5. Press Bksp five times, and notice that both the word *good* and the extra space between *very* and *good* are removed, as shown in **Figure 1**.

6. In the same paragraph, click to position the insertion point just to the left of the word *very*.

7. Press Delete five times, and notice that the word *very* and the extra space are removed, as shown in **Figure 2**.

■ **Continue to the next page to complete the skill**

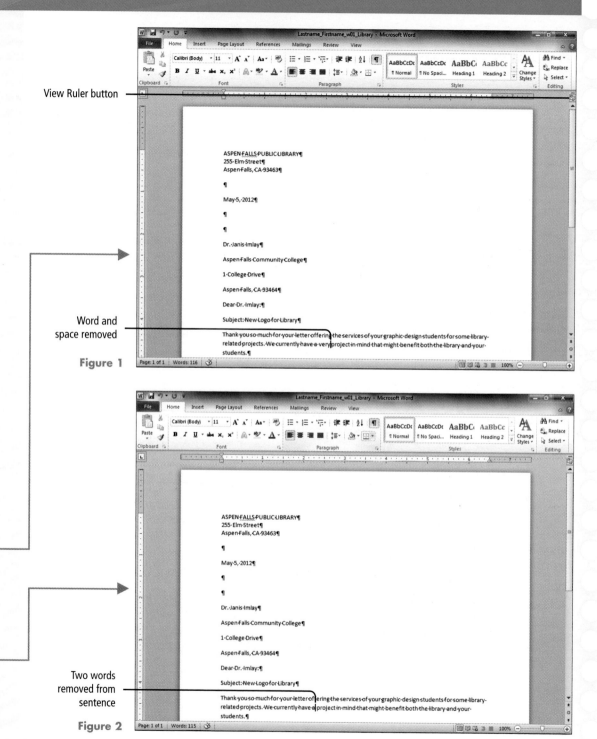

View Ruler button

Word and space removed

Figure 1

Two words removed from sentence

Figure 2

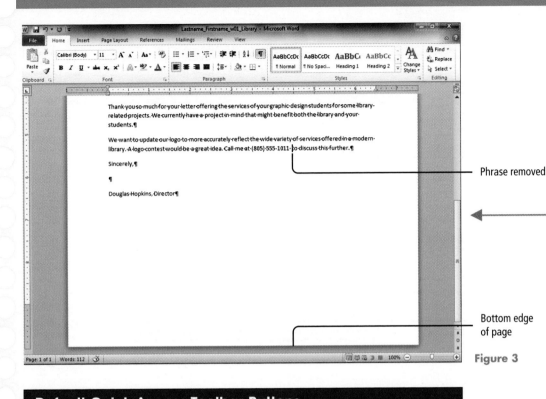

Phrase removed

Bottom edge
of page

Figure 3

Default Quick Access Toolbar Buttons

Button name	Button	Description
Save	🖫	Saves the current document. If the document has not been saved, the button displays the Save As dialog box.
Undo	↶	Reverses the last action or series of actions.
Repeat	↻	Repeats the last action; shares the same button location as the Redo button.
Redo	↷	Displays instead of the Repeat button if the Undo command has been used; reverses the action of the Undo button.

Figure 4

8. Press Ctrl + End to move to the end of the document.

   The insertion point is positioned at the end of the last paragraph, and the bottom edge of the page displays at the bottom of the screen.

9. In the last paragraph of the letter body, which begins *We want to update*, locate the phrase *at any time*. Use either Bksp or Delete to remove the phrase and the extra space, and then compare your screen with **Figure 3**.

10. On the **Quick Access Toolbar**, click the **Save** button 🖫. Alternately, hold down Ctrl, and then press S.

    This new saved version of your file overwrites the previous version.

11. Take a moment to examine the default buttons on the Quick Access Toolbar—your toolbar may display additional buttons—summarized in the table in **Figure 4**.

12. Press Ctrl + Home to move the insertion point to the beginning of the document and display the top edge of the page.

- **You have completed Skill 2 of 10**

▶ To format text, first select the text, and then make formatting changes. You can also select text and then delete it.

▶ You can insert text at the insertion point by typing new text. You can also insert text by selecting existing text and then typing new text.

1. In the first line of the document, point just to the left of *ASPEN*. Hold down the left mouse button, and then drag to the right to select the entire line, including the paragraph mark. Notice that selected text is highlighted.

2. From the Mini toolbar, click the **Center** button to center the first line of text.

3. Repeat this procedure to center the second and third lines of the library address.

4. In the paragraph that begins *Thank you*, in the first line, point to the word *some*, and then double-click. Notice that double-clicking in this manner selects a single word and the Mini toolbar displays, as shown in **Figure 1**.

5. With the word *some* selected, press Delete.

    When you double-click to select and delete a word, the selected word is deleted, along with its following space.

6. In the paragraph *Dr. Janis Imlay*, point to any word and triple-click. Notice that the entire paragraph is selected. On the **Home tab**, in the **Styles group**, click the **No Spacing** button.

7. Repeat this procedure to remove the extra spacing from the two paragraphs below *Dr. Janis Imlay*. Compare your screen with **Figure 2**.

■ **Continue to the next page to complete the skill**

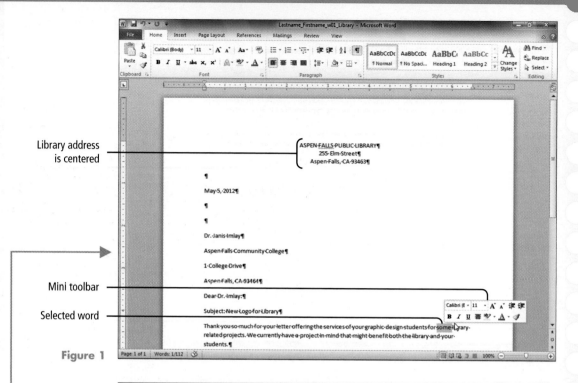

Library address is centered

Mini toolbar

Selected word

Figure 1

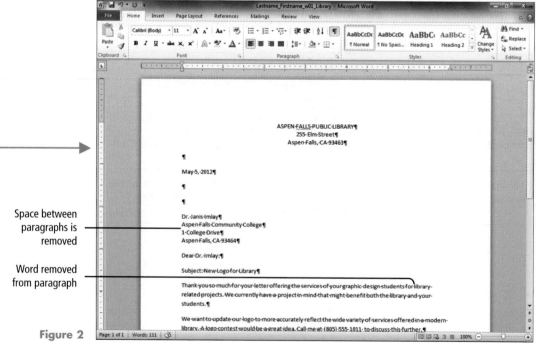

Space between paragraphs is removed

Word removed from paragraph

Figure 2

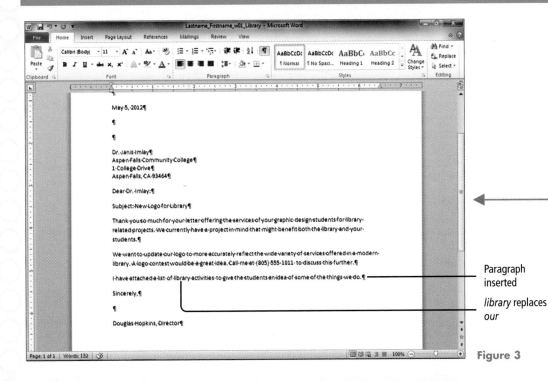

Paragraph
inserted

library replaces
our

Figure 3

8. In the paragraph that begins *We want to,* click to position the insertion point at the end of the paragraph—following the period after *further.*

9. Press Enter one time, and then type I have attached a list of our activities to give the students an idea of some of the things we do.

10. In the same paragraph, double-click the word *our* to select it, type library and then compare your screen with **Figure 3**.

   Recall that when you select a word, phrase, sentence, or paragraph, anything you type will replace all of the selected text.

11. In the paragraph that begins *Thank you,* move the pointer into the left margin area next to the first line of the paragraph. When the 🔎 pointer displays, double-click. Notice that the entire paragraph is selected.

12. Click anywhere in the document to dese-lect the text. Hold down Ctrl, and then press A. Notice that all of the text in the document is selected. Alternately, display the 🔎 pointer in the left margin and triple-click to select the entire document.

13. Press Ctrl + Home.

   Using a keyboard shortcut to move the insertion point also deselects any selected text.

14. **Save** 🖫 the changes, and then take a moment to examine some ways to select text, described in the table in **Figure 4**.

▪ **You have completed Skill 3 of 10**

Selecting Text in a Document

To select	Do this
A portion of text	Hold down the left mouse button and drag from the beginning to the end of the text you want to select.
A word	Double-click the word.
A sentence	Hold down Ctrl, and then click anywhere in the sentence.
A paragraph	Triple-click anywhere in the paragraph.
A line	Move the pointer to the left of the line. When the 🔎 pointer displays, click one time.
The entire document	Hold down Ctrl and press A. Alternately, display the 🔎 pointer in the left margin and triple-click.

Figure 4

► Objects, such as a text file or a graphic, can be inserted into a document.

► Inserted text displays at the insertion point location.

1. Press [Ctrl] + [End] to move the insertion point to the end of the document.

2. Press [Ctrl] + [Enter] to create a page break, as shown in **Figure 1**.

   A *manual page break*—forcing a page to end at a location you specify—is added at the end of Page 1, and a new blank page is created. A manual page break indicator also displays below the text at the bottom of Page 1.

3. Press [Ctrl] + [Home] to move to the top of the document, and then notice that the active page and the number of pages in the document display on the status bar. Press [Ctrl] + [End] to move to the end of the document.

   The insertion point moves to the blank paragraph at the top of Page 2, and the top portion of Page 2 displays near the top of the Word document window.

4. On the Ribbon, click the **Insert tab**.

5. In the **Text group**, click the **Object button arrow**, and then compare your screen with **Figure 2**.

   The Object button is used to insert *objects*—items such as graphics, charts, or spreadsheets created by Word or other programs—or text from another Word file.

■ **Continue to the next page to complete the skill**

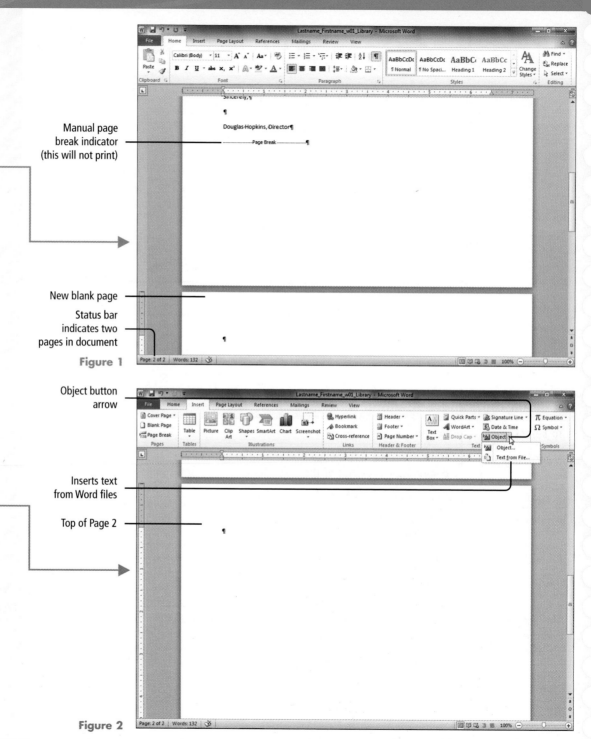

Manual page break indicator (this will not print)

New blank page

Status bar indicates two pages in document

Figure 1

Object button arrow

Inserts text from Word files

Top of Page 2

Figure 2

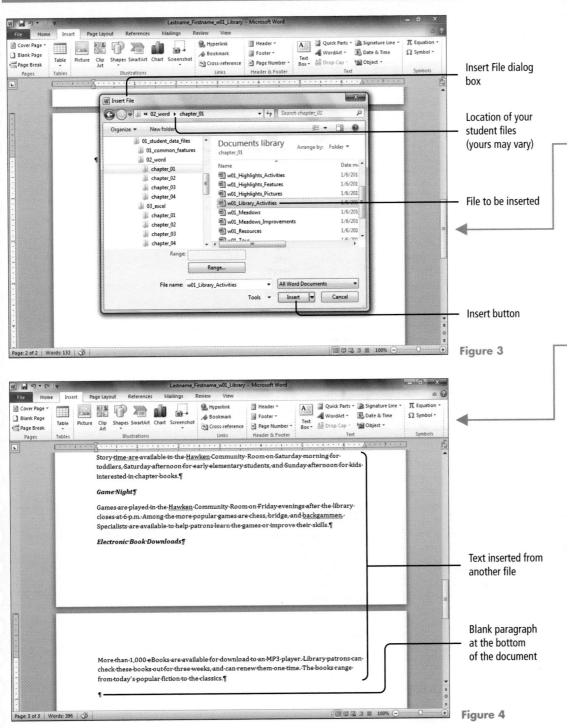

Insert File dialog box

Location of your student files (yours may vary)

File to be inserted

Insert button

Figure 3

Text inserted from another file

Blank paragraph at the bottom of the document

Figure 4

6. From the displayed list, click **Text from File** to display the **Insert File** dialog box.

   The Insert File dialog box is similar to the Open dialog box.

7. Navigate to the location of your student files, and then click the **w01_Library_ Activities** file. Compare your screen with **Figure 3**.

8. In the lower right corner of the **Insert File** dialog box, click the **Insert** button.

   All of the text from the w01_Library_ Activities file is copied into the current document at the insertion point location. The original file remains unchanged. The spelling and grammar errors in the inserted document will be corrected in Skill 7.

9. If necessary, press Ctrl + End to move to the end of the document, and notice that an extra blank paragraph displays, as shown in **Figure 4**.

10. Press Bksp one time to remove the blank paragraph from the end of the document.

11. Press Ctrl + Home to move the insertion point to the beginning of the document, and then **Save** 🔲 the changes.

   ■ **You have completed Skill 4 of 10**

► A *font* is a set of characters with the same design and shape.

► One way to format text is to change the font or font size.

► You can also add bold, italic, or underline emphasis to make text stand out from surrounding text. Bold, italic, and underline are referred to as *font styles*.

1. Click the **Home tab**. In the **Font group**, notice that Word's default font is **Calibri (Body)**, and the default font size is **11**.

   Fonts are measured in *points*, with one point equal to 1/72 of an inch.

2. Scroll so that you can view Page 2, click anywhere in the text, and then notice that the font is **Cambria (Headings)** and the font size is **12**.

3. Press $\boxed{\text{Ctrl}}$ + $\boxed{\text{A}}$ to select all of the text in the document. In the **Font group**, click the **Font arrow** $\boxed{\text{Calibri (Body)} \ \ \cdot}$, and then from the displayed list, point to—but do not click—**Arial Black**. Notice that Live Preview displays what the text would look like if you select the Arial Black font, as shown in **Figure 1**.

4. From the displayed **Font** list, click **Calibri (Body)** to change all of the text in the document to Calibri.

5. With the text still selected, in the **Font** group, click the **Font Size arrow** $\boxed{11 \ \cdot}$, and then click **11**.

6. On Page 2, click anywhere in the text to cancel the selection. Notice the change to the font and font size, as shown in **Figure 2**.

■ **Continue to the next page to complete the skill**

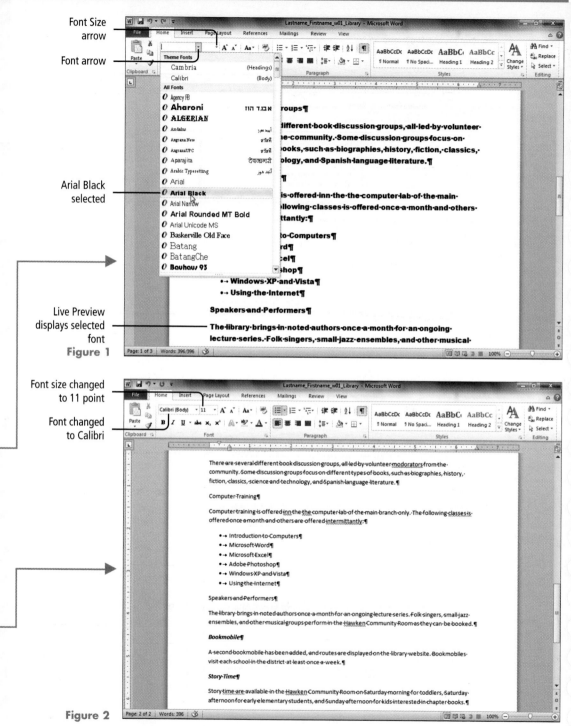

Font Size arrow

Font arrow

Arial Black selected

Live Preview displays selected font

Figure 1

Font size changed to 11 point

Font changed to Calibri

Figure 2

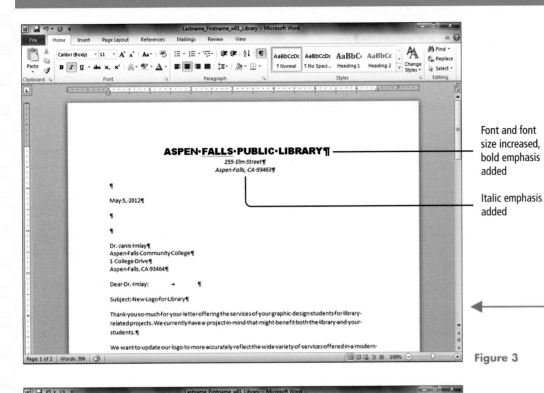

Font and font size increased, bold emphasis added

Italic emphasis added

Figure 3

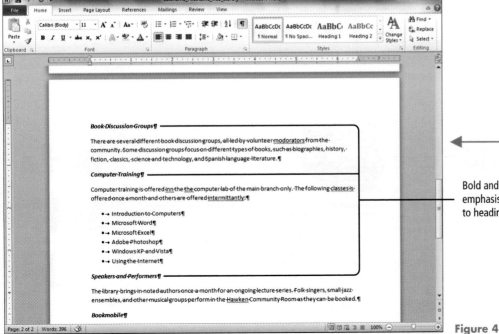

Bold and italic emphasis added to headings

Figure 4

7. Press Ctrl + Home to move to the beginning of the document. Move the pointer to the left of the first letterhead paragraph—the library name—to display the pointer, and then click one time to select the first paragraph.

8. On the Mini toolbar, click the **Font Size arrow**, and then click **16**. With the Mini toolbar still displayed, click the **Bold** button, click the **Font arrow**, and then click **Arial Black**.

9. In the two paragraphs that complete the letterhead, select both paragraphs. On the displayed Mini toolbar, click the **Italic** button. Click anywhere to deselect the text, and then compare your screen with **Figure 3**.

10. Scroll to view the top of Page 2. With the pointer to the left of the one-line paragraph *Book Discussion Groups*, click to select the entire line. On the Mini toolbar, click the **Bold** button, and then click the **Italic** button.

11. Select the heading *Computer Training*, and then hold down Ctrl and select the heading *Speakers and Performers*. On the Mini toolbar, apply **Bold** and **Italic**. Click anywhere to deselect the headings, and then compare your screen with **Figure 4**.

All of the topic headings are formatted consistently.

12. **Save** the document.

▪ **You have completed Skill 5 of 10**

▶ You can insert *clip art*—graphics and images included with Microsoft Office or obtained from other sources—anywhere in a document.

▶ You can also insert pictures that have been saved as files on your computer.

1. Scroll to position the top of Page 2 on your screen, and then click to position the insertion point to the left of the *B* in *Book Discussion Groups.*

2. Click the **Insert tab**. In the **Illustrations group**, click the **Clip Art** button.

3. In the **Clip Art** task pane, in the **Search for** box, type library

4. Click the **Results should be arrow**, and then clear all of the check boxes except **Illustrations**. Select the **Include Office.com content** check box, and then click the **Go** button.

5. Scroll down to display the picture shown in **Figure 1**. If you do not see this image, **Close** the Clip Art task pane. On the **Insert tab**, in the **Illustrations group**, click **Picture**, and navigate to your student files for this chapter. Select and insert the **w01_Library_Logo** file, and skip to **Step 8**.

6. In the **Clip Art** pane, click the library image indicated in Figure 1, and then compare your screen with **Figure 2**.

   The image is inserted at the insertion point location. By default, the image is inserted in the text in exactly the same manner that a character is inserted from the keyboard. Some of the text at the bottom of Page 2 moves to a new Page 3.

7. In the **Clip Art** task pane, click the **Close** button ⊠.

■ **Continue to the next page to complete the skill** ▶

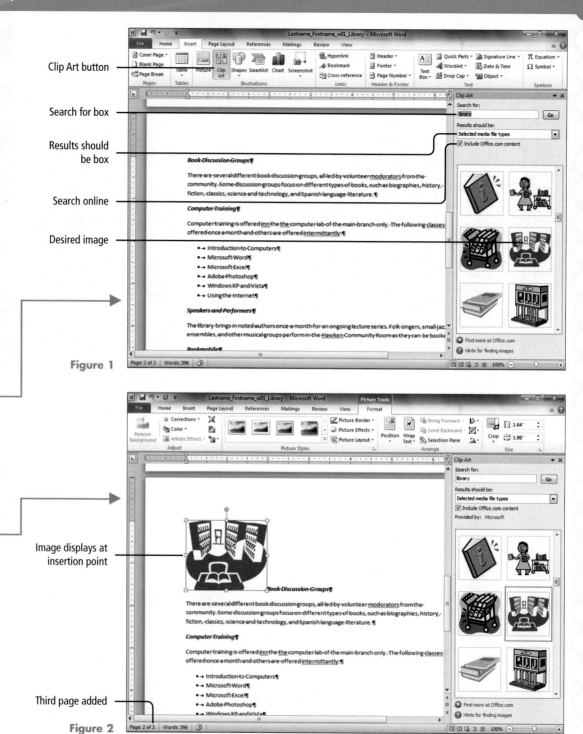

Figure 1

Figure 2

Clip Art button

Search for box

Results should be box

Search online

Desired image

Image displays at insertion point

Third page added

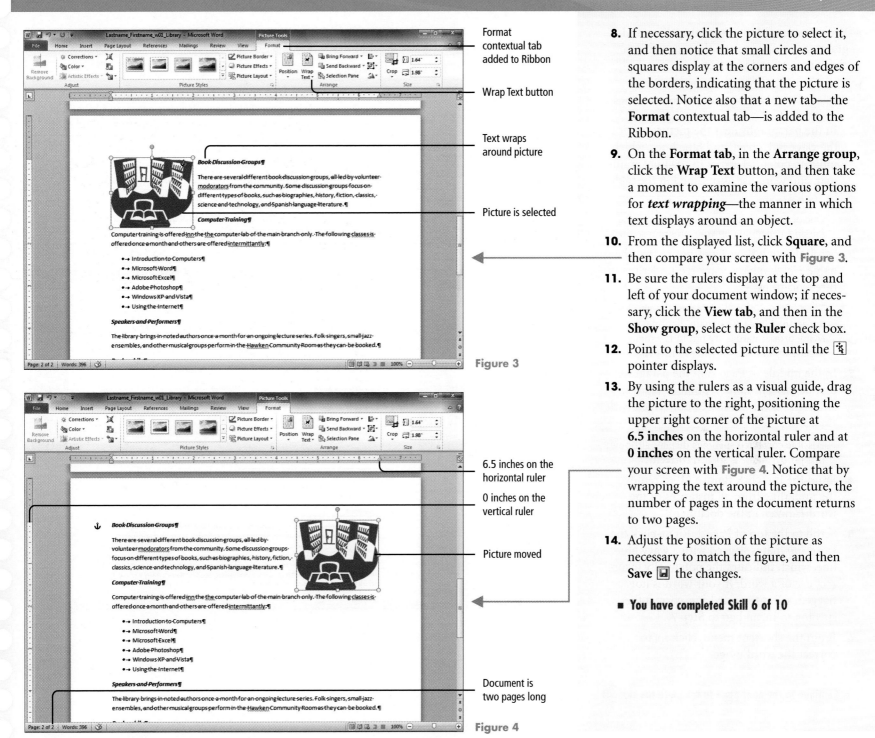

Format contextual tab added to Ribbon

Wrap Text button

Text wraps around picture

Picture is selected

Figure 3

6.5 inches on the horizontal ruler

0 inches on the vertical ruler

Picture moved

Document is two pages long

Figure 4

8. If necessary, click the picture to select it, and then notice that small circles and squares display at the corners and edges of the borders, indicating that the picture is selected. Notice also that a new tab—the **Format** contextual tab—is added to the Ribbon.

9. On the **Format tab**, in the **Arrange group**, click the **Wrap Text** button, and then take a moment to examine the various options for *text wrapping*—the manner in which text displays around an object.

10. From the displayed list, click **Square**, and then compare your screen with Figure 3.

11. Be sure the rulers display at the top and left of your document window; if necessary, click the **View tab**, and then in the **Show group**, select the **Ruler** check box.

12. Point to the selected picture until the [🛉] pointer displays.

13. By using the rulers as a visual guide, drag the picture to the right, positioning the upper right corner of the picture at **6.5 inches** on the horizontal ruler and at **0 inches** on the vertical ruler. Compare your screen with Figure 4. Notice that by wrapping the text around the picture, the number of pages in the document returns to two pages.

14. Adjust the position of the picture as necessary to match the figure, and then **Save** [💾] the changes.

■ **You have completed Skill 6 of 10**

► You can respond to potential spelling and grammar errors one at a time, or you can check the entire document.

► The number of potential grammar errors displayed by Word depends on your settings.

1. In the paragraphs near the picture, notice the wavy red, green, and blue lines, which indicate potential errors in spelling, grammar, and word use as outlined in the table in **Figure 1**.

   One or more of the wavy line colors may be missing, depending on your program settings.

2. Scroll through Page 2 and notice that the name *Hawken* has a wavy red underline in three locations.

   The wavy red underline means the word is not in the Office 2010 main dictionary. Many proper names are not in the main dictionary and are flagged as misspellings.

3. In the middle of Page 2, in the paragraph that begins *The library*, point to *Hawken* and right-click. Compare your screen with **Figure 2**.

   Possible corrected spellings display, although this proper name is spelled correctly.

4. From the list, click **Ignore All** to remove the underline from all instances of the word *Hawken* in the document.

5. Scroll to the top of Page 2. Right-click the word *inn* that is flagged with a wavy blue line, which indicates the potentially incorrect use of a word. If your word is not flagged, select the word *inn*, correct the spelling to **in**, and go to **Step 7**.

6. From the shortcut menu, click *in*, to correct the word usage.

■ **Continue to the next page to complete the skill**

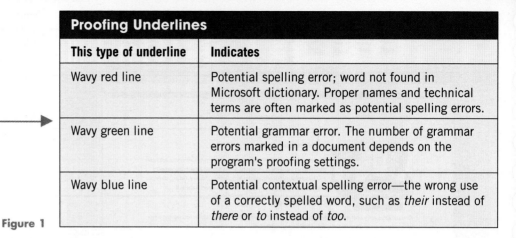

Proofing Underlines	
This type of underline	**Indicates**
Wavy red line	Potential spelling error; word not found in Microsoft dictionary. Proper names and technical terms are often marked as potential spelling errors.
Wavy green line	Potential grammar error. The number of grammar errors marked in a document depends on the program's proofing settings.
Wavy blue line	Potential contextual spelling error—the wrong use of a correctly spelled word, such as *their* instead of *there* or *to* instead of *too*.

Figure 1

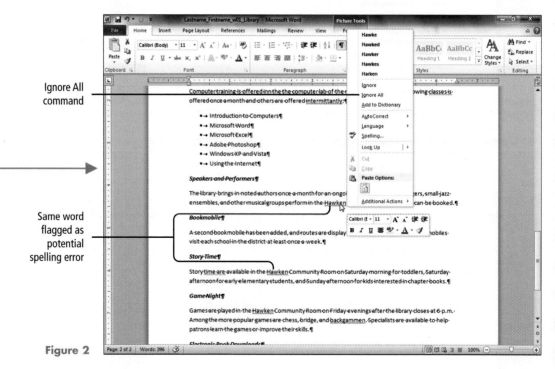

Ignore All command

Same word flagged as potential spelling error

Figure 2

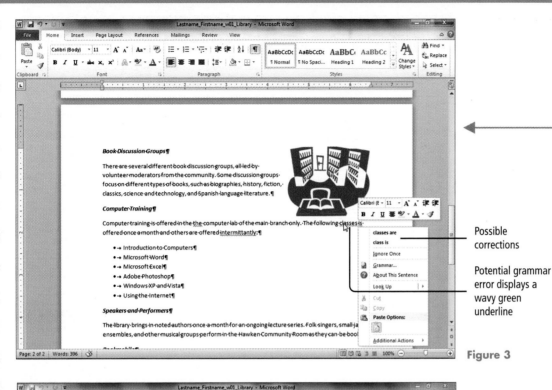

Possible corrections

Potential grammar error displays a wavy green underline

Figure 3

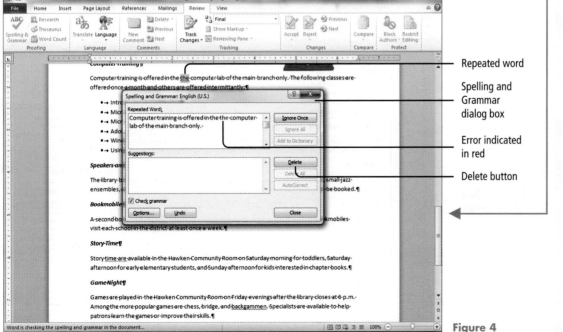

Repeated word

Spelling and Grammar dialog box

Error indicated in red

Delete button

Figure 4

7. Right-click *moderators*, which displays a wavy red line. Click the correct spelling **moderators**.

8. Right-click the text *classes is*, which displays a wavy green line indicating a potential grammar error. Compare your screen with **Figure 3**.

9. From the displayed list, click **classes are** to correct the grammatical error.

10. Scroll down and notice that there are additional spelling and grammar errors in the document. Press Ctrl + Home to move to the beginning of the document. Click the **Review tab**, and then in the **Proofing group**, click the **Spelling & Grammar** button. If a *Verb Confusion* error displays for *ASPEN FALLS*, click **Ignore Once**, and then compare your screen with **Figure 4**.

    The Spelling and Grammar dialog box displays a potential error—a repeated word.

11. In the **Spelling and Grammar** dialog box, click the **Delete** button to delete the repeated word. For the next selected error, notice under **Suggestions** that the correct spelling—*intermittently*—is highlighted. Click the **Change** button to correct the spelling.

12. For the grammatical error *time are*, click **times are**, and then click **Change**.

13. Correct the misspelled word *backgammen* by clicking **Change**.

14. Ignore any other errors, and then when a message indicates that the spelling and grammar check is complete, click **OK**. **Save** 💾 your document.

■ **You have completed Skill 7 of 10**

▶ Proofing tools include Spelling & Grammar checking, a Thesaurus, and Research tools.

▶ You can set proofing options to provide readability statistics for your document.

1. Scroll to the middle of Page 2 and locate the heading *Speakers and Performers*.

2. Double-click anywhere in *Performers* to select the word. On the **Review tab**, in the **Proofing group**, click the **Thesaurus** button. Notice that a **Research** task pane displays lists of similar words, as shown in **Figure 1**.

   A *thesaurus* lists words that have the same or similar meaning to the word you are looking up.

3. In the **Research** task pane, locate and point to *Entertainers*. To the right of the word, click the displayed arrow, and then click **Insert**. Notice that *Entertainers* replaces *Performers*. If an extra space displays to the left of *Entertainers*, remove the space.

4. In the second line of the paragraph that begins *Games are played*, locate and click anywhere in the word *Specialists*. In the **Proofing group**, click the **Thesaurus** button, and use the technique you just practiced to replace *Specialists* with **Experts**. Compare your screen with **Figure 2**.

5. In the **Research** task pane, click the **Close** button ⊠.

6. On the **Review tab**, in the **Proofing group**, click the **Word Count** button. Notice that the document statistics display, and include the number of pages, words, paragraphs, lines, and characters.

■ **Continue to the next page to complete the skill**

Thesaurus button

Research task pane

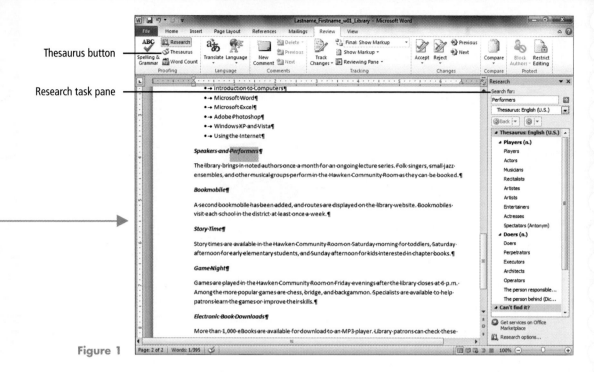

Figure 1

Two words have been changed

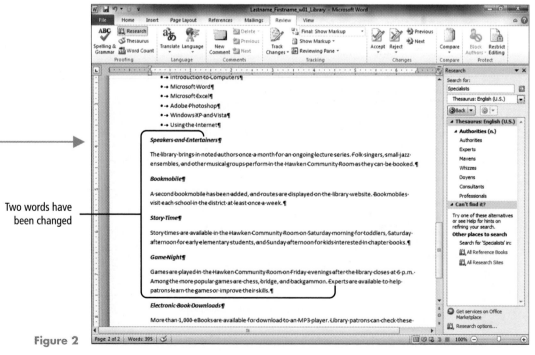

Figure 2

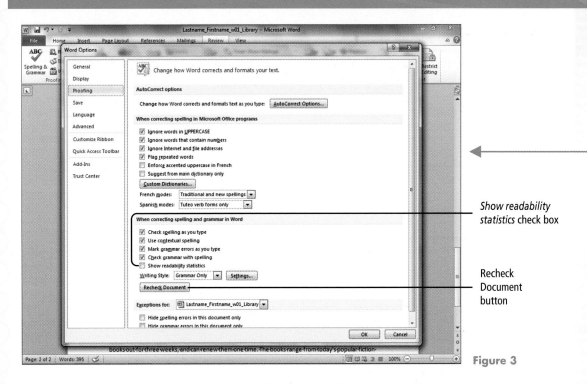

Figure 3

Show readability statistics check box

Recheck Document button

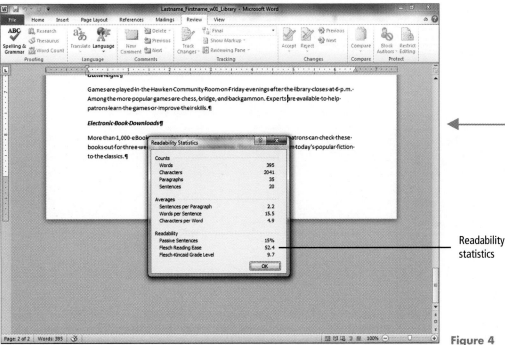

Figure 4

Readability statistics

7. In the **Word Count** dialog box, click the **Close** button.

8. Click the **File tab**. On the left side of the Backstage, click **Help**, and then on the **Help page**, click **Options**. On the left side of the **Word Options** dialog box, click **Proofing**, and then compare your screen with **Figure 3**.

   The Proofing options give you control over which potential spelling and grammar errors will be flagged, and lets you choose which items or rules to ignore.

9. In the **Word Options** dialog box, under **When correcting spelling and grammar in Word**, select the **Show readability statistics** check box, and then near the bottom of the dialog box, click **Recheck Document**.

10. Read the message, and then click **Yes** to recheck the spelling and grammar. Click **OK** to close the Word Options dialog box.

11. In the **Proofing** group, click the **Spelling & Grammar** button, and then ignore any errors that display. Notice that when the check is complete, a **Readability Statistics** dialog box displays, as shown in **Figure 4**.

    The Readability Statistics dialog box includes some of the information found in the Word Count dialog box, but it also includes information on the length of paragraphs, the number of words in sentences, and the reading level—shown at the bottom of the dialog box.

12. **Close** the **Readability Statistics** dialog box. Repeat **Steps 8** and **9**, clear the **Show readability statistics** check box, and then close the dialog box. **Save** the document.

   ■ **You have completed Skill 8 of 10**

► A *header* and *footer* are reserved areas for text, graphics, and fields that display at the top (header) or bottom (footer) of each page in a document.

► Throughout this book, you will insert the document file name in the footer of each document.

1. Press [Ctrl] + [Home] to move to the beginning of the document.

2. Click the **Insert tab**, and then in the **Header & Footer group**, click the **Footer** button. Compare your screen with **Figure 1**.

    Word provides several built-in footers. When you want to enter your own text, the Edit Footer command at the bottom of the gallery is used.

3. In the **Footer** gallery, use the vertical scroll bar to examine the footer formats that are available.

4. Below the **Footer** gallery, click **Edit Footer**. Notice that at the bottom of Page 1, below **Footer**, the insertion point is blinking in the footer, and the **Design** contextual tab displays on the Ribbon, as shown in **Figure 2**.

■ **Continue to the next page to complete the skill**

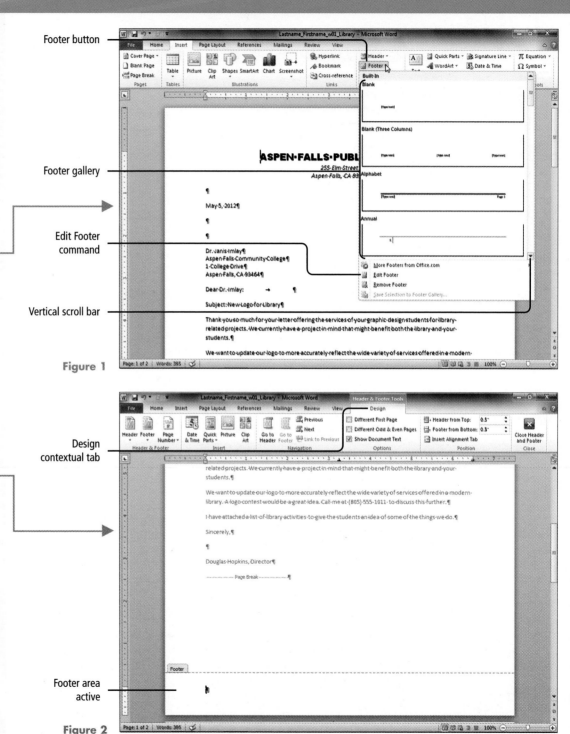

Footer button

Footer gallery

Edit Footer command

Vertical scroll bar

Figure 1

Design contextual tab

Footer area active

Figure 2

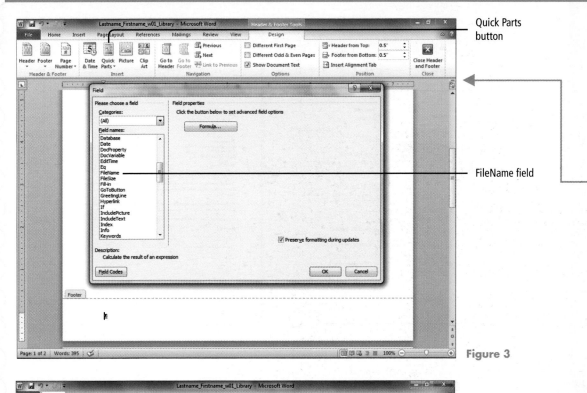

Quick Parts button

FileName field

Figure 3

5. On the **Design tab**, in the **Insert group**, click the **Quick Parts** button.

6. From the displayed list, click **Field**.

A *field* is a category of data—such as a file name, a page number, or the current date—that can be inserted into a document.

7. Under **Field names**, use the vertical scroll bar to see what types of fields are available, and then locate the **FileName** field. Compare your screen with **Figure 3**.

When a field name consists of two or more words, the spaces between the words are removed.

8. Under **Field names**, click **FileName**. Under **Format**, be sure (**none**) is selected, and then at the bottom of the **Field** dialog box, click **OK**.

The file name is added to the footer.

9. On the **Design tab**, in the **Close group**, click the **Close Header and Footer** button.

10. Scroll to display the bottom of Page 1 and the top of Page 2, and then compare your screen with **Figure 4**.

The text in the footer area displays in gray because the footer is inactive; while the document text is active, the footer text cannot be edited. When the footer area is active, the footer text is black, the document text is gray, and the footer text can be edited.

11. Save ▣ the document.

■ **You have completed Skill 9 of 10**

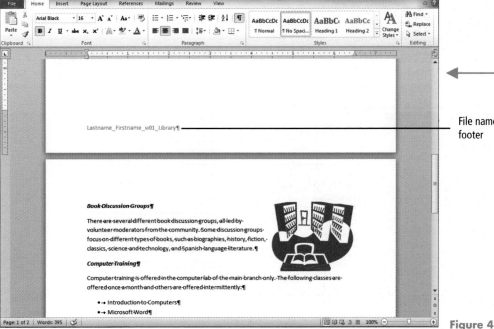

File name in footer

Figure 4

▶ Before you print a document, it is good practice to preview it on your screen so that you can see any final changes that are necessary.

▶ Using the Backstage Print page, you can choose which printer to use, which pages to print, and how many copies of the document to print.

▶ You can save documents in different formats so that people who do not have Word can read them.

1. Press [Ctrl] + [Home] to move to the beginning of the document.

2. Click the **File tab**. On the left side of the **Backstage**, click **Print**, and then compare your screen with **Figure 1.**

   Recall that print settings display on the left side of the Print page, and a preview of the current page of the printed document displays on the right. The Zoom percent displays at the bottom of the preview; yours may vary depending on your screen resolution.

3. Below the document preview, click the **Zoom In** ⊕ button as necessary to change the zoom level of the preview to **100%.**

4. Click the **Zoom percent** to display the **Zoom** dialog box. Under **Zoom to**, select the **Whole Page** option button, and then click **OK.**

5. On the right side of the **Print** page, at the bottom of the vertical scroll bar, click the **arrow** ▼ to display Page 2, as shown in **Figure 2**. Notice that the footer text is no longer gray in the preview.

6. At the top of the vertical scroll bar, click ▲ to display Page 1.

■ **Continue to the next page to complete the skill** ▶

Preview of first page of document

Print tab

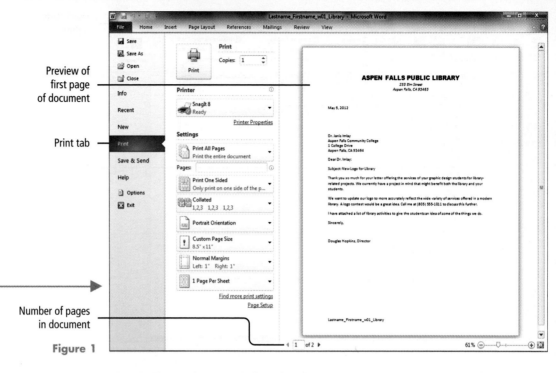

Number of pages in document

Figure 1

Second page of document

Footers display as black text

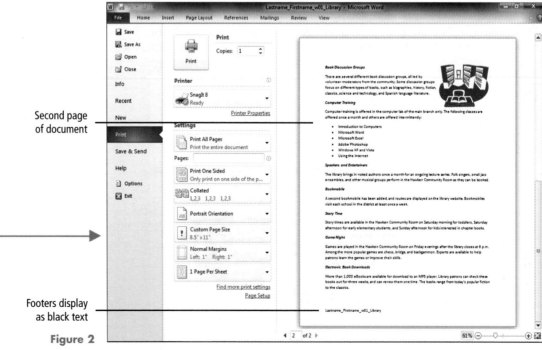

Figure 2

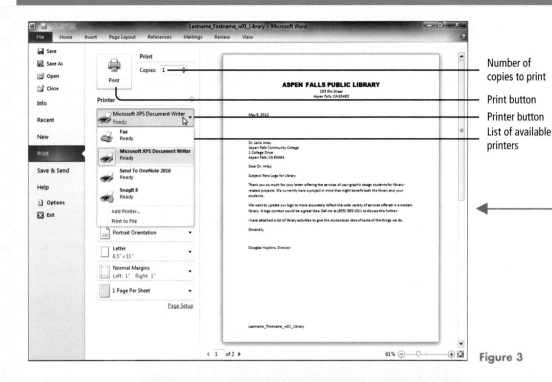

Number of copies to print

Print button

Printer button

List of available printers

Figure 3

7. Under **Printer**, click the **Printer** button, and then compare your screen with **Figure 3**.

   A list of printers that are available to your computer displays, as do other document destinations.

8. From the **Printer** list, select the printer you would like to use.

   You can use the Print page to select a printer, select the number of copies to print, and specify which document pages to print.

9. Be sure that the **Copies** is set to **1**. If you are printing your work for this project, at the top of the **Print** page, click the **Print** button—otherwise, do not click the **Print** button.

10. On the left side of the **Backstage**, click **Save As**. In the **Save As** dialog box, click the **Save as type** box, and then take a moment to examine the most common file formats for Word documents, which are summarized in the table in **Figure 4**.

11. From the list, click **Word 97-2003 Document**. Navigate to the **Word Chapter 1** folder, rename the file Lastname_Firstname_w01_Library_2003 and then click **Save**.

    Saving a document in an older format enables people with older software to open the document.

12. Display the footer area, right-click the file name, and then click **Update Field**. Close the footer area.

13. Click the **File tab**, and then under **Help**, click **Exit**.

14. Submit your printout or files as directed by your instructor.

Word Save As File Formats

Format	Descriptions
Word Document	Saves the document using the Word 2010 file format.
Word Template	Saves the document so that it can be used over and over, without altering the original document.
Word 97-2003 Document	Saves the file in earlier Word formats so that individuals using earlier versions of the program can open the document.
PDF	Saves the document in the popular Portable Document Format (PDF) display format, which can be opened on most computers.
XPS Document	Saves the document in the Microsoft XPS display format.
Other Formats	Lets you save a document as plain text with no formatting, in a universal file format such as Rich Text Format, or as a web page.

Figure 4

Done! You have completed Skill 10 of 10 and your document is complete!

The following More Skills are located at **www.pearsonhighered.com/skills**

More Skills ⑪ Split and Arrange Windows

You can split the Word screen, which lets you look at different parts of the same document at the same time. In a multiple-page document, this is convenient for viewing both the first page and the last page at the same time. You can also view two different documents side by side and make comparisons between the two.

In More Skills 11, you will open a multiple-page document, and split the screen. Then, you will open a second document and view both documents at the same time.

To begin, open your web browser, navigate to www.pearsonhighered.com/skills, locate the name of your textbook, and then follow the instructions on the website.

More Skills ⑫ Insert Symbols

There are many symbols that are used occasionally, but not often enough to put on a standard computer keyboard. Some examples of commonly inserted symbols include copyright and trademark symbols, mathematical operators, and special dashes that are longer than hyphens. These symbols can be found and inserted from the Symbols group on the Insert tab.

In More Skills 12, you will open a document and insert several symbols from the Special Characters list in the Symbol dialog box.

To begin, open your web browser, navigate to www.pearsonhighered.com/skills, locate the name of your textbook, and then follow the instructions on the website.

More Skills ⑬ Use Collect and Paste to Create Documents

To create a document by using text and objects from a variety of different sources, first collect all of the documents and images into the Office Clipboard, and then paste them into a new document.

In More Skills 13, you will open a document, collect two text files and two images on the Office Clipboard, and then construct a document from the collected items.

To begin, open your web browser, navigate to www.pearsonhighered.com/skills, locate the name of your textbook, and then follow the instructions on the website.

More Skills ⑭ Insert Screen Shots into Documents

When you are working on a document, you may want to include a screen shot from your computer—such as a screen from another program or a website—as a graphic in the document.

In More Skills 14, you will use a browser to go to a government website, and then create a copy of the screen and store it in the Clipboard. You will then paste the screen into a document.

To begin, open your web browser, navigate to www.pearsonhighered.com/skills, locate the name of your textbook, and then follow the instructions on the website.

Key Terms

Online Help Skills

1. **Start** 🏁 Word. In the upper right corner of the Word window, click the **Help** button 🔘. In the **Help** window, click the **Maximize** 🔲 button.

2. Click in the search box, type page numbers and then click the **Search** button 🔍. In the search results, click **Add or remove headers, footers, and page numbers**.

3. Read the article's introduction, and then below **What do you want to do?**, click **Add a page number without any other information**. Compare your screen with Figure 1.

Figure 1

4. Read the section to see if you can answer the following: What is a quick way to open a header or footer? How can you show page numbers in the *Page X of Y* format—for example, *Page 3 of 12?*

Matching

Match each term in the second column with its correct definition in the first column by writing the letter of the term on the blank line in front of the correct definition.

____ **1.** A character that indicates a paragraph, tab, or space on your screen, but that does not print when you print a Word document.

____ **2.** The color of the wavy line that indicates a potential spelling error.

____ **3.** The color of the wavy line that indicates a potential grammar error.

____ **4.** Forces a page to end, and places subsequent text at the top of the next page.

____ **5.** Graphics and images included with Microsoft Office or obtained from other sources.

____ **6.** A technology that shows the result of applying a formatting change as you point to it.

____ **7.** A unit of measurement for font sizes.

____ **8.** Automatically moves text from the right edge of a paragraph to the beginning of the next line as necessary to fit within the margins.

____ **9.** A reserved area for text, graphics, and fields that displays at the top of each page in a document.

____ **10.** A category of data—such as a file name, the page number, or the current date—that can be inserted into a document.

A Clip art

B Field

C Formatting mark

D Green

E Header

F Live Preview

G Manual page break

H Point

I Red

J Word wrap

Multiple Choice

Choose the correct answer.

1. Formatting marks such as paragraph symbols and dots for spaces are also called:
   A. Nonprinting characters
   B. Symbols
   C. Objects

2. When you are typing text and a word will not fit within the established right margin, this Word feature moves the entire word to the next line in the paragraph.
   A. AutoComplete
   B. Word wrap
   C. Alignment

3. To delete the character to the left of the insertion point, press:
   A. Bksp
   B. Delete
   C. ←

4. To delete the character to the right of the insertion point, press:
   A. Bksp
   B. Delete
   C. →

5. Pressing a combination of keys—such as Ctrl + Home to move to the top of the document—is referred to as a:
   A. ScreenTip
   B. Live Preview
   C. Keyboard shortcut

6. A potential contextual spelling error is indicated by a wavy underline of this color:
   A. Red
   B. Green
   C. Blue

7. To select a sentence, hold down this key, and then click anywhere in the sentence.
   A. Alt
   B. Ctrl
   C. Shift

8. A thesaurus provides:
   A. Correct word usage
   B. Words with similar meanings
   C. Reading level of the document

9. To change Proofing tool settings, first display the:
   A. References tab
   B. Home tab
   C. Backstage

10. A reserved area for text and graphics that displays at the bottom of each page in a document is a:
    A. Footer
    B. Header
    C. Margin

Topics for Discussion

1. What kind of information do you commonly see in the headers and footers of textbooks and magazines? Why do you think publishers include this type of information? In a report, what other type of information might you put in a header or footer?

2. When you check the spelling in a document, one of the options is to add unrecognized words to the dictionary. If you were working for a large company, what types of words do you think you would add to your dictionary?

Skill Check

To complete this project, you will need the following files:

- New blank Word document
- w01_Donation_Opportunities
- w01_Donation_Photo

You will save your file as:

- Lastname_Firstname_w01_Donation

1. **Start** Word. On the **Home tab**, click the **Show/Hide** button until it displays in gold. In all uppercase letters, type ASPEN FALLS PUBLIC LIBRARY and press [Enter]. Type 255 Elm Street and press [Enter]. Type Aspen Falls, CA 93463 and press [Enter] two times. Complete the beginning of the letter as follows with the information shown in **Figure 1**. ————

2. Press [Enter] and type Thank you so much for your interest in making a donation to the Aspen Falls Public Library. You asked about potential projects for which we need additional resources, so I have attached a list of possible projects. **Press** [Enter] **and type** In answer to your question, our library does not have 501c3 status. However, our Friends of the Library group is a 501c3 organization, and all donations to the library through the Friends group are fully tax deductible. Press [Enter] two times.

3. Type Sincerely, and press [Enter] two times. Type Douglas Hopkins, Director and then move to the top of the document. Select the first two lines of the letterhead. On the **Home tab**, in the **Styles group**, click the **No Spacing** button. Repeat this procedure with the first two lines of the inside address.

4. In the paragraph that begins *Thank you*, use [Bksp] to delete *so much*. In the same paragraph, double-click *potential*, press [Delete], and then compare your screen with **Figure 2**. ————

5. Press [Ctrl] + [End], and then press [Ctrl] + [Enter] to insert a manual page break.

6. Click the **Insert tab**, and then in the **Text group**, click the **Object button arrow**. Click **Text from File**, and then locate and insert the file **w01_Donation_Opportunities**. Press [Bksp] to remove the blank paragraph.

- Continue to the next page to complete this Skill Check

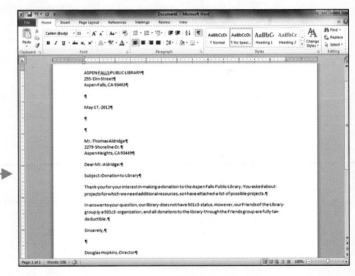

May 17, 2012

Mr. Thomas Aldridge

2279 Shoreline Dr.

Aspen Heights, CA 93449

Dear Mr. Aldridge:

Subject: Donation to the Library

Figure 1

Figure 2

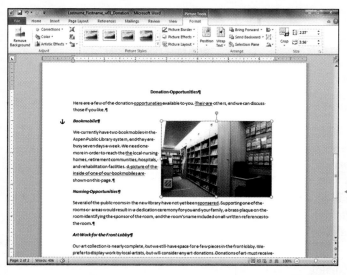

Figure 3

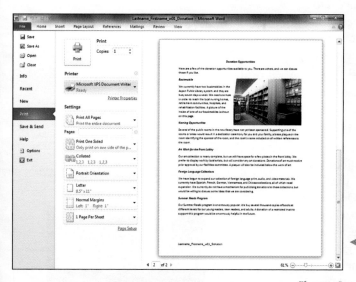

Figure 4

7. Press ⌃Ctrl⌄ + ⌊A⌋. On the **Home tab**, in the **Font group**, change the **Font Size** to **11** and change the **Font** to **Calibri**. At the top of the document, select the library name. On the Mini toolbar, change the **Font** to **Arial Black**, the **Font Size** to **16**, and then click **Bold**.

8. **Save** the document in your **Word Chapter 1** folder as Lastname_Firstname_w01_Donation Display the top of Page 2. Select the heading *Donation Opportunities*, and then on the Mini toolbar, click **Bold** and **Center**.

9. Select the heading *Bookmobile* and from the Mini toolbar, click **Bold**. Select the next heading—*Naming Opportunities*—hold down ⌊Ctrl⌋, and then select the rest of the headings displayed in italic. On the Mini toolbar, click **Bold**.

10. Click to the left of the first *B* in the heading *Bookmobile*. From your student files, insert the picture **w01_Donation_Photo**. With the picture selected, on the **Format tab**, in the **Arrange group**, click the **Wrap Text** button, and then click **Square**. Drag the picture to the right, aligning the right edge at approximately **6.5 inches** on the horizontal ruler and the top edge at approximately **1 inch** on the vertical ruler. Compare your screen with **Figure 3**.

11. Right-click the word, *opportunaties*, that has a wavy red underline, and then click **opportunities**. In the same sentence, right-click *Their are* that displays a wavy blue line, and then click **There are**. Move the insertion point to the top of Page 2.

12. On the **Review tab**, in the **Proofing group**, click the **Spelling & Grammar** button. Make the following corrections—your marked errors may differ: For the repeated word *the*, delete the word. In the sentence that begins *A picture*, change to the suggested correction that ends with the word *is*. Correct the misspelled word *sponsored*, change *too* to *to*, and change *languge* to *language*. Ignore any other changes except words you might have mistyped on Page 1.

13. On the **Insert tab**, in the **Header & Footer** group, click the **Footer** button, and then click **Edit Footer**. On the **Design tab**, in the **Insert group**, click the **Quick Parts** button, and then click **Field**. Under **Field names**, scroll down and click **FileName**. Click **OK**, and then on the **Design tab**, click **Close Header and Footer**.

14. Click **Save**. Click the **File tab**, and then click **Print**. Compare your document with **Figure 4**. Print or submit the file as directed by your instructor. **Exit** Word.

Done! You have completed the Skill Check

Assess Your Skills 1

To complete this document, you will need the following files:

- w01_Meadows
- w01_Meadows_Improvements
- w01_Meadows_Research

You will save your file as:

- Lastname_Firstname_w01_Meadows

1. **Start** Word and display the formatting marks. Click the **File tab**, and then click **Open**. Navigate to your student files. **Open** the file **w01_Meadows**, save it in your **Word Chapter 1** folder as Lastname_Firstname_w01_Meadows and then add the file name to the footer.

2. In the letterhead, select the first line of text and change the **Font** to **Arial Black** and the **Font Size** to **16**. Select the remaining three lines of the letterhead and add **Bold** emphasis.

3. Press Ctrl + End. Type Dear Ms. Jefferson: and press Enter. Type Subject: Aspen Meadows Branch Improvements and press Enter. Type the following paragraph: Thank you for your letter of concern about the Aspen Meadows Branch of the Aspen Falls Public Library. This is our smallest branch, and we are working hard to improve the collection and the services offered to our patrons. We have just completed some improvements, which I have detailed on the attached page. We hope these changes will answer some of your concerns. Press Enter, type Sincerely, and then press Enter two times. Type Douglas Hopkins, Director and then insert a manual page break.

4. On Page 2, insert the file **w01_Meadows_Improvements**. Select all of the text in the new page and change the **Font** to **Calibri**

and the **Font Size** to **11**. Select the report heading that begins *Recent Improvements*, apply **Bold**, change the **Font Size** to **14**, and **Center** the text. Select the three headings on the page—*Collection, Children's Collection, and Research Stations*—and apply **Bold** and **Italic** emphasis.

5. Display the **Spelling and Grammar** dialog box and on Page 2, fix the following problems: Remove the duplicate *to*, change *a* to *an*, and correct the spelling of *severel* to *several* and *suatable* to *suitable*. Ignore other marked words in the document unless you find typing errors that you made on Page 1.

6. In the first line of the last paragraph that begins *We have added*, double-click to select the word *deliver*. Use the **Thesaurus** to change *deliver* to **provide**.

7. Move to the blank line at the bottom of Page 2. Press Enter, and then insert the picture in the file **w01_Meadows_Research**. On the **Home tab**, in the **Paragraph group**, click the **Center** button to center the picture. **Save** the changes, and then compare your document with **Figure 1**. Preview your document, make any necessary changes, and then print or submit the file as directed by your instructor.

Done! You have completed Assess Your Skills 1

ASPEN FALLS PUBLIC LIBRARY
255 Elm St.
Aspen Falls, CA 93463
(805) 555-1011

May 25, 2012

Ms. Ayline Jefferson
1414 Barbary Dr.
Aspen Falls, CA 93464

Dear Ms. Jefferson:

Subject: Aspen Meadows Branch Improvements

Thank you for your letter of concern about the Aspen Meadows Branch of the Aspen Public Library. This is our smallest branch, and we are working hard to improve the collection and the services offered to our patrons. We have just completed some improvements, which I have detailed on the attached page. We hope these changes will answer some of your concerns.

Sincerely,

Douglas Hopkins, Director

Lastname_Firstname_w01_Meadows

Recent Improvements to the Aspen Meadows Branch

Collection

We have added 1,250 volumes to the print collection, nearly 100 titles to the CD collection, over 200 titles to the DVD collection, and a dozen microfilm reels of the Aspen Falls Weekly Herald, covering the period from 1878 to 1889.

Children's Collection

The Friends of the Aspen Falls Public Library just donated an extensive collection of books, stories on CD, and DVDs to be used at the Aspen Meadows Branch. They also included several tables and chairs suitable for young children.

Research Stations

We have added four research stations to the Aspen Meadows Branch. These research stations provide access to a large number of free and subscription databases, including many genealogy resources that were previously available only in the Aspen Falls Main Library. A picture of the research stations is shown below:

Lastname_Firstname_w01_Meadows

Figure 1

Assess Your Skills 3 and 4 can be found at **www.pearsonhighered.com/skills**.

Assess Your Skills 2

To complete this document, you will need the following files:

- w01_Tour
- w01_Tour_Topics

You will save your files as:

- Lastname_Firstname_w01_Tour

1. **Start** Word and display the formatting marks. Open the file **w01_Tour**, save it in your **Word Chapter 1** folder as Lastname_Firstname_w01_Tour and then add the file name to the footer. Select the first line of text and change the **Font** to **Calibri** and the **Font Size** to **36**, and then **Center** and **Bold** the title. Add **Bold** emphasis to the four words on the left side of the memo—TO:, FROM:, DATE:, and RE:.

2. Move to the end of the document, type Jamie:, and then press Enter. Type I have been thinking about the suggestion made at the Board of Trustees meeting the other night that we hire an outside company to design a virtual tour of the library. The virtual tour might consist of several different modules featuring different topics. I have listed some of the more interesting things on the next page. Press Enter, type Let me know what you think. and then press Enter two times. Type Doug and then add a manual page break.

3. In the text you just typed, use Bksp or Delete to remove the phrase *more interesting*. Double-click the next word—*things*—and type topics to replace it. Locate and double-click the first instance of the word *different*— to the left of *modules*—and then press Delete.

4. Position the insertion point at the top of Page 2. Insert the file **w01_Tour_Topics**.

5. On Page 2, select the first line of text, apply **Bold** emphasis, and **Center** the text. Select the five topic titles on the left side of Page 2 and apply **Bold** emphasis. Select all of the text in the document except the title on the first page, and change the **Font Size** to **12**.

6. Move to the top of Page 2. Display the **Spelling and Grammar** dialog box. Delete the repeated word *the*, change *interier* to *interior*, change *databasis* to *databases*, and then change *has* to *have*. Correct any mistakes you made on the first page.

7. Position the insertion point at the bottom of the document. Insert and position the clip art image shown in **Figure 1**. Use *library* as the search term, and search only for **Illustrations**. (Note: If this image is not available, insert the picture in the student file w01_Library_Logo.) **Close** the Clip Art task pane.

8. **Save** the changes and compare your document with **Figure 1**. Preview your document, make any necessary changes, and then print or submit the file as directed by your instructor.

Done! You have completed Assess Your Skills 2

MEMORANDUM

TO: Jamie McArthur, Special Services

FROM: Douglas Hopkins, Director

DATE: June 21, 2012

RE: Virtual Tour of the Library

Jamie:

I have been thinking about the suggestion made at the Board of Trustees meeting the other night that we hire an outside company to design a virtual tour of the library. The virtual tour might consist of several modules featuring different topics. I have listed some of the topics on the next page.

Let me know what you think.

Doug

Lastname_Firstname_w01_Tour

Topics for the Virtual Tour of the New Library

Here is a list I put together of topics I would like to see included if we go ahead with the virtual tour for the Internet:

The Building Exterior

The new building is very striking, and we should have a 360-degree tour of the exterior, including the grounds and the pond. We should also mention the Alvarado architectural firm that we employed to design the building.

The Building Interior

Shots of the interior should include a panorama of our wonderful lobby, and then should move inside to show the collections, the kids' area, the community room, the computer labs, the genealogy room, the office suite, and the board room.

Library Technology

Some of the technology that we show will be physical features, such as computer labs, but some will have to rely on screen shots of technology in action, such as downloading e-books, using the research databases, and some of the adaptive technologies that are available for the disabled. I think it is important that we have a special section that focuses only on the technology. This topic will be of special interest to our youngest and oldest patrons.

Friends of the Aspen Falls Public Library Bookshop

The Friends bookshop is a centerpiece of our new library, and needs to have its own module in the virtual tour.

People

I am not sure we should include any of the staff in the virtual tour. Several of them have already indicated that they do not want to be shown in the tours. If we need one or more people for any of the tour modules, we should probably ask for volunteers.

Lastname_Firstname_w01_Tour

Figure 1

Assess Your Skills Visually

To complete this document, you will need the following file:

- New blank Word document

You will save your document as:

- Lastname_Firstname_w01_Closures

Start Word. Create the document shown in **Figure 1. Save** the file as Lastname_Firstname_w01_Closures in your **Word Chapter 1** folder. To complete this document, use Arial Black sized at 24 points for the title and Cambria sized at 12 points for the rest of the document. After the last paragraph, insert the clip art image shown in **Figure 1** by searching for *holidays*. If you do not see the same image, use any other appropriate clip art. Insert the file name in the footer, and then print or submit the file as directed by your instructor.

Done! You have completed Assess Your Skills Visually

MEMORANDUM

TO:	All Library Staff
FROM:	Douglas Hopkins, Director
DATE:	December 15, 2011
RE:	Library Closings for the 2012 Calendar Year

I have listed the days we are going to close the library in 2012. I have listed the holidays, the in-service days, and the days we will close early.

Holidays

We will be closed on New Year's Day, Easter, Memorial Day, the Fourth of July, Labor Day, Thanksgiving, and Christmas.

In-Service Days

We will be closed on April 15th for a session on library security, and on November 7th for a session that will focus on streamlining the material handling process.

Close Early

We will close early on New Year's Eve, the day before Easter, the day before Thanksgiving, and Christmas Eve.

HAPPY HOLIDAYS!

Lastname_Firstname_w01_Closures

Figure 1

Skills in Context

To complete this document, you will need the following files:

- New blank Word document
- w01_Trustees_Report

You will save your document as:

- Lastname_Firstname_w01_Trustees

Using the information provided, compose a letter from Douglas Hopkins, the Director of the Aspen Falls Public Library, to Fran Darcy, the Chair of the Library Board of Trustees. Use the current date and the address used in Skill 1. The letter is regarding the attached report on library operations for the previous year, and it should include the purpose of the letter and provide a very brief summary of the attached document. Save the document as

Lastname_Firstname_w01_Trustees On a new page, insert the report **w01_ Trustees_Report** and at an appropriate location in the document, insert a representative clip art image. Format the document appropriately. Check the entire document for grammar and spelling, and then insert the file name in the footer. Submit as directed.

Done! You have completed Skills in Context

Skills and You

To complete this document, you will need the following file:

- New blank Word document

You will save your document as:

- Lastname_Firstname_w01_Careers

Using the skills you have practiced in this chapter, compose either a letter or a memo to the director of your college's Career Center inquiring about the skills needed to find a job. Ask if there are upcoming seminars or workshops that you might attend. If you have a picture of yourself, insert it in the memo as a way of introducing yourself. You should include several instances of text

formatting somewhere in the document. Save the document as Lastname_Firstname_w01_Careers Check the entire document for grammar and spelling, and insert the file name in the footer. Print or submit the file as directed by your instructor.

Done! You have completed Skills and You

CHAPTER 2

Format and Organize Text

▶ Format a document to enhance page layout and improve the readability of the text in the document.

▶ Add bulleted and numbered lists to group related information; add headers and footers to display important information on each page.

Your starting screen will look like this:

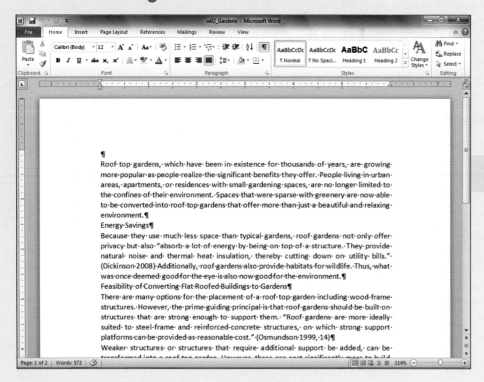

SKILLS

myitlab
Skills 1-10 Training

At the end of this chapter, you will be able to:

Skill 1 Set Document Margins

Skill 2 Align Text and Set Indents

Skill 3 Modify Line and Paragraph Spacing

Skill 4 Format Text Using Format Painter

Skill 5 Find and Replace Text

Skill 6 Create Bulleted and Numbered Lists

Skill 7 Insert and Format Headers and Footers

Skill 8 Insert and Modify Footnotes

Skill 9 Add Citations

Skill 10 Create Bibliographies

MORE SKILLS

More Skills 11 Record AutoCorrect Entries

More Skills 12 Use AutoFormat to Create Numbered Lists

More Skills 13 Format and Customize Lists

More Skills 14 Manage Document Properties

Outcome

Using the skills listed to the left will enable you to create
a document like this:

Page 1

**Roof Gardens:
Advantages and Potential Problems**

By Your Name

March 14, 2012

Roof gardens, which have been in existence for thousands of years, are growing more popular as people realize the significant benefits they offer. People living in urban areas, apartments, or residences with small gardening spaces, are no longer limited to the confines of their environment. Spaces that were sparse with greenery are now able to be converted into roof gardens that offer more than just a beautiful and relaxing environment.

ENERGY SAVINGS

Because they use much less space than typical gardens, roof gardens not only offer privacy but also "absorb a lot of energy by being on top of a structure. They provide natural noise and thermal heat insulation, thereby cutting down on utility bills." (Dickinson 2008) Additionally, roof gardens also provide habitats for wildlife. Thus, what was once deemed good for the eye is also now good for the environment.

FEASIBILITY OF CONVERTING FLAT ROOFED BUILDINGS TO GARDENS

There are many options for the placement of a roof garden including wood-frame structures. However, the primary guiding principal is that roof gardens should be built on structures that are strong enough to support them. "Roof gardens are more ideally suited to steel-frame and reinforced-concrete structures, on which strong support platforms can be provided as reasonable cost." (Osmundson 1999, 14)

Weaker structures or structures that require additional support to be added, can be transformed into a roof garden. However, these can cost significantly more to build depending on the initial weight-bearing capability of that structure.[1]

---
[1] Internal reinforcement is sufficient in most cases.

Page 2

STRUCTURAL REQUIREMENTS

Developing a roof garden does not need to be limited to the concept of a traditional garden that might be seen on top of a downtown apartment building. Instead, creativity is imperative as other structure-types are considered. Some of these alternatives include:

- Garages and sheds[2]
- Balconies and terraces
- Patios or decks

The main consideration when designing a roof garden is to consider whether the structure can withstand not only the weight of the garden but also the water needed to maintain the garden. "The load-bearing potential of a roof or balcony will determine where beds, containers, and other heavy features can be safely placed." (Stevens 1997, 14) In designing the garden, it will be necessary then to understand the weaknesses and strengths of a particular structure and design accordingly to avoid structural issues.[3]

POSSIBLE PROBLEMS

Before getting started, it is important to understand the potential problems that can impact a roof garden. While there are numerous issues to consider, a few of the more important ones include:

1. Rainwater build-up can sacrifice the structural soundness of the roof. Make sure the structure is slightly angled or has proper drainage to allow for water runoff.
2. The structure may be unable to sustain the weight. Consider container gardens which consist of lower weight but offer the same benefits of in-ground plants.
3. Selecting plants that require too much water can add considerable weight to the garden. The best option is to research and understand which flowers and plants thrive in a given area and do not require a lot of water.

Regardless of the type of roof garden, the final touch is to ensure that it is personalized and contains special touches. Add personal touches by using unique objects that show off the gardener's personality. According to one group of designers, "Keep an eye out. Our favorite sources are salvage yards and antique markets, but garage sales, estate sales, and trash are great places to look." (Zimmeth 2008, 83)

---
[2] On structurally weaker buildings, potted plants work best.
[3] Heavier materials should be located near load-bearing walls.

Lastname_Firstname_w02_Gardens   DRAFT   4/24/2010 12:30 PM

Page 3

Bibliography

Dickinson, Marc. *Stunning Roof Gardens Also Have Beautiful Advantages*. 2008. http://www.servicemagic.com/article.show.Stunning-Roof-Gardens-Also-Have-Beautiful-Advantages.13556.html (accessed January 23, 2010).

Osmundson, Theodore H. *Roof Gardens: History, Design and Construction*. New York: W. W. Norton & Company, 1999.

Stevens, David. *Roof Gardens, Balconies & Terraces*. New York: Rizzoli International, 1997.

Zimmeth, Khristi S. "Serenity in the City." *Garden Ideas & Outdoor Living*, Fall 2008: 78-85.

Lastname_Firstname_w02_Gardens   DRAFT   4/24/2010 12:30 PM

You will save this document as:

Lastname_Firstname_w02_Gardens

In this chapter, you will create documents for the Aspen Falls City Hall, which provides essential services for the citizens and visitors of Aspen Falls, California.

Introduction

- ▶ Document margins are the spaces that display on the outer edges of a printed page. All four page margins can be adjusted independently.

- ▶ To make paragraphs stand out, add spacing above and below, change the first line indents, and format subheadings. This helps the reader understand the structure of the document, which increases the document's readability.

- ▶ Lists make information easier to understand. Use numbered lists when information is displayed in a sequence, and use bulleted lists when information can appear in any order.

- ▶ Informal business reports are often formatted using guidelines in *The Gregg Reference Manual* by William A. Sabin. These guidelines cover the way the text is formatted, the way notes display, and the types of citations used.

Time to complete all
10 skills – 60 to 90 minutes

Find your student data files here:

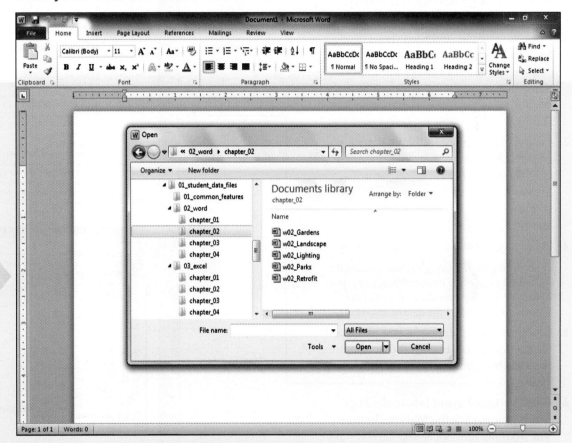

Student data files needed for this chapter:

- New blank Word document
- w02_Gardens

▶ *Margins* are the spaces between the text and the top, bottom, left, and right edges of the paper.

▶ Each of the margins can be adjusted independently of the other margins.

1. **Start** ● Word. Click the **File tab**, click **Open**, navigate to your student files, and then open **w02_Gardens**. If necessary, display the formatting marks.

2. Click the **File tab**, and then click **Save As**. Navigate to the location where you are saving your files, create a folder named Word Chapter 2 and then **Save** the document as Lastname_Firstname_w02_Gardens

3. Press [Enter] five times. In the **Font group**, click the **Font arrow** [Calibri (Body)], and then click **Cambria**. Type Roof Gardens: Advantages and Potential Problems and then press [Enter]. Type By *(Type your name)*, and then press [Enter].

4. Type the current date, and then press [Enter].

   According to *The Gregg Reference Manual*, the first page of an informal business report uses a 2 inch margin above the title, the author's name, and the date of the report.

5. Select the three paragraphs you just typed. On the Mini toolbar, click the **Bold** button [B], and then compare your screen with **Figure 1**.

6. Click the **Page Layout tab**. In the **Page Setup group**, click the **Margins** button. The Margins gallery displays several standard margin settings and the last custom setting (if any), as shown in **Figure 2**.

■ **Continue to the next page to complete the skill**

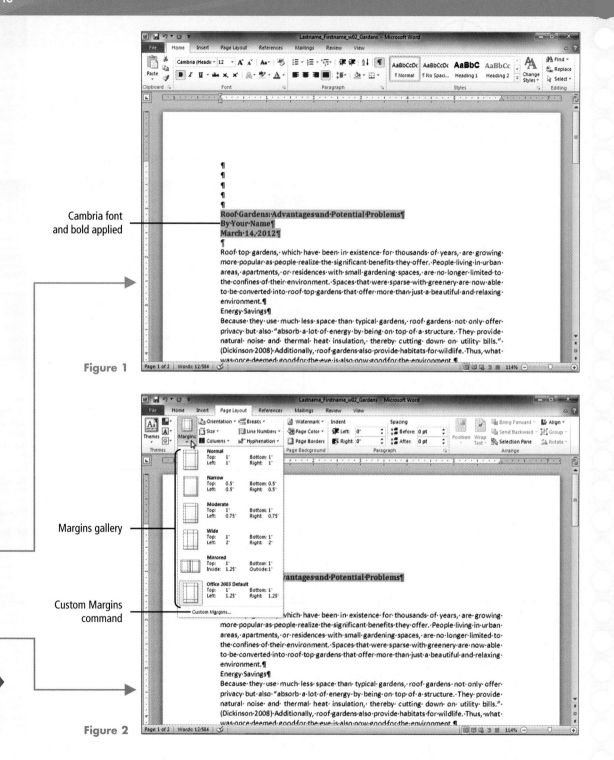

Cambria font and bold applied

Figure 1

Margins gallery

Custom Margins command

Figure 2

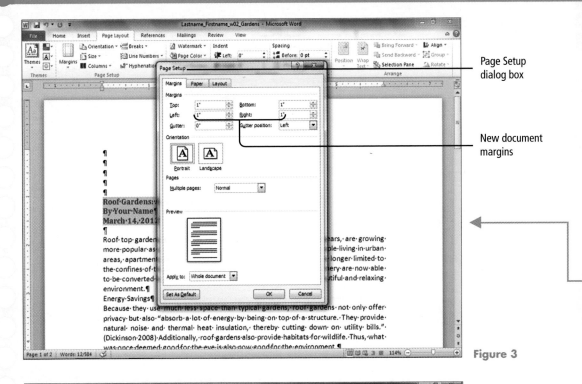

Page Setup
dialog box

New document
margins

Figure 3

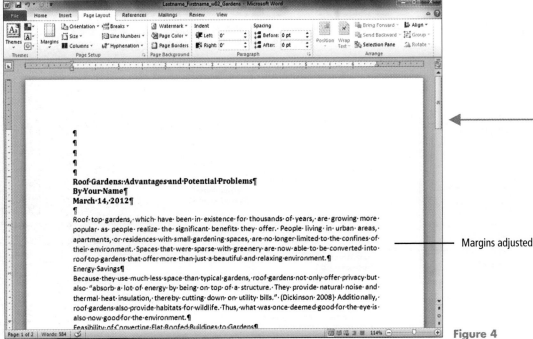

Margins adjusted

Figure 4

7. At the bottom of the **Margins** gallery, click **Custom Margins**.

> The Page Setup dialog box provides you with document formatting options, some of which are not available on the Ribbon.

8. In the **Page Setup** dialog box, be sure the **Margins tab** is selected. Press (Tab) two times. Under **Margins**, in the **Left** box, with *1.25"* selected, click the **down spin arrow** three times to change the left margin to *1"*. Alternately, with the current margin selected, type the new margin in the margin box.

9. Press (Tab), and then repeat this procedure to change the **Right** margin to *1"*. Compare your screen with **Figure 3**.

10. Under **Orientation**, be sure the **Portrait** button is selected. At the bottom of the **Page Setup** dialog box, verify that the **Apply to** box displays *Whole document*, and then click **OK**.

> With *portrait orientation*, the printed page is taller than it is wide; with *landscape orientation*, the printed page width is greater than the page height. Most reports use portrait orientation.

11. Click anywhere in the document to deselect the text. Compare your screen with **Figure 4**, and notice the results of the changes you made to the margins.

12. Save 🖫 the document.

■ **You have completed Skill 1 of 10**

▶ **Indents** are the position of paragraph lines in relation to the page margins.

▶ **Horizontal alignment** is the orientation of the left or right edges of the paragraph—for example, flush with the left or right margins.

1. Position the insertion point anywhere in the first paragraph you typed—the title that begins *Roof Gardens*.

   To align a single paragraph, you need only position the insertion point anywhere in the paragraph.

2. On the **Home tab**, in the **Paragraph group**, click the **Align Right** button to align the title with the right margin.

3. In the **Paragraph** group, click the **Center** button to center the title between the left and right margins.

4. Select the second and third bold title lines. From the Mini toolbar, click the **Center** button , and then compare your screen with **Figure 1**.

5. Below the date title, in the left margin, point to the paragraph that begins *Roof top gardens* and drag down to select that paragraph and the following two paragraphs that begin *Energy Savings* and *Because they use*. Notice that these paragraphs are **justified**—the paragraph text is aligned flush with both the left margin and the right margin.

6. In the **Paragraph** group, click the **Align Left** button . Compare your screen with **Figure 2**, and then click anywhere to deselect the text.

   These paragraphs are no longer justified.

■ **Continue to the next page to complete the skill** ▶

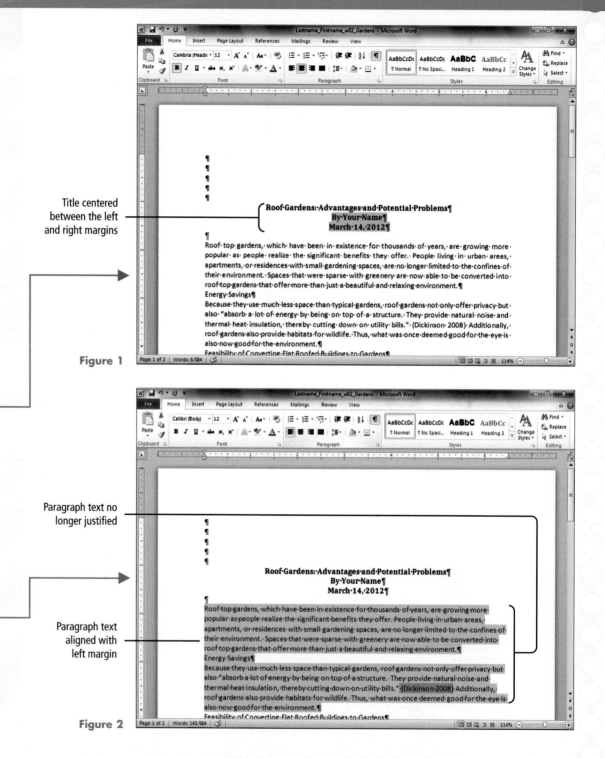

Title centered between the left and right margins

Figure 1

Paragraph text no longer justified

Paragraph text aligned with left margin

Figure 2

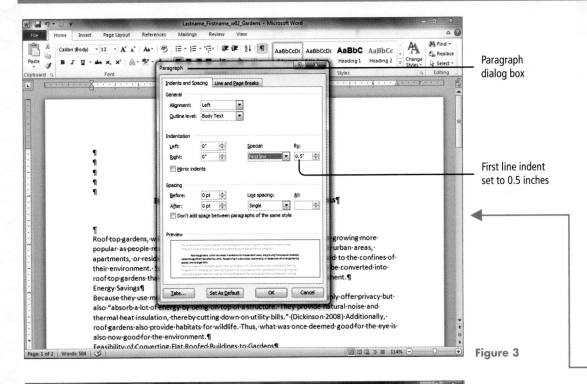

Paragraph dialog box

First line indent set to 0.5 inches

Figure 3

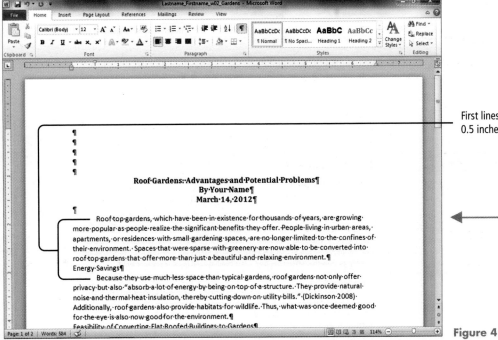

First lines indented 0.5 inches

Figure 4

7. Below the text that you just aligned, click to the left of the paragraph that begins *Feasibility*. Scroll to the end of the document, hold down Shift, and click to the right of the last line in the document. On the **Home tab**, in the **Paragraph group**, click the **Align Left** button.

8. Press Ctrl + Home to move to the top of the document. Below the centered titles, click to position the insertion point anywhere in the paragraph that begins *Roof top gardens*.

9. On the **Home tab**, in the **Paragraph group**, click the **Paragraph Dialog Box Launcher**.

   The Paragraph dialog box displays, which includes commands that are not available on the Ribbon.

10. Under **Indentation**, click the **Special box arrow**, and then click **First line**. Compare your screen with **Figure 3**.

    The *first line indent* is the location of the beginning of the first line of a paragraph in relationship with the left edge of the remainder of the paragraph. In this case, the *By* box displays *0.5"*, which will indent the first line of the current paragraph one-half inch.

11. Click **OK** to indent the first line of the paragraph.

12. Click anywhere in the paragraph that begins *Because they use*, and repeat the procedure just practiced to indent the first line of the paragraph by 0.5 inches. Compare your screen with **Figure 4**.

13. Save the document.

    ■ **You have completed Skill 2 of 10**

► *Line spacing* is the vertical distance between lines of text in a paragraph, and can be adjusted for each paragraph.

► *Paragraph spacing* is the vertical distance above and below each paragraph, and can be adjusted for each paragraph.

1. Below the centered titles, click anywhere in the paragraph that begins *Roof top gardens*.

2. On the **Home tab**, in the **Paragraph group**, click the **Line and Paragraph Spacing** button .

    The current setting is *1.0—single-spacing—*which means that no extra space is added between lines of text. Line spacing of 2.0—*double-spacing*—means that the equivalent of a blank line of text displays between each line of text.

3. In the **Line Spacing** list, point to **2.0**, and with Live Preview, notice that the text takes up twice as much space.

4. In the **Line Spacing** list, click **1.15** to change the line spacing, as shown in Figure 1.

    Text with a line spacing of 1.15 has been found to be easier to read than single-spaced text.

5. Click the **Page Layout tab**. In the **Paragraph group**, under **Spacing**, click the **After up spin arrow** two times to change the spacing after the paragraph to *12 pt*.

6. In the paragraph that begins *Because they use*, repeat the same procedure to set the line spacing to **1.15** and the spacing after to **12 pt**. Notice the change in the spacing between the paragraphs, as shown in Figure 2.

■ **Continue to the next page to complete the skill**

Line and Paragraph Spacing button

Line spacing changed to 1.15

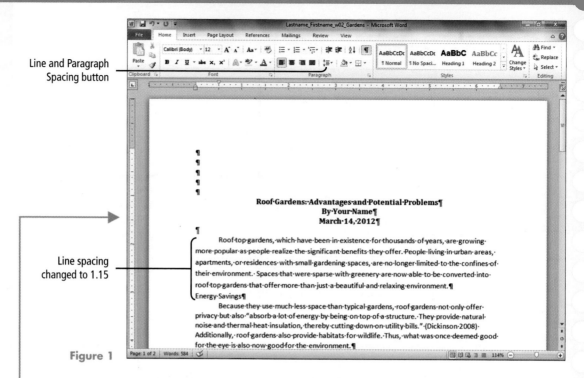

Figure 1

12 point spacing after the paragraph

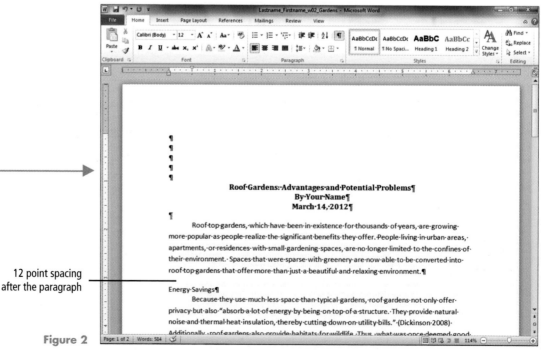

Figure 2

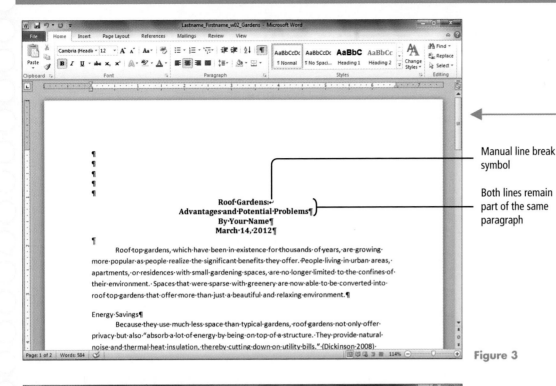

Manual line break symbol

Both lines remain part of the same paragraph

Figure 3

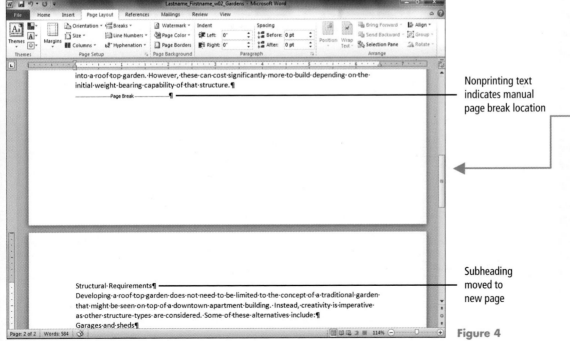

Nonprinting text indicates manual page break location

Subheading moved to new page

Figure 4

7. At the top of the document, in the first title, position the insertion point to the right of *Roof Gardens:*.

8. Press Delete to remove the space, hold down Shift, and then press Enter. Compare your screen with **Figure 3**.

> A ***manual line break***—a line break that moves the remainder of the paragraph to a new line while keeping both lines in the same paragraph—is inserted. The manual line break symbol displays when a manual line break is inserted.

9. In the left margin area, point to the left of the first title to display the pointer, and then drag down to select all of the centered title lines.

10. On the **Page Layout tab**, in the **Paragraph group**, under **Spacing**, click the **After up spin arrow** two times to add 12 points spacing after each paragraph.

> No extra spacing was added after the manual line break because both lines are part of the same paragraph.

11. Near the bottom of Page 1, click to position the insertion point to the left of the subheading that begins *Structural Requirements*. Hold down Ctrl, press Enter, and then compare your screen with **Figure 4**.

> A ***manual page break***—a break that moves the text following it to a new page—is inserted. Here, as line spacing and paragraph spacing is changed on Page 1, the text that follows this manual page break will always start on a new page.

12. Save the document.

■ **You have completed Skill 3 of 10**

▶ Use *Format Painter* to copy text formatting quickly from one place to another.

▶ To use Format Painter on multiple items, double-click the Format Painter button.

1. Near the top of the document, click anywhere in the paragraph that begins *Roof top gardens.*

2. On the **Home tab**, in the **Clipboard group**, click the **Format Painter** button.

3. Scroll down and point anywhere in the paragraph that begins *There are many.* Notice that the pointer displays. Compare your screen with **Figure 1**. ──────

4. Click anywhere in the paragraph. Notice that the formatting from the original paragraph is applied to the new paragraph, and that the pointer no longer displays.

5. Press Ctrl + Home, click anywhere in the title *By Your Name*, and then in the **Clipboard** group, click the **Format Painter** button. In the middle of Page 1, move the pointer to the left of the *Energy Savings* subheading until the pointer displays, and then click. Compare your screen with **Figure 2**. ──────

   The font, bold style, centering, and paragraph spacing from the original paragraph are all applied to the new paragraph.

6. With the *Energy Savings* subheading selected, on the **Home tab**, in the **Paragraph group**, click the **Align Left** button.

7. On the **Home tab**, in the **Font group**, click the **Font Dialog Box Launcher**.

■ **Continue to the next page to complete the skill** ▶

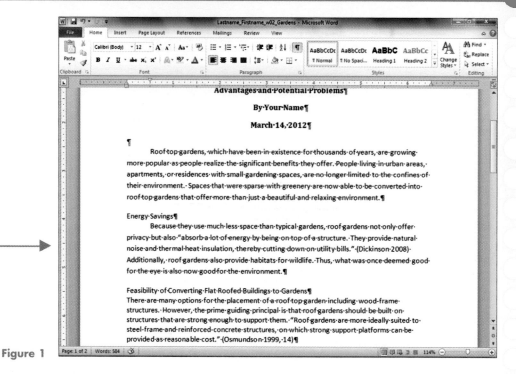

Figure 1

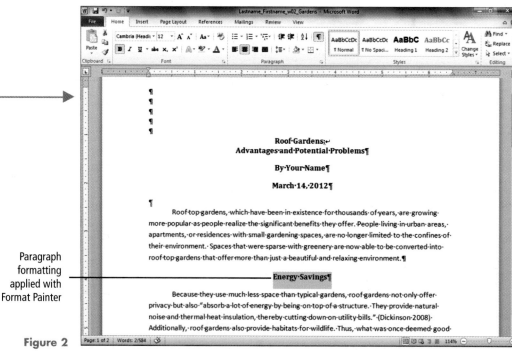

Paragraph formatting applied with Format Painter

Figure 2

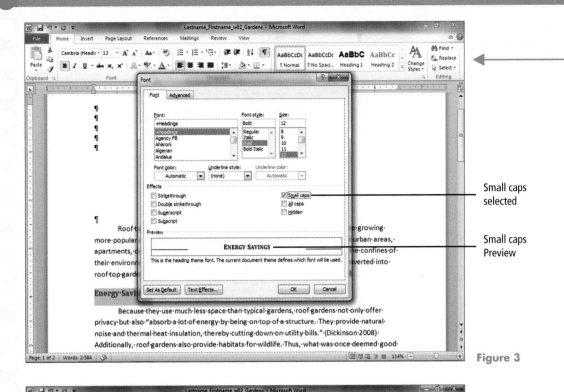

Small caps selected

Small caps Preview

Figure 3

8. In the **Font** dialog box, under **Effects**, select the **Small caps** check box. Compare your screen with **Figure 3**.

9. At the bottom of the **Font** dialog box, click **OK**.

10. With the text still selected, on the **Home tab**, in the **Clipboard group**, *double-click* the **Format Painter** button ⟨⟩.

11. Using the ⟨AI⟩ pointer, select the remaining three subheadings—*Feasibility of Converting, Structural Requirements,* and *Possible Problems.*

    When you double-click the Format Painter button, it remains on until you turn it off. If you accidentally clicked another paragraph, on the Quick Access Toolbar, click the Undo button ⟨⟩ and try again.

12. Press ⟨Esc⟩ to turn off Format Painter. Alternately, click the **Format Painter** button.

13. Move to the top of the document, place the insertion point in the paragraph that begins *Roof top gardens,* and then in the **Clipboard** group, double-click the **Format Painter** button ⟨⟩. At the bottom of Page 1, click in the paragraph that begins *Weaker structures.*

14. Move to Page 2, and then click anywhere in the four paragraphs that begin *Developing a roof, The main consideration, Before getting started,* and the final document paragraph *Regardless of the type.*

15. Press ⟨Esc⟩ to turn off Format Painter, and then compare your screen with **Figure 4**.

16. Save ⟨⟩ the document.

    ■ **You have completed Skill 4 of 10**

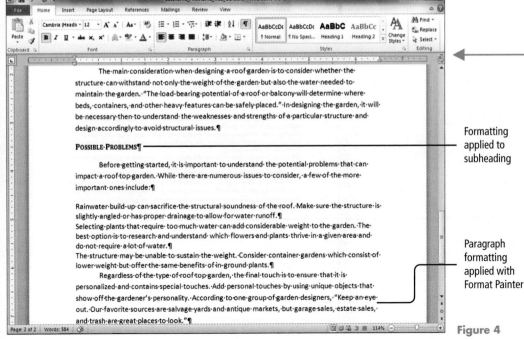

Formatting applied to subheading

Paragraph formatting applied with Format Painter

Figure 4

▶ The Find command is useful if you know a word or phrase is in a document, and you want to locate it quickly.

▶ Using the Replace command, you can find and then replace words or phrases one at a time, or all at once.

1. Press Ctrl + Home to move to the top of the document. On the **Home tab**, in the **Editing group**, click the **Find** button.

2. In the **Navigation Pane Search** box, type space Notice that three instances of the word are highlighted, even though two of them are the plural form of the word—*spaces*. If your screen differs, at the top of the **Navigation Pane**, click the **Browse the results from your current search** button 🔳.

3. In the **Navigation Pane**, click the third instance of the word, and then compare your screen with **Figure 1**.

4. In the **Search** box, select the existing text, type garden and notice that 24 instances of the word are found.

5. In the **Navigation Pane**, use the vertical scroll bar to scroll down the list of *garden* instances. Scroll to the bottom of the list.

   The located instances include *garden, gardens, gardening,* and *gardener.*

6. Click the last item in the list to scroll down to the location of the selected item.

7. On the **Home tab**, in the **Clipboard group**, click the **Cut** button to remove the selected word. In the Navigation Pane, notice that the search results are removed, as shown in **Figure 2**.

■ **Continue to the next page to complete the skill**

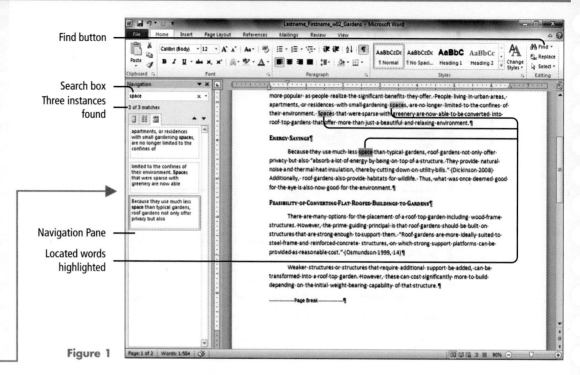

Find button
Search box
Three instances found
Navigation Pane
Located words highlighted

Figure 1

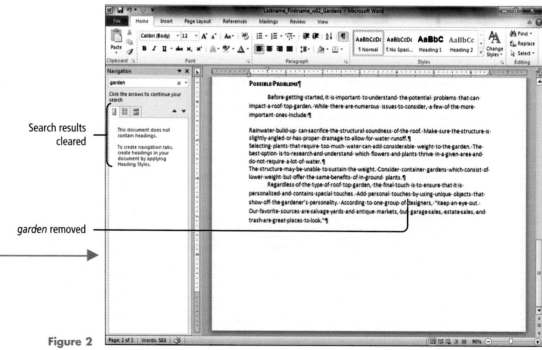

Search results cleared

garden removed

Figure 2

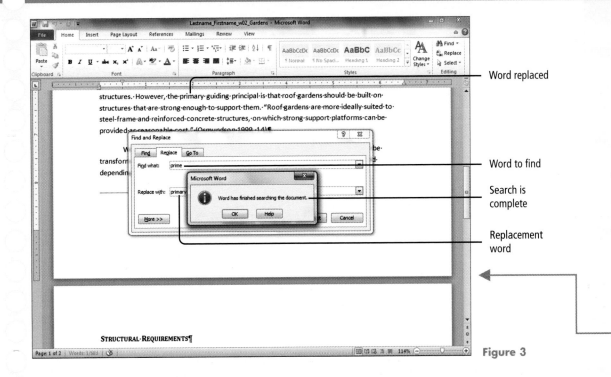

Word replaced

Word to find

Search is complete

Replacement word

Figure 3

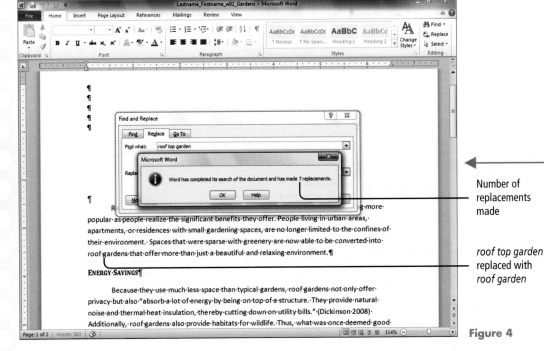

Number of replacements made

roof top garden replaced with *roof garden*

Figure 4

8. At the top of the **Navigation Pane**, click the **Close** button ☒.

9. Press Ctrl + Home. On the **Home tab**, in the **Editing group**, click the **Replace** button. Notice that the Find and Replace dialog box displays with the Replace tab active, and that the previous search term—*garden*—displays in the *Find what* box.

10. In the **Find what** box, select the existing text, type prime and press Tab. In the **Replace with** box, type primary

11. Click the **Find Next** button to find the first instance of *prime*, and then click the **Replace** button. Notice that the word is replaced, and a message box displays showing that there are no more instances of *prime* in the document, as shown in **Figure 3**.

12. In the message box, click **OK**. Click anywhere in the text, and notice that the insertion point remains at the beginning of the document.

13. In the **Find and Replace** dialog box, in the **Find what** box, type roof top garden and in the **Replace with** box, type roof garden

14. In the **Find and Replace** dialog box, click the **Replace All** button. Notice that a message box displays, telling you how many replacements were made, as shown in **Figure 4**.

    When you do not specify any Find and Replace settings, the replaced text will retain the capitalization used in the original word or phrase.

15. **Close** all open dialog boxes, and then **Save** 🖫 the document.

■ **You have completed Skill 5 of 10**

▶ A *bulleted list* is a list of items with each item introduced by a symbol—such as a small circle or check mark—in which the list items can be presented in any order.

▶ A *numbered list* is a list of items with each item introduced by a consecutive number or letter to indicate definite steps, a sequence of actions, or chronological order.

1. Near the top of Page 2, in the left margin area, display the 🔏 pointer to the left of the paragraph *Garages and sheds*, and then drag down to select the three paragraphs up to and including the paragraph *Patios or decks*.

2. On the **Home tab**, in the **Paragraph group**, click the **Bullets** button 🔲. Compare your screen with **Figure 1**.

   The symbols used for your bulleted list may vary, depending on the last bullet type used on your computer.

3. With the bulleted list still selected, on the **Home tab**, in the **Paragraph group**, click the **Line and Paragraph Spacing** button 🔲 , and then click **1.15**.

4. In the **Paragraph group**, click the **Increase Indent** button 🔲 one time.

   The list moves 0.25 inches to the right.

5. With the bulleted list still selected, click the **Page Layout tab**, and then in the **Paragraph group**, under **Spacing**, click the **After up spin arrow** two times to increase the spacing after to *12 pt*.

6. Click anywhere in the document, and notice that the space was added after the *last item* in the list only, as shown in **Figure 2**.

■ **Continue to the next page to complete the skill**

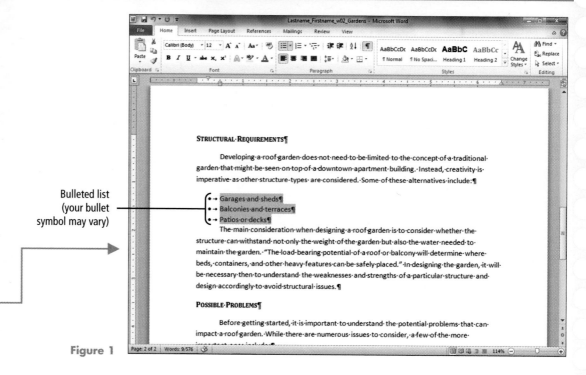

Bulleted list (your bullet symbol may vary)

Figure 1

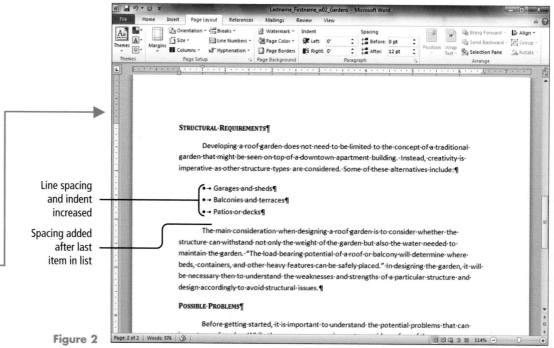

Line spacing and indent increased

Spacing added after last item in list

Figure 2

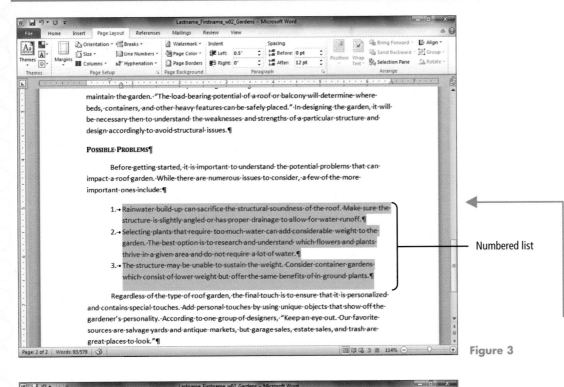

Figure 3

Numbered list

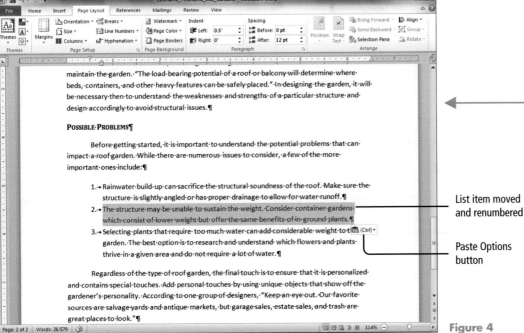

Figure 4

List item moved and renumbered

Paste Options button

7. Scroll to the bottom of Page 2. Select the three paragraphs that begin with *Rainwater build-up* and end with *in-ground plants*.

8. On the **Home tab**, in the **Paragraph group**, click the **Numbering** button. In the **Paragraph group**, click the **Increase Indent** button one time.

9. With the list still selected, in the **Paragraph group**, click the **Line and Paragraph Spacing** button, and then click **1.15**.

10. Click the **Page Layout tab**. In the **Paragraph group**, under **Spacing**, click the **After up spin arrow** two times to change the spacing after the list to *12 pt*. Notice that the space is added only after the last item in the list, as shown in **Figure 3**.

11. In the numbered list, select all of the text in the third item, including the paragraph mark. Do not select the number *3* and, if necessary, press (Esc) to close the Mini toolbar.

12. Move the pointer over the selected text to display the pointer. Drag the selected text up to the left of *Selecting* in the second item in the list. Compare your screen with **Figure 4**.

    Notice that the step text is moved, the numbering is changed, and the space after the list remains at the bottom of the list. Because dragging text treats the text like it was cut and then pasted, a Paste Options button also displays.

13. **Save** the document.

■ **You have completed Skill 6 of 10**

▶ Headers and footers can include not only text, but also graphics and fields—for example, file names and the current date.

▶ You can turn off the headers and footers on the first page of a document.

1. Press `Ctrl` + `Home` to move to the top of the document. Click the **Insert tab**, and then in the **Header & Footer group**, click the **Header** button. Below the **Header** gallery, click **Edit Header**. Notice that the Design contextual tab is added to the Ribbon.

2. On the **Design tab**, in the **Header & Footer** group, click the **Page Number** button, and then point to **Top of Page** to display the Page Number gallery, as shown in **Figure 1**.

3. In the **Page Number** gallery, use the vertical scroll bar to scroll through the page number options. When you are through, scroll to the top of the list. Under **Simple**, click **Plain Number 3** to insert the page number at the right margin.

4. On the **Design tab**, in the **Options group**, select the **Different First Page** check box.

The page number disappears from the header for Page 1, but will display on all other pages of the document.

5. Double-click anywhere in the document to deactivate the header, and then scroll to the top of Page 2. Notice that the page number displays on Page 2, as shown in **Figure 2**.

■ **Continue to the next page to complete the skill**

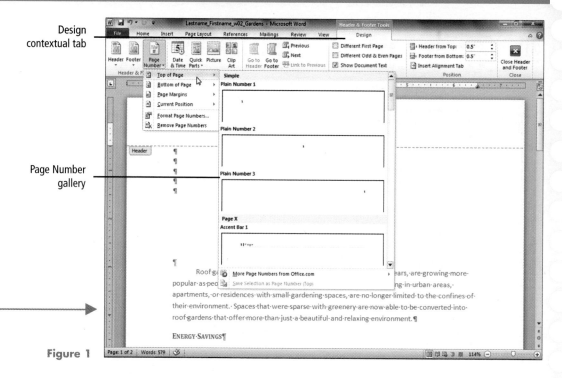

Design contextual tab

Page Number gallery

Figure 1

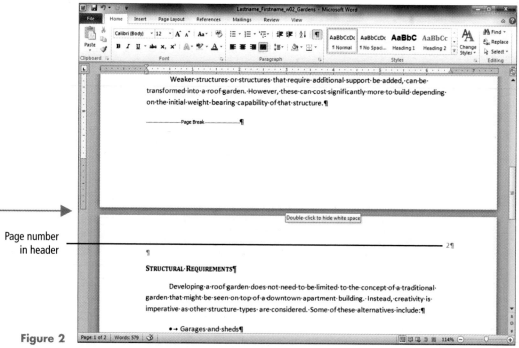

Page number in header

Figure 2

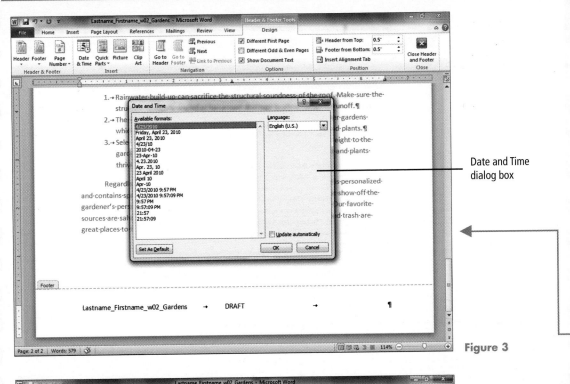

Date and Time
dialog box

Figure 3

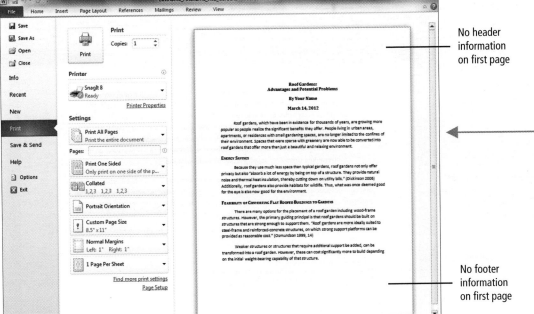

No header
information
on first page

No footer
information
on first page

Figure 4

6. Press Ctrl + Home, and notice that no page number displays on Page 1.

> In most business and research reports, the page number is not included on the first page.

7. Press Ctrl + End to move to the bottom of Page 2. Below the text, near the bottom edge of the page, right-click, and then from the menu, click **Edit Footer** to make the footer active.

8. In the **Insert group**, click the **Quick Parts** button, and then click **Field**. Under **Field names**, scroll down, click **FileName**, and then click **OK**.

9. Press Tab, type DRAFT and then press Tab.

10. On the **Design tab**, in the **Insert group**, click the **Date & Time** button. Compare your screen with **Figure 3**.

11. In the **Date and Time** dialog box, under **Available formats**, click the **1/15/2012 4:15 PM** format—your date and time will vary. Select the **Update automatically** check box, and then click **OK**.

> The date and time are added to the footer, and will be updated every time you open this file. In a business setting, the footer information should be removed when the report is finished.

12. Double-click anywhere in the document to deactivate the footer. Press Ctrl + Home. Click the **File tab**, click **Print**, and notice that the footer text does not display on Page 1, as shown in **Figure 4**.

13. Click the **Home tab**, and then **Save** 🖫 the document.

■ **You have completed Skill 7 of 10**

► A *footnote* is a reference placed at the bottom of the page. An *endnote* is a reference placed at the end of a section or a document.

► You can use either numbers or symbols to label footnotes and endnotes.

1. Scroll to the bulleted list near the top of Page 2. At the end of the first bulleted item—*Garages and sheds*—click to position the insertion point.

2. Click the **References tab**, and then in the **Footnotes group**, click the **Insert Footnote** button.

   A footnote displays at the bottom of the page with a number *1* before the insertion point. A line is also inserted above the footnote area to separate it from the document text.

3. Type On structurally weaker buildings, potted plants work best. Compare your screen with **Figure 1**.

   Footnotes are used to provide supplemental information that does not fit well in the document.

4. Scroll up to the paragraph below the bulleted list that begins *The main consideration*. Position the insertion point at the end of the paragraph.

5. In the **Footnotes group**, click the **Insert Footnote** button. Type Heavier materials should be located near load-bearing walls. Compare your screen with **Figure 2**.

   The second footnote displays below the first, and the footnotes are numbered sequentially.

■ **Continue to the next page to complete the skill**

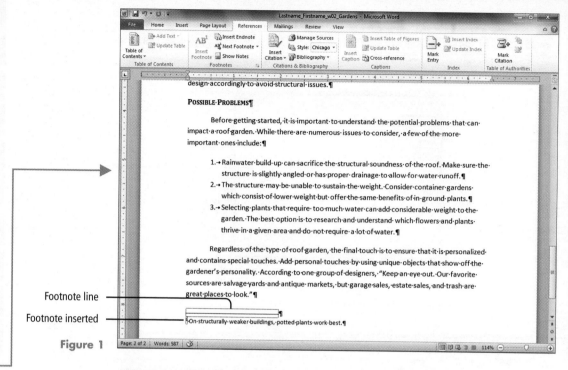

Footnote line

Footnote inserted

Figure 1

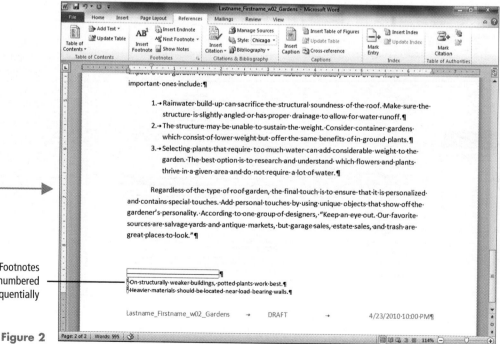

Footnotes numbered sequentially

Figure 2

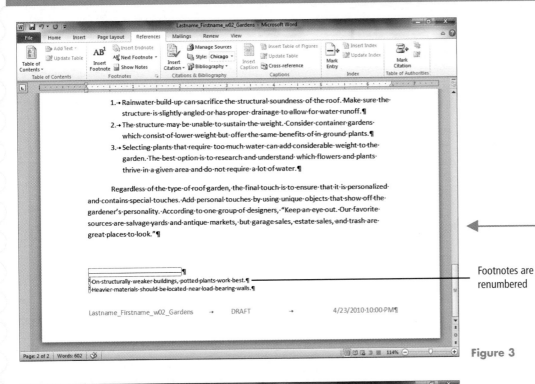

Footnotes are
renumbered

Figure 3

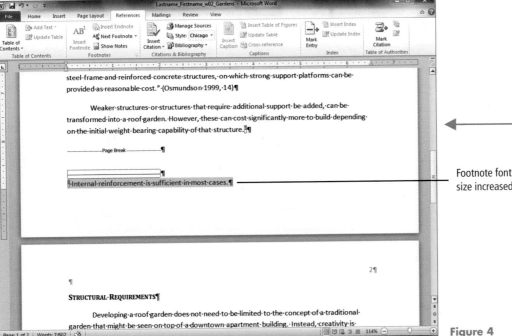

Footnote font
size increased

Figure 4

6. Scroll to the last paragraph on Page 1—
the one that begins *Weaker structures or
structures*. Position the insertion point at
the end of that paragraph.

7. On the **References tab**, in the **Footnotes
group**, click the **Footnotes Dialog Box
Launcher** ▣.

In the Footnote and Endnote dialog box,
you can change footnotes to endnotes or
label the notes with characters other than
numbers.

8. In the **Footnote and Endnote** dialog box,
click **Insert**. Notice that the new footnote
is number *1*, and then type Internal
reinforcement is sufficient in most cases.

9. Scroll to the bottom of Page 2, and then
compare your screen with **Figure 3**.

By default, the footnote font size is smaller
than the font size in the rest of the document. Here, the footnote numbers have
automatically updated to *2* and *3*.

10. At the bottom of Page 2, select both
footnotes. On the Mini toolbar, click the
Font Size arrow ⏷, and then click **12**.

Most style manuals call for the footer text
to be the same size as the document text.

11. Scroll to the bottom of Page 1, select the
footnote, and change the **Font Size** to **12**.
Compare your screen with **Figure 4**.

12. **Save** ▣ the document.

■ **You have completed Skill 8 of 10**

▶ When you use quotations or detailed information from a reference source, you need to specify the source in the document.

▶ A *citation* is a note in the document that refers the reader to a source in the bibliography.

1. Display the lower half of Page 1. Notice that two citations are displayed in parentheses.

   Many business reports use an abbreviated citation, which contains the author's last name, the year of publication, and the page number.

2. On the **References tab**, in the **Citations & Bibliography group**, click the **Manage Sources** button. Compare your screen with **Figure 1.**

   The sources used in the current document display with a check mark on the right.

3. **Close** the Source Manager dialog box. Near the top of Page 2, in the paragraph that begins *The main*, click to the right of the second quotation mark. On the **References tab**, in the **Citations & Bibliography group**, be sure the **Style** is set to **Chicago**. Click the **Insert Citation** button, and then click **Add New Source**.

4. In the **Create Source** dialog box, if necessary click the **Type of Source arrow**, and then click **Book**. In the **Author** box, type Stevens, David In the **Title** box, type Roof Gardens, Balconies & Terraces

5. For the **Year**, type 1997 and for the **City** type Milan For the **Publisher**, type Rizzoli International and then compare your screen with **Figure 2.**

■ **Continue to the next page to complete the skill**

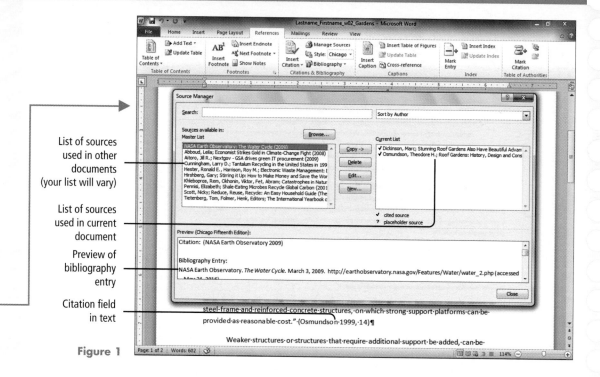

List of sources used in other documents (your list will vary)

List of sources used in current document

Preview of bibliography entry

Citation field in text

Figure 1

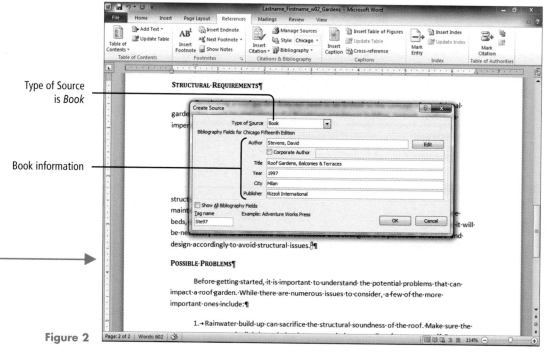

Type of Source is *Book*

Book information

Figure 2

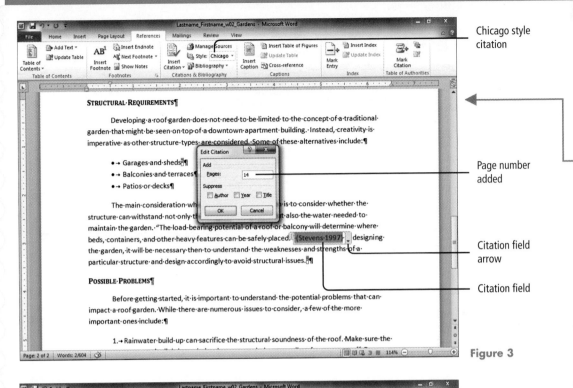

Figure 3

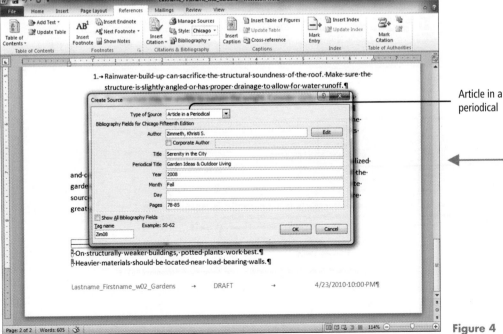

Figure 4

6. In the **Create Source** dialog box, click **OK** to insert an abbreviated citation. Click the citation one time. On the right side of the field, click the **arrow**, and then from the menu, click **Edit Citation**.

7. In the **Edit Citation** dialog box, under **Add**, in the **Pages** box, type 14 to add the page number to the citation. Compare your screen with **Figure 3**.

8. In the **Edit Citation** dialog box, click **OK**. Press Ctrl + End to move to the end of the document. On the **References tab**, in the **Citations & Bibliography group**, click the **Insert Citation** button, and then click **Add New Source**.

9. In the **Create Source** dialog box, click the **Type of Source arrow**, and then click **Article in a Periodical**. In the **Author** box, type Zimmeth, Khristi S. For the **Title**, type Serenity in the City

10. For the **Periodical Title**, type Garden Ideas & Outdoor Living For the **Year**, type 2008 For the **Month** type Fall For the **Pages**, type 78-85 and then compare your screen with **Figure 4**.

11. In the **Create Source** dialog box, click **OK**. Click the citation, click the **arrow**, and then click **Edit Citation**.

12. In the **Edit Citation** dialog box, in the **Pages** box, type 83 and click **OK**.

13. In the **Citations & Bibliography** group, click the **Manage Sources** button. Notice that your new sources are added to the Source Manager.

14. **Close** the dialog box and **Save** 💾 the document.

■ **You have completed Skill 9 of 10**

► A ***bibliography*** is a list of sources referenced in a report, and is listed on a separate page at the end of the report.

► Different styles use different titles for the sources page, including *Works Cited*, *Bibliography*, *References*, or *Sources*.

1. Press Ctrl + End, and then press Ctrl + Enter to insert a manual page break and start a new page. Press Enter two times.

   The bibliography should begin about two inches from the top of the page.

2. On the **References tab**, in the **Citations & Bibliography group**, click the **Bibliography** button to display two built-in bibliographies, as shown in **Figure 1**. ──────────

3. From the gallery, click the **Bibliography** thumbnail to insert a bibliography field. If necessary, scroll up to display the inserted bibliography field. If necessary, close the Navigation pane.

   The bibliography field includes a title and lists the sources cited in the document. The multiple-line references use hanging indents. In a ***hanging indent***, the first line extends to the left of the rest of the paragraph.

4. Right-click the **Bibliography** title, and then on the Mini toolbar, click the **Center** button ▣ to center the title on the page.

5. Click to the right of the title, and then press Enter to add a blank line between the title and the sources. Compare your screen with **Figure 2**. ──────────

6. If necessary, click the **References** tab. In the **Citations & Bibliography group**, click the **Manage Sources** button.

■ **Continue to the next page to complete the skill** ➤

Bibliography gallery

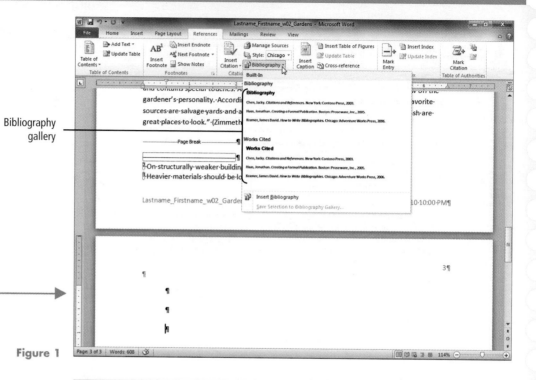

Figure 1

Bibliography field

Title centered

Hanging indent applied to sources

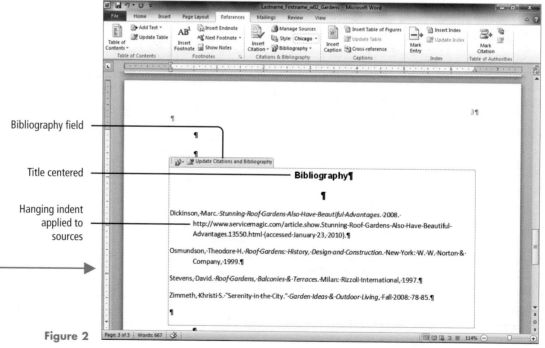

Figure 2

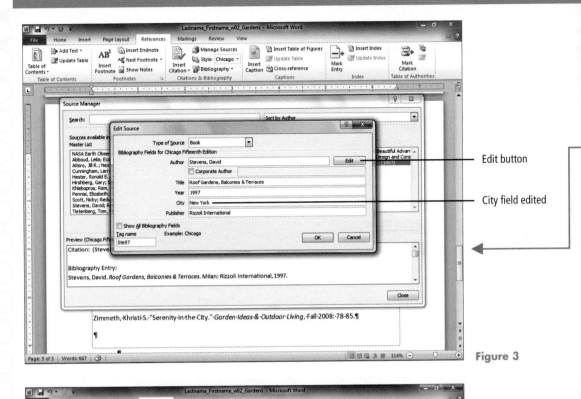

Edit button

City field edited

Figure 3

Click to update field

Bibliography field updated

Figure 4

7. In the **Source Manager** dialog box, under **Current List**, select the *Stevens, David* source. At the bottom of the **Source Manager** dialog box, notice the **Preview**, and then click the **Edit** button.

8. In the **Edit Source** dialog box, in the **City** box, select *Milan*. Type New York and then compare your screen with **Figure 3**.

9. Click **OK** to close the dialog box, read the displayed message, and then click **Yes**.

> The change will be made to both the current document and the master list.

10. In the **Source Manager** dialog box, under **Master List**, select the *Stevens, David* source, and then to the right of the Master List, click the **Delete** button. Use the same procedure to remove the *Zimmeth, Khristi S.* source.

> If you are using a computer in a lab or other public area, it is good practice to restore any permanent changes you make to original settings—in this case, remove the sources from the master list.

11. In the **Source Manager** dialog box, click **Close**. Click in the bibliography. Notice that the change from *Milan* to *New York* has not been made—you must manually update fields when you change them.

12. At the top of the bibliography field, click **Update Citations and Bibliography**. Compare your screen with **Figure 4**.

> The bibliography field is updated to include the change you made in the Source Manager.

13. **Save** ◪ the document. Submit your printout or files electronically as directed by your instructor. **Exit** Word.

Done! You have completed Skill 10 of 10 and your document is complete!

More Skills

The following More Skills are located at **www.pearsonhighered.com/skills**

More Skills Record AutoCorrect Entries

If you enable the AutoCorrect feature in Word, when you misspell a word that is contained in the AutoCorrect list, the misspelling is corrected automatically. You can add words that you commonly misspell as you type, or you can open a dialog box and add words or phrases that you want to be automatically corrected. This feature can also be used to create shortcuts for phrases that you type regularly.

In More Skills 11, you will open a short document and use two methods to add items to the AutoCorrect Options list.

To begin, open your web browser, navigate to www.pearsonhighered.com/skills, locate the name of your textbook, and then follow the instructions on the website.

More Skills Use AutoFormat to Create Numbered Lists

If you create a lot of numbered lists, Word has an AutoFormat feature that lets you start typing the list, and the program will automatically add numbers and formatting to the list as you type.

In More Skills 12, you will open a document, set the AutoFormat options, and then create a numbered list that is formatted automatically.

To begin, open your web browser, navigate to www.pearsonhighered.com/skills, locate the name of your textbook, and then follow the instructions on the website.

More Skills Format and Customize Lists

In this chapter, you create and format numbered and bulleted lists. There are several other formatting changes you can make to lists. You can change the numbering scheme for numbered lists, and you can change the character used for the bullet symbol. You can also increase or decrease the indent of both types of lists.

In More Skills 13, you will open a document and change the numbering on a numbered list. You will also increase the indent on a bulleted list.

To begin, open your web browser, navigate to www.pearsonhighered.com/skills, locate the name of your textbook, and then follow the instructions on the website.

More Skills Manage Document Properties

Document properties are the detailed information about your document that can help you identify or organize your files, including the name of the author, the title, and keywords. Some document properties are added to the document when you create it. You can add others as necessary.

In More Skills 14, you will open a document, open the Document Properties, and add properties where appropriate.

To begin, open your web browser, navigate to www.pearsonhighered.com/skills, locate the name of your textbook, and then follow the instructions on the website.

Key Terms

Online Help Skills

1. Start 🌐 Word. In the upper right corner of the Word window, click the **Help** button 📷. In the **Help** window, click the **Maximize** 📷 button.

2. Under **Getting started with Word 2010**, click **Create a document to be used by previous versions of Word.**

3. Read the article's introduction, and then below **Turn on Compatibility Mode**, read the steps required to create a document in an earlier Word format, and then in the last sentence of the introduction, click **Features that behave differently in earlier versions**. Compare your screen with **Figure 1**.

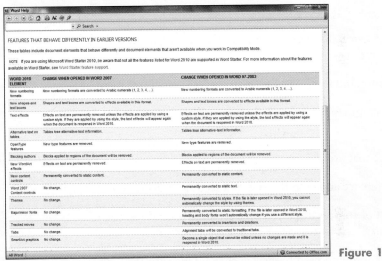

Figure 1

4. Read this information to see if you can answer the following: How do you save a document in an earlier format, such as Word 97-2003? What are three features that work in Word 2010 that do not work properly in Word 97-2003?

Matching

Match each term in the second column with its correct definition in the first column by writing the letter of the term on the blank line in front of the correct definition.

____ **1.** The space between the text and the top, bottom, left, and right edges of the paper when you print the document.

____ **2.** The position of the first line of a paragraph relative to the text in the rest of the paragraph.

____ **3.** The equivalent of a blank line of text displayed between each line of text in a paragraph.

____ **4.** The vertical distance above and below each paragraph in a document.

____ **5.** A command that copies formatting from one place to another.

____ **6.** The command that locates text in a document.

____ **7.** The type of list used for items that are in chronological or sequential order.

____ **8.** A reference added to the end of a section or document.

____ **9.** A list of sources displayed on a separate page at the end of a report.

____ **10.** The command used to display changes made in the Source Manager to a source listed in the bibliography.

A Bibliography

B Double-spacing

C Endnote

D Find

E First line indent

F Format Painter

G Margin

H Numbered

I Paragraph spacing

J Update Field

Multiple Choice

Choose the correct answer.

1. To create your own document margins, use this command at the bottom of the Margins gallery.
   A. Format Paragraph
   B. Document Settings
   C. Custom Margins

2. The placement of paragraph text relative to the left and right document margins is called paragraph:
   A. Alignment
   B. Margins
   C. Orientation

3. The vertical distance between lines in a paragraph is called:
   A. Spacing after
   B. Line spacing
   C. Text wrapping

4. This alignment is used to position paragraph text an equal distance between the left and right margin:
   A. Justify
   B. Center
   C. Middle

5. This type of alignment positions the text so that it is aligned with both the left and right margins.
   A. Justify
   B. Center
   C. Left

6. Hold down [Ctrl] + [Enter] to insert one of these:
   A. Manual line break
   B. Manual paragraph break
   C. Manual page break

7. Items that can be listed in any order are best presented using which of the following?
   A. Bulleted list
   B. Numbered list
   C. Outline list

8. In a bibliography, this type of indent is used for each reference:
   A. Hanging indent
   B. First line indent
   C. Left alignment

9. To place a note on the same page as the reference source, use which of these?
   A. Footnote
   B. Endnote
   C. Citation

10. This refers to an entry in a bibliography.
    A. Footnote
    B. Citation
    C. Endnote

Topics for Discussion

1. You can build and save a list of master sources you have used in research papers and reports and display them using Manage Sources. What are the advantages of storing sources over time?

2. Paragraph text can be left aligned, centered, right aligned, or justified. Left alignment is the most commonly used. In what situations would you use centered text? Justified text? Can you think of any situations where you might want to use right alignment?

Skill Check

To complete this document, you will need the following file:

- w02_Landscape

You will save your document as:

- Lastname_Firstname_w02_Landscape

1. **Start** Word. Open **w02_Landscape**. **Save** the document in your **Word Chapter 2** folder as Lastname_Firstname_w02_Landscape

2. On the **Page Layout tab**, in the **Page Setup group**, click the **Margins** button, and then click **Custom Margins**. Under **Margins**, change the **Left** and **Right** margins to **1**, and then click **OK**. In the second title line, to the right of *By*, type your name.

3. Press **Ctrl** + **A**. On the **Home tab**, in the **Paragraph group**, change the **Line spacing** to **1.15**. On the **Page Layout tab**, in the **Paragraph group**, change the spacing **After** to **12 pt**.

4. Click in the paragraph that begins *Landscaping can be*. On the **Home tab**, in the **Paragraph group**, change the alignment to **Align Left**. In the **Paragraph group**, display the **Paragraph** dialog box. Under **Indentation**, set the **Special** box to **First line**, and then click **OK**. Compare your screen with **Figure 1**.

5. On the **Home tab**, in the **Clipboard group**, double-click the **Format Painter** button, and then copy the current paragraph formatting to the paragraphs that begin *When designing*, *Landscape garden*, *Time is*, *Landscape design*, and *In addition*; also the last three paragraphs in the document. Press **Esc** to turn off Format Painter.

6. Near the top of the document, select the subheading *Landscaping as a Weather Barrier*. In the **Font group**, click the **Dialog Box Launcher** to display the **Font** dialog box. Apply **Bold** emphasis and **Small caps**, and then click **OK**. Copy the formatting of this subheading to the other two subheadings: *Landscaping that Attracts Butterflies*, and *Landscaping to Minimize Water Use*.

7. Press **Ctrl** + **Home**. On the **Home tab**, in the **Editing group**, click the **Replace** button. In the **Find what** box, type insure In the **Replace with** box, type ensure and then click **Replace All**. **Save** the document, and then compare your screen with **Figure 2**.

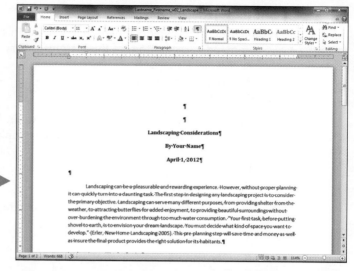

Figure 1

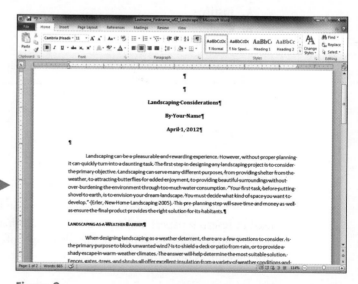

Figure 2

 **Continue to the next page to complete this Skill Check**

8. Near the bottom of Page 1, locate and select the three tree names, beginning with *Willow hybrid*. In the **Paragraph group**, apply **Bullets**, and then click the **Increase Indent** button.

9. Near the top of Page 2, locate and select the four nonindented paragraphs, beginning with *Planting nectar flowers*. In the **Paragraph group**, apply **Numbering**, and then click the **Increase Indent** button.

10. Press ⌃Ctrl + Home. On the **Insert tab**, in the **Header & Footer group**, click **Header**, and then click **Edit Header**. On the **Design tab**, in the **Header & Footer group**, click the **Page Number** button, and then point to **Top of Page**. Under **Simple**, click **Plain Number 3**. Move to the footer. In the **Insert group**, click the **Quick Parts** button, and then click **Field**. Under **Field Names**, click **FileName**, and then click **OK**. In the **Options group**, select the **Different First Page** check box.

11. In the bulleted list, click to the right of *Willow hybrid*. On the **References tab**, in the **Footnotes group**, insert the following footnote: These trees grow quickly but do not live very long. On Page 2, at the end of the second item in the numbered list, insert the following footnote: Local nurseries can help you determine which flowers to use. Compare your screen with **Figure 3**.

12. On the **Home tab**, in the **Editing group**, click the **Find** button. In the **Navigation Pane**, in the search box, type creating and notice that there is only one instance of the word. In the document, double-click the highlighted word, and then type developing to replace the word. **Close** the Navigation Pane.

13. Press ⌃Ctrl + Home. In the first paragraph below the title, that begins *Landscaping can be*, locate and click anywhere in the *Erler* citation. Click the citation **arrow**, and then from the menu, click **Edit Citation**. Under **Add**, in the **Pages** box, type 2 and then click **OK**. Click the citation **arrow** again, and then click **Edit Source**. In the **Edit Source** dialog box, change the title of the book from *New Home Landscaping* to New Complete Home Landscaping and then click **OK**.

14. Press ⌃Ctrl + End, and then press ⌃Ctrl + Enter to add a new page. Press Enter two times.

15. On the **References tab**, in the **Citations & Bibliography group**, click the **Bibliography** button, and then click the **Bibliography** thumbnail. Select the *Bibliography* title. From the Mini toolbar, click the **Center** button. Press End and then press Enter.

16. **Save** the document, and then submit as directed. Compare your document with **Figure 4**.

Done! You have completed the Skill Check

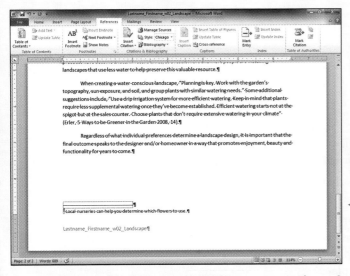

Figure 3

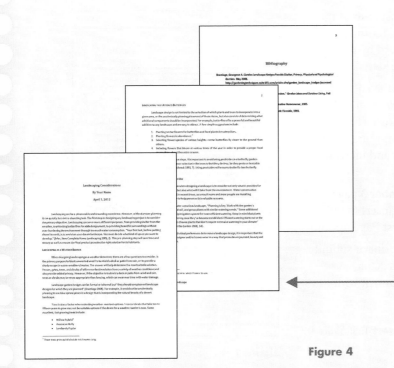

Figure 4

Assess Your Skills 1

To complete this document, you will need the following file:

- w02_Lighting

You will save your document as:

- Lastname_Firstname_w02_Lighting

1. **Start** Word. Locate and open **w02_Lighting**, and then **Save** it in your **Word Chapter 2** folder as Lastname_Firstname_w02_Lighting Set the document's **Top** margin to **1"**, and the **Left** and **Right** margins to **1.3"**.

2. Press Enter three times and type Home Lighting For the second title, type By and your name, and then for the third title, type May 25, 2012 Add a blank line following the date.

3. Select *all* of the text in the document. Change the spacing after the paragraphs to *6 pt* and change the **Line Spacing** to **1.15**. Change the paragraph alignment from *Justify* to **Align Left. Center** all three titles and change their **Font** to **Arial Black.**

4. Near the top of the document, locate the four questions that begin *What is the function.* Change the four questions to a numbered list, and increase the indent one time. Further down the page, select the four lines starting *provide decorative lighting* and ending *substitute for sunlight* and apply a bulleted list with the indent increased one time. At the bottom of the report, repeat this procedure with the three paragraphs (five lines) that begin *Installing* and *Turning lights* and *Understanding.*

5. Near the top of the document, locate the *Interior Lighting* subheading. Add **Bold** emphasis and **Small Caps**, and change the

Font to **Arial Black.** Apply the same format to the other two subheadings: *Exterior Lighting* and *Lighting for Energy Efficiency.*

6. For the seven remaining paragraphs that are not titles or lists, indent the first line by *0.5".*

7. Click the **Find** button and search for *lightning*—not *lighting*—and notice how many misuses of the word are found in the document. Display the **Find and Replace** dialog box, and change each instance of *lightning* to *lighting*

8. On Page 1, at the end of the last item in the bulleted list, add the following footnote: The color temperature produced by the lighting units needs to be considered.

9. Near the bottom of Page 1, at the end of the paragraph that begins *Consider what the room,* add the following footnote: These can include both permanent and movable light fixtures. Select both footnotes and increase the **Font Size** to **11** points.

10. On Page 1, insert a **Plain Number 3** page number header. In the footer, insert the file name. Select the **Different First Page** option.

11. **Save** the document, and then print or submit the file as directed by your instructor. Compare your completed document with Figure 1.

Done! You have completed Assess Your Skills 1

Figure 1

Assess Your Skills 2

Assess Your Skills 3 and 4 can be found at **www.pearsonhighered.com/skills**.

To complete this document, you will need the following file:

- w02_Retrofit

You will save the document as:

- Lastname_Firstname_w02_Retrofit

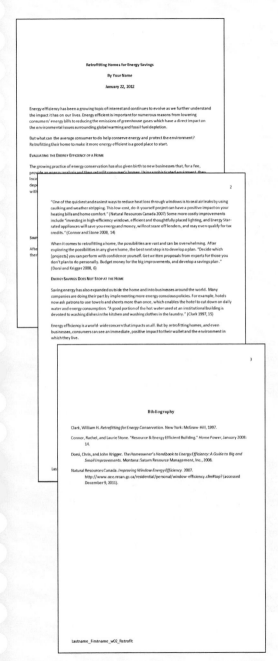

Figure 1

1. **Start** Word. Locate and open **w02_Retrofit**, and then **Save** it in your **Word Chapter 2** folder as Lastname_Firstname_w02_Retrofit Set the document's **Left** and **Right** margins to *1"*.

2. Type your name in the second title line to the right of *By*.

3. Select all of the text in the document. Change the spacing after all paragraphs to *12 pt* and change the **Line Spacing** to **1.15**. Change the paragraph alignment from *Justify* to **Align Left**. **Center** the three titles and add **Bold** emphasis.

4. For the three subheadings that begin *Evaluating the Energy* and *Simple Ways* and *Energy Savings Does Not*, apply **Bold** emphasis and the **Small Caps** style.

5. On Page 1, select the three paragraphs that begin *Check for drafts*, change them to a numbered list, and then increase the indent one time. Further down the page, select the four paragraphs that begin *Replace light bulbs*, change them to a bulleted list, and then increase the indent one time.

6. At the top of Page 2, click to the right of the quotation mark at the end of the paragraph that ends *credits*. Using the **Chicago** style, insert a new **Article in a Periodical** citation. In the **Author** box, type Connor, Rachel; Stone, Laurie The **Title** is Resource & Energy Efficient Building The **Periodical Title** is

Home Power The **Year** is 2008 The **Month** is January The **Pages** are 14 (one-page article). Edit the citation field to include the source's page number.

7. Near the bottom of the report, click at the end of the paragraph that begins *Saving energy*. Insert a new **Book** citation. In the **Author** box, type Clark, William H. The **Title** is Retrofitting for Energy Conservation The **Year** is 1997 The **City** is New York The **Publisher** is McGraw-Hill Edit the citation to add 15 as the page number of the quotation.

8. At the end of the document, use a manual page break to create a new page. At about 2 inches from the top edge of the last page, insert the built-in **Bibliography**. **Center** the title and add a blank line between the title and the sources. Select the title *Bibliography*, change the **Font Size** to **11** and the **Font Color** to **Black**.

9. On Page 1, insert the **Plain Number 3** page number header. In the footer, insert the file name, and then select the **Different First Page** option.

10. **Save** the document, and then print or submit the file as directed by your instructor. Compare your completed document with **Figure 1**.

Done! You have completed Assess Your Skills 2

Assess Your Skills Visually

To complete this document, you will need the following file:

- w02_Parks

You will save your document as:

- Lastname_Firstname_w02_Parks

Open the file **w02_Parks**, and then save it in your **Word Chapter 2** folder as Lastname_ Firstname_w02_Parks Create the document shown in **Figure 1**.

To complete this document, set the left and right margins to 1.3 inches. The first title should start at approximately 2 inches on the vertical ruler. All of the text is 12-point Calibri. The list should align with the first line of the indented paragraphs. Because this is a very short document with only one reference—at the end of the second-to-last paragraph—it is placed in a footnote as shown in **Figure 1**. Line spacing should be 1.15, with six points of spacing after paragraphs. Below the file name in the footer, add the current date field. Print or submit the file as directed by your instructor.

Done! You have completed Assess Your Skills Visually

Park Designs

By Your Name

March 15, 2012

Parks offer numerous benefits, from providing habitats for local animals and plants to serving as a psychological benefit to its occupants. The benefits of open spaces and fresh air have been well documented. Visiting a park can be relaxing and refreshing, and can even help relieve stress. Parks should be designed to accommodate local needs and conditions. Thus, when designing a park, it is important to consider:

- Who will be using the park?
- What kinds of wildlife will live in the park?
- What kinds of plant life are indigenous to the area?

ECOLOGICAL IMPACTS

When considering the ecological aspect of a park, it is critical to understand who will be the natural habitants of the park and what structures or plants would foster their well-being? Gaining a thorough understanding and conduction real world observations are recommended in order to understand the local wildlife and how their presence influences the design of the park.

PARK SIZE

The available space can have a huge impact on the design of a park. Small parks "can provide a place away from but close to home, a place that is not too isolated, and a place that avoids some of the problems that can occur in larger parks, crimes, for example."[1]

One additional step in designing a park is to get the opinions and suggestions of the people living in the community. In doing so, it will help to ensure that the final park is something that they have helped to design and will encourage use.

---

[1] Ann Forsyth and Laura Mussacchio, *Designing Small Parks: A Manual for Addressing Social and Ecological Concerns*, Wiley & Sons, New Jersey, 2005, p. 14.

Lastname_Firstname_w02_Parks
September 12, 2012

Figure 1

Skills in Context

To complete this document, you will need the following file:

- New blank Word document

You will save your document as:

- Lastname_Firstname_w02_National_Parks

The City of Aspen Falls Planning Department is working with the Travel and Tourism Bureau to explore ways to use the city as the base of operation for tourists who want to visit important sites within a day's drive. Using the skills you practiced in this chapter, create a report on the nearby major nature attractions. These could include Yosemite National Park (250 miles), Death Valley National Park (200 miles), Sequoia National Forest (180 miles), and the Channel Islands National Park (40 miles). Research three of these (or other) national sites, and write the highlights of what a visitor might find at each. Your report should include at least two footnotes and two citations, one list for each site, and a bibliography. The lists should contain between three and six items each. Format the report in the style practiced in the chapter.

Save the document as Lastname_Firstname_ w02_National_Parks Insert the file name and current date in the footer, and check the entire document for grammar and spelling. Print or submit the file as directed by your instructor.

Done! You have completed Skills in Context

Skills and You

To complete this document, you will need the following file:

- New blank Word document

You will save your document as:

- Lastname_Firstname_w02_My_Home

Using the skills you have practiced in this chapter, compose a document about your hometown (or county, region, state, or province). The document should include a top margin of two inches; other margins of one inch each, and a title and subtitle appropriately formatted. You should include three paragraphs of text, with appropriate line spacing and spacing after the paragraphs, with the text left aligned and the first lines indented. You should also include a list of things to see or do in the area, and at least three informational footnotes. If you need to use quotations, include references and a bibliography.

Add the file name and date to the footer. Save the document as Lastname_Firstname_w02_My_Home Check the entire document for grammar and spelling. Print or submit the file as directed by your instructor.

Done! You have completed Skills and You

CHAPTER 3

Work with Graphics, Tabs, and Tables

▶ You can add graphics to a document to enhance the effectiveness of your message or to make your document more attractive.

▶ You can use tables to present data in a format of rows and columns, which can make complex information easy to understand at a glance.

Your starting screen will look similar to this:

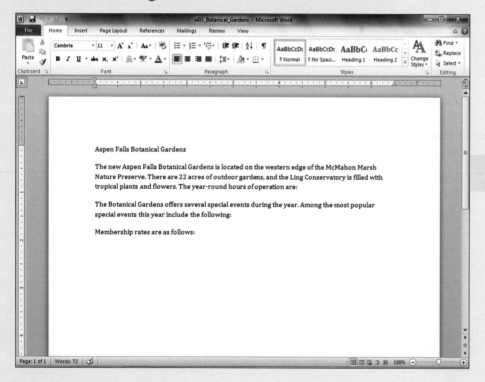

SKILLS

Skills 1-10 Training

At the end of this chapter, you will be able to:

Skill 1 Insert Pictures from Files

Skill 2 Resize and Move Pictures

Skill 3 Format Pictures Using Styles and Artistic Effects

Skill 4 Set Tab Stops

Skill 5 Enter Text with Tab Stops

Skill 6 Apply Table Styles

Skill 7 Create Tables

Skill 8 Add Rows and Columns to Tables

Skill 9 Format Text in Table Cells

Skill 10 Format Tables

MORE SKILLS

More Skills 11 Insert Text Boxes

More Skills 12 Format with WordArt

More Skills 13 Create Tables from Existing Lists

More Skills 14 Insert Drop Caps

Outcome

Using the skills listed to the left will enable you to create a document like this:

Aspen Falls Botanical Gardens

The new Aspen Falls Botanical Gardens is located on the western edge of the McMahon Marsh Nature Preserve. There are 22 acres of outdoor gardens, and the Ling Conservatory is filled with tropical plants and flowers. The year-round hours of operation are:

Day...Hours
Monday-Wednesday...10 to 5
Thursday-Friday ....10 to 6
Saturday ....8 to 5
Sunday ....Noon to 5

The Botanical Gardens offers several special events during the year. Among the most popular special events this year include the following:

Event	Month(s)	Description
Butterflies	May and June	Conservatory display of butterflies from around town and around the world
Rainforest	January to April	Wonders of the rain forests are displayed
Photograph Nature	July and August	Nature photography contest for kids, teens, and adults—photos must be from Aspen Falls area
Holiday Decorations	December	Decorations and model trains

Membership rates are as follows:

Memberships		
Group	Ages	Cost
Children	Under 12	Free
Students	Under 18	$ 8.00
Adults	18 to 60	25.00
Seniors	Over 60	12.50

Lastname_Firstname_w03_Botanical

You will save your file as:

Lastname_Firstname_w03_Botanical

In this chapter, you will create documents for the Aspen Falls City Hall, which provides essential services for the citizens and visitors of Aspen Falls, California.

Introduction

▶ Digital images—such as those you have scanned or taken with a digital camera—can be added to a document and formatted using distinctive borders and other interesting and attractive effects.

▶ You can organize lists in rows and columns by using tabs.

▶ The table feature in Word lets you organize lists and data in columns and rows without needing to create tab settings.

▶ You can use tables to summarize and emphasize information in an organized arrangement of rows and columns that are easy to read.

▶ You can format tables manually or apply a number of different formats quickly using built-in styles.

Time to complete all
10 skills – 55 minutes

Find your student data files here:

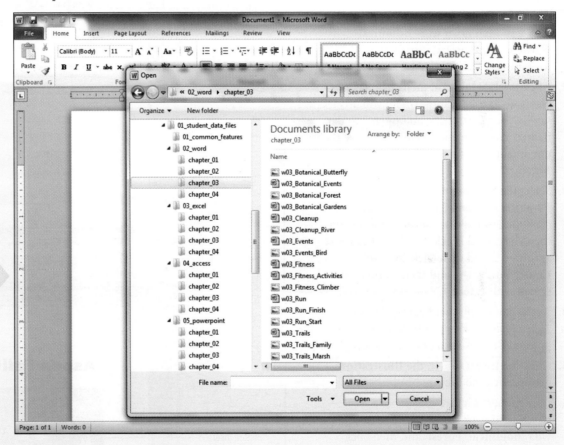

Student data files needed for this chapter:

- w03_Botanical_Gardens
- w03_Botanical_Forest
- w03_Botanical_Butterfly
- w03_Botanical_Events

▶ Recall that pictures are inserted at the insertion point location and are positioned in the paragraph in the same manner as a letter or a number.

▶ You can insert pictures that you have scanned or downloaded from the Web, or pictures from your digital camera.

1. **Start** ⊛ Word. Click the **File tab**, and then click **Open**. Navigate to your student files, and then open **w03_Botanical_ Gardens**. If necessary, display the formatting marks.

2. Click the **File tab**, and then click **Save As**. Navigate to the location where you are saving your files, create and open a folder named Word Chapter 3 and then **Save** the document as Lastname_Firstname_w03_ Botanical

3. Select the document title *Aspen Falls Botanical Gardens*. On the Mini toolbar, click the **Font arrow** [Calibri (Body) ▾], locate and then click **Arial Black**. Click the **Font Size arrow** [11 ▾], and then click **26**. Click the **Center** button [≡], and then compare your screen with **Figure 1**.

4. In the paragraph that begins *The new Aspen Falls*, click to position the insertion point at the beginning of the paragraph.

5. Click the **Insert tab**. In the **Illustrations group**, click the **Picture** button.

6. In the **Insert Picture** dialog box, navigate to your student files, select **w03_Botanical_Forest**, and then click **Insert**. Compare your screen with **Figure 2**.

■ **Continue to the next page to complete the skill** ▶

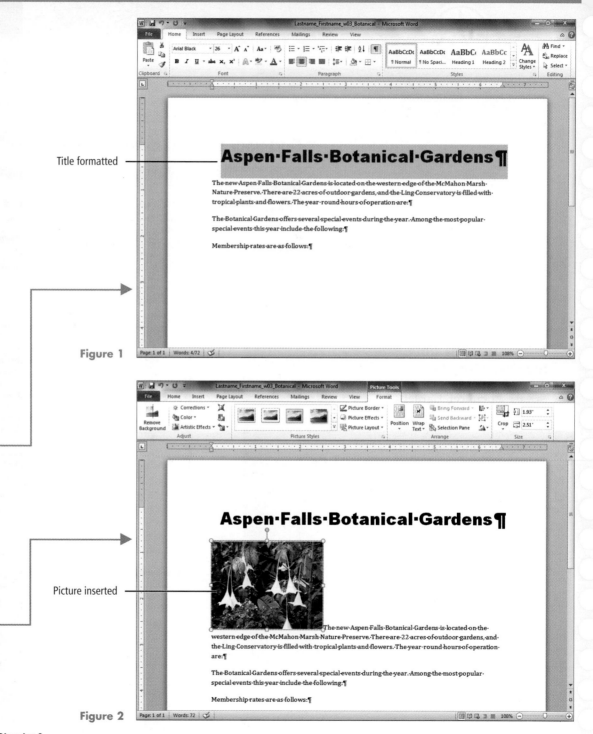

Title formatted

Figure 1

Picture inserted

Figure 2

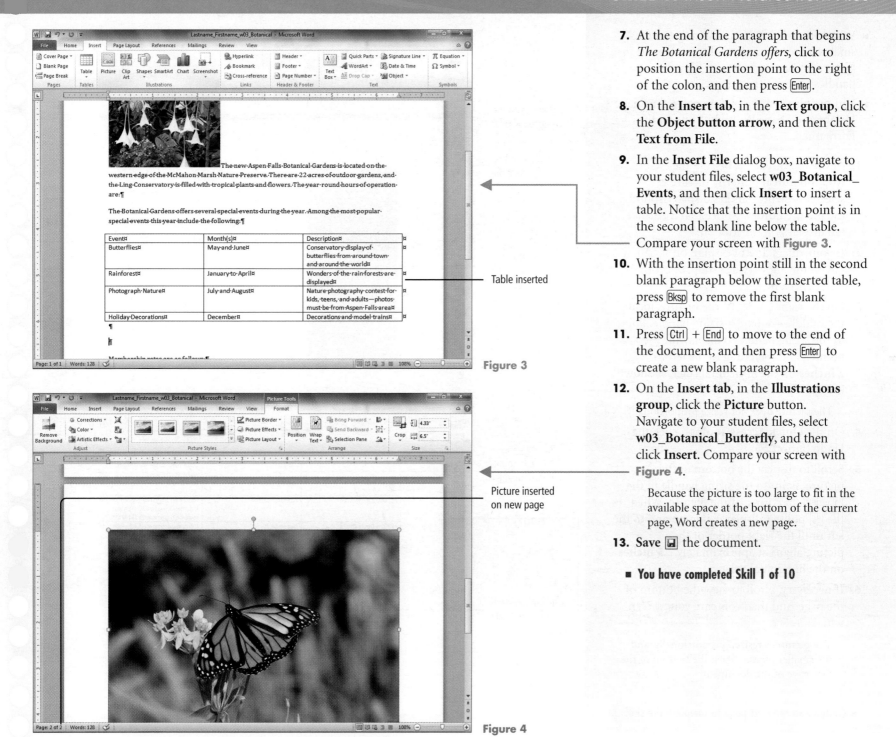

Figure 3

Table inserted

Figure 4

Picture inserted
on new page

7. At the end of the paragraph that begins *The Botanical Gardens offers*, click to position the insertion point to the right of the colon, and then press Enter.

8. On the **Insert tab**, in the **Text group**, click the **Object button arrow**, and then click **Text from File**.

9. In the **Insert File** dialog box, navigate to your student files, select **w03_Botanical_ Events**, and then click **Insert** to insert a table. Notice that the insertion point is in the second blank line below the table. Compare your screen with **Figure 3**.

10. With the insertion point still in the second blank paragraph below the inserted table, press Bksp to remove the first blank paragraph.

11. Press Ctrl + End to move to the end of the document, and then press Enter to create a new blank paragraph.

12. On the **Insert tab**, in the **Illustrations group**, click the **Picture** button. Navigate to your student files, select **w03_Botanical_Butterfly**, and then click **Insert**. Compare your screen with **Figure 4**.

    Because the picture is too large to fit in the available space at the bottom of the current page, Word creates a new page.

13. **Save** 🖫 the document.

■ **You have completed Skill 1 of 10**

▶ When you select a picture, *sizing handles*—small squares or circles—display around the picture border, and you can drag these handles to resize the picture.

▶ You can also resize a picture using the Shape Height and Shape Width buttons on the Format tab.

1. At the top of Page 2, be sure the **w03_Botanical** butterfly picture is selected—sizing handles display around the picture border. Notice that a Format tab displays on the Ribbon.

2. If your rulers do not display, on the View tab, in the Show/Hide group, select the Ruler check box.

3. On the right border of the picture, locate the middle—square—sizing handle. Point to the sizing handle to display the ⟷ pointer, and then drag to the left to **2 inches** on the horizontal ruler, as shown in **Figure 1**.

    The picture does not resize proportionally.

4. On the **Quick Access Toolbar**, click the **Undo** button.

5. Scroll to display the bottom of the picture. Point to the sizing handle in the lower right corner of the picture. When the ⬉ pointer displays, drag up and to the left until the right border of the picture aligns at approximately **2.5 inches** on the horizontal ruler.

6. If necessary, scroll to view the bottom of the page, and then compare your screen with **Figure 2**.

    The picture is resized proportionally, and the smaller picture fits at the bottom of the first page of the document.

■ **Continue to the next page to complete the skill**

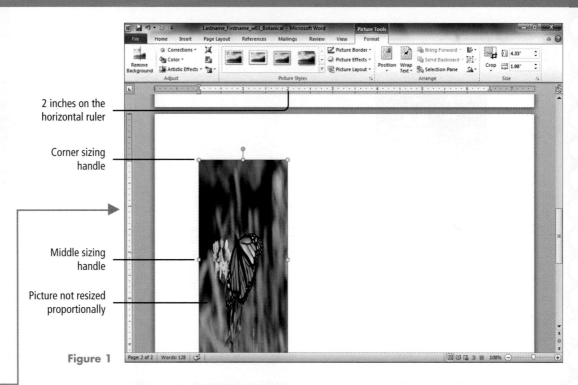

2 inches on the horizontal ruler

Corner sizing handle

Middle sizing handle

Picture not resized proportionally

Figure 1

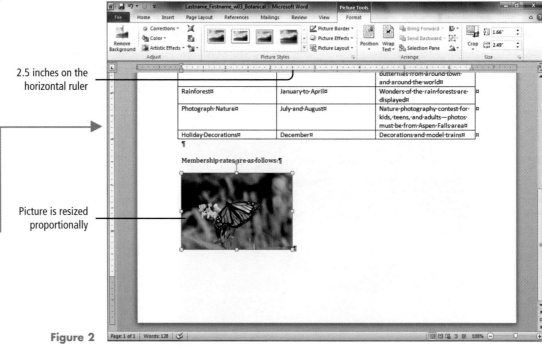

2.5 inches on the horizontal ruler

Picture is resized proportionally

Figure 2

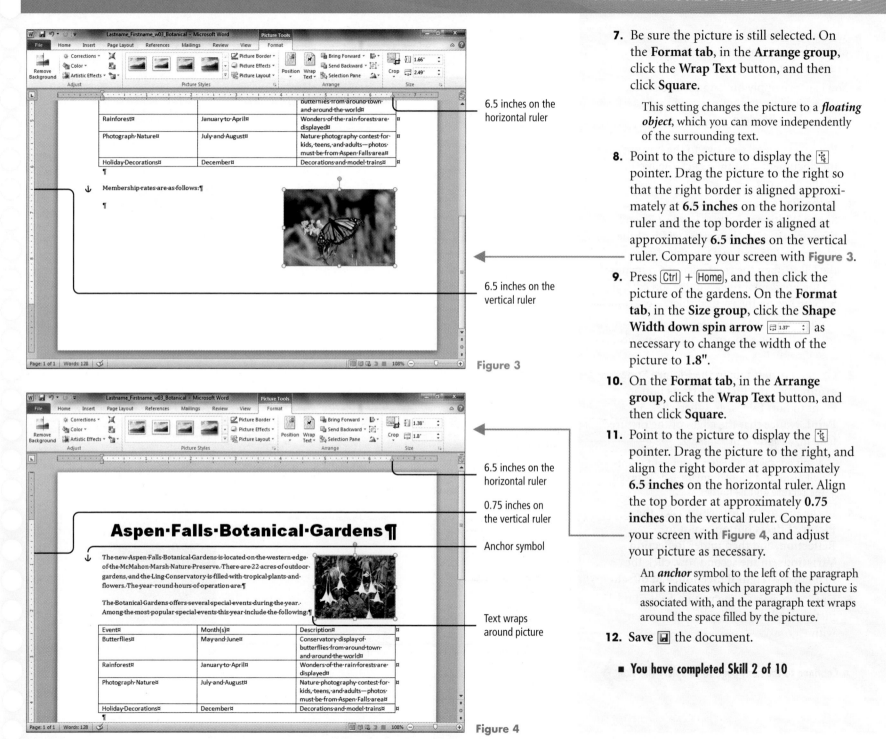

Figure 3

6.5 inches on the horizontal ruler

6.5 inches on the vertical ruler

Figure 4

6.5 inches on the horizontal ruler

0.75 inches on the vertical ruler

Anchor symbol

Text wraps around picture

7. Be sure the picture is still selected. On the **Format tab**, in the **Arrange group**, click the **Wrap Text** button, and then click **Square**.

> This setting changes the picture to a *floating object*, which you can move independently of the surrounding text.

8. Point to the picture to display the pointer. Drag the picture to the right so that the right border is aligned approximately at **6.5 inches** on the horizontal ruler and the top border is aligned at approximately **6.5 inches** on the vertical ruler. Compare your screen with **Figure 3**.

9. Press Ctrl + Home, and then click the picture of the gardens. On the **Format tab**, in the **Size group**, click the **Shape Width down spin arrow** as necessary to change the width of the picture to **1.8"**.

10. On the **Format tab**, in the **Arrange group**, click the **Wrap Text** button, and then click **Square**.

11. Point to the picture to display the pointer. Drag the picture to the right, and align the right border at approximately **6.5 inches** on the horizontal ruler. Align the top border at approximately **0.75 inches** on the vertical ruler. Compare your screen with **Figure 4**, and adjust your picture as necessary.

> An *anchor* symbol to the left of the paragraph mark indicates which paragraph the picture is associated with, and the paragraph text wraps around the space filled by the picture.

12. Save the document.

- **You have completed Skill 2 of 10**

► You can add special effects to the texture of a picture to make it look more like a drawing or a painting.

► You can also apply built-in picture styles, such as borders and frames, and then format those borders.

1. Press [Ctrl] + [End] to move to the bottom of the document, and then click the picture of the butterfly.

2. In the **Size group**, select the value in the **Shape Width** box ⬚ 1.37″ ⬚, type 2.75 and then press [Enter] to change the width of the picture to 2.75 inches. Drag the picture to the left to align the right edge at **6.5 inches** on the horizontal ruler and the top edge at **5.25 inches** on the vertical ruler.

   When you need a size that cannot be entered using spin arrows, type the number in the spin box.

3. On the **Format tab**, in the **Picture Styles group**, click the **Picture Effects** button. Point to **Soft Edges**, and then click **5 Point**. Notice that the edges of the picture fade in, as shown in **Figure 1**. ———

   A soft edge with a higher number of points will result in a more dramatic fade between the picture and its border.

4. In the **Picture Styles group**, click the **Picture Effects** button, point to **Reflection**, and then under **Reflection Variations**, in the second row, click the first effect—**Tight Reflection, 4 pt offset**.

5. Click anywhere in the text to deselect the picture, and then compare your screen with **Figure 2**. ———

■ **Continue to the next page to complete the skill**

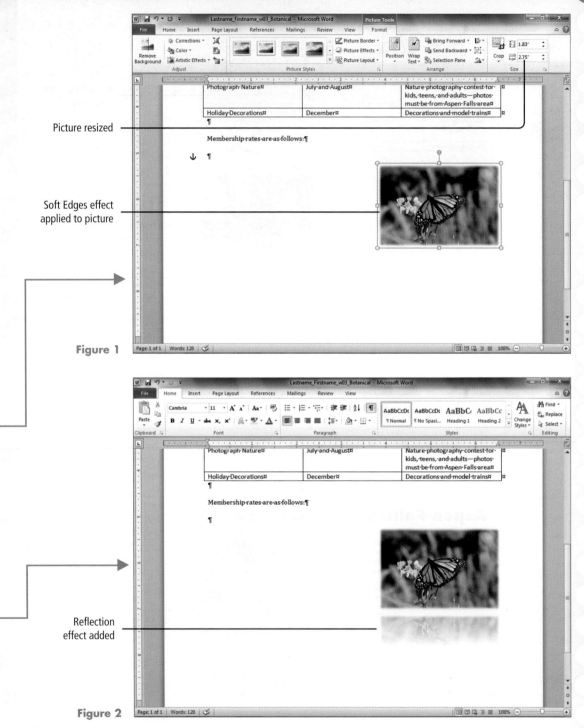

Picture resized

Soft Edges effect applied to picture

Figure 1

Reflection effect added

Figure 2

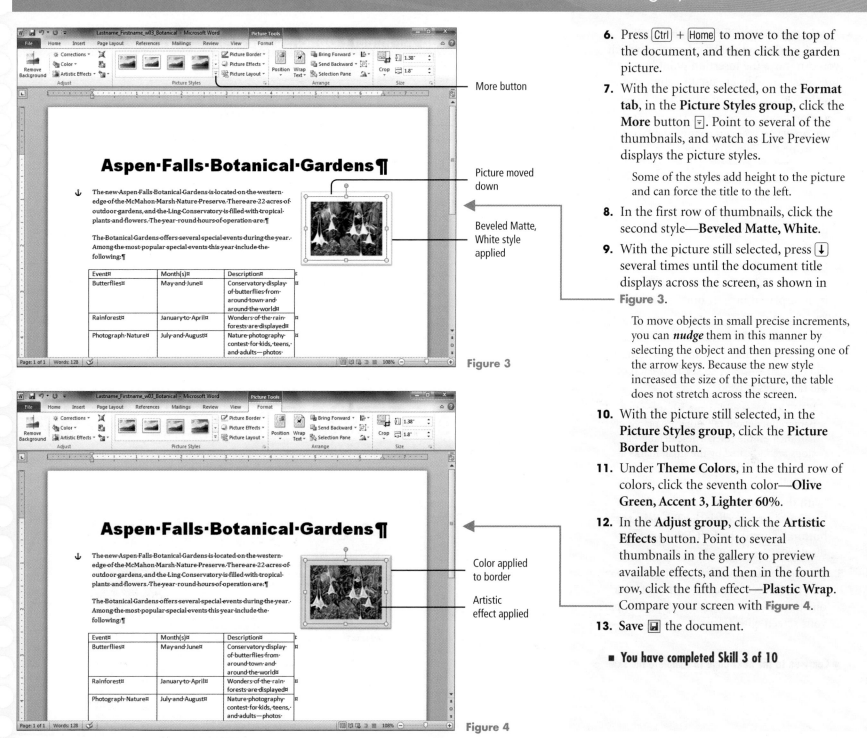

More button

Picture moved down

Beveled Matte, White style applied

Figure 3

Color applied to border

Artistic effect applied

Figure 4

6. Press [Ctrl] + [Home] to move to the top of the document, and then click the garden picture.

7. With the picture selected, on the **Format tab**, in the **Picture Styles group**, click the **More** button ⊡. Point to several of the thumbnails, and watch as Live Preview displays the picture styles.

   Some of the styles add height to the picture and can force the title to the left.

8. In the first row of thumbnails, click the second style—**Beveled Matte, White**.

9. With the picture still selected, press [↓] several times until the document title displays across the screen, as shown in **Figure 3**.

   To move objects in small precise increments, you can *nudge* them in this manner by selecting the object and then pressing one of the arrow keys. Because the new style increased the size of the picture, the table does not stretch across the screen.

10. With the picture still selected, in the **Picture Styles group**, click the **Picture Border** button.

11. Under **Theme Colors**, in the third row of colors, click the seventh color—**Olive Green, Accent 3, Lighter 60%**.

12. In the **Adjust group**, click the **Artistic Effects** button. Point to several thumbnails in the gallery to preview available effects, and then in the fourth row, click the fifth effect—**Plastic Wrap**. Compare your screen with **Figure 4**.

13. Save 📄 the document.

   ■ **You have completed Skill 3 of 10**

► A *tab stop* is a specific location on a line of text marked on the Word ruler to which you can move the insertion point by pressing [Tab]. Tabs are used to align and indent text.

► Tab stop types are set when you insert the stop; however, you can change the tab stop type using the Tabs dialog box.

1. Near the top of the document, click at the end of the paragraph that begins *The new Aspen Falls*, and then press [Enter]. Notice that the table expands to the width of the page.

2. On the left end of the horizontal ruler, notice the **Tab Selector** button ⬜—the icon displayed in your button may vary.

3. Click the button several times to view the various tab types available. Pause at each tab stop type, and view the information in the table in **Figure 1** to see how each of the tab types is used.

   If you have not added any tab stops to a paragraph, default tab stops are placed every half inch on the ruler. These default tab stops are indicated by the small marks at every half inch just below the white area of the ruler.

4. With the insertion point still in the blank paragraph, click the **Tab Selector** button ⬜ until the **Left Tab** icon ⬜ displays.

5. On the horizontal ruler, point to the mark that indicates **0.5 inches**, and then click one time to insert a left tab stop. Compare your screen with **Figure 2.**

■ **Continue to the next page to complete the skill**

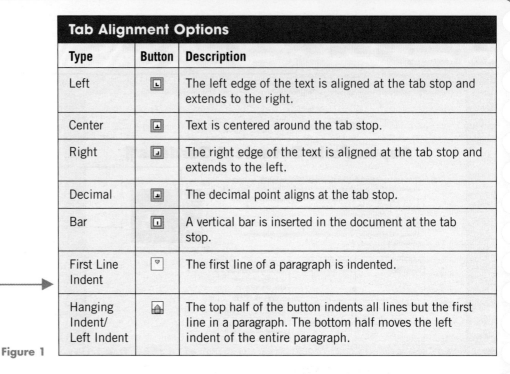

Tab Alignment Options

Type	Button	Description
Left	⬜	The left edge of the text is aligned at the tab stop and extends to the right.
Center	⬜	Text is centered around the tab stop.
Right	⬜	The right edge of the text is aligned at the tab stop and extends to the left.
Decimal	⬜	The decimal point aligns at the tab stop.
Bar	⬜	A vertical bar is inserted in the document at the tab stop.
First Line Indent	▽	The first line of a paragraph is indented.
Hanging Indent/ Left Indent	⬛	The top half of the button indents all lines but the first line in a paragraph. The bottom half moves the left indent of the entire paragraph.

Figure 1

Tab Selector displays Left Tab icon

Left tab stop on horizontal ruler

Figure 2

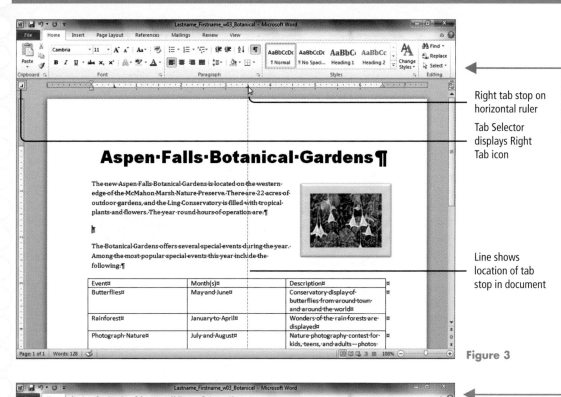

Right tab stop on horizontal ruler

Tab Selector displays Right Tab icon

Line shows location of tab stop in document

Figure 3

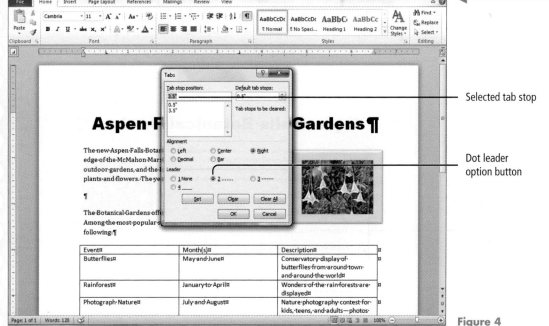

Selected tab stop

Dot leader option button

Figure 4

6. Click the **Tab Selector** button ⬜ two times to display the **Right Tab** icon ⬜.

7. On the ruler, point to the mark that indicates **3.5 inches**. Click and hold down the mouse button. Notice that a dotted line indicates the tab location in the document, as shown in **Figure 3**. In this manner, you can determine whether the tab stop is exactly where you want it.

8. Release the mouse button to insert the right tab stop.

9. On the **Home tab**, click the **Paragraph Dialog Box Launcher** ⬜. At the bottom of the displayed **Paragraph** dialog box, click the **Tabs** button.

10. In the **Tabs** dialog box, under **Tab stop position**, select the tab stop at **3.5"**. Under **Leader**, select the **2** option button to add a dot leader to the selected tab stop. Near the bottom of the dialog box, click the **Set** button, and then compare your screen with **Figure 4**.

    A *leader* is a series of characters that form a solid, dashed, or dotted line that fills the space preceding a tab stop; a *leader character* is the symbol used to fill the space. A *dot leader* is a series of evenly spaced dots that precede a tab stop.

11. In the **Tabs** dialog box, click **OK**, and then **Save** ⬜ the document.

    ■ **You have completed Skill 4 of 10**

► The Tab key is used to move to the next tab stop in a line of text.

► When you want to relocate a tab stop, you can drag the tab stop marker to a new location on the horizontal ruler.

1. Be sure your insertion point is still in the blank paragraph and the tab stops you entered display on the horizontal ruler.

2. Press `Tab` to move the insertion point to the first tab stop you placed on the ruler. Type Day and press `Tab` to move to the right tab with the dot leader that you created.

3. Type Hours and press `Enter`. Compare your screen with **Figure 1**.

   When your insertion point is positioned at a right tab stop and you begin to type, the text moves to the left. When you press `Enter`, the new paragraph displays the same tab stop markers on the ruler as the previous paragraph.

4. Press `Tab`, type Monday-Wednesday and then press `Tab`. Type 10 to 5 and then press `Enter`.

5. Press `Tab`, type Thursday-Friday and then press `Tab`. Type 10 to 6 and then press `Enter`.

6. Press `Tab`, type Saturday and then press `Tab`. Type 8 to 5 and then press `Enter`.

7. Press `Tab`, type Sunday and then press `Tab`. Type Noon to 5 and compare your screen with **Figure 2**.

8. Select the first line of the tabbed list, and then from the Mini toolbar, click the **Bold** button `B`.

■ **Continue to the next page to complete the skill** ➤

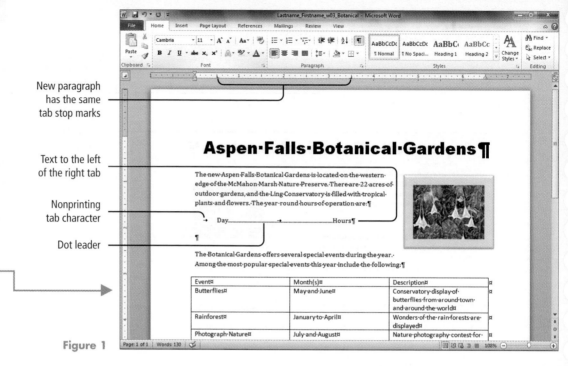

New paragraph has the same tab stop marks

Text to the left of the right tab

Nonprinting tab character

Dot leader

Figure 1

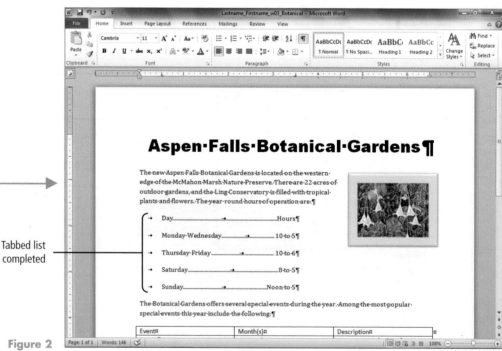

Tabbed list completed

Figure 2

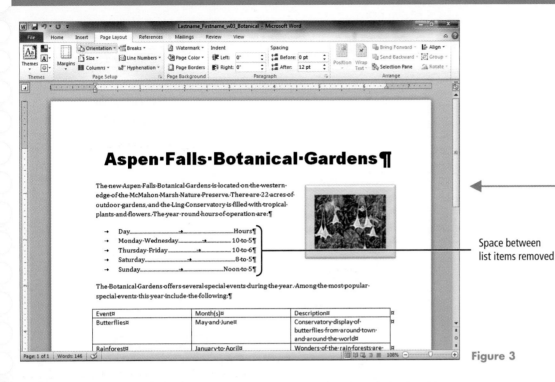

Figure 3

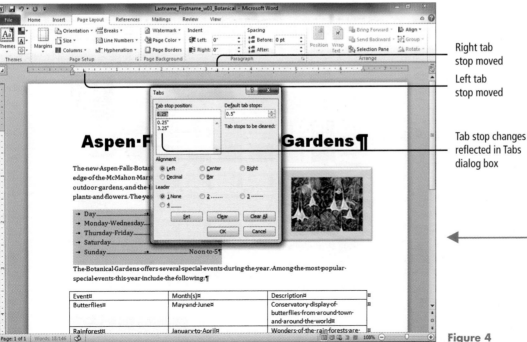

Figure 4

9. Select the first four lines of the tabbed list. Do not select the paragraph that begins *Sunday.*

10. Click the **Page Layout tab**. In the **Paragraph group**, under **Spacing**, click the **After down spin arrow** two times to change the space after the selected paragraphs to **0 pt**. Click anywhere in the document to deselect the text, and then compare your screen with **Figure 3**.

11. To the left of *Day*, point in the margin area to display the ◿ pointer. Then drag down to select all five items in the tabbed list.

12. On the horizontal ruler, point to the left tab mark at **0.5 inches** on the horizontal ruler. When the ScreenTip *Left Tab* displays, drag left to move the tab mark to **0.25 inches** on the horizontal ruler to move each selected line to the new tab location.

13. With the five lines still selected, on the horizontal ruler, point to the right tab mark at **3.5 inches** on the horizontal ruler. When the ScreenTip *Right Tab* displays, drag left to move the tab mark to **3.25 inches** on the horizontal ruler.

14. On the horizontal ruler, point to the right tab mark again. When the ScreenTip *Right Tab* displays, double-click to display the **Tabs** dialog box. Notice that the new tab stop position values display, as shown in **Figure 4**.

15. Click **Cancel** to close the dialog box, and then **Save** 🖫 the document.

■ **You have completed Skill 5 of 10**

▶ A *table* consists of rows and columns of text or numbers. Tables summarize data effectively and efficiently.

▶ You can format each table element individually, or you can apply table styles to the entire table.

1. Scroll as needed to display the table.

    The table contains five rows and three columns. Recall that the intersection of a row and a column in a table is called a *cell*.

2. Click in any cell in the table, and then click the **Design tab**. In the **Table Styles group**, notice that a number of predesigned styles are available.

3. Point to the third style—**Light Shading - Accent 1**—to view the Live Preview of that style, as shown in **Figure 1**.

    Because the styles in the first row of the Table Styles gallery display the styles that were used most recently, your first row of thumbnails may vary.

4. In the **Table Styles group**, click the **More** button ⊡.

5. In the **Table Styles** gallery, use the vertical scroll bar to scroll to the bottom of the gallery. Locate the **Medium Grid 3 - Accent 3** style, and then point to it, as shown in **Figure 2**.

6. Click one time to apply the **Medium Grid 3 - Accent 3** style.

    You do not have to select the entire table to apply a built-in style.

■ **Continue to the next page to complete the skill**

Predefined table styles

Live Preview displays *Light Shading - Accent 1* style

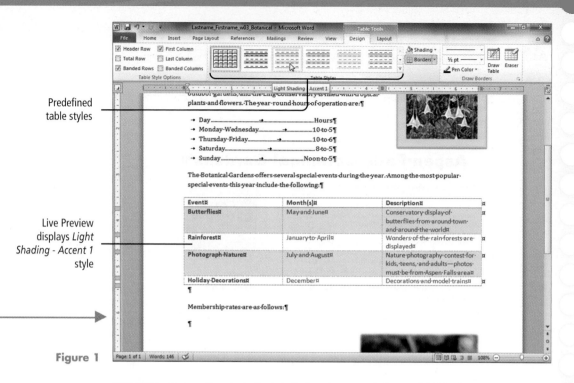
Figure 1

Medium Grid 3 - Accent 3 style

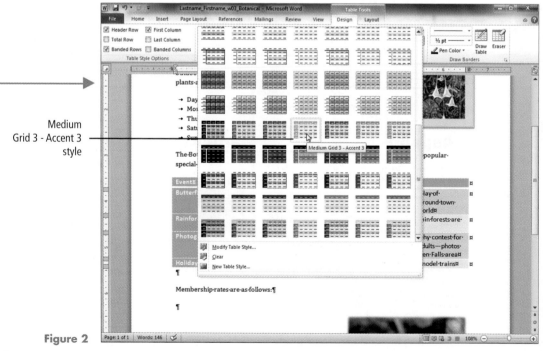
Figure 2

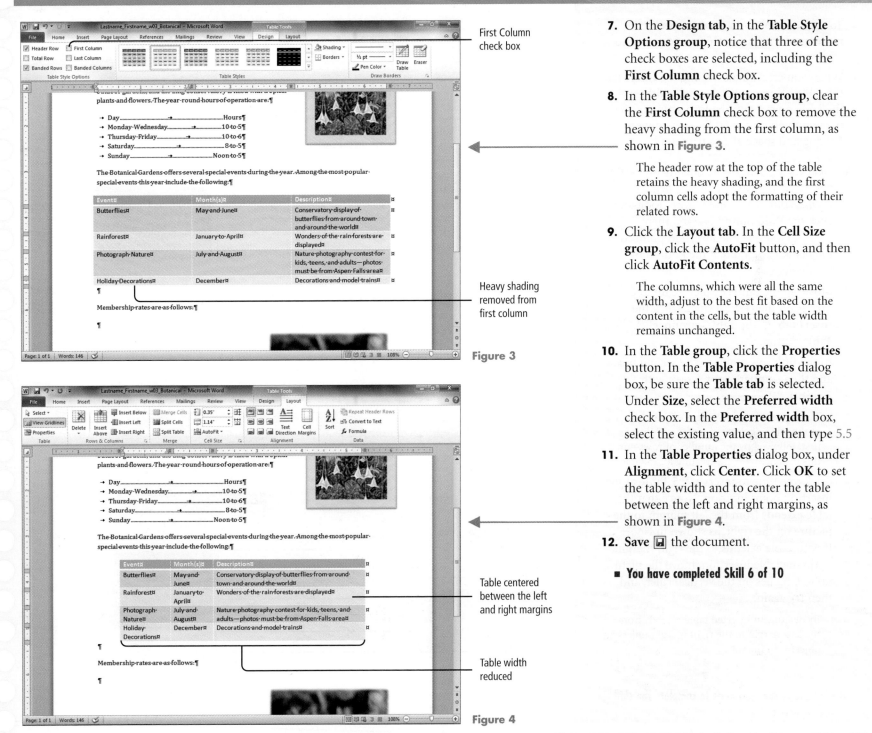

First Column check box

Heavy shading removed from first column

Figure 3

Table centered between the left and right margins

Table width reduced

Figure 4

7. On the **Design tab**, in the **Table Style Options group**, notice that three of the check boxes are selected, including the **First Column** check box.

8. In the **Table Style Options group**, clear the **First Column** check box to remove the heavy shading from the first column, as shown in **Figure 3**.

   The header row at the top of the table retains the heavy shading, and the first column cells adopt the formatting of their related rows.

9. Click the **Layout tab**. In the **Cell Size group**, click the **AutoFit** button, and then click **AutoFit Contents**.

   The columns, which were all the same width, adjust to the best fit based on the content in the cells, but the table width remains unchanged.

10. In the **Table group**, click the **Properties** button. In the **Table Properties** dialog box, be sure the **Table tab** is selected. Under **Size**, select the **Preferred width** check box. In the **Preferred width** box, select the existing value, and then type 5.5

11. In the **Table Properties** dialog box, under **Alignment**, click **Center**. Click **OK** to set the table width and to center the table between the left and right margins, as shown in **Figure 4**.

12. Save 💾 the document.

   ■ **You have completed Skill 6 of 10**

▶ To create a table, you need to specify the number of rows and columns you want to start with.

▶ When you create a table using the Insert tab, the table columns are of equal width, and the table rows retain the formatting of the paragraph above the table—including line spacing and space after a paragraph.

1. Near the bottom of the document, locate and select the paragraph that begins *Membership rates*. On the Mini toolbar, click the **Bold** button ⒝, and then press ⬇ to move the insertion point to the blank paragraph at the bottom of the document.

2. **Move** ⌖ the butterfly picture up to **6 inches** on the vertical ruler. Click the **Insert tab**. In the **Tables group**, click the **Table** button.

3. In the fifth row, point to the second box, and then compare your screen with **Figure 1**.

   The top of the Table gallery displays the size of the table, with the number of columns first, followed by the number of rows—in this instance, you are creating a 2x5 table.

4. Click one time to insert a **2x5 Table** at the insertion point location. Notice that the table extends from the left margin to the picture on the right, as shown in **Figure 2**. If your table extends to the right margin, undo the table insertion, move the picture up to 6 inches on the vertical ruler, and then try again.

   By default, an inserted table extends from the left margin to the right margin unless an object is in the way.

■ **Continue to the next page to complete the skill** ➤

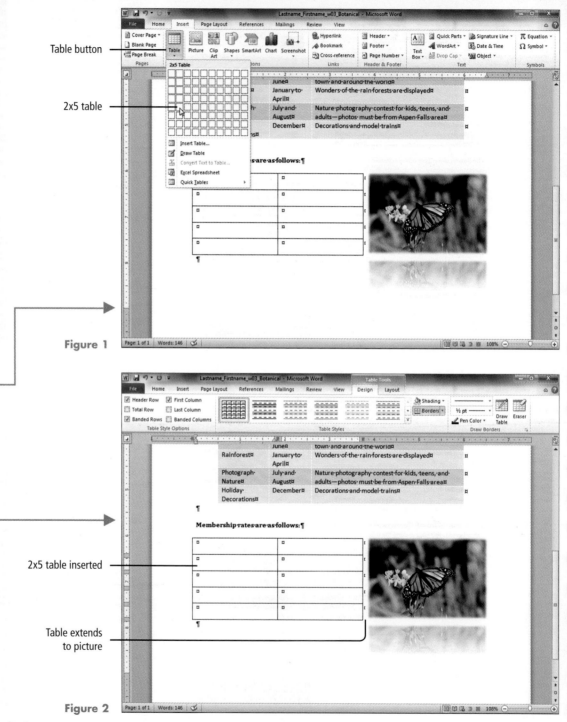

Table button

2x5 table

Figure 1

2x5 table inserted

Table extends to picture

Figure 2

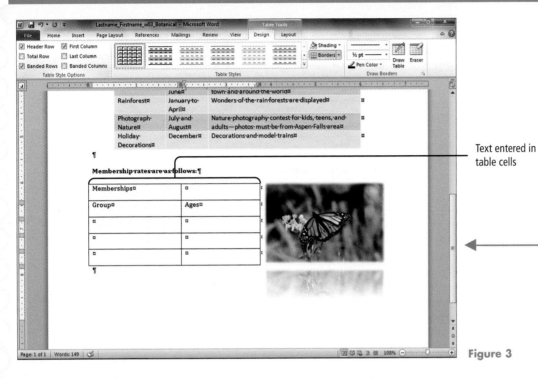

Text entered in table cells

Figure 3

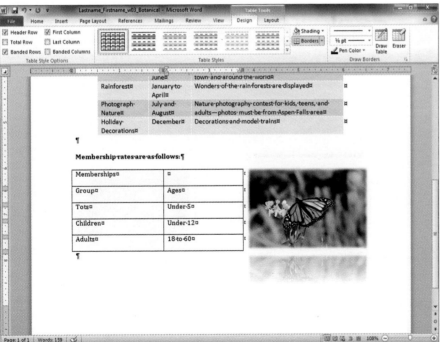

Figure 4

5. Be sure the insertion point is located in the upper left cell of the new table. Type Memberships and then press Tab. Notice that the column widths adjust as you type.

You can use Tab or the arrow keys to move among cells in a table. When you press Enter, a second line in the same cell is created. If this happens, you can press Bksp or ↩ to remove the inserted paragraph.

6. Press Tab again to move to the first cell in the second row.

7. Type Group and then press Tab. Type Ages and then press Tab. Compare your screen with **Figure 3**.

8. With the insertion point in the first cell of the third row, type Tots and then press Tab. Type Under 5 and then press Tab. Do not be concerned if the widths of the columns continue to change while you are typing.

9. In the first cell of the fourth row, type Children and then press Tab. Type Under 12 and then press Tab.

10. In the first cell of the last row, type Adults and then press Tab. Type 18 to 60 and then compare your screen with **Figure 4**.

11. **Save** 💾 the document.

■ **You have completed Skill 7 of 10**

- ► You can add rows to the beginning, middle, or end of a table, and you can delete one or more rows if necessary.
- ► You can add columns to the left or right of the column that contains the insertion point.

1. In the third row of the table, click anywhere in the *Tots* cell.

   To delete a row, you need only position the insertion point anywhere in the row.

2. Click the **Layout tab**, and then in the **Rows & Columns group**, click the **Delete** button. From the displayed list, click **Delete Rows**. If you accidentally click Delete Columns, in the Quick Access Toolbar, click the Undo button 🔄 and try again.

3. Be sure the insertion point is in the *Children* cell. In the **Rows & Columns group**, click the **Insert Below** button. Notice that a blank row is added below the row that contains the insertion point.

4. Type Students and then notice that although the entire row was selected when you started typing, the text was entered into the row's first cell. Press Tab, and then type Under 18 Press Tab, and then compare your screen with **Figure 1**.

5. In the last row of the table, in the second column, click to the right of *18 to 60*.

6. Press Tab to insert a new row at the bottom of the table.

7. Type Seniors and then press Tab. Type Over 60 and then compare your screen with **Figure 2**.

■ **Continue to the next page to complete the skill** ▶

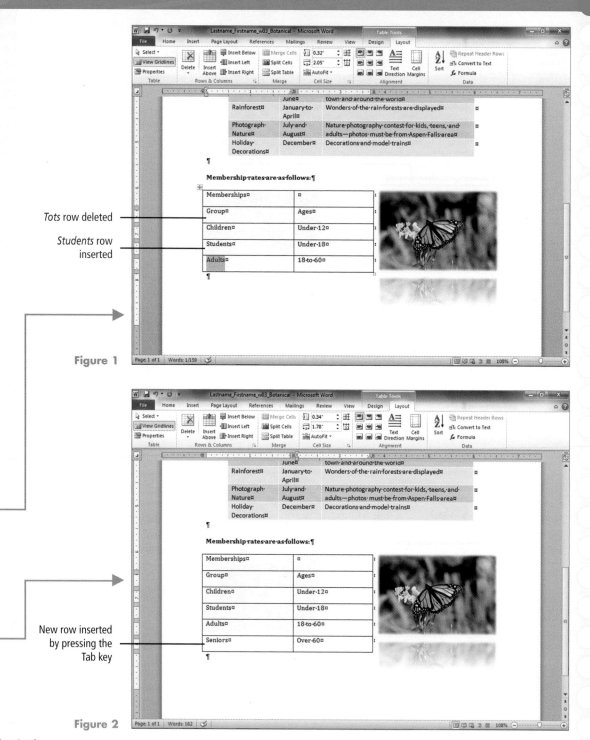

Tots row deleted

Students row inserted

Figure 1

New row inserted by pressing the Tab key

Figure 2

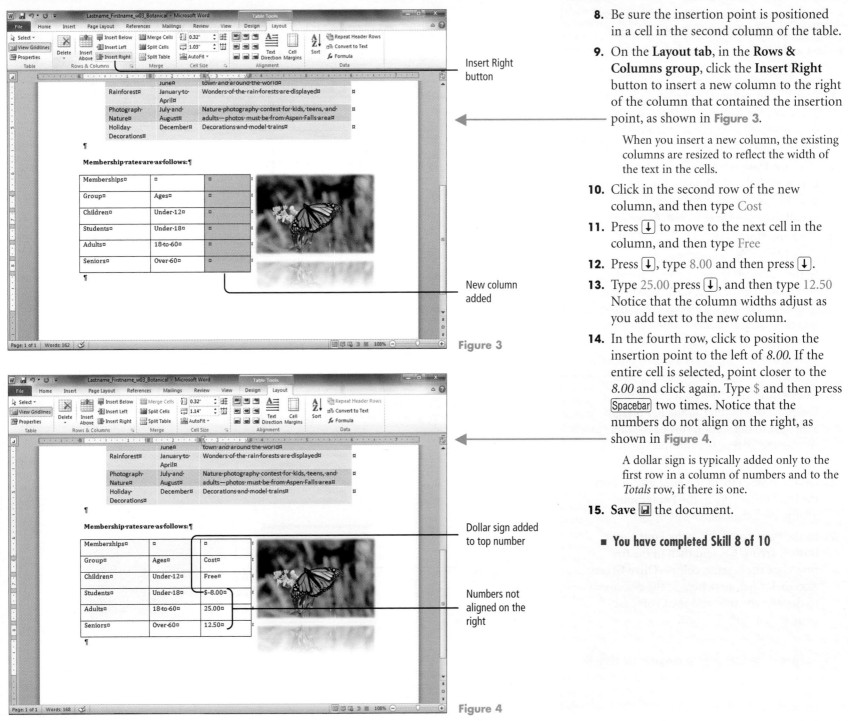

Insert Right button

New column added

Figure 3

Dollar sign added to top number

Numbers not aligned on the right

Figure 4

8. Be sure the insertion point is positioned in a cell in the second column of the table.

9. On the **Layout tab**, in the **Rows & Columns group**, click the **Insert Right** button to insert a new column to the right of the column that contained the insertion point, as shown in **Figure 3**.

   When you insert a new column, the existing columns are resized to reflect the width of the text in the cells.

10. Click in the second row of the new column, and then type Cost

11. Press ↓ to move to the next cell in the column, and then type Free

12. Press ↓, type 8.00 and then press ↓.

13. Type 25.00 press ↓, and then type 12.50 Notice that the column widths adjust as you add text to the new column.

14. In the fourth row, click to position the insertion point to the left of *8.00*. If the entire cell is selected, point closer to the *8.00* and click again. Type $ and then press Spacebar two times. Notice that the numbers do not align on the right, as shown in **Figure 4**.

   A dollar sign is typically added only to the first row in a column of numbers and to the *Totals* row, if there is one.

15. **Save** 🖫 the document.

■ **You have completed Skill 8 of 10**

► You can format text in tables in the same manner you format text in a document.

► Text and numbers can also be aligned in columns.

1. Position the pointer in the left margin to the left of the first row of the new table to display the 📐 pointer, and then click one time to select the row.

2. Click the **Design tab**. In the **Table Styles group**, click the **Shading button arrow** 🖌️, and then in the first row, click the seventh color—**Olive Green, Accent 3**.

3. Click the **Home tab**, and then click the **Font Dialog Box Launcher** 🗔.

4. In the **Font** dialog box, under **Font style**, click **Bold**. Under **Size**, scroll down, and then click **14**. Click the **Font color arrow**, and then under **Theme Colors**, click the first color in the first row—**White, Background 1**. Compare your screen with Figure 1.

5. Click **OK** to close the Font dialog box. Position your pointer in the left margin area next to the second row of the table to display the 📐 pointer, and then click one time to select the row.

6. On the **Home tab**, in the **Font group**, click the **Bold** button 🅱️. In the **Paragraph group**, click the **Center** button 🎚️.

7. In the **Font group**, click the **Font Color button arrow** 🅰️, and then in the first row, click the seventh color—**Olive Green, Accent 3**. Click anywhere in the document to deselect the row, and then compare your screen with Figure 2.

■ **Continue to the next page to complete the skill** ➤

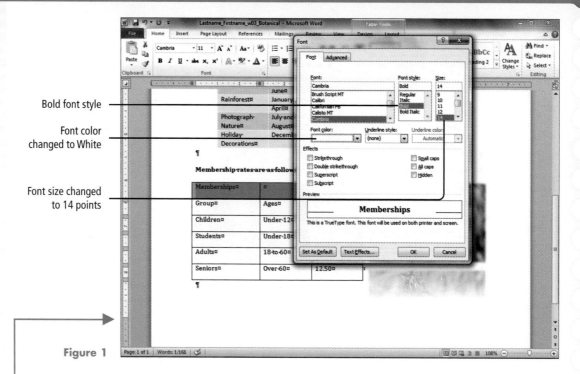

Bold font style

Font color changed to White

Font size changed to 14 points

Figure 1

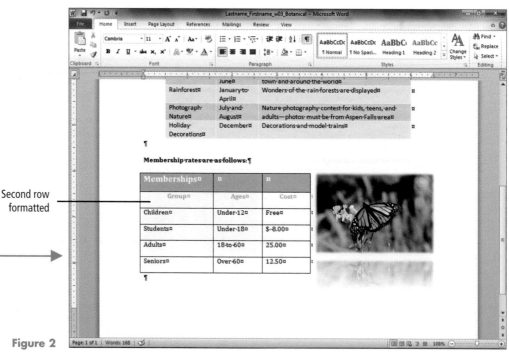

Second row formatted

Figure 2

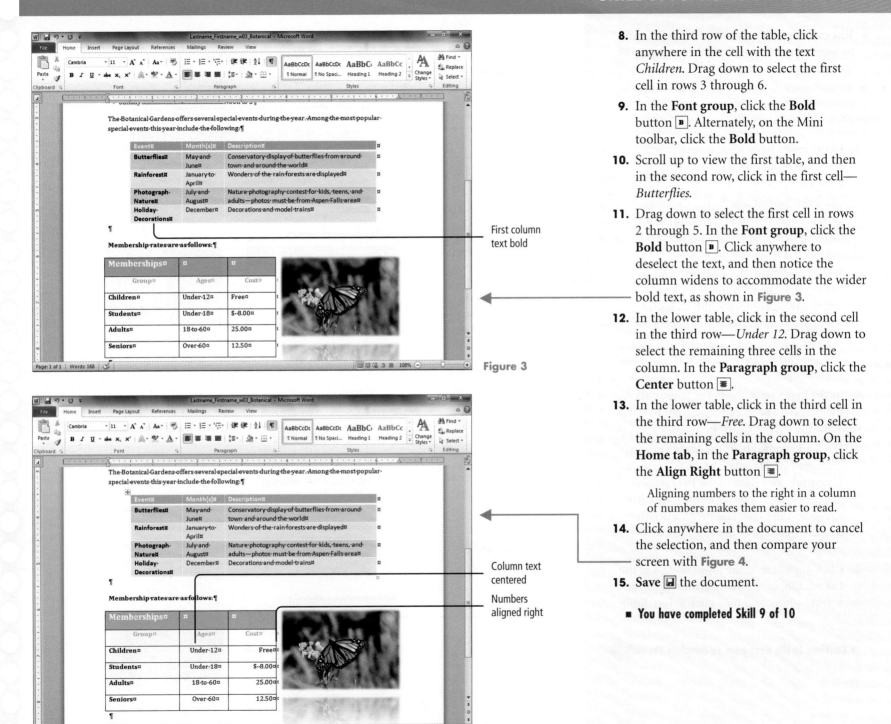

Figure 3

Figure 4

First column
text bold

Column text
centered

Numbers
aligned right

8. In the third row of the table, click anywhere in the cell with the text *Children*. Drag down to select the first cell in rows 3 through 6.

9. In the **Font group**, click the **Bold** button [B]. Alternately, on the Mini toolbar, click the **Bold** button.

10. Scroll up to view the first table, and then in the second row, click in the first cell—*Butterflies.*

11. Drag down to select the first cell in rows 2 through 5. In the **Font group**, click the **Bold** button [B]. Click anywhere to deselect the text, and then notice the column widens to accommodate the wider bold text, as shown in **Figure 3**.

12. In the lower table, click in the second cell in the third row—*Under 12*. Drag down to select the remaining three cells in the column. In the **Paragraph group**, click the **Center** button [≡].

13. In the lower table, click in the third cell in the third row—*Free*. Drag down to select the remaining cells in the column. On the **Home tab**, in the **Paragraph group**, click the **Align Right** button [≡].

Aligning numbers to the right in a column of numbers makes them easier to read.

14. Click anywhere in the document to cancel the selection, and then compare your screen with **Figure 4**.

15. **Save** [💾] the document.

■ **You have completed Skill 9 of 10**

► You can change the width of table columns by using the AutoFit Contents command or by changing the column widths manually.

► To accommodate a title that spans multiple columns, you can merge cells to create one wide cell.

1. In the lower table, click to position the insertion point anywhere in the first column.

2. Click the **Layout tab**. In the **Cell Size group**, click the **Table Column Width down spin arrow** as needed to narrow the first column to **1.5"**.

3. Repeat the technique just practiced to change the second column width to **1.1"** and the third column width to **0.8"**. Compare your screen with **Figure 1**.

    When you manually resize table columns, it is good practice to resize the columns from left to right.

4. In the first row of the lower table, click in the first cell and drag to the right to select all of the cells in the row.

5. On the **Layout tab**, in the **Merge group**, click the **Merge Cells** button. Click the **Home tab**, and then in the **Paragraph group**, click the **Center** button. Click to deselect the text, and then notice that the text spans all of the columns, as shown in **Figure 2**.

6. Click anywhere in the lower table. On the **Layout tab**, in the **Table group**, click the **Select** button, and then click **Select Table**.

■ **Continue to the next page to complete the skill**

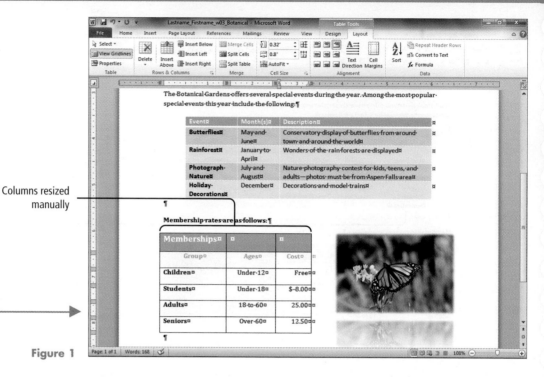

Columns resized manually

Figure 1

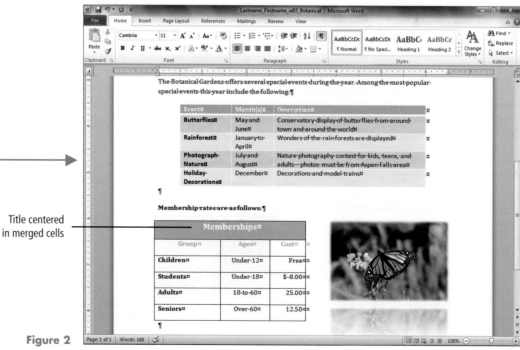

Title centered in merged cells

Figure 2

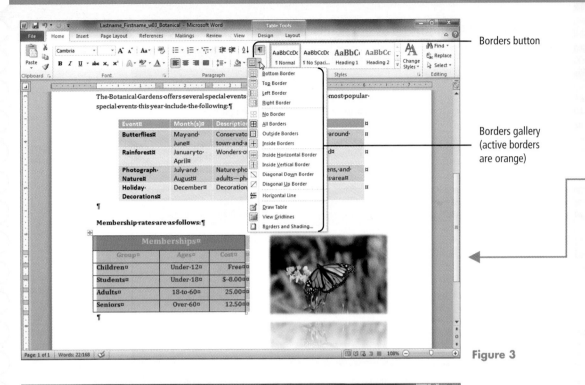

Borders button

Borders gallery (active borders are orange)

Figure 3

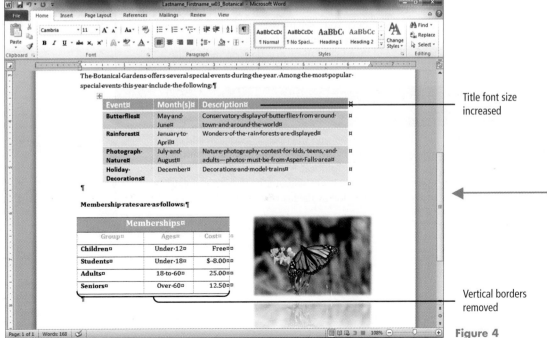

Title font size increased

Vertical borders removed

Figure 4

7. With the lower table still selected, on the **Page Layout tab**, in the **Paragraph group**, click the **Spacing After down spin arrow** one time to reduce the spacing after to **6 pt**.

8. On the **Home tab**, in the **Paragraph group**, click the **Borders button arrow**, and then examine the **Borders** gallery. Notice that the borders that are active display in orange, as shown in **Figure 3**.

9. In the **Borders** gallery, click **Left Border**, and notice that the left border is removed from the selected cells.

10. Repeat the same technique to remove the **Right Border** and the **Inside Vertical Border**. Click anywhere in the document to deselect the text.

   Your program may be set to display light, nonprinting grid lines where borders have been removed.

11. In the upper table, select the first row. On the **Home tab**, in the **Font group**, click the **Font Size arrow** 11 ▾, and then click **14**.

   Consistent formatting helps documents look professional. Here, the font size for the two table titles now matches.

12. Click anywhere in the document to deselect the row, and then compare your screen with **Figure 4**.

13. Add the file name to the footer. **Save** 💾 the document. Print or submit the file as directed by your instructor. **Exit** Word.

Done! You have completed Skill 10 of 10 and your document is complete!

More Skills

The following More Skills are located at **www.pearsonhighered.com/skills**

More Skills Insert Text Boxes

Text boxes are floating objects that can be placed anywhere in a document. They are useful when you want to present text in a different orientation from other text. Text boxes function as a document within a document, and they can be resized or moved. Text in a text box wraps in the same manner it wraps in any document.

In More Skills 11, you will open a document and create a text box. You will also resize and format the text box.

To begin, open your web browser, navigate to www.pearsonhighered.com/skills, locate the name of your textbook, and then follow the instructions on the website.

More Skills Format with WordArt

When you create a flyer or a newsletter, you might want to use a distinctive and decorative title. Word provides a feature called WordArt that you can use to change text into a decorative title.

In More Skills 12, you will open a document and create a title that uses WordArt.

To begin, open your web browser, navigate to www.pearsonhighered.com/skills, locate the name of your textbook, and then follow the instructions on the website.

More Skills Create Tables from Existing Lists

You can create a new table by using the Table button on the Insert tab. You can also use the Table button to convert a tabbed list into a table.

In More Skills 13, you will open a document and convert a tabbed list into a table. You will also format the table.

To begin, open your web browser, navigate to www.pearsonhighered.com/skills, locate the name of your textbook, and then follow the instructions on the website.

More Skills Insert Drop Caps

Word provides a number of methods to format text distinctively. To give text the professional look you often see in books and magazines, you can use a large first letter to begin the first paragraph of the document.

In More Skills 14, you will open a document and create a drop cap for the first character of the first paragraph.

To begin, open your web browser, navigate to www.pearsonhighered.com/skills, locate the name of your textbook, and then follow the instructions on the website.

Key Terms

Online Help Skills

1. **Start** 🟢 Word. In the upper right corner of the Word window, click the **Help** button 🔘. In the **Help** window, click the **Maximize** 🔲 button.

2. Click in the search box, type page numbers and then click the **Search** button 🔍. In the search results, click **Add or remove headers, footers, and page numbers**.

3. Read the article's introduction, and then below **What do you want to do?**, click **Add a page number without any other information**. Compare your screen with **Figure 1**.

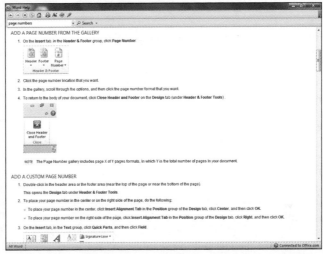

Figure 1

4. Read the section to see if you can answer the following: What is a quick way to open a header or footer? How can you show page numbers in the *Page X of Y* format—for example, *Page 3 of 12*?

Matching

Match each term in the second column with its correct definition in the first column by writing the letter of the term on the blank line in front of the correct definition.

____ **1.** The feature used to change a picture to a floating object so that it can be moved independently of a paragraph.

____ **2.** The type of sizing handle used to resize a picture proportionally.

____ **3.** The formatting feature that makes a picture's edges appear to fade into the picture.

____ **4.** A specific location in the document, marked on the Word ruler, to which you can move using Tab key.

____ **5.** A series of characters that form a solid, dashed, or dotted line that fills the space preceding a tab stop.

____ **6.** Information presented in rows and columns to summarize and present data effectively and efficiently.

____ **7.** A set of predefined table formats.

____ **8.** When you create a table using the Insert tab, the table columns will all be of this width.

____ **9.** With the insertion point in the last cell in the table, the key used to create a new row at the bottom of the table.

____ **10.** The command used to make the size of the table columns reflect the data in the columns.

A AutoFit Contents

B Corner

C Equal

D Leader

E Soft Edges

F Tab

G Tab Stop

H Table

I Table Styles

J Wrap Text

Multiple Choice

Choose the correct answer.

1. When you select a picture, use these to change the picture height or width.
   A. Arrow keys
   B. Sizing handles
   C. `PgUp` or `PgDn`

2. The symbol that indicates which paragraph a picture is associated with.
   A. Anchor
   B. Paragraph mark
   C. Em dash

3. To move a selected picture small distances using an arrow key.
   A. Drag
   B. Bump
   C. Nudge

4. A series of evenly spaced dots that precede a tab.
   A. Ellipsis
   B. Tab stop position
   C. Dot leader

5. When you make a change to a tab stop in the Tabs dialog box, click this button to apply the changes.
   A. Set
   B. Clear
   C. Apply

6. The intersection of a row and column in a table.
   A. Banded row
   B. Cell
   C. Banded column

7. The command used to change a picture to make it look more like a drawing or a painting.
   A. Artistic Effects
   B. Picture Styles
   C. Picture Effects

8. Use this key to move from one part of a table to another.
   A. `Alt`
   B. `Tab`
   C. `Ctrl`

9. How many columns are in a 3x7 table?
   A. 3
   B. 7
   C. 21

10. Numbers in a table are typically aligned this way.
    A. Left
    B. Center
    C. Right

Topics for Discussion

1. Tables have largely taken the place of tabs in most documents. Can you think of any situations where you might want to use tabs instead of tables? What would you have to do to a table to make it look like a tabbed list?

2. Pictures add interest to your documents when used in moderation. What guidelines would you recommend for using pictures—or any other type of graphics—in a document?

Skill Check

To complete this document, you will need the following files:

- w03_Fitness
- w03_Fitness_Activities
- w03_Fitness_Climber

You will save your document as:

- Lastname_Firstname_w03_Fitness

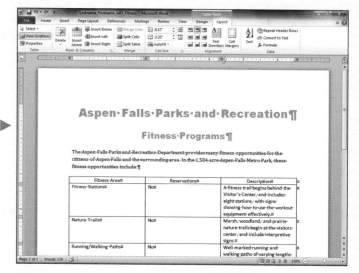

Figure 1

1. **Start** Word. Click the **File tab**, and then click **Open**. Navigate to your student files, and open **w03_Fitness**. Click the **File tab**, click **Save As**, navigate to your **Word Chapter 3** folder, **Save** the document as Lastname_Firstname_w03_Fitness and then add the file name to the footer.

2. In the paragraph that begins *The following*, click to position the insertion point at the beginning of the paragraph. On the **Insert tab**, in the **Text group,** click the **Object button arrow**, and then click **Text from File**. Locate and insert **w03_Fitness_Activities**.

3. Click in the first row of the inserted table. On the **Layout tab**, in the **Rows & Columns group**, click the **Insert Above** button. Right-click the new row. On the Mini toolbar, click the **Center** button. In the first cell, type Fitness Area and press Tab. In the second cell, type Reservations and press Tab. In the third cell, type Description and then compare your screen with **Figure 1**.

4. Click the **Design tab**. In the **Table Styles group**, click the **More** button, and then under **Built-In**, in the first row, click the last style—**Light Shading - Accent 6**.

5. On the **Layout tab**, in the **Cell Size group**, click the **AutoFit** button, and then click **AutoFit Contents**.

6. In the **Table group**, click the **Properties** button. In the **Table Properties** dialog box, set the **Preferred Width** to 6", and then under **Alignment**, **Center** the table. Click **OK**, and then compare your screen with **Figure 2**. **Save** the document.

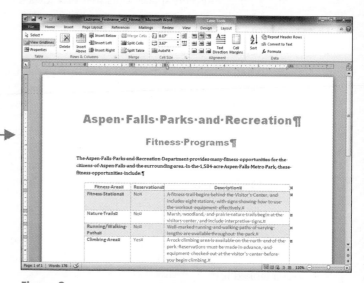

Figure 2

7. At the end of the paragraph that begins *The following*, position the insertion point after the colon, and then press Enter to create a blank line.

8. Click the **Insert tab**. In the **Tables group**, click the **Table** button, and then insert a **2x6** table.

➤ Continue to the next page to complete this Skill Check

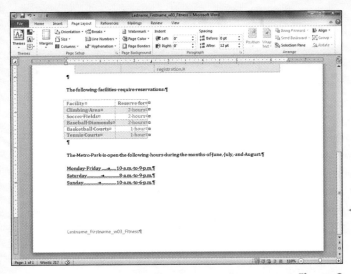

Figure 3

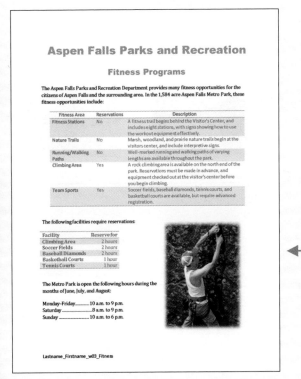

Figure 4

9. Enter the following information in the table:

Facility	Reserve for
Climbing Area	2 hours
Soccer Fields	2 hours
Baseball Diamonds	2 hours
Basketball Courts	1 hour
Tennis Courts	1 hour

10. On the **Design tab**, apply the same table style you applied to the upper table— **Light Shading - Accent 6**. On the **Layout tab**, in the **Cell Size group**, click the **AutoFit** button, and then click **AutoFit Contents**.

11. Select the five cells that contain numbers. On the **Home tab**, in the **Paragraph group**, click the **Align Right** button.

12. Press ⌨ Ctrl + End to position the insertion point at the end of the document. On the left side of the horizontal ruler, click the **Tab Selector** button to display the Right Tab icon. Insert a right tab at **2.5 inches** on the horizontal ruler.

13. Double-click the tab mark. In the **Tabs** dialog box, under **Leader**, select **2**, click **Set**, and then click **OK**. Type the following tabbed list, pressing Tab before typing the text in the *second* column:

Monday-Friday	10 a.m. to 9 p.m.
Saturday	8 a.m. to 9 p.m.
Sunday	10 a.m. to 6 p.m.

14. Select the first two items in the tabbed list. On the **Page Layout tab**, in the **Paragraph group**, set the **Spacing After** to **0 pt**. Press Ctrl + End, and then compare your screen with **Figure 3**.

15. On the **Insert tab**, in the **Illustrations group**, click the **Picture** button, and then locate and **Insert** the **w03_Fitness_Climber** picture. On the **Format tab**, in the **Size group**, select the number in the **Shape Width** box, type 2.5 and then press Enter. In the **Arrange group**, apply **Square** wrapping.

16. On the **View tab**, in the **Zoom group**, click the **Two Pages** button. Drag the picture to page 1 so that the upper edge aligns at about **5.25 inches** on the vertical ruler and the right edge aligns at about **6.5 inches** on the horizontal ruler. Adjust the picture position as necessary.

17. On the **Format tab**, in the **Picture Styles group**, click the **Picture Effects** button, point to **Soft Edges**, and then click **10 point**. On the **View tab**, in the **Zoom group**, click the **100%** button.

18. Click anywhere to deselect the picture, and then compare your document with **Figure 4**. **Save** the document, and submit it as directed. **Exit** Word.

Done! You have completed the Skill Check

Assess Your Skills 1

To complete this document, you will need the following files:

- w03_Run
- w03_Run_Start
- w03_Run_Finish

You will save your document as:

- Lastname_Firstname_w03_Run

1. **Start** Word. Locate and open **w03_Run**, and then save it in your **Word Chapter 3** folder as Lastname_Firstname_w03_Run

2. Add a new third column to the table. In the first cell of the new column, type Start Time and then complete the column with the following:

10:00 a.m.	11:30 a.m.	1:00 p.m.
10:30 a.m.	12:00 p.m.	
11:00 a.m.	12:30 p.m.	

3. Click in the first row of the table, and add a new row above the first row. In the first cell of the new row, type Waves for 10K Run

4. Select the table, and then apply the **Light Shading - Accent 6** table style. Apply **AutoFit Contents** formatting. **Align Right** all of the cells in the third column. Apply **Bold** formatting to the titles in row 2.

5. **Merge** the cells in the first row of the table, and then **Center** the text. Select the table, and increase the **Font Size** to **14** points. **Center** the table.

6. Move to the end of the document, and press Enter. Type: There are several requirements for registration in Waves A through E, and these can be found on the attached registration form. Each participant will receive a T-shirt package after the race. Press Enter.

7. Insert a left tab stop at **2 inches** and a right tab stop at **4.5 inches** on the horizontal ruler. Add a dot leader to the right tab stop. Enter the following text to create a tabbed list. *Be sure to press Tab before the first item in each row.*

Category	Cost
Men	$40
Women	40
Children (12 & under)	20
Seniors (62 & older)	25

8. In the first row of the list, **Bold** the titles. For the first four rows in the list, change the **Spacing After** to **0 pt**.

9. Insert the **w03_Run_Start** picture, apply **Square** text wrapping, change the **Width** to **2.8"**, and then position the left edge of the picture at the left margin and the top of the picture at **7 inches** on the vertical ruler. Repeat this procedure with the **w03_Run_Finish** picture, except position the picture at the right margin.

10. Add the file name to the footer. **Save** the document, and then print or submit the file as directed by your instructor. Compare your completed document with **Figure 1**.

Done! You have completed Assess Your Skills 1

Aspen Falls 10K Run

Information

The Aspen Falls Parks and Recreation Department is once again sponsoring the Spring 10K Run. This year, instead of closing down the main streets in town, the entire run will take place in the Aspen Falls Metro Park. The race will start on the boardwalk that separates the lake from the swamp, and will end at the south end of the mid-lake trail. Because of the anticipated increase in runners, we have expanded the number of waves to seven. When you register, be sure to register for the correct wave!

Waves for 10K Run		
Wave	10K Time	Start Time
A	sub 40:00	10:00 a.m.
B	sub 45:00	10:30 a.m.
C	sub 50:00	11:00 a.m.
D	sub 55:00	11:30 a.m.
E	sub 60:00	12:00 p.m.
F	60:00 - 90:00	12:30 p.m.
G	90:00 +	1:00 p.m.

There are several requirements for registration in Waves A through E, and these can be found on the attached registration form. Each participant will receive a T-shirt package after the race.

Category	Cost
Men	$40
Women	40
Children (12 & under)	20
Seniors (62 & older)	25

Lastname_Firstname_w03_Run

Figure 1

Assessment

Assess Your Skills 3 and 4 can be found at
www.pearsonhighered.com/skills.

Assess Your Skills 2

To complete this document, you will need the following files:

- w03_Cleanup
- w03_Cleanup_River

You will save your document as:

- Lastname_Firstname_w03_Cleanup

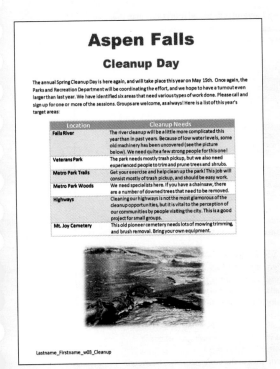

Aspen Falls

Cleanup Day

The annual Spring Cleanup Day is here again, and will take place this year on May 15th. Once again, the Parks and Recreation Department will be coordinating the effort, and we hope to have a turnout even larger than last year. We have identified six areas that need various types of work done. Please call and sign up for one or more of the sessions. Groups are welcome, as always! Here is a list of this year's target areas:

Location	Cleanup Needs
Falls River	The river cleanup will be a little more complicated this year than in past years. Because of low water levels, some old machinery has been uncovered (see the picture below). We need quite a few strong people for this one!
Veterans Park	The park needs mostly trash pickup, but we also need experienced people to trim and prune trees and shrubs.
Metro Park Trails	Get your exercise and help clean up the park! This job will consist mostly of trash pickup, and should be easy work.
Metro Park Woods	We need specialists here. If you have a chainsaw, there are a number of downed trees that need to be removed.
Highways	Cleaning our highways is not the most glamorous of the cleanup opportunities, but it is vital to the perception of our communities by people visiting the city. This is a good project for small groups.
Mt. Joy Cemetery	This old pioneer cemetery needs lots of mowing trimming, and brush removal. Bring your own equipment.

Lastname_Firstname_w03_Cleanup

Figure 1

1. **Start** Word. Locate and open **w03_Cleanup**, and then save it in your **Word Chapter 3** folder as Lastname_Firstname_w03_Cleanup **Center** both document titles, change the **Font** to **Arial Black**, and then change the **Font Color** to the last color under Theme Colors—**Orange, Accent 6, Darker 50%**. Change the **Font Size** of the first title to **36** points and the **Font Size** of the second title to **24** points. Change the **Spacing After** the first title to **0 pt**.

2. Select the table, and then apply the last table style in the fourth row—**Medium Shading 1 - Accent 6**. Insert a new row at the bottom of the table, and in the new row, type Mt. Joy Cemetery Press Tab, and then type This old pioneer cemetery needs lots of mowing, trimming, and brush removal. Bring your own equipment.

3. Set the **Width** of the first column to **1.5"**. Use the **Table Properties** dialog box to set the **Preferred Width** of the table to **5.5 inches** and to **Center** the table.

4. In the first row of the table, change the **Font Size** to **14** points, and then **Center** the table titles.

5. At the end of the document, insert the picture **w03_Cleanup_River**. Change the height of the picture to **2.5"**. Apply **Square** text wrapping, and then drag the picture so that it is centered under the table and the top edge is about 0.25 inches below the table. If you accidentally drag the picture into the table, click the Undo button and try again. If the picture moves to the second page, switch to Two Pages view.

6. With the picture still selected, apply a **Soft Edges** picture effect of **10 Points**, and then apply the second artistic effect in the fourth row—**Texturizer Artistic Effect**.

7. Add the file name to the footer. **Save** the document, and then print or submit the file as directed by your instructor. Compare your completed document with **Figure 1**.

Done! You have completed Assess Your Skills 2

Assess Your Skills Visually

To complete this document, you will need the following files:

- New blank Word document
- w03_Trails
- w03_Trails_Family
- w03_Trails_Marsh

You will save your document as:

- Lastname_Firstname_w03_Trails

Open a new Word document, and then save it in your **Word Chapter 3** folder as Lastname_Firstname_w03_Trails Create the document shown in **Figure 1**.

To complete this document, add the titles and opening paragraph. The titles are in **Arial Rounded MT Bold 24** point and **16** point, and the space between the titles is **0 pt**. Insert the table from the **w03_Trails** file, and format it as shown, with the **Header Row** formatting removed, the width of the first column set at **1.6"**, and the table width **6"**. The font colors are **Automatic**, and the titles are the last color in the last column under Theme Colors—**Orange, Accent 6, Darker 50%**. Add the **w03_Trails_Family** and **w03_Trails_Marsh** pictures, and then size and position the pictures as shown in **Figure 1**. The Marsh picture has the **Paint Brush** Artistic Effect applied. Add the file name to the footer, **Save** the document, and then print or submit the file as directed by your instructor.

Done! You have completed Assess Your Skills Visually

City of Aspen Falls
Self-Guided Tours

The Aspen Falls Parks and Recreation Department has created several self-guided tours that cover the history of the city and the local environment. Brochures for each of the tours are available at City Hall, all of the park offices, all local schools, and the area libraries.

Historic Houses	Take a walking tour through the historic district of Aspen Falls. Use the self-guided tour guide to learn about the history and architecture of some of our more interesting buildings.
Flower Gardens	Take a tour through the houses in the older part of town, and see some spectacular flower gardens. Because these gardens are on private property, the tours are open only on Sunday afternoons from 1 to 4 p.m.
Bird Watching	Both the nature trails in the Metro Park and the shoreline trails along the ocean offer you plenty of opportunity for birding. The best time of the day is the very early morning.
Marsh Life	A meandering boardwalk trail through the marsh area in the Metro Park gives you the opportunity to see the wide varieties of plant, animal, and insect life in the marsh.
Waterfalls and Rapids	There are actually two trails, along the Falls River and Aspen Creek, that can be walked individually or together, passing a number of small waterfalls and rapids—great for pictures!
Geological Formations	Take a look at the physical evidence of the strike-slip zone between the North American Plate and the Pacific Plate. Interpretive signs are placed at interesting locations along this shoreline trail.

Lastname_Firstname_w03_Trails

Figure 1

Skills in Context

To complete this document, you will need the following files:

- New blank Word document
- w03_Events
- w03_Events_Bird

You will save your document as:

- Lastname_Firstname_w03_Events

Each month, the City of Aspen Falls Parks and Recreation Department hosts events throughout the city. Using the information in the file **w03_Events**, create a flyer that describes and lists the events that will be held during the month of May. Begin with a title and a subtitle, followed by a short descriptive paragraph about the events. Then create the table of events that are going to take place during the specified month. You will need to determine the appropriate number of columns. In the table, include column headings; at the top of the table, include a table title that spans all of the columns. Use an appropriate table style to make the table attractive. Locate and insert a picture or a clip art image that is related to one of the events in some way; you can use the included w03_Events_Bird picture if you want. Format the picture using appropriate picture styles.

Save the document as Lastname_Firstname_w03_Events Insert the file name in the footer, and be sure to check the entire document for grammar and spelling. Print or submit the file as directed by your instructor.

Done! You have completed Skills in Context

Skills and You

To complete this project, you will need the following file:

- New blank Word document

You will save your document as:

- Lastname_Firstname_w03_Resume

Using the skills you have practiced in this chapter, create a resume using a table for the structure. To find information on what to include in a resume, find a book in your library or search for *resume* on the web. To complete your resume, you will need to hide most, if not all, of the table borders. (Hint: In this chapter, you merged cells across a row. In the resume, you will probably want to merge cells in a column several times.)

Save the document as Lastname_Firstname_w03_Resume Check the entire document for grammar and spelling. Add the file name to the footer. Print or submit electronically as directed by your instructor.

Done! You have completed Skills and You

CHAPTER 4

Apply Special Text, Paragraph, and Document Formats

▶ Text used in a flyer is commonly displayed in two or three columns.
▶ Clip art is included with Microsoft Office and is treated in much the same way as pictures are.
▶ You can use the mail merge feature in Word to create mailing labels to distribute flyers or brochures.

Your starting screen will look like this:

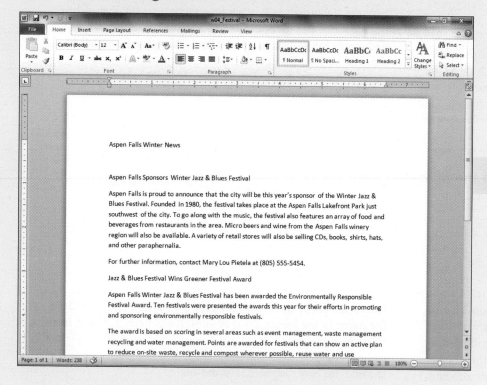

SKILLS

Skills 1-10 Training

At the end of this chapter, you will be able to:

Skill 1   Create Multiple-Column Text
Skill 2   Insert a Column Break
Skill 3   Apply and Format Text Effects
Skill 4   Use and Create Quick Styles
Skill 5   Add Borders and Shading to Paragraphs and Pages
Skill 6   Insert and Format Clip Art Graphics
Skill 7   Insert SmartArt Graphics
Skill 8   Format SmartArt Graphics
Skill 9   Create Labels Using Mail Merge
Skill 10 Preview and Print Mail Merge Documents

MORE SKILLS

More Skills 11 Create Resumes from Templates
More Skills 12 Create Outlines
More Skills 13 Prepare Documents for Distribution
More Skills 14 Preview and Save Documents as Web Pages

Outcome

Using the skills listed to the left will enable you to create documents like this:

Aspen Falls Winter News

ASPEN FALLS SPONSORS WINTER JAZZ & BLUES FESTIVAL

Aspen Falls is proud to announce that the city will be this year's sponsor of the Winter Jazz & Blues Festival. Founded in 1980, the festival takes place at the Aspen Falls Lakefront Park just southwest of the city. To go along with the music, the festival also features an array of food and beverages from restaurants in the area. Micro beers and wine from the Aspen Falls winery region will also be available. A variety of retail stores will also be selling CDs, books, shirts, hats, and other paraphernalia.

For further information, contact Mary Lou Pietela at (805) 555-5454.

JAZZ & BLUES FESTIVAL WINS GREENER FESTIVAL AWARD

Aspen Falls Winter Jazz & Blues Festival has been awarded the Environmentally Responsible Festival Award. Ten festivals were presented the awards this year for their efforts in promoting and sponsoring environmentally responsible festivals.

The award is based on scoring in several areas such as event management, waste management recycling and water management. Points are awarded for festivals that can show an active plan to reduce on-site waste, recycle and compost wherever possible, reuse water and use sustainable power.

Some of the Jazz & Blues Festival efforts include the promotion of Refuse, Reuse, Reduce, Recycle, only allow recyclable materials within the festival site, observing the 'leave no trace' program and using parking income to help protect the nearby wetlands.

Refuse

Reuse

Reduce

Recycle

Lastname_Firstname_w04_Festival

First Name	Last Name	Address 1	Address 2	City	State	Zip	Phone
Leslie	Spurgeon	1187 Ripple Street		Aspen Falls	CA	93463	(805) 555-0194
Carrol	Bruno	161 Bei Meadow Drive		Aspen Falls	CA	93464	(805) 555-4909
Irma	Knowles	173 New Street		Aspen Falls	CA	93464	(805) 555-1821
Mark	Cole	803 Jett Lane	#320	Aspen Falls	CA	93464	(805) 555-7209
		703 Willison Street	#8	Aspen Falls	CA	93464	(805) 555-0277
		358 Maryland Avenue		Aspen Falls	CA	93463	(805) 555-8182
		892 Lightning Point Drive		Aspen Falls	CA	93463	(805) 555-6360
		646 School House Road	#352	Aspen Falls	CA	93463	(805) 555-6201
		626 Desert Broom Court	#320	Aspen Falls	CA	93463	(805) 555-2675
		936 Losh Lane	#1550	Aspen Falls	CA	93464	(805) 555-4712
		40 Turkey Pen Lane		Aspen Falls	CA	93463	(805) 555-2737
		808 Oakridge Farm Lane		Aspen Falls	CA	93464	(805) 555-3419
		311 Gore Street		Aspen Falls	CA	93464	(805) 555-7152
		934 Davisson Street		Aspen Falls	CA	93463	(805) 555-4049
		078 Raccoon Run		Aspen Falls	CA	93463	(805) 555-6926
		333 Conference Center Way		Aspen Falls	CA	93464	(805) 555-6645
		36 Saint Clair Street	#D	Aspen Falls	CA	93464	(805) 555-2835
		442 Ingram Road	#G	Aspen Falls	CA	93463	(805) 555-6814
		571 Lucy Lane		Aspen Falls	CA	93463	(805) 555-5391
		514 Public Works Drive	#1442	Aspen Falls	CA	93463	(805) 555-8206
		772 Patterson Road		Aspen Falls	CA	93464	(805) 555-7333
		1 Green Acres Road		Aspen Falls	CA	93463	(805) 555-4261
		401 Buena Vista Avenue	#D	Aspen Falls	CA	93464	(805) 555-0185
		98 Spring Street		Aspen Falls	CA	93463	(805) 555-4550
		894 Bullpen Road		Aspen Falls	CA	93464	(805) 555-1853

Festival_Addresses

Kristin Arnold
740 Turkey Pen Lane
Aspen Falls, CA 93463

Robert Bingham
536 Saint Clair Street
#D
Aspen Falls, CA 93464

Dessie Broadnay
4808 Oakridge Farm Lane
Aspen Falls, CA 93464

...runo
...Meadow Drive
...lls, CA 93464

Mark Cole
803 Jett Lane
#320
Aspen Falls, CA 93464

Bryan Crum
1078 Raccoon Run
Aspen Falls, CA 93463

...ugley
...blic Works Drive
...lls, CA 93463

Abraham Garza
1626 Desert Broom Court
#320
Aspen Falls, CA 93463

Michael Hammonds
1936 Losh Lane
#1550
Aspen Falls, CA 93464

...Howard
... Acres Road
...lls, CA 93463

Marsha Keelin
2934 Davisson Street
Aspen Falls, CA 93463

Irma Knowles
173 New Street
Aspen Falls, CA 93464

...McArthur
...llpen Road
...lls, CA 93464

Willie Mench
4442 Ingram Road
#G
Aspen Falls, CA 93463

Tracy Michael
4311 Gore Street
Aspen Falls, CA 93464

...wkirk
...hool House Road
...lls, CA 93463

Margaret Peavey
4571 Lucy Lane
Aspen Falls, CA 93463

Ilda Pinto
198 Spring Street
Aspen Falls, CA 93464

...mirez
...htning Point Drive
...lls, CA 93463

Cassie Simpson
1333 Conference Center Way
Aspen Falls, CA 93464

Leslie Spurgeon
1187 Ripple Street
Aspen Falls, CA 93463

...Stevenson
...ryland Avenue
...lls, CA 93463

William Tapper
1703 Willison Street
#8
Aspen Falls, CA 93464

James Tomlinson
1772 Patterson Road
Aspen Falls, CA 93464

...Vincent
...ena Vista Avenue
...lls, CA 93464

Firstname_w04_Festival_Merged

You will save your files as:

Lastname_Firstname_w04_Festival
Lastname_Firstname_w04_Festival_Addresses
Lastname_Firstname_w04_Festival_Labels
Lastname_Firstname_w04_Festival_Merged

In this chapter, you will create documents for the Aspen Falls City Hall, which provides essential services for the citizens and visitors of Aspen Falls, California.

Introduction

- ► You can convert text from one column to two or three columns, which in a newsletter or flyer is often easier to read.

- ► Clip art and SmartArt graphics display information visually and can add a professional look to a document.

- ► To draw attention to a small amount of text, you can add a border and shading to the paragraph.

- ► You can take an existing list of names and addresses from any Office application and use the mail merge feature in Word to create mailing labels.

Time to complete all
10 skills – 60 minutes

Find your student data files here:

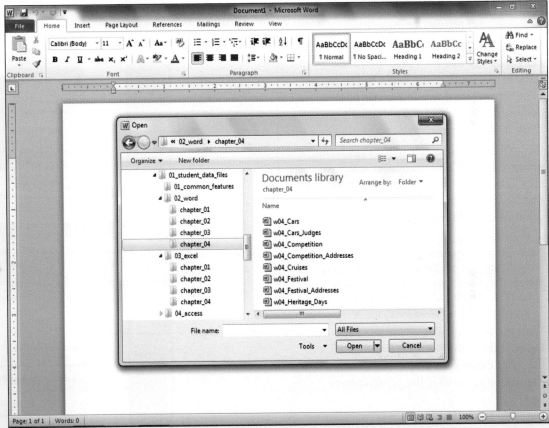

Student data files needed for this chapter:

- New blank Word document
- w04_Festival
- w04_Festival_Addresses

▶ In a brochure or flyer, using multiple columns make text easier to read.

▶ Two or three columns are typically used on a standard 8 1/2" x 11" page.

1. **Start** ⏺ Word. Open **w04_Festival**, create a folder named Word Chapter 4 and then **Save** the document as Lastname_Firstname_w04_Festival Add the file name to the footer. If necessary, display formatting marks.

2. Locate the paragraph that begins *Aspen Falls Sponsors*, and then position the 🔏 pointer to the left of the first word in the paragraph. Drag down to the end of the document—including the paragraph mark in the last paragraph.

3. Click the **Page Layout tab**. In the **Page Setup group**, click the **Columns** button, and then click **Two**. If necessary, scroll up, and notice that the text is formatted in two uneven columns, as shown in **Figure 1**.

   A section break displays above the two-column text. A **section** is a portion of a document that can be formatted differently from the rest of the document. A **section break** marks the end of one section and the beginning of another section.

4. With the text still selected, on the **Page Layout tab**, in the **Paragraph group**, click the **After down spin arrow** one time to change the space after the paragraphs to **6 pt**.

5. Click the **Home tab**. In the **Font group**, click the **Font arrow** [Calibri (Body) ▾], and then scroll down and select **Comic Sans MS**. Click the **Font Size arrow** [11 ▾], and then click **11**. Compare your screen with **Figure 2**.

■ **Continue to the next page to complete the skill**

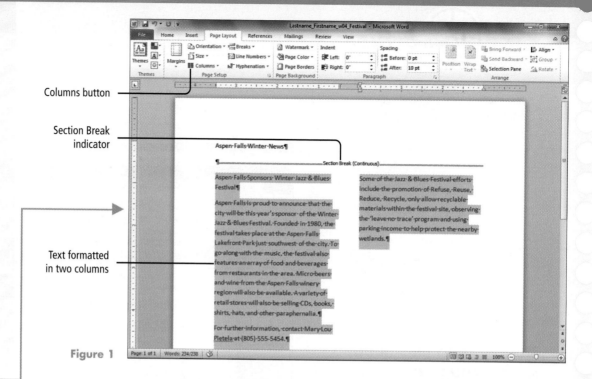

Columns button

Section Break indicator

Text formatted in two columns

Figure 1

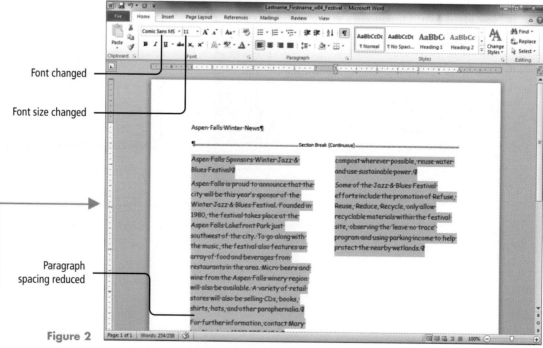

Font changed

Font size changed

Paragraph spacing reduced

Figure 2

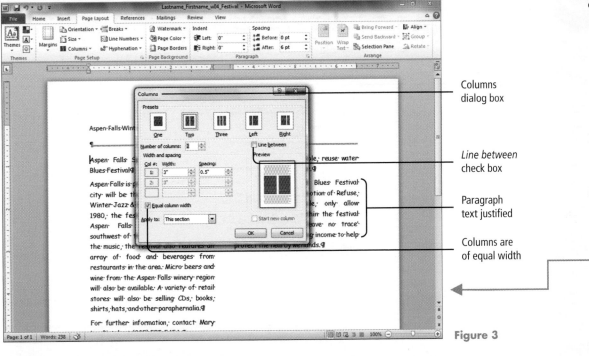

Columns dialog box

Line between check box

Paragraph text justified

Columns are of equal width

Figure 3

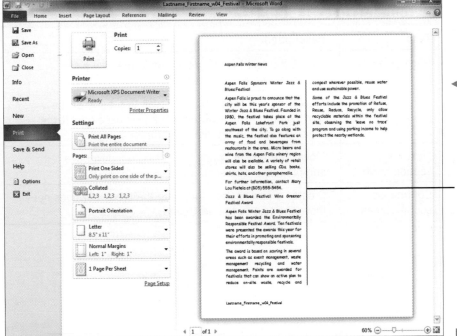

Line between columns

Figure 4

6. With the two-column text still selected, on the **Home tab**, in the **Paragraph group**, click the **Justify** button ▤.

Both the left and right margins of the two columns are aligned. Justified text is often used in documents with multiple columns, although some wide gaps can occur in the text.

7. Click anywhere in the two-column text to deselect the text, and then click the **Page Layout tab**.

8. In the **Page Setup group**, click the **Columns** button, and then below the **Columns** gallery, click **More Columns** to display the Columns dialog box. Compare your screen with **Figure 3**.

The number of columns and the distance between the columns display. By default, the columns are of equal width with 0.5 inches of space between them.

9. In the **Columns** dialog box, select the **Line between** check box, and then click **OK** to insert a line between the two columns.

10. Click the **File tab**, and then click **Print** to preview the document. Compare your screen with **Figure 4**.

11. Click the **Home tab** to return to the document.

12. Save ▤ the document.

■ **You have completed Skill 1 of 10**

▶ A *column break* forces the text following the break to the top of the next column but does not automatically create a new page.

▶ You can increase or decrease the space between the columns to adjust the document layout.

1. On the **Page Layout tab**, in the **Page Setup group**, click the **Margins** button, and then below the **Margins** gallery, click **Custom Margins** to display the Page Setup dialog box.

2. In the **Page Setup** dialog box, under **Margins**, use the **down spin arrows** to change the **Top** and **Bottom** margins to **0.8"**.

3. Under **Preview**, click the **Apply to arrow**, and then click **Whole document**. At the bottom of the dialog box, click **OK** to close the dialog box.

   If the document has multiple sections, by default actions from the Page Setup dialog box apply only to the current section.

4. Near the bottom of the document, in the left column, click to position the insertion point to the left of the paragraph that begins *The award is based.*

5. On the **Page Layout tab**, in the **Page Setup group**, click the **Breaks** button, and then compare your screen with **Figure 1**.

6. Take a moment to examine common types of breaks displayed in the Breaks gallery and described in the table in **Figure 2**. Notice that the breaks are divided into two categories—Page Breaks and Section Breaks.

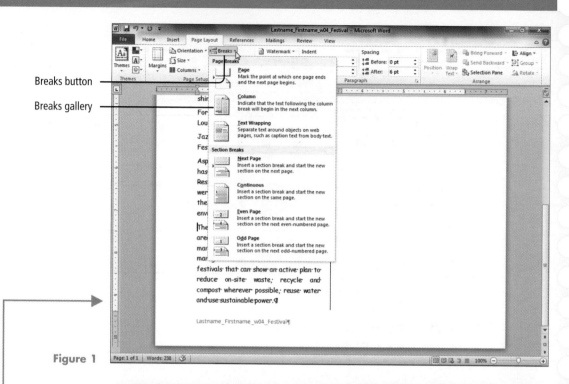

Breaks button

Breaks gallery

Figure 1

Figure 2

Common Types of Breaks	
Type	**Description**
Page break	Moves the text following the break to a new page; does not create a new section.
Column break	Moves the text following the break to the top of the next column, which will create a new page only if the break is made in the right column of a page.
Next Page section break	Moves the text following the break to a new page and creates a new section.
Continuous section break	Creates a new section following the break but does not move the text to the next page.

■ **Continue to the next page to complete the skill** ▶

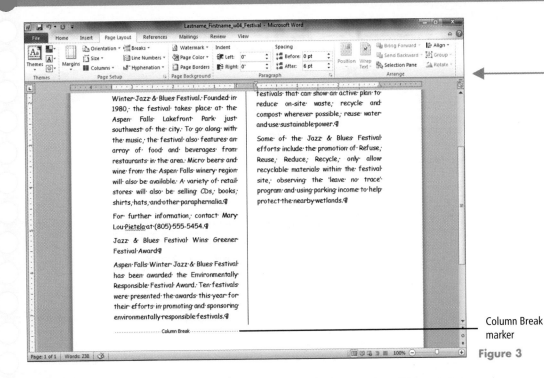

Column Break marker

Figure 3

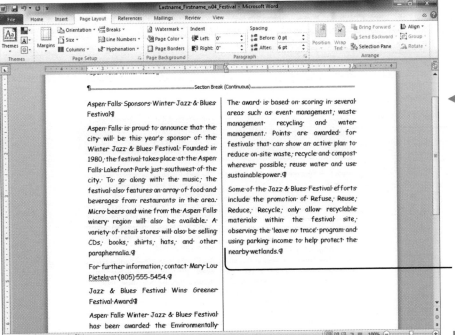

Spacing reduced between columns

Figure 4

7. Click **Column** to insert a column break at the insertion point location. Notice the Column Break marker at the bottom of the first column, as shown in **Figure 3**.

8. If necessary, scroll up until you can see the top of the two-column text, and notice that the paragraph to the right of the insertion point moved to the top of Column 2 and the following paragraphs moved down.

   Creating an uneven column break will enable you to insert a graphic or another object. You can also break a column in the middle of a paragraph.

9. Be sure the insertion point is located in either of the two columns. On the **Page Layout tab**, in the **Page Setup group**, click the **Columns** button, and then below the **Columns** gallery, click **More Columns**.

10. Under **Width and spacing**, click the first **Spacing down spin arrow** two times to change the spacing between the columns to **0.3"**.

    Both columns will remain of equal width because the *Equal column width* check box is selected. When you decrease the spacing between columns, the width of each column is increased, in this case from 3.0" to 3.1".

11. Be sure the **Apply to** box displays *This section*, and then at the bottom of the **Columns** dialog box, click **OK**. Compare your screen with **Figure 4**.

12. **Save** 🖫 the document.

■ **You have completed Skill 2 of 10**

▶ *Text effects* are decorative formats, such as outlines, shadows, text glow, and colors, that make text stand out in a document.

▶ You should use text effects sparingly in a document, typically just for titles or subtitles.

1. Move to the top of the document. Move the pointer to the left of the *Aspen Falls Winter News* title to display the pointer, and then click one time to select the title and the paragraph mark.

2. On the **Home tab**, in the **Font group**, click the **Text Effects** button. Compare your screen with **Figure 1**.

   A Text Effects gallery displays as well as several other text formatting options.

3. In the **Text Effects** gallery, in the first row, click the fourth thumbnail—**Fill - White, Outline - Accent 1**.

4. With the title text still selected, on the **Home tab**, in the **Font group**, click the **Font arrow**, and then click **Arial Rounded MT Bold**.

   The font changes, but the text effect is still applied.

5. In the **Font group**, click in the **Font Size** box to select the existing value. Type 38 and then press Enter.

   By typing the font size, you are not restricted to the displayed sizes when you click the Font Size arrow.

6. On the **Home tab**, in the **Paragraph group**, click the **Center** button, and then compare your screen with **Figure 2**.

▪ **Continue to the next page to complete the skill**

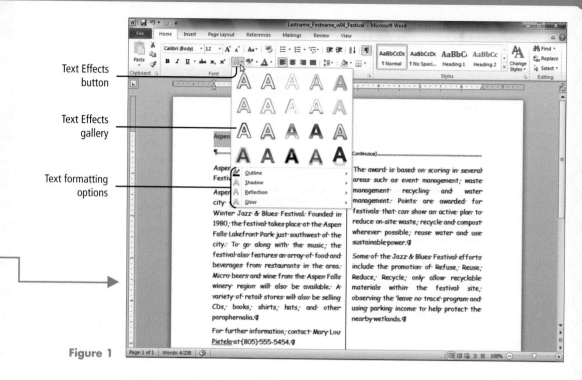

Text Effects button

Text Effects gallery

Text formatting options

Figure 1

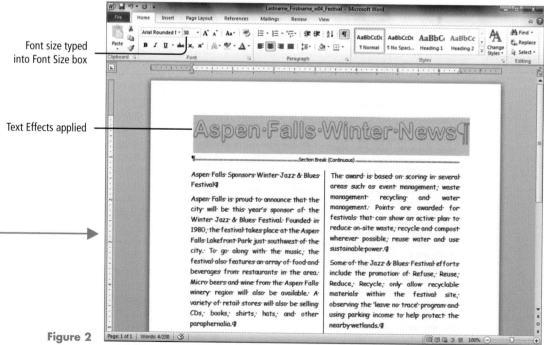

Font size typed into Font Size box

Text Effects applied

Figure 2

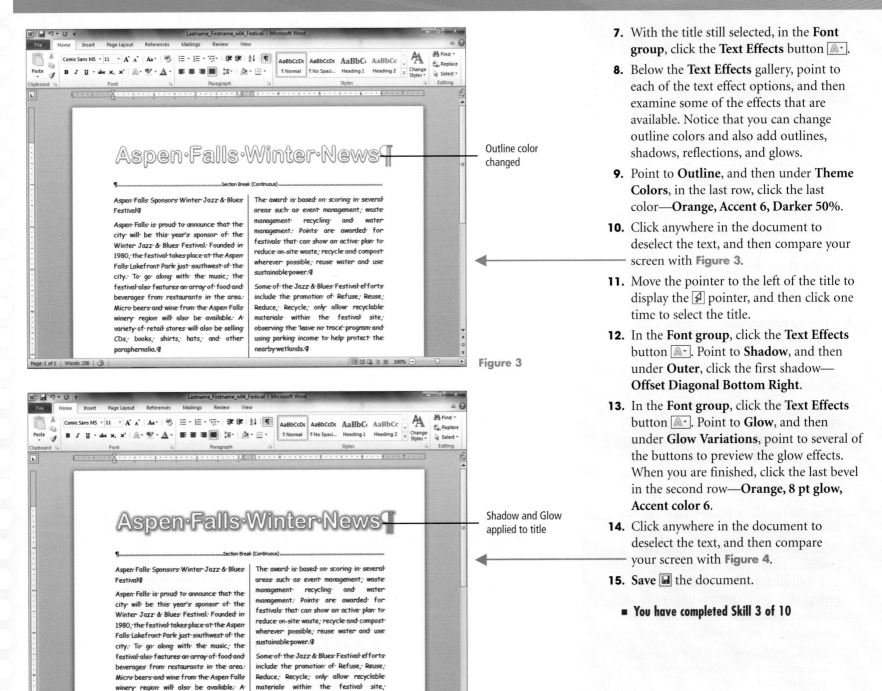

Outline color changed

Figure 3

Shadow and Glow applied to title

Figure 4

7. With the title still selected, in the **Font group**, click the **Text Effects** button.

8. Below the **Text Effects** gallery, point to each of the text effect options, and then examine some of the effects that are available. Notice that you can change outline colors and also add outlines, shadows, reflections, and glows.

9. Point to **Outline**, and then under **Theme Colors**, in the last row, click the last color—**Orange, Accent 6, Darker 50%**.

10. Click anywhere in the document to deselect the text, and then compare your screen with **Figure 3**.

11. Move the pointer to the left of the title to display the pointer, and then click one time to select the title.

12. In the **Font group**, click the **Text Effects** button. Point to **Shadow**, and then under **Outer**, click the first shadow—**Offset Diagonal Bottom Right**.

13. In the **Font group**, click the **Text Effects** button. Point to **Glow**, and then under **Glow Variations**, point to several of the buttons to preview the glow effects. When you are finished, click the last bevel in the second row—**Orange, 8 pt glow, Accent color 6**.

14. Click anywhere in the document to deselect the text, and then compare your screen with **Figure 4**.

15. Save the document.

■ **You have completed Skill 3 of 10**

▶ A *style* is a predefined set of formats that can be applied to text, a paragraph, a table cell, or a list.

▶ A *Quick Style* is a style that can be accessed from a Ribbon gallery of thumbnails.

▶ When you create your own Quick Style based on existing text formatting, the new Quick Style is added to the Ribbon.

1. At the top of the left column, move the pointer to the left of the subtitle that begins *Aspen Falls Sponsors* to display the ⌐ pointer, and then drag down to select both lines of text.

2. On the **Home tab**, in the **Styles group**, point to **Heading 1**. Compare your screen with **Figure 1**. ────────

   Live Preview displays the title using the Heading 1 Quick Style. The Quick Style is not applied until you click the Quick Style button.

3. In the **Styles group**, click the **More** button ⧩ to display the **Quick Styles** gallery.

4. Point to several of the Quick Styles. Notice the different formats that are available, and also notice that the subtitle font changes with the different styles but the text in the rest of the document remains the same.

5. From the **Quick Styles** gallery, click the **Heading 2** style.

6. With the text still selected, in the **Font group**, click the **Font Size arrow** ⎡11 ⎤, and then click **16**. In the **Paragraph group**, click the **Center** button ▤. Click anywhere to deselect the title, and then compare your screen with **Figure 2**. ────

   The black square to the left of the subtitle indicates that it will always stay with the next paragraph.

■ **Continue to the next page to complete the skill**

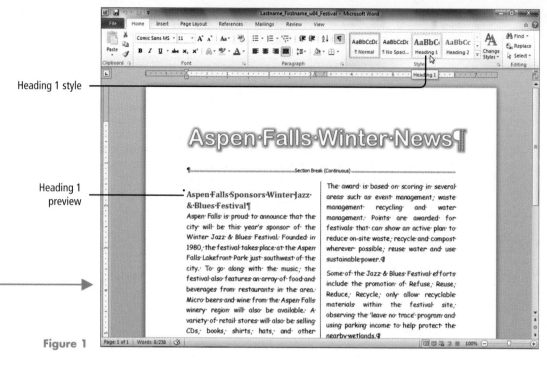

Heading 1 style

Heading 1 preview

Figure 1

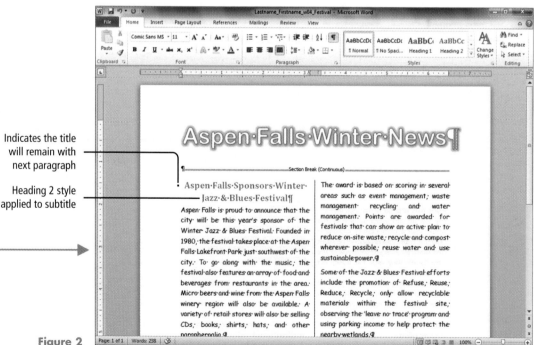

Indicates the title will remain with next paragraph

Heading 2 style applied to subtitle

Figure 2

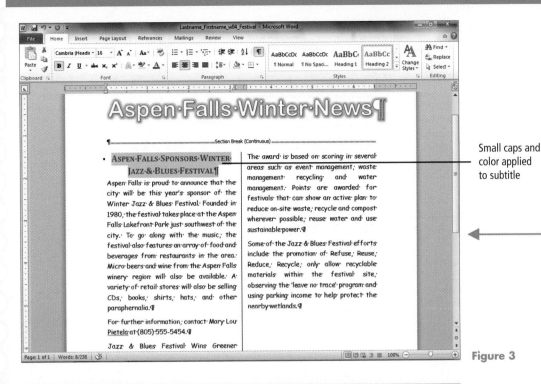

Small caps and color applied to subtitle

Figure 3

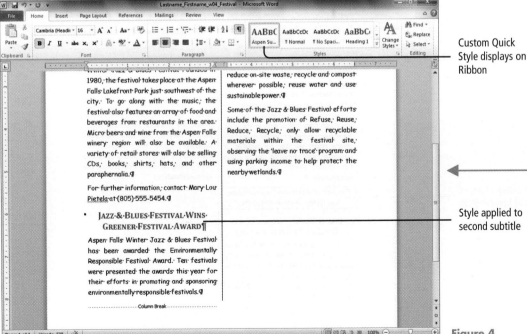

Custom Quick Style displays on Ribbon

Style applied to second subtitle

Figure 4

7. Move the pointer to the left of the subtitle that begins *Aspen Falls Sponsors* to display the 🔏 pointer, and then drag down to select both lines of text.

8. On the **Home tab**, in the **Font group**, click the **Font Dialog Box Launcher** 🔳. In the **Font** dialog box, under **Effects**, select the **Small caps** check box.

9. Click the **Font Color arrow**. Under **Theme Colors**, in the last row, click the last color—**Orange, Accent 6, Darker 50%**. Click **OK**, and then compare your screen with **Figure 3**.

10. With the text still selected, in the **Paragraph group**, click the **Line Spacing** button 🔲, and then click **1.0** to move the subtitle lines closer together. On the **Page Layout tab**, in the **Paragraph group**, click the **After up spin arrow** one time.

11. With the subtitle text still selected, on the **Home tab**, in the **Styles group**, click the **More** button 🔻, and then below the **Styles** gallery, click **Save Selection as a New Quick Style**.

12. In the **Create New Style from Formatting** dialog box, under **Name**, type Aspen Subtitle and then click **OK**. In the **Quick Styles** gallery, notice that the new style displays as the first style.

13. Locate the second subtitle, which begins *Jazz & Blues Festival*. Click anywhere in the subtitle.

14. On the **Home tab**, in the **Styles group**, click the **Aspen Subtitle** Quick Style to apply the formatting from the first subtitle to the second subtitle, as shown in **Figure 4**.

15. Save 🔲 the document.

■ **You have completed Skill 4 of 10**

► To make a paragraph stand out in a document, add a paragraph border. Add shading and color for even more impact.

► You can use page borders to frame flyers or posters, giving the document a more professional look.

1. Scroll to display the middle of the first column. Select the last paragraph in the first article, beginning with *For further information.* Be sure to include the paragraph mark to the right of the telephone number.

2. On the **Home tab**, in the **Paragraph group**, click the **Borders button arrow** ⊞▾.

3. From the **Borders** gallery, click **Outside Borders**, and then compare your screen with **Figure 1.**

4. With the text still selected, in the **Paragraph group**, click the **Center** button ▤. In the **Font group**, click the **Bold** button **B**.

5. In the **Font group**, click the **Font Color arrow** ▲▾, and then under **Theme Colors**, in the last row, click the last color—**Orange, Accent 6, Darker 50%**. Click anywhere in the document to deselect the text, and then compare your screen with **Figure 2.**

    The font color matches the document title and subtitles.

6. Select all of the bordered text, including the paragraph mark. On the **Home tab**, in the **Paragraph group**, click the **Shading button arrow** ▧▾. Under **Theme Colors**, click the last color in the third row—**Orange, Accent 6, Lighter 60%**.

■ **Continue to the next page to complete the skill**

Borders button arrow

Border added to paragraph

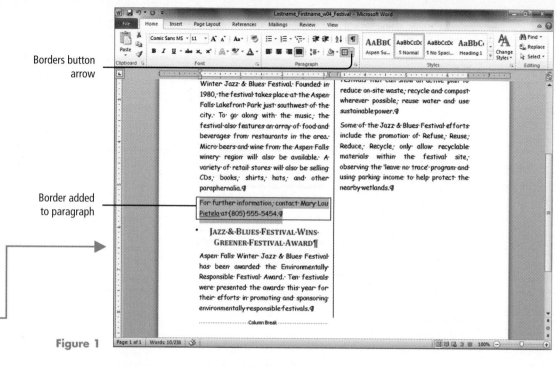

Figure 1

Font color changed and text centered

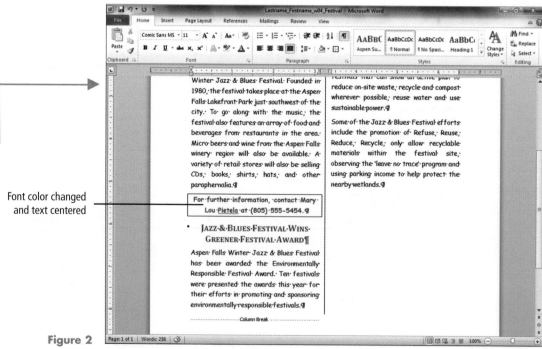

Figure 2

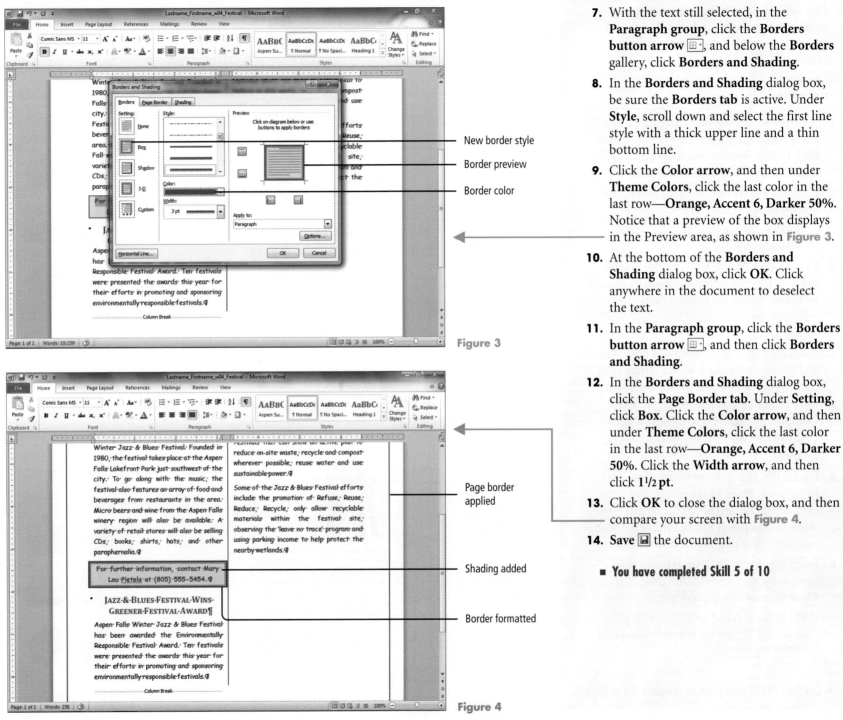

New border style

Border preview

Border color

Figure 3

Page border applied

Shading added

Border formatted

Figure 4

7. With the text still selected, in the **Paragraph group**, click the **Borders button arrow** ⊞▾, and below the **Borders** gallery, click **Borders and Shading**.

8. In the **Borders and Shading** dialog box, be sure the **Borders tab** is active. Under **Style**, scroll down and select the first line style with a thick upper line and a thin bottom line.

9. Click the **Color arrow**, and then under **Theme Colors**, click the last color in the last row—**Orange, Accent 6, Darker 50%**. Notice that a preview of the box displays in the Preview area, as shown in **Figure 3**.

10. At the bottom of the **Borders and Shading** dialog box, click **OK**. Click anywhere in the document to deselect the text.

11. In the **Paragraph group**, click the **Borders button arrow** ⊞▾, and then click **Borders and Shading**.

12. In the **Borders and Shading** dialog box, click the **Page Border tab**. Under **Setting**, click **Box**. Click the **Color arrow**, and then under **Theme Colors**, click the last color in the last row—**Orange, Accent 6, Darker 50%**. Click the **Width arrow**, and then click **1½ pt**.

13. Click **OK** to close the dialog box, and then compare your screen with **Figure 4**.

14. Save 🖫 the document.

■ **You have completed Skill 5 of 10**

► *Clip art* is a set of images, drawings, photographs, videos, and sound included with Microsoft Office or accessed from Microsoft Office Online.

► You insert clip art from the Clip Art task pane.

1. Near the top of the first column, in the paragraph that begins *Aspen Falls is proud*, click to position the insertion point at the beginning of the paragraph.

2. Click the **Insert tab**. In the **Illustrations group**, click the **Clip Art** button.

   The Clip Art task pane displays on the side of the screen.

3. In the **Clip Art** task pane, in the **Search for** box, type jazz Click the **Results should be arrow**, select the **Illustrations** check box, and then clear all of the other check boxes.

4. Click anywhere in the **Clip Art** task pane, and then be sure the **Include Office.com content** check box is selected. Near the top of the **Clip Art** task pane, click **Go**. Compare your screen with **Figure 1**.

   The position of your clip art images may vary.

5. Locate the *Jazz & Blues* image identified in **Figure 1**. Point to the image, and then click the image arrow. If you do not have access to Microsoft Office Online, choose another image and adjust it as necessary.

6. From the menu, click **Insert**, and then compare your screen with **Figure 2**. **Close** ☒ the Clip Art task pane.

   The image is placed at the insertion point as an *inline* image—as if it were a character from the keyboard.

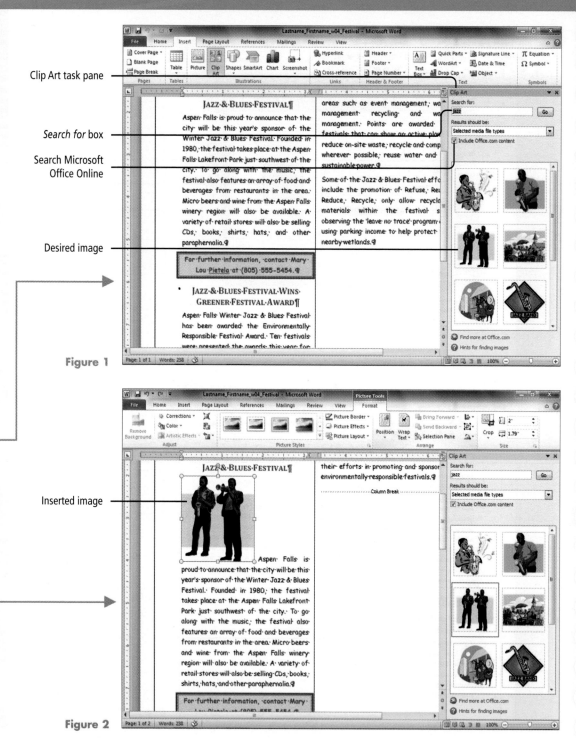

Clip Art task pane

Search for box

Search Microsoft Office Online

Desired image

Figure 1

Inserted image

Figure 2

■ **Continue to the next page to complete the skill** ➤

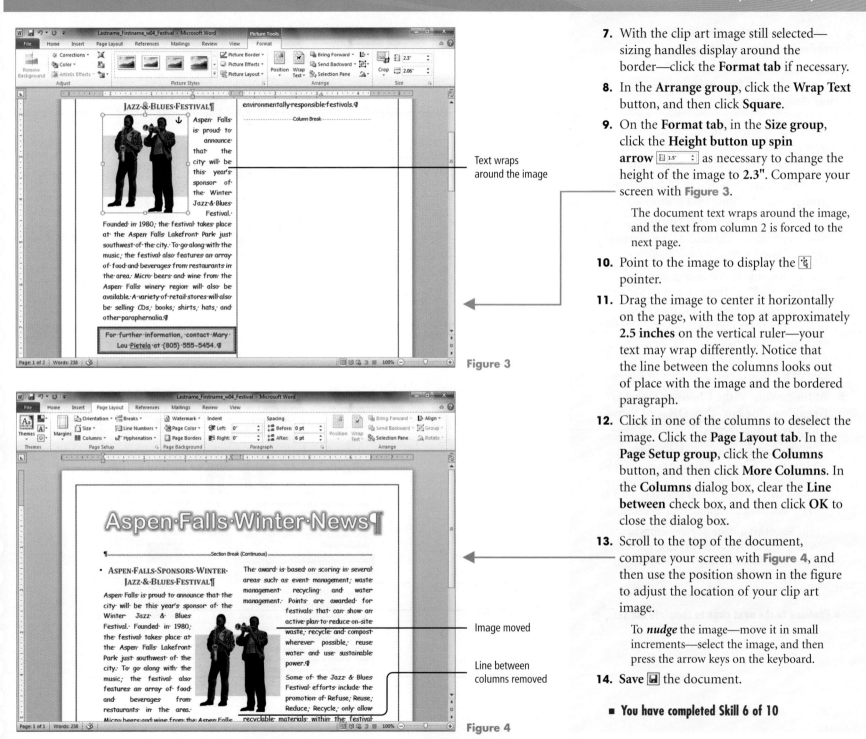

Text wraps around the image

Figure 3

Image moved

Line between columns removed

Figure 4

7. With the clip art image still selected—sizing handles display around the border—click the **Format tab** if necessary.

8. In the **Arrange group**, click the **Wrap Text** button, and then click **Square**.

9. On the **Format tab**, in the **Size group**, click the **Height button up spin arrow** as necessary to change the height of the image to **2.3"**. Compare your screen with **Figure 3**.

   The document text wraps around the image, and the text from column 2 is forced to the next page.

10. Point to the image to display the pointer.

11. Drag the image to center it horizontally on the page, with the top at approximately **2.5 inches** on the vertical ruler—your text may wrap differently. Notice that the line between the columns looks out of place with the image and the bordered paragraph.

12. Click in one of the columns to deselect the image. Click the **Page Layout tab**. In the **Page Setup group**, click the **Columns** button, and then click **More Columns**. In the **Columns** dialog box, clear the **Line between** check box, and then click **OK** to close the dialog box.

13. Scroll to the top of the document, compare your screen with **Figure 4**, and then use the position shown in the figure to adjust the location of your clip art image.

   To *nudge* the image—move it in small increments—select the image, and then press the arrow keys on the keyboard.

14. **Save** the document.

■ **You have completed Skill 6 of 10**

► A *SmartArt graphic* is a visual representation of information.

► You can choose from many different SmartArt layouts to communicate your message or ideas.

1. Press Ctrl + End to move the insertion point to the end of the document, and then press Enter to create a blank line.

2. Click the **Insert tab**. In the **Illustrations group**, click the **SmartArt** button.

3. In the **Choose a SmartArt Graphic** dialog box, scroll down and look at the various types of layouts that are available.

4. On the left side of the dialog box, click **Process**. Click the third layout in the sixth row—**Vertical Process** (the exact location of this SmartArt may vary). Notice that a preview and a description of the layout display in the preview area on the right side of the dialog box, as shown in **Figure 1**.

5. At the bottom of the **Choose a SmartArt Graphic** dialog box, click **OK**, and then compare your screen with **Figure 2**.

   The Vertical Process SmartArt graphic displays at the insertion point, with the graphic width equal to the width of the column. Two SmartArt Tools contextual tabs are added to the Ribbon—a Design tab and a Format tab.

   The SmartArt outline displays sizing handles, which consist of a series of dots, and a Text Pane button, which displays on the left of the SmartArt border.

■ **Continue to the next page to complete the skill**

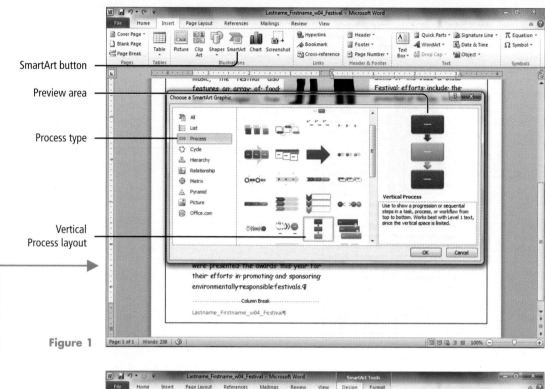

SmartArt button
Preview area
Process type
Vertical Process layout

Figure 1

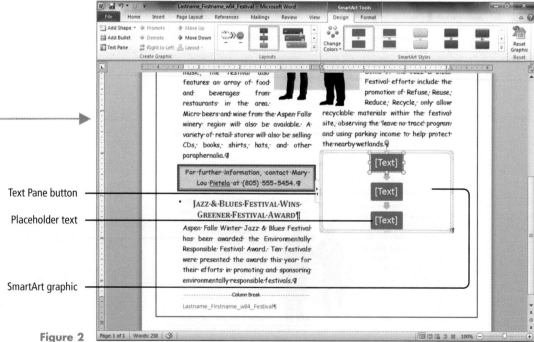

Text Pane button
Placeholder text
SmartArt graphic

Figure 2

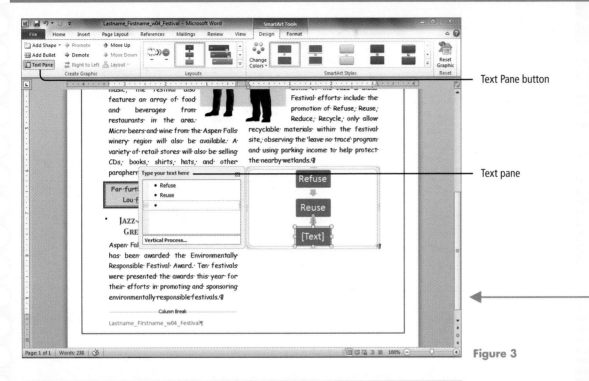

Text Pane button

Text pane

Figure 3

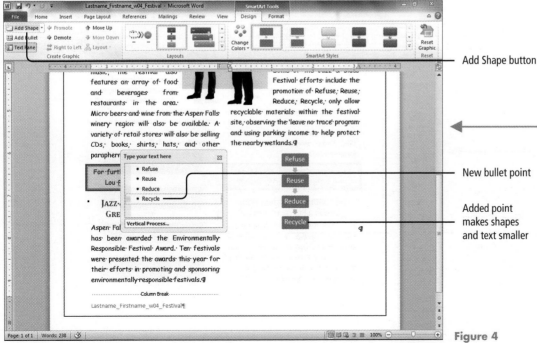

Add Shape button

New bullet point

Added point
makes shapes
and text smaller

Figure 4

6. Click in the top [**Text**] shape, type Refuse and then notice that the shape resizes as you type. The font size also adjusts automatically.

> [Text] is *placeholder text*—reserved space in shapes into which you enter your own text. If no text is entered, the placeholder text will not print.

7. In the second shape, click the [**Text**] placeholder, and then type Reuse

> To move to the next [Text] shape, you must click in the shape—you cannot use Tab to move from one shape to the next.

8. On the **Design tab**, in the **Create Graphic group**, click the **Text Pane** button. Notice that the items in the shapes are displayed as a bulleted list, as shown in **Figure 3**.

9. In the **Text** pane, if necessary, click in the third [**Text**] placeholder, and then type Reduce Notice that while you type in the bulleted list, the text also displays in the third SmartArt shape.

> To move to the next [Text] shape in the Text pane, you can also press ↑ or ↓.

10. On the **Design tab**, in the **Create Graphic group**, click the **Add Shape** button to display another bullet point. Type Recycle and then compare your screen with **Figure 4**. Notice that the shapes and the text in the shapes became smaller when you added an item to the list.

11. Close ⊠ the Text pane, and then **Save** 🖫 the document.

■ **You have completed Skill 7 of 10**

► When you change the height or width of a SmartArt graphic, the shapes and the text will automatically adjust to fit the available space.

► In a SmartArt graphic, you can also format the text, the backgrounds, and the borders of the shapes.

1. Click the border of the SmartArt graphic to select it. On the **Format tab**, click the **Size** button.

2. In the displayed list, click the **Height box up spin arrow** as necessary to increase the height of the graphic to **3"**. Compare your screen with **Figure 1**.

   When you change the height or width of a SmartArt graphic, the graphic width is not resized proportionally; however, the text font size increases to fit the new shape size.

3. Click anywhere on the border of the top shape—*Refuse*. Hold down Ctrl, and then click the other three shapes to select all four shapes in the SmartArt graphic.

4. With all four shapes selected, click the **Size** button. Click the **Width box up spin arrow** as necessary to increase the width of the graphic to **2.5"**.

5. In the **Shape Styles group**, click the **Shape Fill** button. Under **Theme Colors**, click the last color in the last row—**Orange, Accent 6, Darker 50%**.

6. In the **WordArt Styles group**, click the **Text Fill** button. Under **Theme Colors**, click the last color in the third row—**Orange, Accent 6, Lighter 60%**. Compare your screen with **Figure 2**.

■ **Continue to the next page to complete the skill**

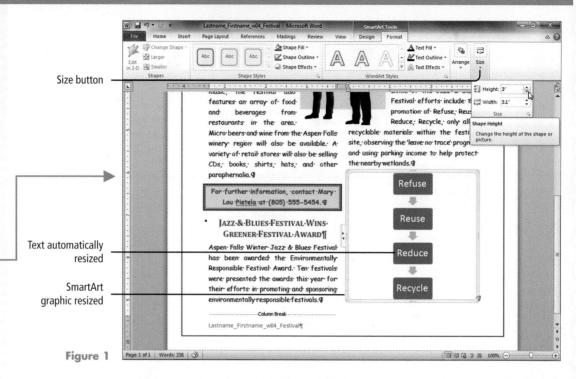

Size button

Text automatically resized

SmartArt graphic resized

Figure 1

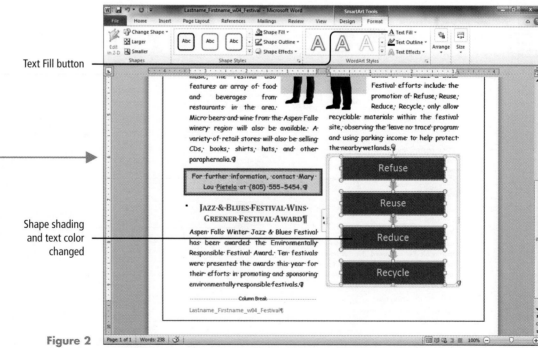

Text Fill button

Shape shading and text color changed

Figure 2

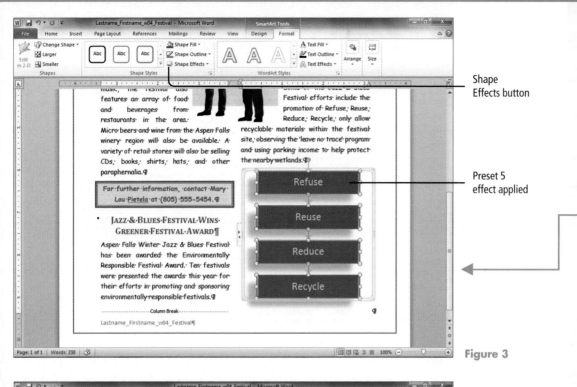

Shape Effects button

Preset 5 effect applied

Figure 3

7. With all four shapes still selected, in the **Shape Styles group**, click the **Shape Effects** button.

8. Take a moment to point to several of the categories, and then point to some of the effects and watch as Live Preview shows you what your layout would look like using each effect.

9. Point to **Preset**, and then under **Presets**, click the first effect in the second row—**Preset 5**. Compare your screen with **Figure 3**.

10. With all four shapes still selected, in the **WordArt Styles group**, click the **Text Effects** button. Point to **Reflection**, and then under **Reflection Variations**, click the first effect in the first row—**Tight Reflection, touching**.

11. Click anywhere in the text in one of the columns to deselect the SmartArt graphic.

12. On the **View tab**, in the **Zoom group**, click the **One Page** button. Compare your screen with **Figure 4**. If necessary, adjust the location of the clip art image and the size of the SmartArt graphic to match the ones in the figure.

13. In the **Zoom group**, click the **100%** button. **Save** 🖫 the document.

14. Print or submit the file as directed by your instructor, and then **Exit** Word.

■ **You have completed Skill 8 of 10**

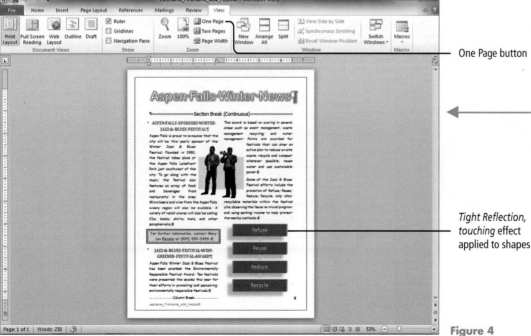

One Page button

Tight Reflection, touching effect applied to shapes

Figure 4

► The *mail merge* feature in Word is used to customize letters or labels by combining a main document with a data source.

► The *main document* contains the text that remains constant; the *data source* contains the information—such as names and addresses—that changes with each letter or label.

1. **Start** Word. Click the **File tab**, **Open** the document **w04_Festival_Addresses**, and then **Save** the document in your **Word Chapter 4** folder as Lastname_Firstname_w04_Festival_Addresses Add the file name to the footer.

2. Take a moment to examine the table of names and addresses.

   This table will be the data source for the mailing labels you will create to use with the festival flyer you created earlier in this chapter.

3. Scroll to the bottom of the table. Right-click in the bottom row of the table. From the shortcut menu, point to **Insert**, and then click **Insert Rows Below**. Enter the information for Duncan McArthur 1894 Bullpen Road Aspen Falls CA 93464 (805) 555-1853 and then compare your screen with **Figure 1**. **Save** the document and **Exit** Word.

4. **Start** Word. **Save** the document in your **Word Chapter 4** folder as Lastname_Firstname_w04_Festival_Labels If necessary, display formatting marks.

5. Click the **Mailings tab**. In the **Start Mail Merge group**, click the **Start Mail Merge** button, and then click **Labels** to open the Label Options dialog box, as shown in **Figure 2**.

■ **Continue to the next page to complete the skill**

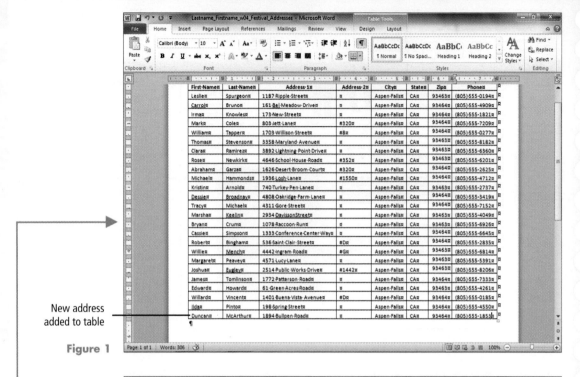

New address added to table

Figure 1

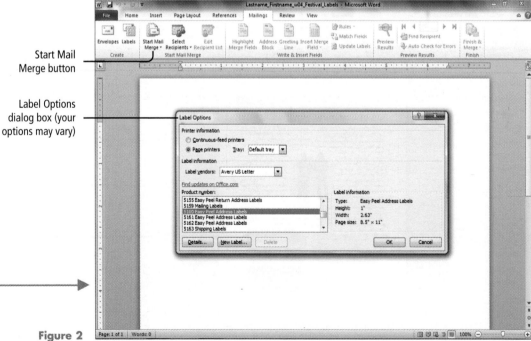

Start Mail Merge button

Label Options dialog box (your options may vary)

Figure 2

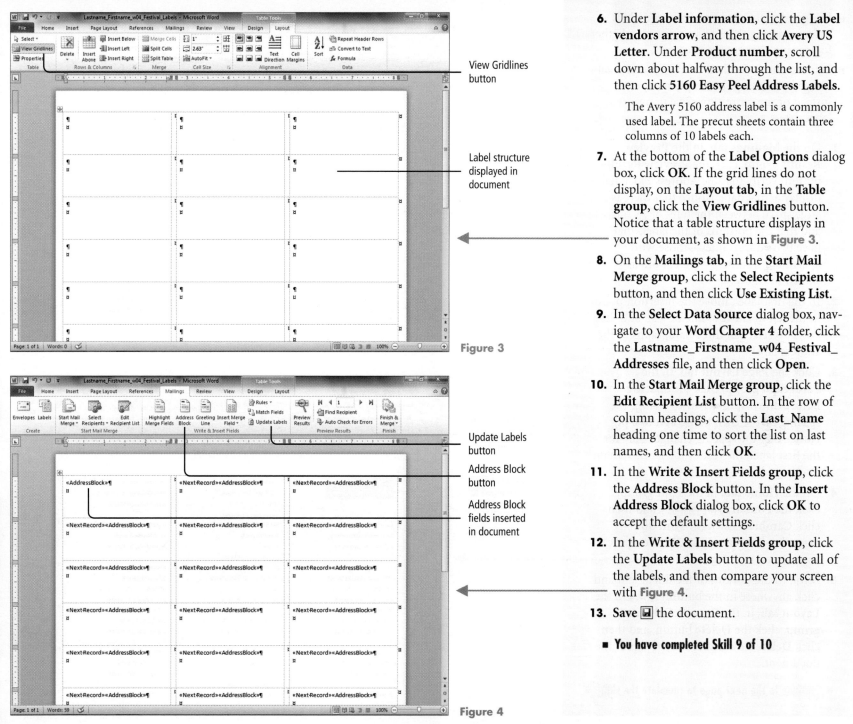

View Gridlines
button

Label structure
displayed in
document

Figure 3

Update Labels
button

Address Block
button

Address Block
fields inserted
in document

Figure 4

6. Under **Label information**, click the **Label vendors arrow**, and then click **Avery US Letter**. Under **Product number**, scroll down about halfway through the list, and then click **5160 Easy Peel Address Labels**.

    The Avery 5160 address label is a commonly used label. The precut sheets contain three columns of 10 labels each.

7. At the bottom of the **Label Options** dialog box, click **OK**. If the grid lines do not display, on the **Layout tab**, in the **Table group**, click the **View Gridlines** button. Notice that a table structure displays in your document, as shown in **Figure 3**.

8. On the **Mailings tab**, in the **Start Mail Merge group**, click the **Select Recipients** button, and then click **Use Existing List**.

9. In the **Select Data Source** dialog box, navigate to your **Word Chapter 4** folder, click the **Lastname_Firstname_w04_Festival_ Addresses** file, and then click **Open**.

10. In the **Start Mail Merge group**, click the **Edit Recipient List** button. In the row of column headings, click the **Last_Name** heading one time to sort the list on last names, and then click **OK**.

11. In the **Write & Insert Fields group**, click the **Address Block** button. In the **Insert Address Block** dialog box, click **OK** to accept the default settings.

12. In the **Write & Insert Fields group**, click the **Update Labels** button to update all of the labels, and then compare your screen with **Figure 4**.

13. Save 🖫 the document.

■ **You have completed Skill 9 of 10**

▶ It is good practice to preview your labels before printing them so you can see whether formatting changes are necessary.

▶ You can check the final results of your mail merge by printing first to plain paper instead of the more expensive preprinted label sheets.

1. On the **Mailings tab**, in the **Preview Results group**, click the **Preview Results** button. Verify that the Address Block fields display actual data. Notice that there is a large space between the lines of each label and that the bottoms of the labels that have two address lines—those with apartment numbers—are cut off, as shown in **Figure 1**.

2. In the first label, move the insertion point to the left of the first line of text, and drag down to select all three paragraphs of the address label.

3. Click the **Page Layout tab**. In the **Paragraph group**, click the **Spacing Before down spin arrow** to change the spacing before each paragraph to **0 pt**. Notice that the spacing changes only for the first label; the rest of the labels remain unchanged.

4. On the **Home tab**, in the **Font group**, click the **Font arrow** Calibri (Body) ▼, and then click **Cambria**. Click the **Font Size arrow** 11 ▼, and then click **12**. Compare your screen with **Figure 2**.

5. Scroll to the bottom of the document and click anywhere in the bottom row. On the **Layout tab**, in the **Rows & Columns group**, click the **Delete** button, and then click **Delete Rows**. Move to the top of the document.

■ **Continue to the next page to complete the skill**

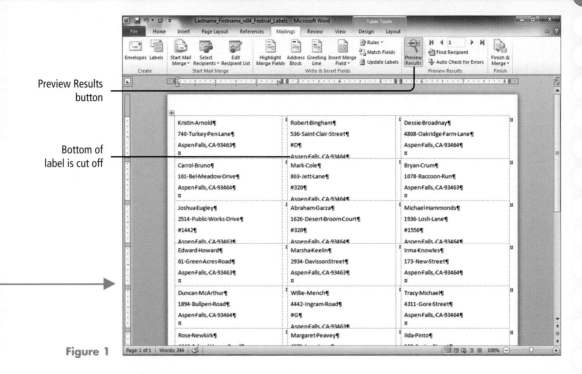

Preview Results button

Bottom of label is cut off

Figure 1

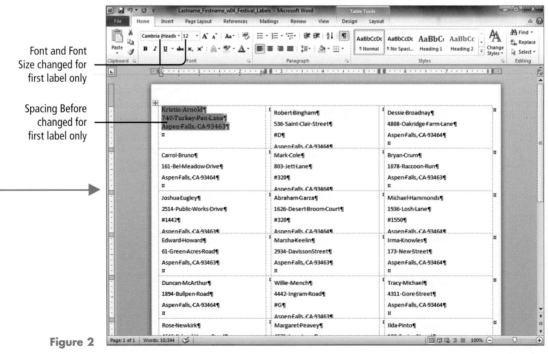

Font and Font Size changed for first label only

Spacing Before changed for first label only

Figure 2

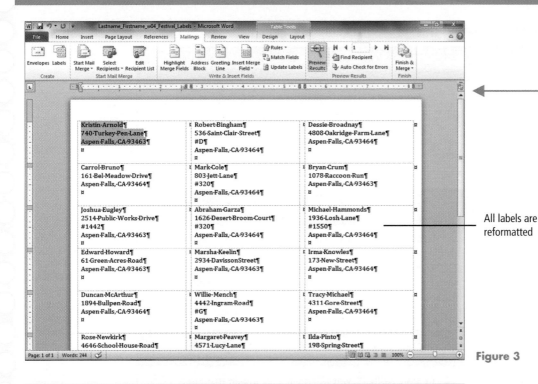

All labels are reformatted

Figure 3

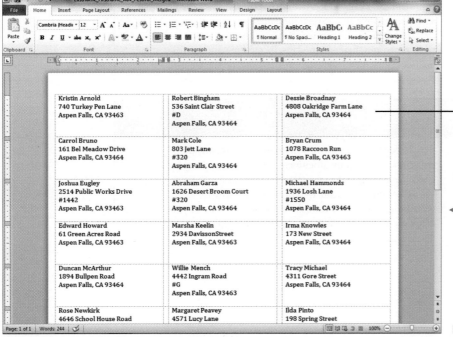

New file merges main document and data source

Figure 4

6. On the **Mailings tab**, in the **Write & Insert Fields group**, click the **Update Labels** button to apply the formatting of the original address block to all of the labels, as shown in **Figure 3**.

To reformat labels, you can first change the *original* address block, and then update the remaining labels in this manner, or you can select all of the labels and make the changes.

7. On the **Mailings tab**, in the **Finish group**, click the **Finish & Merge** button, and then click **Edit Individual Documents**. In the **Merge to New Document** dialog box, click **OK**. Notice that a new document named *Labels1* is created.

The *Labels1* document has merged two documents—the main document and the data source. Combining the two enables you to work in a single document.

8. Click the **Save** button 💾, and then save the document in your **Word Chapter 4** folder as Lastname_Firstname_w04_ Festival_Merged Add the file name to the footer.

9. On the **Home tab**, in the **Paragraph group**, click the **Show/Hide** button ¶ to turn off the formatting marks. Press Ctrl + Home, and then compare your screen with **Figure 4**.

10. **Save** 💾, and then **Close** the merged document. **Close** Lastname_ Firstname_w04_Festival_Labels but do not save or submit. Print or submit the files as directed by your instructor. **Exit** Word.

Done! You have completed Skill 10 of 10 and your document is complete!

The following More Skills are located at **www.pearsonhighered.com/skills**

More Skills 11 Create Resumes from Templates

Templates are predesigned document structures that enable you to create a new document quickly. Word templates are available for many document types, including memos, letters, business cards, and fax cover sheets. Several different resume templates are also available.

In More Skills 11, you will open a resume template, and then complete the resume.

To begin, open your web browser, navigate to www.pearsonhighered.com/skills, locate the name of your textbook, and then follow the instructions on the website.

More Skills 12 Create Outlines

When you work with a document, assigning outline levels to various parts of the text can be helpful. When you use outline levels, you can move blocks of text around in a document just by moving an outline item—all associated text moves with the outline item.

In More Skills 12, you will open a document, switch to Outline view, create outline levels, and move outline text.

To begin, open your web browser, navigate to www.pearsonhighered.com/skills, locate the name of your textbook, and then follow the instructions on the website.

More Skills 13 Prepare Documents for Distribution

Before sharing a document with colleagues, it is good practice to remove any hidden data or personal information embedded in the document. Word can inspect your document and remove any features that you do not want to share.

In More Skills 13, you will open a document that has comments and other document properties, inspect the document, and then remove all personal information.

To begin, open your web browser, navigate to www.pearsonhighered.com/skills, locate the name of your textbook, and then follow the instructions on the website.

More Skills 14 Preview and Save Documents as Web Pages

You can preview a document to see what it would look like as a web page. When you have the document formatted the way you want, you can save the document in a format that can be used on the web.

In More Skills 14, you will open a document, add a hyperlink to text in the document, preview the document as a web page, and finally save the document as a web page.

To begin, open your web browser, navigate to www.pearsonhighered.com/skills, locate the name of your textbook, and then follow the instructions on the website.

Key Terms

Online Help Skills

1. **Start** ⊕ Word. In the upper right corner of the Word window, click the **Help** button ▣. In the **Help** window, click the **Maximize** ▭ button.

2. Click in the search box, type mail merge and then click the **Search** button ▣. In the search results, click **Use mail merge to create and print letters and other documents**.

3. Read the article's introduction, and then click the blue text in step. **Add placeholders**. Compare your screen with **Figure 1**.

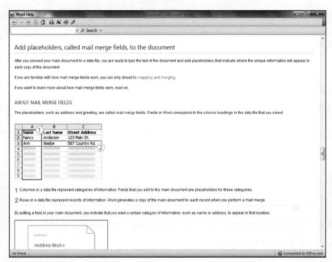

Figure 1

4. Read the section to see if you can answer the following: What fields are included in an address block? How would you add individual fields, such as a first name or last name, to a form letter?

Matching

Match each term in the second column with its correct definition in the first column by writing the letter of the term on the blank line in front of the correct definition.

____ **1.** In mail merge, the command used to modify all labels based on changes made to the original label.

____ **2.** In the Columns gallery, the command that displays the Columns dialog box.

____ **3.** A style displayed on the Ribbon.

____ **4.** A set of decorative formats that make text stand out in a document.

____ **5.** A portion of a document that can be formatted differently from the rest of the document.

____ **6.** A format that makes a paragraph stand out from the rest of the text.

____ **7.** A set of images, photographs, videos, and sound provided by Microsoft that is available on your computer or online.

____ **8.** To move an object in small increments by selecting the object, and then pressing one of the arrow keys.

____ **9.** Text that reserves space in a SmartArt shape but does not print.

____ **10.** A feature that combines a main document and a data source to create customized letters or tables.

A Border

B Clip art

C Mail merge

D More Columns

E Nudge

F Placeholder

G Quick Style

H Section

I Text effects

J Update Labels

Multiple Choice

Choose the correct answer.

1. The default width assigned to columns.
   A. Proportional
   B. Equal
   C. Unbalanced

2. A predefined set of text formats that can be applied from the Ribbon.
   A. Quick Style
   B. SmartArt
   C. Clip art

3. A picture is inserted into a document using this format.
   A. Centered
   B. Text wrapped
   C. Inline

4. Moves the text to the right of the insertion point to the top of the next column.
   A. Page break
   B. Column break
   C. Continuous break

5. A type of break that is used to create a new section that can be formatted differently from the rest of the document.
   A. Page
   B. Column
   C. Continuous

6. To change the color of the background in a paragraph, add this to the text background.
   A. Shading
   B. A border
   C. Text emphasis

7. Reserved spaces in shapes into which you enter your own text.
   A. Text effects
   B. Placeholder text
   C. Data sources

8. A graphic visual representation of information.
   A. Text effects
   B. Clip art
   C. SmartArt

9. Used by a mail merge document, this file contains information such as names and addresses.
   A. Data source
   B. Main document
   C. Merge document

10. In a mail merge document, this document contains the text that remains constant.
    A. Data source
    B. Main document
    C. Merge document

Topics for Discussion

1. In this chapter, you practiced inserting a clip art image in a document. When do you think clip art images are most appropriate, and in what kind of documents might clip art images be inappropriate. If you had to create a set of rules for using clip art in a document, what would the top three rules be?

2. In this chapter, you used the mail merge feature in Word to create labels and name tags. With mail merge, you can also insert one field at a time—and the fields do not have to be just names and addresses. Can you think of any situations where you might want to insert fields in a letter or another document?

Skill Check

To complete this document, you will need the following files:

- w04_Cars
- w04_Cars_Judges

You will save your documents as:

- Lastname_Firstname_w04_Cars
- Lastname_Firstname_w04_Cars_Labels

1. **Start** Word, and open **w04_Cars**. **Save** the document in your **Word Chapter 4** folder as Lastname_Firstname_w04_Cars Add the file name to the footer.

2. Locate the paragraph *This Year's Show*, and then select the document text from that point to the end of the document. On the **Home tab**, in the **Paragraph group**, **Justify** the text. On the **Page Layout tab**, in the **Page Setup group**, click the **Columns** button, and then click **Two**.

3. Position the insertion point at the beginning of the paragraph *Featured Cars*. On the **Page Layout tab**, in the **Page Setup group**, click the **Breaks** button, and then click **Column**. Compare your screen with **Figure 1**. ⎯⎯⎯

4. Select the document title. On the **Home tab**, in the **Styles group**, click the **More** button, and then click **Title**.

5. In the **Font group**, click the **Text Effects** button, and then in the fourth row of the gallery, click the first thumbnail—**Gradient Fill - Blue, Accent 1, Outline - White, Glow - Accent 2**. **Center** the title, and then change the **Font Size** to **42** pt.

6. Select the subtitle *This Year's Show*. In the **Font group**, click the **Dialog Box Launcher**. Under **Font style**, click **Bold**. Under **Size**, click **16**. Click the **Font Color arrow**, and then under **Theme Colors**, click the sixth color in the first row—**Red Accent 2**. Under **Effects**, select the **Small caps** check box, and then click **OK**. In the **Paragraph group**, click the **Center** button.

7. In the **Styles group**, click the **More** button, and then click **Save selection as a New Quick Style**. In the **Create New Style from Formatting** dialog box, under **Name**, type Cars Subtitle and then press [Enter].

8. Select the second subtitle—*Featured Cars*. On the **Home tab**, in the **Styles group**, click the **Cars Subtitle** Quick Style. Compare your screen with **Figure 2**. ⎯⎯⎯

Figure 1

Figure 2

 ■ Continue to the next page to complete this Skill Check

9. Click anywhere in the document. On the **Insert tab**, in the **Illustrations group**, click the **Clip Art** button.

10. In the **Clip Art** task pane, in the **Search for** box, type sports car and then click **Go**. Click the image shown in **Figure 3** (or a similar image if this one is not available). Close the **Clip Art** pane. On the **Format tab**, in the **Arrange group**, click the **Wrap Text** button, and then click **Tight**. On the **Format tab**, in the **Size group**, change the **Width** to 2.5". Move the image to the position shown in **Figure 3**.

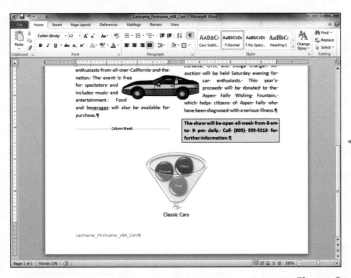

11. Select the last paragraph in the document. In the **Paragraph group**, click the **Borders button arrow**, and then click **Outside Borders**. In the **Paragraph group**, click the **Shading button arrow**. Under **Theme Colors**, click the second color in the sixth column—**Red, Accent 2, Lighter 80%**.

12. Click anywhere in the document. On the **Insert tab**, in the **Illustrations group**, click the **SmartArt** button. Click **Process**, click the **Funnel** layout—the fourth layout in the tenth row—and then click **OK**. Click the border of the SmartArt image. On the **Format tab**, click the **Arrange** button. Click the **Position** button, and then under **With Text Wrapping**, in the third row, click the second button. Click the **Size** button, and increase the **Height** to 2.2".

Figure 3

13. On the **Design tab**, in the **SmartArt Styles group**, click the **More** button, and then click the first style under **3-D**—Polished. In the **Create Graphic group**, click the **Text Pane** button. For the four bullets, type Chevy and Chrysler and Ford and Classic Cars and then **Close** the Text pane. Deselect the SmartArt graphic, and then compare your document with **Figure 3**. **Save** and **Exit** Word.

14. **Start** Word. On the **Mailings tab**, in the **Start Mail Merge group**, click the **Start Mail Merge** button, and then click **Labels**. Under **Label information**, select **Avery US Letter**. Under **Product number**, click **5160**, and then click **OK**. In the **Start Mail Merge group**, click **Select Recipients**, click **Use Existing List**, and then locate and open **w04_Cars_Judges**.

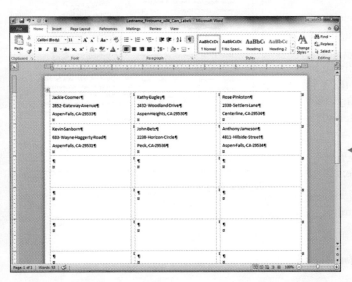

15. In the **Write & Insert Fields** group, click the **Address Block** button, and then click **OK**. In the **Write & Insert Fields group**, click the **Update Labels** button.

16. In the **Preview Results group**, click the **Preview Results** button. In the **Finish group**, click the **Finish & Merge** button, click **Edit Individual Documents**, and then click **OK**. Delete the last row in the table. **Save** the document in your **Word Chapter 4** folder as Lastname_Firstname_w04_Cars_Labels and add the file name to the footer. Compare your document with **Figure 4**.

Figure 4

17. **Save** and then submit your documents as directed. **Exit** Word but do not save changes to any other documents.

Done! You have completed the Skill Check

Assess Your Skills 1

To complete this document, you will need the following file:

- w04_Cruises

You will save your document as:

- Lastname_Firstname_w04_Cruises

1. **Start** Word. Locate and open **w04_Cruises**, save it in your **Word Chapter 4** folder as Lastname_Firstname_w04_Cruises and then add the file name to the footer. Select the title *Aspen Lake Cruises*—including the paragraph mark—and then on the **Home tab**, apply the **Intense Quote** Quick Style.

2. With the title still selected, change the title font size to **36** points. Apply the **Gradient Fill - Blue, Accent 1** text effect—the fourth effect in the third row. Then apply an **Offset Diagonal Bottom Left** text effect shadow—under **Outer**, the third effect in the first row.

3. Starting with the *Aspen Lake Nature Cruise* subtitle, select all of the text to the end of the document, and then change it to a two-column format. **Justify** the two-column text. Display the **Columns** dialog box, and then change the **Spacing** between the columns to **0.3".** At the left side of the *Valentine's Day Cruise!* subtitle, insert a column break.

4. Select the *Aspen Lake Nature Cruise* subtitle, and then apply **Bold, Italic,** and **Center** alignment. Change the font size to **16** points, the font color to **Blue, Accent 1,** and then apply the **Small Caps** effect.

5. Create a new **Quick Style** named Cruise Subtitle based on the subtitle you just formatted. Apply the **Cruise Subtitle** Quick Style to the *Valentine's Day Cruise!* subtitle.

6. Position the insertion point at the beginning of the last paragraph, which begins *Book online or call.* Use the **Clip Art** task pane to search the Clip Art media type for cruise ship and then insert the image shown in **Figure 1**.

7. Change the width of the clip art image to **2.5".** Change the **Wrap Text** to **Top and Bottom,** and then center the image horizontally in the column, as shown in **Figure 1.**

8. At the bottom of the first column, select the last paragraph, including the paragraph mark. Add an **Outside Border** to the paragraph. Display the **Borders and Shading** dialog box. Change the border width to **1½ pt,** the border color to **Dark Blue, Text 2,** and the shading fill to **Blue, Accent 1, Lighter 80%**—the fifth color in the second row.

9. Add a **Box** style page border that is **½ pt** wide, with a **Color** of **Dark Blue, Text 2.**

10. Compare your document with **Figure 1**. **Save** your document, and then submit it as directed.

Done! You have completed Assess Your Skills 1

Figure 1

Aspen Falls Classic Car Competition

THIS YEAR'S SHOW

Aspen Falls will be sponsoring this year's classic car show, which will be held in the convention center downtown.

The Aspen Falls Classic Car Show attracts enthusiasts from all over California and the nation. The event is free for spectators and includes music and entertainment. Food and beverages will also be available for purchase.

THIS YEAR'S COMPETITION

For the first time ever, the Aspen Falls Classic Car Show will have a car competition. Awards will be given to the best cars in three categories:

Vintage Cars—Pre World War II
Classic Cars—Post World War II to 1980
Hot Rods—Cars modified for racing

There will also be a Best In Show award presented, which will be chosen from among the winners in each of the three categories.

For entry forms and further information, call Gail Lipscomb at (805) 555-5213.

Lastname_Firstname_w04_Competition

Leslie Spurgeon 1187 Ripple Street Aspen Falls, CA 29534	Carrol Bruno 161 Bel Meadow Drive Aspen Falls, CA 29531	Irma Knowles 173 New Street Aspen Falls, CA 29533
Mark Cole 809 Jett Lane #320 Aspen Falls, CA 29531	William Tapper 1703 Willison Street #8 Aspen Falls, CA 29534	Thomas Stevenson 3358 Maryland Avenue Aspen Falls, CA 29531
Clara Ramirez 3892 Lightning Point Drive Aspen Falls, CA 29533	Rose Newkirk 4646 School House Road #352 Aspen Falls, CA 29534	Abraham Garza 1626 Desert Broom Court #320 Aspen Falls, CA 29531
Michael Hammonds 1936 Losh Lane #1550 Aspen Falls, CA 29534	Kristin Arnold 740 Turkey Pen Lane Aspen Falls, CA 29531	Dessie Broadnay 4808 Oakridge Farm Lane Aspen Falls, CA 29534
Tracy Michael 4311 Gore Street Aspen Falls, CA 29533	Marsha Keelin 2934 Davisson Street Aspen Falls, CA 29531	Bryan Crum 1078 Raccoon Run Aspen Falls, CA 29534
Cassie Simpson 1333 Conference Center Way Aspen Falls, CA 29533	Robert Bingham 536 Saint Clair Street #D Aspen Falls, CA 29534	Willie Mench 4442 Ingram Road #6 Aspen Falls, CA 29533
Margaret Peavey 4571 Lucy Lane Aspen Falls, CA 29534	Joshua Eugley 2514 Public Works Drive #1442 Aspen Falls, CA 29531	James Tomlinson 1772 Patterson Road Aspen Falls, CA 29534
Edward Howard 61 Green Acres Road Aspen Falls, CA 29531	Willard Vincent 1401 Buena Vista Avenue #D Aspen Falls, CA 29533	Ilda Pinto 198 Spring Street Aspen Falls, CA 29531

Lastname_Firstname_w04_Competition_Labels

Figure 1

Assess Your Skills 2

Assess Your Skills 3 and 4 can be found at **www.pearsonhighered.com/skills**.

To complete this document, you will need the following files:

- w04_Competition
- w04_Competition_Addresses

You will save your documents as:

- Lastname_Firstname_w04_Competition
- Lastname_Firstname_w04_Competition_Labels

1. **Start** Word. Locate and open **w04_Competition**, save it in your **Word Chapter 4** folder as Lastname_Firstname_w04_Competition and then add the file name to the footer.

2. Select the document title. Change the title text to **Arial Black, 42** points, and **Center** the text. Change the *title* **Line Spacing** to **1.0**, and the **Spacing After** to **0 pt**. With the title still selected, apply the **Gradient Fill - Orange, Accent 6, Inner Shadow** text effect—the second effect in the fourth row. Apply an **Orange, 5 pt glow, Accent color 6 Glow** text effect—the last Glow effect in the first row.

3. Press Ctrl + End to move to the end of the document. Insert a **Cycle** SmartArt graphic using the **Radial Cycle** layout—the first style in the third row. In the center circle, type Best in Show

4. Display the **Text Pane**, and then fill in the empty bullet points with the following text:

   Vintage
   Classic
   Hot Rod
   Custom

5. **Close** the Text pane. Change the SmartArt **Height** to **3"** and the **Width** to **6.5"**. On the **Design tab**, apply the **Cartoon SmartArt Style**—the third style under 3-D.

6. With the SmartArt graphic still selected, **Change Colors** to **Colorful - Accent Colors**—the first style under Colorful.

7. Insert a **Shadow** page border with the **Orange, Accent 6, Darker 50%** color and a width of **3 pt**. **Save** your document, and then **Exit** Word.

8. Create a new blank document. Start the mail merge process to create **Labels** using **Avery US Letter, Product number 5160**. Use the **w04_Competition_Addresses** document as the data source. Add an **Address Block**, and accept all address block defaults, and then **Update Labels**. In the first label, remove the spacing before the address block. **Update Labels** and then preview the results. Merge all the labels into a single document. Delete the two bottom rows of the table.

9. **Save** the mail merge document in your **Word Chapter 4** folder as Lastname_Firstname_w04_Competition_Labels and then add the file name to the footer. Compare your completed documents with **Figure 1**. **Exit** Word—do not save the original mail merge document. Print or submit your documents as directed.

Done! You have completed Assess Your Skills 2

Assess Your Skills Visually

To complete this document, you will need the following file:

■ w04_Heritage_Days

You will save your document as:

■ Lastname_Firstname_w04_Heritage_Days

Start Word, and open **w04_Heritage_Days**. Create a flyer as shown in **Figure 1**. **Save** the file as Lastname_Firstname_w04_Heritage_Days in your **Word Chapter 4** folder.

To complete this document, apply the **Title** Quick Style, with a font size of **26 pt**. Break the column as indicated. In the bordered text, apply the **Dark Blue, Text 2** text and border colors, and **Blue, Accent 1, Lighter 80%** shading. Use the same border color for the page border. Set all border widths to **3 pt**. Insert the **Clip Art** image shown in **Figure 1** using old west as the search term, and change its **Height** to **2"**.

For the subtitles, use an **18** point font size, **Small caps**, and **Center** the titles. Use the same color you used for the borders. For the SmartArt graphic, in the **Relationship** category, apply the **Converging Radial** layout. Adjust the graphic to **6.5"** wide and **3"** high, and then apply the **White Outline** SmartArt style. Insert the file name in the footer, and then print or submit it electronically as directed.

Done! You have completed Assess Your Skills Visually

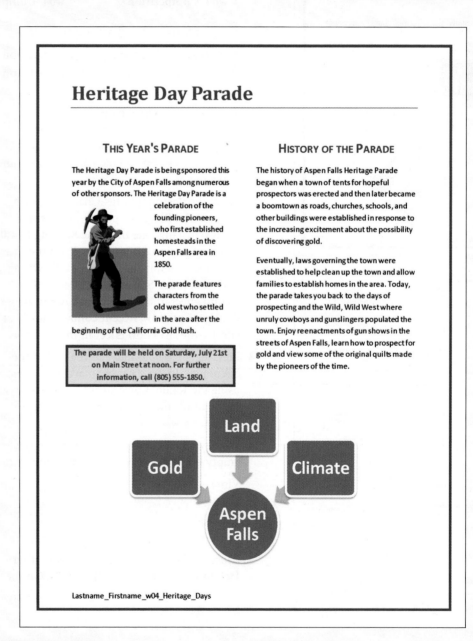

Figure 1

Skills in Context

To complete this document, you will need the following file:

- New blank Word document

You will save your document as:

- Lastname_Firstname_w04_Attractions

Create a flyer about the attractions around Aspen Falls. Use the web to research northern California for ideas—you could research attractions such as sailing, nature trails, bird watching, waterfalls, wineries, and so on. The flyer should have a formatted title and a subtitle, and then two-column text describing the area's attractions. Your completed document should include a page border, a paragraph or paragraphs with a paragraph border and shading, a clip art image, and a SmartArt graphic of your choice. You can include a picture if you would like to do so.

Save the document as Lastname_Firstname_w04_Attractions Insert the file name in the footer, and be sure to check the entire document for grammar and spelling. Print or submit the file electronically as directed.

Done! You have completed Skills in Context

Skills and You

To complete this document, you will need the following file:

- New blank Word document

You will save your document as:

- Lastname_Firstname_w04_Family

Using the skills you have practiced in this chapter, create a flyer to send to family members about family events coming up during the next year. The flyer should have a formatted title and a subtitle, and then two-column text describing the various events. Your completed document should include a page border, a paragraph with a paragraph border and shading, a clip art image, and a SmartArt graphic of your choice.

Save the document as Lastname_Firstname_w04_Family Check the entire document for grammar and spelling. Print or submit the file electronically as directed.

Done! You have completed Skills and You

CHAPTER 1

Create Workbooks with Excel 2010

▶ Microsoft Office Excel 2010 is used worldwide to create workbooks and to analyze data that is organized into columns and rows.

▶ After data is entered into Excel, you can perform calculations on the numerical data and analyze the data to make informed decisions.

Your starting screen will look similar to this:

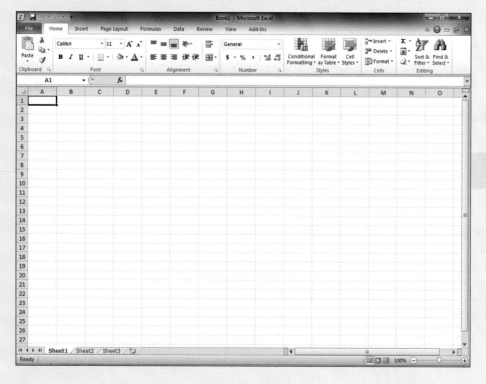

SKILLS

Skills 1-10 Training

At the end of this chapter, you will be able to:

Skill 1 Create and Save New Workbooks

Skill 2 Enter Worksheet Data and Merge and Center Titles

Skill 3 Construct Addition and Subtraction Formulas

Skill 4 Construct Multiplication and Division Formulas

Skill 5 Adjust Column Widths and Apply Cell Styles

Skill 6 Use the SUM Function

Skill 7 Copy Formulas and Functions Using the Fill Handle

Skill 8 Format, Edit, and Check the Spelling of Data

Skill 9 Create Footers and Change Page Settings

Skill 10 Display and Print Formulas and Scale Worksheets for Printing

MORE SKILLS

More Skills 11 Create New Workbooks from Templates

More Skills 12 Use Range Names in Formulas

More Skills 13 Change Themes

More Skills 14 Manage Document Properties

Outcome

Using the skills listed to the left will enable you to create a worksheet like this:

Aspen Falls Parks and Recreation							
Bike Rentals at Aspen Lake Recreation Area							
Location	Children	Adult	Total	Difference	Rental Fee		Total Fees
North	139	51	190	88	$	6	$ 1,140
South	108	60	168	48		7	1,176
Central	153	93	246	60		7	1,722
East	175	82	257	93		10	2,570
West	246	170	416	76		7	2,912
Total	**821**	**456**	**1277**				$ 9,520
Percent of Adult Bikes Rented							
North	26.8%						
South	35.7%						
Central	37.8%						
East	31.9%						
West	40.9%						

Lastname_Firstname_e01_Bikes.xlsx   4/29/2010   Parks and Recreation

You will save your workbook as:

Lastname_Firstname_e01_Bikes

In this chapter, you will create documents for the Aspen Falls City Hall, which provides essential services for the citizens and visitors of Aspen Falls, California.

Introduction

- ► Excel is used to perform calculations on numbers. When you make changes to one or more number values, you can immediately see the effect of those changes in totals and charts that rely on those values.

- ► An Excel workbook can contain a large amount of data—up to 16,384 columns and 1,048,576 rows.

- ► The basic skills you need to work efficiently with Excel include entering and formatting data, and navigating within Excel.

- ► When planning your worksheet, think about what information will form the rows and what information will form the columns. Generally, rows are used to list the items and columns to group or describe the items in the list.

Time to complete all
10 skills – 50 to 90 minutes

Find your student data files here:

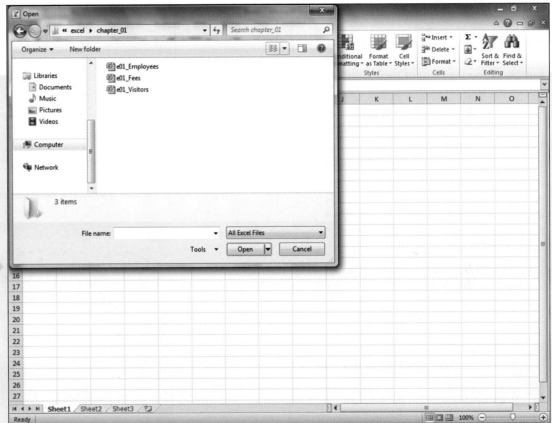

**Student data file needed
for this chapter:**

■ **New blank Excel workbook**

▶ Starting Excel displays a new blank *workbook*—a file that you can use to organize various kinds of related information. A workbook contains *worksheets*, also called *spreadsheets*—the primary document that you use in Excel to store and work with data.

▶ The worksheet forms a grid of vertical columns and horizontal rows. The small box where one column and one row meet is a cell.

1. Start ⊕ Microsoft Excel 2010. In the lower right, if necessary, click the **Normal** button ▦. To the right of the button, notice the zoom—magnification level.

> Your zoom level should be 100%, but most figures in this chapter are zoomed to 130%.

2. Verify the cell in the upper left corner is the *active cell*—the cell outlined in black in which data is entered when you begin typing. Notice that columns have alphabetical headings across the top, and rows have numerical headings down the left side, as shown in **Figure 1**.

> When a cell is active, the headings for the column and row in which the cell is located are highlighted. The column letter and row number that identify a cell is the *cell address*, also called the *cell reference*.

3. In cell **A1**, type Aspen Falls Parks and Recreation and then press Enter to store the entry.

4. In cell **A2**, type Bike Rentals at Aspen Lake Area and then press Enter. Compare your screen with **Figure 2**.

■ **Continue to the next page to complete the skill**

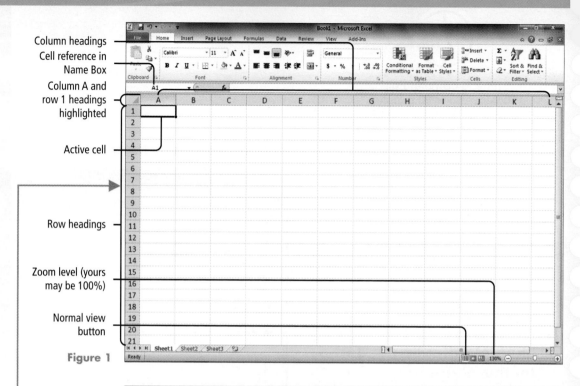

Column headings
Cell reference in Name Box
Column A and row 1 headings highlighted
Active cell
Row headings
Zoom level (yours may be 100%)
Normal view button

Figure 1

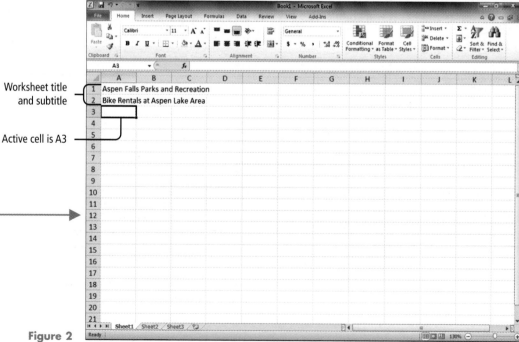

Worksheet title and subtitle
Active cell is A3

Figure 2

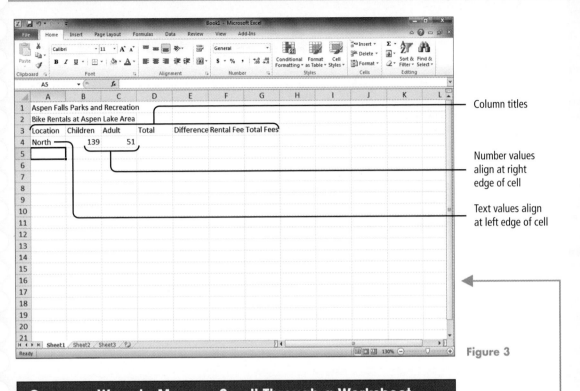

Figure 3

Common Ways to Move or Scroll Through a Worksheet

Press	Description
Enter	Move down one row.
Tab	Move one column to the right.
Shift + Tab	Move one column to the left.
↓ ↑ → ←	Move one cell in the direction of the arrow.
Ctrl + Home	Move to cell A1.
Ctrl + End	Move to the lowest row and the column farthest to the right that contains data.

Figure 4

5. Type Location and press Tab to make the cell to the right—**B3**—active.

6. With cell **B3** the active cell, type the following titles, pressing Tab between each title:

Children
Adult
Total
Difference
Rental Fee
Total Fees

> Titles above columns help readers understand the data.

> To correct typing errors, click a cell and retype the data—the new typing will replace the existing data.

7. Click cell **A4**, type North and then press Tab. Type 139 and press Tab. Type 51 and then press Enter.

> Data in a cell is called a *value*. You can have a *text value* (*North*) or a *number value* (*139*). A text value is also referred to as a *label*.

8. Notice that the text values align at the left cell edge, and number values align at the right cell edge, as shown in **Figure 3**.

9. On the Quick Access Toolbar, click **Save** 🔲. In the **Save As** dialog box, navigate to the location where you are saving your files. Click **New folder**, type Excel Chapter 1 and then press Enter two times. In the **File name** box, using your own name, name the workbook Lastname_ Firstname_e01_Bikes and then press Enter.

> Common methods to move between cells in an Excel worksheet are summarized in the table in **Figure 4**.

■ **You have completed Skill 1 of 10**

► Multiple cells can be selected by dragging so that the selection can be edited, formatted, copied, or moved.

1. In cell **A5**, type Soutth and press [Tab]. (You will correct the spelling in Skill 8.)

2. In cell **B5**, type 108 and press [Tab]. In cell **C5**, type 60 and press [Enter].

3. In row 6 and row 7, enter the following data:

   Easst   75   32
   West   246   170

4. In cell **A8**, type Total and press [Enter]. Compare your screen with **Figure 1**.

5. Click cell **B1**, type Worksheet and press [Enter]. Notice that the text in cell A1 is **truncated**—cut off.

   When text is too long to fit in a cell and the cell to the right of it contains data, the text will be truncated.

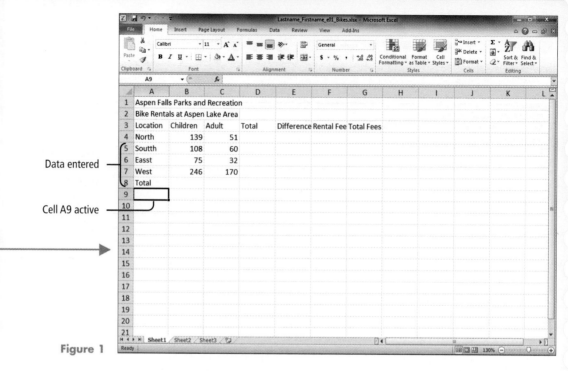

Data entered

Cell A9 active

Figure 1

6. Click cell **A1**, and then above column D, locate the **formula bar**—a bar below the Ribbon that displays the value contained in the active cell and is used to enter or edit values or formulas. Compare your screen with **Figure 2**.

   Data displayed in a cell is the **displayed value**. Data displayed in the formula bar is the **underlying value**. Displayed values often do not match their underlying values.

7. On the Quick Access Toolbar, click the **Undo** button to remove the text in cell B1. Notice that the text in cell A1 now overlaps the cells to the right because those cells are empty.

■ **Continue to the next page to complete the skill**

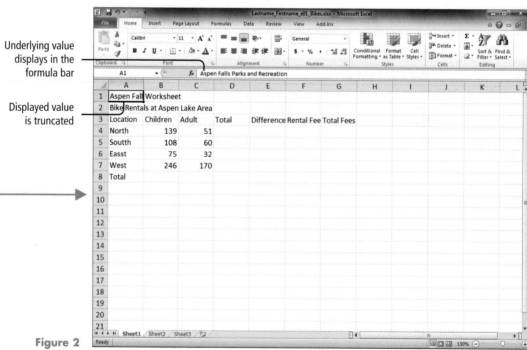

Underlying value displays in the formula bar

Displayed value is truncated

Figure 2

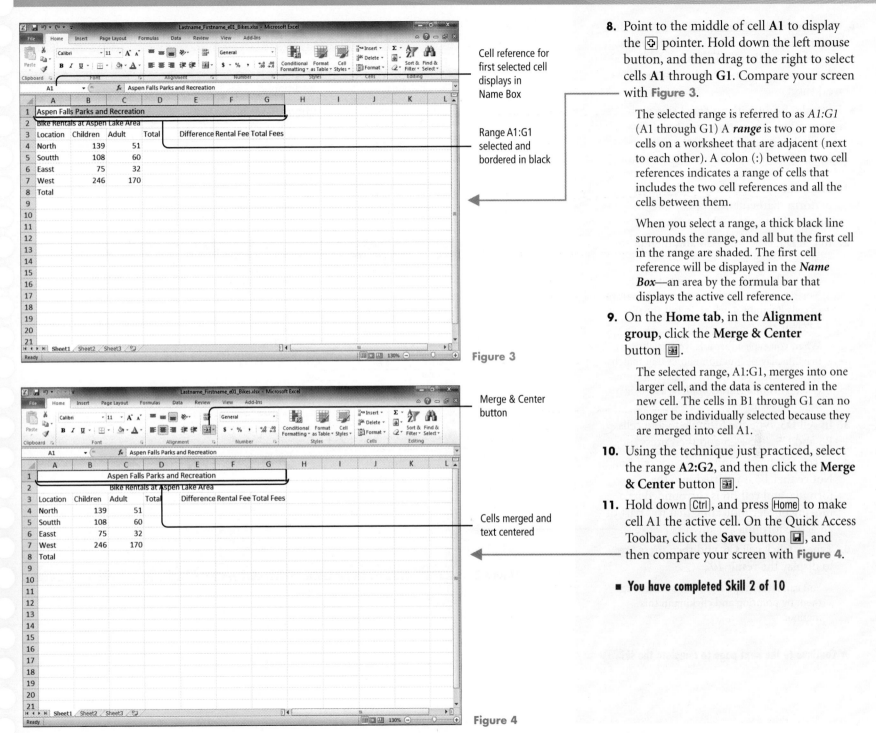

Cell reference for first selected cell displays in Name Box

Range A1:G1 selected and bordered in black

Figure 3

Merge & Center button

Cells merged and text centered

Figure 4

8. Point to the middle of cell **A1** to display the ⊕ pointer. Hold down the left mouse button, and then drag to the right to select cells **A1** through **G1**. Compare your screen with **Figure 3**.

   The selected range is referred to as *A1:G1* (A1 through G1) A *range* is two or more cells on a worksheet that are adjacent (next to each other). A colon (:) between two cell references indicates a range of cells that includes the two cell references and all the cells between them.

   When you select a range, a thick black line surrounds the range, and all but the first cell in the range are shaded. The first cell reference will be displayed in the *Name Box*—an area by the formula bar that displays the active cell reference.

9. On the **Home tab**, in the **Alignment group**, click the **Merge & Center** button ⊞.

   The selected range, A1:G1, merges into one larger cell, and the data is centered in the new cell. The cells in B1 through G1 can no longer be individually selected because they are merged into cell A1.

10. Using the technique just practiced, select the range **A2:G2**, and then click the **Merge & Center** button ⊞.

11. Hold down Ctrl, and press Home to make cell A1 the active cell. On the Quick Access Toolbar, click the **Save** button 🖫, and then compare your screen with **Figure 4**.

   ▪ **You have completed Skill 2 of 10**

▶ A cell's underlying value can be a text value, a number value, or a formula. A *formula* is an equation that performs mathematical calculations on number values in the worksheet.

▶ Formulas begin with an equal sign and often include an *arithmetic operator*— a symbol that specifies a mathematical operation such as addition or subtraction.

1. Study the symbols that Excel uses to perform mathematical operations, as summarized in the table in **Figure 1**.

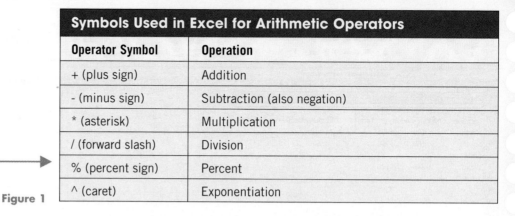

Symbols Used in Excel for Arithmetic Operators

Operator Symbol	Operation
+ (plus sign)	Addition
- (minus sign)	Subtraction (also negation)
* (asterisk)	Multiplication
/ (forward slash)	Division
% (percent sign)	Percent
^ (caret)	Exponentiation

Figure 1

2. In cell **D4**, type =B4+C4 and then press Enter.

The total number of bikes rented for the North location equals the sum of the values in cells B4 and C4, which is *190*, the sum of 139 and 51.

When you type a formula, you might see a brief display of function names that match the first letter you type. This Excel feature, called *Formula AutoComplete*, assists in inserting formulas.

3. In cell **D5**, type the formula to add cells B5 and C5, =B5+C5 and then press Enter.

4. In cell **D6**, type = and then click cell **B6**. Notice that *B6* is inserted into the formula, and cell **B6** is surrounded by a moving border indicating that it is part of an active formula as shown in **Figure 2**.

5. Type + Click cell **C6**, and then press Enter to display the result *107*.

You can either type formulas or construct them by pointing and clicking in this manner.

Displayed values in D4 and D5

Moving border around B6

Beginning of formula in D6

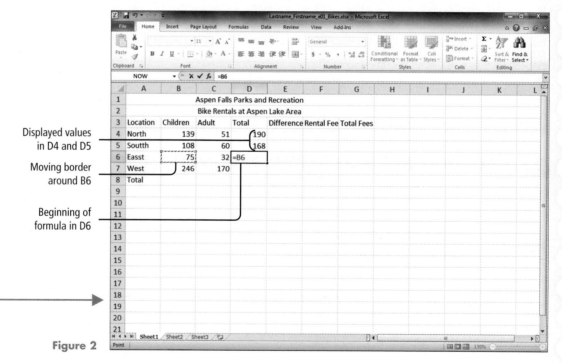

Figure 2

■ **Continue to the next page to complete the skill**

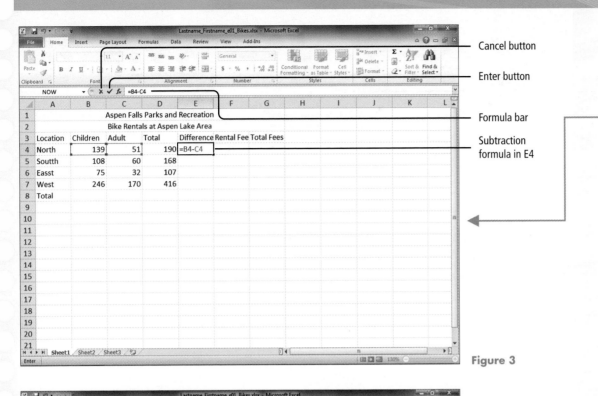

Cancel button

Enter button

Formula bar

Subtraction formula in E4

Figure 3

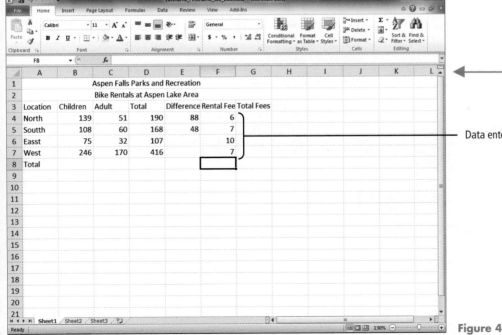

Data entered

Figure 4

6. In cell **D7**, use point and click to construct a formula that adds cells **B7** and **C7**.

7. In cell **E4**, type =B4-C4 On the **formula bar**, notice that the Cancel and Enter buttons display to the left of the formula as shown in **Figure 3**.

   If you make an error entering a formula, you can click the Cancel button and then start over. Alternately, you can press the (Esc) key.

8. On the **formula bar**, click the **Enter** button ☑ to confirm the entry while keeping cell **E4** the active cell. Notice that the underlying value for cell E4 displays as a formula in the formula bar and the display value, 88, displays in the cell as a result of the formula.

9. In cell **E5**, use point and click to enter the formula =B5-C5 to display the difference for the South location. (You will complete the column E formulas in Skill 7.)

10. Type the following data using the ⬇ to move to the next row, and then compare your screen with **Figure 4**.

Cell	Value
F4	6
F5	7
F6	10
F7	7

11. **Save** 🖫 the workbook.

   ■ **You have completed Skill 3 of 10**

► The four most common operators for addition (+), subtraction (-), multiplication (*), and division (/) can be found on the number keypad at the right side of a standard keyboard.

1. In cell **G4**, type =D4*F4—the formula that multiplies the total North bikes rented by its rental fee. On the **formula bar**, click the **Enter** button ✓, and then compare your screen with **Figure 1**.

   The *underlying formula*—the formula as displayed in the formula bar—multiplies the value in cell D4 (*190*) by the value in cell F4 (*6*) and displays the result in cell G4 (*1140*).

2. In the range **G5:G7**, enter the following formulas:

Cell	Formula
G5	=D5*F5
G6	=D6*F6
G7	=D7*F7

3. In cell **A11**, type Percent of Adult Bikes Rented and then press Enter.

4. Select cells **A11:B11**. On the **Home tab**, in the **Alignment group**, click the **Merge & Center button arrow**, and then on the displayed list, click **Merge Across**. Compare your screen with **Figure 2**.

   Merge Across will merge the selected cells without centering.

■ **Continue to the next page to complete the skill**

Underlying value in the formula bar

Displayed value in G4

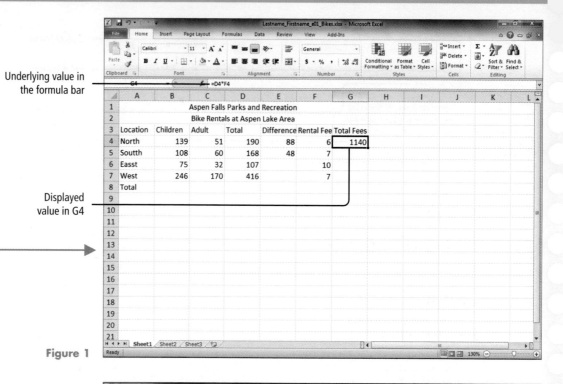

Figure 1

Formulas entered into G4:G7

A11:B11 merged with text truncated

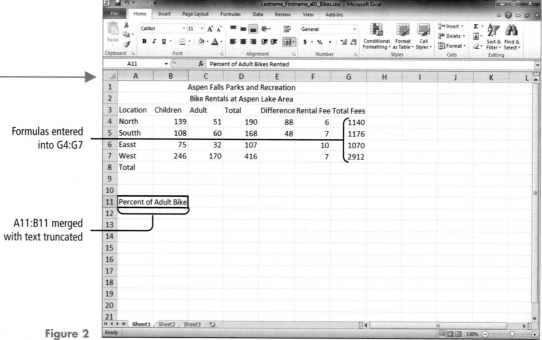

Figure 2

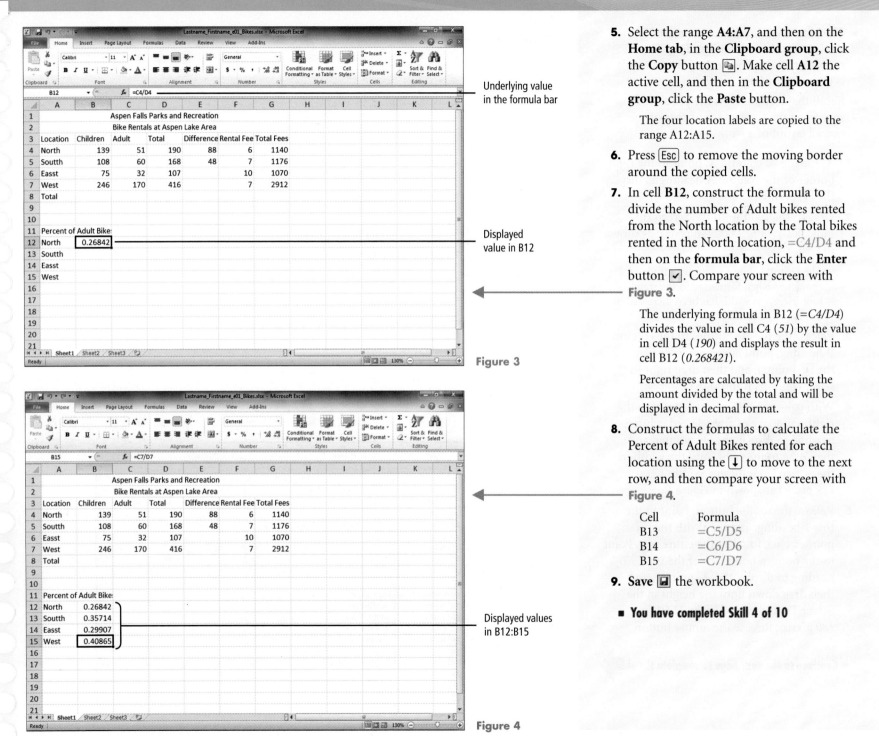

Underlying value in the formula bar

Displayed value in B12

Figure 3

Displayed values in B12:B15

Figure 4

5. Select the range **A4:A7**, and then on the **Home tab**, in the **Clipboard group**, click the **Copy** button. Make cell **A12** the active cell, and then in the **Clipboard group**, click the **Paste** button.

   The four location labels are copied to the range A12:A15.

6. Press Esc to remove the moving border around the copied cells.

7. In cell **B12**, construct the formula to divide the number of Adult bikes rented from the North location by the Total bikes rented in the North location, =C4/D4 and then on the **formula bar**, click the **Enter** button ✔. Compare your screen with **Figure 3**.

   The underlying formula in B12 (=C4/D4) divides the value in cell C4 (51) by the value in cell D4 (190) and displays the result in cell B12 (0.268421).

   Percentages are calculated by taking the amount divided by the total and will be displayed in decimal format.

8. Construct the formulas to calculate the Percent of Adult Bikes rented for each location using the ↓ to move to the next row, and then compare your screen with **Figure 4**.

Cell	Formula
B13	=C5/D5
B14	=C6/D6
B15	=C7/D7

9. **Save** the workbook.

▪ **You have completed Skill 4 of 10**

▶ The letter that displays at the top of a column is the ***column heading***. The number that displays at the left of a row is the ***row heading***.

▶ Recall that formatting is the process of specifying the appearance of cells or the overall layout of a worksheet.

1. At the top of column **A**, point to the right border of the column **A** heading to display the ⊞ pointer.

2. Drag to the right until the ScreenTip indicates *Width: 13.00 (96 pixels)* as shown in **Figure 1**.

   The default column width will display 8.43 characters when formatted in the standard font. Here, the width has been increased to display more characters.

3. Release the mouse button. In the column **B** heading, point anywhere to display the ⬇ pointer, and then drag right to select columns **B** through **G**.

4. With columns **B:G** selected, point to the right boundary of any selected column heading to display the ⊞ pointer, and then drag to the right until the width in the ScreenTip indicates *Width: 12.00 (89 pixels)* as shown in **Figure 2**.

5. Release the mouse button. Point to the row **1** heading, and then with the ➡ pointer, click to select the entire row. Point to the bottom boundary of the row heading to display the ⊞ pointer, and then drag down until the height in the ScreenTip indicates *Height 22.50 (30 pixels)*. Release the mouse button.

■ **Continue to the next page to complete the skill** ▶

Column headings
ScreenTip
⊞ pointer

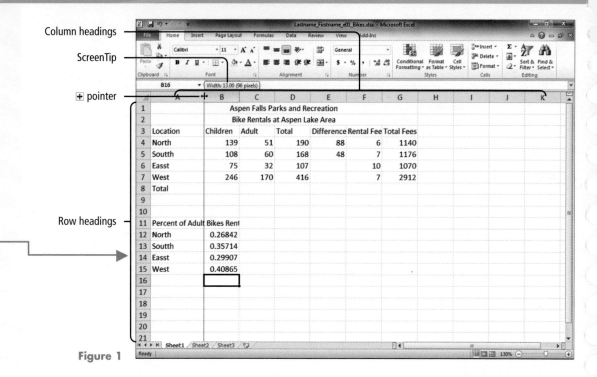

Row headings

Figure 1

ScreenTip
⊞ pointer

Columns
B:G selected

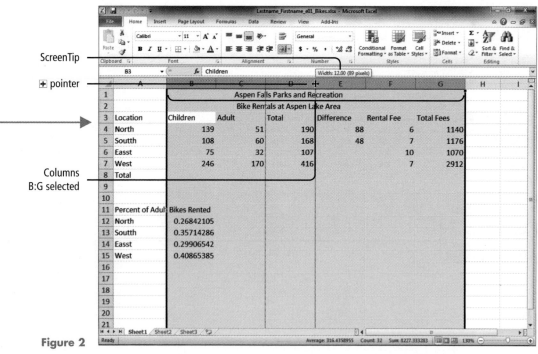

Figure 2

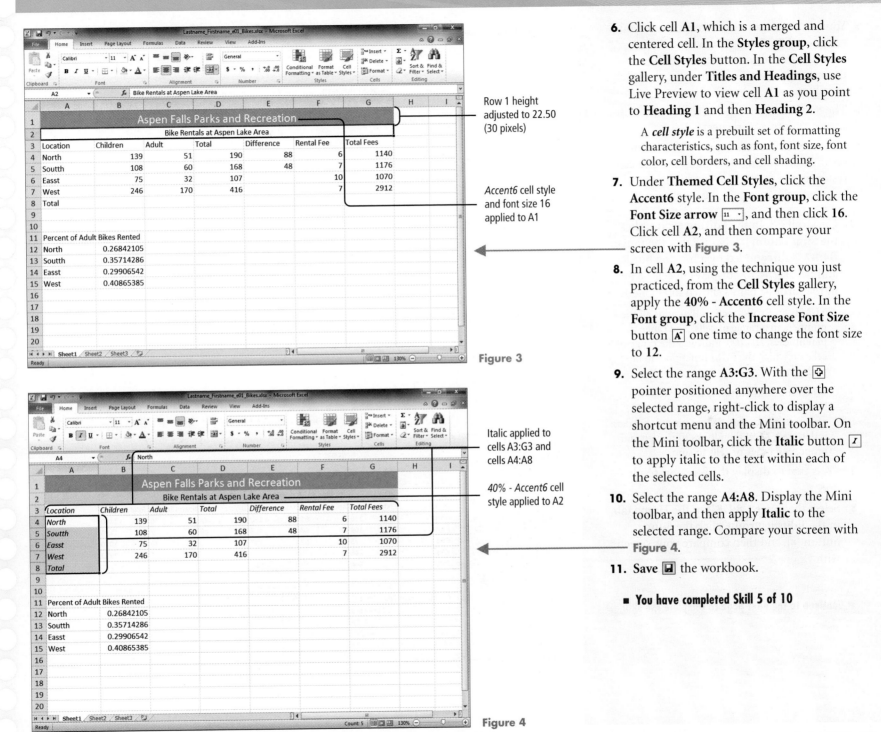

Row 1 height adjusted to 22.50 (30 pixels)

Accent6 cell style and font size 16 applied to A1

Figure 3

Italic applied to cells A3:G3 and cells A4:A8

40% - Accent6 cell style applied to A2

Figure 4

6. Click cell **A1**, which is a merged and centered cell. In the **Styles group**, click the **Cell Styles** button. In the **Cell Styles** gallery, under **Titles and Headings**, use Live Preview to view cell **A1** as you point to **Heading 1** and then **Heading 2**.

   A *cell style* is a prebuilt set of formatting characteristics, such as font, font size, font color, cell borders, and cell shading.

7. Under **Themed Cell Styles**, click the **Accent6** style. In the **Font group**, click the **Font Size arrow** , and then click **16**. Click cell **A2**, and then compare your screen with **Figure 3**.

8. In cell **A2**, using the technique you just practiced, from the **Cell Styles** gallery, apply the **40% - Accent6** cell style. In the **Font group**, click the **Increase Font Size** button one time to change the font size to **12**.

9. Select the range **A3:G3**. With the pointer positioned anywhere over the selected range, right-click to display a shortcut menu and the Mini toolbar. On the Mini toolbar, click the **Italic** button to apply italic to the text within each of the selected cells.

10. Select the range **A4:A8**. Display the Mini toolbar, and then apply **Italic** to the selected range. Compare your screen with **Figure 4**.

11. **Save** the workbook.

   ■ **You have completed Skill 5 of 10**

▶ You can create your own formulas, or you can use a *function*—a prewritten Excel formula that takes a value or values, performs an operation, and returns a value or values.

▶ The Sum button is used to insert common functions into a worksheet.

▶ When cell references are used in a formula or function, editing the values in those cells results in the formula or function automatically recalculating a new result.

1. Click cell **B8**. In the **Editing group**, click the **Sum** button Σ. Notice that the range **B4:B7** is surrounded by a moving border, and =*SUM(B4:B7)* displays in cell B8 and in the formula bar as shown in **Figure 1**.

   SUM is an Excel function that adds all the numbers in a range of cells. The range in parentheses, *(B4:B7)*, indicates the range of cells on which the SUM function will be performed.

   When the Sum button is used, Excel first looks *above* the selected cell for a suitable range of cells to sum. When no suitable data is detected, Excel then looks to the *left* and proposes a range of cells to sum.

2. Press Enter to display the function result—*568*.

3. Select the range **C8:D8**. On the **Home tab**, in the **Editing group**, click the **Sum** button Σ, and then compare your screen with **Figure 2**.

■ **Continue to the next page to complete the skill**

Sum button

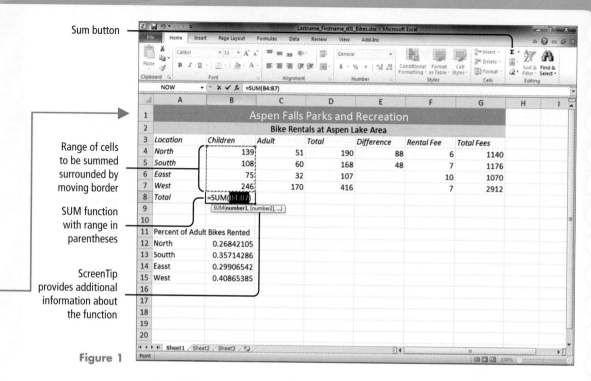

Range of cells to be summed surrounded by moving border

SUM function with range in parentheses

ScreenTip provides additional information about the function

Figure 1

Result of SUM function displays in cells

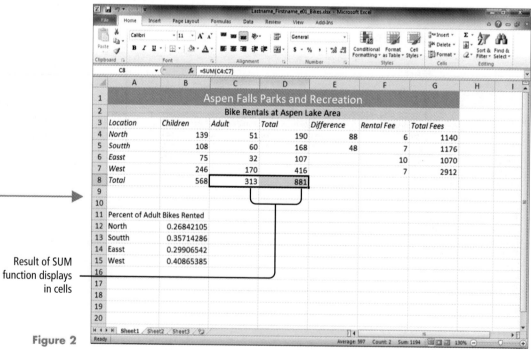

Figure 2

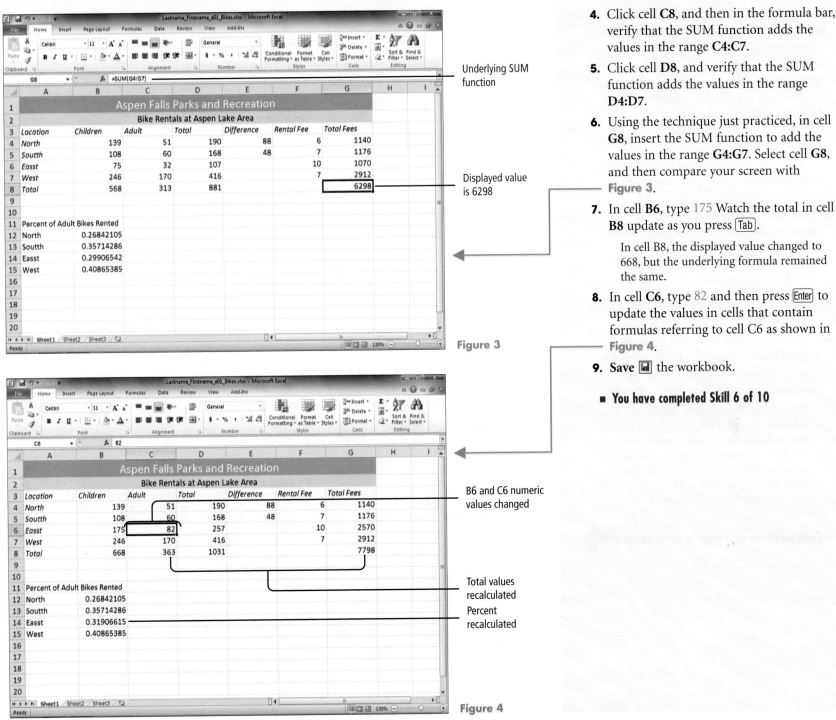

Underlying SUM function

Displayed value is 6298

Figure 3

B6 and C6 numeric values changed

Total values recalculated

Percent recalculated

Figure 4

4. Click cell **C8**, and then in the formula bar, verify that the SUM function adds the values in the range **C4:C7**.

5. Click cell **D8**, and verify that the SUM function adds the values in the range **D4:D7**.

6. Using the technique just practiced, in cell **G8**, insert the SUM function to add the values in the range **G4:G7**. Select cell **G8**, and then compare your screen with **Figure 3**.

7. In cell **B6**, type 175 Watch the total in cell **B8** update as you press Tab.

   In cell B8, the displayed value changed to 668, but the underlying formula remained the same.

8. In cell **C6**, type 82 and then press Enter to update the values in cells that contain formulas referring to cell C6 as shown in **Figure 4**.

9. Save 🖫 the workbook.

■ **You have completed Skill 6 of 10**

► Text, numbers, formulas, and functions can be copied down rows and also across columns to insert formulas and functions quickly.

► When a formula is copied to another cell, Excel adjusts the cell references relative to the new location of the formula.

1. Click cell **E5**.

   To use the fill handle, first select the cell that contains the content you want to copy—here the formula =*B5-C5*.

2. With cell **E5** selected, point to the *fill handle*—the small black square in the lower right corner of the selection—until the ⊞ pointer displays as shown in **Figure 1**.

3. Drag the ⊞ pointer down to cell **E7,** and then release the mouse button.

4. Click cell **E6**, and verify the formula copied from E5 is =*B6-C6*. Click cell **E7,** and verify the copied formula is =*B7-C7* as shown in **Figure 2**.

   In each row, Excel copied the formula but adjusted the cell references *relative to the* row number—B5 changed to B6 and then to B7. This adjustment is called a *relative cell reference* because it refers to cells based on their position *in relation to* (relative to) the cell that contains the formula.

■ **Continue to the next page to complete the skill**

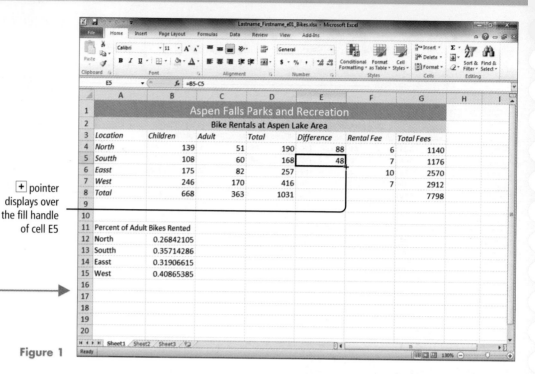

⊞ pointer displays over the fill handle of cell E5

Figure 1

B5 changed to B7 and C5 changed to C7

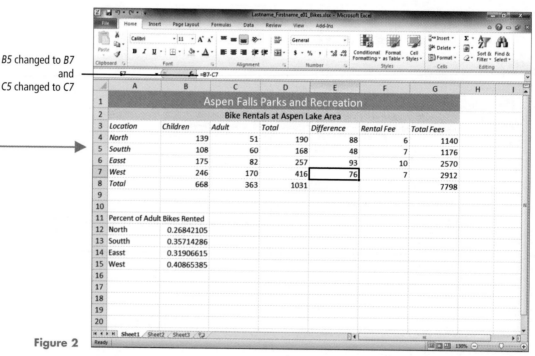

Figure 2

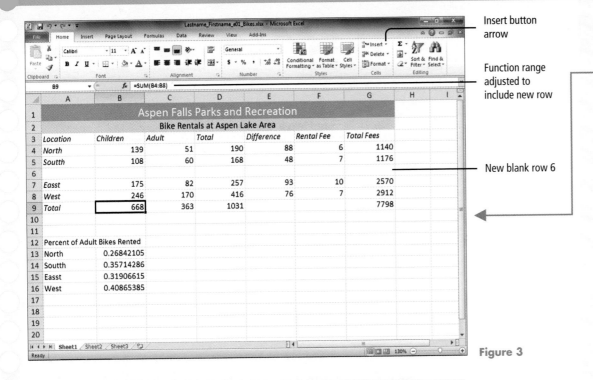

Insert button arrow

Function range adjusted to include new row

New blank row 6

Figure 3

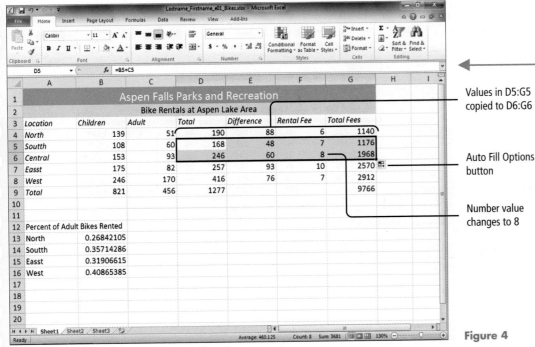

Values in D5:G5 copied to D6:G6

Auto Fill Options button

Number value changes to 8

Figure 4

5. Click cell **A6**. In the **Cells group**, click the **Insert button arrow**, and then click **Insert Sheet Rows**. Click cell **B9**, and then compare your screen with **Figure 3**.

> The function in cell B9 automatically updates to include the new row.

> When you insert a new row or column, the cell references and the ranges in formulas or in functions adjust to include the new row or column.

6. In cell **A6**, type Central and then press Tab. Notice that the formatting (italic) from cell A7 was applied to the inserted row.

7. In cell **B6**, type 153 and then press Tab to enter the value and update the column total in cell B9 to *821*.

8. In cell **C6**, type 93 and press Tab.

9. Select cells **D5:G5**. Point to the fill handle so that the ⊞ pointer displays, and then drag the ⊞ pointer down one row. Release the mouse button, and notice the Auto Fill Options button ⊞ displays as shown in **Figure 4**.

> When you copy number values using the fill handle, the numbers automatically increment for each row or column. Here, the number value in cell F5 increased by one when it was copied to cell F6.

10. Click the **Auto Fill Options** button ⊞, and then click **Copy Cells**.

> With the Copy Cells option, number values are literally copied and do not increment. Here, the number value in cell F6 changes to 7.

11. Save 🖫 the workbook.

■ **You have completed Skill 7 of 10**

▶ Always check spelling after you have finished formatting and editing your worksheet data.

1. Click cell **A15**, and repeat the technique used previously to insert a new row.

2. In cell **A15**, type Central and then press Enter. Click cell **B14**, and then use the fill handle to copy the formula down to cell **B15**. Compare your screen with **Figure 1**.

3. Click cell **A2**. Click in the **formula bar**, and then use the arrow keys to move to the left of the word *Area*. Type Recreation Add a space as needed, and then press Enter.

4. Click cell **F4**, and then with the ⊕ pointer, drag right from cells **F4** to **G4**. Hold down Ctrl, and then click cell **G9**.

> You can select nonadjacent ranges by holding down Ctrl.

5. In the **Styles group**, click the **Cell Styles** button, and then under **Number Format**, click **Currency [0]**.

6. Select the range **B13:B17**. In the **Number group**, click the **Percent Style** button %, and then click the **Increase Decimal** button one time.

> The Increase Decimal and Decrease Decimal buttons do not actually add or remove decimals, but they change how the underlying decimal values *display* in the cells.

7. Select the range **B9:D9**. Hold down Ctrl, and then click cell **G9**. In the **Styles group**, click the **Cell Styles** button. Under **Titles and Headings**, click the **Total** style. Click cell **A10**, and then compare your screen with **Figure 2**.

■ **Continue to the next page to complete the skill**

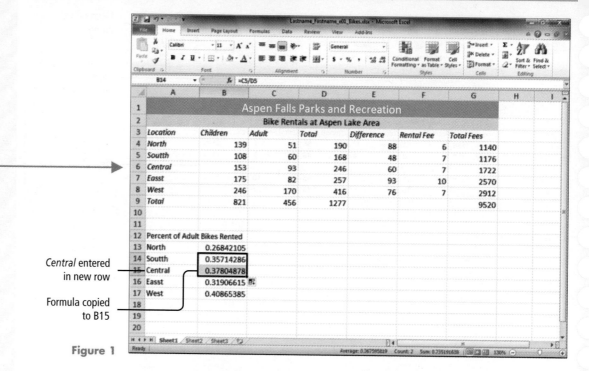

Central entered in new row

Formula copied to B15

Figure 1

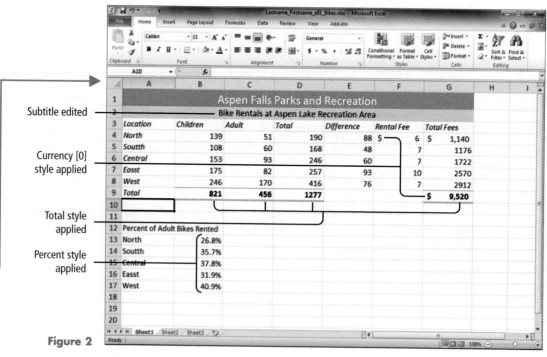

Subtitle edited

Currency [0] style applied

Total style applied

Percent style applied

Figure 2

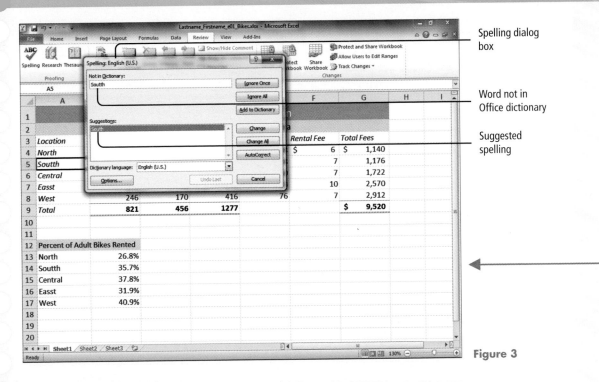

Spelling dialog box

Word not in Office dictionary

Suggested spelling

Figure 3

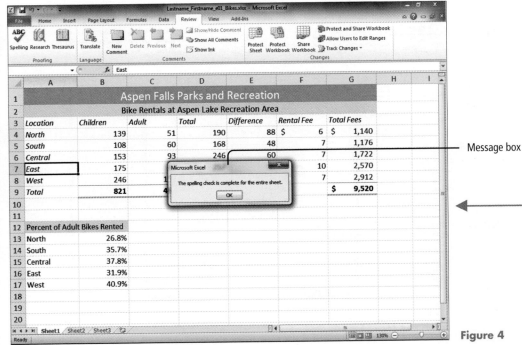

Message box

Figure 4

8. Select the range **G5:G8**. Click the **Cell Styles** button, and then under **Number Format**, click **Comma [0]**. Select cell **A12**. Click the **Cell Styles** button, and then click **40% - Accent6**.

9. Press Ctrl + Home to make cell **A1** active. On the **Review tab**, in the **Proofing group**, click the **Spelling** button.

    The Spelling checker starts with the active cell and moves to the right and down, so making cell A1 the active cell before beginning is useful.

10. In the **Spelling** dialog box, under **Not in Dictionary**, notice the word *Soutth*, as shown in **Figure 3**.

    This word is not in the Office dictionary; however, words not in the dictionary are not necessarily misspelled. Many proper nouns or less commonly used words are not in the Office dictionary.

11. Under **Suggestions**, verify that the correct spelling, *South*, is selected, and then click the **Change** button to correct the spelling and to move to the next word not in the Office dictionary.

12. Under **Suggestions**, verify that the correct spelling, *East*, is selected, and then click the **Change All** button to correct its spelling in the entire worksheet.

13. Continue to use the Spelling checker to correct any remaining errors. When the message **The spelling check is complete for the entire sheet** displays, as shown in **Figure 4**, click **OK**.

    When words you use often are not in the Office dictionary, you can click *Add to Dictionary* to add them.

14. Save 💾 the workbook.

   ■ **You have completed Skill 8 of 10**

► In Excel, *Page Layout view* is used to change the page orientation, work with page headers and footers, or set margins for printing.

1. Click the **Insert tab**, and then in the **Text group**, click the **Header & Footer** button to switch to **Page Layout view** and to open the Header area.

2. On the **Design tab**, in the **Navigation group**, click the **Go to Footer** button to move to the Footer area. Click just above the word *Footer* to place the insertion point in the left section of the Footer area. Compare your screen with **Figure 1**.

3. In the **Header & Footer Elements group**, click the **File Name** button to insert the *&[File]* placeholder into the left section of the Footer area.

   Predefined headers and footers insert placeholders with instructions for printing. Here, the *&[File]* placeholder instructs Excel to insert the file name when the worksheet is printed.

4. Click in the middle section of the Footer area, and then click the **Current Date** button. Click the right section of the Footer area, and type Parks and Recreation Click in a cell just above the footer to exit the Footer area.

5. Click the **Page Layout tab**. In the **Sheet Options group**, under **Gridlines**, select the **Print** check box. In the **Page Setup group**, click the **Margins** button, and then below the **Margins** gallery, click **Custom Margins**. In the **Page Setup** dialog box, under **Center on page**, select the **Horizontally** check box, and then compare your screen with **Figure 2**.

■ **Continue to the next page to complete the skill**

Header & Footer Tools Design contextual tab

File Name button

Footer area

Edges of paper display in Page Layout view

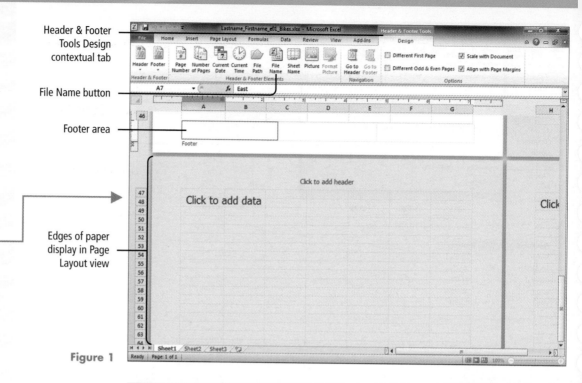

Figure 1

Margins button

Page Setup dialog box

Horizontally check box selected

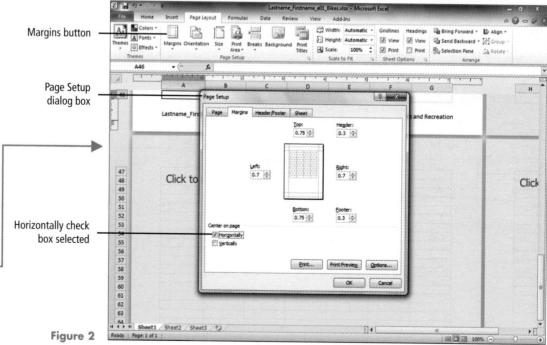

Figure 2

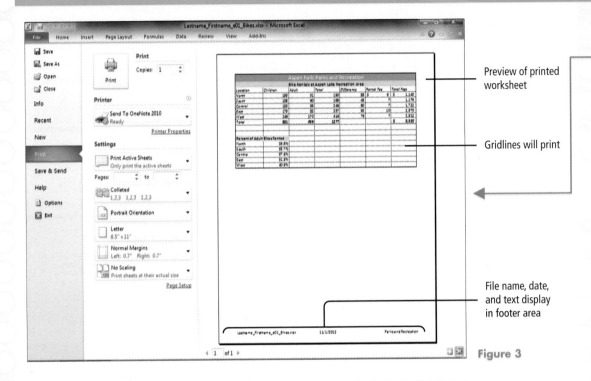

Preview of printed worksheet

Gridlines will print

File name, date, and text display in footer area

Figure 3

6. In the **Page Setup** dialog box, click **Print Preview,** and then compare your screen with **Figure 3**.

   In the Backstage, the Print page displays a preview of the worksheet and is used to modify print settings.

7. Click the **Home** tab. On the lower right side of the status bar, click the **Normal** button ⊞ to return to Normal view, and then press Ctrl + Home.

   Normal view maximizes the number of cells visible on the screen. The page break—the dotted line between columns G and H— indicates where one page ends and a new page begins.

8. At the bottom of your worksheet, click the **Sheet2 sheet tab** to display **Sheet2**. Hold down Ctrl, and then click the **Sheet3 sheet tab**. On the **Home tab**, in the **Cells group**, click the **Delete button arrow**, and then click **Delete Sheet**.

   Deleting unused worksheets saves storage space and removes any doubt that additional information is in the workbook. When you delete a worksheet with data, Excel displays a warning so you can cancel the deletion.

9. At the bottom of your worksheet, right-click the **Sheet1 sheet tab**, and then from the shortcut menu, click **Rename**. Type Bike Rentals and then press Enter. Compare your screen with **Figure 4**.

10. **Save** ⊞ the workbook. Click the **File tab**, and then click **Print**. If you are directed by your instructor to print, click the Print button.

   ■ **You have completed Skill 9 of 10**

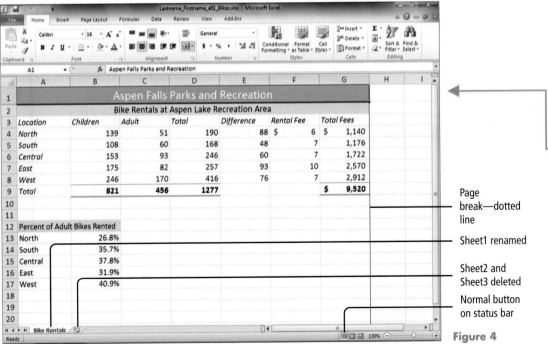

Page break—dotted line

Sheet1 renamed

Sheet2 and Sheet3 deleted

Normal button on status bar

Figure 4

▶ Underlying formulas and functions can be displayed and printed.

▶ When formulas are displayed in cells, the orientation and worksheet scale might need to be changed so that the worksheet prints on a single page.

1. Click the **Formulas tab**, and then in the **Formula Auditing group**, click the **Show Formulas** button to display the underlying formulas in the cells as shown in **Figure 1.**

    Columns often become wider when formulas are displayed. Here, the printed worksheet extends to a second page.

2. Display the **Page Layout tab**. Click the **Page Setup Dialog Box Launcher** 📷. In the **Page Setup** dialog box, click the **Print Preview** button.

    Below the preview of the printed page, *1 of 3* indicates that the worksheet will print on three pages.

3. In the Backstage, on the bottom of the Print page, click the **Next Page** button ▶ two times to view the second and the third pages. Compare your screen with **Figure 2.**

4. On the **Print** page, under **Settings**, click the **Portrait Orientation** button, and then click **Landscape Orientation** so that the orientation will be wider than it is tall.

▪ **Continue to the next page to complete the skill**

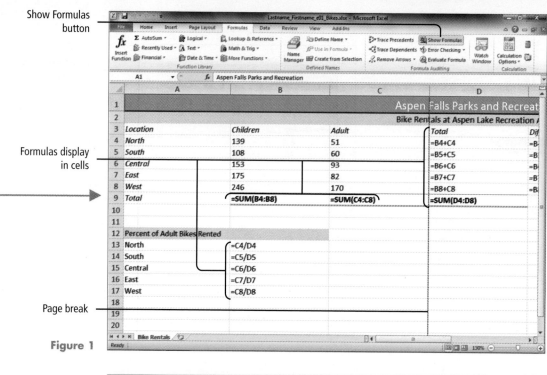

Show Formulas button

Formulas display in cells

Page break

Figure 1

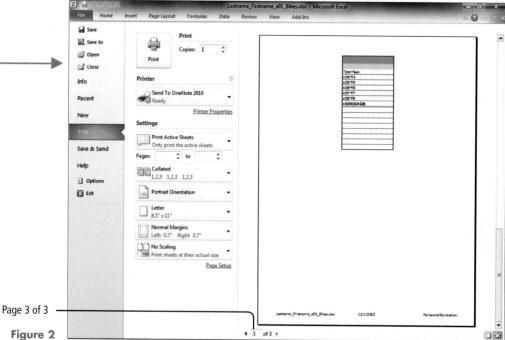

Page 3 of 3

Figure 2

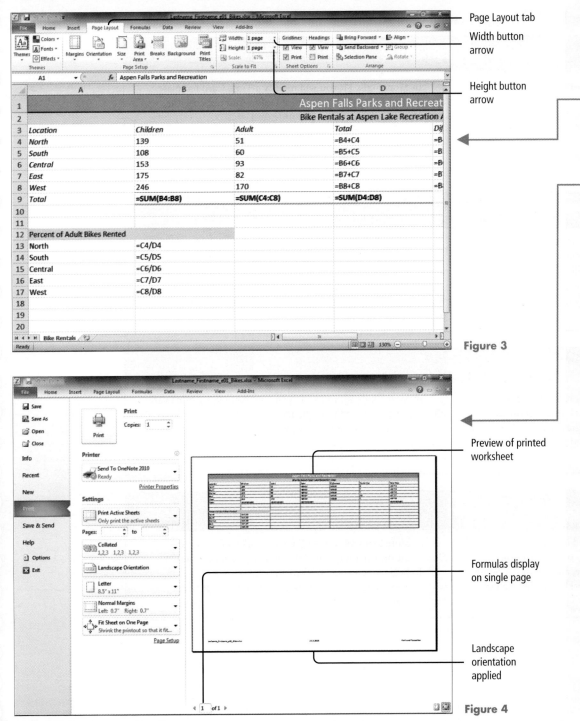

Figure 3

Figure 4

5. Click the **Page Layout tab**. In the **Scale to Fit group**, click the **Width button arrow**, and then click **1 page**. Click the **Height button arrow**, and then click **1 page**. The scaling is one page wide by one page tall as shown in **Figure 3**.

> Scaling adjusts the size of the printed worksheet to fit on the number of pages that you specify.

6. Click the **File tab**, and then click **Print**. Compare your screen with **Figure 4**.

> *1 of 1* displays at the bottom middle of the Print page to notify you that the worksheet will now print on one page.

7. If you are directed by your instructor to submit a printout of your formulas, click the **Print** button.

8. Click the **Formulas** tab. In the **Formula Auditing** group, click the **Show Formulas** button.

> The values are displayed.

9. **Save** 🖫 the workbook, and then **Close** Excel.

10. Submit your printouts or file as directed by your instructor.

Done! You have completed Skill 10 of 10 and your document is complete!

The following More Skills are located at **www.pearsonhighered.com/skills**

More Skills ⓫ Create New Workbooks from Templates

Templates are used to build workbooks without having to start from scratch. You can save one of your own workbooks as a template to use again, or you can download one of many predefined templates from Microsoft Office Online.

In More Skills 11, you will modify a Time Card template downloaded from Microsoft Office Online and then use the template to create a new weekly time card.

To begin, open your web browser, navigate to www.pearsonhighered.com/skills, locate the name of your textbook, and then follow the instructions on the website.

More Skills ⓬ Use Range Names in Formulas

Instead of using cell references in formulas and functions, you can assign names that refer to the same cell or range. Range names can be easier to remember than cell references, and they can add meaning to formulas, making them easier for you and others to understand.

In More Skills 12, you will open a workbook and practice various ways to name cell ranges. You will then use the names in formulas.

To begin, open your web browser, navigate to www.pearsonhighered.com/skills, locate the name of your textbook, and then follow the instructions on the website.

More Skills ⓭ Change Themes

Office themes are used to apply a coordinated set of colors, fonts, and graphic effects with a single click. You can use the Office themes, which were developed by graphics professionals, to provide a consistent and polished look and feel for all of your worksheets.

In More Skills 13, you will open a workbook, examine various Office themes, and then change the theme of the worksheet.

To begin, open your web browser, navigate to www.pearsonhighered.com/skills, locate the name of your textbook, and then follow the instructions on the website.

More Skills ⓮ Manage Document Properties

Document properties are the detailed information about your workbook that can help you identify or organize your files, including the name of the author, the title, and keywords. Some workbook properties are added to the workbook when you create it. You can add others as necessary.

In More Skills 14, you will open a workbook, open the Document Information Panel, and add document properties.

To begin, open your web browser, navigate to www.pearsonhighered.com/skills, locate the name of your textbook, and then follow the instructions on the website.

Key Terms

Online Help Skills

1. Start ● Excel. In the upper right corner of the Excel window, click the Help button ◉. In the Help window, click the Maximize ▭ button.

2. Click in the search box, type insert columns and then click the Search button ⌕. In the search results, click **Insert or delete cells, rows, and columns**.

3. Read the article's introduction, and then below in this article, click **Insert columns on a worksheet**. Compare your screen with **Figure 1**.

Figure 1

4. Read the section to see if you can answer the following: Explain how to insert multiple columns and why you might use this feature.

Matching

Match each term in the second column with its correct definition in the first column by writing the letter of the term on the blank line in front of the correct definition.

____ **1.** An Excel file that contains one or more worksheets.

____ **2.** The primary document that you use in Excel to store and work with data, and which is formatted as a pattern of uniformly spaced horizontal and vertical lines.

____ **3.** Another name for a worksheet.

____ **4.** The cell, surrounded by a black border, ready to receive data or be affected by the next Excel command.

____ **5.** The identification of a specific cell by its intersecting column letter and row number.

____ **6.** Data in a cell—text or numbers.

____ **7.** Data in a cell made up of text only.

____ **8.** Data in a cell made up of numbers only.

____ **9.** Another name for a text value.

____ **10.** An Excel window area that displays the address of a selected cell.

A Active cell

B Cell reference

C Label

D Name Box

E Number value

F Spreadsheet

G Text value

H Value

I Workbook

J Worksheet

Multiple Choice

Choose the correct answer.

1. The data displayed in a cell.
   A. Viewed value
   B. Inspected value
   C. Displayed value

2. An equation that performs mathematical calculations on number values.
   A. Method
   B. Formula
   C. System

3. A view that maximizes the number of cells visible on the screen.
   A. Page Layout view
   B. Standard view
   C. Normal view

4. The column letter and row number that identify a cell.
   A. Cell window
   B. Cell address
   C. Cell file name

5. An Excel window area that displays the value contained in the active cell.
   A. Formula bar
   B. Workbook
   C. Name Box

6. Symbols that specify mathematical operations such as addition or subtraction.
   A. Hyperlinks
   B. Bookmarks
   C. Arithmetic operators

7. The number that displays at the left of a row.
   A. Row heading
   B. Row name
   C. Row border

8. A prewritten Excel formula.
   A. A formula
   B. A function
   C. An exponent

9. The small black square in the lower right corner of the active cell.
   A. Border
   B. Fill handle
   C. Edge

10. Page headers and footers can be changed in this view.
    A. Print preview
    B. Page Layout view
    C. Normal view

Topics for Discussion

1. What is the advantage of using cell references instead of actual number values in formulas and functions?

2. What are some things you can do to make your worksheet easier for others to read and understand?

According to the Introduction to this chapter, how do you decide which information to put in columns and which to put in rows?

Skill Check

To complete this project, you will need the following file:

- New blank Excel document

You will save your workbook as:

- Lastname_Firstname_e01_Sales

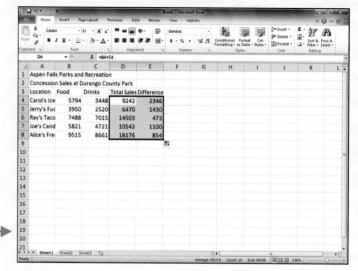

Figure 1

1. **Start** Excel. In cell **A1**, type Aspen Falls Parks and Recreation and then in cell **A2**, type Concession Sales at Durango County Park In cell **A3**, type Location and then pressing Tab after each title, type Food, Drinks, Total Sales, and Difference.

2. In rows **4** through **8**, enter the following data starting in cell **A4**:

Carol's Ice Cream	5794	3448	Joe's Candy	5821	4721
Jerry's Fudge	3950	2520	Alice's Fresh Fruit	9515	8661
Ray's Tacos	7488	7015			

3. In cell **D4**, type =B4+C4 and then in cell **E4**, type =B4-C4 Select the range **D4:E4**. Point to the fill handle, and then drag down through row **8**. Compare your screen with **Figure 1**.

4. **Save** the workbook in your **Excel Chapter 1** folder with the name Lastname_ Firstname_e01_Sales

5. On the **Insert tab**, in the **Text group**, click the **Header & Footer** button. In the **Navigation group**, click the **Go to Footer** button, and then click in the left footer. In the **Header & Footer Elements group**, click the **File Name** button. Click in a cell just above the footer. On the lower right side of the status bar, click the **Normal** button. Press Ctrl + Home.

6. In cell **A9**, type Totals and then select the range **B9:D9**. On the **Home tab**, in the **Editing group**, click the **Sum** button.

7. Select cell **A7**. In the **Cells group**, click the **Insert button arrow**, and then click **Insert Sheet Rows**. In the new row **7**, type the data David's Biscotti, 7183, and 5492

8. Select the range **D6:E6**, and then use the fill handle to copy the formulas down one row.

9. In cell **A13**, type Drinks as a Percent of Total Sales

10. Select the range **A4:A9**, and then on the **Home tab**, in the **Clipboard group**, click the **Copy** button. Click cell **A14**, and then in the **Clipboard group**, click the **Paste** button. Press Esc, and then compare your screen with **Figure 2**.

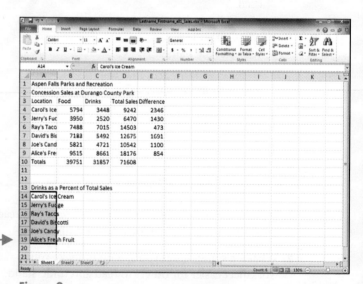

Figure 2

- Continue to the next page to complete this Skill Check

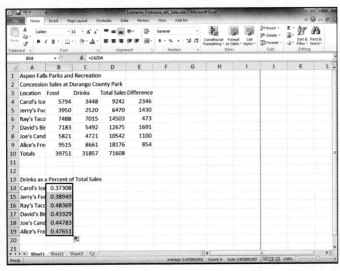

Figure 3

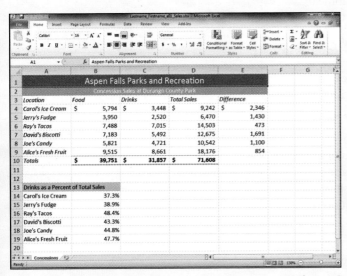

Figure 4

11. In cell **B14**, type =C4/D4 and then on the formula bar, click the **Enter** button. In cell **B14**, use the fill handle to copy the formula down through row **19**. Compare your screen with **Figure 3**.

12. Select the range **A1:E1**, and then on the **Home tab**, in the **Alignment group**, click the **Merge & Center** button. In the **Styles group**, click the **Cell Styles** button, and then click **Accent4**. In the **Font group**, click the **Font Size arrow**, and then click **16**. Select the range **A2:E2**, and then in the **Alignment group**, click the **Merge & Center** button. Click the **Cell Styles** button, and then click **60% - Accent4**.

13. Select columns **A:E**, point to the right boundary of any selected column heading, drag to a column width of *16.00 (117 pixels)*, and then release the mouse button.

14. Select the range **A3:E3**. Hold down Ctrl, and then select the range **A4:A10**. In the **Font group**, click the **Italic** button.

15. Select range **B4:E4**. Hold down Ctrl, and then select the range **B10:D10**. In the **Styles group**, click the **Cell Styles** button, and then click **Currency [0]**. Select the range **B10:D10**. Click the **Cell Styles** button, and then click the **Total** style. Select the range **B5:E9**, click the **Cell Styles** button, and then click **Comma [0]**.

16. Select the range **A13:B13**. In the **Alignment group**, click the **Merge & Center button arrow**, and then click **Merge Across**. Click the **Cell Styles** button, and then click **40% - Accent4**.

17. Select the range **B14:B19**. In the **Number group**, click the **Percent Style** button, and then click the **Increase Decimal** button one time.

18. Press Ctrl + Home. On the **Review tab**, in the **Proofing group**, click the **Spelling** button, and then correct any spelling errors.

19. Click the **Sheet2 sheet tab**. Hold down Ctrl, and then click the **Sheet3 sheet tab**. On the **Home tab**, in the **Cells group**, click the **Delete button arrow**, and then click **Delete Sheet**.

20. Right-click the **Sheet1 sheet tab**, and from the shortcut menu, click **Rename**. Type Concessions and then press Enter. **Save**, and then compare your screen with **Figure 4**. If asked by your instructor, print the worksheet. If asked by your instructor, display and format the worksheet formulas as described in Skill 10, and then print the worksheet.

21. **Exit** Excel. Submit the printouts or file as directed by your instructor.

Done! You have completed the Skill Check

Assess Your Skills 1

To complete this project, you will need the following file:

- e01_Fees

You will save your workbook as:

- Lastname_Firstname_e01_Fees

1. **Start** Excel. From your student data files, open **e01_Fees**. Save the workbook in your **Excel Chapter 1** folder as Lastname_Firstname_e01_Fees Add the file name to the worksheet's left footer, add the current date to the center footer, and then type **Tax Rates** in the right footer. Return to **Normal** view.

2. For the range **A1:E1**, merge and center and apply the **Accent5** cell style. Increase the font size to **18** points. For the range **A2:E2**, merge and center and apply the **40% - Accent5** cell style. Widen column **A** to *20.00 (145 pixels)*. For all column and row titles, apply **Italic**.

3. For the range **E5:E13**, insert the **SUM** function to add the three fees for each row. In the range **B14:E14**, insert the **SUM** function to provide totals for each column.

4. Select the nonadjacent ranges **B5:E5** and **B14:E14**. Apply the **Currency** [0] cell style.

5. Select the range **B6:E13**, and then apply the **Comma** [0] cell style. Select the range **B14:E14**, and then apply the **Total** cell style.

6. Insert a new row above row **7**. In cell **A7**, type Silkworth Hiking Area and as the fees for the new location, type 14257 and 9625 and 10925 Use the fill handle to copy the formula in cell **E6** to cell **E7**.

7. **Copy** the location names from the range **A5:A14** to the range **A20:A29**.

8. In cell **B19**, type New Tax Rate In cells **B20** and **B21**, type .03 In cells **B22** and **B23**, type .05 and in cell **B24**, type .06 Use the fill handle to copy the value in cell **B24** down through cell **B29**. Select the range **B20:B29**, and then apply the **Percent Style** number format.

9. In cell **C19**, type New Tax Collections In cell **C20**, enter a formula that calculates the new tax charged by the city by multiplying cell **E5** by cell **B20**. In cell **C20**, use the fill handle to copy the formula down through cell **C29**.

10. Rename the **Sheet1** sheet tab as City Fees and then delete **Sheet2** and **Sheet3**.

11. Use **Page Setup** to center the worksheet **Horizontally**. Set the **Gridlines** to print.

12. Check and correct any spelling errors, ignoring the proper names.

13. Print or submit the workbook electronically as directed by your instructor. If you are instructed to do so, display the worksheet formulas, scale the worksheet to print on one page, and then print.

14. Compare your completed worksheet with **Figure 1**. **Save** the workbook, and then **Exit** Excel.

Done! You have completed Assess Your Skills 1

Figure 1

Assess Your Skills 2

Assess Your Skills 3 and 4 can be found at **www.pearsonhighered.com/skills**.

To complete this project, you will need the following file:

- e01_Visitors

You will save your workbook as:

- Lastname_Firstname_e01_Visitors

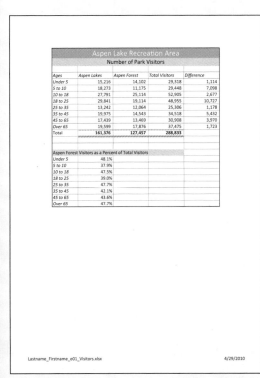

Lastname_Firstname_e01_Visitors.xlsx   4/29/2010

Figure 1

1. **Start** Excel. From the student data files, open **e01_Visitors**. Save the workbook in your **Excel Chapter 1** folder as Lastname_Firstname_e01_Visitors Add the file name to the worksheet's left footer, and then add the Current Date to the right footer. Return to **Normal** view.

2. In cell **D5**, construct a formula to add cells **B5** and **C5**. In cell **E5**, construct a formula to subtract cell **C5** from **B5**. Use the fill handle to copy the formulas in **D5:E5** down through row **11**.

3. In cell **A12**, type Total and then in row **12**, insert the SUM function to total columns **B:D**.

4. Insert a new row above row **7**, and then in the new cell, **A7**, type 10 to 18 In cell **B7**, type 27791 and in cell **C7** type 25114

5. Use the fill handle to copy the formulas in the range **D6:E6** down one row.

6. Merge and center the range **A1:E1**, and then apply the **Accent3** cell style. Increase the font size to **18**. Merge and center the range **A2:E2**, and then apply the **40%-Accent3** cell style. Increase the font size to **14**.

7. Widen column **A** to *10.00 (75 pixels)*, and then widen columns **B:E** to *14.00 (103 pixels)*.

8. For the column and row titles, apply **Italic**. In the range **B5:E13**, apply the **Comma [0]** cell style, and then in range **B13:D13**, apply the **Total** cell style.

9. In cell **A16**, type Aspen Forest Visitors as a Percent of Total Visitors For the range **A16:D16**, apply the **Merge Across** alignment and the **40%-Accent3** cell style.

10. **Copy** the age groups from the range **A5:A12**, and **Paste** them to the range **A17:A24**.

11. In cell **B17**, construct a formula to divide *Aspen Forest* visitors—cell **C5** by *Total Visitors*—cell **D5**. In cell **B17**, apply the **Percent** number style and display one decimal. Use the fill handle to copy the formula down through row **24**.

12. Rename the sheet tab Park Visitors and then delete the worksheets **Sheet2** and **Sheet3**.

13. Check and correct any spelling errors.

14. Use Page Setup to center the page **Horizontally**. Set the **Gridlines** to print, and then **Save** the workbook.

15. Print or submit the workbook electronically as directed by your instructor. If you are instructed to do so, display the worksheet formulas, scale the worksheet to print on one page, and then print.

16. Compare your completed worksheet with **Figure 1**. **Save** and then **Exit** Excel.

Done! You have completed Assess Your Skills 2

Assess Your Skills Visually

To complete this project, you will need the following file:

- New blank Excel workbook

You will save your workbook as:

- Lastname_Firstname_e01_Boats

Open a new blank workbook, and then **Save** the workbook as Lastname_Firstname_e01_Boats Create the worksheet shown in **Figure 1**. The width of column A is 14.00 (103 pixels) and the width of columns B:F is 11.00 (82 pixels). Construct formulas that display the results shown in columns D and F, row 11, and the range B15:B21. The title uses the **Accent6** cell style, and the font size is **14.** The subtitle uses the **40%-Accent6** cell style, and the font size is 12. The title and subtitle should be merged and centered. Using **Figure 1** as your guide, apply the **Currency[0]** cell style, the **Comma [0]** cell style, the **Total** cell style, the **Percent** number style, and the **Italic** format. On the range **A14:C14**, use Merge Across and apply the **40%-Accent6** cell style. Rename the Sheet1 sheet tab as Boat Rentals and delete any unused worksheets. Check and correct any spelling errors. Add the file name to the left footer. **Save** the workbook, and then print or submit the file as directed by your instructor.

Done! You have completed Assess Your Skills Visually

Aspen Falls Parks and Recreation						
Hourly Boat Rentals at Aspen Lake Recreation Area						
Location	Canoes	Kayaks	Total Hours	Hourly Fee	Total Fees	
North	178	175	353	$ 50	$ 17,650	
South	251	158	409	60	24,540	
Central	112	148	260	75	19,500	
Main Entrance	401	370	771	80	61,680	
Kid's Corner	491	296	787	40	31,480	
East	292	189	481	50	24,050	
West	143	193	336	50	16,800	
Total	1,868	1,529	3,397		$ 195,700	

Canoe Hours as a Percent of Total Hours	
North	50.4%
South	61.4%
Central	43.1%
Main Entrance	52.0%
Kid's Corner	62.4%
East	60.7%
West	42.6%

Lastname_Firstname_e01_Boats.xlsx

Figure 1

Skills in Context

To complete this project, you will need the following file:

■ e01_Employees

You will save your workbook as:

■ Lastname_Firstname_e01_Employees

Open the workbook **e01_Employees**, and then save the workbook as Lastname_Firstname_e01_Employees The city of Aspen Falls wants to total and compare the number of employees at its recreation areas. Using the skills you practiced in this chapter, insert formulas that calculate the total workers for each park, the total workers in each job category, and the Aspen Lakes employees as a percentage of the total employees. Format the worksheet as appropriate, and adjust column widths as necessary to display all data. Insert the file name in the footer, and check for spelling errors. Save the workbook, and then print or submit the file as directed by your instructor.

Done! You have completed Skills in Context

Skills and You

To complete this project, you will need the following file:

■ New blank Excel workbook

You will save your workbook as:

■ Lastname_Firstname_e01_My_College

Select six popular courses at your college, for example, *Algebra, Introduction to Computers, Biology, American History*, and so on. Consult your college's course schedule, and note the number of sections for each course that are offered in the Fall term and in the Spring term. Using the skills you have practiced in this chapter, create a worksheet to calculate the total number of sections for each course. SUM the total number of courses for the Fall term and for the Spring term. Below this data, calculate the Fall sections of each course as a percentage of the total courses offered by your school. Add appropriate titles and formatting. Save the workbook as Lastname_Firstname_e01_My_College and then add the file name to the left footer. Delete unused worksheets, check the worksheet for spelling, and then save the workbook. Print or submit the file as directed by your instructor.

Done! You have completed Skills and You

CHAPTER 2

Create Charts

▶ After data is entered into Excel, you can create a visual representation of the data in the form of charts. Excel provides various types of charts that can make your data easier to understand—for example, pie charts show the size of items proportional to the sum of the items.

▶ Charts can be enhanced with effects such as 3-D and soft shadows to create compelling graphical summaries.

Your starting screen will look similar to this:

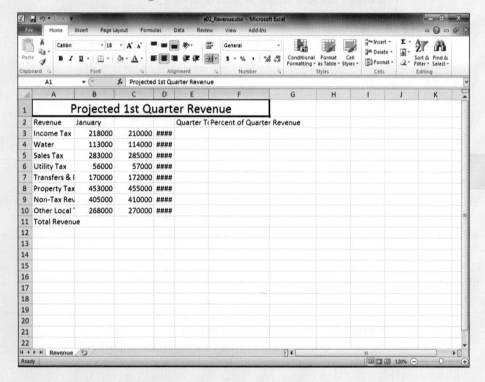

SKILLS

Skills 1-10 Training

At the end of this chapter, you will be able to:

Skill 1 Open Existing Workbooks and Align Text

Skill 2 Construct and Copy Formulas Containing Absolute Cell References

Skill 3 Format Numbers

Skill 4 Create Column Charts

Skill 5 Format Column Charts

Skill 6 Create Pie Charts and Chart Sheets

Skill 7 Apply 3-D Effects and Rotate Pie Chart Slices

Skill 8 Explode and Color Pie Slices, and Insert Text Boxes

Skill 9 Update Charts and Insert WordArt

Skill 10 Prepare Chart Sheets for Printing

MORE SKILLS

More Skills 11 Insert and Edit Comments

More Skills 12 Change Chart Types

More Skills 13 Copy Excel Data to Word Documents

More Skills 14 Fill Series Data into Worksheet Cells

Outcome

Using the skills listed to the left will enable you to create a worksheet and charts like these:

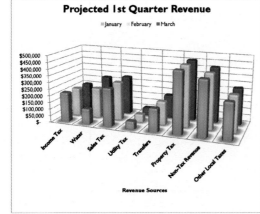

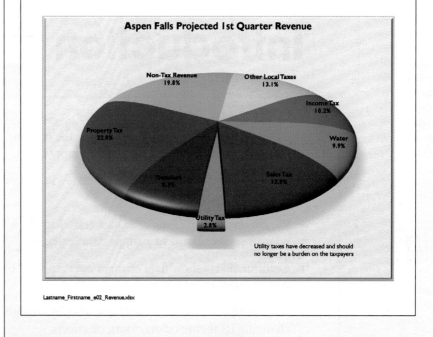

You will save your workbook as:

Lastname_Firstname_e02_Revenue

In this chapter, you will create documents for the Aspen Falls City Hall, which provides essential services for the citizens and visitors of Aspen Falls, California.

Introduction

- Excel helps you find errors by displaying error values, such as #### when a column is not wide enough to display the content, or #DIV/0! when a formula's divisor is 0 or refers to an empty cell.

- Excel provides various number formats so that you can format the worksheet with proper accounting format.

- Pie charts illustrate how each part relates to the whole. Pie charts display the relative sizes of items in a single data series.

- Column charts show data changes over a period of time or illustrate comparisons among items.

- A spreadsheet can be quickly formatted by changing its overall theme or by changing its theme colors, fonts, or effects.

**Time to complete all
10 skills – 50 to 90 minutes**

Find your student data files here:

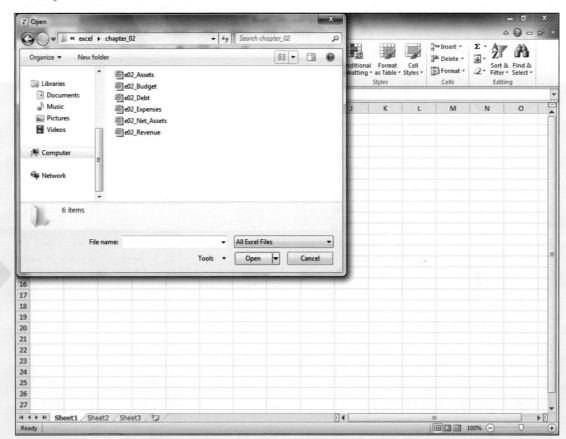

**Student data file needed
for this chapter:**

- e02_Revenue

▶ The *Text wrap* format displays text on multiple lines within a cell.

▶ A *document theme*—a set of design elements that provides a unified look for colors, fonts, and graphics—can be applied to a workbook.

1. Start ● Excel. Click the **File tab**, and then click **Open**. In the **Open** dialog box, navigate to your student data files. Select **e02_Revenue**, and then click the **Open** button. Compare your screen with **Figure 1**.

2. Click the **File tab**, and then click **Save As**. Navigate to the location where you are saving your files, create a folder named Excel Chapter 2 and then **Save** the workbook as Lastname_Firstname_e02_Revenue

3. Click the **Insert tab**, and then in the **Text group**, click the **Header & Footer** button. In the **Navigation group**, click the **Go to Footer** button. Click just above the word **Footer**, and then in the **Header & Footer Elements group**, click the **File Name** button. Click a cell above the footer. On the status bar, click the **Normal** button ▦, and then press Ctrl + Home.

4. In the column heading area, point to the right boundary of column **A** to display the ⊞ pointer, as shown in **Figure 2**.

5. With the ⊞ pointer displayed, double-click to *AutoFit* the column—automatically change the column width to accommodate the longest entry.

■ **Continue to the next page to complete the skill** ▶

Cell E2 text is truncated

Column is too narrow to display values

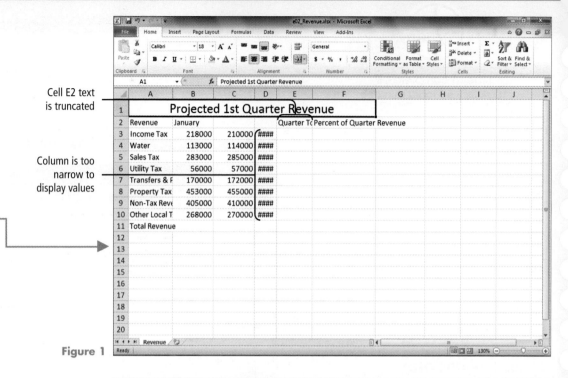

Figure 1

Right column boundary and ⊞ pointer

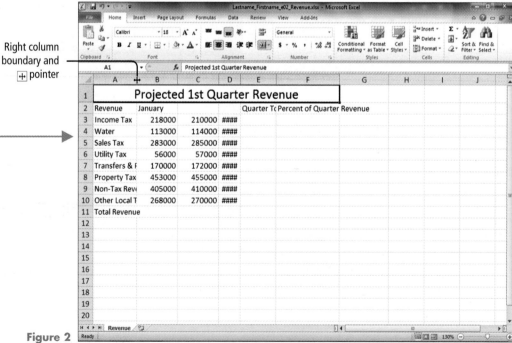

Figure 2

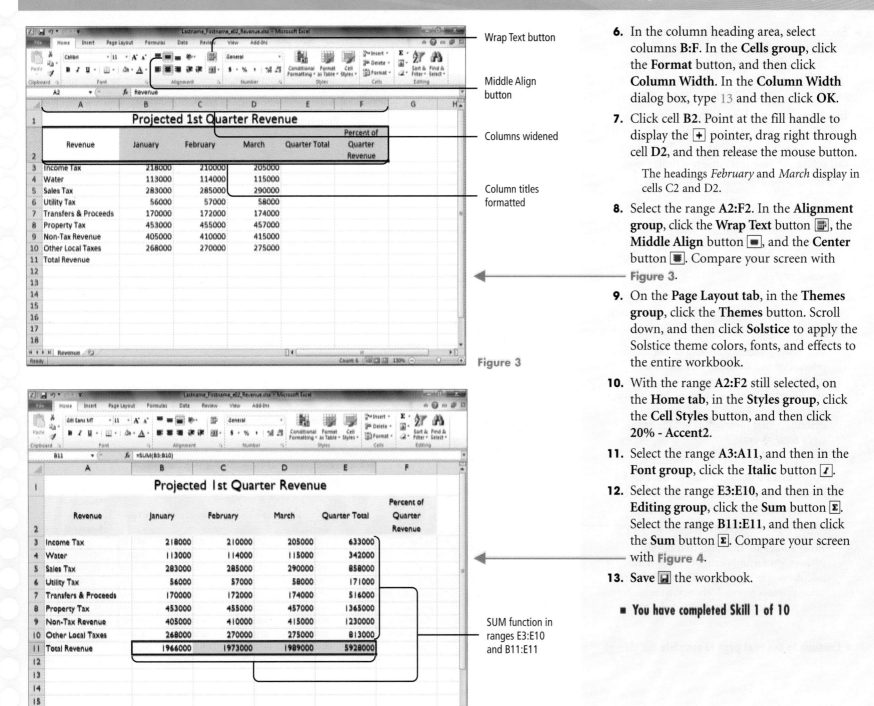

Wrap Text button

Middle Align button

Columns widened

Column titles formatted

Figure 3

SUM function in ranges E3:E10 and B11:E11

Figure 4

6. In the column heading area, select columns **B:F**. In the **Cells group**, click the **Format** button, and then click **Column Width**. In the **Column Width** dialog box, type 13 and then click **OK**.

7. Click cell **B2**. Point at the fill handle to display the ⊞ pointer, drag right through cell **D2**, and then release the mouse button.

   The headings *February* and *March* display in cells C2 and D2.

8. Select the range **A2:F2**. In the **Alignment group**, click the **Wrap Text** button 🔳, the **Middle Align** button 🔳, and the **Center** button 🔳. Compare your screen with **Figure 3**.

9. On the **Page Layout tab**, in the **Themes group**, click the **Themes** button. Scroll down, and then click **Solstice** to apply the Solstice theme colors, fonts, and effects to the entire workbook.

10. With the range **A2:F2** still selected, on the **Home tab**, in the **Styles group**, click the **Cell Styles** button, and then click **20% - Accent2**.

11. Select the range **A3:A11**, and then in the **Font group**, click the **Italic** button 🔳.

12. Select the range **E3:E10**, and then in the **Editing group**, click the **Sum** button 🔳. Select the range **B11:E11**, and then click the **Sum** button 🔳. Compare your screen with **Figure 4**.

13. **Save** 🔳 the workbook.

■ **You have completed Skill 1 of 10**

► Excel uses rules to check for formula errors. When a formula breaks one of the rules, the cell displays an *error indicator*—a green triangle that indicates a possible error in a formula.

► In a formula, an *absolute cell reference* is a cell reference that remains the same when it is copied or filled to other cells. To make a cell reference absolute, insert a dollar sign before the row and column reference.

1. Click cell **F3**, and then type =E3/E11 On the **formula bar**, click the **Enter** button ✓ to display *0.106781377*. In the **Number group**, click the **Percent Style** button % to display *11%*.

2. Double-click cell **F3** to display the range finder, and then compare your screen with **Figure 1**.

   The *range finder* outlines all of the cells referenced in a formula. It is useful for verifying which cells are used in a formula and for editing formulas. Here, *Income Tax* revenue is divided by *Total Revenue* to determine that Income Tax is 11% of the city's total revenue.

3. Press Esc to leave the range finder while keeping cell F3 active. Point to the cell **F3** fill handle, drag down through cell **F10**, and then release the mouse button. Compare your screen with **Figure 2**.

   Error values are messages that display whenever a formula cannot perform the calculations in a formula. The *#DIV/0!* error value displays in a cell whenever the underlying formula attempts to divide by zero.

■ **Continue to the next page to complete the skill** ▶

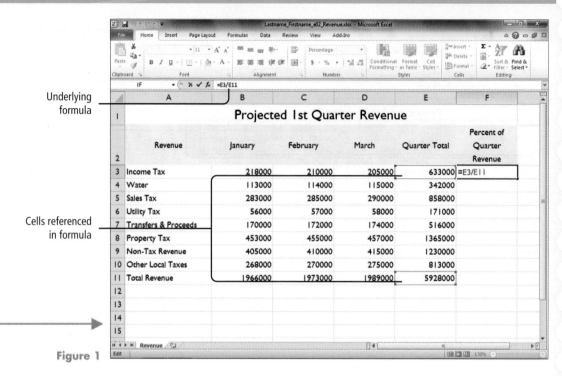

Underlying formula

Cells referenced in formula

Figure 1

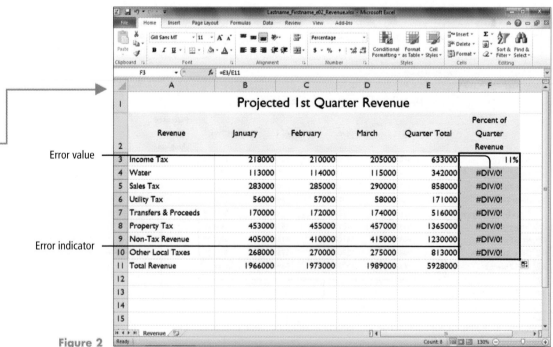

Error value

Error indicator

Figure 2

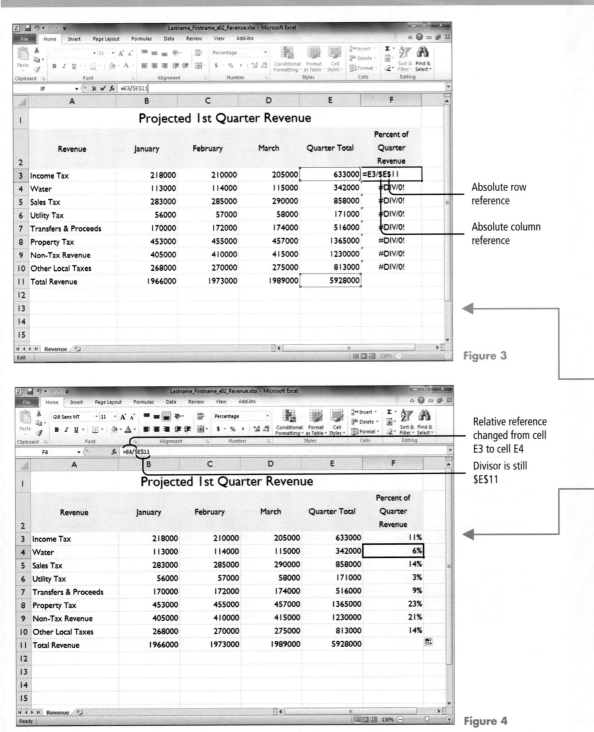

Figure 3

Figure 4

4. Click cell **F4**. To the left of the cell, point to the displayed **Error Message** button 🔷 ▾ to display the ScreenTip—*The formula or function used is dividing by zero or empty cells.*

5. Double-click cell **F4** to display the range finder.

   The formula was copied with a relative cell reference. In the copied formula, the cell reference to cell E4 is correct, but the formula is dividing by the value in cell E12, an empty cell. In this calculation, the divisor must always be cell E11.

6. Press ⎋, and then double-click cell **F3**. Move the insertion point to the end of the formula—to the right of *E11*—and then press ⌷F4⌷ to make the cell reference absolute. Notice that a dollar sign is inserted in front of the column reference *E* and that a dollar sign is inserted in front of the row reference *11*, as shown in Figure 3.

7. On the **formula bar**, click the **Enter** button ✔. In cell **F3**, point to the fill handle, and then drag the fill handle to copy the formula down through cell **F10**.

8. Click cell **F4**. Notice that the divisor refers to cell E11, as shown in Figure 4.

   The cell reference for the *Water Quarter Total* changed relative to its row; however, the value used as the divisor—*Total Revenue* in cell E11—remained absolute.

9. Press the ↓ repeatedly, and notice that the divisor remains constant—$E$11—while the quotient changes relative to the row.

10. Save 🖫 the workbook.

   ■ **You have completed Skill 2 of 10**

▶ A *number format* is a specific way that Excel displays numbers. By default, Excel displays the *General format*—a number format that does not display commas or trailing zeros to the right of a decimal point.

▶ The *Accounting number format* applies comma separators where appropriate, inserts a fixed dollar sign aligned at the left edge of the cell, applies two decimal places, and leaves a small amount of space at both the right and left edges of the cell to accommodate parentheses for negative numbers.

▶ The *Comma cell style* adds commas where appropriate and applies the same formatting as the Accounting number format but without a dollar sign.

1. Click cell **B3**, and then on the **Home tab**, in the **Number group**, notice that *General* displays, as shown in **Figure 1**.

2. Select the range **B3:E3**, hold down Ctrl, and then select the range **B11:E11**.

3. With the two nonadjacent ranges selected, on the **Home tab**, in the **Number group**, click the **Accounting Number Format** button $ ▾, and then click the **Decrease Decimal** button two times to remove the decimal places. Compare your screen with **Figure 2**.

  Financial worksheets typically display dollar signs only in the first row and in the total row.

■ **Continue to the next page to complete the skill**

General number format

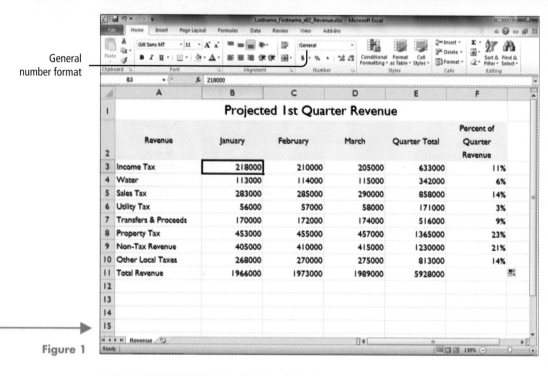

Figure 1

Accounting Number Format button

Decrease Decimal button

Nonadjacent ranges selected and format applied

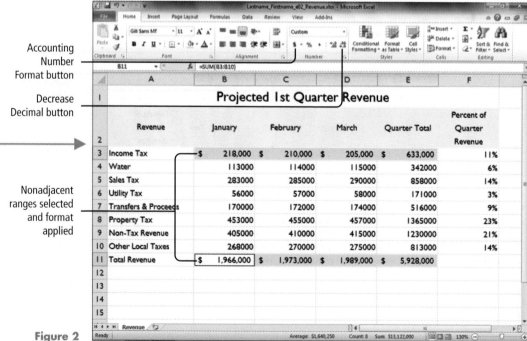

Figure 2

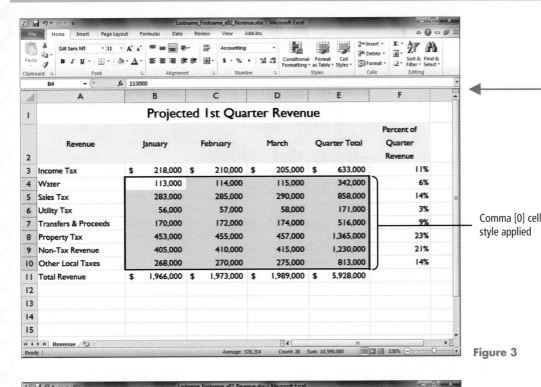

Comma [0] cell style applied

Figure 3

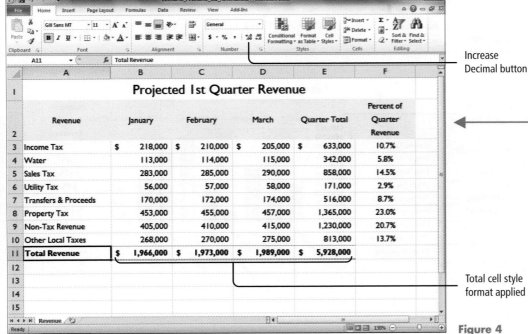

Increase Decimal button

Total cell style format applied

Figure 4

4. Select the range **B4:E10**. In the **Styles group**, click the **Cell Styles** button, and then under **Number Format**, click **Comma[0]**. Compare your screen with **Figure 3**.

The Comma[0] cell style inserts commas and rounds the values so that no decimals display.

5. Select the range **F3:F10**. In the **Number group**, click the **Increase Decimal** button one time to add one decimal to the applied Percent style. In the **Alignment group**, click the **Center** button.

6. Select the range **B11:E11**. In the **Styles group**, click the **Cell Styles** button, and then under **Titles and Headings**, click **Total**.

The *Total cell style* applies a single top border, which indicates that calculations were performed on the numbers above, and a double bottom border, which indicates that the calculations are complete.

7. Right-click cell **A11** to select the cell and to display the Mini toolbar. On the Mini toolbar, click the **Bold** button. Compare your screen with **Figure 4**.

8. Save the workbook.

■ **You have completed Skill 3 of 10**

▶ A *chart* is a graphic representation of data used to show comparisons, patterns, and trends.

▶ A *column chart* is useful for illustrating comparisons among related numbers.

1. Select the range **A2:D10**—do *not* include the *Quarter Total* column or the *Total Revenue* row in your selection. On the **Insert tab**, in the **Charts group**, click the **Column** button to display the Chart gallery, as shown in **Figure 1**.

2. In the **Chart** gallery, under **2-D Column**, click the first chart—**Clustered Column**. On the Ribbon, under **Chart Tools**, notice that the Design, Layout, and Format contextual tabs display as shown in **Figure 2**.

    When you insert a chart, borders surround the chart data and an embedded chart is inserted. An *embedded chart* is a chart that is placed on the worksheet containing the data. Embedded charts are beneficial when you want to view or print a chart with its source data.

3. Along the bottom of the chart, locate the names of the revenue categories.

    An *axis* is a line bordering the chart plot area used as a frame of reference for measurement. The *category axis* is the axis that displays the category labels. A *category label* is nonnumeric text that identifies the categories of data. Here, the worksheet's row titles are used for the category labels. For column charts, the category axis is the *x-axis*—the horizontal axis of a chart.

■ **Continue to the next page to complete the skill**

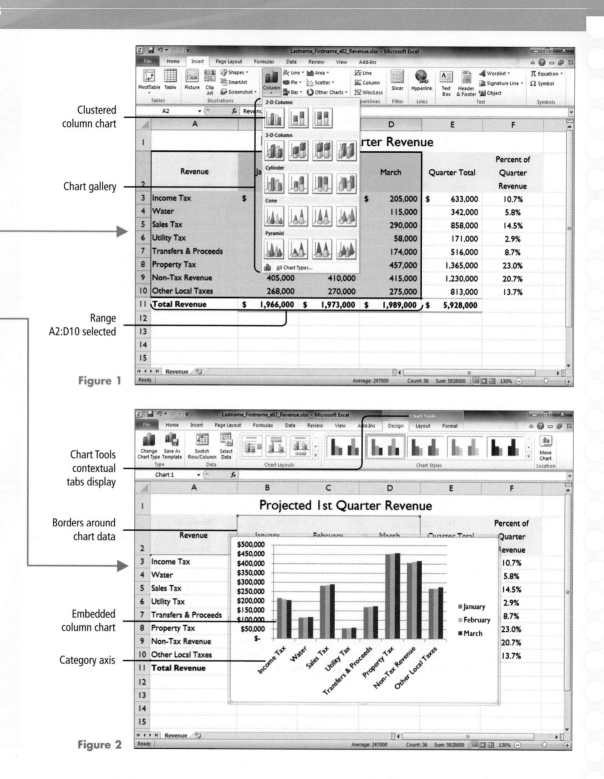

Clustered column chart

Chart gallery

Range A2:D10 selected

Figure 1

Chart Tools contextual tabs display

Borders around chart data

Embedded column chart

Category axis

Figure 2

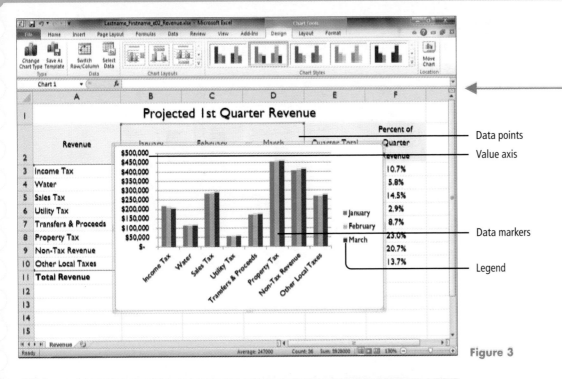

Data points

Value axis

Data markers

Legend

Figure 3

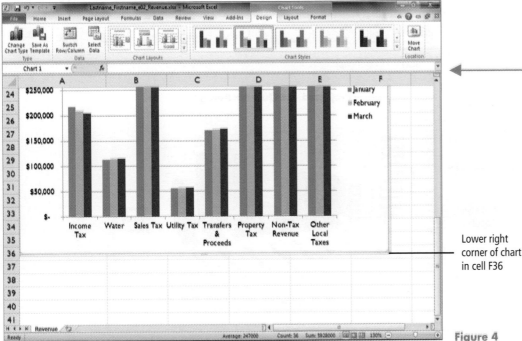

Lower right corner of chart in cell F36

Figure 4

4. On the left side of the chart, locate the numerical scale, and then on the right side, locate the months displayed in the legend. Compare your screen with **Figure 3**.

In the worksheet, each cell bordered in blue is referred to as a **data point**—a chart value that originates in a worksheet cell. Each data point is represented in a chart by a **data marker**—a column, a bar, an area, a dot, a pie slice, or another symbol that represents a single data point.

The **value axis** is the axis that displays the worksheet's numeric data. In a column chart, the value axis is the **y-axis**—the vertical axis of a chart.

Data points that are related to one another form a **data series**, and each data series has a unique color or pattern represented in the chart **legend**—a box that identifies the patterns or colors that are assigned to the data series or categories in the chart. Here, each month is a different data series, and the legend shows the color assigned to each month.

5. Point to the upper border of the chart to display the ⊞ pointer, and then move the chart to position its upper left corner in cell **A14**.

6. Scroll down to display row **36**, and then point to the lower right corner of the chart. With the ⬔ pointer, drag to position the lower right corner in the middle of cell **F36**, as shown in **Figure 4**.

7. Save ⊟ the workbook.

■ **You have completed Skill 4 of 10**

▶ You can customize individual chart elements by using the buttons on the Chart Tools contextual tabs.

▶ You can modify the look of a chart by applying a ***chart layout***—a prebuilt set of chart elements that can include a title, a legend, or labels—or by applying a ***chart style***—a prebuilt chart format that applies an overall visual look to a chart by modifying its graphic effects, colors, and backgrounds.

1. If necessary, click the border of the chart to select the chart. On the **Design tab**, in the **Type group**, click the **Change Chart Type** button. In the displayed **Change Chart Type** dialog box, under **Column**, click **3-D Column**, and then click **OK**.

    The chart is changed from a two-dimensional chart to a three-dimensional chart. ***3-D***, which is short for ***three-dimensional***, refers to an image that appears to have all three spatial dimensions—length, width, and depth.

2. In the **Chart Layouts group**, click the **More** button ⊡, and then click **Layout 9** to add the chart title and the axis titles as shown in **Figure 1**.

3. At the top of the chart, click the text *Chart Title*, and type Projected 1st Quarter Revenue Notice the text is inserted in the formula bar. Verify that your text replaced any text, and then press Enter to accept the text.

4. In the **Chart Styles group**, click the **More** button ⊡, and then click **Style 26**. Compare your screen with **Figure 2**.

■ **Continue to the next page to complete the skill**

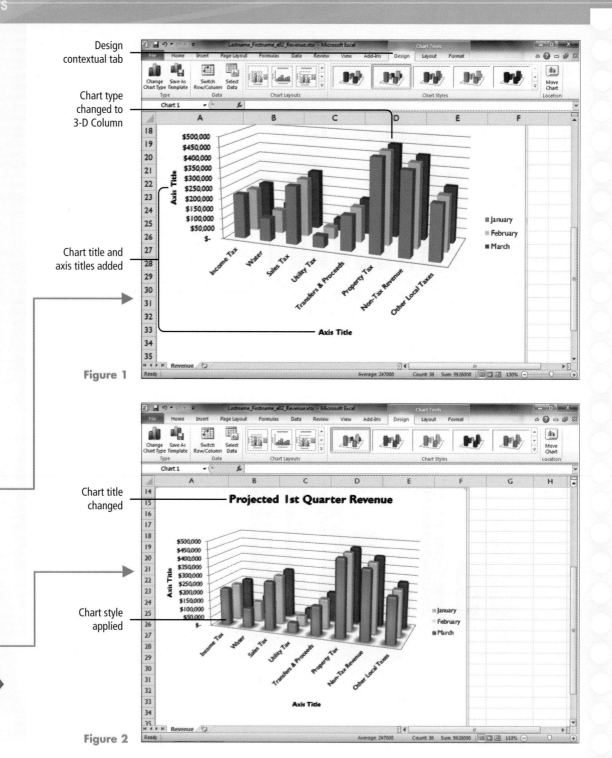

Design contextual tab

Chart type changed to 3-D Column

Chart title and axis titles added

Figure 1

Chart title changed

Chart style applied

Figure 2

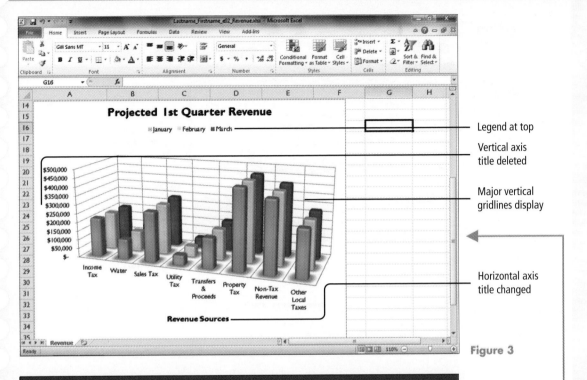

Legend at top

Vertical axis title deleted

Major vertical gridlines display

Horizontal axis title changed

Figure 3

Chart Types Commonly Used in Excel

Chart type	Use to
Column	Illustrate data changes over a period of time or illustrate comparisons among items.
Line	Illustrate trends over time, with time displayed along the horizontal axis and the data point values connected by a line.
Pie	Illustrate the relationship of parts to a whole.
Bar	Illustrate comparisons among individual items.
Area	Emphasize the magnitude of change over time.

Figure 4

5. Below the horizontal axis, click the text *Axis Title*. Type Revenue Sources Verify that your text displays in the formula bar, and then press Enter.

6. In the chart, right-click the *Revenue Sources* axis title to display the shortcut menu and the Mini toolbar. On the Mini toolbar, click the **Font Size** arrow 11 ▾, and then click **12**.

7. To the left of the vertical axis, click the text *Axis Title*. Press Delete to delete the vertical axis title.

> The vertical axis title is deleted, and the chart automatically resizes to use the additional space.

8. On the **Layout tab**, in the **Labels group**, click the **Legend** button. From the displayed list, click **Show Legend at Top** to move the legend to the top of the chart.

> When you move chart elements such as the legend, the chart automatically resizes.

9. In the **Axes group**, click the **Gridlines** button. Point to **Primary Vertical Gridlines**, and then click **Major Gridlines** to display vertical grid lines between each category.

10. Click cell **G16** to deselect the chart. **Save** 🖫 the workbook, and then compare your screen with Figure 3.

11. Take a moment to examine the various types of charts available in Excel, as summarized in Figure 4.

■ **You have completed Skill 5 of 10**

► A *pie chart* displays the relationship of parts to a whole.

► A *chart sheet* is a workbook sheet that contains only a chart and is useful when you want to view a chart separately from the worksheet data.

1. Select the range **A3:A10**. Hold down Ctrl, and then select the range **E3:E10** to select the nonadjacent quarter totals.

2. On the **Insert tab**, in the **Charts group**, click the **Pie** button. Under **3-D Pie**, click the first chart—**Pie in 3-D**.

   The row labels in the range A3:A10 identify the slices of the pie chart. The quarter totals in the range E3:E10 are the data series that determines the size of each pie slice.

3. On the **Design tab**, in the **Location group**, click the **Move Chart** button. In the **Move Chart** dialog box, select the **New sheet** option button. In the **New sheet** box, replace the highlighted text *Chart1* by typing Revenue Chart as shown in **Figure 1**. ————

4. In the **Move Chart** dialog box, click **OK** to move the pie chart to a chart sheet.

5. On the **Design tab**, in the **Chart Layouts group**, click the **More** button ⏷, and then click **Layout 5**. Compare your screen with **Figure 2**. ————

   With Chart Layout 5, the chart title displays at the top of the chart, the legend is deleted, and the category names display in each pie slice.

6. Use the technique practiced earlier to change the **Chart Title** to Aspen Falls Projected 1st Quarter Revenue

■ **Continue to the next page to complete the skill** ▶

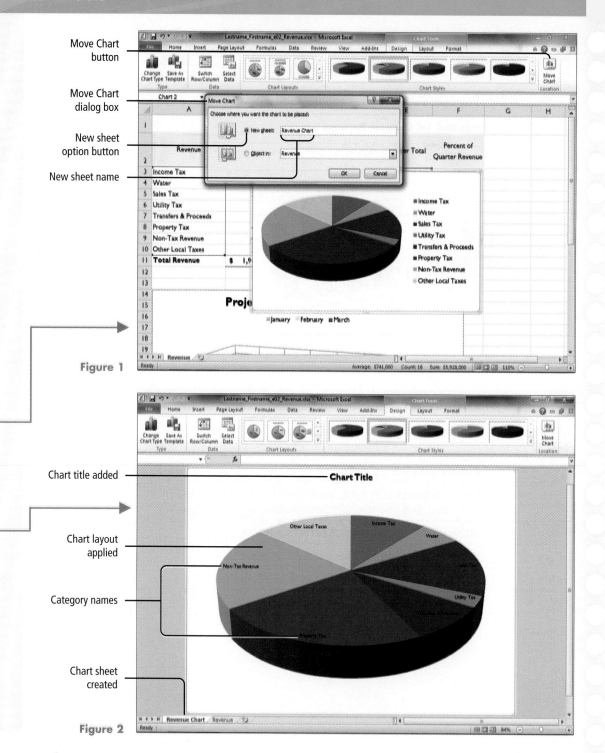

Move Chart button
Move Chart dialog box
New sheet option button
New sheet name

Figure 1

Chart title added
Chart layout applied
Category names
Chart sheet created

Figure 2

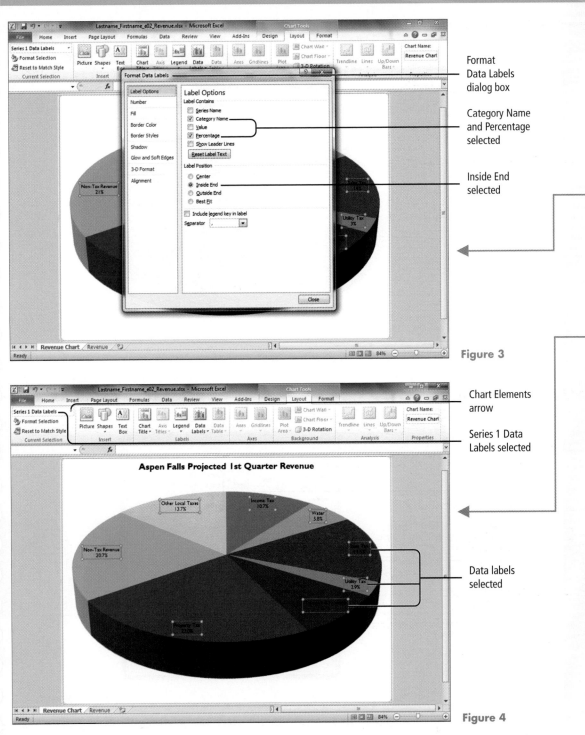

Format Data Labels dialog box

Category Name and Percentage selected

Inside End selected

Figure 3

Chart Elements arrow

Series 1 Data Labels selected

Data labels selected

Figure 4

7. On the **Layout tab**, in the **Labels group**, click the **Data Labels** button, and then click **More Data Label Options**.

8. In the **Format Data Labels** dialog box, on the right, under **Label Contains**, verify that the **Category Name** check box is selected, and then select the **Percentage** check box. Clear any other check boxes in this group. Under **Label Position**, select the **Inside End** option button, and then compare your screen with **Figure 3**.

9. In the left side of the **Format Data Labels** dialog box, click **Number**. Under **Category**, click **Percentage**. In the **Decimal places** box, replace the value with 1 and then click **Close**.

10. In the **Current Selection group**, verify that *Series 1 Data Labels* displays as shown in **Figure 4**. If necessary, click the Chart Elements arrow, and then click Series 1 Data Labels.

   You can use the Chart Elements list to select any chart element.

11. Right-click any of the selected data labels to display the Mini toolbar, click the **Bold** button B, and then change the **Font Size** to **12**.

12. On the **Insert tab**, in the **Text group**, click the **Header & Footer** button. In the **Page Setup** dialog box, click the **Custom Footer** button. Verify that the insertion point is in the **Left section** box, and then click the **Insert File Name** button. Click **OK** two times to insert a footer that will display when the chart sheet is printed.

13. **Save** the workbook.

   ■ **You have completed Skill 6 of 10**

► You can modify chart elements by changing the fill color or texture, or by adding an effect such as a shadow, glow, reflection, or bevel.

► You can rotate pie chart slices to present a different visual perspective of the chart.

1. Click the edge of any pie slice to deselect the data labels and to select all of the pie slices—*Series 1*. Compare your screen with **Figure 1.**

2. On the **Format tab**, in the **Shape Styles group**, click the **Shape Effects** button. Point to **Bevel**, and then at the bottom of the Bevel gallery, click **3-D Options**.

3. In the **Format Data Series** dialog box, under **Bevel**, click the **Top** button. In the gallery, under **Bevel**, point to the first thumbnail to display the ScreenTip *Circle*, and then click the **Circle** thumbnail. Click the **Bottom** button, and then click the **Circle** thumbnail.

4. Under **Bevel**, in the four **Width** and **Height** spin boxes, replace the existing value with 512 pt and then compare your screen with **Figure 2.**

5. In the **Format Data Series** dialog box, under **Surface**, click the **Material** button, and then under **Standard**, click the third thumbnail—**Plastic**. In the lower right corner of the dialog box, click the **Close** button.

6. On the **Format tab**, in the **Shape Styles group**, click the **Shape Effects** button, and then point to **Shadow**. At the bottom of the Shadow gallery, under **Perspective**, click the third thumbnail—**Below**.

■ **Continue to the next page to complete the skill**

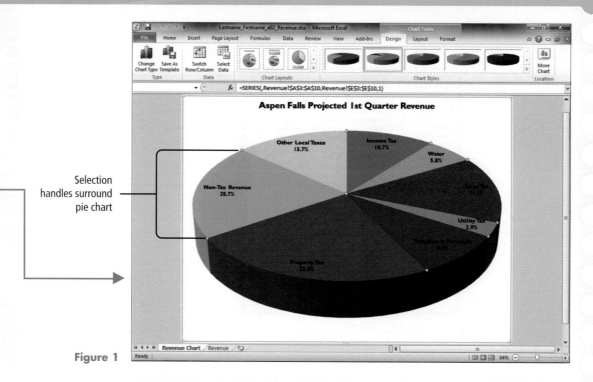

Selection handles surround pie chart

Figure 1

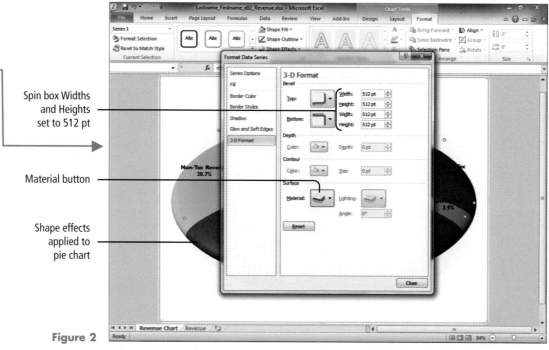

Spin box Widths and Heights set to 512 pt

Material button

Shape effects applied to pie chart

Figure 2

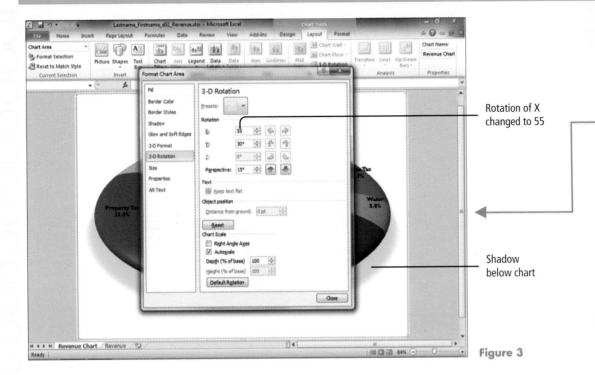

Rotation of X changed to 55

Shadow below chart

Figure 3

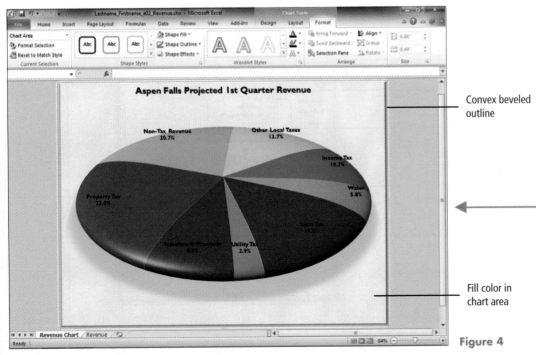

Convex beveled outline

Fill color in chart area

Figure 4

7. Notice the position of the **Utility Tax** slice in the chart. On the **Layout tab**, in the **Background group**, click the **3-D Rotation** button. In the **Format Chart Area** dialog box, under **Rotation**, in the **X** spin box, replace the value with 55 as shown in **Figure 3**.

8. In the **Format Chart Area** dialog box, click the **Close** button.

> The order in which the data series is plotted is determined by the order of the data on the worksheet. The pie chart slices can be rotated up to 360 degrees. Here, the slices were rotated to bring the *Utility Tax* slice to the front of the pie chart.

9. On the **Format tab**, in the **Current Selection group**, verify that the **Chart Elements** box displays the text *Chart Area*. In the **Shape Styles group**, click the **Shape Effects** button, point to **Bevel**, and then under **Bevel**, click the third thumbnail in the second row—**Convex**.

> This effect adds a convex beveled frame around the entire chart.

10. On the **Format tab**, in the **Current Selection group**, click the **Format Selection** button. In the **Format Chart Area** dialog box, select the **Solid fill** option button. Click the **Color button arrow**, and then under **Theme Colors**, click the sixth color in the third row—**Gold, Accent 2, Lighter 60%**. Click the **Close** button, and then compare your screen with **Figure 4**.

11. Save 💾 the workbook.

■ **You have completed Skill 7 of 10**

► You can *explode*—pull out one or more slices—of a 3-D pie chart to emphasize a specific slice or slices in a pie chart.

1. Click in the shaded area outside the pie chart to deselect all elements. On the pie chart, click the outer edge of the **Utility Tax** slice once to select the entire pie chart, and then click the **Utility Tax** slice again to select only the one pie slice.

2. Point to the **Utility Tax** slice to display the 🕂 pointer, and then drag the slice away from the center of the pie, as shown in **Figure 1**.

3. Release the mouse button to see the Utility Tax pie slice exploded—pulled away from the pie.

4. With the **Utility Tax** slice still selected, on the **Format tab**, in the **Current Selection group**, click the **Format Selection** button. In the left side of the **Format Data Point** dialog box, click **Fill**. On the right, select the **Solid fill** option button. Click the **Color button arrow**, and then under **Theme Colors**, click the ninth color in the fourth row—**Brown, Accent 5, Lighter 40%**. Compare your screen with **Figure 2**.

5. In the dialog box, click the **Close** button.

6. Click the inner edge of the **Water** pie slice to select only that pie slice. Use the technique just practiced to change the *Water* pie slice solid fill color to the last color in the fourth row—**Indigo, Accent 6, Lighter 40%**. Click the **Close** button.

■ **Continue to the next page to complete the skill**

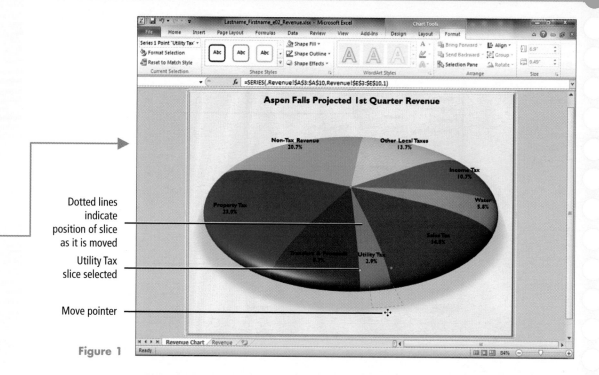

Dotted lines indicate position of slice as it is moved

Utility Tax slice selected

Move pointer

Figure 1

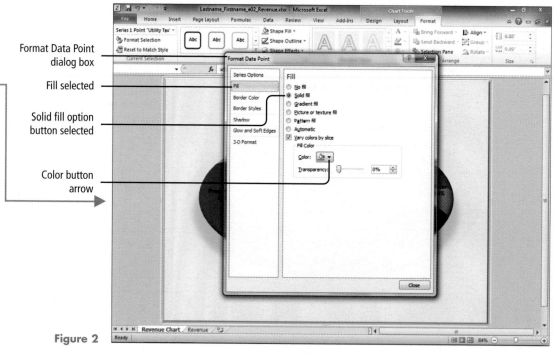

Format Data Point dialog box

Fill selected

Solid fill option button selected

Color button arrow

Figure 2

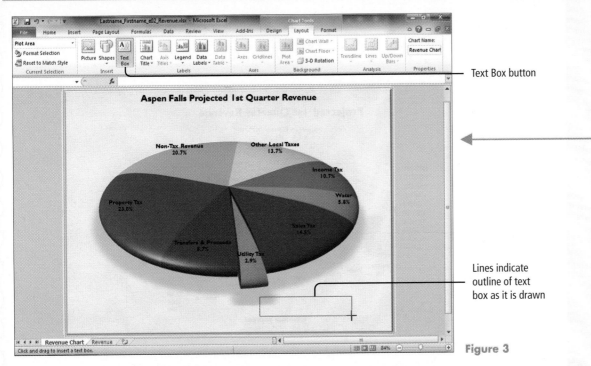

Text Box button

Lines indicate outline of text box as it is drawn

Figure 3

7. On the **Layout tab**, in the **Insert group**, click the **Text Box** button.

8. Position the displayed ⬇ pointer just under and to the right of the **Utility Tax** pie slice. Hold down the left mouse button, and then drag down and to the right to draw the text box approximately as shown in **Figure 3**.

9. Release the mouse button to insert the text box. With the insertion point blinking inside the text box, type Utility taxes have decreased and should no longer be a burden on the taxpayers

10. Select all the text in the text box, and then right-click the text to display the Mini toolbar. On the Mini toolbar, click the **Font Size arrow** 11 ⬝, and then click **12**. If necessary, resize the text box to display all the text.

11. Click in the Chart Area to deselect the text box. On the chart, click the **Utility Tax** category label once to select all data labels, and then click the **Utility Tax** data label again to select only that one data label. Point to the *Utility Tax* data label's bottom border, and then with the 🔧 pointer, drag the Utility Tax data label to the edge of the exploded slice as shown in **Figure 4**. Adjust the size and position of the data label or text box as needed.

12. **Save** 💾 the workbook.

■ **You have completed Skill 8 of 10**

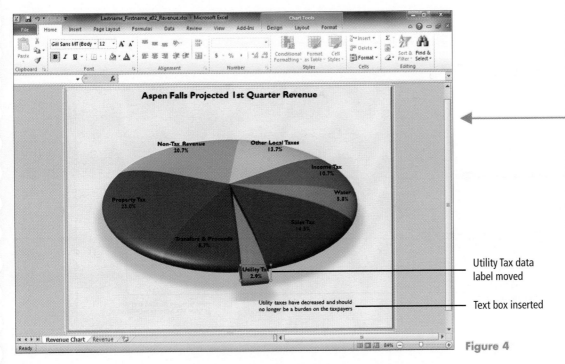

Utility Tax data label moved

Text box inserted

Figure 4

▶ Recall that a chart's data series and category labels are linked to the source data in the worksheet. When worksheet values are changed, the chart is automatically updated.

▶ *Sheet tabs* are the labels along the lower border of the workbook window that identify each worksheet or chart sheet.

1. In the sheet tab area at the bottom of the workbook, click the **Revenue** sheet tab to display the worksheet. If necessary, scroll down, and in the column chart, note the height of the Water data markers for February and March.

2. Click cell **C4**, type 225000 and then press Enter to accept the new value. If necessary, scroll down to view the chart. Notice the *Water* value for the month of *February* is updated as shown in **Figure 1**.

   The data marker—the column—representing this data point is updated on the column chart.

3. Click cell **D4**, type 275000 and then press Enter. In cell **F4**, notice the Water revenue now represents 9.9% of the projected 1st Quarter Revenue.

4. Click the **Revenue Chart** sheet tab to display the pie chart and then move the Utility tax data label to the edge of the slice. Verify that in the pie chart, the slice for *Water* displays *9.9%* as shown in **Figure 2**.

   When underlying data is changed, the pie chart percentages and pie slices are automatically recalculated and resized.

■ **Continue to the next page to complete the skill** ▶

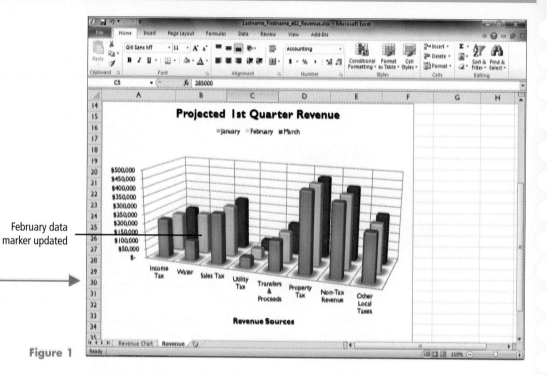

February data marker updated

Figure 1

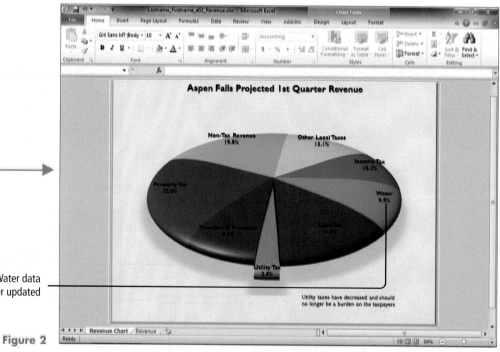

Water data marker updated

Figure 2

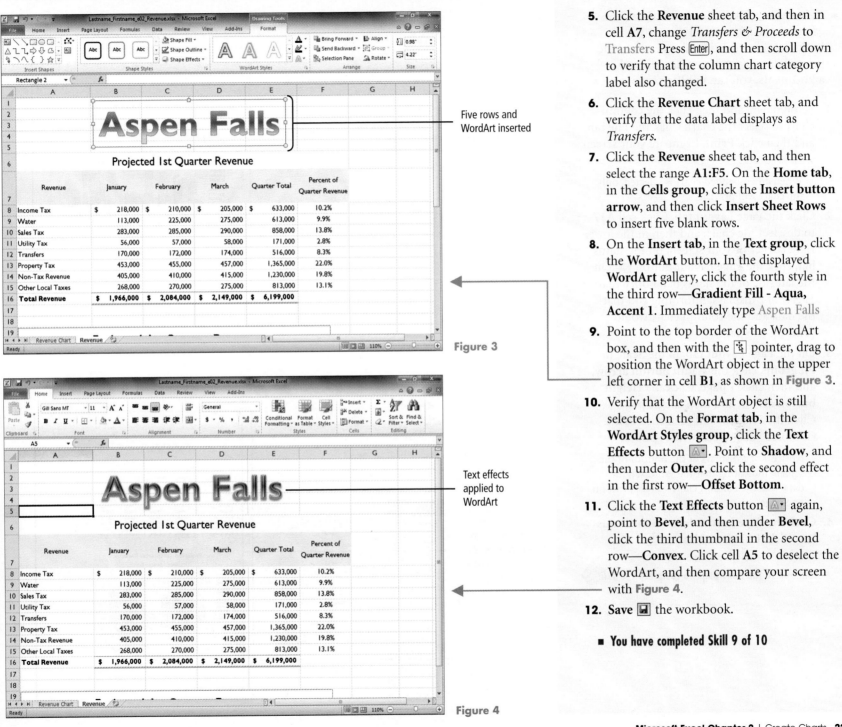

Five rows and
WordArt inserted

Figure 3

Text effects
applied to
WordArt

Figure 4

5. Click the **Revenue** sheet tab, and then in cell **A7**, change *Transfers & Proceeds* to Transfers Press Enter, and then scroll down to verify that the column chart category label also changed.

6. Click the **Revenue Chart** sheet tab, and verify that the data label displays as *Transfers*.

7. Click the **Revenue** sheet tab, and then select the range **A1:F5**. On the **Home tab**, in the **Cells group**, click the **Insert button arrow**, and then click **Insert Sheet Rows** to insert five blank rows.

8. On the **Insert tab**, in the **Text group**, click the **WordArt** button. In the displayed **WordArt** gallery, click the fourth style in the third row—**Gradient Fill - Aqua, Accent 1**. Immediately type Aspen Falls

9. Point to the top border of the WordArt box, and then with the 🔁 pointer, drag to position the WordArt object in the upper left corner in cell **B1**, as shown in **Figure 3**.

10. Verify that the WordArt object is still selected. On the **Format tab**, in the **WordArt Styles group**, click the **Text Effects** button Ⓐ▾. Point to **Shadow**, and then under **Outer**, click the second effect in the first row—**Offset Bottom**.

11. Click the **Text Effects** button Ⓐ▾ again, point to **Bevel**, and then under **Bevel**, click the third thumbnail in the second row—**Convex**. Click cell **A5** to deselect the WordArt, and then compare your screen with **Figure 4**.

12. **Save** 🖫 the workbook.

■ **You have completed Skill 9 of 10**

► Before you print an Excel worksheet, you can click the File tab and then in the Backstage use the Print tab to preview the printed document. If you need to make adjustments, you can use Page Layout view.

1. Scroll down, and then click the column chart to select the chart. Click the **File tab**, and then click **Print**. Compare your screen with **Figure 1**.

   When an embedded chart is selected, only the chart will print.

2. Click the **Page Layout tab**. Click cell **A17** to deselect the chart, and then in the lower right corner of your screen, on the status bar, click the **Page Layout** button ▣. On the left side of the status bar, notice that *Page 1 of 2* displays, informing you that the data and the column chart would print on two pages.

3. On the **Page Layout tab**, in the **Scale to Fit group**, click the **Width button arrow**, and then click **1 page**. Click the **Height button arrow**, and then click **1 page**. Click the **File tab**, and then click **Print**. Compare your screen with **Figure 2**.

   Notice *1 of 1* displays at the bottom of the screen, indicating that the WordArt, the data, and the column chart will all print on one page.

4. Click the **Page Layout tab**. On the status bar, click the **Normal** button ▥.

■ **Continue to the next page to complete the skill**

Only the column chart displays in preview of printed page

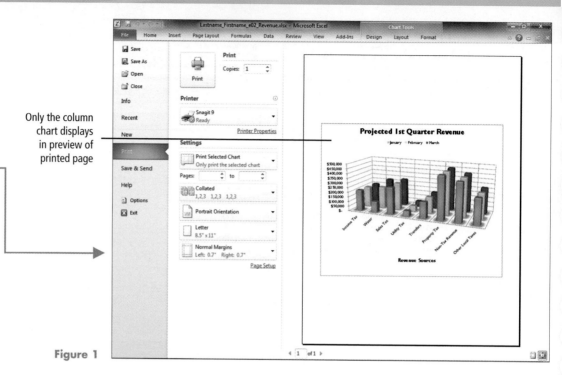

Figure 1

WordArt, data, and chart display on one page

Page 1 of 1

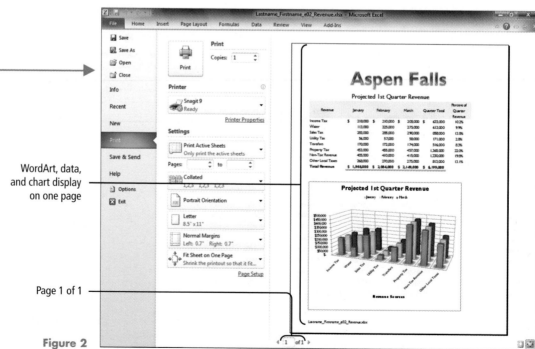

Figure 2

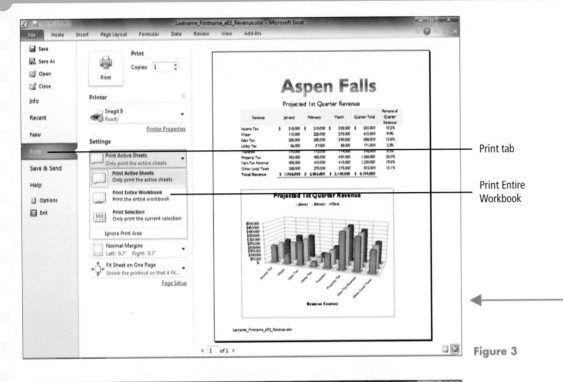

Print tab

Print Entire Workbook

Figure 3

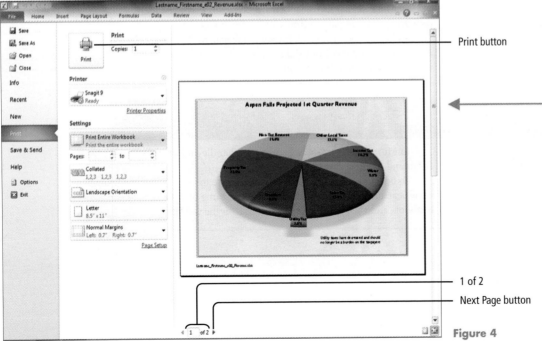

Print button

1 of 2

Next Page button

Figure 4

5. In the **Page Setup group**, click the **Margins** button, and then click **Custom Margins**. In the **Page Setup** dialog box, under **Center on page**, select the **Horizontally** check box, and then click **OK**.

6. Press Ctrl + Home to make cell **A1** the active cell. On the **Review tab**, in the **Proofing group**, click the **Spelling** button, and then check the spelling of the worksheet. When the message *The spelling check is complete for the entire sheet* displays, click **OK**.

7. **Save** 🖫 the workbook.

8. Click the **File tab**, and then click **Print**. Under **Settings**, click the first button as shown in **Figure 3**.

9. On the displayed list, click **Print Entire Workbook**. Notice at the bottom of the screen, *1 of 2* displays, and the chart sheet with the pie chart is the first page, as shown in **Figure 4**.

10. At the bottom of the screen, click the **Next Page** button ▶ to preview the worksheet containing your WordArt, the data, and the column chart. Print the workbook, or submit the file as directed by your instructor. If you are instructed to do so, display and format the worksheet formulas, and then print the formulas.

11. **Close** ⊠ the workbook, and then **Exit** Excel.

Done! You have completed Skill 10 of 10 and your document is complete!

The following More Skills are located at **www.pearsonhighered.com/skills**

More Skills Insert and Edit Comments

You can add comments to cells in a worksheet to provide reminders, to display clarifying information about data within the cells, or to document your work. When you point to a cell that contains a comment, the comment and the name of the person who created the comment display.

In More Skills 11, you will read, create, and edit comments.

To begin, open your web browser, navigate to www.pearsonhighered.com/skills, locate the name of your textbook, and then follow the instructions on the website.

More Skills Change Chart Types

After you create a chart, a different chart type might be easier for the readers of your chart to understand. For example, you can change a column chart to a bar chart. Both a column chart and a bar chart are good choices to illustrate comparisons among items; however, a bar chart might be a better choice when the axis labels are lengthy.

In More Skills 12, you will create a column chart and then change the chart type to a bar chart.

To begin, open your web browser, navigate to www.pearsonhighered.com/skills, locate the name of your textbook, and then follow the instructions on the website.

More Skills Copy Excel Data to Word Documents

You can copy the data and objects created in one application to another application, saving time and providing accuracy because data is entered only one time.

In More Skills 13, you will create a chart in Excel and then copy the chart and paste it into a Word document.

To begin, open your web browser, navigate to www.pearsonhighered.com/skills, locate the name of your textbook, and then follow the instructions on the website.

More Skills 14 Fill Series Data into Worksheet Cells

Instead of entering data manually, you can use the fill handle or the fill command to enter data that follow a pattern or series—for example, hours, days of the week, or numeric sequences such as even numbers.

In More Skills 14, you will use the fill handle and the fill command to enter data in cells.

To begin, open your web browser, navigate to www.pearsonhighered.com/skills, locate the name of your textbook, and then follow the instructions on the website.

Key Terms

Online Help Skills

1. **Start** Excel. In the upper right corner of the Excel window, click the **Help** button . In the Help window, click the **Maximize** button.

2. Click in the search box, type create charts and then click the **Search** button . In the search results, click **Available chart types**.

3. Read the article's introduction, and then below in this article, click **Column charts**. Compare your screen with **Figure 1**.

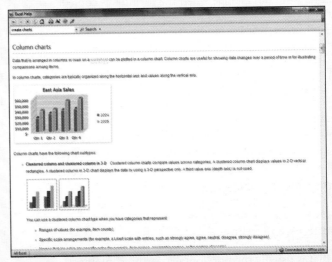

Figure 1

4. Read the section and then scroll down and read the section on Pie Charts to see if you can answer the following: A pie chart is more useful than a column chart for showing what type of data?

Matching

Match each term in the second column with its correct definition in the first column by writing the letter of the term on the blank line in front of the correct definition.

___ **1.** A command with which you can display text on multiple lines within a cell.

___ **2.** A cell reference that refers to a cell by its fixed position in a worksheet and that does not change when the formula is copied.

___ **3.** A specific way that Excel displays numbers.

___ **4.** The default format that Excel applies to numbers—whatever you type in the cell will display, with the exception that trailing zeros to the right of a decimal point will not display.

___ **5.** The Excel number format that applies a comma separator where appropriate, inserts a fixed dollar sign aligned at the left edge of the cell, applies two decimal places, and leaves a small amount of space at both the right and left edges of the cell to accommodate parentheses for negative numbers.

___ **6.** A graphic representation of data in a worksheet that shows comparisons, patterns, and trends.

___ **7.** The chart axis that is usually the horizontal axis and contains categories.

___ **8.** The chart axis that is usually the vertical axis and contains data.

___ **9.** To pull out one or more slices of a 3-D pie chart to emphasize a specific slice or slices.

___ **10.** A set of design elements that provides a unified look for colors, fonts, and graphics.

A Absolute cell reference

B Accounting number format

C Category axis

D Chart

E Explode

F General format

G Number format

H Theme

I Text wrap

J Value axis

Multiple Choice

Choose the correct answer.

1. Automatically changing the column width to accommodate the longest column entry is called:
   - A. Drag and drop
   - B. AutoFit
   - C. Auto adjust

2. A green triangle that indicates a possible error in a formula is called:
   - A. An error indicator
   - B. A message
   - C. A Dialog Box Launcher

3. The Excel feature that outlines all of the cells referenced in a formula is the:
   - A. Formula finder
   - B. Cell finder
   - C. Range finder

4. A chart type useful for illustrating comparisons among related numbers is called:
   - A. A pie chart
   - B. An area chart
   - C. A column chart

5. A chart placed on a worksheet with the source data is:
   - A. A chart sheet
   - B. A column chart
   - C. An embedded chart

6. The chart data points related to one another are known as a:
   - A. Column
   - B. Data series
   - C. Chart point

7. The box that identifies the patterns or colors assigned to the data series in a chart is called a:
   - A. Legend
   - B. Dialog box
   - C. Message box

8. A predesigned combination of chart elements is referred to as a:
   - A. 3-D chart
   - B. Chart layout
   - C. Chart

9. The chart type that displays the relationship of parts to a whole is:
   - A. A pie chart
   - B. An area chart
   - C. A column chart

10. A worksheet that contains only a chart is referred to as a:
    - A. Worksheet
    - B. Chart area
    - C. Chart sheet

Topics for Discussion

1. Search some current newspapers and magazines for examples of charts. Which charts catch your eye and why? Do the charts appeal to you because of their color or format? Is something intriguing revealed to you in the chart that you have never considered before? What are some formatting changes that you think make a chart interesting and valuable to a reader?

2. Why is it important to present accounting and financial information in a manner that is attractive and easy to read? What are some of the ways that Excel can help you do so?

Skill Check

To complete this project, you will need the following file:

- e02_Expenses

You will save your workbook as:

- Lastname_Firstname_e02_Expenses

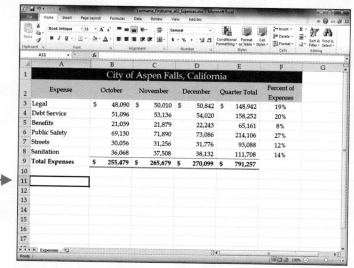

1. **Start** Excel, and open the file **e02_Expenses**. **Save** the file in your **Excel Chapter 2** folder as Lastname_Firstname_e02_Expenses Insert the file name in the left footer and then return to **Normal** view.

2. On the **Page Layout tab**, in the **Themes group**, click the **Themes** button, and then click **Hardcover**.

3. Click cell **B2**, and then use the fill handle to fill the months into the range **C2:D2**. Select the range **A2:F2**. On the **Home tab**, in the **Alignment group**, click the **Wrap Text**, **Middle Align**, and **Center** buttons.

4. Select **E3:E8**, and then in the **Editing** group, click the **SUM** button. In the range **B9:E9**, use the **SUM** function to calculate the *Total Expenses*.

5. In cell **F3**, type =E3/$E$9 and then on the formula bar, click the **Enter** button. Use the fill handle to fill the formula down through cell **F8**. With the range **F3:F8** still selected, in the **Number group**, click the **Percent Style** button. In the **Alignment group**, click the **Center** button.

6. Select the range **B3:E3**, hold down Ctrl, and then select the range **B9:E9**. In the **Number group**, click the **Accounting Number Format** button, and then click the **Decrease Decimal** button two times. Select the range **B4:E8**. In the **Styles group**, click the **Cell Styles** button, and then click **Comma [0]**. Select the range **B9:E9**, click the **Cell Styles** button, and then click **Total**. Click cell **A11**, and then compare your screen with **Figure 1**. ──────

Figure 1

7. Select the range **A2:D8**. On the **Insert tab**, in the **Charts group**, click the **Column** button, and then click **3-D Column**. Move the chart below the data, and then resize the chart to display in approximately the range **A11:F30**. On the **Design tab**, in the **Chart Layouts group**, click **Layout 1**. Click the **Chart Title**, type Expenses and then press Enter. Compare your screen with **Figure 2**. ──────

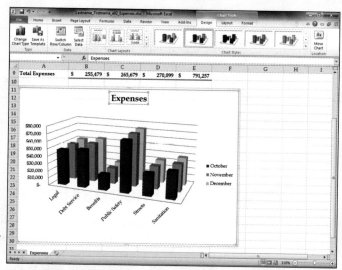

Figure 2

- Continue to the next page to complete this Skill Check

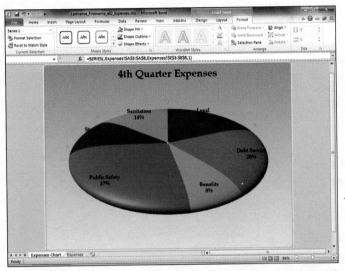

Figure 3

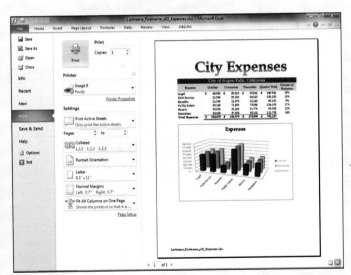

Figure 4

8. Select the nonadjacent ranges **A3:A8** and **E3:E8**. On the **Insert tab**, in the **Charts group**, click the **Pie** button, and then click **Pie in 3-D**.

9. On the **Design tab**, in the **Location group**, click the **Move Chart** button. In the **Move Chart** dialog box, select the **New sheet** option button, type the sheet name Expenses Chart and then click **OK**.

10. For the pie chart, apply the **Layout 1** chart layout, and then change the **Chart Title** to 4th Quarter Expenses Right-click the chart title, and from the Mini toolbar, change the **Font Size** to **28**.

11. Right-click any of the data labels, and use the Mini toolbar to change the **Font Size** to **14** and to apply the **Bold** format.

12. Click the **Chart Area**. On the **Layout tab**, in the **Current Selection group**, click the **Format Selection** button. In the **Format Chart Area** dialog box, select the **Gradient Fill** option button, and then click **Close**.

13. Click the edge of a pie slice to select all of the slices. On the **Format tab**, in the **Shape Styles group**, click the **Shape Effects** button, point to **Bevel**, and then click **3-D Options**. Click the **Top** button, and then click the **Circle** thumbnail. Click the **Bottom** button, and then click the **Circle** thumbnail. Set the four Bevel **Width** and **Height** spin boxes to 250 pt and then click **Close**. Compare your screen with **Figure 3**.

14. On the **Insert tab**, in the **Text group**, click the **Header & Footer** button. In the **Page Setup** dialog box, click the **Custom Footer** button. Verify that the insertion point is in the Left section, click the **Insert File Name** button, and then click **OK** two times.

15. Click the **Expenses** sheet tab. Select the range **A1:F6**. On the **Home tab**, in the **Cells group**, click the **Insert button arrow**, and then click **Insert Sheet Rows**. On the **Insert tab**, in the **Text group**, click the **WordArt** button, and then in the third row, click the fourth thumbnail—**Gradient Fill - Dark Red, Accent 1**. Immediately type City Expenses and then move the WordArt to the top of the worksheet.

16. Click the **Page Layout tab**. In the **Scale to Fit group**, click the **Width** arrow, and then click **1 page**. In the **Page Setup group**, click the **Margins** button, and then click **Custom Margins**. In the **Page Setup** dialog box, select the **Horizontally** check box, and then click the **Print Preview** button.

17. Compare your screen with **Figure 4**. **Save** the workbook, and then print or submit the file as directed by your instructor.

Done! You have completed the Skill Check

Assess Your Skills 1

To complete this project, you will need the following file:

- e02_Assets

You will save your workbook as:

- Lastname_Firstname_e02_Assets

1. **Start** Excel, and open the file **e02_Assets**. **Save** the workbook in your **Excel Chapter 2** folder as Lastname_Firstname_e02_Assets Add the file name in the worksheet's left footer, and then return to **Normal** view.

2. In the ranges **D4:D10** and **B11:D11**, use the **SUM** function to total the rows and the columns. Select the ranges **B4:D4** and **B11:D11**, apply the **Accounting** number format, and format the range so that no decimals display. For the range **B5:D10**, apply the **Comma [0]** cell style. In the range **B11:D11**, apply the **Total** cell style.

3. Insert a **3-D Clustered Column** chart based on the range **A3:C10**. Move the chart below the data, and then resize the chart to approximately the range **A13:D30**. Apply chart **Style 36**, and then show the legend at the top of the chart. Change the legend font size to **12**.

4. Insert a **Pie in 3-D** chart based on the non-adjacent ranges **A4:A10** and **D4:D10**. Move the pie chart to a chart sheet named Capital Assets Chart and then apply **Layout 1**. Change the chart title to Capital Assets

5. For the data labels, apply **Bold**, and then change the **Font Size** to **14**.

6. Format the **Chart Area** with **Solid fill**, and then change the **Color** to **Red**, **Accent 2**, **Lighter 60%**.

7. For all the slices—in Series 1, change the **3-D Rotation** of **X** to **140**, and then explode the **Collections** pie slice. Verify that all data labels display on a pie slice. If necessary, move the Collections pie slice back toward the center of the pie to display the labels on the slices. Display the **3-D Format** settings in the **Format Data Series** dialog box. Change the top bevel to Circle and then change the top bevel width and height to 1000 pt. Change the **Material** setting to **Metal**.

8. For the chart sheet, add a footer with the file name in the left section. Compare your worksheet and chart sheet with **Figure 1**. **Save** the workbook, and then print or submit the file as directed by your instructor.

Done! You have completed Assess Your Skills 1

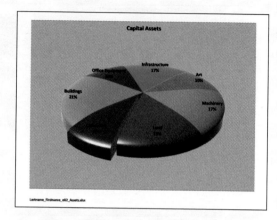

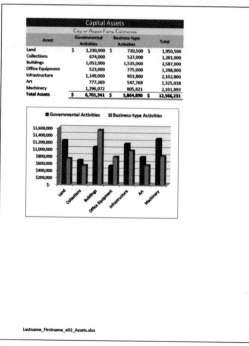

Figure 1

Assess Your Skills 3 and 4 can be found at
www.pearsonhighered.com/skills.

Assess Your Skills 2

To complete this project, you will need the following file:

- e02_Debt

You will save your workbook as:

- Lastname_Firstname_e02_Debt

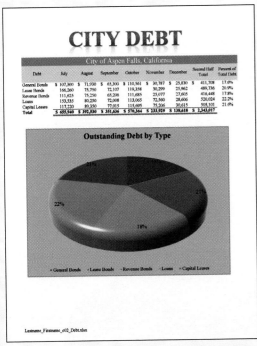

CITY DEBT

Lastname_Firstname_e02_Debt.xlsx

Figure 1

1. **Start** Excel, and open the file **e02_Debt**. **Save** the workbook in your **Excel Chapter 2** folder as Lastname_Firstname_e02_Debt Add the file name in the worksheet's left footer, and then return to **Normal** view.

2. Apply the **Newsprint** theme. In cell **B2**, type July and then Auto Fill the months through cell **G2**.

3. In cell **I4**, calculate the *Percent of Total Debt*. In the formula, use an absolute cell reference when referring to cell **H8**. Copy the formula down through cell **I7**, and then format the results as percentages with one decimal place. Center the results in the cell.

4. Select the ranges **B3:H3** and **B8:H8**, and then apply the **Accounting** number format and display zero decimal places. In the range **B4:H7**, apply the **Comma [0]** cell style, and in the range **B8:H8**, apply the **Total** cell style.

5. Insert a **Pie in 3-D** chart based on the non-adjacent ranges **A3:A7** and **H3:H7**. Move the pie chart below the data, and then resize the chart so that it displays approximately in the range **A11:I38**. Apply **Layout 2**.

6. Change the **Chart Title** to Outstanding Debt by Type and then change the chart title **Font Size** to **20**. Right-click the data labels, and then change the **Font Size** to **14**. Right-click the legend, and then change the **Font Size** to **12**. Display the legend at the bottom of the chart.

7. Format the **Chart Area** to display a **Solid fill** using the ninth color in the third row—**Blue-Gray, Accent 5, Lighter 60%**.

8. Display the **Format Data Series** dialog box. Set a Top **Divot** 3-D Bevel, set the Top **Width** and **Height** to 50 pt and change the **Material** setting to **Soft Edge**.

9. Insert seven sheet rows at the top of the worksheet. Insert a **WordArt**, using the style **Gradient Fill - Blue-Gray, Accent 4, Reflection**. Change the WordArt text to City Debt and then move the WordArt to the top of the worksheet, centering it in the seven blank rows.

10. View the worksheet in **Print Layout** view. Verify that the WordArt, data, and pie chart all print on one page. If necessary, adjust the Scale to Fit to fit all objects on one page.

11. **Save** the workbook, and then print or submit the file as directed by your instructor. Compare your completed workbook with **Figure 1**.

Done! You have completed Assess Your Skills 2

Assess Your Skills Visually

To complete this project, you will need the following file:

- e02_Net_Assets

You will save your workbook as:

- Lastname_Firstname_e02_Net_Assets

Start Excel, and open the file **e02_Net_Assets**. **Save** the workbook in your **Excel Chapter 2** folder as Lastname_Firstname_e02_Net_Assets Create the worksheet and chart sheet as shown in **Figure 1**. Apply the **Solstice** theme. Auto Fill the months in row 4. Insert totals using the **SUM** function. Calculate the *Percent of Total Net Assets* using an absolute cell reference and then format the values as shown. Create the 3-D pie chart, and move the chart to a chart sheet as shown in the figure. Apply the Layout 1 chart layout and then format the chart title and data labels as shown. Format the 3-D pie chart with the **Circle** bevel 3-D shape effect on both the top and bottom, with all the widths and heights set to 512 pt Use the **Metal** surface, and add a shadow and chart area fill. Explode the *Power* pie slice, and rotate the pie chart as shown. Insert the text box shown in the figure. Insert the file name in the left footer of both sheets. Check the spelling of the worksheet. **Save** the file, and then print or submit it as directed by your instructor.

Done! You have completed Assess Your Skills Visually

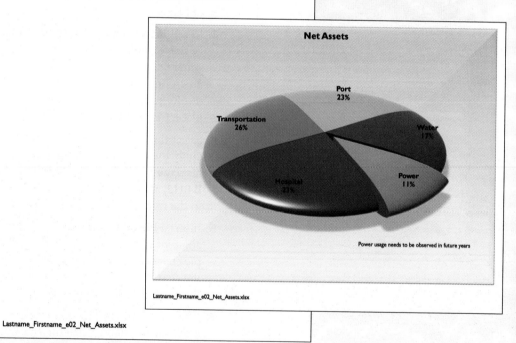

Figure 1

Skills in Context

To complete this project, you will need the following file:

- e02_Budget

You will save your workbook as:

- Lastname_Firstname_02_Budget

During the fourth quarter of this year, the Accounting Department developed a summary of the proposed Aspen Falls budget. Open the file **e02_Budget**, and then save the workbook in your **Excel Chapter 2** folder as Lastname_Firstname_e02_Budget Apply a theme of your choice. Compute the totals and the percentage by which each budget item makes up the total budget. Use an absolute cell reference when computing the percentages. Format the values appropriately. Create an embedded column chart that effectively compares the budget data for the three

months in the fourth quarter. Create an attractive pie chart on a separate chart sheet that describes the quarter percentages. Insert blank rows at the top of the worksheet, and then insert a WordArt with the text Proposed Budget Format the WordArt appropriately. Insert the file name in the left footer of both sheets. Save the workbook, and then print or submit the workbook file as directed by your instructor.

Done! You have completed Skills in Context

Skills and You

To complete this project, you will need the following file:

- New blank Excel workbook

You will save your workbook as:

- Lastname_Firstname_e02_Personal_Budget

What items in your monthly budget might you be able to reduce? A pie chart can point out items on which you might be overspending without realizing it. Create a worksheet for a month's worth of your expenses. Total the expenses, and then create a pie chart to show the percentage by which each item makes up your monthly budget. Format the pie chart appropriately. Insert the filename in the left

footer of the worksheet, and then return to **Normal** view. Save the workbook as Lastname_Firstname_e02_Personal_Budget and print or submit the workbook electronically as directed by your instructor.

Done! You have completed Skills and You

CHAPTER 3

Manage Multiple Worksheets

▶ In an Excel workbook, you can insert and move worksheets, or you can group any number of worksheets and then edit or format the data in all of the worksheets at the same time.

▶ Multiple math operators can be used in one formula, and a formula can refer to a cell in another worksheet.

Your starting screen will look similar to this:

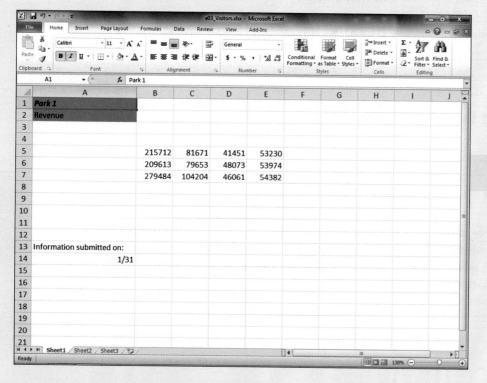

SKILLS

Skills 1-10 Training

At the end of this chapter, you will be able to:

Skill 1 Work with Sheet Tabs

Skill 2 Enter and Format Dates

Skill 3 Clear Cell Contents and Formats

Skill 4 Move, Copy, Paste, and Paste Options

Skill 5 Work with Grouped Worksheets

Skill 6 Use Multiple Math Operators in a Formula

Skill 7 Format Grouped Worksheets

Skill 8 Insert and Move Worksheets

Skill 9 Construct Formulas That Refer to Cells in Other Worksheets

Skill 10 Create Clustered Bar Charts

MORE SKILLS

More Skills 11 Create Organization Charts

More Skills 12 Create Line Charts

More Skills 13 Set and Clear Print Areas

More Skills 14 Insert Hyperlinks

Outcome

Using the skills listed to the left will enable you to create
a workbook containing worksheets like this:

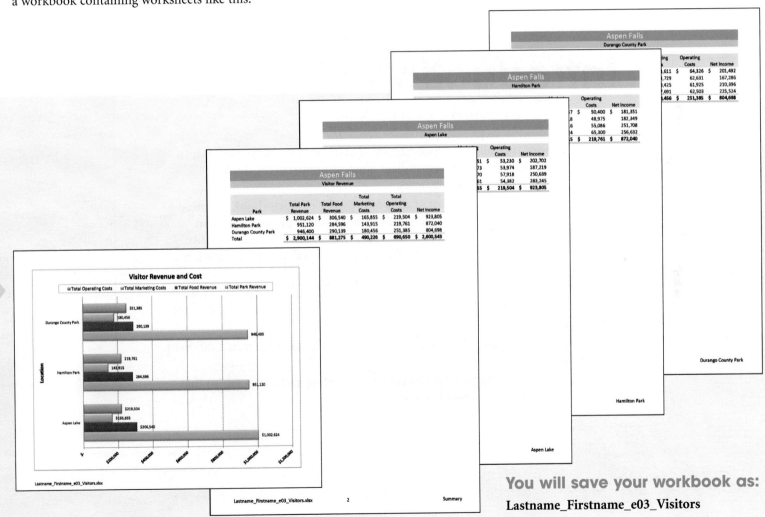

You will save your workbook as:

Lastname_Firstname_e03_Visitors

In this chapter, you will create documents for the Aspen Falls City Hall, which provides essential services for the citizens and visitors of Aspen Falls, California.

Introduction

- ▶ Organizations typically create workbooks that contain multiple worksheets. In such a workbook, the first worksheet often summarizes the detailed information in the other worksheets.

- ▶ When you have a large amount of data to organize in a workbook, dividing the data into logical elements such as locations or time periods and then placing each element in a separate worksheet makes sense. In other words, design a *system* of worksheets instead of trying to fit all of the information on a single worksheet.

- ▶ By grouping worksheets, you can edit and format data in multiple worksheets simultaneously. Data that you edit on the active sheet is reflected in all of the selected sheets.

- ▶ You can copy information from one worksheet and then paste it in a different worksheet.

- ▶ You can manage multiple worksheets by color coding each sheet tab so that you can quickly locate the detailed information.

Time to complete all
10 skills – 50 to 90 minutes

Find your student data files here:

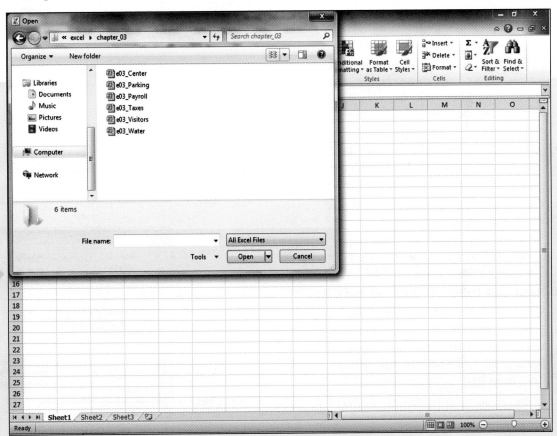

Student data file needed for this chapter:

- e03_Visitors

► When a workbook contains more than one worksheet, you can navigate (move) among worksheets by clicking the sheet tabs.

► To view sheet tabs, use the four ***tab scrolling buttons***—the buttons to the left of the sheet tabs used to display Excel sheet tabs that are not in view.

1. **Start** ● Excel, and then open **e03_Visitors**. Click the **File tab**, and then click **Save As**. In the **Save As** dialog box, navigate to the location where you are saving your files. Click **New folder**, type Excel Chapter 3 and then press [Enter] two times. In the **File name** box, using your own name, type Lastname_Firstname_ e03_Visitors and then press [Enter].

2. Along the bottom of the Excel window, click the **Sheet2 sheet tab**, and then compare your screen with **Figure 1**.

3. Click the **Sheet1 sheet tab**. In cell **A1**, notice the text *Park 1*.

   The first worksheet becomes the active sheet, and cell A1, which is formatted with a green background, displays *Park 1*.

4. Right-click the **Sheet1 sheet tab**, and then compare your screen with **Figure 2**.

5. From the shortcut menu, click **Rename**. On the **Sheet1 sheet tab**, verify the tab name is selected, and then type Aspen Lake Press [Enter].

   You can use up to 31 characters in a sheet tab name. Strive for a short but meaningful name.

■ **Continue to the next page to complete the skill**

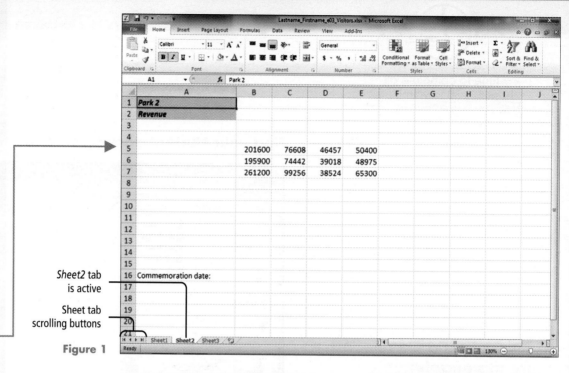

Sheet2 tab is active

Sheet tab scrolling buttons

Figure 1

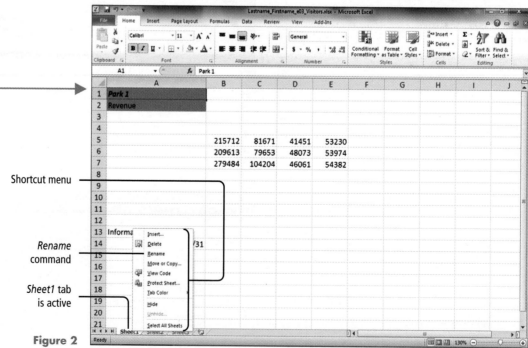

Shortcut menu

Rename command

Sheet1 tab is active

Figure 2

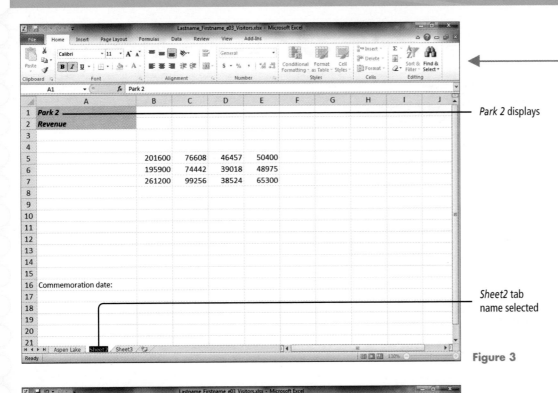

Park 2 displays

Sheet2 tab name selected

Figure 3

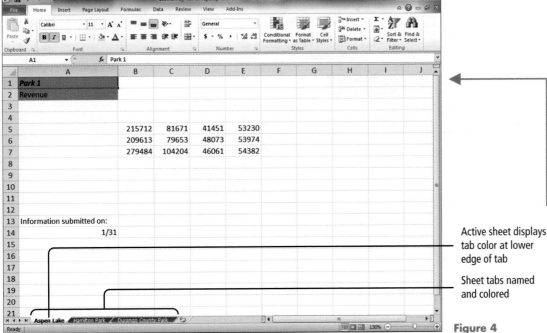

Active sheet displays tab color at lower edge of tab

Sheet tabs named and colored

Figure 4

6. Double-click the **Sheet2 sheet tab** to make it the active sheet and to select the sheet name, as shown in **Figure 3**.

7. With the *Sheet2* sheet tab name selected, type Hamilton Park and then press Enter.

8. Using either of the two methods just practiced, rename the **Sheet3 sheet tab** as Durango County Park and then press Enter.

9. Verify that the *Durango County Park* sheet is the active worksheet. On the **Page Layout tab**, in the **Themes group**, click the **Colors** button. Scroll down, and then click **Metro** to change the theme colors for this workbook.

10. On the **Home tab**, in the **Cells group**, click the **Format** button, and then point to **Tab Color** to display the colors associated with the *Metro* theme colors. Click the fourth color in the first row—**Blue-Gray, Text 2**. Alternately, right-click the sheet tab, and then point to Tab Color.

   When a worksheet is active, the sheet tab color displays only along the lower edge of the sheet tab. When a worksheet is not active, the entire sheet tab is filled with the selected color.

11. Use the technique just practiced to change the sheet tab color of the **Hamilton Park tab** to the sixth color in the first row—**Pink, Accent 2**.

12. Change the sheet tab color of the **Aspen Lake sheet tab** to the last color in the first row—**Teal, Accent 6**. Compare your screen with **Figure 4**.

13. **Save** 💾 the workbook.

■ **You have completed Skill 1 of 10**

► When you enter a date, it is assigned a *serial number*—a sequential number.

► Dates are stored as sequential serial numbers so they can be used in calculations. By default, January 1, 1900 is serial number 1. January 1, 2012 is serial number 40909 because it is 40,908 days after January 1, 1900. Serial numbers make it possible to perform calculations on dates, for example, to find the number of days between two dates by subtracting the older date from the more recent date.

► When you type any of the following values into cells, Excel interprets them as dates: *7/4/10, 4-Jul, 4-Jul-10, Jul-10*. When typing in these date formats, the ⁻ (hyphen) key and the / (forward slash) key function identically.

► You can enter months using the entire name or the first three characters. Years can be entered as two digits or four digits. When you leave the year off, the current year will be inserted.

1. On the **Aspen Lake sheet**, click cell **A14**, and then notice that in the cell the date displays as *1/31*. In the **formula bar**, notice that the underlying value displays as *1/31/2012*, as shown in **Figure 1**.

2. On the **Home tab**, in the **Number group**, click the **Number Format arrow**, as shown in **Figure 2**.

   Here you can select popular date, time, and number formats, or click *More Number Formats* at the bottom of the list to display additional built-in number formats.

■ **Continue to the next page to complete the skill**

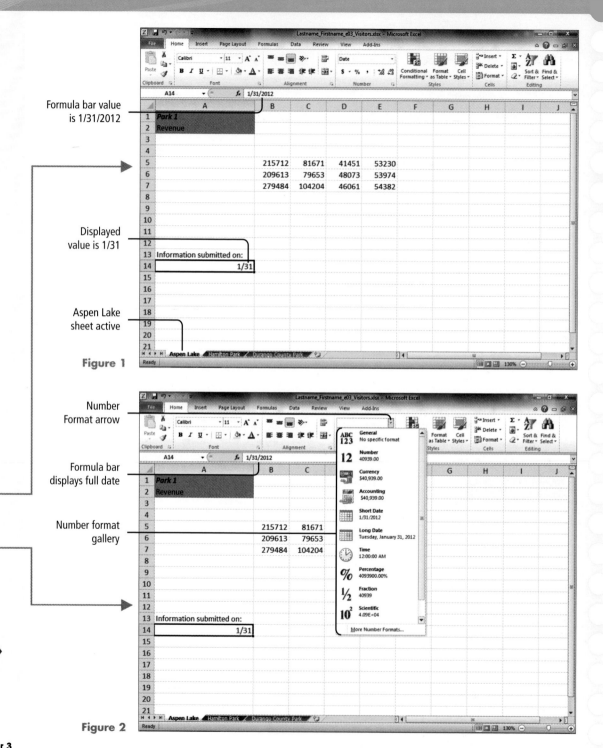

Formula bar value is 1/31/2012

Displayed value is 1/31

Aspen Lake sheet active

Figure 1

Number Format arrow

Formula bar displays full date

Number format gallery

Figure 2

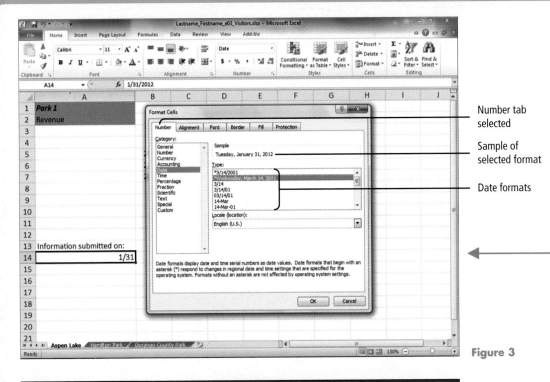

Figure 3

Date Format AutoComplete

Date Typed As	Completed by Excel As
7/4/11	7/4/2011
7-4-98	7/4/1998
7/4 or 7-4	4-Jul (current year assumed)
July 4 or Jul 4	4-Jul (current year assumed)
Jul/4 or Jul-4	4-Jul (current year assumed)
July 4, 1998	4-Jul-98
July 2012	Jul-12
July 1998	Jul-98

Figure 4

3. At the bottom of the Number Format list, click **More Number Formats**. In the displayed **Format Cells** dialog box, on the **Number tab**, under **Type**, click ***Wednesday, March 14, 2001** to show a sample of the selected date format, as shown in **Figure 3**.

> The date *Wednesday, March 14, 2001* will not display in your worksheet. This is a sample of a format that can be applied to your current date.

4. Under **Type**, scroll down, click **March 14, 2001**, and then click **OK**.

> The date January 31, 2012 displays in cell A14.

5. Click the **Hamilton Park sheet tab** to make it the active worksheet, and then click cell **A17**. Type 8/11/98 and then on the **formula bar**, click the **Enter** button ✔.

> In cell A17, the year changed from *98* to *1998*. When a two-digit year between 30 and 99 is entered, a 20th-century date is assumed.

6. Click the **Durango County Park sheet tab**, and then click cell **A17**. Hold down (Ctrl) and press (;)—the semicolon key. Press (Enter) to confirm the entry.

> The (Ctrl) + (;) shortcut enters the current date, obtained from your computer, into the selected cell using the default date format. The table in **Figure 4** summarizes how Excel interprets various date formats.

7. Save 🖫 the workbook.

- **You have completed Skill 2 of 10**

▶ Cells can contain formatting, comments, and *contents*—underlying formulas and data.

▶ You can clear the contents of a cell, the formatting of a cell, or both.

1. Click the **Aspen Lake sheet tab** to make it the active worksheet, and then click cell **A1**. On the **Home tab**, in the **Editing group**, click the **Clear** button ◿, and then click **Clear Contents**.

   Alternately, you can press Delete to clear the contents of a cell.

2. Look at cell **A1**, and verify that text has been cleared but that the fill color applied to the cell still displays, as shown in **Figure 1**.

   Deleting the contents of a cell does *not* delete the formatting of the cell.

3. In cell **A1**, type Aspen Lake and then on the **formula bar**, click the **Enter** button ✓.

4. With cell **A1** still selected, in the **Editing group**, click the **Clear** button ◿, and then click **Clear Formats**. Compare your screen with **Figure 2**.

   Clear Formats deletes the formatting from the cell but does not delete the cell contents.

■ **Continue to the next page to complete the skill**

Contents cleared, formatting not cleared

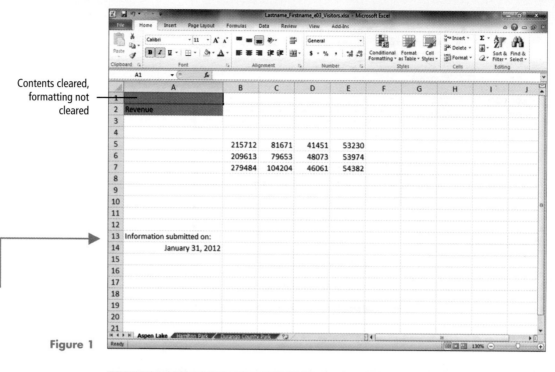

Figure 1

Cell formats cleared, contents not cleared

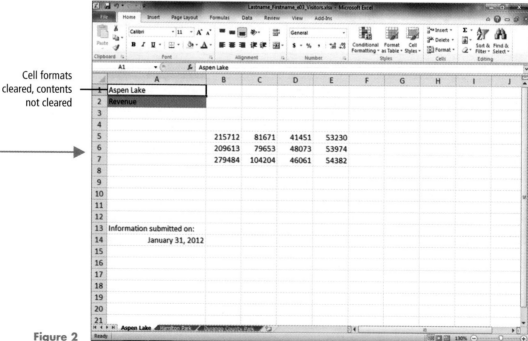

Figure 2

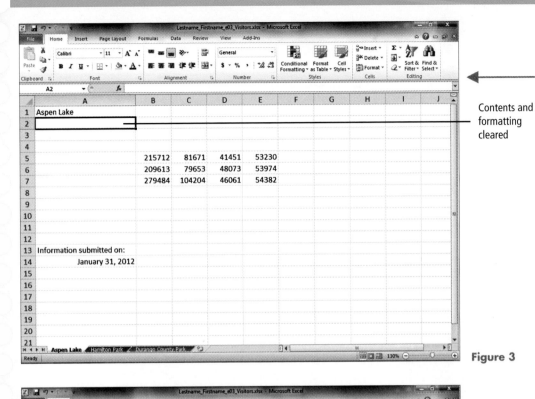

Contents and formatting cleared

Figure 3

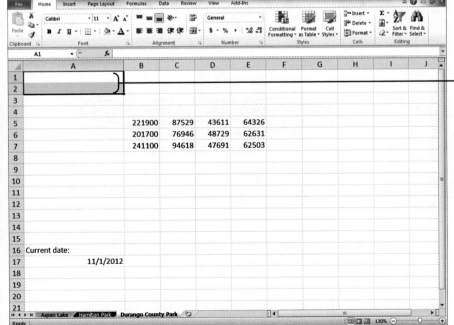

Cell contents and formats cleared

Figure 4

5. Select cell **A2**. On the **Home tab**, in the **Editing group**, click the **Clear** button, and then click **Clear All**. Compare your screen with **Figure 3**.

Clear All deletes both the cell contents and the formatting.

6. In cell **A14**, use the technique just practiced to clear the formatting from the cell. In the **Number group**, verify that *General* displays as the number format of the cell. Notice that the date format is removed from the cell and that the underlying serial number—a sequential number—displays.

The date, *January 31, 2012*, displays as 40939—the number of days since the reference date of January 1, 1900.

7. In the **Number group**, click the **Number Format arrow**, click **Long Date**, and then verify that the serial number in cell A14 again displays as a date.

The long date format is applied to the date—*Tuesday, January 31, 2012*.

8. Display the **Hamilton Park sheet**, and then select the range **A1:A2**. In the **Editing group**, click the **Clear** button, and then click **Clear All**.

9. Display the **Durango County Park sheet**. Select the range **A1:A2**. In the **Editing group**, click the **Clear** button, and then click **Clear All**. Compare your screen with **Figure 4**.

10. Make **Aspen Lake** the active worksheet, and then **Save** the workbook.

■ **You have completed Skill 3 of 10**

► Data from cells and ranges can be copied and then pasted to other cells in the same worksheet, to other worksheets, or to worksheets in another workbook.

► The *Clipboard* is a temporary storage area for text and graphics. When you perform either the Copy command or the Cut command, the selected data is placed in the Clipboard, from which the data is available for pasting.

1. Select the range **A13:A14**. Point to the lower edge of the black border surrounding the selected range until the pointer displays. Drag downward until the ScreenTip displays *A16:A17*, as shown in **Figure 1**, and then release the mouse button to complete the move.

    Drag and drop is a method of moving objects in which you point to the selection and then drag it to a new location.

2. Click cell **A4**, type Visitor Type and then press [Tab]. Type the following titles in row **4**, pressing [Tab] after each title: Park Revenue, Food Revenue, Marketing Costs, Operating Costs, Net Income

3. Select columns **B:F**. In the **Cells group**, click the **Format** button, and then click **Column Width**. In the **Column Width** dialog box, select the displayed number, type 12 and then click **OK**. Compare your screen with **Figure 2**.

4. Select the range **A4:F4**. In the **Styles group**, click the **Cell Styles** button, and then click **20% - Accent6**. In the **Alignment group**, click the **Wrap Text** button and the **Center** button.

■ **Continue to the next page to complete the skill**

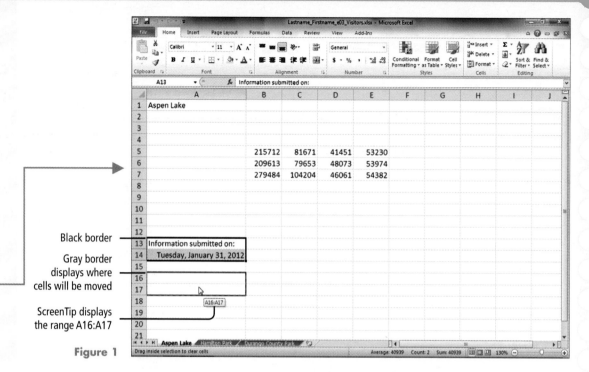

Black border
Gray border displays where cells will be moved
ScreenTip displays the range A16:A17

Figure 1

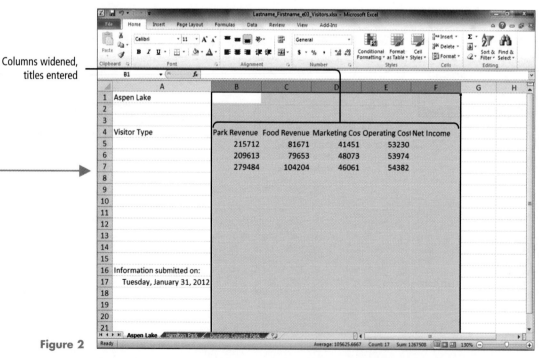

Columns widened, titles entered

Figure 2

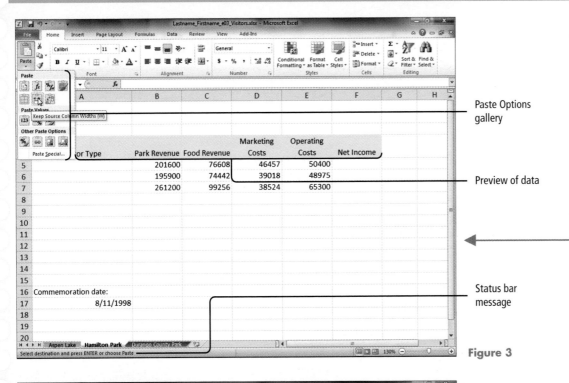

Paste Options gallery

Preview of data

Status bar message

Figure 3

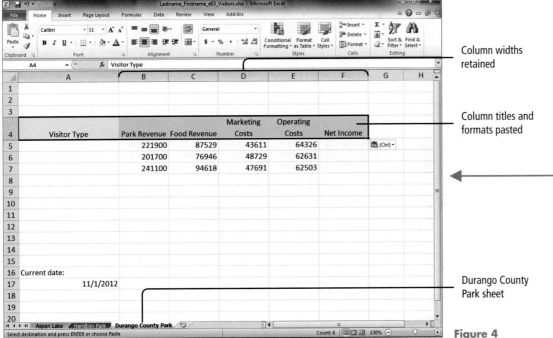

Column widths retained

Column titles and formats pasted

Durango County Park sheet

Figure 4

5. With the range **A4:F4** still selected, in the **Clipboard group**, click the **Copy** button.

A moving border surrounds the selected range, and a message on the status bar indicates *Select destination and press ENTER or choose Paste*, confirming that your selected range has been copied to the Clipboard.

6. Display the **Hamilton Park sheet**, and then click cell **A4**. In the **Clipboard group**, click the lower half of the **Paste** button to display the **Paste Preview** gallery. Point at the various Paste Options to preview the pasted text, as shown in **Figure 3**.

7. In the **Paste Options** gallery, click the second option in the second row— **Keep Source Column Widths**.

The column titles are pasted, and the column widths from the source worksheet are retained.

When pasting a range of cells, you need to select only the cell in the upper left corner of the *paste area*—the target destination for data that has been cut or copied. When an item is pasted, it is not removed from the Clipboard, as indicated by the status bar message.

8. Display the **Durango County Park** worksheet, and then click cell **A4**. Using the technique just practiced, paste the column titles using the Paste Option **Keep Source Column Widths**. Compare your screen with **Figure 4**.

9. Display the **Aspen Lake sheet**, and then Save the workbook.

■ **You have completed Skill 4 of 10**

► You can group any number of worksheets in a workbook. After the worksheets are grouped, you can edit data or format cells in all the grouped worksheets at the same time.

► Grouping worksheets is useful when you are creating or modifying a set of worksheets that are similar in purpose and structure.

1. Right-click the **Aspen Lake sheet tab**, and then from the shortcut menu, click **Select All Sheets**.

2. At the top of the screen, on the title bar, verify that *[Group]* displays, as shown in **Figure 1**.

   All the worksheets are selected, as indicated by *[Group]* on the title bar, and the sheet tab names are underlined in the sheet tab color. An underline on a worksheet tab indicates that the worksheet is active or selected within a group.

3. Click cell **A5**, type Local and then press [Enter]. In cell **A6**, type Domestic and then press [Enter]. In cell **A7**, type International and then press [Enter].

4. Select the range **A5:A7**. In the **Styles group**, click the **Cell Styles** button, and then under **Titles and Headings**, click **40% - Accent6**.

5. Display the **Hamilton Park sheet**, and verify that the row labels and formats you entered on the **Aspen Lake sheet** display. Compare your screen with **Figure 2**.

   Data and formats are entered on all grouped worksheets.

■ **Continue to the next page to complete the skill** ▶

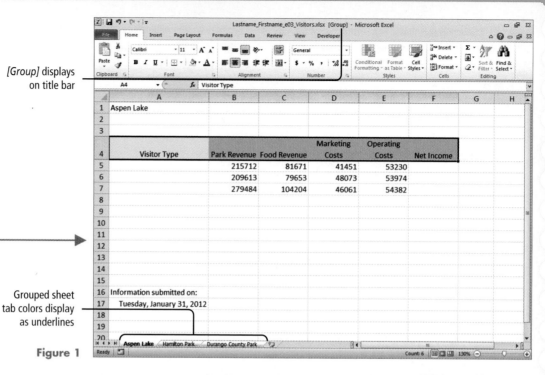

[Group] displays on title bar

Grouped sheet tab colors display as underlines

Figure 1

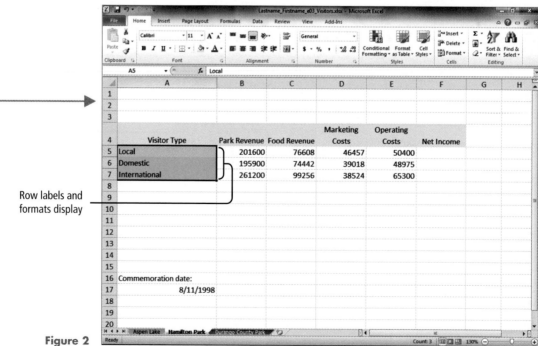

Row labels and formats display

Figure 2

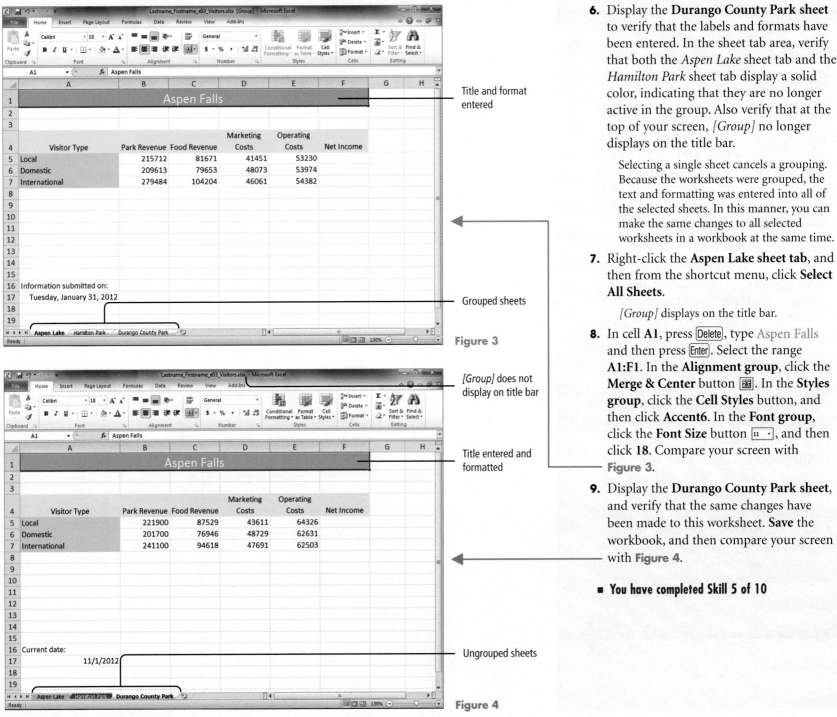

Title and format entered

Grouped sheets

Figure 3

[Group] does not display on title bar

Title entered and formatted

Ungrouped sheets

Figure 4

6. Display the **Durango County Park sheet** to verify that the labels and formats have been entered. In the sheet tab area, verify that both the *Aspen Lake* sheet tab and the *Hamilton Park* sheet tab display a solid color, indicating that they are no longer active in the group. Also verify that at the top of your screen, *[Group]* no longer displays on the title bar.

Selecting a single sheet cancels a grouping. Because the worksheets were grouped, the text and formatting was entered into all of the selected sheets. In this manner, you can make the same changes to all selected worksheets in a workbook at the same time.

7. Right-click the **Aspen Lake sheet tab**, and then from the shortcut menu, click **Select All Sheets**.

[Group] displays on the title bar.

8. In cell **A1**, press Delete, type Aspen Falls and then press Enter. Select the range **A1:F1**. In the **Alignment group**, click the **Merge & Center** button ⊞. In the **Styles group**, click the **Cell Styles** button, and then click **Accent6**. In the **Font group**, click the **Font Size** button ⒒ ▾, and then click **18**. Compare your screen with **Figure 3**.

9. Display the **Durango County Park sheet**, and verify that the same changes have been made to this worksheet. **Save** the workbook, and then compare your screen with **Figure 4**.

■ **You have completed Skill 5 of 10**

▶ When you combine several math operators in a single formula, Excel follows a set of mathematical rules for performing calculations within a formula, called **operator precedence.** First, expressions within parentheses are calculated. Second, multiplication and division are performed before addition and subtraction.

▶ When a formula contains operators with the same precedence level, Excel evaluates the operators from left to right. Multiplication and division are considered to be on the same level of precedence. Addition and subtraction are considered to be on the same level of precedence.

1. Display the **Aspen Lake sheet**. Click cell **A2**, type Aspen Lake and then press (Enter). Display the **Hamilton Park sheet**. Click cell **A2**, type Hamilton Park and then press (Enter). Display the **Durango County Park sheet**. Click cell **A2**, type Durango County Park and then press (Enter). Compare your screen with **Figure 1.**

2. Right-click the **Durango County Park sheet tab**, and then click **Select All Sheets**.

3. Select the range **A2:F2**, and then in the **Alignment group**, click the **Merge & Center** button. In the **Styles group**, click the **Cell Styles** button, and then click **40% - Accent6**.

4. Click cell **A13**, type Submitted by: and then press (Enter). In cell **A14**, using your first and last names, type Your Name and then press (Enter). Compare your screen with **Figure 2.**

■ **Continue to the next page to complete the skill**

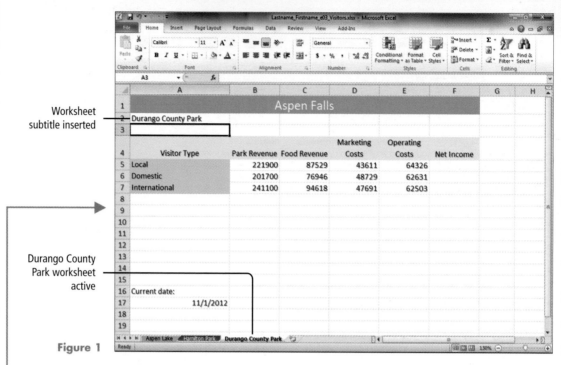

Worksheet subtitle inserted

Durango County Park worksheet active

Figure 1

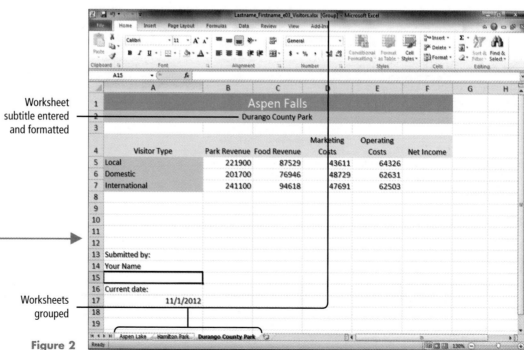

Worksheet subtitle entered and formatted

Worksheets grouped

Figure 2

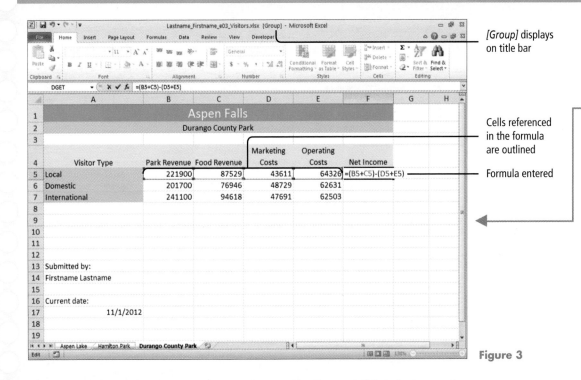

[Group] displays on title bar

Cells referenced in the formula are outlined

Formula entered

Figure 3

5. Verify that *[Group]* still displays on the title bar. If necessary, right-click a sheet tab, and click **Select All Sheets**. Click cell **F5**, enter the formula =(B5+C5)-(D5+E5) and then compare your screen with **Figure 3**.

   The formula *Net Income = Total Revenue – Total Cost* is represented by *(Park Revenue + Food Revenue) – (Marketing Costs + Operating Costs)*. By placing parentheses in the formula, the revenue is first added, the costs are added next, and then the total costs are subtracted from the total revenues. Without the parentheses, the formula would give an incorrect result.

6. On the **formula bar**, click the **Enter** button ✓. Use the **fill handle** to copy the formula down through cell **F7**.

   Recall that because the worksheets are grouped, the formulas have been entered on all three worksheets.

7. Verify that the formula results display in the **Hamilton Park** and **Aspen Lake** sheets.

8. Click the **Durango County Park sheet tab** to make it the active worksheet, and verify that the worksheets are no longer grouped. Click cell **A17**, and then point to the upper edge of the black border surrounding the cell until the ⬚ pointer displays. Drag up to move the cell contents up to cell **A16**. In the message box *Do you want to replace the contents of the destination cells?* click **OK**. Compare your screen with **Figure 4**.

9. Save ⬚ the workbook.

■ **You have completed Skill 6 of 10**

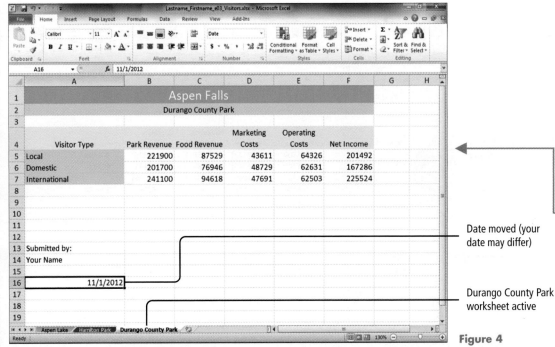

Date moved (your date may differ)

Durango County Park worksheet active

Figure 4

► When worksheets are grouped, any changes made to a single worksheet are made to each worksheet in the group. For example, if you change the width of a column or add a row, all the worksheets in the group are changed in the same manner.

1. Right-click the **Hamilton Park sheet tab**, and then click **Select All Sheets**.

2. In the row heading area, point to row **7** to display the ➡ pointer. Right-click, and then compare your screen with **Figure 1**.

3. From the shortcut menu, click **Insert** to insert a new blank row above the *International* row. In cell **A7**, type Families and press Tab.

4. Click the **Aspen Lake sheet tab** to make it the active worksheet and to cancel the grouping of the worksheets. Beginning in cell **B7**, enter the following *Families* data for Aspen Lake:

   297815   41012   30270   57918

5. Click the **Hamilton Park sheet tab**, and then beginning in cell **B7**, enter the following *Families* data for Hamilton Park:

   292420   34290   19916   55086

6. Click the **Durango County Park sheet tab**, and then beginning in cell **B7**, enter the following *Families* data for **Durango County Park**:

   281700   31046   40425   61925

7. Click each of the sheet tabs, and then verify that you entered the values correctly. Click the **Durango County Park sheet tab**, and then compare your screen with **Figure 2**.

■ **Continue to the next page to complete the skill**

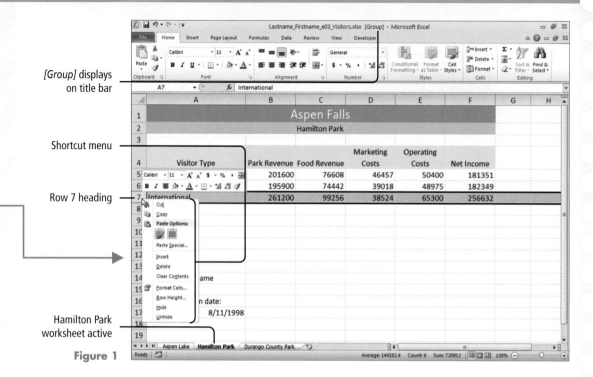

[Group] displays on title bar

Shortcut menu

Row 7 heading

Hamilton Park worksheet active

Figure 1

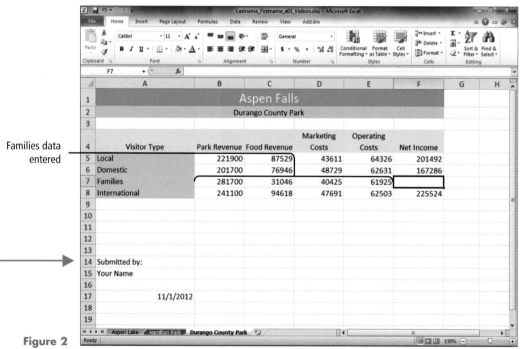

Families data entered

Figure 2

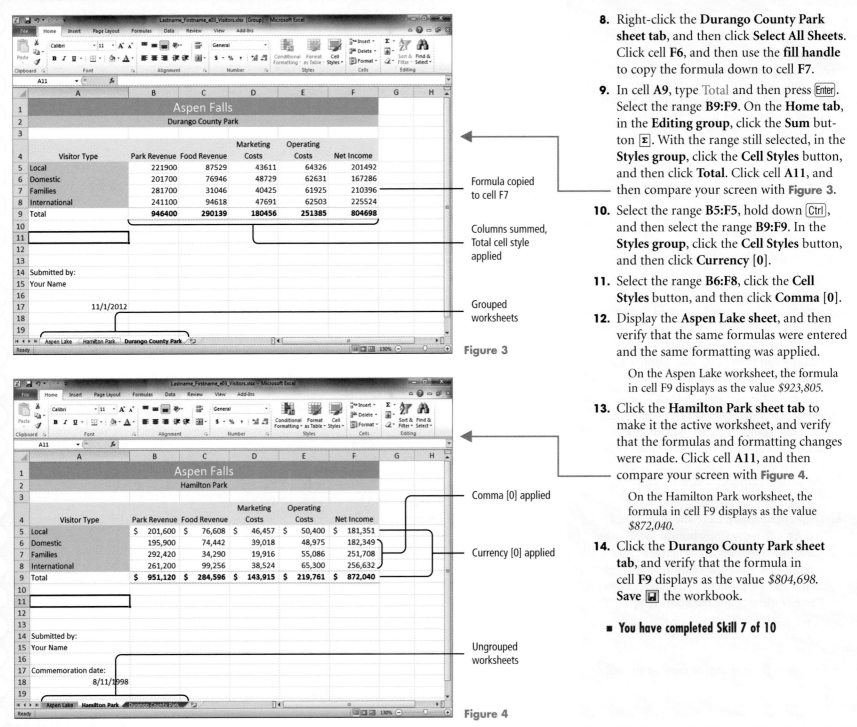

Figure 3

Figure 4

8. Right-click the **Durango County Park sheet tab**, and then click **Select All Sheets**. Click cell **F6**, and then use the **fill handle** to copy the formula down to cell **F7**.

9. In cell **A9**, type Total and then press Enter. Select the range **B9:F9**. On the **Home tab**, in the **Editing group**, click the **Sum** button Σ. With the range still selected, in the **Styles group**, click the **Cell Styles** button, and then click **Total**. Click cell **A11**, and then compare your screen with **Figure 3**.

10. Select the range **B5:F5**, hold down Ctrl, and then select the range **B9:F9**. In the **Styles group**, click the **Cell Styles** button, and then click **Currency [0]**.

11. Select the range **B6:F8**, click the **Cell Styles** button, and then click **Comma [0]**.

12. Display the **Aspen Lake sheet**, and then verify that the same formulas were entered and the same formatting was applied.

    On the Aspen Lake worksheet, the formula in cell F9 displays as the value *$923,805*.

13. Click the **Hamilton Park sheet tab** to make it the active worksheet, and verify that the formulas and formatting changes were made. Click cell **A11**, and then compare your screen with **Figure 4**.

    On the Hamilton Park worksheet, the formula in cell F9 displays as the value *$872,040*.

14. Click the **Durango County Park sheet tab**, and verify that the formula in cell **F9** displays as the value *$804,698*. Save 🔲 the workbook.

■ **You have completed Skill 7 of 10**

► To organize a workbook, you can move sheet tabs into any order you desire.

► You can add new worksheets to accommodate new information.

1. To the right of the **Durango County Park sheet tab**, click the **Insert Worksheet** button.

   A new blank worksheet is inserted with a unique name such as *Sheet1* or *Sheet2*.

2. Double-click the **sheet tab** just inserted, type Summary and then press Enter. Compare your screen with **Figure 1**.

3. In cell **A4**, type Park and then press Tab. In cell **B4**, type Total Park Revenue and then press Tab. In cell **C4**, type Total Food Revenue and then press Tab. In cell **D4**, type Total Marketing Costs and then press Tab. In cell **E4**, type Total Operating Costs and then press Tab. In cell **F4**, type Net Income and then press Enter. Compare your screen with **Figure 2**.

4. Select cell **A1**, and then in the **Cells group**, click the **Format** button, and then click **Column Width**. In the **Column Width** dialog box, type 20 and then click **OK**. Select columns **B:F**, and then using the same technique, widen the columns to *12*.

5. Display the **Aspen Lake sheet**, and click cell **A4**. Click the Copy button. Display the **Summary sheet**, and then select the range **A4:F4**. Click the **Paste button arrow**. In the **Paste Options** gallery, under **Other Paste Options**, click **Formatting**.

   The formatting is applied to the range A4:F4.

■ **Continue to the next page to complete the skill**

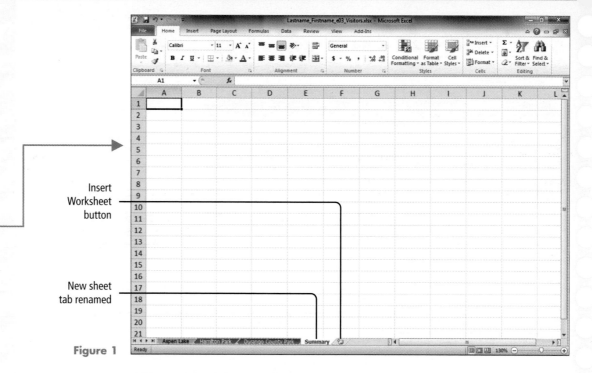

Insert Worksheet button

New sheet tab renamed

Figure 1

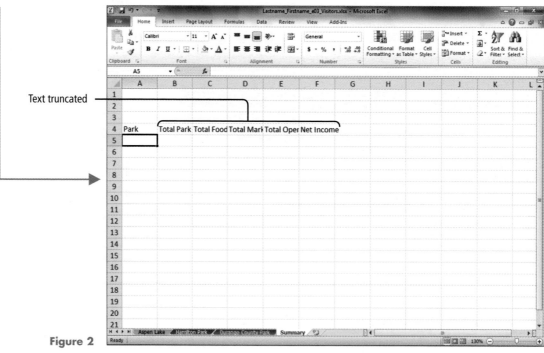

Text truncated

Figure 2

6. In cell **A5**, type Aspen Lake and then press Enter. In cell **A6**, type Hamilton Park and then in cell **A7**, type Durango County Park

7. Display the **Aspen Lake sheet**, and click cell **A1**. In the **Clipboard group**, click the **Copy** button. Display the **Summary sheet**, and click cell **A1**. In the **Clipboard group**, click the **Paste** button.

   The cell contents, including both the text *Aspen Falls* and the formatting, are pasted.

8. On the **Summary sheet**, in cell **A2**, type Visitor Revenue and press Enter. Display the **Aspen Lake sheet**, and click cell **A2**. Click the **Copy** button. Display the **Summary sheet**, and click cell **A2**. In the **Clipboard group**, click the **Paste button arrow**. In the **Paste Options** gallery, under **Other Paste Options**, click **Formatting**, and then compare your screen with **Figure 3**.

   Only the cell formatting is pasted.

9. Right-click the **Summary sheet tab**, click **Tab Color**, and then click the seventh color in the first row—**Gold, Accent 3**.

10. Point to the **Summary sheet tab**, hold down the left mouse button to display a small black triangle—a caret—and then notice that a small paper icon attaches to the mouse pointer.

11. Drag to the left until the caret and mouse pointer are to the left of the **Aspen Lake tab**, as shown in **Figure 4**.

12. Release the left mouse button to complete the worksheet move.

13. **Save** the workbook.

■ **You have completed Skill 8 of 10**

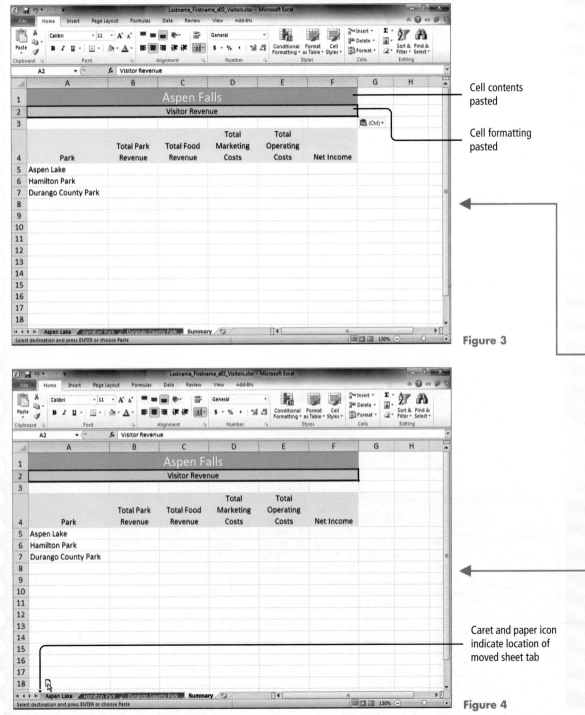

Cell contents pasted

Cell formatting pasted

Figure 3

Caret and paper icon indicate location of moved sheet tab

Figure 4

▶ A **summary sheet** is a worksheet that displays and summarizes totals from other worksheets. A **detail sheet** is a worksheet with cells referred to by summary sheet formulas.

▶ Changes made to the detail sheets that affect their totals will automatically recalculate and display on the summary sheet.

1. On the **Summary sheet**, click cell **B5**. Type = and then click the **Aspen Lake sheet tab**. On the **Aspen Lake sheet**, click cell **B9**, and then press Enter.

   The Summary worksheet displays the value from cell B9 in the Aspen Lake worksheet.

2. Click cell **B5**. In the **formula bar**, notice that the cell reference in the underlying formula includes both a worksheet reference and a cell reference, as shown in **Figure 1**.

   By using a formula of this type, changes made to cell B9 of the *Aspen Lake* worksheet will be automatically updated in this *Summary* worksheet.

3. Click cell **B6**, type = and then click the **Hamilton Park sheet tab**. On the **Hamilton Park sheet**, click cell **B9**, and then press Enter.

4. On the **Summary sheet**, repeat the technique just practiced to place the value in cell **B9** from the **Durango County Park sheet** in cell **B7** of the **Summary sheet**.

5. On the **Summary sheet**, select the range **B5:B7**. Point to the **fill handle**, and then drag to the right to fill the formulas through column **F**. Click cell **F7**, and compare your screen with **Figure 2**.

■ **Continue to the next page to complete the skill**

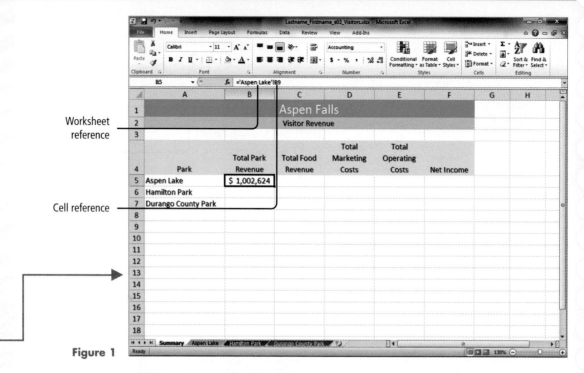

Worksheet reference

Cell reference

Figure 1

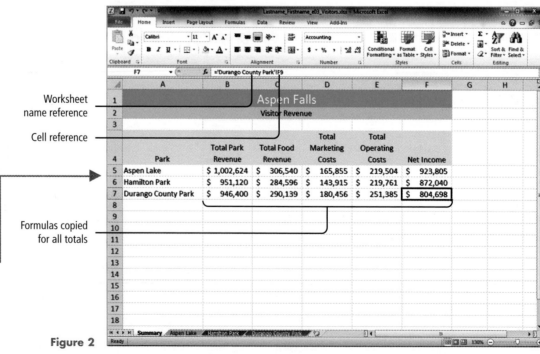

Worksheet name reference

Cell reference

Formulas copied for all totals

Figure 2

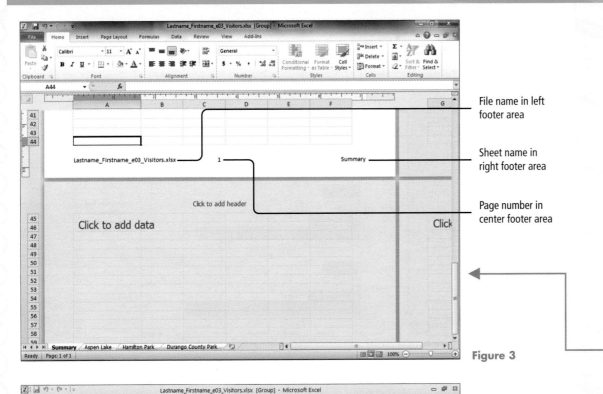

File name in left footer area

Sheet name in right footer area

Page number in center footer area

Figure 3

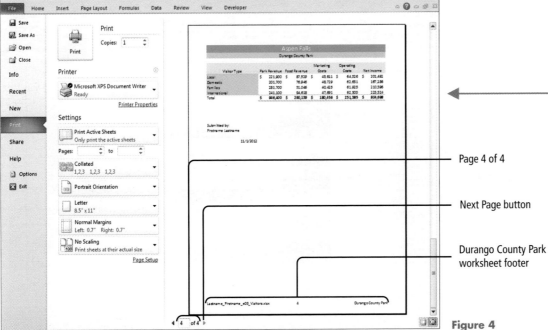

Page 4 of 4

Next Page button

Durango County Park worksheet footer

Figure 4

6. On the **Summary sheet**, in cell **A8**, type Total and then select the range **B8:F8**. In the **Editing group**, click the **Sum** button Σ, and then apply the **Total** cell style. Select the range **B6:F7**, and then apply the **Comma [0]** cell style.

7. Right-click the **Summary sheet tab**, and then click **Select All Sheets**. On the **Insert tab**, in the **Text group**, click the **Header & Footer** button. Insert the **File Name** in the left footer.

8. Click the **center section** of the footer, and then in the **Header & Footer Elements group**, click the **Page Number** button. Click the right section of the footer, and then in the **Header & Footer Elements group**, click the **Sheet Name** button. Click in a cell just above the footer to exit the **Footer area**, and then compare your screen with **Figure 3**.

9. On the lower right side of the status bar, click the **Normal** button. Hold down Ctrl, and press Home. Click the **File tab**, and then click **Print**. At the bottom of the screen, click the **Next Page** button ▶ three times to view each of the four worksheets, and then compare your screen with **Figure 4**.

   Because the worksheets are grouped, all four worksheets will be previewed and the footer will display in each worksheet.

10. Click the **Home tab**. Right-click the **Summary sheet tab**, and then click **Ungroup Sheets**.

11. **Save** the workbook.

■ **You have completed Skill 9 of 10**

► A *clustered bar chart* is a chart type that is useful when you want to compare values across categories; bar charts organize categories along the vertical axis and values along the horizontal axis.

1. On the **Summary sheet**, select the range **A4:E7**. On the **Insert tab**, in the **Charts group**, click the **Bar** button, and then under **2-D Bar**, click **Clustered Bar**.

2. On the **Design tab**, in the **Location group**, click the **Move Chart** button. In the **Move Chart** dialog box, select the **New sheet** option button, type Revenue and Cost Chart and then click **OK**.

   The chart is moved to a chart sheet.

3. On the **Design tab**, in the **Data group**, click the **Switch Row/Column** button. Compare your screen with **Figure 1**.

   Because you want to look at revenue and costs by location, displaying the locations on the vertical axis is useful.

4. In the **Chart Layouts group**, click the **More** button ⊡, and then click **Layout 8**. In the **Chart Styles group**, click the **More** button ⊡, and then click **Style 26**.

5. On the **Layout tab**, in the **Axes group**, click the **Axes** button. Point to **Primary Horizontal Axis**, and then click **More Primary Horizontal Axis Options**. On the left side of the **Format Axis** dialog box, click **Alignment**, and then on the right, in the **Custom angle box**, type -40 Click **Close**, and then compare your screen with **Figure 2**.

■ **Continue to the next page to complete the skill**

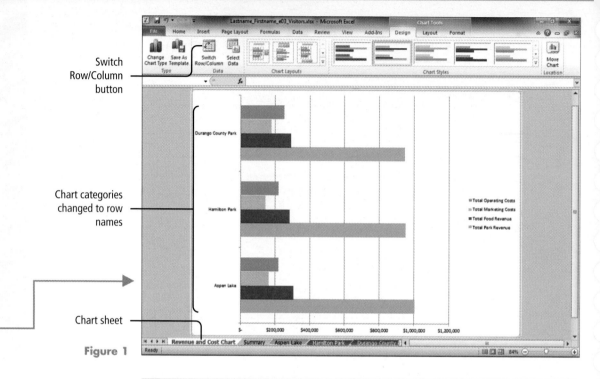

Switch Row/Column button

Chart categories changed to row names

Chart sheet

Figure 1

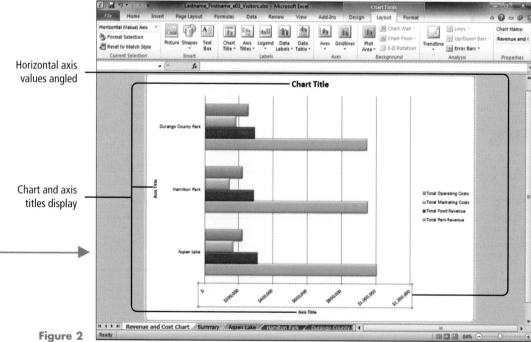

Horizontal axis values angled

Chart and axis titles display

Figure 2

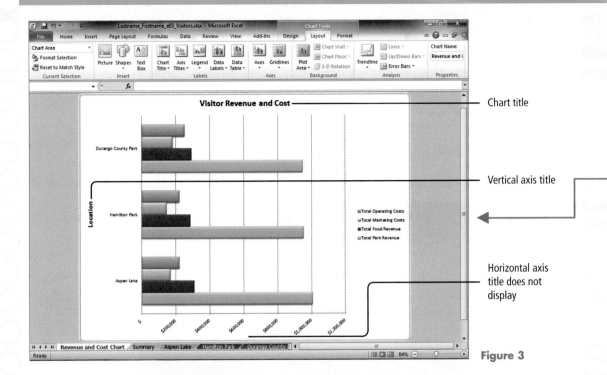

Chart title

Vertical axis title

Horizontal axis title does not display

Figure 3

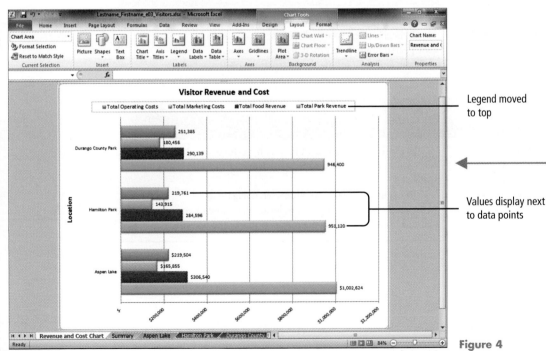

Legend moved to top

Values display next to data points

Figure 4

6. Click the **Chart Title**. Type Visitor Revenue and Cost and then press Enter.

7. On the left side of the chart, click the vertical **Axis Title**. Type Location and then press Enter. Right-click the *Location* title, and then on the Mini toolbar, change the **Font Size** to **14**. At the bottom of the chart, click the horizontal **Axis Title**, press Delete, and then compare your screen with **Figure 3**.

8. On the **Layout tab**, in the **Labels group**, click the **Legend** button, and then click **More Legend Options**. In the **Format Legend** dialog box, under **Legend Position**, select the **Top** option button. On the left, click **Border Color**, and then on the right, select the **Solid line** option button. Click **Close**. Right-click the legend, and then on the Mini toolbar, change the **Font Size** to **12**.

9. In the **Labels group**, click the **Data Labels** button, and then click **Outside End**. Compare your screen with **Figure 4**.

10. On the **Insert tab**, in the **Text group**, click the **Header & Footer** button. In the **Page Setup** dialog box, click the **Custom Footer** button. Click the **Insert File Name** button, and then click **OK** two times.

11. **Save** the workbook. Print or submit your file as directed by your instructor. To print, click the **File tab**, and then click **Print**. Under Settings, click **Print Active Sheets**, and then click **Print Entire Workbook**. Click the **Print** button. **Exit** Excel.

Done! You have completed Skill 10 of 10 and your document is complete!

The following More Skills are located at **www.pearsonhighered.com/skills**

More Skills Create Organization Charts

You can add SmartArt graphics to a worksheet to create timelines, illustrate processes, or show relationships. When you click the SmartArt button on the Ribbon, you can select from among a broad array of graphics, including an organization chart. An organization chart graphically represents the relationships between individuals and groups in an organization.

In More Skills 11, you will insert and modify a SmartArt graphic organization chart.

To begin, open your web browser, navigate to www.pearsonhighered.com/skills, locate the name of your textbook, and then follow the instructions on the website.

More Skills Create Line Charts

Use a line chart when you want to compare more than one set of values over time. Time is displayed along the bottom axis and the data point values are connected with a line. The curves and directions of the lines make trends obvious to the reader.

In More Skills 12, you will create a line chart comparing three sets of values.

To begin, open your web browser, navigate to www.pearsonhighered.com/skills, locate the name of your textbook, and then follow the instructions on the website.

More Skills Set and Clear Print Areas

If you are likely to print the same portion of a particular worksheet over and over again, you can save time by setting a print area.

In More Skills 13, you will set print areas in a worksheet.

To begin, open your web browser, navigate to www.pearsonhighered.com/skills, locate the name of your textbook, and then follow the instructions on the website.

More Skills Insert Hyperlinks

You can insert a hyperlink in a worksheet that can link to a file, a location in a file, a web page on the World Wide Web, or a web page on an organization's intranet. Creating a hyperlink in a workbook is a convenient way to provide quick access to related information.

In More Skills 14, you will insert hyperlinks to related information on the web and to other worksheets in the workbook.

To begin, open your web browser, navigate to www.pearsonhighered.com/skills, locate the name of your textbook, and then follow the instructions on the website.

Key Terms

Online Help Skills

1. **Start** Excel. In the upper right corner of the Excel window, click the **Help** button. In the Help window, click the **Maximize** button.

2. Click in the search box, type move formula and then click the **Search** button. In the search results, click **Move or copy a formula**. Compare your screen with **Figure 1**.

Figure 1

3. Read the article's introduction, and then read the sections **Move a formula** and **Copy a formula** to see if you can answer the following: What can happen to a cell reference when you move or copy a formula?

Matching

Match each term in the second column with its correct definition in the first column by writing the letter of the term on the blank line in front of the correct definition.

____ **1.** The labels along the lower border of the workbook window that identify each worksheet.

____ **2.** Buttons to the left of the sheet tabs used to display Excel sheet tabs that are not in view.

____ **3.** A sequential number assigned to a date.

____ **4.** A temporary storage area for text and graphics.

____ **5.** A method of moving or copying the content of selected cells in which you point to the selection and then drag it to a new location.

____ **6.** The target destination for data that has been cut or copied using the Clipboard.

____ **7.** The mathematical rules for performing calculations within a formula.

____ **8.** A worksheet that displays and summarizes totals from other worksheets in a workbook.

____ **9.** A worksheet that contains the detailed information in a workbook.

____ **10.** A chart type that is useful when you want to compare values across categories; categories are typically organized along the vertical axis, and the values along the horizontal axis.

A Clipboard

B Clustered bar chart

C Detail sheet

D Drag and drop

E Operator precedence

F Paste area

G Serial number

H Sheet tabs

I Summary sheet

J Tab scrolling buttons

Multiple Choice

Choose the correct answer.

1. In an Excel workbook, you can do this.
   - A. Insert only one worksheet
   - B. Move worksheets
   - C. Move only one worksheet

2. Grouped worksheets can be edited and formatted in this way.
   - A. All at the same time
   - B. Only one worksheet at a time
   - C. Only once

3. Deleting the contents of a cell also deletes this.
   - A. Only the contents
   - B. Only the format
   - C. Both contents and format

4. When pasting a range of cells, this cell needs to be selected in the paste area.
   - A. Bottom right cell
   - B. Center cell
   - C. Top left cell

5. When grouping worksheets in a workbook, you can group this number of worksheets.
   - A. Only two
   - B. Only three
   - C. Any number

6. If a workbook contains grouped worksheets, this word will display on the title bar.
   - A. [Collection]
   - B. [Set]
   - C. [Group]

7. When a formula contains operators with the same precedence level, the operators are evaluated in this order.
   - A. Left to right
   - B. Right to left
   - C. From the center out

8. Addition and this mathematical operator are considered to be on the same precedence level.
   - A. Multiplication
   - B. Division
   - C. Subtraction

9. Changes made in a detail worksheet will automatically recalculate and display on this sheet.
   - A. Summary
   - B. Final
   - C. Outline

10. In a chart, the legend can be located here.
    - A. The detail sheet
    - B. The top of the chart
    - C. The summary sheet

Topics for Discussion

1. Think of the various departments and discipline areas at your college. What might be an example of workbooks that would contain data that could be organized into identically structured worksheets and then summarized in a summary sheet? Can you think of any examples specifically for your college athletic department?

2. Illustrate some examples of how a formula's results will be incorrect if parentheses are not used to group calculations in the order they should be performed. Think of averaging three test scores and how you would write the formula to get a correct result.

Skill Check

To complete this workbook, you will need the following file:

- e03_Payroll

You will save your workbook as:

- Lastname_Firstname_e03_Payroll

1. **Start** Excel, and open the file **e03_Payroll**. **Save** the workbook in your **Excel Chapter 3** folder as Lastname_Firstname_e03_Payroll

2. Double-click the **Sheet1 sheet tab**, type Courthouse and then press Enter. Right-click the **Courthouse sheet tab**, click **Tab Color**, and then click **Ice Blue, Accent 5**. Use the same technique to rename **Sheet2** as City Center and then apply the tab color **Gold, Accent 4**. Rename **Sheet3** as Community Center and then apply the tab color **Red, Accent 3**.

3. Right-click a **sheet tab**, and then click **Select All Sheets**. Add the file name in the worksheets left footer, and then add the sheet name in the right footer. Return to **Normal** view.

4. In cell **A4**, type Job Title and then press Tab. In cell **B4**, type Total Gross Pay In cell **C4**, type Income Tax In cell **D4**, type Social Security (FICA) Tax In cell **E4**, type Health Insurance In cell **F4**, type Net Pay

5. Select the range **A4:F4**, and then apply the cell style **40% - Accent3**. In the **Alignment group**, click the **Wrap Text** and the **Center** buttons. Click cell **A10**, and then compare your screen with **Figure 1**. ————————

6. Verify that the worksheets are still grouped. In cell **F5**, type =B5-(C5+D5+E5) and then press Enter to construct the formula to compute the Net Pay as *Total Gross Pay – (Income Tax + Social Security (FICA) Tax + Health Insurance)*. In cell **F5**, use the **fill handle** to copy the formula down through cell **F8**.

7. Select the range **B9:F9**. In the **Editing group**, click the **Sum** button, and then apply the **Total** cell style. Select the nonadjacent ranges **B5:F5** and **B9:F9**, and then apply the **Currency [0]** cell style. In the range **B6:F8**, apply the **Comma [0]** cell style. Right-click a **sheet tab**, and then click **Ungroup Sheets**. Click cell **A10**, and then compare your screen with **Figure 2**. ————————

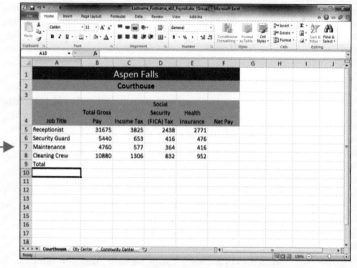

Figure 1

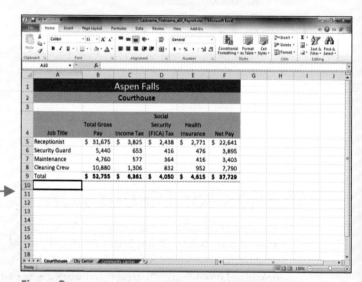

Figure 2

■ Continue to the next page to complete this Skill Check

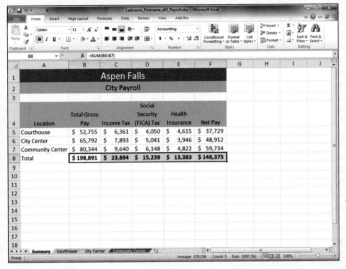

Figure 3

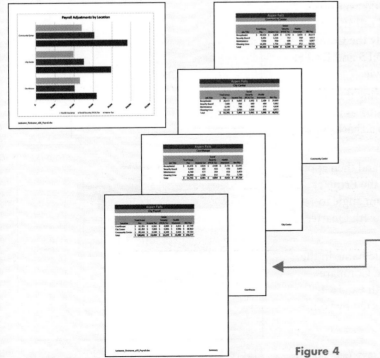

Figure 4

8. Insert a new worksheet. Rename the new sheet tab Summary and then change the **Tab Color** to **Orange, Accent 1**. Move the **Summary sheet** to the first position in the workbook.

9. Display the **Courthouse sheet**, select the range **A1:F4**, and then click **Copy**. Display the **Summary sheet** and then click cell **A1**. Click the **Paste button arrow** and then click **Keep Source Column Widths**. In cell **A2**, type City Payroll and then in cell **A4**, type Location In cell **A5**, type Courthouse In cell **A6**, type City Center In cell **A7**, type Community Center and then in cell **A8**, type Total

10. Click **B5**, type = and then click the **Courthouse sheet tab**. On the **Courthouse sheet**, click cell **B9**, and then press Enter. Use the same technique in cells **B6** and **B7** to place the *Total Gross Pay* amounts from the *City Center* and the *Community Center* worksheets on the *Summary* worksheet.

11. On the **Summary sheet**, select the range **B5:B7**, and then use the **fill handle** to copy the formulas to the right through column **F**. Select the range **B8:F8**. In the **Editing group**, click the **Sum** button, and then apply the **Total** cell style. Compare your screen with **Figure 3**.

12. On the **Summary sheet**, select the nonadjacent ranges **A4:A7** and **C4:E7**. On the **Insert tab**, in the **Charts group**, click the **Bar** button, and then click **Clustered Bar**. On the **Design tab**, in the **Location group**, click the **Move Chart** button. Rename the chart sheet Payroll Chart

13. On the **Design tab**, in the **Data group**, click the **Switch Row/Column** button. In the **Chart Styles group**, click the **More** button, and then click **Style 13**. In the **Chart Layouts group**, click **Layout 3**. Click the **Chart Title**, type Payroll Adjustments by Location and then press Enter. On the **Layout tab**, in the **Axes group**, click the **Axes** button, point to **Primary Horizontal Axis**, and then click **More Primary Horizontal Axis Options**. On the left, click **Alignment**. In the **Custom angle** box, type -40 and then click **Close**.

14. On the **Insert tab**, in the **Text group**, click the **Header & Footer** button. In the **Page Setup** dialog box, click the **Custom Footer** button, and then in the **Left section**, click the **Insert File Name** button. Click **OK** two times.

15. **Save** the workbook. Group the worksheets. Click the **File tab**, and then click **Print**. Click the **Next Page** button to view the five sheets. Compare your workbook with **Figure 4**. Print or submit the file as directed by your instructor.

Done! You have completed the Skill Check

Assess Your Skills 1

To complete this workbook, you will need the following file:

- e03_Water

You will save your workbook as:

- Lastname_Firstname_e03_Water

1. **Start** Excel, and open the file **e03_Water**. **Save** the workbook in your **Excel Chapter 3** folder as Lastname_Firstname_e03_Water Rename **Sheet1** as October and then apply the sheet tab color **Dark Red, Accent 2**.

2. Group the sheets. In cell **F5**, construct a formula to compute *Net Revenue = (Water Usage * Rate) + (City Sales Tax + Water Tax)*. Copy the formula down. In row **9**, sum the columns. In the range **B9:F9**, apply the **Total** cell style.

3. In the nonadjacent ranges **C5:F5** and **C9:F9**, apply the **Currency [0]** cell style, and then in the ranges **B5:B9** and **C6:F8**, apply the **Comma [0]** cell style.

4. Insert a new worksheet. Rename the new sheet tab Summary and apply the sheet tab color **Orange, Accent1**. Move the new sheet tab to make it the first worksheet in the workbook.

5. Group the sheets. Add the file name in the left footer and the sheet name in the right footer. Return to **Normal View**, and then ungroup the sheets.

6. Copy the range **A1:F4** from any of the other worksheets, and then on the **Summary sheet**, click cell **A1**. Click the **Paste button arrow**, and then click the **Keep Source Column Widths** button. Change the title of cell **A2** to Water Revenue: 4th Quarter and then change the title in cell **A4** to Month In cell **A5**, type

October and then use the fill handle to fill cells **A6** and **A7** with *November* and *December*. In cell A8, type Total

7. In the *Summary* worksheet, enter a formula in cell **B5** setting the cell equal to cell **B9** in the *October* worksheet. Enter the *Water Usage* total from the *November* and the *December* worksheets in cells **B6** and **B7**. In the *Summary* worksheet, select the range **B5:B7**, and then use the **fill handle** to copy the formulas to the right through column **F**.

8. In row **8**, sum column **B** and the columns **D:F**, and then apply the **Total** cell style to the cells. In the range **D6:F7**, apply the **Comma [0]** cell style. In the ranges **D5:F5** and **D8:F8**, apply the **Currency [0]** cell style.

9. Insert a **Clustered Bar** chart using the non-adjacent ranges **A4:A7** and **D4:E7** as the source data. Move the chart to a chart sheet with the sheet name Tax Chart

10. Apply the **Style 28** chart style, and then apply the **Layout 1** chart layout. For the **Primary Horizontal Axis**, set the **Custom angle** to -40°. Change the **Chart Title** to 4th Quarter Taxes

11. On the **chart sheet**, add the file name in the left footer. **Save** the workbook. Compare your completed workbook with **Figure 1**. Print or submit the file as directed by your instructor.

Done! You have completed Assess Your Skills 1

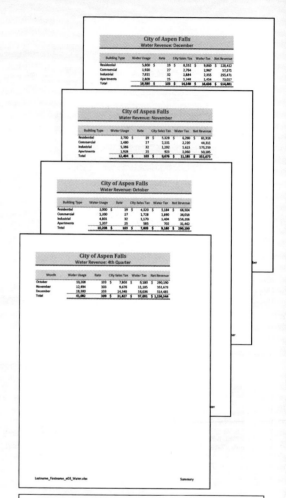

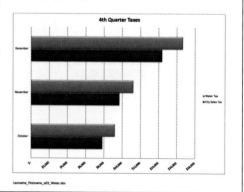

Figure 1

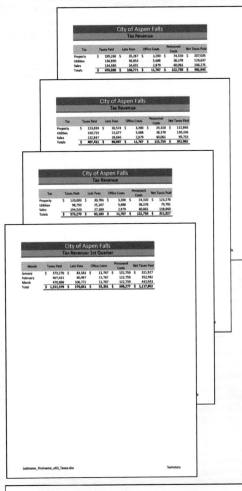

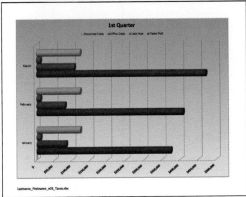

Figure 1

Assess Your Skills 2

Assess Your Skills 3 and 4 can be found at **www.pearsonhighered.com/skills**.

To complete this workbook, you will need the following file:

- e03_Taxes

You will save your workbook as:

- **Lastname_Firstname_e03_Taxes**

1. **Start** Excel, and open the file **e03_Taxes**. **Save** the workbook in your **Excel Chapter 3** folder as Lastname_Firstname_e03_Taxes

2. Rename the **Sheet1** sheet tab as January and then apply the sheet tab color **Pink, Text 2**. In cell **A13**, using your first and last names, type Your Name and then in cell **A14** enter the current date.

3. Group the sheets. In cell **F5**, construct a formula to compute *Net Taxes = (Taxes Paid + Late Fees) − (Office Costs + Personnel Costs)*. Copy the formula down, and then in row **8**, sum the columns.

4. In the ranges **B5:F5** and **B8:F8**, apply the **Currency [0]** cell style; in the range **B8:F8**, apply the **Total** cell style; and then in the range **B6:F7**, apply the **Comma [0]** cell style.

5. Insert a new sheet, rename the sheet tab Summary and then change the sheet tab color to **Black, Text 1**. Move the sheet to the first position in the workbook. Copy the range **A1:F4** from another sheet, and then paste the range into the *Summary* sheet using the **Keep Source Column Widths** button.

6. Group the sheets. Add the file name in the left footer and the sheet name in the right footer. Return to **Normal** view, and then ungroup the sheets.

7. On the **Summary sheet**, change the title in cell **A2** to Tax Revenue: 1st Quarter and then change the title in cell **A4** to Month In the

range **A5:A7**, enter the months January, February, and March and in cell **A8**, type Total

8. In cell **B5**, enter a formula setting the cell equal to cell **B8** in the *January* worksheet. Enter the total *Taxes Paid* from the *February* and the *March* worksheets in cells **B6** and **B7** of the **Summary sheet**. In the *Summary* worksheet, copy the range **B5:B7** to the right through column **F**.

9. In the range **B8:F8**, sum the columns, and then apply the **Total** cell style. In the range **B6:F7**, apply the **Comma [0]** cell style.

10. Select the range **A4:E7**, and then from the **Bar Chart** gallery, insert a **Clustered Horizontal Cylinder** chart. Move the chart to a chart sheet with the sheet tab name Tax Chart In the **Data group**, click the **Switch Row/Column** button. Apply the **Layout 1** chart layout and the **Style 26** chart style. Change the chart title to 1st Quarter

11. Show the **Legend** at the top of the chart. For the **Primary Horizontal Axis**, set the **Alignment** to **Custom angle** of **-40°**. Right-click the **Chart Area**, click **Format Chart Area**, and then select the **Gradient fill** option button. Add the file name in the left footer of the chart sheet.

12. **Save** the workbook. Print or submit the file as directed by your instructor. Compare your completed workbook with **Figure 1**.

Done! You have completed Assess Your Skills 2

Assess Your Skills Visually

To complete this workbook, you will need the following file:

- e03_Parking

You will save your workbook as:

- Lastname_Firstname_e03_Parking

Open the file **e03_Parking**, and save the workbook in your **Excel Chapter 3** folder as Lastname_Firstname_e03_Parking Complete the three details sheets as shown in **Figure 1**. To compute the *Net Income*, group the worksheets, and then use the formula *Net Income = (Parking Meters + Parking Tickets) − (Maintenance Cost + Personnel Costs)*. Sum the columns, and then apply appropriate number formats. Create the summary sheet for the 2nd Quarter with the totals from each month and the titles as shown in the figure. Insert a **Clustered Bar chart**, and then move the chart to a chart sheet with the sheet tab name Parking Chart Apply the **Style 27** chart style and the **Layout 1** chart layout. For the chart title, type Parking Revenue and Cost and show the legend at the top. Angle the primary horizontal axis at **-40°**. On all worksheets, add a footer with the file name in the left section and the sheet name in the right section. **Save** the workbook, and then print or submit the workbook electronically as directed by your instructor.

Done! You have completed Assess Your Skills Visually

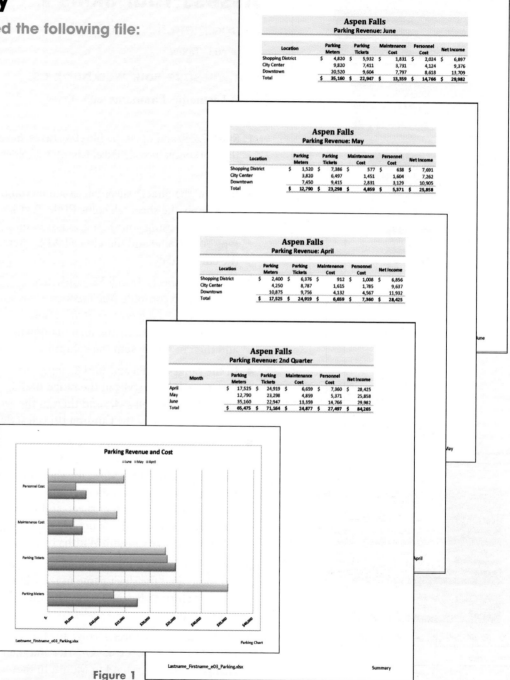

Figure 1

Skills in Context

To complete this workbook, you will need the following file:

- e03_Center

You will save your workbook as:

- Lastname_Firstname_e03_Center

During each quarter, the city tracked the rental revenue at the City Center. Open the file **e03_Center**, and then save the workbook in your **Excel Chapter 3** folder as Lastname_Firstname_ e03_Center For each quarter, compute the net income using the formula *Net Income = Income − (Indirect Costs + Direct Costs)*. Total the columns, and format the numbers appropriately. Create a worksheet named Summary containing the totals for each quarter. Use the same column titles that are on the detail worksheets in the range B4:E4, and change the row titles in the range A4:A7. Total and format the numbers on the *Summary* worksheet. Insert a clustered bar chart, and move the chart to a chart sheet. Format the chart appropriately. On all sheets, insert the file name in the left footer and the sheet name in the right footer. Save the workbook, and then print or submit the workbook electronically as directed by your instructor.

Done! You have completed Skills in Context

Skills and You

To complete this workbook, you will need the following file:

- New blank Excel workbook

You will save your workbook as:

- Lastname_Firstname_e03_Repairs

How much does it cost your family to own, operate, and maintain more than one vehicle? Recording the cost of owning each vehicle and then comparing the costs might reveal that one or more of your vehicles are costing more in repairs or gasoline than you want to spend. Create a worksheet for each vehicle your family uses. Use months as the row names, and use *Payment, Insurance, Gasoline,* and *Maintenance and Repairs* as the column names. Record three months of data, and then format the data appropriately. Create a summary sheet for the vehicles. Create a clustered bar chart, and move the chart to a chart sheet. Switch the rows and columns as necessary so that the vehicles form the vertical axis. You might find that one or more vehicles is using much more gasoline or costing more in repairs and maintenance than you realized. Save the workbook in your **Excel Chapter 3** folder as Lastname_Firstname_e03_Repairs and submit the workbook as directed by your instructor.

Done! You have completed Skills and You

CHAPTER 4

Use Excel Functions and Tables

▸ The Excel Function Library contains hundreds of special functions that perform complex calculations quickly. Some of the categories in the Function Library include statistical, financial, logical, date and time, and math and trigonometry.

▸ Excel tables help you manage information by providing many ways to sort, filter, analyze, format, and generate charts from the data in a table.

Your starting screen will look similar to this:

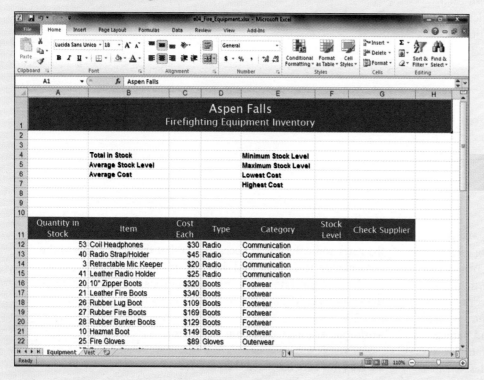

SKILLS

Skills 1–10 Training

At the end of this chapter, you will be able to:

Skill 1 Use the SUM and AVERAGE Functions
Skill 2 Use the MIN and MAX Functions
Skill 3 Move Ranges with Functions, Add Borders, and Rotate Text
Skill 4 Use the IF Function
Skill 5 Apply Conditional Formatting with Custom Formats, Data Bars, and Sparklines
Skill 6 Use Find and Replace and Insert the NOW Function
Skill 7 Freeze and Unfreeze Panes
Skill 8 Create and Sort Excel Tables
Skill 9 Use the Search Filter in Excel Tables
Skill 10 Convert Tables to Ranges, Hide Rows and Columns, and Format Large Worksheets

MORE SKILLS

More Skills 11 Apply Conditional Color Scales with Top and Bottom Rules
More Skills 12 Use the Payment (PMT) Function
More Skills 13 Create PivotTable Reports
More Skills 14 Use Goal Seek

Outcome

Using the skills listed to the left will enable you to create
a workbook like this:

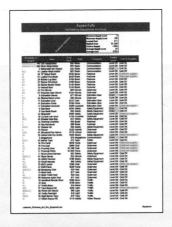

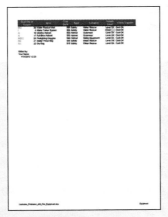

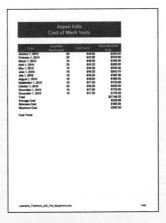

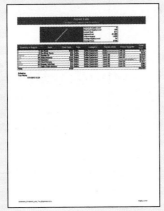

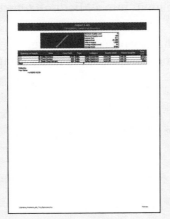

You will save your workbook as:

Lastname_Firstname_e04_Fire_Equipment

In this chapter, you will create documents for the Aspen Falls City Hall, which provides essential services for the citizens and visitors of Aspen Falls, California.

Introduction

- ▶ Functions are prewritten formulas that have two parts: the name of the function and the arguments that specify the values or cells to be used by the function.
- ▶ Conditional formatting helps you see important trends and highlight exceptions in your data by applying various formats such as colored gradients, data bars, or icons.
- ▶ You can convert data organized in rows and columns into a Microsoft Office Excel table.
- ▶ Excel tables allow you to add data analysis such as sorting and filtering, summary rows, and calculated columns, and you can format the tables using a large library of table styles.

**Time to complete all
10 skills – 50 to 90 minutes**

Find your student data files here:

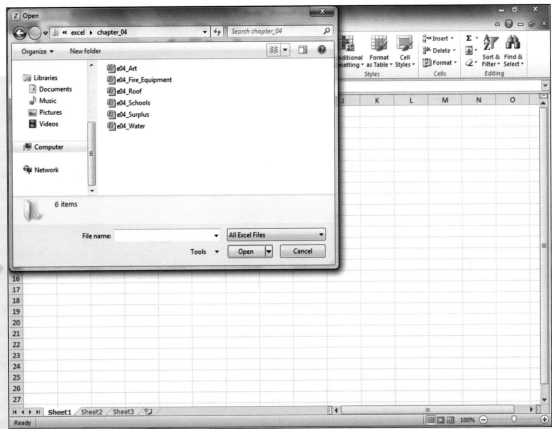

**Student data file needed
for this chapter:**

- e04_Fire_Equipment

► A *function* is a prewritten formula that takes input, performs an operation, and returns a value. Functions are used to simplify and shorten formulas.

► *Statistical functions* are predefined formulas that describe a collection of data—for example, totals, counts, and averages.

► The *AVERAGE function* adds a group of values and then divides the result by the number of values in the group.

1. **Start** ● Excel, and then open **e04_Fire_ Equipment**. Click the **File tab**, and then click **Save As**. In the **Save As** dialog box, navigate to the location where you are saving your files. Click **New folder**, type Excel Chapter 4 and then press Enter two times. In the **File name** box, type Lastname_Firstname_e04_Fire_ Equipment and then press Enter.

2. Click cell **C4**. On the **Home tab**, in the **Editing group**, click the **Sum** button Σ, and then compare your screen with **Figure 1**.

3. With the insertion point in the function parentheses, click cell **A12**, and then press Ctrl + Shift + ↓ to select the range **A12:A70**. On the formula bar, click the **Enter** button ✓ to display the result *1745*, as shown in **Figure 2**.

   The range in parentheses is the function *argument*—the values that a function uses to perform operations or calculations. The arguments each function uses are specific to that function. Common arguments include numbers, text, cell references, and range names.

■ **Continue to the next page to complete the skill**

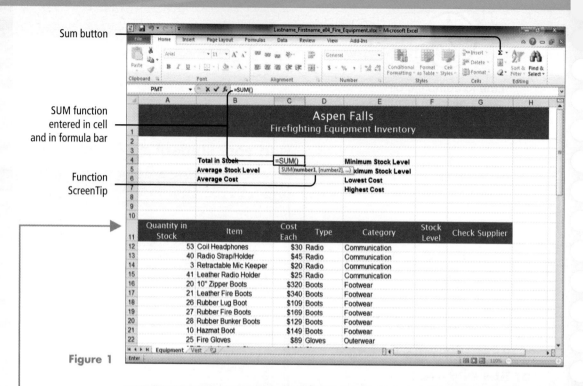

Sum button

SUM function entered in cell and in formula bar

Function ScreenTip

Figure 1

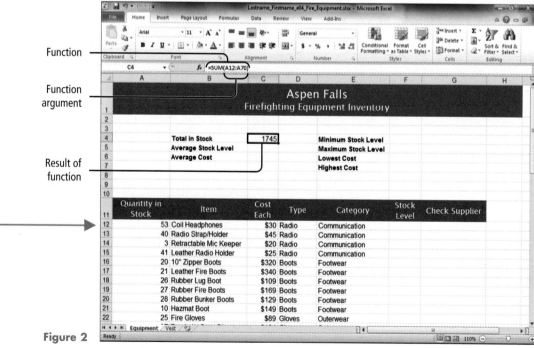

Function

Function argument

Result of function

Figure 2

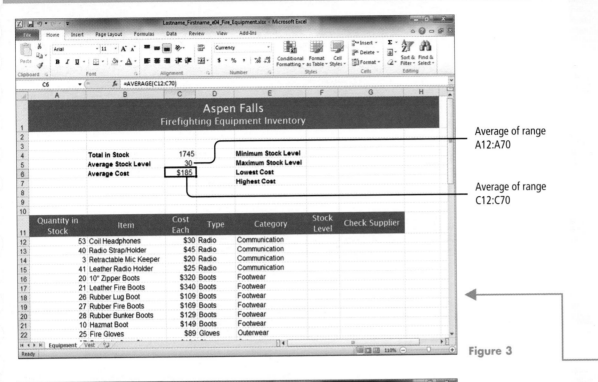

Average of range
A12:A70

Average of range
C12:C70

Figure 3

4. Click cell **C5**. In the **Editing group**, click the **Sum button arrow** Σ, and then in the list of functions, click **Average**. In the formula bar and in the cell, notice that Excel proposes to average the value in cell *C4*.

> When data is above or to the left of a selected cell, a function will suggest a range. Often, you will need to edit a suggested range.

5. With cell **C4** highlighted in the function argument, select the range **A12:A70**, and then on the formula bar, click the **Enter** button ☑ to display the result *29.5763*. In the **Styles group**, click the **Cell Styles** button, and then click **Comma [0]**.

6. Click cell **C6**. In the **Editing group**, click the **Sum button arrow** Σ, and then in the list, click **Average**. Select the range **C12:C70**, and then click the **Enter** button ☑. Scroll up to display the result *$185*, as shown in **Figure 3**.

7. Click the **Vest** sheet tab, and then click cell **D17**. Using the techniques just practiced, enter the **SUM** function using the argument range **D5:D16**, and then press Enter. In cell **D18**, enter the **AVERAGE** function using the argument range **D5:D16**, and then click the **Enter** button ☑. Verify that cell **D17** is not included in the Average range. Compare your sheet to **Figure 4**.

8. Right-click the sheet tab, and then click **Select All Sheets**. Display the worksheet footers, insert the **File Name** in the left footer and the **Sheet Name** in the right footer. Return to **Normal** view and then press Ctrl + Home.

9. Save ☐ the workbook.

■ **You have completed Skill 1 of 10**

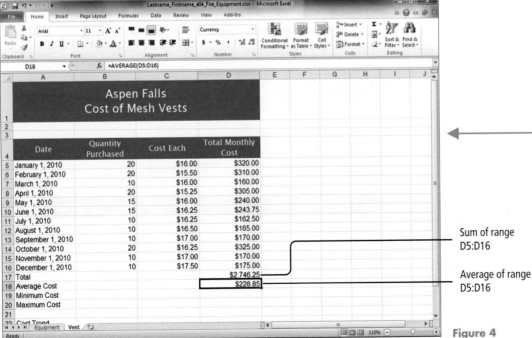

Sum of range
D5:D16

Average of range
D5:D16

Figure 4

▶ The **MIN function** returns the smallest value in a range of cells.

▶ The **MAX function** returns the largest value in a range of cells.

1. Make the **Equipment** sheet the active sheet. Click cell **F4**. In the **Editing group**, click the **Sum button arrow** Σ, and then in the list, click **Min**. With the insertion point blinking in the function, select the range **A12:A70**, and then on the formula bar, click the **Enter** button ✔ to display the result *3*.

> The MIN function evaluates all of the values in the range A12:A70 and then returns *3*, the lowest value found in the range.

2. Click cell **F5**. In the **Editing group**, click the **Sum button arrow** Σ, and then in the list, click **Max**.

> The function automatically suggests the argument F4 because the cell above contains a value.

3. With cell **F4** selected in the function argument, select the range **A12:A70**, and then on the formula bar, click the **Enter** button ✔ to display the result *90*, as shown in **Figure 1**.

> The MAX function evaluates all of the values in the range A12:A70 and then returns the highest value found.

4. Click cell **A12**, type *146* and then press `Enter`. In cell **A13**, type *2* and then press `Enter`. Verify that the MIN and MAX functions in cells **F4** and **F5** now display the lowest and highest values in the range **A12:A70**. Verify that the SUM and AVERAGE functions also automatically recalculated, as shown in **Figure 2**.

■ **Continue to the next page to complete the skill**

Result of MIN function

Result of MAX function

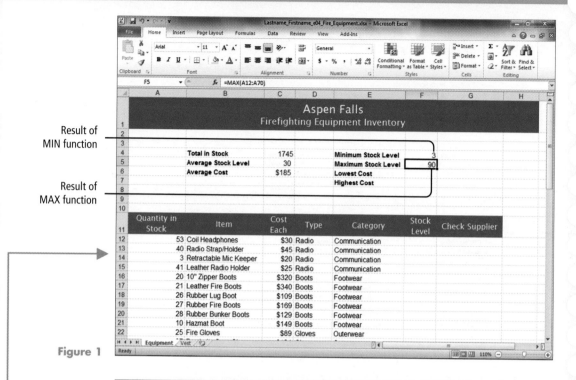

Figure 1

Function results recalculated

Value changed to *146*

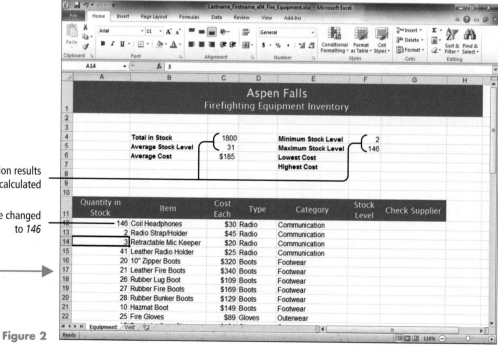

Figure 2

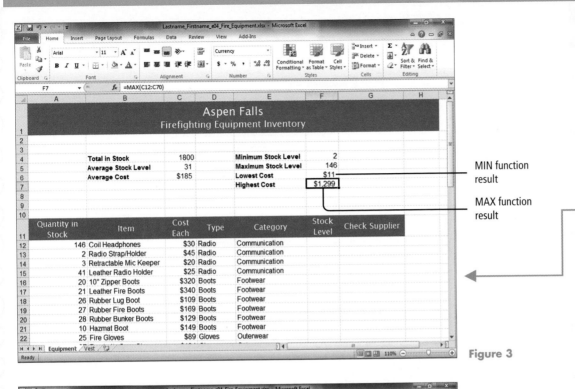

MIN function result

MAX function result

Figure 3

5. In cell **F6**, repeat the technique just practiced to insert the **MIN** function using the range **C12:C70** as the argument in the parentheses. Verify that the result is *$11*.

6. In cell **F7**, insert the **MAX** function to return the highest cost in the range **C12:C70**. Verify that the result is *$1,299*. Scroll down to view the worksheet, and verify that the lowest and highest values in column **C** were selected from each of the ranges for the MIN and MAX functions. Compare your screen with **Figure 3**.

7. Make the **Vest** worksheet the active sheet.

8. In cell **D19**, insert the MIN function to evaluate the lowest monthly cost in the range **D5:D16** as the argument in the parentheses. Do not include the *Total* or *Average Cost* values in the range. Verify that the result is *$160.00*.

9. In cell **D20**, insert the MAX function to evaluate the highest monthly cost in the range **D5:D16** as the argument. Verify that the result is *$325.00*, as shown in **Figure 4**.

10. **Save** 🖫 the workbook.

■ **You have completed Skill 2 of 10**

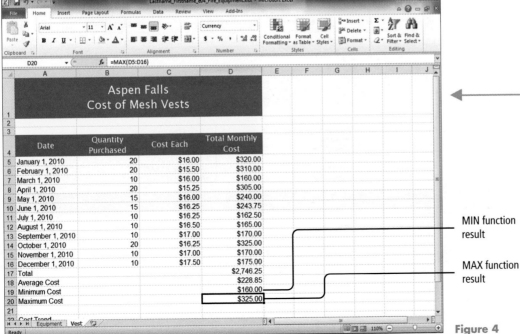

MIN function result

MAX function result

Figure 4

► You can move a range of cells containing formulas or functions without changing the cell references in those formulas or functions.

► Borders and shading emphasize a cell or a range of cells, and rotated or angled text draws attention to text on a worksheet.

1. Make the **Equipment** worksheet the active sheet. Select the range **E4:F7**. Point to the top edge of the selected range to display the 🔭 pointer. Drag the selected range up until the ScreenTip displays the range *E3:F6*, as shown in **Figure 1**, and then release the mouse button to complete the move.

2. Select the range **B4:C6**, and then using the technique you just practiced, move the range to **E7:F9**.

3. On the **Formulas tab**, in the **Formula Auditing group**, click the **Show Formulas** button to display the functions in the cells. Scroll to the right, and then click cell **F2**. Notice that the cell references in the functions did not change, as shown in **Figure 2**.

4. In the **Formula Auditing group**, click the **Show Formulas** button to display the function results in the cells.

5. Select the range **F3:F4**. Hold down [Ctrl], and then select the range **F7:F8**. With the nonadjacent cells selected, on the **Home tab**, in the **Styles group**, click the **Cell Styles** button, and then click **Comma [0]**.

6. Select the range **A11:G11**. On the **Home tab**, in the **Font group**, click the **Border button arrow** ⊞▾, and then click **Thick Bottom Border**.

■ Continue to the next page to complete the skill

ScreenTip indicates range E3:F6

Outline indicates destination of range

Border displays around range being moved

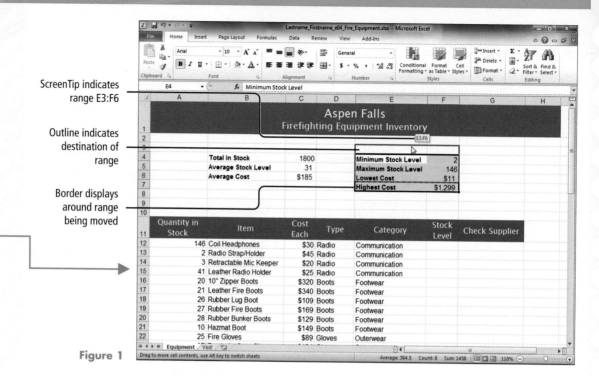

Figure 1

Cell references remain unchanged

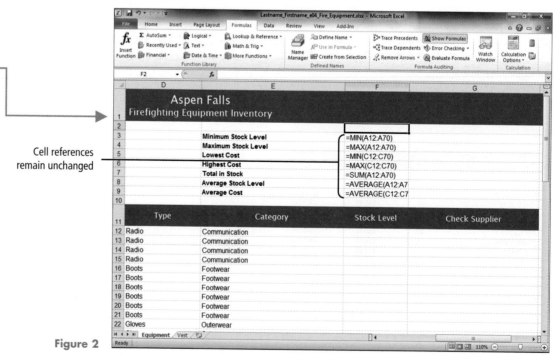

Figure 2

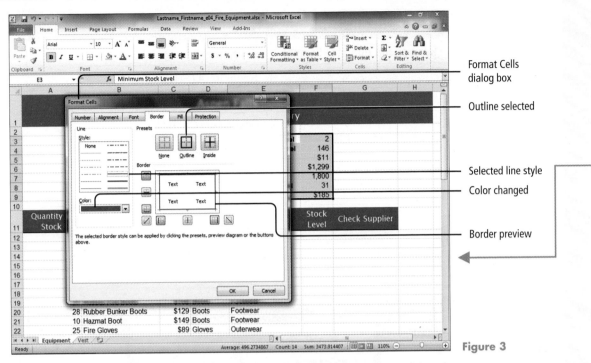

Format Cells dialog box

Outline selected

Selected line style

Color changed

Border preview

Figure 3

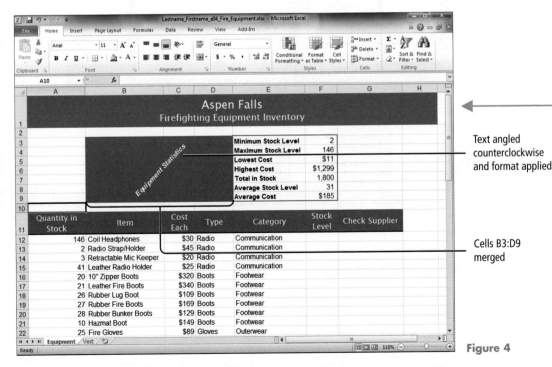

Text angled counterclockwise and format applied

Cells B3:D9 merged

Figure 4

7. Select the range **E3:F9**. In the **Font group**, click the **Border button arrow** , and then at the bottom of the gallery, click **More Borders**. In the left of the **Format Cells** dialog box, under **Style**, click the fifth line style in the second column. Click the **Color arrow**, and then click the sixth color in the first row—**Red, Accent 2**. Under **Presets**, click **Outline**, and then compare your screen with **Figure 3**.

The Format Cells dialog box displays a preview of formatting.

8. At the bottom of the **Format Cells** dialog box, click **OK**. Click cell **B3** to view the border around the range E3:F9.

9. In cell **B3**, type Equipment Statistics and then press Enter.

10. Select the range **B3:D9**. On the **Home tab**, in the **Alignment group**, click the **Merge & Center** button . In the **Alignment group**, click the **Middle Align** button . In the **Font group**, click the **Fill Color button arrow** , and then click the sixth color in the first row—**Red, Accent 2**. Click the **Font Color button arrow** , and then click the first color in the first row—**White, Background 1**. Apply the **Bold** and **Italic** format.

11. With the merged cell still selected, in the **Alignment group**, click the **Orientation** button , and then click **Angle Counterclockwise**. Click cell **A10**, and then compare your screen with **Figure 4**.

12. **Save** the workbook.

■ **You have completed Skill 3 of 10**

▶ A *logical test* is any value or expression that can be evaluated as TRUE or FALSE.

▶ A *logical function* applies a logical test to determine whether a specific condition is met. *Criteria* are the conditions specified in the logical test.

▶ The *IF Function* checks whether criteria are met and then returns one value when the condition is TRUE and another value when the condition is FALSE.

1. Click cell **F12**. On the **Formulas tab**, in the **Function Library group**, click the **Logical** button, and then on the list, point to **IF**. Read the ScreenTip, and then click **IF** to display the **Function Arguments** dialog box.

2. With the insertion point in the **Logical_test** box, type A12<10

   The logical test *A12<10* will look at the value in cell A12 and then determine whether the value is less than 10. The expression *<10* includes the < comparison operator, which means *less than*. A *comparison operator* compares two values and returns either TRUE or FALSE. The table in **Figure 1** lists commonly used comparison operators.

3. Press [Tab] to move the insertion point to the **Value_if_true** box, and then type Order

4. Press [Tab] to move the insertion point to the **Value_if_false** box, type Level OK and then compare your screen with **Figure 2**.

   Quotation marks display around *Order* and will automatically be inserted around *Level OK* after you click OK. In function arguments, text values are surrounded by quotation marks.

■ **Continue to the next page to complete the skill**

Figure 1

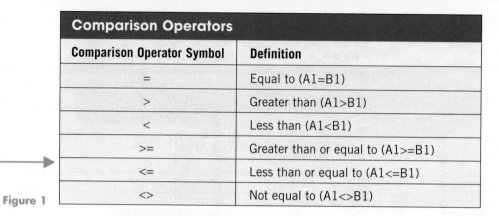

Comparison Operator Symbol	Definition
=	Equal to (A1=B1)
>	Greater than (A1>B1)
<	Less than (A1<B1)
>=	Greater than or equal to (A1>=B1)
<=	Less than or equal to (A1<=B1)
<>	Not equal to (A1<>B1)

Logical test argument

Value if true argument with quotation marks indicating text

Value if false argument

Figure 2

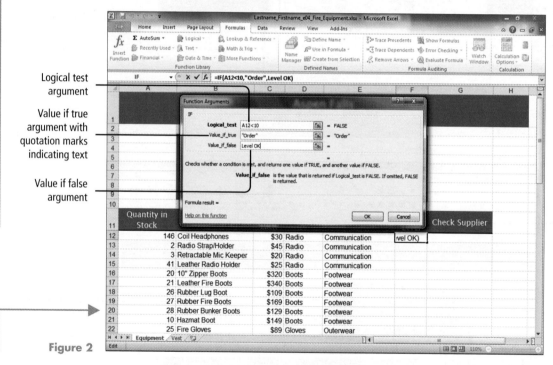

5. Click **OK** to display the result *Level OK* in cell **F12**.

The IF function tests whether cell A12 is less than 10. If this condition were TRUE, *Order* would display. Because cell A12 contains the value *146*, the condition is FALSE, and *Level OK* displays in cell F12.

6. In cell **F12**, point to the fill handle to display the ⊞ pointer, and then double-click to copy the function down through cell **F70**. Click cell **F13**, and then compare your screen with **Figure 3**.

When a function has multiple arguments, each argument is separated by a comma.

When the function was copied down to cell F13, the cell reference changed from A12 to A13.

7. Click cell **G12**. In the **Function Library group**, click the **Logical** button, and then click **IF**. In the **Logical_test** box, type C12>300 and then press Tab. In the **Value_if_true** box, type Check new supplier and then press Tab. In the **Value_if_false** box, type Cost OK and then click the **OK** button. In cell **G12**, point to the fill handle to display the ⊞ pointer, and then double-click to copy the function down through cell **G70**. Compare your screen with **Figure 4**.

In each row, the function evaluates the value in column C. When the value in column C is greater than $300, the text *Check new supplier* displays. Otherwise, the text *Cost OK* displays.

8. Save 🖫 the workbook.

■ **You have completed Skill 4 of 10**

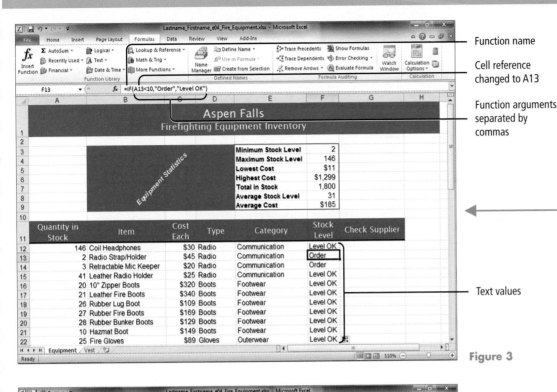

Function name

Cell reference changed to A13

Function arguments separated by commas

Text values

Figure 3

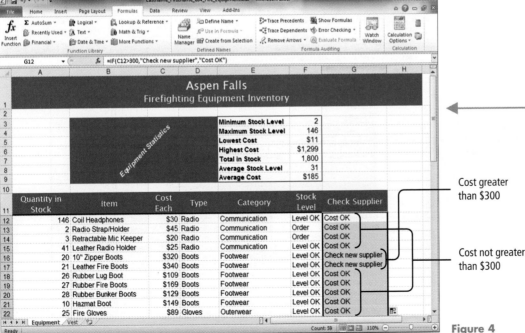

Cost greater than $300

Cost not greater than $300

Figure 4

▶ *Conditional formatting* is a format, such as cell shading or font color, that is applied to cells when a specified condition is true.

▶ Conditional formatting makes analyzing data easier by emphasizing cell values.

1. Click cell **F12**. Press Ctrl + Shift + ↓ to select the range **F12:F70**.

2. On the **Home tab**, in the **Styles group**, click the **Conditional Formatting** button. On the list, point to **Highlight Cells Rules**, and then click **Text that Contains**. In the **Text That Contains** dialog box, with the insertion point in the first box, type Order as shown in **Figure 1**.

3. In the **Text That Contains** dialog box, click **OK**.

   Within the range F12:F70, cells that contain the text *Order* display with light red fill and dark red text formatting.

4. Using the technique just practiced, select the range **G12:G70**. Click the **Conditional Formatting** button, point to **Highlight Cells Rules**, and then click **Text that Contains**. In the first box, type Check new supplier Click the second box arrow, and on the list, click **Yellow Fill with Dark Yellow Text**. Compare your screen with **Figure 2**.

   The Text That Contains dialog box is used to specify the formatting to apply when the condition is true—here, if the cell contains the text *Check new supplier*. Within the selected range, if a cell contains the text *Check new supplier*, the conditional format is applied.

■ **Continue to the next page to complete the skill**

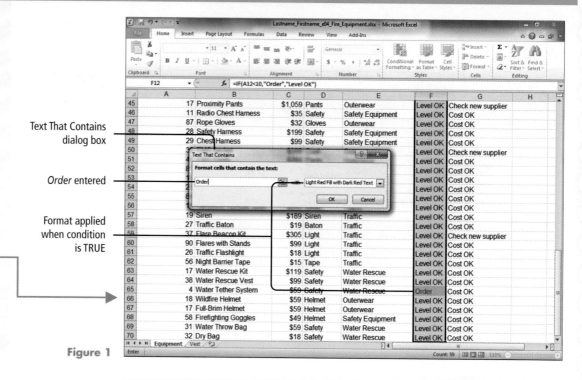

Text That Contains dialog box

Order entered

Format applied when condition is TRUE

Figure 1

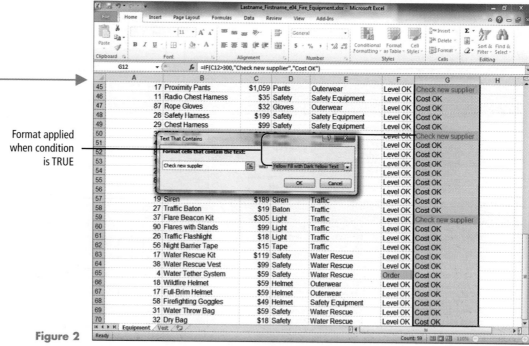

Format applied when condition is TRUE

Figure 2

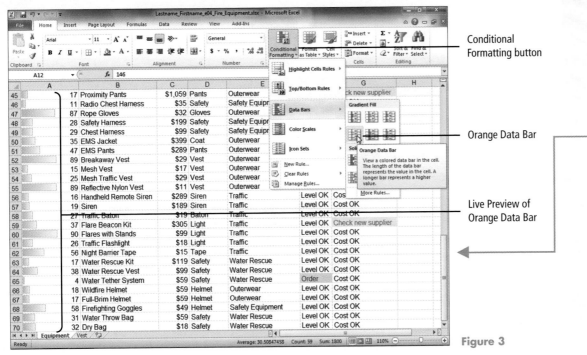

Conditional Formatting button

Orange Data Bar

Live Preview of Orange Data Bar

Figure 3

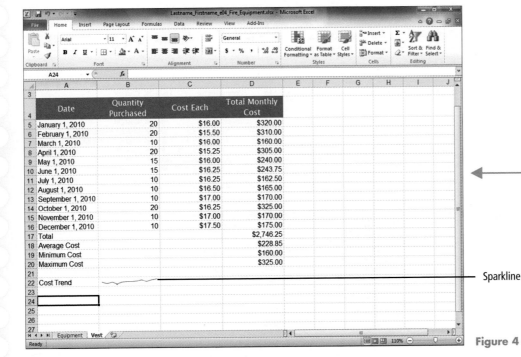

Sparkline

Figure 4

5. In the **Text That Contains** dialog box, click **OK**.

6. Select the range **A12:A70**. In the **Styles group**, click the **Conditional Formatting** button. On the list, point to **Data Bars**, and then in the gallery, under Gradient Fill, point at **Orange Data Bar**, as shown in **Figure 3**.

A *data bar* provides a visual cue about the value of a cell relative to other cells in a range. Data bars are useful to quickly identify higher and lower numbers within a large group of data, such as very high or very low levels of inventory.

7. Click **Orange Data Bar**, and then click cell **A13**, type 190 and then press Enter.

The data bar in cell A13 is longer than in other cells—a visual indicator that the cell contains a higher value.

8. Make the **Vest** sheet the active sheet. Select the range **C5:C16**. On the **Insert tab**, in the **Sparklines group**, click the **Line** button. In the **Create Sparklines** dialog box, in the **Location Range** box, type B22 and then click **OK**.

9. On the **Design tab**, in the **Show group**, select the **Low Point** check box. In the **Style group**, click the **Sparkline Color** button, and then click **Red, Accent 2**. Click cell **A24**, and then compare your screen with **Figure 4**.

A *sparkline* is a tiny chart used to show data trends.

10. Save the workbook.

■ **You have completed Skill 5 of 10**

▶ The ***Find and Replace*** command finds and then replaces a character or string of characters in a worksheet or in a selected range.

▶ The ***NOW function*** returns the serial number of the current date and time. Recall from Chapter 3 that a serial number is a sequential number.

1. Make **Equipment** the active sheet. Press Ctrl + Home. On the **Home tab**, in the **Editing group**, click the **Find & Select** button, and then click **Replace**.

2. In the **Find and Replace** dialog box, in the **Find what** box, type Removal and then press Tab. In the **Replace with** box, type Extrication and then compare your screen with **Figure 1**.

3. Click the **Find Next** button, and then verify that cell **B24** is highlighted. In the **Find and Replace** dialog box, click the **Replace** button. Verify that the first occurrence of *Removal* was replaced with *Extrication* and that the second occurrence—in cell **B26**—is automatically located.

   The Replace option will replace a single occurrence of a character or string of characters with the replacement value.

4. Click the **Replace All** button, and then in the message box, notice that **3 replacements** were made, as shown in **Figure 2**.

   The Replace All option replaces all matches of an occurrence of a character or string of characters with the replacement value.

5. Click **OK**, and then click the **Close** button.

6. Press Ctrl + Home.

■ **Continue to the next page to complete the skill**

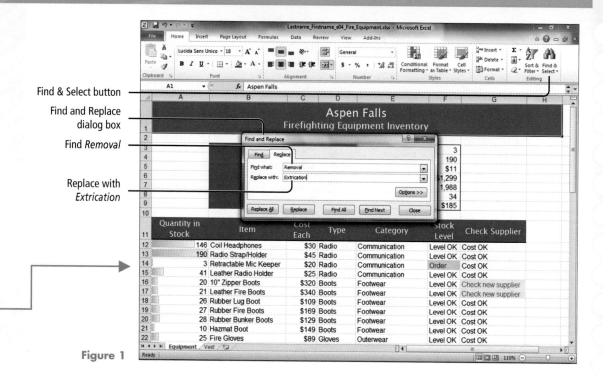

Find & Select button
Find and Replace dialog box
Find *Removal*
Replace with *Extrication*

Figure 1

Replacements made

Figure 2

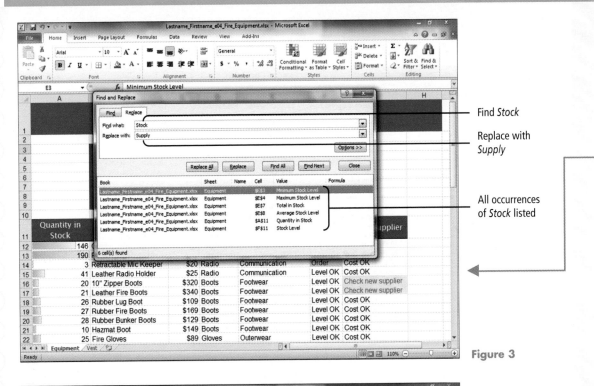

Find *Stock*

Replace with *Supply*

All occurrences of *Stock* listed

Figure 3

7. In the **Editing group**, click the **Find & Select** button, and then click **Replace**. In the **Find and Replace** dialog box, in the **Find what** box, replace *Removal* with Stock and then press Tab. In the **Replace with** box, replace *Extrication* with Supply and then click the **Find All** button. Resize the **Find and Replace** dialog box as necessary to view the data as shown in **Figure 3**.

> The Find All option finds all occurrences of the search criteria.

8. In the lower portion of the **Find and Replace** dialog box, in the **Cell** column, click **$E$8** to make cell **E8** the active cell, and then click the **Replace** button.

> The word *Stock* in cell E8 is replaced with the word *Supply*.

9. Click the **Replace All** button. Read the message, and then click **OK**. In the **Find and Replace** dialog box, click the **Close** button.

10. Scroll down, click cell **A73**, type Edited by: and then press Enter. In cell **A74**, using your first and last names, type Your Name and then press Enter.

11. On the **Formulas tab**, in the **Function Library group**, click the **Date & Time** button, and then click **NOW**. Read the message, and then compare your screen with **Figure 4**.

> The NOW function takes no arguments, and the result is *volatile*—the date and time will not remain as entered but rather will be updated each time this workbook is opened.

12. Click **OK** to enter the date and time. Save the workbook.

■ **You have completed Skill 6 of 10**

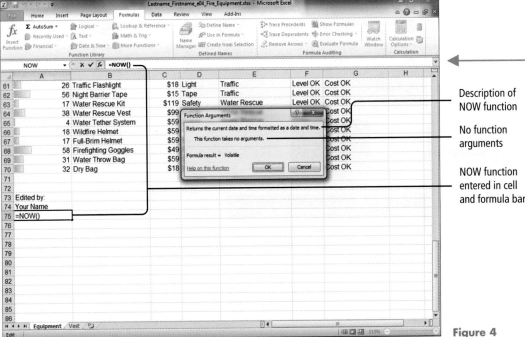

Description of NOW function

No function arguments

NOW function entered in cell and formula bar

Figure 4

► The **Freeze Panes** command keeps rows or columns visible when you are scrolling in a worksheet. The frozen rows and columns become separate panes.

► When you freeze panes, you determine the specific rows or columns that you want to remain visible when scrolling. You will likely find it easier to work with large worksheets when you can always view the identifying row or column labels.

1. Press Ctrl + Home, and then scroll down until row **50** displays at the bottom of your window and the column labels are out of view, as shown in **Figure 1**.

   When you scroll in large worksheets, the column and row labels may not be visible, which can make identifying the purpose of each row or column difficult. You may see different rows depending on the zoom level.

2. Press Ctrl + Home, and then click cell **C15**. On the **View tab**, in the **Window group**, click the **Freeze Panes** button, and then click **Freeze Panes**.

   By selecting cell C15, the rows above and the columns to the left of C15 are frozen. A line displays along the upper border of row 15 and on the left border of column C.

3. Click the **Scroll Down** ▼ and **Scroll Right** ► arrows to display cell **M80**, and then notice that the top and left panes remain frozen, as shown in **Figure 2**.

■ **Continue to the next page to complete the skill**

Column titles cannot be seen

Row 50 displays at the bottom of the window

Figure 1

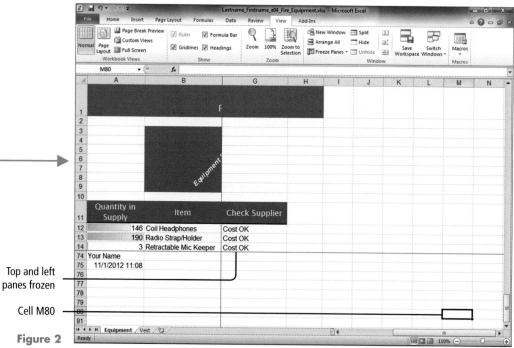

Top and left panes frozen

Cell M80

Figure 2

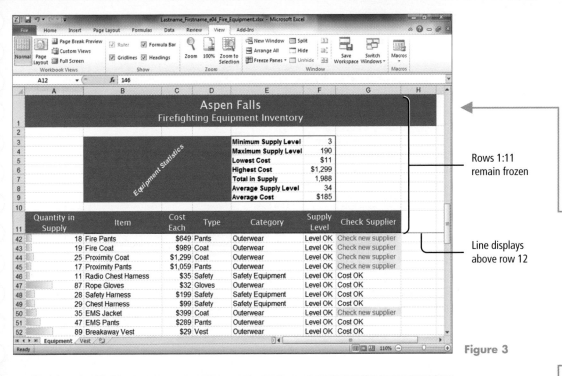

Rows 1:11 remain frozen

Line displays above row 12

Figure 3

4. In the **Window group**, click the **Freeze Panes** button, and then click **Unfreeze Panes**.

   The rows and columns are no longer frozen, and the border no longer displays on row 15 and on column C.

5. Click cell **A12**. In the **Window group**, click the **Freeze Panes** button, and then click **Freeze Panes**.

6. Watch the row numbers below row **11** as you scroll down to row **50**. Compare your screen with **Figure 3**.

   The titles in row 1 through row 11 stay frozen while the remaining rows of data continue to scroll.

7. Right-click the **Equipment** sheet tab, and then from the list, click **Move or Copy**. In the **Move or Copy** dialog box, click (**move to end**), and then select the **Create a copy** check box. Compare your screen with **Figure 4**.

8. In the **Move or Copy** dialog box, click **OK**.

   A copy of the *Equipment* worksheet is created, and the new sheet tab is named *Equipment (2)*.

9. Right-click the **Equipment (2)** sheet tab, click **Rename**, type Sort by Cost and then press Enter. In the **Window group**, click the **Freeze Panes** button, and then click **Unfreeze Panes**. Click the **Equipment** sheet tab, and verify that on this worksheet, the panes are still frozen.

10. Save the workbook.

■ **You have completed Skill 7 of 10**

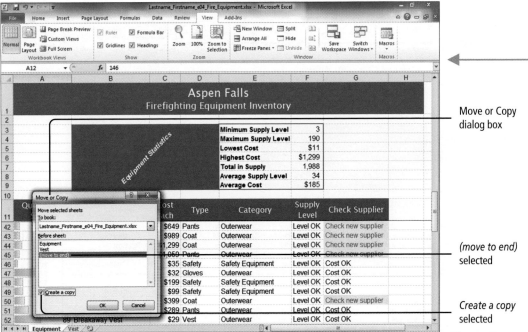

Move or Copy dialog box

(move to end) selected

Create a copy selected

Figure 4

▶ To analyze a group of related data, you can convert a range into an ***Excel table***—a series of rows and columns that contain related data. Data in an Excel table are managed independently from the data in other rows and columns in the worksheet.

▶ Data in Excel tables can be sorted in a variety of ways—for example, in ascending order or by color.

1. Click the **Sort by Cost** sheet tab, and then click cell **A11**. On the **Insert tab**, in the **Tables group**, click the **Table** button. In the **Create Table** dialog box, under **Where is the data for your table?** verify that the range =$A$11:$G$70 displays. If necessary, select the *My table has headers* check box, as shown in **Figure 1**.

   The range A11:G70 is automatically selected because there are no blank rows or columns in the range.

2. In the **Create Table** dialog box, click **OK** to convert the range into an Excel table.

   In the Excel table, formatting is applied and the header row displays filter arrows in each column.

3. On the **Design tab**, in the **Table Styles group**, click the **More** button ⊡, and then under **Light**, click **Table Style Light 10**. Click cell **H11**, type Total Cost and then press Enter to automatically include the column in the Excel table.

4. In **H12**, type =A12*C12 and then press Enter to create a ***calculated column***— a column in an Excel table that uses a single formula that adjusts for each row—as shown in **Figure 2**.

■ **Continue to the next page to complete the skill**

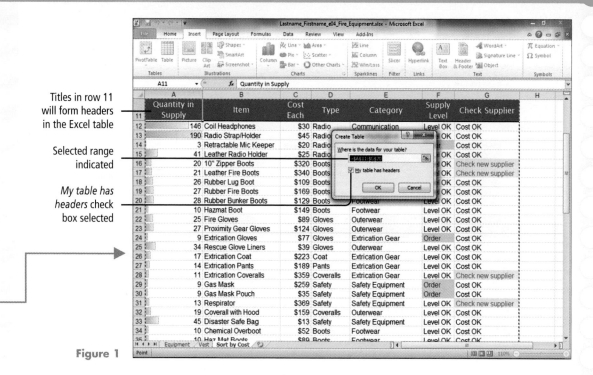

Titles in row 11 will form headers in the Excel table

Selected range indicated

My table has headers check box selected

Figure 1

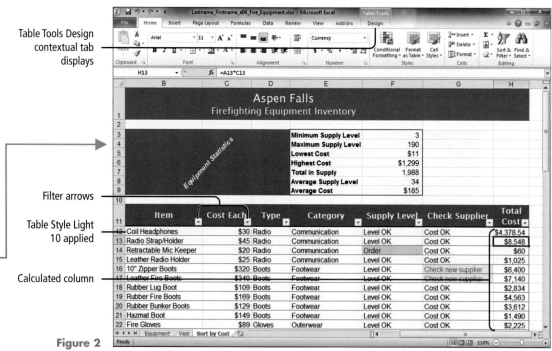

Table Tools Design contextual tab displays

Filter arrows

Table Style Light 10 applied

Calculated column

Figure 2

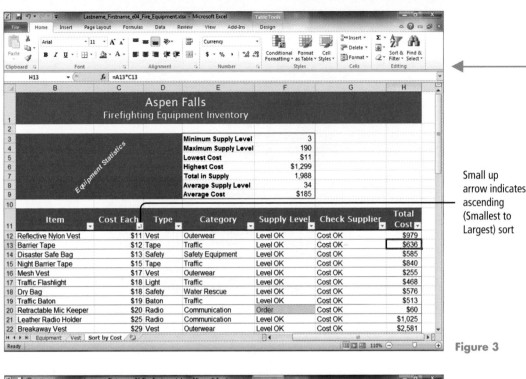

Small up arrow indicates ascending (Smallest to Largest) sort

Figure 3

5. In the header row of the Excel table, click the **Cost Each filter arrow**, and then from the list, click **Sort Smallest to Largest**. Compare your screen with **Figure 3**.

The rows in the table are sorted by the *Cost Each* values, from the lowest to the highest, as indicated by the up arrow on the column's filter button.

6. In the header row, click the **Total Cost filter arrow**, and then click **Sort Largest to Smallest**.

The rows in the table are now sorted from the highest to lowest *Total Cost* value, and the small arrow in the Total Cost filter arrow points down, indicating a descending sort. The previous sort on the *Cost Each* column no longer displays.

7. Right-click the **Sort by Cost** sheet tab, and then click **Move or Copy**. In the **Move or Copy** dialog box, click (**move to end**), select the **Create a copy** check box, and then click **OK**.

8. Right-click the **Sort by Cost (2)** sheet tab, click **Rename**, type Supply Level and then press Enter.

9. In the **Supply Level** worksheet, click the **Supply Level filter arrow**, and then point to **Sort by Color**. Notice that the color formats in column **F** display in the list, as shown in **Figure 4**.

If you have applied manual or conditional formatting to a range of cells, you can sort by these colors.

10. In the **Sort by Color** list, under **Sort by Cell Color**, click the **pink tile** to display the six items that need to be ordered first in the Excel table.

11. Save the workbook.

■ **You have completed Skill 8 of 10**

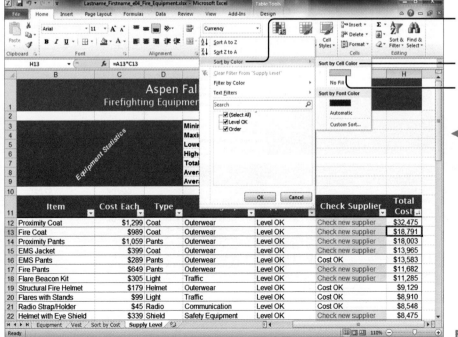

Sort by Color

Sort by Cell Color

Pink tile

Figure 4

► You can *filter* data to display only the rows of a table that meet specified criteria. Filtering temporarily hides rows that do not meet the criteria.

1. On the **Supply Level** worksheet, click the **Category filter arrow**. From the menu, clear the (**Select All**) check box to clear all the check boxes. Select the **Safety Equipment** check box, and then click **OK**. Compare your screen with **Figure 1**.

    In the *Category* column, only the rows containing *Safety Equipment* display. The rows not meeting this criteria are hidden from view.

2. On the **Design tab**, in the **Table Style Options group**, select the **Total Row** check box.

    The *total row* displays as the last row in an Excel table and provides functions in drop-down lists for each column. Here, *Total* displays in cell A71. In cell H71, the number *$33,816* indicates the SUM of the Total Cost column for the filtered rows.

3. In the Total row, click cell **C71**, and then click the arrow that displays to the right of the selected cell. In the list, click **Average**. Compare your screen with **Figure 2**.

    Excel averages only the visible rows in column C—here, *$150* is the average cost.

4. In the header row, click the **Type filter arrow**. From the menu, clear the **Helmet** and the **Shield** check boxes, and then click **OK**.

    Filters can be applied to more than one column. Here, both the Type and Category columns are filtered.

■ **Continue to the next page to complete the skill** ➤

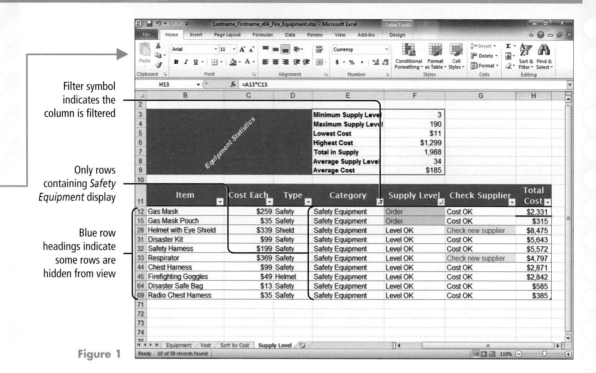

Filter symbol indicates the column is filtered

Only rows containing *Safety Equipment* display

Blue row headings indicate some rows are hidden from view

Figure 1

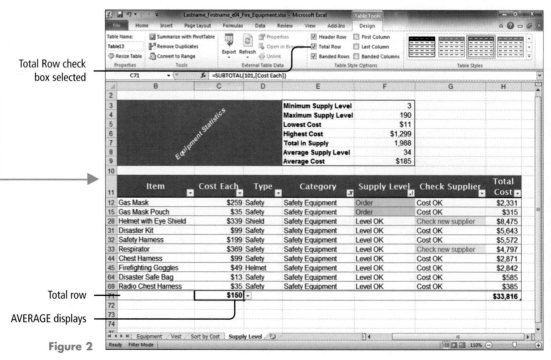

Total Row check box selected

Total row

AVERAGE displays

Figure 2

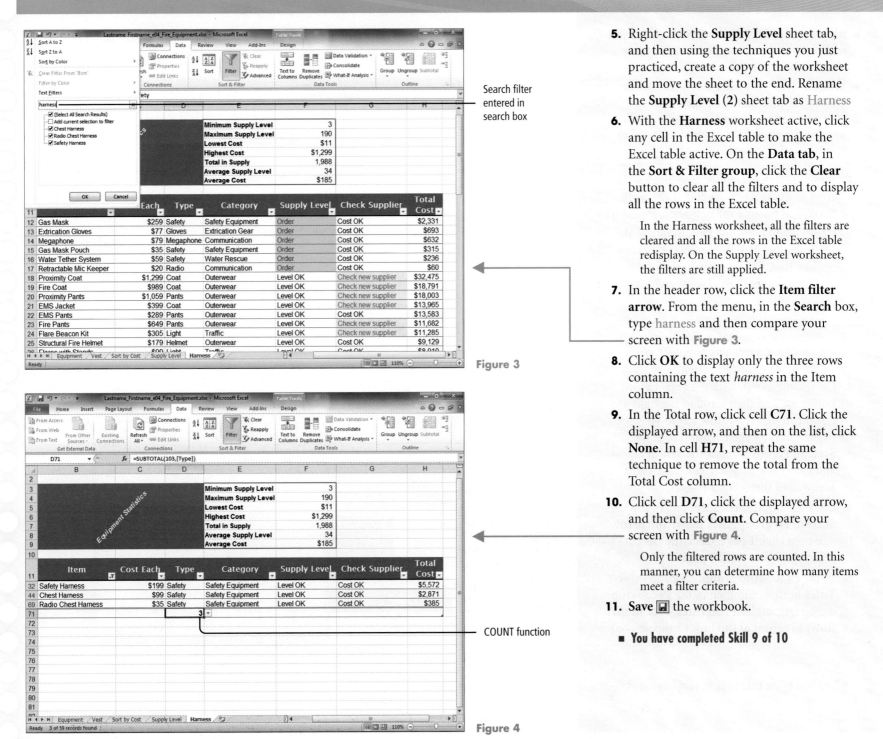

Search filter entered in search box

Figure 3

COUNT function

Figure 4

5. Right-click the **Supply Level** sheet tab, and then using the techniques you just practiced, create a copy of the worksheet and move the sheet to the end. Rename the **Supply Level (2)** sheet tab as Harness

6. With the **Harness** worksheet active, click any cell in the Excel table to make the Excel table active. On the **Data tab**, in the **Sort & Filter group**, click the **Clear** button to clear all the filters and to display all the rows in the Excel table.

   In the Harness worksheet, all the filters are cleared and all the rows in the Excel table redisplay. On the Supply Level worksheet, the filters are still applied.

7. In the header row, click the **Item filter arrow**. From the menu, in the **Search** box, type harness and then compare your screen with **Figure 3**.

8. Click **OK** to display only the three rows containing the text harness in the Item column.

9. In the Total row, click cell **C71**. Click the displayed arrow, and then on the list, click **None**. In cell **H71**, repeat the same technique to remove the total from the Total Cost column.

10. Click cell **D71**, click the displayed arrow, and then click **Count**. Compare your screen with **Figure 4**.

    Only the filtered rows are counted. In this manner, you can determine how many items meet a filter criteria.

11. **Save** 🖫 the workbook.

■ **You have completed Skill 9 of 10**

▶ After sorting, filtering, and totaling an Excel table, you can convert the Excel table into a range.

▶ When a large worksheet is too wide or too long to print on a single page, row and column headings can be printed on each page or the worksheet can be formatted to print on a single page.

1. Right-click the **Harness** sheet tab, create a copy of the sheet at the end of the workbook, and rename the new sheet Inventory

2. Click cell **A11**. On the **Design tab**, in the **Tools group**, click the **Convert to Range** button. Read the message box, click **Yes**, and then compare your screen with **Figure 1.**

   When converting an Excel table into a range, all filters are removed and the heading row no longer displays filter buttons. Any existing sorts and formatting remain.

3. On the status bar, click the **Page Layout** button, and then scroll to the right and down through the worksheet to view the pages. On the **Page Layout tab**, in the **Scale to Fit group**, click the **Width arrow**, and then click **1 page**. Click the **Height arrow**, and then click **1 page**.

4. Click the **Equipment** sheet tab. In the **Scale to Fit group**, click the **Width arrow**, and then click **1 page**. Click the **Height arrow**, and then click **2 pages**.

5. In the **Page Setup group**, click the **Print Titles** button, and then in the **Page Setup** dialog box, under **Print titles**, click in the **Rows to repeat at top** box. Compare your screen with **Figure 2.**

■ **Continue to the next page to complete the skill**

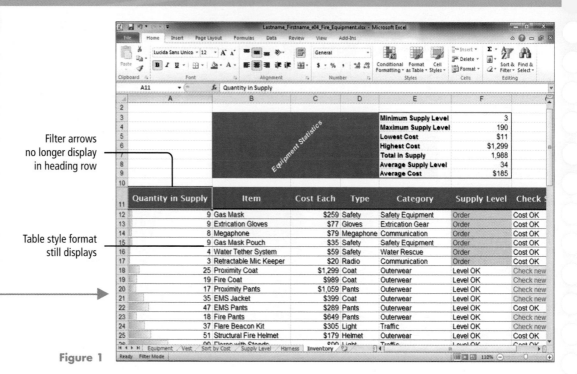

Filter arrows no longer display in heading row

Table style format still displays

Figure 1

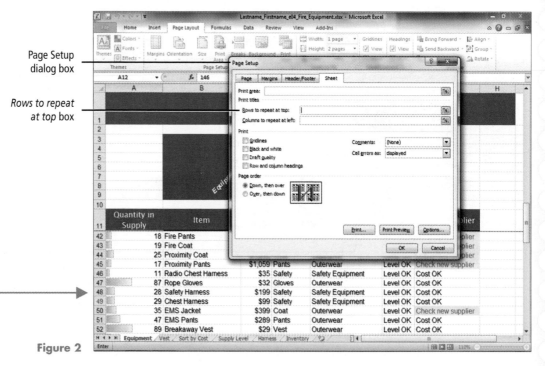

Page Setup dialog box

Rows to repeat at top box

Figure 2

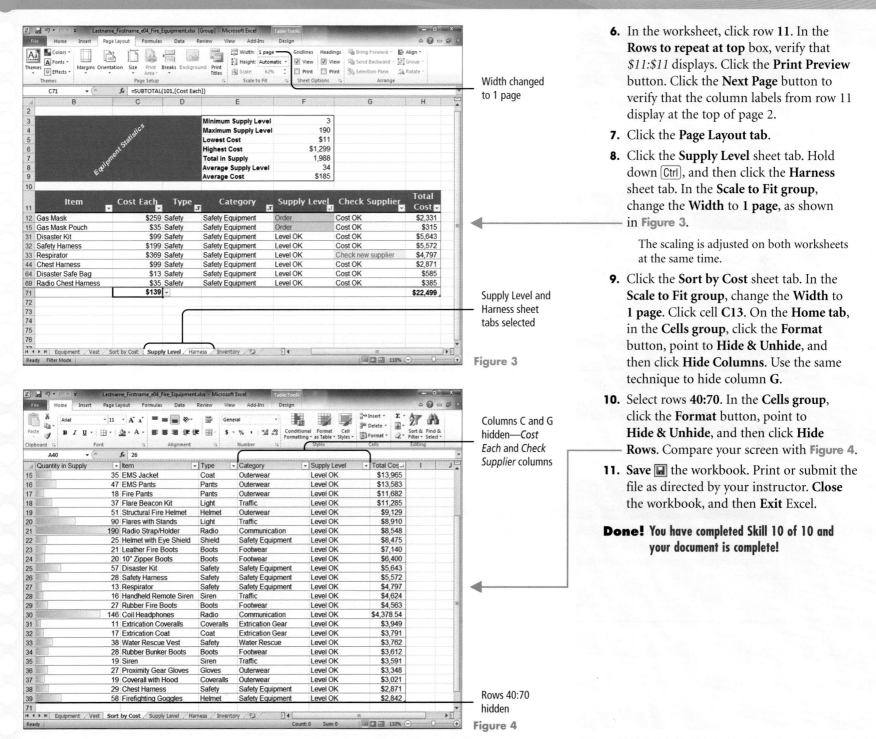

Width changed to 1 page

Supply Level and Harness sheet tabs selected

Figure 3

Columns C and G hidden—*Cost Each* and *Check Supplier* columns

Rows 40:70 hidden

Figure 4

6. In the worksheet, click row **11**. In the **Rows to repeat at top** box, verify that *$11:$11* displays. Click the **Print Preview** button. Click the **Next Page** button to verify that the column labels from row 11 display at the top of page 2.

7. Click the **Page Layout tab.**

8. Click the **Supply Level** sheet tab. Hold down Ctrl, and then click the **Harness** sheet tab. In the **Scale to Fit group**, change the **Width** to **1 page**, as shown in **Figure 3**.

   The scaling is adjusted on both worksheets at the same time.

9. Click the **Sort by Cost** sheet tab. In the **Scale to Fit group**, change the **Width** to **1 page**. Click cell **C13**. On the **Home tab**, in the **Cells group**, click the **Format** button, point to **Hide & Unhide**, and then click **Hide Columns**. Use the same technique to hide column **G**.

10. Select rows **40:70**. In the **Cells group**, click the **Format** button, point to **Hide & Unhide**, and then click **Hide Rows**. Compare your screen with **Figure 4**.

11. **Save** 🖫 the workbook. Print or submit the file as directed by your instructor. **Close** the workbook, and then **Exit** Excel.

Done! You have completed Skill 10 of 10 and your document is complete!

The following More Skills are located at **www.pearsonhighered.com/skills**

More Skills (11) Apply Conditional Color Scales with Top and Bottom Rules

In addition to the conditional formats you have applied in this chapter, you can apply color scales, which apply different colors to the cells, and top/bottom rules, which format the highest or lowest values.

In More Skills 11, you will apply the additional types of conditional formats.

To begin, open your web browser, navigate to www.pearsonhighered.com/skills, locate the name of your textbook, and then follow the instructions on the website.

More Skills (12) Use the Payment (PMT) Function

The PMT function calculates the periodic payment for any loan given the loan amount, interest rate, and length of the loan. When you borrow money from a bank, the amount charged for your use of the borrowed money is called interest, and the interest amount is included in the PMT function.

In More Skills 12, you will use the PMT function to calculate various loan payments.

To begin, open your web browser, navigate to www.pearsonhighered.com/skills, locate the name of your textbook, and then follow the instructions on the website.

More Skills (13) Create PivotTable Reports

A PivotTable report is an interactive way to summarize large amounts of data quickly, to analyze numerical data in depth, and to answer unanticipated questions about your data.

In More Skills 13, you will create a PivotTable report, pivot the data, and then filter the data.

To begin, open your web browser, navigate to www.pearsonhighered.com/skills, locate the name of your textbook, and then follow the instructions on the website.

More Skills (14) Use Goal Seek

Goal Seek is a method to find a specific value for a cell by adjusting the value of another cell. With Goal Seek, you work backward from the desired outcome to find the necessary input to achieve your goal.

In More Skills 14, you will use Goal Seek to determine how much money can be borrowed to achieve a specific monthly payment.

To begin, open your web browser, navigate to www.pearsonhighered.com/skills, locate the name of your textbook, and then follow the instructions on the website.

Key Terms

Online Help Skills

1. **Start** 🔘 Excel. In the upper right corner of the Excel window, click the **Help** button 🔘. In the **Help** window, click the **Maximize** 🔲 button.

2. Click in the search box, type sparklines and then click the **Search** button 🔍. In the search results, click **Use sparklines to show data trends**. Compare your screen with **Figure 1**.

Figure 1

3. Read the article to see if you can answer the following: What are some benefits of using sparklines compared to charts?

Matching

Match each term in the second column with its correct definition in the first column by writing the letter of the term on the blank line in front of the correct definition.

_____ **1.** A prewritten formula that performs calculations by using specific values in a particular order or structure.

_____ **2.** A column in an Excel table that uses a single formula that adjusts for each row.

_____ **3.** The Excel function that adds a group of values and then divides the result by the number of values in the group.

_____ **4.** In an Excel function, the values in parentheses used to perform calculations or operations.

_____ **5.** A type of function that summarizes a group of measurements.

_____ **6.** The function that returns the serial number of the current date and time.

_____ **7.** An Excel function that determines the smallest value in a selected range of values.

_____ **8.** An Excel function that determines the largest value in a selected range of values.

_____ **9.** The type of function that tests for specific conditions and typically uses conditional tests to determine whether specified conditions are TRUE or FALSE.

_____ **10.** Conditions that you specify.

A Arguments

B AVERAGE

C Calculated column

D Criteria

E Function

F Logical functions

G MAX

H MIN

I NOW

J Statistical functions

Multiple Choice

Choose the correct answer.

1. This type of test has an outcome of TRUE or FALSE.
   A. Logical
   B. Rational
   C. Normal

2. This function checks whether criteria are met and returns one value if TRUE and another value if FALSE.
   A. BRANCH
   B. TRUE
   C. IF

3. After sorting, filtering, and totaling an Excel table, an Excel table can be converted into this.
   A. Link
   B. Pane
   C. Range

4. This word describes a format, such as cell shading, that is applied to cells when a specified condition is true.
   A. Filtered
   B. Conditional
   C. Calculated

5. This word describes a function that is updated each time the workbook is opened.
   A. Volatile
   B. Changeable
   C. Unstable

6. This command ensures that header rows and columns remain visible when a worksheet is scrolled.
   A. Total Panes
   B. Excel Panes
   C. Freeze Panes

7. This term refers to related data organized in rows and columns that is managed independently from other data in the worksheet.
   A. Pane
   B. Excel table
   C. Window

8. This command displays only the rows of a table that meet specified criteria.
   A. Filter
   B. Standard
   C. Chart

9. This row displays as the last row in an Excel table and provides summary statistics.
   A. Total
   B. Sorted
   C. Changeable

10. These symbols are inserted into logical functions to determine whether a condition is true or false—(<) and (=), for example.
    A. Comparison operators
    B. Mathematical operators
    C. Logical symbols

Topics for Discussion

1. Think about current news stories, including sports stories, and identify one or more in which statistical functions, such as AVERAGE, MIN, or MAX play an important part. For example, when reporting about home prices, the average home price is frequently quoted.

2. Sorting and filtering are two of the most valuable ways to analyze data. If you were presented with an Excel table containing names and addresses, what are some of the ways you might sort or filter the data? If you were presented with an Excel table of a day's cash transactions at your college's cafeteria, what are some ways you could sort, filter, and total?

Skill Check

To complete this project, you will need the following file:

- e04_Surplus

You will save your workbook as:

- **Lastname_Firstname_e04_Surplus**

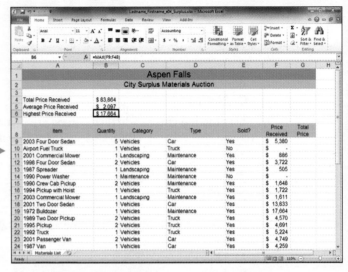

1. **Start** Excel, and then open the file **e04_Surplus**. Save the workbook in the **Excel Chapter 4** folder as Lastname_Firstname_e04_Surplus Insert the file name in the worksheet's left footer and the sheet name in the right footer. Return to **Normal** view.

2. Click cell **B4**, and then on the **Home tab**, in the **Editing group**, click the **Sum** button. With the insertion point in the function parentheses, select the range **F9:F48**, and then press [Enter]. With cell **B5** active, in the **Editing group**, click the **Sum button arrow**, and then click **Average**. Select the range **F9:F48**, and then press [Enter]. Using the same range, in cell **B6**, enter the **MAX** function. Compare your screen with **Figure 1**.

Figure 1

3. Select the range **A4:B6**. Point to the right edge of the selected range, and then drag the cells to **D4:E6**. With the range still selected, in the **Font group**, click the **Border button arrow**, and then click **Outside Borders**.

4. In cell **B4**, type Surplus and then merge and center the title in the range **B4:C6**. In the **Alignment group**, click the **Middle Align** button. Click the **Orientation** button, and then click **Angle Counterclockwise**. Click the **Fill Color button arrow**, and then click the color in the fourth row and sixth column— **Blue, Accent 2, Lighter 40%**.

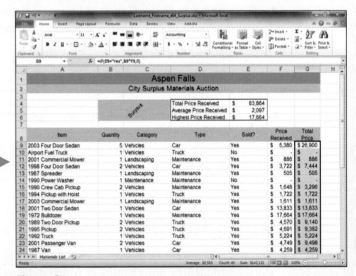

5. Click cell **G9**. On the **Formulas tab**, in the **Function Library group**, click **Logical**, and then click **IF**. In the **Logical_test** box, type E9="Yes" In the **Value_if_true** box, type B9*F9 In the **Value_if_false** box, type 0 and then click **OK**. Copy the function down through cell **G48**, and then on the **Home tab**, in the **Styles group**, click the **Cell Styles** button and apply **Currency [0]** to the range. Compare your screen with **Figure 2**.

Figure 2

■ Continue to the next page to complete this Skill Check

6. Select cell **A1**. On the **Home tab**, in the **Editing group**, click the **Find & Select** button, and then click **Replace**. In the **Find what** box, type Sedan In the **Replace with** box, type Car and then click **Replace All**. Click **OK**, and then **Close** the dialog box.

7. Click cell **A9**. On the **View tab**, in the **Window group**, click the **Freeze Panes** button, and then click **Freeze Panes**.

8. Right-click the **Materials List** sheet tab, and then click **Move or Copy**. In the **Move or Copy** dialog box, click (**move to end**), select the **Create a copy** check box, and then click **OK**. Rename the new sheet tab as Price by Car

9. With the *Price by Car* worksheet active, in the **Window group**, click the **Freeze Panes** button, and then click **Unfreeze Panes**. On the **Insert tab**, in the **Tables group**, click the **Table** button. Verify that the **My table has headers** check box is selected, and then click **OK**. On the **Design tab**, in the **Table Styles group**, click the **More** button, and then under **Light**, click **Table Style Light 17**.

10. Click the **Type filter arrow**, and then clear the (**Select All**) check box. Select the **Car** check box, and then click **OK**. Click the **Total Price filter arrow**, and then click **Sort Largest to Smallest**. On the **Design tab**, in the **Table Style Options group**, select the **Total Row** check box. Click cell **B49**, click the arrow that displays, and from the list, click **Sum**.

11. Select the range **F9:F48**. On the **Home tab**, in the **Styles group**, click the **Conditional Formatting** button, point to **Data Bars**, and then click the first choice in the second row—**Orange Data Bar**. Click cell **A9**, and then compare your screen with **Figure 3**.

12. Create a copy of the *Price by Car* worksheet, and then rename the new sheet tab Pickups On the **Data tab**, in the **Sort & Filter group**, click the **Clear** button. Click the **Item filter arrow**. In the **Search** box, type Pickup and then click **OK**.

13. Right-click the sheet tab, and then click **Select All Sheets**. On the **Page Layout tab**, in the **Page Setup group**, click the **Orientation** button, and then click **Landscape**. In the **Scale to Fit group**, change the **Width** to **1 page**.

14. Click the **Materials List** sheet tab, and then in the **Page Setup group**, click the **Print Titles** button. In the **Page Setup** dialog box, click in the **Rows to repeat at top** box, click row **8**, and then press Enter.

15. **Save** the workbook. Click the **File tab**, and then click the **Print tab**. Under **Settings**, click the button, and then click **Print Entire Workbook**. Compare your workbook with **Figure 4**. Print or submit the file as directed by your instructor. **Close** the workbook. **Exit** Excel.

Done! You have completed the Skill Check

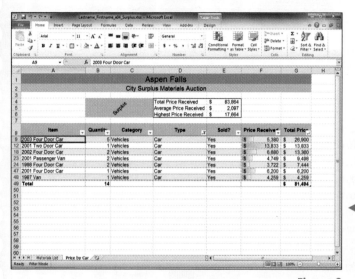

Figure 3

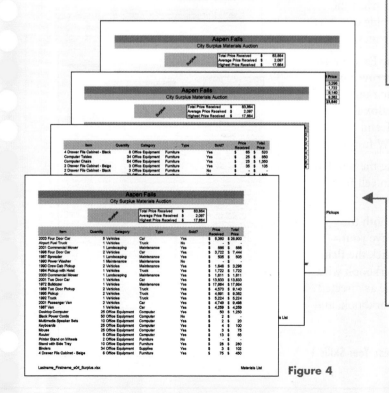

Figure 4

Assess Your Skills 1

To complete this project, you will need the following file:

- e04_Water

You will save your workbook as:

- **Lastname_Firstname_e04_Water**

1. **Start** Excel, and open the file **e04_Water**. Save the workbook in the **Excel Chapter 4** folder as Lastname_Firstname_e04_Water Insert the file name in the worksheet's left footer and the sheet name in the right footer. Return to **Normal** view.

2. Click cell **F4**. From the **Editing group**, insert the **AVERAGE** function using the range **F12:F41** as the argument. For each cell in the range **F5:F7**, insert the appropriate **Statistical** functions using the values in column **G** as the function arguments.

3. In cell **H12**, insert the **IF** function with the following logical arguments. For the logical test, check whether the **Farm Water** result is greater than the **MCL, TT,** or **MRDL** value in the same row. If the logical test is true, Yes should display. If the logical test is false, No should display. **Center** the result in the cell, and then copy the function down through cell **H41**.

4. Verify that the range **H12:H41** is selected, and then apply a **Highlight** conditional format that will display any cells that indicate Yes formatted with **Light Red Fill with Dark Red Text**.

5. Convert the range **A11:H41** to an Excel table, and then apply the **Table Style Light 16** table style.

6. Create a copy of the *Water* worksheet, and then rename the new sheet tab **Chlorine**. On the *Chlorine* worksheet, filter the table to display only the contaminant Chlorine For the Excel table, display the **Total Row**. In cell **E42**, display the **AVERAGE**, and then in cell **H42**, select **None**. In cell **A42**, change the title to Average

7. Create a copy of the *Chlorine* worksheet, and then rename the new sheet tab Farm Water In the *Farm Water* worksheet, convert the Excel table to a range, and then hide columns C and G. In cell **A12**, freeze the panes.

8. Click the **Water** sheet tab. In the Excel table, click the **Contaminants filter arrow**, and then click **Sort A to Z**. Select the range **D4:F7**, and then apply a **Thick Box Border**. Click cell **A43**, type High Test Trend and then in cell **A44**, insert the **NOW** function.

9. Select the range **G12:G41**. Using the selected range, insert a **Line Sparkline** in cell **B43**, and then display its **High Point**.

10. Select all the worksheets. Scale both the **Width** and **Height** to **1 page**. **Save** your workbook. Click the **File tab**, click the **Print tab**, and then compare your workbook with **Figure 1**. Print or submit the file as directed by your instructor. **Close** the workbook, and then **Exit** Excel.

Done! You have completed Assess Your Skills 1

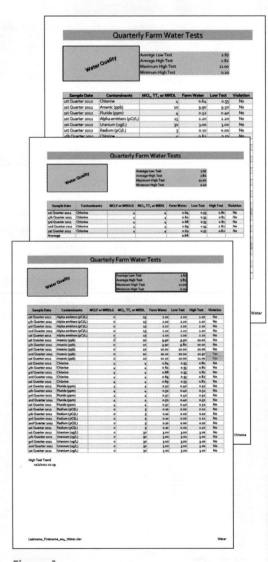

Figure 1

Assessment

Assess Your Skills 3 and 4 can be found at **www.pearsonhighered.com/skills**.

Assess Your Skills 2

To complete this project, you will need the following file:

- e04_Roof

You will save your workbook as:

- Lastname_Firstname_e04_Roof

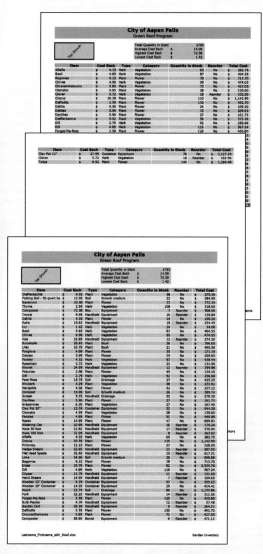

Lastname_Firstname_e04_Roof.xlsx   Garden Inventory

Figure 1

1. **Start** Excel, and open the file **e04_Roof**. Save the workbook in the **Excel Chapter 4** folder as Lastname_Firstname_e04_Roof Insert the file name in the worksheet's left footer and the sheet name in the right footer. Return to **Normal** view.

2. In the range **B4:B7**, insert the appropriate statistical functions using the appropriate ranges. Move the range **A4:B7** to **D4:E7**.

3. In cell **A4**, type Top Growth and then merge and center the cell across the range **A4:A7**. In the merged cell, apply **Middle Align**, a **Thick Box Border**, the **Fill Color Dark Green, Accent 4, Lighter 60%**, and then change the orientation to **Angle Counterclockwise**.

4. In cell **F10**, insert the **IF** function with the following logical arguments. For the logical test, check whether the **Quantity in Stock** is greater than **20**. If the logical test is true, No should display. If the logical test is false, Reorder should display. **Center** the result in the cell.

5. Copy the function in cell **F10** down through cell **F68**. In the range **F10:F68**, apply a **Highlight** conditional format that will display any cells that indicate *Reorder* formatted with **Light Red Fill**.

6. Find and replace all occurrences of Ground Cover with Herb

7. Convert the range **A9:F68** to an Excel table, and then apply the **Table Style Medium 12** table style. In cell **G9**, type Total Cost and then in cell **G10**, enter the formula to calculate the *Cost Each* multiplied by the *Quantity in Stock*. In columns **A:G**, AutoFit the column width.

8. Scale the page **Width** to **1 page** and the page **Height** to **2 pages**, and then set the titles in row **9** to repeat on each printed page.

9. Create a copy of the worksheet, and then rename the new sheet tab Plants On the *Plants* worksheet, filter the Excel table to display the categories **Bush, Flower,** and **Vegetation**. Sort the table in alphabetical order by **Item**.

10. Display the **Total Row**, and then in **E69**, display the column's **SUM**.

11. **Save** your workbook. Compare your workbook with **Figure 1**. Print or submit the file as directed by your instructor. **Close** the workbook, and then **Exit** Excel.

Done! You have completed Assess Your Skills 2

Assess Your Skills Visually

To complete this project, you will need the following file:

- e04_Art

You will save your workbook as:

- **Lastname_Firstname_e04_Art**

Open the file **e04_Art**, and save the workbook in the **Excel Chapter 4** folder as Lastname_Firstname_e04_Art Add the file name in the worksheet's left footer and the sheet name in the right footer. In the range **E4:E7**, apply appropriate functions to calculate the results shown. In column **F**, use the **IF** logical function indicating *Insure* for art with a value greater than $50,000. Apply conditional formatting to the **Insurance** column, as shown in **Figure 1**. Create a copy of the worksheet, and rename the new sheet tab Paintings Convert the data to an Excel table, and format with the **Table Style Light 14**. Filter the table to show only the **Painting** category, and sort the table by **Location**. Insert the **Total Row** as shown in **Figure 1**. **Save** the workbook. Print or submit the file as directed by your instructor.

Done! You have completed Assess Your Skills Visually

Aspen Falls

City Artwork

Artwork

Highest Value	$	74,482
Lowest Value	$	25,631
Average Value	$	53,375
Total Value	$	1,120,866

Artist	Name of Art	Value	Location	Category	Insurance
Margaret Voboril	Spring in Aspen Falls	$ 74,482	Aspen Falls Courthouse	Painting	Insure
Margaret Voboril	Aspen Falls Spring	$ 49,293	Convention Center	Sculpture	No
Margaret Voboril	Aspen Falls in Blue	$ 48,180	Aspen Falls Courthouse	Painting	No
Jennifer Grube	Aspen Falls in Green	$ 45,448	Aspen Falls Courthouse	Painting	No
Margaret Voboril	Autumn in Aspen Falls	$ 59,571	Durango County Center	Painting	Insure
Becky Spiegel	Durango Park Geese	$ 64,687	Durango County Center	Sculpture	Insure
Becky Spiegel	Durango Park View	$ 38,794	Durango County Center	Painting	No
Margaret Voboril	Aspen Falls Winter	$ 41,377	Aspen Falls Courthouse	Sculpture	No
Margaret Voboril	Winter in Aspen Falls	$ 25,631	Aspen Falls Courthouse	Painting	No
Lisa Junker	Aspen Lakes at Sunset	$ 59,387	Convention Center	Painting	Insure
Lisa Junker	Aspen Lakes	$ 71,663	Convention Center	Sculpture	Insure
Jennifer Grube	Aspen Falls in Scarlet	$ 57,417	Convention Center	Sculpture	Insure
Margaret Voboril	Summer in Aspen Falls	$ 36,789	Aspen Falls Courthouse	Painting	No
Becky Spiegel	Durango Park Lake	$ 68,837	Convention Center	Painting	Insure
Lisa Junker	Aspen Lakes at Dawn	$ 72,698	Durango County Center	Painting	Insure
Lisa Junker	Aspen Lakes at Night	$ 29,306	Durango County Center	Painting	No
Jennifer Grube	Aspen Falls in Gold	$ 54,372	Convention Center	Painting	Insure
Becky Spiegel	Durango Park Children	$ 36,786	Aspen Falls Courthouse	Painting	No
Lisa Junker	Aspen Lakes at Noon	$ 71,084	Aspen Falls Courthouse	Painting	Insure
Becky Spiegel	Durango Park Water	$ 43,139	Durango County Center	Painting	No
Jennifer Grube	Aspen Falls in Yellow	$ 71,925	Aspen Falls Courthouse	Painting	Insure

Lastname_Firstname_e04_Art.xlsx Art Inventory

Aspen Falls

City Artwork

Artwork

Highest Value	$	74,482
Lowest Value	$	25,631
Average Value	$	53,375
Total Value	$	1,120,866

Artist	Name of Art	Value	Location	Category	Insurance
Margaret Voboril	Spring in Aspen Falls	$ 74,482	Aspen Falls Courthouse	Painting	Insure
Margaret Voboril	Aspen Falls in Blue	$ 48,180	Aspen Falls Courthouse	Painting	No
Jennifer Grube	Aspen Falls in Green	$ 45,448	Aspen Falls Courthouse	Painting	No
Margaret Voboril	Winter in Aspen Falls	$ 25,631	Aspen Falls Courthouse	Painting	No
Margaret Voboril	Summer in Aspen Falls	$ 36,789	Aspen Falls Courthouse	Painting	No
Becky Spiegel	Durango Park Children	$ 36,786	Aspen Falls Courthouse	Painting	No
Lisa Junker	Aspen Lakes at Noon	$ 71,084	Aspen Falls Courthouse	Painting	Insure
Jennifer Grube	Aspen Falls in Yellow	$ 71,925	Aspen Falls Courthouse	Painting	Insure
Lisa Junker	Aspen Lakes at Sunset	$ 59,387	Convention Center	Painting	Insure
Becky Spiegel	Durango Park Lake	$ 68,837	Convention Center	Painting	Insure
Jennifer Grube	Aspen Falls in Gold	$ 54,372	Convention Center	Painting	Insure
Margaret Voboril	Autumn in Aspen Falls	$ 59,571	Durango County Center	Painting	Insure
Becky Spiegel	Durango Park View	$ 38,794	Durango County Center	Painting	No
Lisa Junker	Aspen Lakes at Dawn	$ 72,698	Durango County Center	Painting	Insure
Lisa Junker	Aspen Lakes at Night	$ 29,306	Durango County Center	Painting	No
Becky Spiegel	Durango Park Water	$ 43,139	Durango County Center	Painting	No
Total		$ 836,429			

Lastname_Firstname_e04_Art.xlsx Paintings

Figure 1

Skills in Context

To complete this project, you will need the following file:

- e04_Schools

You will save your workbook as:

- Lastname_Firstname_e04_Schools

Open the file **e04_Schools**, and save the workbook in your **Excel Chapter 4** folder as Lastname_Firstname_e04_Schools Add the file name in the worksheet's left footer. View the worksheet, and decide how best to summarize the data effectively. Add titles and statistical functions similar to those you used in this chapter. In column D, use a logical function to calculate whether a class needs a Teacher Aide—a class needs a Teacher Aide if the class size is greater than 30. Format the data as an Excel table, add a total row, and sort the Excel table from largest to smallest class

size. Set the titles in row 12 to repeat on each page. Copy the worksheet, and then in the new worksheet, apply a filter to display the classes that need a teacher aide. Rename the new sheet tab with a worksheet name that describes the filter. Save your workbook, and then print or submit the file as directed by your instructor.

Done! You have completed Skills in Context

Skills and You

To complete this project, you will need the following file:

- New blank Excel workbook

You will save your workbook as:

- Lastname_Firstname_e04_Budget

Do you ever try to figure out where your money goes? Make a list of major spending categories, such as Housing, Transportation, Food, Clothing, Entertainment, Gifts, Personal Care, and so on. Within each category, make a list of Types. For example, within Clothing, you might have Work Clothes, Leisure Clothes, or Special Occasion Clothes. Next, for a one-week or a one-month period, keep an exact record of every financial transaction you make. In an Excel worksheet, use a new row for every transaction.

Record the amount and a description of the transaction, and assign a type and a category. Use Excel's table feature to sort and filter your information to see how much you are spending for specific types of expenses. Save your workbook as Lastname_Firstname_e04_Budget and submit the workbook as directed by your instructor.

Done! You have completed Skills and You

CHAPTER 1

Work with Databases and Create Tables

▶ Microsoft Access is an application used to store, organize, access, and update data.

▶ To build a database, you first save the database file and then create tables to store the information you need.

Your starting screen will look like this:

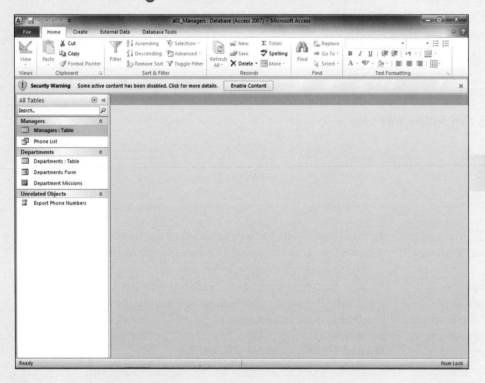

SKILLS

Skills 1-10 Training

At the end of this chapter, you will be able to:

Skill 1   Open and Organize Existing Databases

Skill 2   Enter and Edit Table Data

Skill 3   Create Forms and Enter Data

Skill 4   Filter Data in Queries

Skill 5   Create, Preview, and Print Reports

Skill 6   Create Databases and Tables

Skill 7   Change Data Types and Other Field Properties

Skill 8   Create Tables in Design View

Skill 9   Relate Tables

Skill 10 Enter Data in Related Tables

MORE SKILLS

More Skills 11 Compact and Repair Databases

More Skills 12 Import Data from Excel

More Skills 13 Work with the Attachment Data Type

More Skills 14 Work with the Hyperlink and Yes/No Data Types

Outcome

Using the skills listed to the left will enable you to create database objects like this:

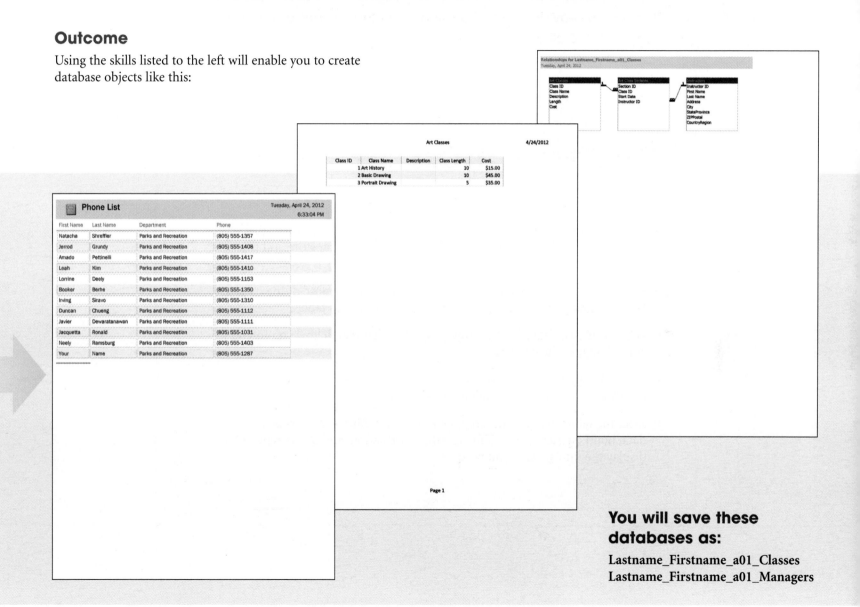

You will save these databases as:

Lastname_Firstname_a01_Classes
Lastname_Firstname_a01_Managers

In this chapter, you will create documents for the Aspen Falls City Hall, which provides essential services for the citizens and visitors of Aspen Falls, California.

Introduction

▶ A single Access file contains many objects, including tables, forms, queries, and reports. Each object has a special purpose to help you store and track information.

▶ When you create a database, you first determine the purpose of the database. You can then plan how to organize the information into tables.

▶ When you create tables, you assign properties that match how you intend to enter data into the database.

▶ After creating tables, you establish the relationships between them and then test those relationships by adding sample data.

▶ After the table relationships are tested, you are ready to add forms to enter data, build queries to search for specific information, and create reports to display the information you need.

Time to complete all
10 skills – 50 to 75 minutes

Find your data files here:

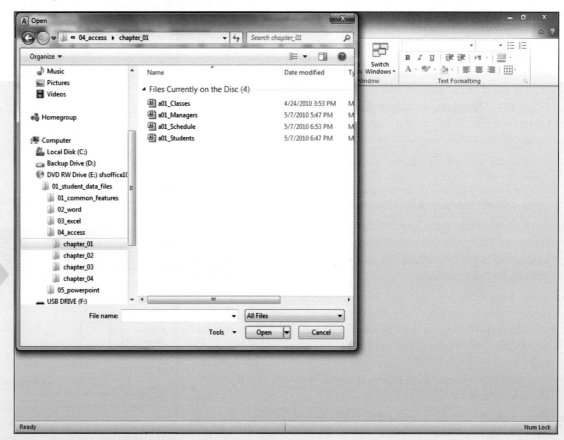

**Student data file needed
for this chapter:**

- a01_Managers

► A *database* is a structured collection of related information about people, events, and things.

1. Click the **Start** button ⊕. From the **Start** menu, locate and then click **Microsoft Access 2010**. If necessary, Maximize ▭ the window.

2. If necessary, insert the Student CD that came with this book.

3. On the left side of the Backstage, click **Open**. In the **Open** dialog box, navigate to your student data files and display the student files for this chapter. Select **a01_Managers**, and then click the **Open** button. Compare your screen with **Figure 1.**

   A security warning may display so that you can verify that the database file came from a trusted source. In the Navigation Pane, several database objects are listed.

4. Click the **File tab**, and then click **Save Database As**. In the **Save As** dialog box navigation pane, display the file list where you are saving your files.

5. In the **Save As** dialog box, click **New folder**, type Access Chapter 1 and then press Enter two times. In the **File name** box, using your own name, name the file Lastname_Firstname_a01_Managers Compare your screen with **Figure 2**, and then click **Save**.

6. If the Security Warning message displays, click the Enable Content button.

■ **Continue to the next page to complete the skill**

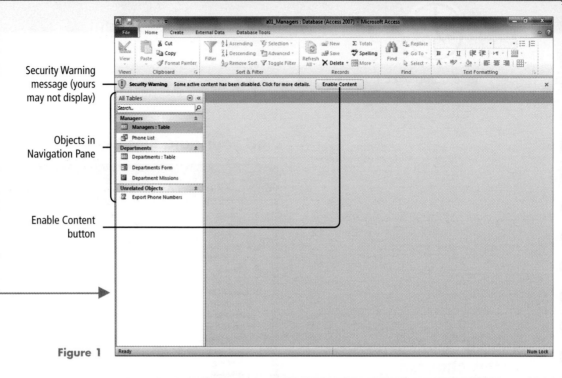

Security Warning message (yours may not display)

Objects in Navigation Pane

Enable Content button

Figure 1

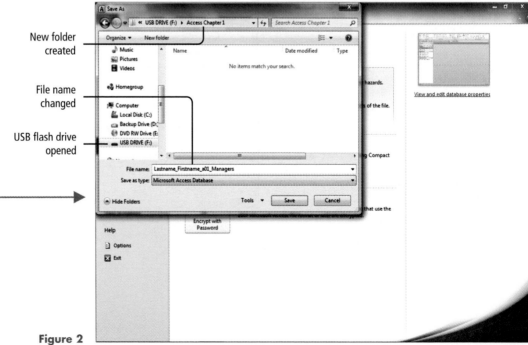

New folder created

File name changed

USB flash drive opened

Figure 2

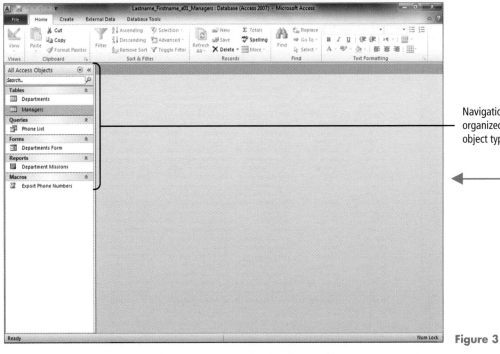

Navigation Pane organized by object type

Figure 3

Common Access Database Objects	
Object	**Purpose**
Table	Store the data in rows and columns.
Form	Enter new records, delete records, or update existing records.
Query	Display a subset of the data in response to a specific question.
Report	Display table data or query results on the screen or in printed form.
Macro	Store a sequence of commands that can be performed as one task.

Figure 4

7. Click the **Navigation Pane arrow**, and then, in the list, click **Managers** to list only the objects related to the Managers data.

 The Navigation Pane can display the objects by type. *Database objects*—or *objects*—are the basic parts of a database that you work with. Here, two tables, a query, a form, a report, and a macro are listed.

8. Click the **Navigation Pane arrow**, and then, in the list, click **Object Type**. Compare your screen with **Figure 3**.

 Database objects work together to provide a *database management system (DBMS)*—software used to manage and interact with the database. The purpose of each database object is summarized in the table in **Figure 4**.

9. In the **Navigation Pane**, under **Forms**, double-click **Departments Form** to open the form.

10. In the **Navigation Pane**, under **Reports**, double-click **Department Missions** to open the report.

11. In the upper-right corner of the **Department Missions** report, click the **Close** button.

12. In the upper-right corner of **Departments Form**, click the **Close** button.

 In this manner, database objects are opened and closed.

13. Leave the database open for the next skill.

■ **You have completed Skill 1 of 10**

▶ Databases store information in tables by organizing data into rows and columns.

▶ You can open tables to view the data that it stores and then make changes to that data.

1. In the **Navigation Pane**, under **Tables**, double-click the **Managers** table to open the table.

2. Click the **Shutter Bar Open/Close** button ⟨«⟩ to close the **Navigation Pane**, and then compare your screen with **Figure 1**.

The *table*—the database object that stores the data—opens in Datasheet view. A *datasheet* displays records in rows and fields in columns similar to a Microsoft Excel spreadsheet. A *record* is the collection of related information that displays in a single row of a database table, and a *field* is a set of common characteristics around which a table is organized.

3. Point to the right of the **Position** column header. When the ⊞ pointer displays, double-click to resize the column width automatically to fit its contents.

4. On the Quick Access Toolbar, click **Save** 🖫. Compare your screen with **Figure 2**.

With Access objects, design changes should be saved. Here, the wider column settings are saved.

5. In the **First Name** column of the first row—the **First Name** field in the first record—double-click *Jake* to select the value, and then type Jack Press ⟨Enter⟩ to accept the change and move to the next field.

■ **Continue to the next page to complete the skill**

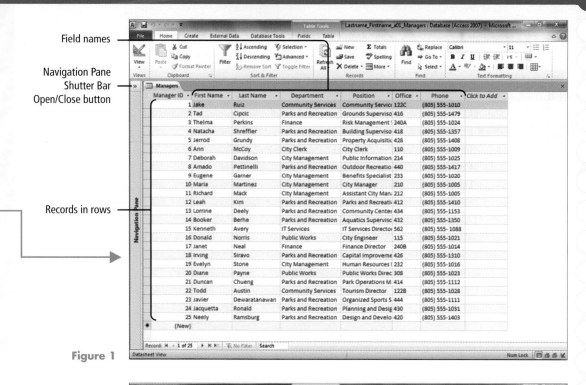

Field names

Navigation Pane Shutter Bar Open/Close button

Records in rows

Figure 1

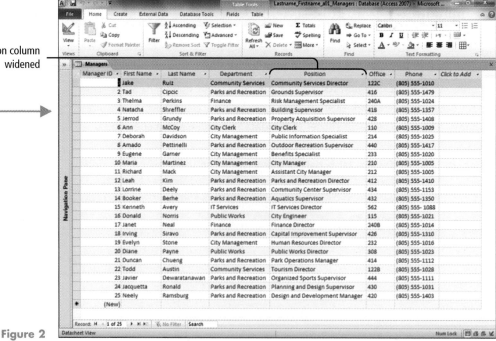

Position column widened

Figure 2

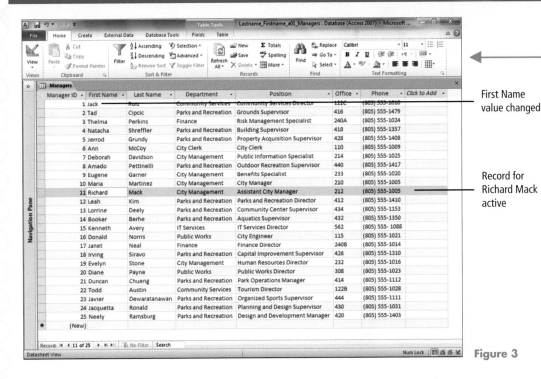

First Name value changed

Record for Richard Mack active

Figure 3

Department	Position	Office	Phone
Community Services	Development Director	122A	(805) 555-1015

Figure 4

6. Click anywhere in the 11th row—the record for Richard Mack. Compare your screen with **Figure 3**.

   When you change data, the new data is saved automatically when you click or navigate to a different record. Here, the new name entered in the previous step has been saved.

7. With the record for Richard Mack active, on the **Home tab**, in the **Records group**, click the **Delete button arrow**, and then click **Delete Record**. Read the message that displays, and then click **Yes**.

8. In the lower-left corner of the datasheet, click the **New (blank) record** button ▶ to move to the datasheet *append row*—a blank row in which a new record is entered.

9. Press Enter to move to the **First Name** column, and then watch the **Manager ID** column as you type Julia

   Manager ID is an *AutoNumber*—a field that automatically enters a unique, numeric value when a record is created. The number is assigned as soon as you begin adding data to a new record. Once an AutoNumber value has been assigned, it cannot be changed. When your AutoNumber values differ from the ones shown in figures, do not try to change yours to match.

10. Press Enter to move to the **Last Name** column, type Wagner and then press Enter. Repeat this technique to enter the data shown in **Figure 4**.

11. When you are done, press Enter to move to a new append row and to save the record. **Close** ✕ the table.

   ■ **You have completed Skill 2 of 10**

► Access *forms* are created so that you can modify or add to the data stored in tables.

1. **Open** ≫ the **Navigation Pane**. If necessary, in the Navigation Pane, under **Tables**, click **Managers** one time to select it.

2. On the **Create tab**, in the **Forms group**, click the **Form** button to create a form for the **Managers** table. Compare your screen with **Figure 1**. If necessary, close the Property Sheet ✕.

   The Form tool creates a form for the table that you selected in the Navigation Pane.

3. Click **Save** 🖫, and then, in the **Save As** dialog box, accept the suggested name for the form by clicking **OK**. In the **Navigation Pane**, notice that the **Managers** form is listed under **Forms**.

4. On the **Design tab**, in the **Themes group**, click the **Themes** button. In the **Themes** gallery, point to—do not click—thumbnails to see their **Live Preview**. Under **Built-In**, click the third thumbnail—**Angles**—to apply the theme.

5. On the **Design tab**, in the **Views group**, click the **View button** to switch to **Form** view. Click **Save** 🖫 to save the design changes, and then compare your screen with **Figure 2**.

   Most forms use the *single form layout*, a layout that displays one record at a time. Here, the form shows the first record from the Managers table. The navigation bar in the lower-left corner of the form is used to move to other records.

■ **Continue to the next page to complete the skill** ▶

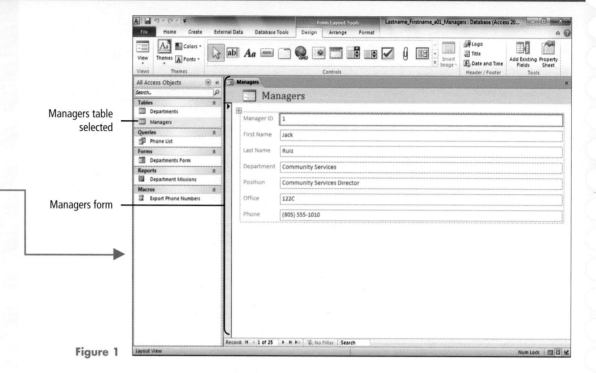

Managers table selected

Managers form

Figure 1

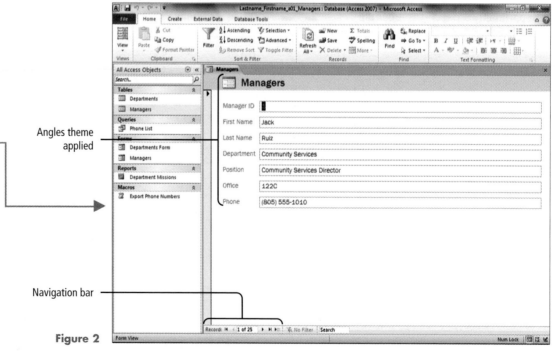

Angles theme applied

Navigation bar

Figure 2

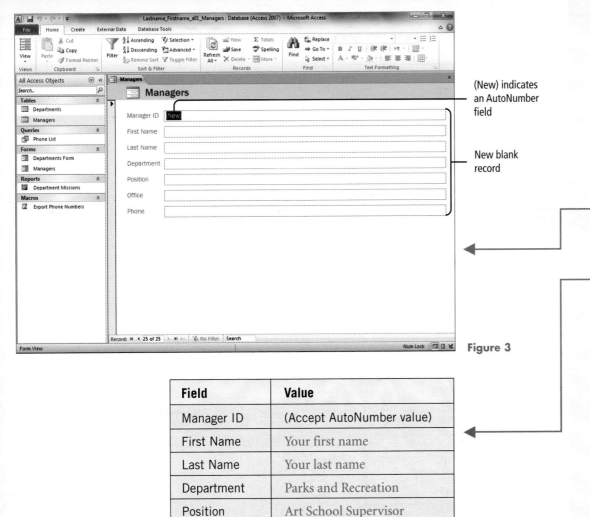

(New) indicates an AutoNumber field

New blank record

Figure 3

Field	Value
Manager ID	(Accept AutoNumber value)
First Name	Your first name
Last Name	Your last name
Department	Parks and Recreation
Position	Art School Supervisor
Office	442
Phone	(805) 555-1287

Figure 4

6. On the **Navigation bar**, click the **Next record** button ▶ to move to the second record—record 2 of 25.

7. In the **Records group**, click the **Delete button arrow**, and then click **Delete Record**. Read the message that displays, and then click **Yes** to remove the record for Tad Cipcic from the Managers table.

8. On the **Navigation bar**, click the **New (blank) record** button ▶ to create a new record. Compare your screen with **Figure 3**.

9. Click in the **First Name** text box, and then type your own first name. Using Enter to move to each field, enter the data shown in **Figure 4**.

10. With the insertion point still in the **Phone** field, press Tab.

    Pressing Enter or Tab when you are in the last field of the last record creates a new, blank record.

11. Press Enter, and then type Kevin Press Esc, and notice that the record returns to a blank record.

    You can cancel entering data into a new record by pressing Esc. This technique is helpful when you are entering data into a record, and you need to start over.

12. **Close** ☒ the **Managers** form.

    Recall that data is saved automatically as you complete each record. Access had already saved the data that you entered, and it did not ask you to save changes when you closed the form.

■ **You have completed Skill 3 of 10**

▶ A *query* displays a subset of the data in response to a specific question.

▶ Queries are modified in *Design view*—a view in which the structure and behavior of Access database objects are modified—and they display their results in Datasheet view.

1. In the **Navigation Pane**, under **Queries**, double-click **Phone List** to open the query datasheet. Compare your screen with **Figure 1**.

Queries display the subset of data in Datasheet view. Here, the query displays the records of the four City Management Department managers from the Managers table.

2. In the **Views** group, click the upper half of the **View** button to switch to **Design** view. Compare your screen with **Figure 2**.

The upper half of the Query tab—the *query design workspace*—lists the available tables and fields that the query should use. The lower half of the query tab—the *design grid*—lists the fields that will display in the query results.

In Access, *criteria* are the conditions used to select the records that you are looking for. Here, the Department field must equal the text *City Management*.

■ **Continue to the next page to complete the skill**

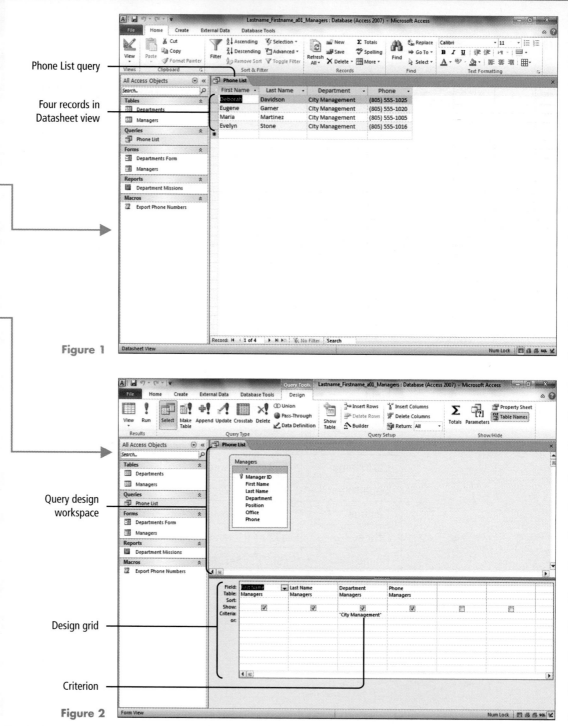

Phone List query

Four records in Datasheet view

Figure 1

Query design workspace

Design grid

Criterion

Figure 2

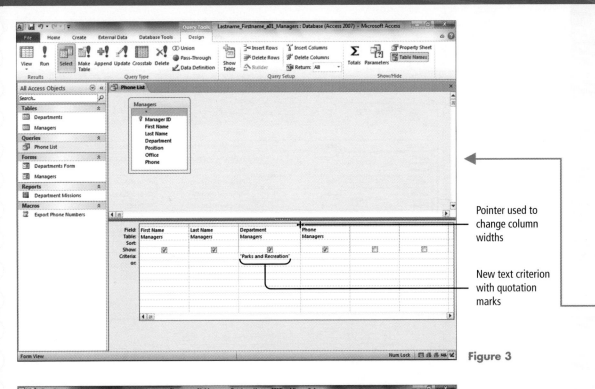

Figure 3

Pointer used to change column widths

New text criterion with quotation marks

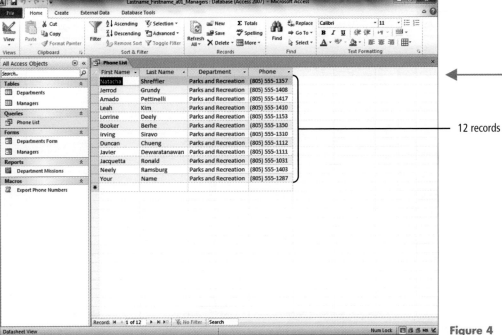

12 records

Figure 4

3. In the **Department** column, in the **Criteria** box, drag to select *"City Management"*, and then press Delete to remove the criterion.

4. In the **Results group**, click the **Run** button to display the phone numbers for all 25 city managers.

5. In the **Views group**, click the **View** button to switch to **Design** view. Click the **Department** column **Criteria** box, and then type "Parks and Recreation"

6. On the right of the **Department** column header, point to the line, and then, with the ⊞ pointer, drag to widen the column so that you can see the entire criterion just typed. Compare your screen with **Figure 3**.

When a query criterion is a text value, the text value needs to be in quotation marks.

7. In the **Results group**, click the **Run** button to display the phone numbers for the 12 managers from the Parks and Recreation Department. Compare your screen with **Figure 4**.

8. On the **Quick Access Toolbar**, click the **Save** button 🔒.

When you widen datasheet columns or change query criteria, you need to save the changes.

9. **Close** ⊠ the Phone List query.

■ **You have completed Skill 4 of 10**

▶ *Reports* display the results of a query or the data in a table.

▶ Reports are often printed and cannot be used to change data.

1. If necessary, in the Navigation Pane, click the Phone List query one time to select it.

2. On the **Create tab**, in the **Reports** group, click the **Report** button to create a report for the selected query.

3. Click **Save** 🔲. In the **Save As** box, accept the name provided by clicking **OK**.

4. **Close** ◀ the **Navigation Pane**, and then compare your screen with **Figure 1**. ──────

When you first create a report using the Report tool, it displays in *Layout view*—a view used to format a report or form while being able to view a sample of the data. Here, the report has the Angles theme because that was the theme last assigned in this database.

The dashed line near the right edge of the report indicates when one printed page will end and another will begin.

5. On the **Home tab**, in the **Views group,** click the lower half of the **View** button— the **View button arrow**, and then click **Print Preview**.

6. On the **Print Preview tab**, in the **Zoom group**, click the **Two Pages** button, and then compare your screen with **Figure 2**. ──

Print Preview is a view used to work with a report that will be printed. Here, the preview indicates that the phone numbers will be printed on two different pages.

■ **Continue to the next page to complete the skill** ▶

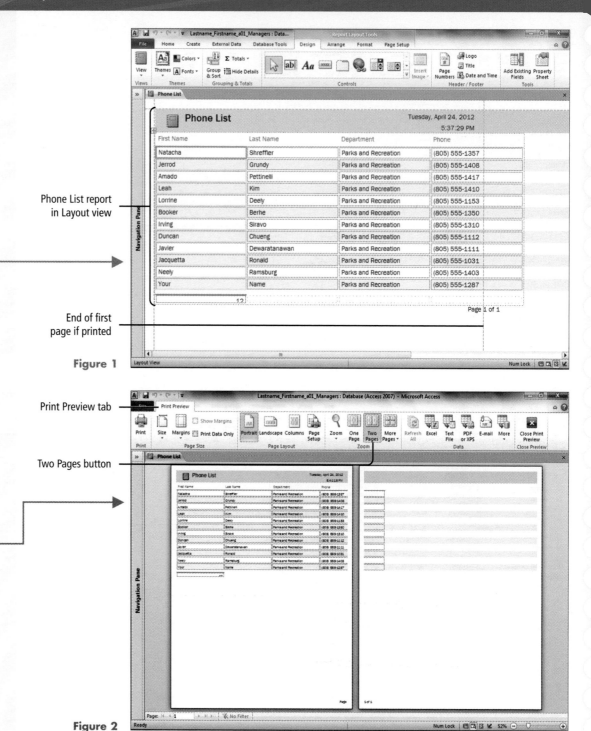

Phone List report in Layout view

End of first page if printed

Figure 1

Print Preview tab

Two Pages button

Figure 2

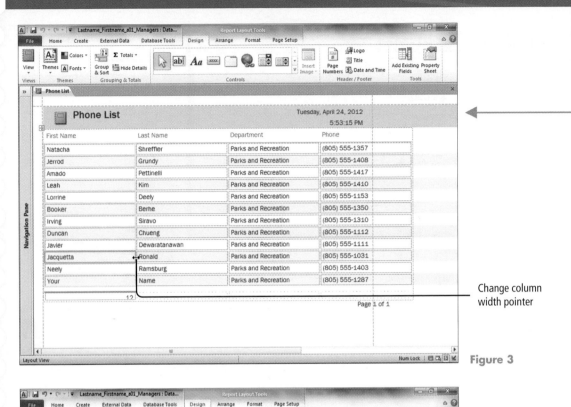

Change column
width pointer

Figure 3

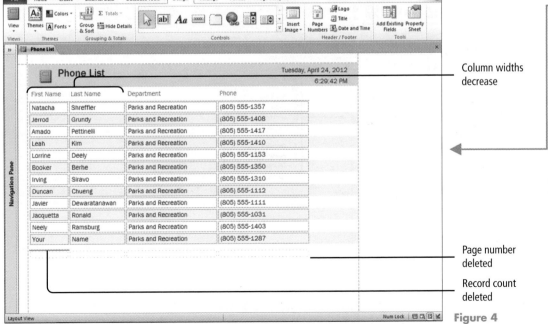

Column widths
decrease

Page number
deleted

Record count
deleted

Figure 4

7. Click the **Close Print Preview** button to return to **Layout** view. In the third to last record, click in the **First Name** field with the value *Jacquetta*. Point to the right edge of the selected field to display the ↔ pointer, as shown in **Figure 3**.

8. With the ↔ pointer, drag to the left to decrease the width of the **First Name** column so that it is slightly wider than the text *Jacquetta*.

9. Repeat the technique just practiced to decrease the width of the **Last Name** column so that it is slightly wider than the text *Dewaratanawan*.

10. Click a field in the **First Name** column. On the **Design tab**, in the **Grouping & Totals group**, click the **Totals** button, and click **Count Records** so that it is no longer selected.

11. At the lower-right edge of the report, click the text *Page 1 of 1*, and the press Delete to remove the page number. Compare your screen with **Figure 4**.

12. On the **Home tab**, in the **Views group**, click the **View button arrow**, and then click **Print Preview**.

13. On the **Print Preview tab**, in the **Page Layout group**, click the **Zoom** button to display the entire report.

14. In the **Print group**, click the **Print** button. If your instructor has asked you to print your work for this chapter, click OK. Otherwise, click Cancel.

15. Click **Save** 🖫, and then **Close** ✕ the **Phone List Report** tab. Open » the **Navigation Pane**.

16. Click **File**, and then click **Exit**.

■ **You have completed Skill 5 of 10**

► Before you create a new database, you assign a name and location for the database file. You can then add objects such as tables, queries, forms, and reports.

► When you save design changes to the objects that you add to a database, they become part of the database file that you created.

1. **Start** ⚫ Access. On the right side of the **New tab**, click in the **File Name** box, and then type Lastname_Firstname_a01_ Classes

2. Click the **Browse** button 🖼, and then navigate to your **Access Chapter 1** folder. Compare your screen with **Figure 1**.

3. Click **OK**, and then on the right side of the **New tab**, click the **Create** button.

   When you create a blank database, a new table is automatically created. The table's ID field is an AutoNumber designated as the table's **primary key**—a field that uniquely identifies each record in a table.

4. Double-click the **ID** column header, and then type Instructor ID Press Enter, and then compare your screen with **Figure 2**.

   When you move to the Click to Add column, a list of basic data types displays. The **Data Type** specifies the type of information that a field will hold; for example, text, number, date, and currency.

5. In the list of data types, click **Text**, and then type First Name

   The **Text data type** stores up to 255 characters of text.

6. Press Enter. In the list of data types, click **Text**, and then type Last Name

■ **Continue to the next page to complete the skill**

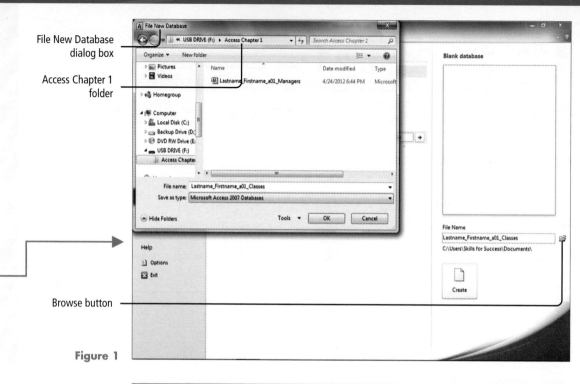

File New Database dialog box

Access Chapter 1 folder

Browse button

Figure 1

Field name changed

List of common data types

Figure 2

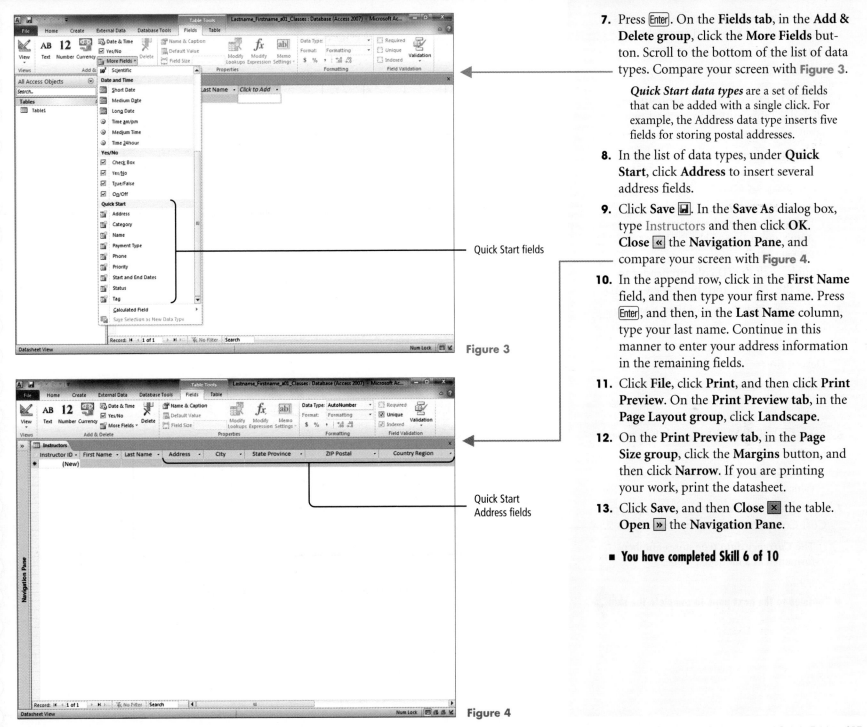

Quick Start fields

Figure 3

Quick Start
Address fields

Figure 4

7. Press Enter. On the **Fields tab**, in the **Add & Delete group**, click the **More Fields** button. Scroll to the bottom of the list of data types. Compare your screen with **Figure 3**.

   Quick Start data types are a set of fields that can be added with a single click. For example, the Address data type inserts five fields for storing postal addresses.

8. In the list of data types, under **Quick Start**, click **Address** to insert several address fields.

9. Click **Save** 🔲. In the **Save As** dialog box, type Instructors and then click **OK**. **Close** « the **Navigation Pane**, and compare your screen with **Figure 4**.

10. In the append row, click in the **First Name** field, and then type your first name. Press Enter, and then, in the **Last Name** column, type your last name. Continue in this manner to enter your address information in the remaining fields.

11. Click **File**, click **Print**, and then click **Print Preview**. On the **Print Preview tab**, in the **Page Layout group**, click **Landscape**.

12. On the **Print Preview tab**, in the **Page Size group**, click the **Margins** button, and then click **Narrow**. If you are printing your work, print the datasheet.

13. Click **Save**, and then **Close** ⊠ the table. **Open** » the **Navigation Pane**.

   ■ **You have completed Skill 6 of 10**

▶ Field properties define the characteristics of the data that can be added to a field.

▶ In addition to Data Type and Name, you can change several other field properties.

1. On the **Create tab**, in the **Tables group**, click the **Table** button to create a new table.

2. Click **Save** 🖫. In the **Save As** dialog box, type Art Classes and then press Enter. Compare your screen with **Figure 1**.

   Recall that when you create a table in Datasheet view, the first column is an AutoNumber that will be the table's primary key.

3. Double-click the **ID** column header to select the text *ID*, and then type Class ID

4. Press Enter, click **Text**, and then type Class Name

5. Press Enter, click **Memo**, and then type Description

   The *Memo data type* stores up to 65,535 characters of text data and the formatting assigned to that text.

6. Press Enter, click **Number**, and then type Length

   The *Number data type* stores numeric values.

7. Press Enter, click **Currency**, and then type Cost Compare your screen with **Figure 2**.

   The *Currency data type* stores numbers formatted as a monetary value.

■ **Continue to the next page to complete the skill**

Table saved as Art Classes

Primary key AutoNumber

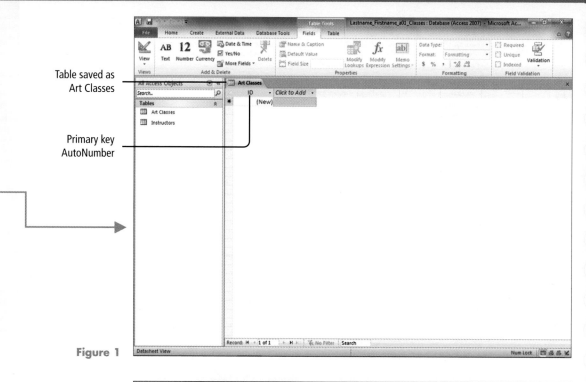

Figure 1

Fields added to table

Currency data type applied

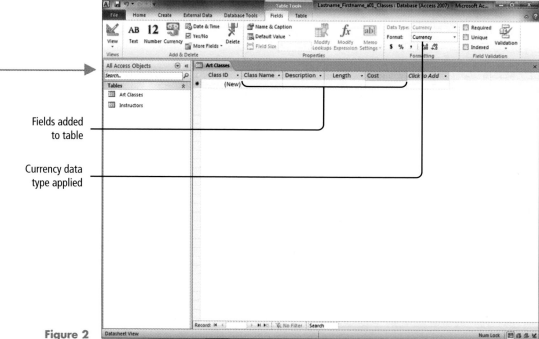

Figure 2

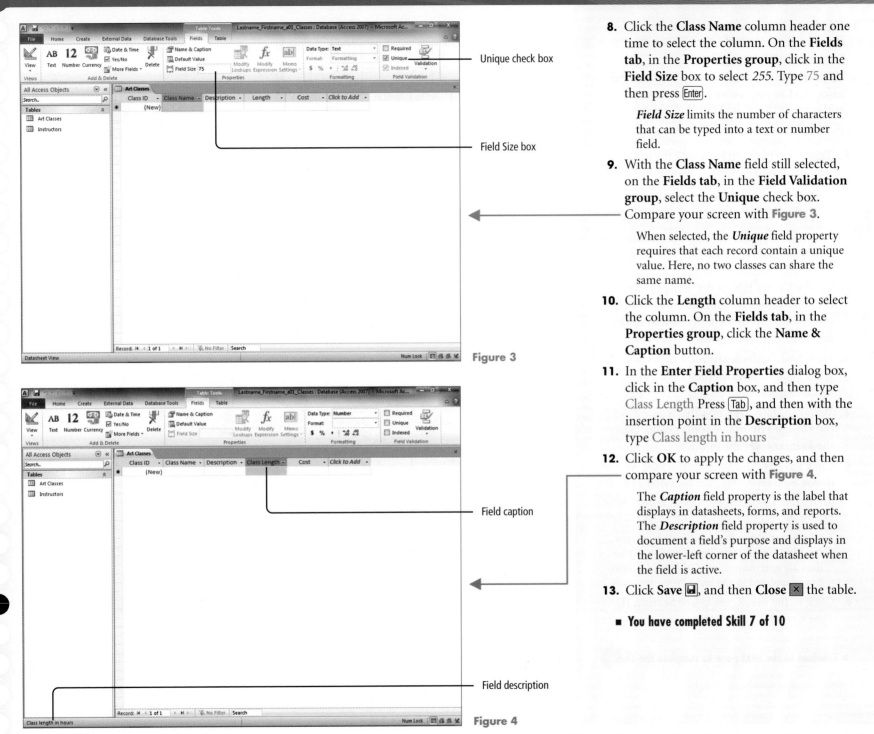

Unique check box

Field Size box

Figure 3

Field caption

Field description

Figure 4

8. Click the **Class Name** column header one time to select the column. On the **Fields tab**, in the **Properties group**, click in the **Field Size** box to select *255*. Type 75 and then press Enter.

   Field Size limits the number of characters that can be typed into a text or number field.

9. With the **Class Name** field still selected, on the **Fields tab**, in the **Field Validation group**, select the **Unique** check box. Compare your screen with **Figure 3**.

   When selected, the *Unique* field property requires that each record contain a unique value. Here, no two classes can share the same name.

10. Click the **Length** column header to select the column. On the **Fields tab**, in the **Properties group**, click the **Name & Caption** button.

11. In the **Enter Field Properties** dialog box, click in the **Caption** box, and then type Class Length Press Tab, and then with the insertion point in the **Description** box, type Class length in hours

12. Click **OK** to apply the changes, and then compare your screen with **Figure 4**.

   The *Caption* field property is the label that displays in datasheets, forms, and reports. The *Description* field property is used to document a field's purpose and displays in the lower-left corner of the datasheet when the field is active.

13. Click **Save** 💾, and then **Close** ❌ the table.

   ▪ **You have completed Skill 7 of 10**

▶ Database designers often sketch the database they need and then follow that plan to create tables.

▶ In a *relational database*, you can place the same field in two tables and then join the tables using the related fields. A *relationship* joins tables using common fields.

1. Take a few moments to study the entity relationship diagram in **Figure 1**.

   An *entity relationship diagram*, or **ERD**, is a visual model used to plan a database. An ERD shows the tables and their fields. Each field's data type is also displayed. The lines between the tables show how each table will be related.

2. On the **Create tab**, in the **Tables group**, click the **Table Design** button. With the insertion point in the first column of the first row, type Section ID

3. Press Enter. In the **Section ID** row, click the **Data Type** arrow, and then click **AutoNumber**.

4. With the **Data Type** box still selected, on the **Design tab**, in the **Tools group**, click the **Primary Key** button.

5. Click **Save** 🔲, and then, in the **Save As** dialog box, type Art Class Sections and then press Enter. Compare your screen with **Figure 2**.

   When working with a table in Design view, the Field Name, Data Type, and Description data are entered in rows. Other field properties are entered in the Field Properties pane.

6. Click in the blank row below **Section ID**. Type Class ID

■ **Continue to the next page to complete the skill**

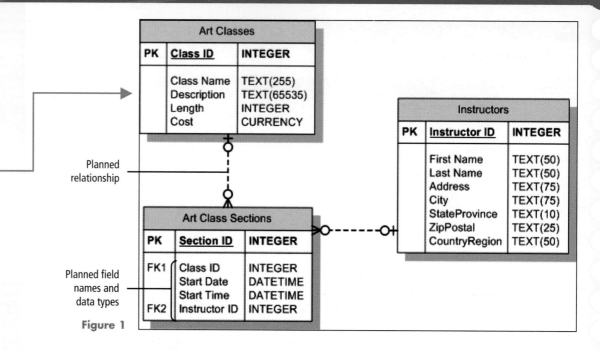

Planned relationship

Planned field names and data types

Figure 1

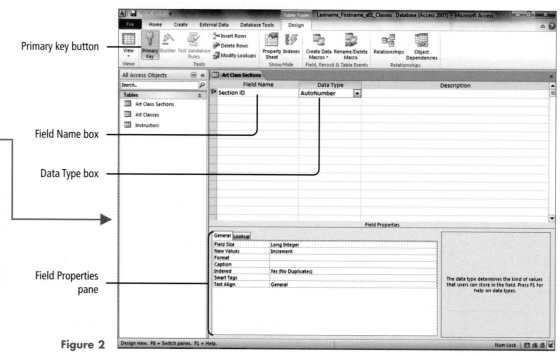

Primary key button

Field Name box

Data Type box

Field Properties pane

Figure 2

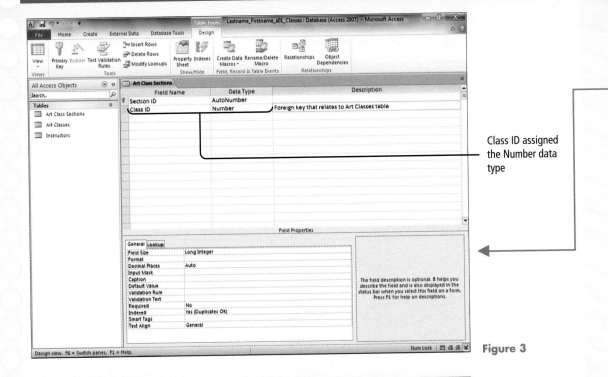

Figure 3

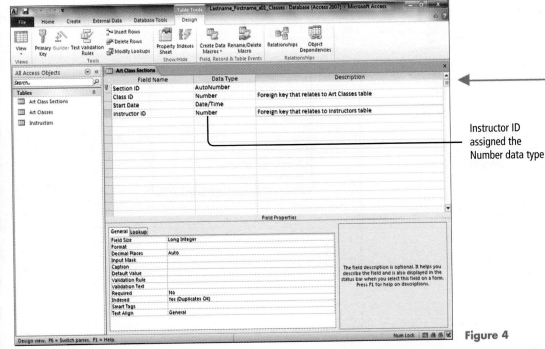

Figure 4

7. Press Enter, click the **Data Type arrow**, and then click **Number**.

8. Press Enter. In the **Description** box, type Foreign key that relates to Art Classes table Compare your screen with **Figure 3**.

   A *foreign key* is a field that is also in another related table. The field in the other table is usually that table's primary key. Here, Class ID is the primary key of the Art Classes table. The Class ID field will be used to join the Art Class Sections and Art Classes tables.

   When you join tables, the common fields must share the same data type. Because the Art Classes table automatically assigns a number to each record, the Class ID field should be assigned the Number data type.

9. Press Enter to move to a new row, and then type Start Date Press Enter, and then type the letter D to assign the **Date/Time** data type.

   The *Date/Time data type* stores numbers in the date or time format.

10. Press Enter two times to move to a new row, and then type Instructor ID Press Enter, and then assign the **Number** data type.

11. In the **Instructor ID Description** box, type Foreign key that relates to Instructors table Compare your screen with **Figure 4**.

   Instructor ID needs to be a number so that it can be joined to the Instructor ID AutoNumber values assigned to records in the Instructors table.

12. Click **Save**, and then **Close** the table.

■ **You have completed Skill 8 of 10**

Class ID assigned the Number data type

Instructor ID assigned the Number data type

▶ Tables are typically joined in a *one-to-many relationship*—a relationship where a record in the first table can have many associated records in the second table.

▶ One-to-many relationships enforce *referential integrity*—the principle that a rule keeps related values synchronized. For example, the foreign key value must match one of the primary key values in the other table.

1. On the **Database Tools tab**, in the **Relationships group**, click the **Relationships** button.

2. In the **Show Table** dialog box, double-click **Art Classes** to add it to the **Relationships** tab. In the **Show Table** dialog box, double-click **Art Class Sections**, double-click **Instructors**, and then click the **Close** button. Compare your screen with **Figure 1**.

3. From the **Art Classes** table, drag **Class ID** to the **Class ID** in the **Art Class Sections** table. When the pointer displays, release the mouse button.

4. In the **Edit Relationships** dialog box, select the **Enforce Referential Integrity** check box. Select the **Cascade Update Related Fields** and **Cascade Delete Related Records** check boxes, and then compare your screen with **Figure 2**.

   With a *cascading update*, you can edit the primary key values in a table, and all the related records in the other table will update accordingly.

   With a *cascading delete*, you can delete a record on the *one* side of the relationship, and all the related records on the *many* side will also be deleted.

■ **Continue to the next page to complete the skill**

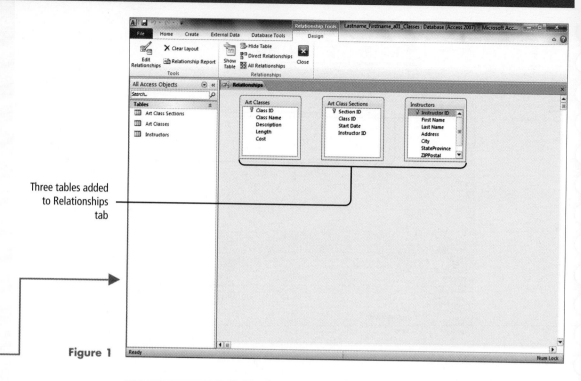

Three tables added to Relationships tab

Figure 1

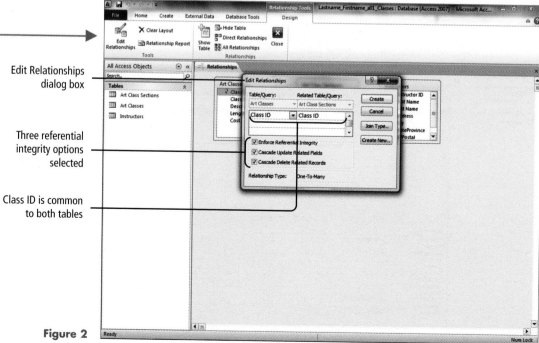

Edit Relationships dialog box

Three referential integrity options selected

Class ID is common to both tables

Figure 2

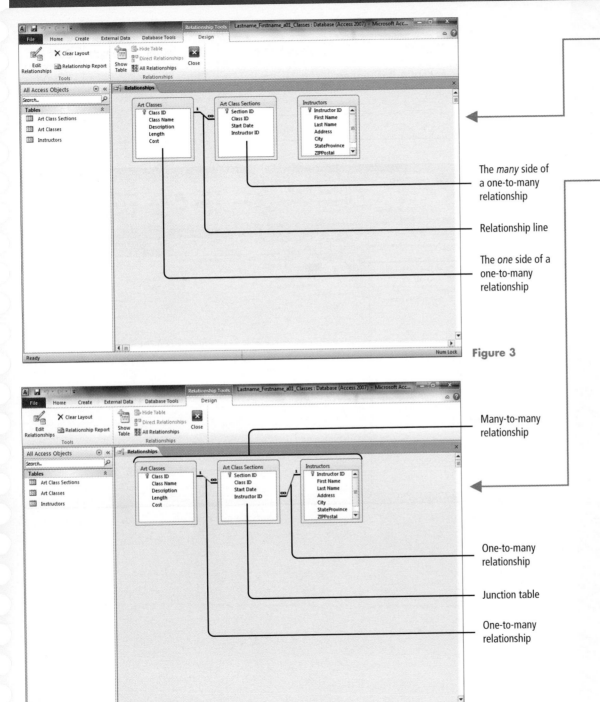

The *many* side of a one-to-many relationship

Relationship line

The *one* side of a one-to-many relationship

Figure 3

Many-to-many relationship

One-to-many relationship

Junction table

One-to-many relationship

Figure 4

5. Click **Create**, and then compare your screen with **Figure 3**.

6. From the **Instructors** table, drag **Instructor ID** to the **Instructor ID** in the **Art Class Sections** table. When the pointer displays, release the mouse button.

7. In the **Edit Relationships** dialog box, select all three referential integrity options, and then click **Create**. Compare your screen with **Figure 4**.

    The three tables are joined to create a *many-to-many relationship*—a relationship where one record in either of the outer tables can have many associated records in the other outer table.

    A many-to-many relationship is created by placing the primary keys from the outer tables into a middle table called a *junction table*. Here, Art Class Sections is a junction table for Art Classes and Instructors. An art class can have several sections assigned and an instructor can be assigned to teach several different sections.

8. Click **Save**. On the **Design tab**, in the **Tools group**, click the **Relationship Report** button to create a report showing the database relationships.

9. If your instructor asks you to print your work for this chapter, print the report.

10. Click **Save**. In the **Save As** dialog box, accept the report name by clicking **OK**.

11. **Close** the report, and then **Close** the **Relationships tab**.

    ▪ **You have completed Skill 9 of 10**

▶ After relating two tables, it is a good idea to enter sample data into both tables.

▶ When you enter data in related tables, referential integrity rules are applied. For example, a foreign key value must have a matching value in the related table.

1. In the **Navigation Pane**, double-click **Instructors** to open its datasheet.

2. Note the number assigned to the **Instructor ID** record with your name. Later in this skill, you will need to enter this value in another table.

3. **Close** ☒ the **Instructors** table. In the **Navigation Pane**, double-click **Art Classes** to open its datasheet. In the append row, enter the three records shown in **Figure 1**.

4. Point to the line to the right of the **Class Name** column header, and then with the ⊞ pointer, double-click to size the column automatically.

5. In the first record, click the **Expand** button ⊞, and then compare your screen with **Figure 2**.

> When a table is on the one side of a relationship, a subdatasheet is available. A **subdatasheet** displays related records from the table on the many side of the relationship.

6. In the subdatasheet append row for the **Art History** class, click in the **Start Date** column.

> Fields that have been assigned the Date/Time data type display the **Date Picker**—a feature used to enter dates by clicking dates on a calendar.

■ **Continue to the next page to complete the skill** ▶

Figure 1

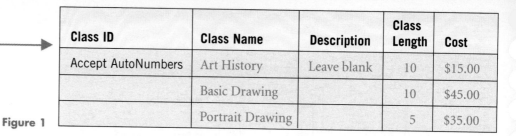

Class ID	Class Name	Description	Class Length	Cost
Accept AutoNumbers	Art History	Leave blank	10	$15.00
	Basic Drawing		10	$45.00
	Portrait Drawing		5	$35.00

Subdatasheet expanded

Figure 2

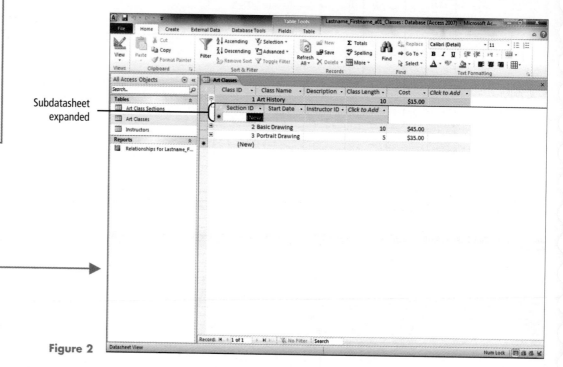

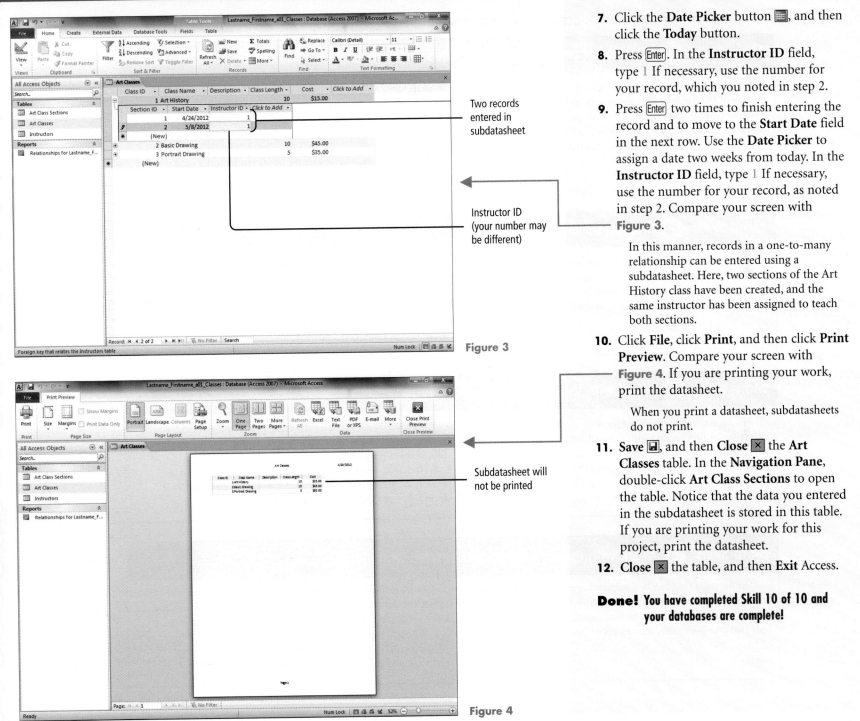

Two records
entered in
subdatasheet

Instructor ID
(your number may
be different)

Figure 3

Subdatasheet will
not be printed

Figure 4

7. Click the **Date Picker** button ▦, and then click the **Today** button.

8. Press Enter. In the **Instructor ID** field, type 1 If necessary, use the number for your record, which you noted in step 2.

9. Press Enter two times to finish entering the record and to move to the **Start Date** field in the next row. Use the **Date Picker** to assign a date two weeks from today. In the **Instructor ID** field, type 1 If necessary, use the number for your record, as noted in step 2. Compare your screen with **Figure 3**.

   In this manner, records in a one-to-many relationship can be entered using a subdatasheet. Here, two sections of the Art History class have been created, and the same instructor has been assigned to teach both sections.

10. Click **File**, click **Print**, and then click **Print Preview**. Compare your screen with **Figure 4**. If you are printing your work, print the datasheet.

    When you print a datasheet, subdatasheets do not print.

11. Save ▦, and then **Close** ☒ the **Art Classes** table. In the **Navigation Pane**, double-click **Art Class Sections** to open the table. Notice that the data you entered in the subdatasheet is stored in this table. If you are printing your work for this project, print the datasheet.

12. **Close** ☒ the table, and then **Exit** Access.

Done! You have completed Skill 10 of 10 and your databases are complete!

The following More Skills are located at **www.pearsonhighered.com/skills**

More Skills 11 Compact and Repair Databases

As tables, forms, queries, and reports are created and deleted, the size of the database file can grow quite large. Access provides a tool that rebuilds database files so that data and these objects are stored more efficiently. Applying the Compact and Repair tool decreases the size of a database file and improves database performance.

In More Skills 11, you will view the file size for a database before and after deleting several forms and reports. You will then compact and repair the database and observe the resulting change in file size.

To begin, open your web browser, navigate to www.pearsonhighered.com/skills, locate the name of your textbook, and follow the instructions on the website.

More Skills 12 Import Data from Excel

You can build Access tables by importing tables from Excel. You can also add data from Excel to an existing Access table. When you import data from Excel, the worksheet needs to be organized with records in rows and fields in columns.

In More Skills 12, you will import data from Excel into an existing Access table. You will then import a different Excel worksheet to create a new Access table.

To begin, open your web browser, navigate to www.pearsonhighered.com/skills, locate the name of your textbook, and follow the instructions on the website.

More Skills 13 Work with the Attachment Data Type

In Access, tables can store files such as Microsoft Word files, Excel files, or files created with a digital camera. Access provides a method to attach specific files to specific records. The attached files can then be opened and viewed in the application that created them.

In More Skills 13, you will create an Attachment field, attach several files to two records, and then open one of these attached files in other programs.

To begin, open your web browser, navigate to www.pearsonhighered.com/skills, locate the name of your textbook, and follow the instructions on the website.

More Skills 14 Work with the Hyperlink and Yes/No Data Types

In Access, a field can be used to store a hyperlink to a web page or file. These fields use the Hyperlink data type. Another data type, called Yes/No, can be assigned to a field that will have only two possible values, such as Yes or No.

In More Skills 14, you will create a new field, assign it the Hyperlink data type, and enter a web address into a record. You will then create a Yes/No field and enter a Yes value into a record.

To begin, open your web browser, navigate to www.pearsonhighered.com/skills, locate the name of your textbook, and follow the instructions on the website.

Key Terms

Online Help Skills

1. **Start** Access. In the upper right corner of the Access window, click the **Help** button. In the **Help** window, click the **Maximize** button.

2. Click in the search box, type templates and then click the **Search** button. In the search results, click **Where do I find templates**. Compare your screen with **Figure 1**.

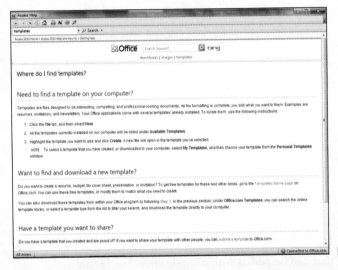

Figure 1

3. Read the article to see if you can answer the following: What is a template and where can you find them?

Matching

Match each term in the second column with its correct definition in the first column by writing the letter of the term on the blank line in front of the correct definition.

____ **1.** The basic part of a database that you work with; for example, tables, queries, forms, and reports.

____ **2.** The collection of related information that displays in a single row of a database table.

____ **3.** A form that displays one record at a time uses this type of layout.

____ **4.** A data type that automatically assigns a unique, numeric value to a field.

____ **5.** A database object used to enter new records, delete records, or update existing records.

____ **6.** The conditions used in a query to select the records that you are looking for.

____ **7.** This specifies the kind of information that a field will hold; for example, text or numbers.

____ **8.** A set of fields that can be added with a single click. For example, the Address data type inserts five fields for storing postal addresses.

____ **9.** An Access field property that prevents a field in a table from having two of the same values.

____ **10.** A database that consists of two or more tables that are related by sharing a field common to both tables.

A AutoNumber

B Criteria

C Data type

D Database object

E Form

F Quick Start

G Record

H Relational database

I Single Form

J Unique

Multiple Choice

Choose the correct answer.

1. A structured collection of related information about people, events, and things.
   A. Database
   B. Database management system
   C. Database object

2. The computer software that allows people to interact with a database.
   A. Database
   B. Database management system
   C. Database object

3. An Access view that displays records in rows and fields in columns.
   A. Database
   B. Data grid
   C. Datasheet

4. Each individual characteristic in a record that displays as a single column in a datasheet.
   A. Field
   B. Record
   C. Subset

5. A database object that displays a subset of data in response to a specific question.
   A. Form
   B. Query
   C. Table

6. A database object used to display the results of a query or the contents of a table on the screen or in printed form.
   A. Form
   B. Macro
   C. Report

7. The blank row at the end of a datasheet used to add records to a table.
   A. Append
   B. Data entry
   C. New record

8. An Access field property that limits the number of characters that can be typed into a text or number field.
   A. Character Limit
   B. Character Size
   C. Field Size

9. A rule that keeps related values synchronized.
   A. Data duplication
   B. Data redundancy
   C. Referential integrity

10. An Access view that displays tools to modify the format of a report or form while being able to view the data that it is intended to display.
    A. Layout
    B. Print Preview
    C. Report

Topics for Discussion

1. What kind of information do you think a small business or organization would organize into a database?

2. Each database object has a special purpose. For example, a query is used to filter and sort records. Why do you think that the filter and sort tools are also available when you work with tables, forms, and reports?

Skill Check

To complete this database, you will need the following file:

- a01_Students

You will save your databases as:

- Lastname_Firstname_a01_Councils
- Lastname_Firstname_a01_Students

1. **Start** Access, and then click **Open**. In the **Open** dialog box, navigate to the student files for this chapter, and then open **a01_Students**.

2. Click the **File tab**, and then click **Save Database As**. In the **Save As** dialog box, navigate to your **Access Chapter 1** folder and then, using your own name, save the database as Lastname_Firstname_a01_Students If the Security Warning displays, click the Enable Content button.

3. In the **Navigation Pane**, double-click **Student Data Entry Form**. In the Navigation bar, click the **New (blank) record** button. In the new blank record, enter the information shown in **Figure 1**. Use Enter to move to each text box, and be sure to use your own name where indicated. **Close** the form.

4. In the **Navigation Pane**, under **Queries**, double-click **Central Neighborhood**. In the **Views group**, click the **View** button to switch to **Design** view.

5. In the **Neighborhood** column, in the **Criteria** box, change the criteria to "Central"

6. In the **Results group**, click the **Run** button to display 10 records. **Save** the query design, and then **Close** the query.

7. In the **Navigation Pane**, double-click **Central Students Report**. In the **Views group**, click the **View button arrow**, and then click **Print Preview**. Compare your screen with **Figure 2**. ⎯⎯⎯⎯

8. If your instructor asks you to print your work for this project, print the report. **Close** the report, and then **Exit** Access.

9. **Start** Access. On the **New tab**, in the **File Name** box, type Lastname_Firstname_a01_Councils

10. Click the **Browse** button, and then navigate to your **Access Chapter 1** folder. Click **OK** and then click **Create**.

11. In **Table1**, double-click the **ID** field, type Member ID and then press Enter.

Student ID:	(Accept AutoNumber value)
First Name:	First name
Last Name:	Last name
Street:	8446 W Marvelo St
City:	Aspen Falls
State:	CA
Zip:	93464
Neighborhood:	Central

Figure 1

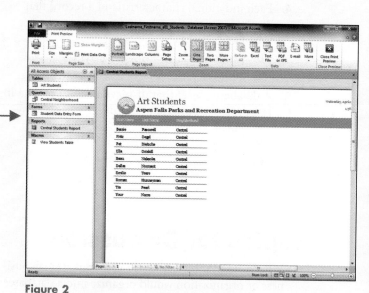

Figure 2

▪ **Continue to the next page to complete this Skill Check**

12. In the list of fields, click **Text**, type First Name and then press ⏎. Click **Text**, and then type Last Name Press ⏎, click **Number**, and then type Council ID

13. Click the **First Name** column. In the **Properties group**, click the **Field Size** box, type 50 and then press ⏎. Repeat this technique to change the **Last Name** field size to 50

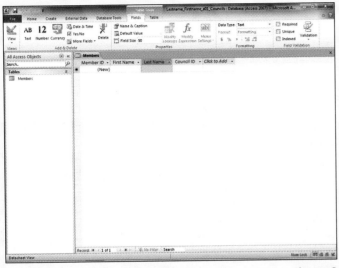

14. Click **Save**, type Members and then press ⏎. Compare your screen with **Figure 3**.

15. **Close** the table. On the **Create tab**, in the **Tables group**, click **Table Design**.

16. In the first **Field Name** box, type Council ID Press ⏎, and then set the **Data Type** to **AutoNumber**. With the first row still active, on the **Tools** group, click the **Primary Key** button.

17. In the second **Field Name** box, type Council Name Press ⏎ two times, and then click **Save**. In the **Save As** dialog box, type Councils and then press ⏎. **Close** the table.

18. On the **Database Tools tab**, click the **Relationships** button. In the **Show Table** dialog box, double-click to add each table to the **Relationships tab**, and then click **Close**.

19. Drag **Council ID** from the **Councils** table to **Council ID** in the **Members** table. In the **Edit Relationships** dialog box, select **Enforce Referential Integrity**, and then click **Create**. Compare your screen with **Figure 4**.

Figure 3

20. On the **Design tab**, in the **Tools group**, click **Relationship Report**. If you are printing this project, print the report. Click **Save**, and then click **OK**. **Close** the report, and then **Close** the **Relationships tab**.

21. In the **Navigation Pane**, double-click **Councils** to open the table. In the **Council Name** column, type Parks & Recreation Council Double-click the line to the right of the **Council Name** column header to resize the column.

22. Press ⏎ two times, and then type City Council Repeat this technique to add the Planning Council and Public Works Commission

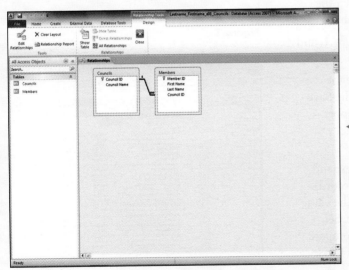

23. Expand the **Public Works Commission** subdatasheet. In the subdatasheet append row, click in the **First Name** column, and then type your own first name. Press ⏎, and then type your last name.

24. If you are printing this project, print the datasheet. **Save**, and then **Close** the table.

25. In the **Navigation Pane**, double-click the **Members** table. If you are printing this project, print the datasheet. **Close** the table.

26. **Exit** Access. Submit your printouts or database files as directed by your instructor.

Figure 4

Done! You have completed the Skill Check

Assess Your Skills 1

To complete this database, you will need the following file:

- a01_Schedule

You will save your database as:

- Lastname_Firstname_a01_Schedule

1. **Start** Access, and then open the student data file **a01_Schedule**. Save the database in your **Access Chapter 1** folder with the name Lastname_Firstname_a01_Schedule

2. Open the **Outings Form**, and then add a new record. Accept the **AutoNumber** value, and then type the **Outing Name**, Rattlesnake Snowshoe The **Ages** field is 18 & over and the **Fee** is 20 **Close** the form.

3. Open the **Adult Outings** query to display 12 records, and then **Close** the query.

4. Open the **Adult Outings Report**, and then switch to **Print Preview**. If asked by your instructor, print the report. **Close** the report.

5. Create a new table in datasheet view. Rename the **ID** field Leader ID Add two new **Text** fields named First Name and Last Name

6. Click the **Click to Add** column, and then add the **Address Quick Start** fields. **Save** the table with the name Leaders

7. In the append row, enter a record using your own name and contact information. Note the **AutoNumber** value that is assigned to your record, and then **Close** the table.

8. Create a new table in **Design** view. Name the first field Schedule ID Assign it the **AutoNumber** data type, and then make it the **Primary Key**. Name the second field Outing ID and assign the **Number** data type. Name the third field Leader ID and assign

the **Number** data type. Name the fourth field Outing Date and assign the **Date/Time** data type.

9. **Save** the table as Scheduled Outings and then **Close** the table.

10. Open the **Relationships tab** and then add all three tables to the tab. Create a relationship that enforces referential integrity between the **Outings** and **Scheduled Outings** tables using the fields common to both tables. Create a similar relationship between the **Leaders** and **Scheduled Outings** tables.

11. Arrange the tables as shown in **Figure 1**, and then click **Save**.

12. Create a **Relationship Report**. **Save** the report with the name provided in the **Save As** dialog box. If asked, print the report. **Close** the report, and then **Close** the **Relationships tab**.

13. Open the **Outings** table, and then expand **Family Fun Canoe Paddle**. In the record's subdatasheet, set the **Leader ID** to the value assigned to you in the Leaders table. Set **Outing Date** to the current date. Compare your screen with **Figure 2**, and then **Close** the table.

14. If asked, print the Scheduled Outings datasheet. **Exit** Access. Submit your printouts or database file as directed.

Done! You have completed Assess Your Skills 1

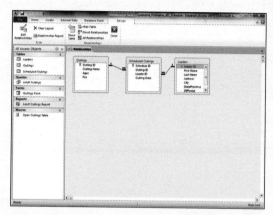

Figure 1

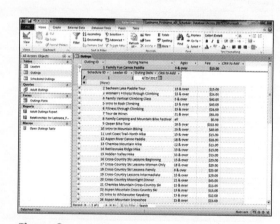

Figure 2

Assessment

▶ Assess Your Skills 3 and 4 can be found at **www.pearsonhighered.com/skills**.

Assess Your Skills 2

To complete this database, you will need the following file:

- New blank Access database

You will save your database as:

- Lastname_Firstname_a01_Camps

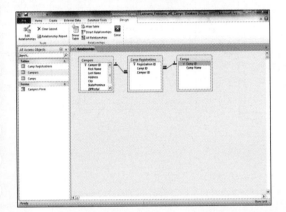

Figure 1

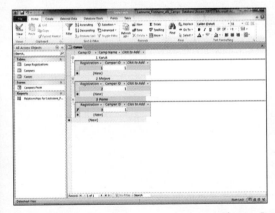

Figure 2

1. **Start** Access. Create a new database with the name Lastname_Firstname_a01_Camps and save it in your **Access Chapter 1** folder.

2. In the new table, rename the **ID** field Camper ID Add two new **Text** fields named First Name and Last Name

3. Click the **Click to Add** column, and then add the **Address Quick Start** fields. For all fields except **Camper ID**, change the **Field Size** to 50 **Save** the table with the name Campers and then **Close** the table.

4. Select the **Campers** table, and then, on the **Create tab**, in the **Forms group**, click the **Form** button. Use the form to add yourself as a camper. Include your own contact information. **Save** the form as Campers Form Note the **Camper ID** value, and then **Close** the form.

5. Create a new table in **Datasheet** view. Rename the **ID** field Camp ID Add a new **Text** field named Camp Name **Save** the table as **Camps** and then **Close** the table.

6. Create a new table in **Design** view. Name the first field Registration ID Assign it the **AutoNumber** data type, and then make it the **Primary Key**. Name the second field Camp ID and assign the **Number** data type. Name the third field Camper ID and assign the **Number** data type.

7. **Save** the table as Camp Registrations and then **Close** the table.

8. Open the **Relationships tab**, and then add all three tables to the tab. Create a relationship that enforces referential integrity between the **Camps** and **Camp Registrations** tables using their common field. Create a similar relationship between the **Campers** and **Camp Registrations** tables.

9. Arrange the tables as shown in **Figure 1**, and then click **Save**.

10. Create a **Relationship Report**. **Save** the report with the name provided in the **Save As** dialog box. If asked, print the report. **Close** the report and **Close** the **Relationships tab**.

11. Open the **Camps** table, and add these three camps: Karuk and Mojave and Pomo Open each record's subdatasheet, and then enter your **Camper ID** value to add yourself as a registered camper in all three camps. Compare your screen with **Figure 2**.

12. **Close** the table. With the **Camps** table still selected, on the **Create tab**, in the **Reports group**, click the **Report** button to create a report for the table. In the **Grouping & Totals group**, click **Totals**, and then click **Count Records**. **Save** the report as Camps Report If asked, print the report. **Close** the report.

13. If asked, print the Camp Registrations datasheet. **Exit** Access. Submit your printouts or database file as directed.

Done! You have completed Assess Your Skills 2

Assess Your Skills Visually

To complete this database, you will need the following file:

- New blank Access database

You will save your database as:

- Lastname_Firstname_a01_Race

Create a new, blank database and **Save** it in your **Access Chapter 1** folder with the name Lastname_Firstname_a01_Race Create the tables shown in **Figure 1**. For each table, assign the primary key as indicated. For each table, rename the primary key, and then add the fields shown in **Figure 1**. For any field that will be on the many side of a one-to-many relationship, assign the **Number** data type. For the **Year** field, assign the **Number** data type. For the remaining fields, assign the data type appropriate for the type of data it will store. Create the many-to-many relationship shown in **Figure 1**. Create a relationships report and then **Save** the report using the name suggested by Access.

Print the report or submit the database file as directed by your instructor.

Done! You have completed Assess Your Skills Visually

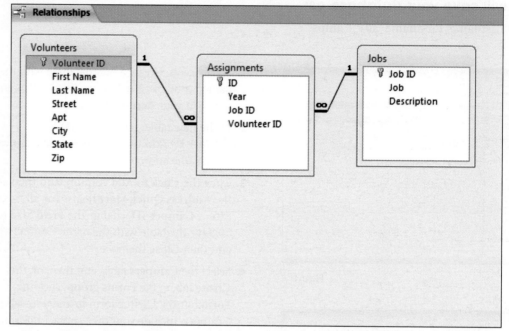

Figure 1

Skills in Context

To complete this database, you will need the following file:

- New blank Access database

You will save your database as:

- Lastname_Firstname_a01_Volunteers

Create a new database named Lastname_Firstname_a01_Volunteers and save it in your **Access Chapter 1** folder. Create a table to store the data in the table to the right. Add an AutoNumber primary key and assign appropriate field names. Consider the type of data that is being stored, and then assign appropriate data types and field sizes. Name the table Volunteers

Create a form for the table and then apply the theme of your choice. Use the form to enter the following contacts:

Your First Name	Virginia	Nancy
Your Last Name	Pipe	Warns
3924 S Williams St	9218 NE North St	53893 SE Park St
Aspen Falls	Marshall	Paulden
CA	CA	AZ
93464	94940	86334
Your phone number	(992) 555-2259	(928) 555-9512
Your date of birth	2/15/1986	8/6/1954

Print the table datasheet or submit the database file as directed by your instructor.

Done! You have completed Skills in Context

Skills and You

To complete this database, you will need the following file:

- New blank Access database

You will save your database as:

- Lastname_Firstname_a01_Contacts

Using the skills you have practiced in this chapter, create a database named Lastname_Firstname_a01_Contacts Create a table that can be used to store personal contacts. Include fields for names, addresses, e-mail addresses, and phone numbers. Use the table to enter at least 10 contacts, and include your own contact information. Print the datasheet or submit the database file electronically as directed by your instructor.

Done! You have completed Skills and You

CHAPTER 2

Manage Datasheets and Create Queries

▶ Filtering, sorting, and formatting tables or queries are techniques used to present data in more meaningful ways.

▶ Queries are used to display fields from several tables, apply complex filters, or calculate new values based on the data in the query.

Your starting screen will look similar to this:

SKILLS
Skills 1-10 Training

At the end of this chapter, you will be able to:

Skill 1 Find and Replace Data

Skill 2 Filter and Sort Datasheets

Skill 3 Use the Simple Query Wizard

Skill 4 Format Datasheets

Skill 5 Add Date and Time Criteria

Skill 6 Create Queries in Design View

Skill 7 Add Calculated Fields to Queries

Skill 8 Work with Logical Criteria

Skill 9 Add Wildcards to Query Criteria

Skill 10 Group and Total Queries

MORE SKILLS

More Skills 11 Export Queries to Other File Formats

More Skills 12 Find Duplicate Records

More Skills 13 Find Unmatched Records

More Skills 14 Create Crosstab Queries

Outcome

Using the skills listed to the left will enable you to create database objects like these:

Instructor Assignments   4/28/2012

Class Title	First Name	Last Name	Start Date	Start Time
Art History	Your	Name	6/18/2012	1:00 PM
Basic Drawing	Bradford	Andrzejczyk	6/19/2012	1:00 PM
Beginning Watercolors	Chasidy	Trowery	6/20/2012	1:00 PM
Impressionism in Art	Larry	Moyerman	6/21/2012	1:00 PM

Discounts

First Name	Last Name	Class Title	Fee	Discount	Discounted Fee
William	Smith	Tour of Aspen Falls	$5.00	25%	$3.75
Geraldo	Colver	Tour of Aspen Falls	$5.00	25%	$3.75
Vivan	Fosnough	Tour of Aspen Falls	$5.00	25%	$3.75
Romona	Springate	Impressionism in Art	$15.00	50%	$7.50
Glen	Urda	Impressionism in Art	$15.00	50%	$7.50
Your	Name	Basic Drawing	$35.00	75%	$8.75
Dane	Rhinehardt	Impressionism in Art	$15.00	25%	$11.25
German	Mulnix	Impressionism in Art	$15.00	25%	$11.25
Phillis	Lacerda	Basic Drawing	$45.00	75%	$11.25
Bertram	Ciucci	Perspective Drawing	$35.00	50%	$17.50
Greta	Voetsch	Perspective Drawing	$35.00	25%	$26.25
Geraldo	Colver	Perspective Drawing	$35.00	25%	$26.25
Norris	Corriher	Basic Drawing	$35.00	25%	$26.25
Eugene	Warring	Perspective Drawing	$35.00	25%	$26.25
Tuan	Gruhn	Beginning Watercolors	$45.00	25%	$33.75
Daisy	Harbison	Beginning Watercolors	$55.00	25%	$41.25
William	Smith	Beginning Watercolors	$55.00	25%	$41.25
Clotilde	Mostero	Beginning Watercolors	$55.00	25%	$41.25

Enrollments   4/28/2012

Class Title	Start Date	Enrollment	Total Fee
Art History	1/9/2012	6	$90.00
Portrait Drawing	1/9/2012	5	$175.00
Basic Drawing	1/10/2012	12	$420.00
Beginning Watercolors	1/11/2012	14	$770.00
Impressionism in Art	1/12/2012	10	$150.00
Perspective Drawing	1/14/2012	14	$490.00
Art History	3/5/2012	6	$90.00
Basic Drawing	3/6/2012	9	$405.00
Beginning Watercolors	3/7/2012	6	$270.00
Impressionism in Art	3/8/2012	12	$180.00
Perspective Drawing	3/9/2012	11	$385.00
Portrait Drawing	3/13/2012	7	$245.00
Tour of Aspen Falls	5/12/2012	10	$50.00

You will save your database as:

Lastname_Firstname_a02_Classes

In this chapter, you will create documents for the Aspen Falls City Hall, which provides essential services for the citizens and visitors of Aspen Falls, California.

Introduction

▸ Tables and queries are displayed in datasheets. You can organize these datasheets to derive information from the data.

▸ You can filter datasheets to display a subset of the data, and you can sort the records in alphabetical or numeric order.

▸ When you need to display fields from more than one table in a single datasheet, you can add those fields to a query.

▸ In queries, you can write expressions to filter the information you need, calculate values based on other fields, and provide statistics that summarize your data.

Time to complete all
10 skills – 50 to 75 minutes

Find your student data files here:

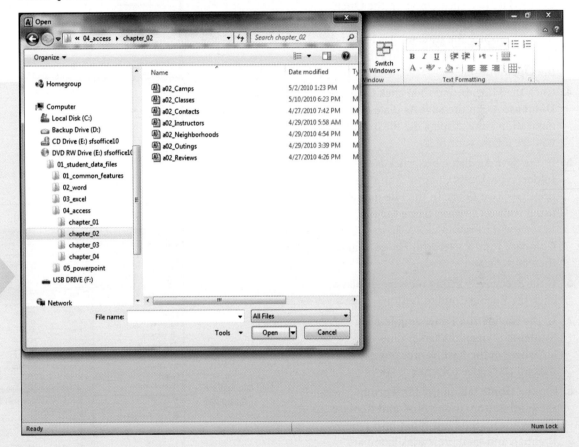

Student data files needed for this chapter:

- a02_Classes

► Specific information can be located using the Find tool, and data can be searched and changed using Find and Replace.

1. **Start** ⊙ Access. If necessary, **Maximize** ▣ the window.

2. If necessary, insert the Student CD that came with this book.

3. On the **File tab**, click **Open**. In the **Open** dialog box, navigate to your student data files and display the student files for this chapter. Select **a02_Classes**, and then click the **Open** button.

4. Click the **File tab**, and then click **Save Database As**. In the **Save As** dialog box navigation pane, display the file list where you are saving your files.

5. In the **Save As** dialog box, click **New folder**, type Access Chapter 2 and then press [Enter] two times. In the **File name** box, using your own name, name the file Lastname_Firstname_a02_Classes Compare your screen with **Figure 1**, and then click **Save**.

6. If the Security Warning message displays, click the Enable Content button.

7. In the **Navigation Pane**, double-click **Students** to open the table. Click anywhere in the **Last Name** column to make it the active column.

8. On the **Home tab**, in the **Find group**, click the **Find** button. In the **Find and Replace** dialog box, in the **Find What** box, type Brennan and then press [Enter]. Compare your screen with **Figure 2**.

   Access searches the Last Name field for the text *Brennan*. The record for Eliseo Brennan displays with the text *Brennan* selected.

■ **Continue to the next page to complete the skill**

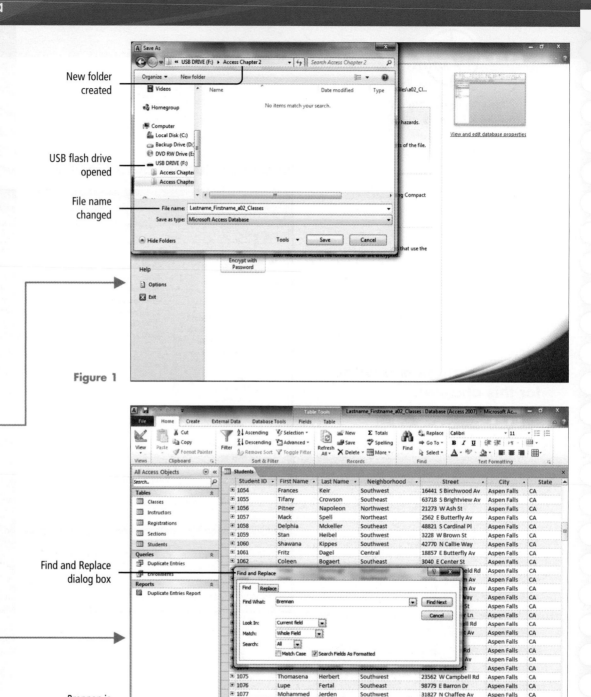

New folder created

USB flash drive opened

File name changed

Figure 1

Find and Replace dialog box

Brennan is selected

Figure 2

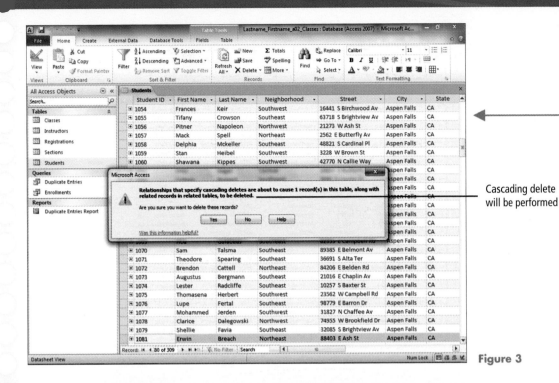

Figure 3

Cascading delete will be performed

Search item not found

Figure 4

9. **Close** [x] the **Find and Replace** dialog box. Be sure that the text *Brennan* is still selected. In the **Records group**, click the **Delete button arrow**, and then click **Delete Record**. Compare your screen with **Figure 3**, and then click **Yes**.

   The Students table is related to other tables with the cascading delete referential integrity option. Here, any records for Eliseo Brennan in related tables will also be deleted.

10. Click anywhere in the **Neighborhood** column, and then, in the **Find group**, click the **Replace** button.

11. In the **Find What** box, type SW In the **Replace With** box, type Southwest

12. In the **Find and Replace** dialog box, click the **Find Next** button. Notice that the first instance of *SW* is selected, and then click the **Replace** button.

    When you click the Replace button, the old value is replaced and the next instance of the old value is located.

13. Continue clicking the **Replace** button until the message shown in **Figure 4** displays.

14. Read the message, and then click **OK**. **Close** [x] the **Find and Replace** dialog box.

15. Repeat the techniques just practiced to **Find** the record for *Kisha Algeo*, and then change that record's first and last name to your own first and last name.

16. Leave the table open for the next skill.

    Recall that the data you changed was saved automatically as you made changes. The table does not need to be saved.

■ **You have completed Skill 1 of 10**

▶ Information can be sorted by one or more columns. Sorting arranges data in ways that make it more useful.

▶ The Filter tool displays a list of all values for the active column. In the filter list, you can display or hide that value by clicking its check box.

1. **Close** « the **Navigation Pane** to make more room for the **Students** datasheet.

2. Scroll to the top of the datasheet, and then compare your screen with **Figure 1.**

    By default, the records are sorted by the **Student ID** field.

3. Scroll the datasheet to the right, and click the **Birth Date** column header to select the column. In the **Sort & Filter group**, click the **Ascending** button to sort the records by date.

4. Scroll down to display the last four records. Notice that the records are sorted by birth date in chronological order and that students born in the same year are grouped together.

5. In the **Sort & Filter group**, click the **Remove Sort** button to return the datasheet to its original sort order.

6. Select the **Last Name** column. In the **Sort & Filter group**, click the **Ascending** button.

7. Select the **Neighborhood** column. In the **Sort & Filter group**, click the **Ascending** button. Compare your screen with **Figure 2.**

    The records are now sorted by Neighborhood, and within each group of neighborhoods, the records remain sorted by Last Name.

■ **Continue to the next page to complete the skill**

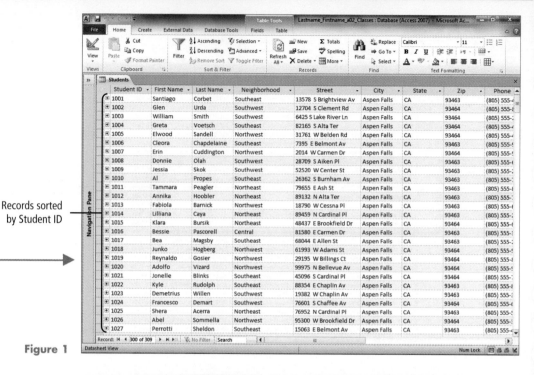

Records sorted by Student ID

Figure 1

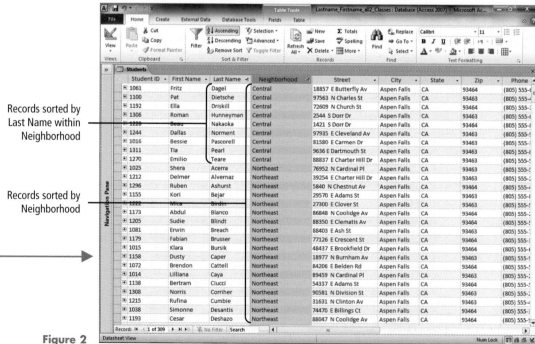

Records sorted by Last Name within Neighborhood

Records sorted by Neighborhood

Figure 2

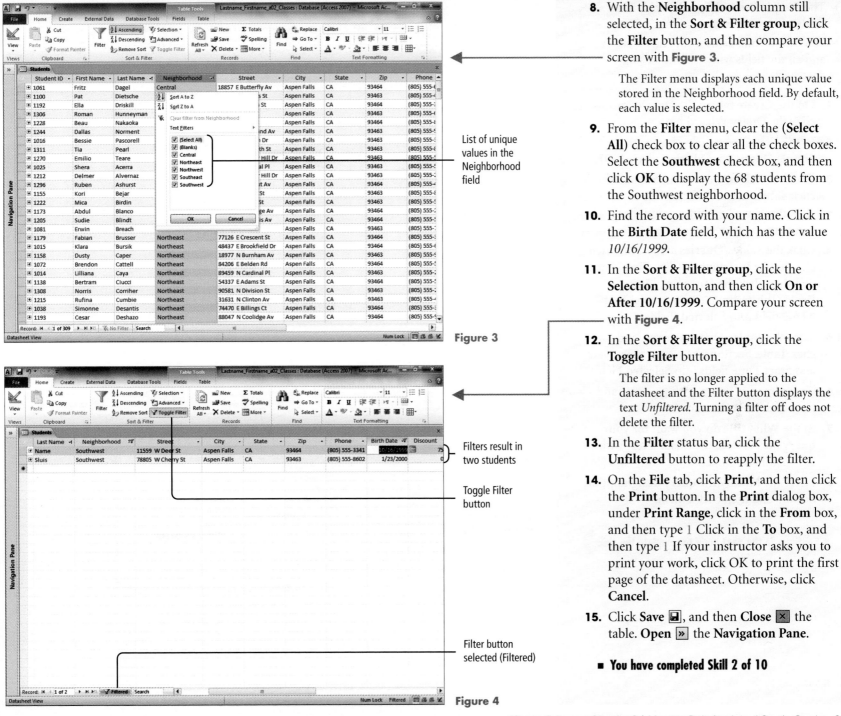

List of unique
values in the
Neighborhood
field

Figure 3

Filters result in
two students

Toggle Filter
button

Filter button
selected (Filtered)

Figure 4

8. With the **Neighborhood** column still selected, in the **Sort & Filter group**, click the **Filter** button, and then compare your screen with **Figure 3**.

   The Filter menu displays each unique value stored in the Neighborhood field. By default, each value is selected.

9. From the **Filter** menu, clear the **(Select All)** check box to clear all the check boxes. Select the **Southwest** check box, and then click **OK** to display the 68 students from the Southwest neighborhood.

10. Find the record with your name. Click in the **Birth Date** field, which has the value *10/16/1999*.

11. In the **Sort & Filter group**, click the **Selection** button, and then click **On or After 10/16/1999**. Compare your screen with **Figure 4**.

12. In the **Sort & Filter group**, click the **Toggle Filter** button.

    The filter is no longer applied to the datasheet and the Filter button displays the text *Unfiltered*. Turning a filter off does not delete the filter.

13. In the **Filter** status bar, click the **Unfiltered** button to reapply the filter.

14. On the **File** tab, click **Print**, and then click the **Print** button. In the **Print** dialog box, under **Print Range**, click in the **From** box, and then type 1 Click in the **To** box, and then type 1 If your instructor asks you to print your work, click OK to print the first page of the datasheet. Otherwise, click **Cancel**.

15. Click **Save** 🖫, and then **Close** ✕ the table. **Open** » the **Navigation Pane**.

■ **You have completed Skill 2 of 10**

► The *Simple Query Wizard* quickly adds fields to a new query.

► You can include fields from related tables and all the fields will display in a single datasheet.

1. On the **Create tab**, in the **Queries group**, click the **Query Wizard** button.

2. In the **New Query** dialog box, with **Simple Query Wizard** selected, click **OK**.

3. Click the **Tables/Queries arrow**, and then click **Table: Classes**. Click **Class Title**, click the **Move** ► button, and then compare your screen with **Figure 1**.

4. Click the **Tables/Queries arrow**, and then click **Table: Instructors**. Click **First Name**, and then click the **Move** ► button. Repeat this technique to move the **Last Name** field into **Selected Fields**.

5. Click the **Tables/Queries arrow**, and then click **Table: Sections**. Move the **Start Date** and **Start Time** fields into **Selected Fields**.

6. Compare your screen with **Figure 2**, and then click **Next** two times.

7. In the **What title do you want for your query** box, replace the existing text with Instructor Assignments

8. Select the **Modify the query design** option button, and then click **Finish**.

■ **Continue to the next page to complete the skill** ▶

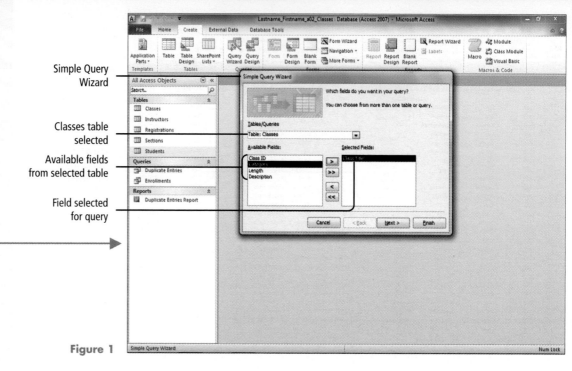

Simple Query Wizard

Classes table selected

Available fields from selected table

Field selected for query

Figure 1

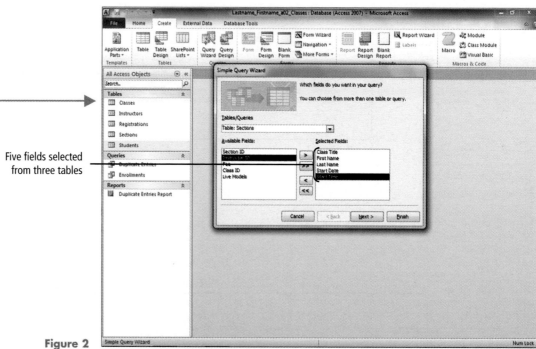

Five fields selected from three tables

Figure 2

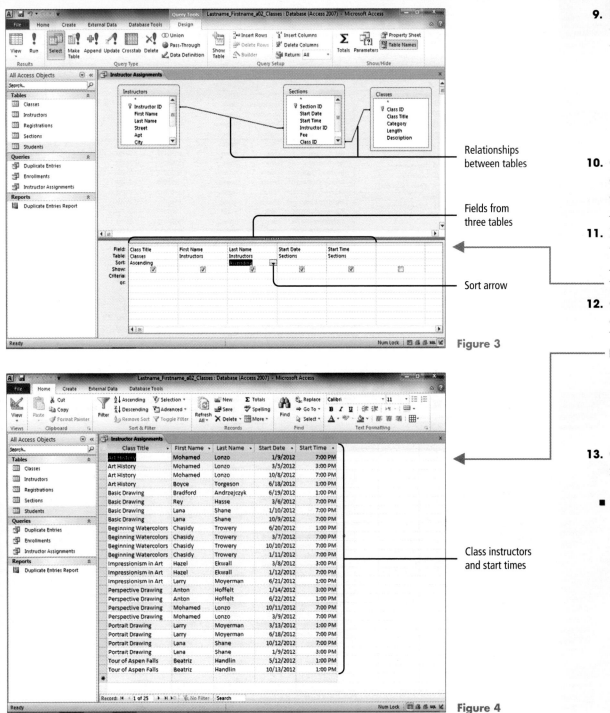

Relationships
between tables

Fields from
three tables

Sort arrow

Figure 3

Class instructors
and start times

Figure 4

9. In the query design workspace, point to the **Classes** table title bar and then drag it to the right of the **Sections** table.

When you choose fields from multiple tables in a query, the relationships defined in the Relationships tab will also apply to the query. Here, an instructor can be assigned to teach many sections, and a class can be assigned to many sections.

10. Click the **Class Title** column **Sort** box to display its arrow. Click the **Class Title** column **Sort arrow**, and then click **Ascending**.

11. Repeat the technique just practiced so that the **Last Name** column is sorted in **Ascending** order. Compare your screen with **Figure 3**.

12. On the **Design tab**, in the **Results group**, click the **Run** button. Alternately, click the View button. Compare your screen with **Figure 4.**

Recall that queries show subsets of the data to answer a question. Here, the query shows fields from three related tables and answers the question: *When do classes start and who is assigned to teach them?*

13. Click **Save** 🖫, and leave the query open for the next skill.

■ **You have completed Skill 3 of 10**

▶ Datasheets—for tables or for queries—can be formatted to make the data easier to read.

1. If necessary, open the Instructor Assignments query datasheet.

2. On the **Home tab**, in the **Text Formatting group**, click the **Font arrow**. Scroll to the top of the list of fonts, and then click **Arial Narrow**.

3. On the **Home tab**, in the **Text Formatting group**, click the **Font Size arrow**, and then click **12**. Compare your screen with **Figure 1**. ─────────────

When you change the font size or font, the changes are applied to the entire datasheet.

4. In the upper-left corner of the datasheet, click the **Select All** button. Place the pointer on the line between any two column headers. With the ⊞ pointer, double-click to resize all the columns automatically.

5. Click in any cell to deselect the datasheet, and then compare your screen with **Figure 2**. ─────────────

■ **Continue to the next page to complete the skill**

Font arrow

Font Size arrow

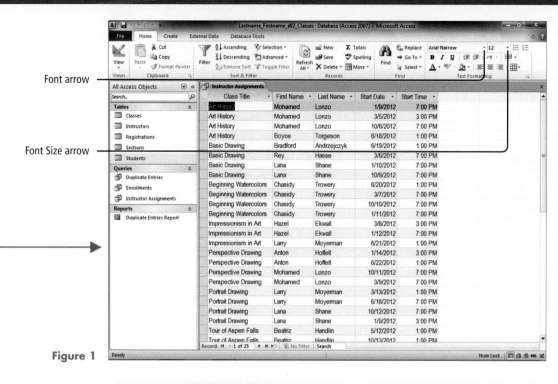

Figure 1

Columns resized

Select All button

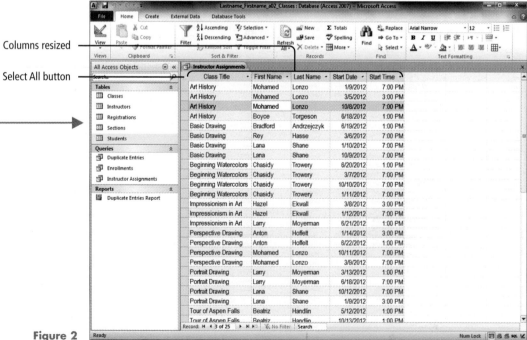

Figure 2

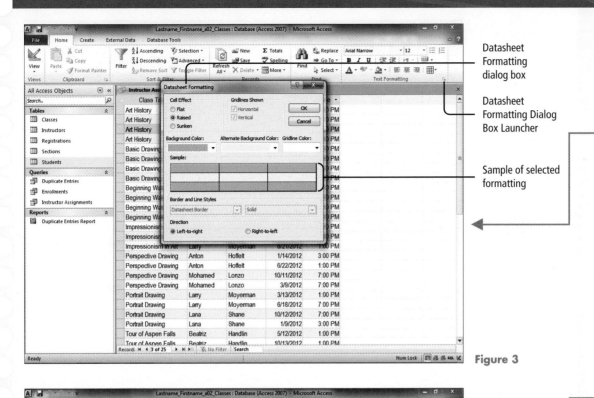

Datasheet
Formatting
dialog box

Datasheet
Formatting Dialog
Box Launcher

Sample of selected
formatting

Figure 3

6. In the **Text Formatting group**, click the **Datasheet Formatting Dialog Box Launcher** ⌐.

7. In the **Datasheet Formatting** dialog box, under **Cell Effect**, select the **Raised** option button. Compare your screen with **Figure 3**.

   In the Datasheet Formatting dialog box, a sample of the selected formatting displays.

8. In the **Datasheet Formatting** dialog box, click the **Background Color arrow**. In the gallery, click **Automatic**.

9. In the **Datasheet Formatting** dialog box, click the **Alternate Background Color arrow**. In the gallery, under **Theme Colors**, click the sixth color in the second row—**Aqua, Accent 2, Lighter 80%**.

10. Click the **Gridline Color arrow**. In the gallery, under **Theme Colors**, click the eighth color in the first row—**Gray-50%, Accent 4**. Compare your screen with **Figure 4**.

11. Click **OK** to apply the changes and to close the dialog box.

12. Click the **Save** 🖫 button to save the design changes that you made. Leave the query open for the next skill.

■ **You have completed Skill 4 of 10**

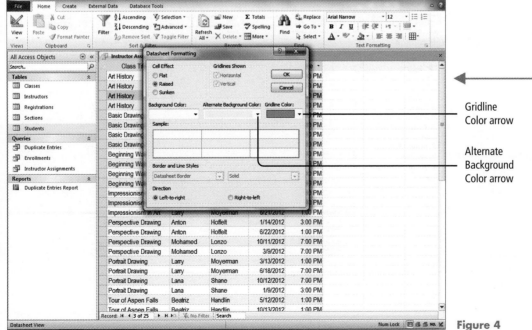

Gridline
Color arrow

Alternate
Background
Color arrow

Figure 4

▶ In Access, dates and times are stored as numbers. The underlying numbers display as dates in database objects. For example, the number 37979 displays as *12/24/2003* if the Short Date format is assigned to the Date/Time field.

▶ When dates are used as query criteria, they are surrounded by number signs (#).

1. With the **Instructor Assignments** query still open, click the **View** button to switch to Design view.

2. Click in the **Start Time** column **Criteria** box, and then type 1:00 PM Compare your screen with **Figure 1**. ────────

    As you type in a date criteria box, *IntelliSense*—Quick Info, ToolTips, and AutoComplete—display. *AutoComplete* is a menu of commands that match the characters you type. The *Quick Info* box explains the purpose of the selected AutoComplete. Here, the suggested command—Pmt—is not needed and should be ignored.

3. On the **Design tab**, in the **Results group**, click the **Run** button. Verify that the eight classes that start at 1:00 PM display, and then switch to Design view. Compare your screen with **Figure 2**. ────────

    When you do not type the number symbols that surround dates or times, Access inserts them before running the query.

■ **Continue to the next page to complete the skill**

IntelliSense AutoComplete box

IntelliSense Quick Info box

Figure 1

Number signs surround date or time criterion

Figure 2

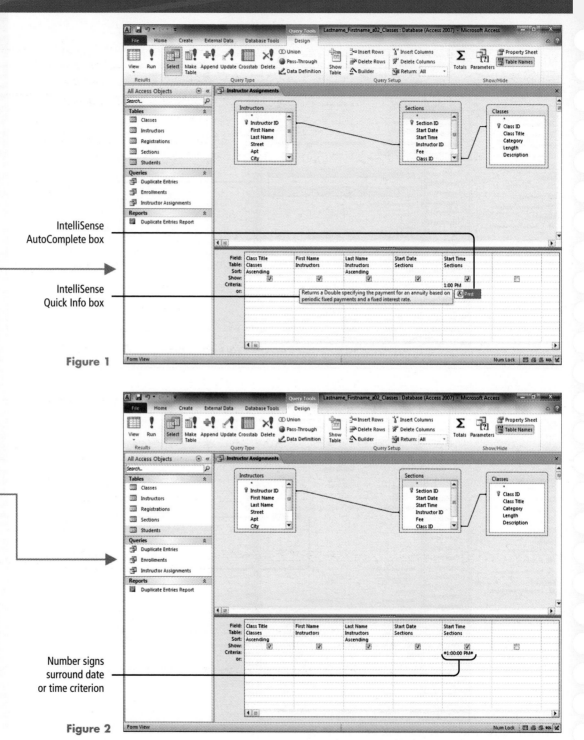

Common Comparison Operators

Operator	Purpose
=	Is true when the field's value is equal to the specified value
<>	Is true when the field's value does not equal the specified value
<	Is true when the field's value is less than the specified value
<=	Is true when the field's value is less than or equal to the specified value
>	Is true when the field's value is greater than the specified value
>=	Is true when the field's value is greater than or equal to the specified value

Figure 3

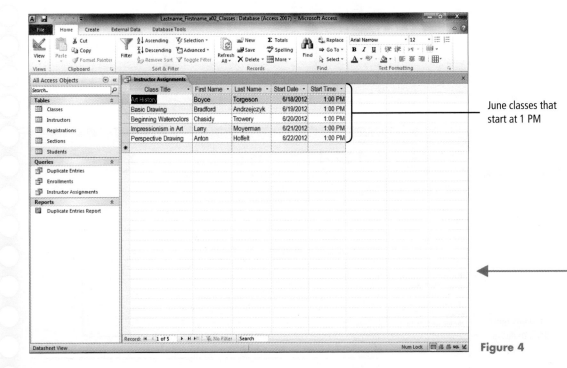

June classes that start at 1 PM

Figure 4

4. In the **Start Date** column **Criteria** box, type >4/1/2012 **Run** the query to display the seven classes that start after April 1, 2012 and start at 1:00 PM.

   Dates, times, and other numeric criteria often use **comparison operators**—operators used to compare two values—for example, = (equal to) and < (less than). Common comparison operators are listed in the table in **Figure 3**.

5. Switch to Design view. In the **Start Date** column **Criteria** box, replace the existing criterion with Between 6/1/2012 And 6/30/2012 With the ⊞ pointer, increase the width of the **Start Date** column to display all its criteria.

   The **Between...And operator** finds all numbers or dates between and including two values. Here, all the June classes that start at 1:00 PM will display in the query.

   When you widen a query column in the design grid, the column will return to its original width when the query is closed.

6. Save 💾, and then **Run** the query to display the June classes that start at 1:00 PM. Compare your screen with **Figure 4**.

7. In the first record, change the name *Boyce Torgeson* to your own first and last name. If you are printing your work, print the datasheet.

8. **Close** ✕ the query.

   ■ **You have completed Skill 5 of 10**

► To create a query in Design view, you first add the tables you will need to the query design workspace. You then add the fields you want to use to the design grid. Finally, you add criteria and run the query.

1. On the **Create tab**, in the **Queries group**, click the **Query Design** button.

2. In the **Show Table** dialog box, double-click **Classes** to add the table to the query design workspace. Alternately, select the table in the dialog box, and then click the Add button.

3. Repeat the technique just practiced to add the **Sections** and **Registrations** tables. Compare your screen with **Figure 1**, and then **Close** the **Show Table** dialog box.

4. In the **Navigation Pane**, point to the **Students** table. Drag the table from the **Navigation Pane** to the right of the **Registrations** table in the query design workspace. Compare your screen with **Figure 2**.

Tables can be added to the query design workspace using the Show Table dialog box or by dragging them from the Navigation Pane.

This query needs to ask the question: *Which students receive a discount?* To answer this question, fields from three tables are needed. The Registrations table has been added to the query to join Sections and Students in a many-to-many relationship.

■ **Continue to the next page to complete the skill** ▶

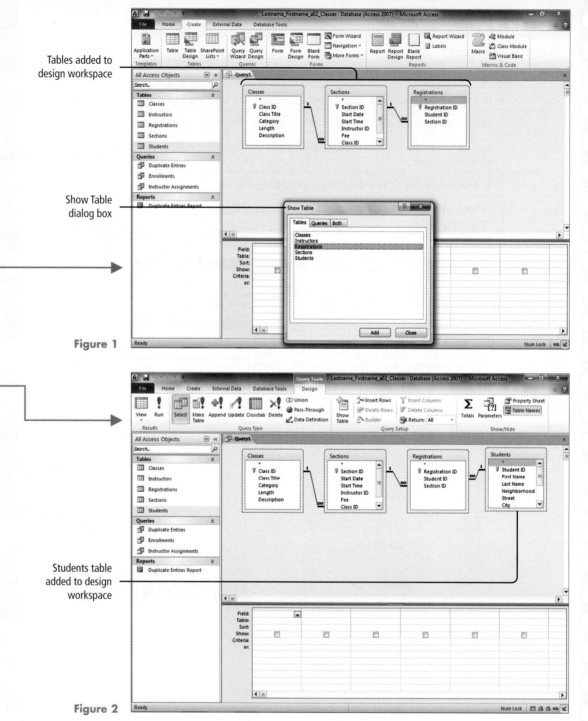

Tables added to design workspace

Show Table dialog box

Figure 1

Students table added to design workspace

Figure 2

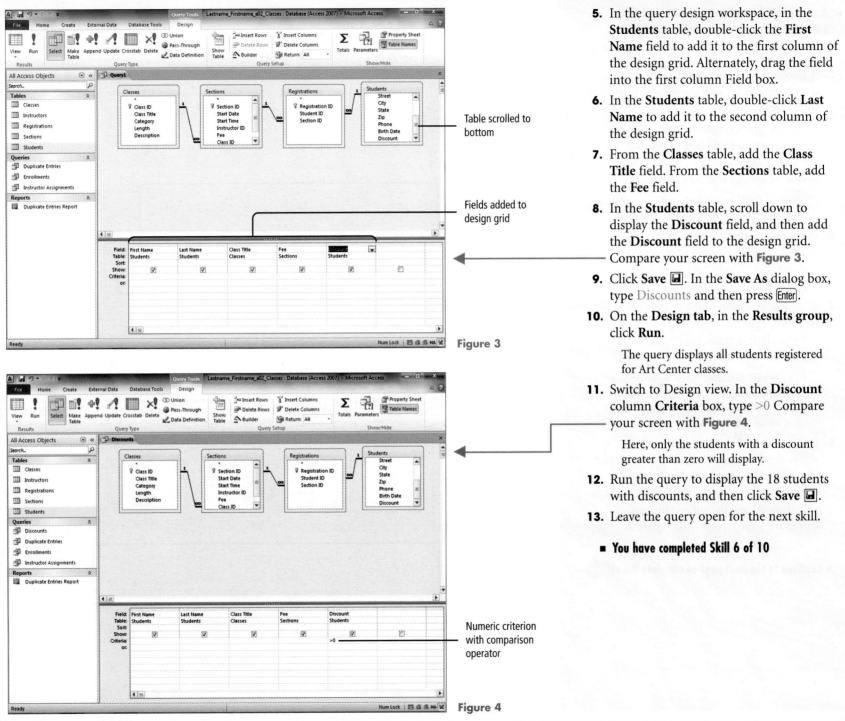

Table scrolled to bottom

Fields added to design grid

Figure 3

Numeric criterion with comparison operator

Figure 4

5. In the query design workspace, in the **Students** table, double-click the **First Name** field to add it to the first column of the design grid. Alternately, drag the field into the first column Field box.

6. In the **Students** table, double-click **Last Name** to add it to the second column of the design grid.

7. From the **Classes** table, add the **Class Title** field. From the **Sections** table, add the **Fee** field.

8. In the **Students** table, scroll down to display the **Discount** field, and then add the **Discount** field to the design grid. Compare your screen with **Figure 3**.

9. Click **Save** 🖫. In the **Save As** dialog box, type Discounts and then press Enter.

10. On the **Design tab**, in the **Results group**, click **Run**.

    The query displays all students registered for Art Center classes.

11. Switch to Design view. In the **Discount** column **Criteria** box, type >0 Compare your screen with **Figure 4**.

    Here, only the students with a discount greater than zero will display.

12. Run the query to display the 18 students with discounts, and then click **Save** 🖫.

13. Leave the query open for the next skill.

    ■ **You have completed Skill 6 of 10**

► A *calculated field* is a column added to a query that derives its value from other fields.

1. If necessary, open the Discounts query datasheet. Click the **View** button to switch to Design view.

2. **Close** « the **Navigation Pane**. Click in the first empty **Field** box to the right of the **Discount** column. Click the **Field arrow** to display the field list.

   Clicking fields in the Field list is an alternate method of selecting fields in queries.

3. Press Esc to close the field list.

   In this Field box, you will create a new field that derives its value from two different fields—Fee and Discount.

4. With the insertion point in the first blank field box, type Discounted Fee followed by a colon (:). Compare your screen with **Figure 1**.

   In a query, calculated fields begin with a descriptive label that ends with a colon. Here, Discounted Fee will be the column label when the query is run.

5. Point to the line to the right and slightly above the **Discounted Fee** column. When the ⊞ pointer displays, drag to the right to the middle of the second blank column and then release the mouse button. Compare your screen with **Figure 2**.

■ **Continue to the next page to complete the skill**

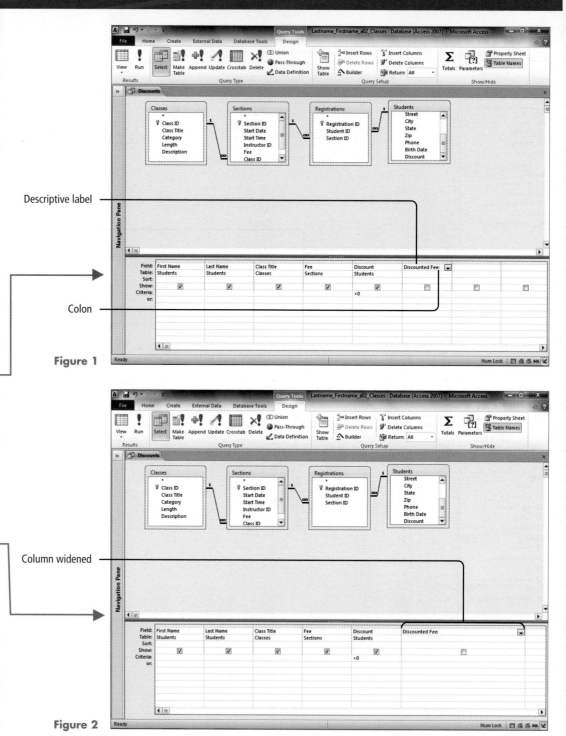

Descriptive label

Colon

Figure 1

Column widened

Figure 2

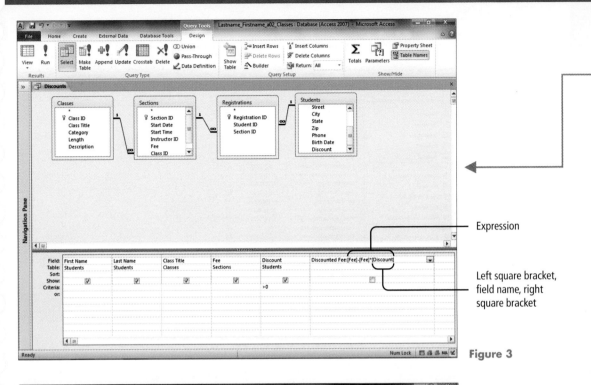

Expression

Left square bracket, field name, right square bracket

Figure 3

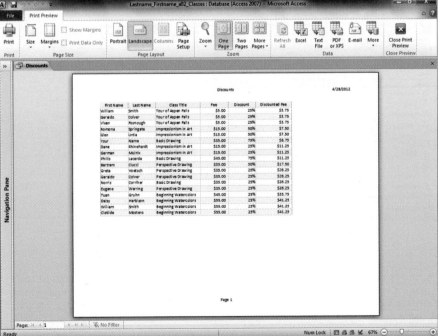

Figure 4

6. With the insertion point to the right of the colon, type the following expression: [Fee]-[Fee]*[Discount] Compare your screen with **Figure 3**.

> An *expression* is a combination of fields, mathematical operators, and prebuilt functions that calculates values in tables, forms, queries, and reports.

> In expressions, field names are always enclosed between a left square bracket and a right square bracket. Here, the expression multiplies the fee by the discount to determine the discount amount. To determine the discounted fee, the discount amount is subtracted from the original fee.

7. In the **Results group**, click **Run**. If the Enter Parameter Value dialog box or any other dialog box displays, close the dialog box, and then carefully check the placement of the colon and square brackets, and check that you spelled the field names correctly. Then run the query again.

8. With the ⊞ pointer, double-click to resize the **Discounted Fee** column automatically.

9. Click anywhere in the **Discounted Fee** column, and then, on the **Home tab**, in the **Sort & Filter group**, click the **Ascending** button.

10. Click **File**, click **Print**, and then click **Print Preview**. In the **Page Layout group**, click **Landscape**. Compare your screen with **Figure 4**.

11. Click **Save** 🖫. If you are printing this project, print the datasheet.

12. **Close** ☒ the datasheet, and then **Open** ≫ the **Navigation Pane**.

■ **You have completed Skill 7 of 10**

► When criteria are in more than one column, the placement of the criteria in the design grid rows determines if one or both of the criteria must be true for the record to display.

1. On the **Create tab**, in the **Queries group**, click the **Query Design** button. In the **Show Table** dialog box, add the **Classes** table, add the **Sections** table, and then **Close** the dialog box.

2. In the design workspace, point to the bottom edge of the **Sections** table. With the ⬍ pointer, drag down so that all the table fields display, and then release the mouse button.

3. From the **Classes** table, add the **Class Title** field to the design grid. From the **Sections** table, add the **Start Date** and **Live Models** fields to the design grid.

4. Click **Save** 💾, type Adults Only Classes and then click **OK**.

5. In the **Results group**, click the **Run** button, and then compare your screen with **Figure 1**. ──────

The Live Models field has been assigned the **Yes/No data type**—a data type used to store values that can have one of two possible values—for example, yes and no, or true and false.

6. Click the **View** button to switch to Design view. In the **Live Models** column **Criteria** box, type =Yes **Run** the query, and then compare your results with **Figure 2**. ──────

When a check box in a Yes/No field is selected, the value *Yes* is stored in the field. When the check box is cleared, the value *No* is stored in that field.

■ **Continue to the next page to complete the skill** ▶

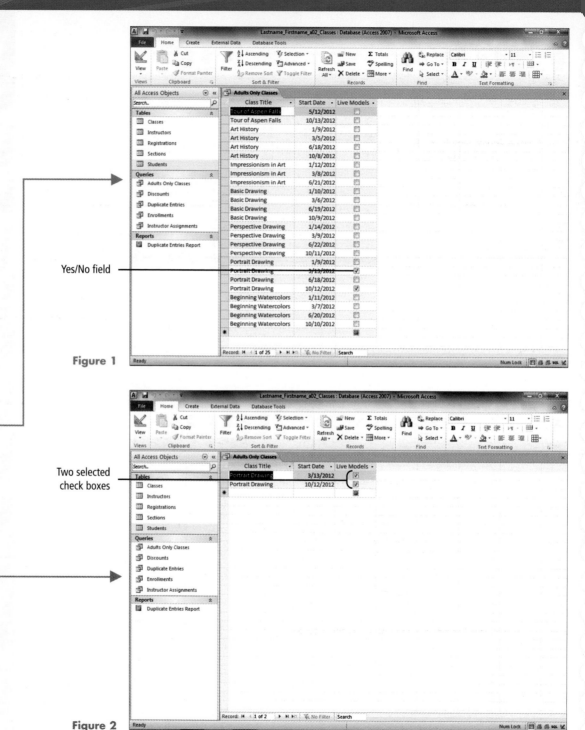

Yes/No field ────

Figure 1

Two selected check boxes ────

Figure 2

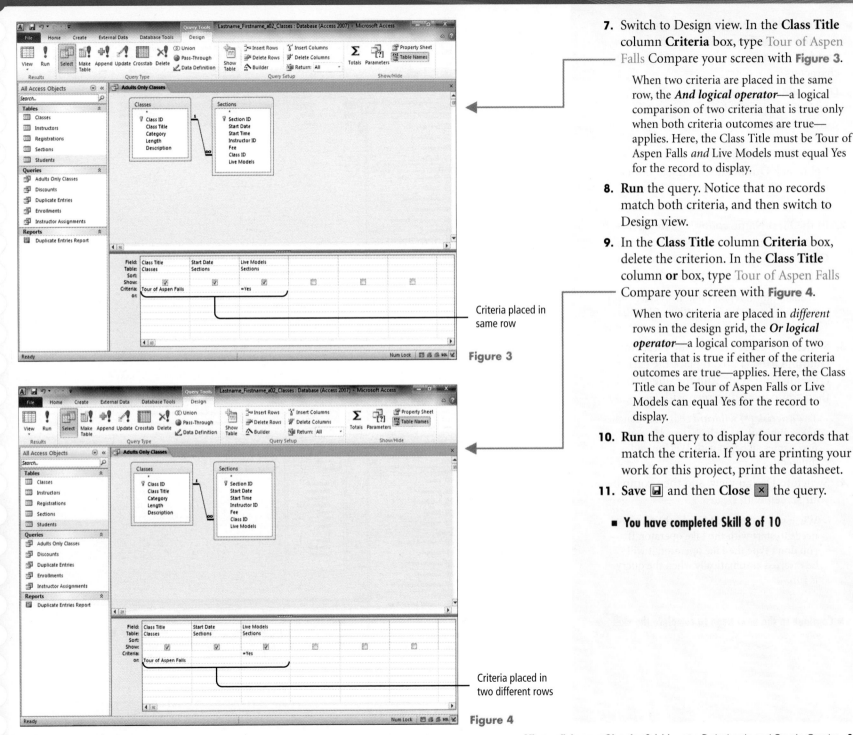

Criteria placed in same row

Figure 3

Criteria placed in two different rows

Figure 4

7. Switch to Design view. In the **Class Title** column **Criteria** box, type Tour of Aspen Falls Compare your screen with **Figure 3**.

When two criteria are placed in the same row, the ***And logical operator***—a logical comparison of two criteria that is true only when both criteria outcomes are true—applies. Here, the Class Title must be Tour of Aspen Falls *and* Live Models must equal Yes for the record to display.

8. **Run** the query. Notice that no records match both criteria, and then switch to Design view.

9. In the **Class Title** column **Criteria** box, delete the criterion. In the **Class Title** column **or** box, type Tour of Aspen Falls Compare your screen with **Figure 4**.

When two criteria are placed in *different* rows in the design grid, the ***Or logical operator***—a logical comparison of two criteria that is true if either of the criteria outcomes are true—applies. Here, the Class Title can be Tour of Aspen Falls or Live Models can equal Yes for the record to display.

10. **Run** the query to display four records that match the criteria. If you are printing your work for this project, print the datasheet.

11. **Save** 🖫 and then **Close** ⊠ the query.

■ **You have completed Skill 8 of 10**

► A *wildcard* is a special character, such as an asterisk, used in query criteria to allow matches for any combination of letters or characters.

► Using wildcards, you can expand your search criteria to find a more accurate subset of the data.

1. In the **Navigation Pane**, under **Queries**, right-click **Duplicate Entries**, and then, from the shortcut menu, click **Design View**.

2. In the **First Name** column **Criteria** box, type William In the **Last Name** column **Criteria** box, type Smith **Run** the query to display the record for William Smith.

   William Smith reports that he receives four copies of every Art Center flyer. With the current criteria, his record is listed one time.

3. Switch to Design view. In the **First Name** column **Criteria** box, replace the existing criterion with Will* **Run** the query, and then compare your screen with **Figure 1**. ─────

   The *asterisk (*) wildcard* character matches any combination of characters. Here, the first names all begin with *Will* but end differently.

4. Switch to Design view, and then compare your screen with **Figure 2**. ─────

   When you include wildcards, the criterion needs to start with the Like operator. If you don't type the Like operator, it will be inserted automatically when the query is run.

■ **Continue to the next page to complete the skill**

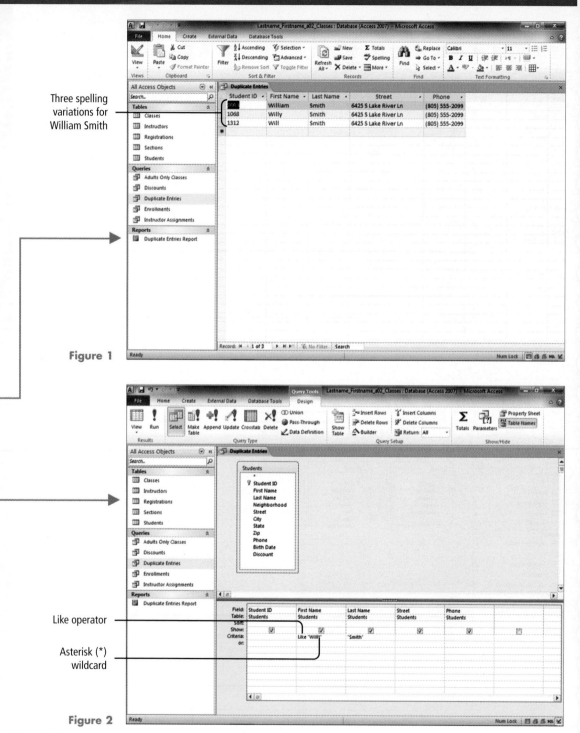

Three spelling variations for William Smith

Figure 1

Like operator

Asterisk (*) wildcard

Figure 2

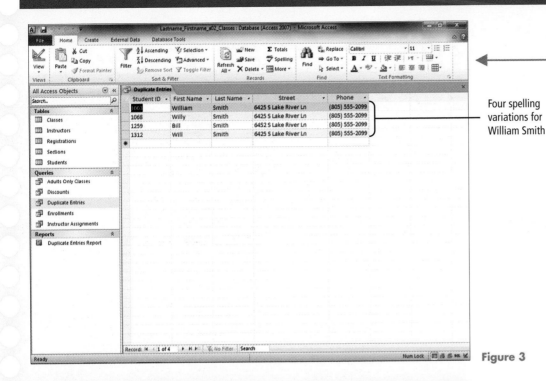

Four spelling variations for William Smith

Figure 3

Common Access Wildcard Characters		
Character	**Description**	**Example**
*	Matches any number of characters.	Don* matches Don and Donna, but not Adonna.
?	Matches any single alphabetic character.	D?n matches Don and Dan, but not Dean.
[ ]	Matches any single character in the brackets.	D[ao]n matches Dan and Don, but not Den.
#	Matches any single numeric character.	C-#PO matches C-3PO, but not C-DPO.

Figure 4

5. In the **First Name** column **Criteria** box, replace the existing criterion with Like "?ill*" **Run** the query to display the four duplicate records for William Smith. Compare your screen with **Figure 3**.

   The *question mark (?) wildcard* character matches any single character. Common wildcard characters supported by Access are summarized in the table in **Figure 4**.

6. **Save** 🔲, and then **Close** ❌ the query.

7. In the **Navigation Pane**, under **Reports**, double-click **Duplicate Entries Report**. If you are printing this project, print the report.

   Recall that reports are often used to display the results of queries. Here, the report displays the results of the Duplicate Entries query.

8. **Close** ❌ the report.

   Because you did not make any design changes to the report, you do not need to save it.

■ **You have completed Skill 9 of 10**

▶ A *summary statistic* is a calculation for a group of data such as a total, an average, or a count.

▶ When summary statistics are added to a query, the query calculates statistics for a group of data.

1. In the **Navigation Pane**, under **Queries**, right-click **Enrollments**, and then, from the shortcut menu, click **Design View**.

2. In the query design workspace, in the **Classes** table, double-click **Class Title** to add it to the design grid. Repeat this technique to insert the **Start Date, Student ID**, and **Fee** fields.

3. Change the **Start Date** column **Sort** box to **Ascending**. **Run** the query, and then compare your screen with **Figure 1**.

   The query lists each class and its starting date, the Student ID of each student enrolled in the class, and the normal Fee charged to each student.

4. Switch to Design view. On the **Design tab**, in the **Show/Hide group**, click the **Totals** button to insert the **Total** row in the design grid.

5. Click in the **Student ID** column **Total** box to display its arrow. Click the **Student ID** column **Total arrow**, and then click **Count**. Repeat this technique to change the **Fee** column **Total** box to **Sum**. Compare your screen with **Figure 2**.

   The Total row is used to determine how queries should be grouped and summarized. Here, two columns have been designated as columns to group by and the other two columns have been designated to calculate statistics—count and sum.

▪ **Continue to the next page to complete the skill** ▶

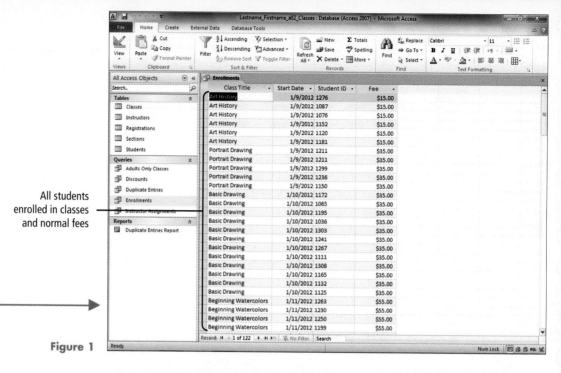

All students enrolled in classes and normal fees

Figure 1

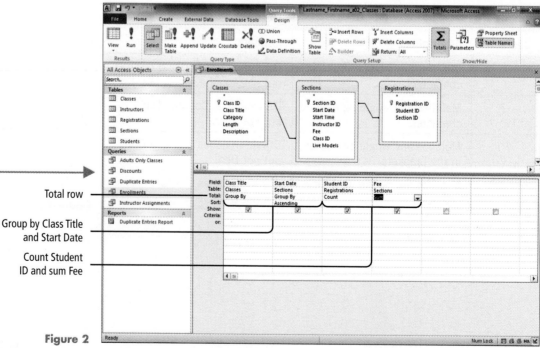

Total row

Group by Class Title and Start Date

Count Student ID and sum Fee

Figure 2

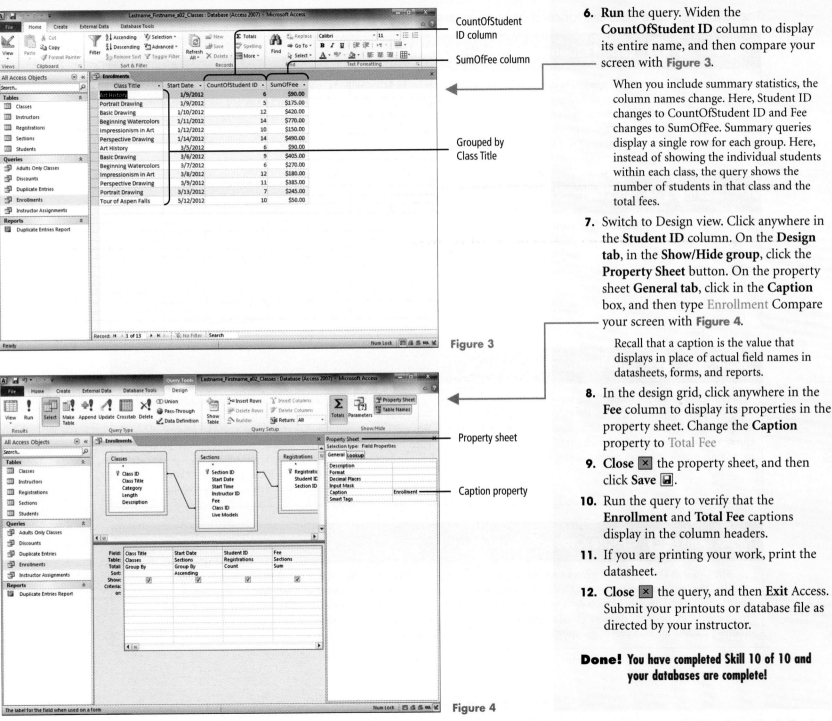

CountOfStudent ID column

SumOfFee column

Grouped by Class Title

Figure 3

Property sheet

Caption property

Figure 4

6. **Run** the query. Widen the **CountOfStudent ID** column to display its entire name, and then compare your screen with **Figure 3**.

When you include summary statistics, the column names change. Here, Student ID changes to CountOfStudent ID and Fee changes to SumOfFee. Summary queries display a single row for each group. Here, instead of showing the individual students within each class, the query shows the number of students in that class and the total fees.

7. Switch to Design view. Click anywhere in the **Student ID** column. On the **Design tab**, in the **Show/Hide group**, click the **Property Sheet** button. On the property sheet **General tab**, click in the **Caption** box, and then type Enrollment Compare your screen with **Figure 4**.

Recall that a caption is the value that displays in place of actual field names in datasheets, forms, and reports.

8. In the design grid, click anywhere in the **Fee** column to display its properties in the property sheet. Change the **Caption** property to Total Fee

9. **Close** ✕ the property sheet, and then click **Save** 🖫.

10. Run the query to verify that the **Enrollment** and **Total Fee** captions display in the column headers.

11. If you are printing your work, print the datasheet.

12. **Close** ✕ the query, and then **Exit** Access. Submit your printouts or database file as directed by your instructor.

Done! You have completed Skill 10 of 10 and your databases are complete!

The following More Skills are located at **www.pearsonhighered.com/skills**

More Skills Export Queries to Other File Formats

There are times when you need to work with data in a table or query using another application. Access can export database tables and queries into several file formats that are used by other applications. For example, you can export a table to a Word document or an Excel spreadsheet, or to a web page.

In More Skills 11, you will export a query to an Excel spreadsheet and to a file that can be opened with a web browser.

To begin, open your web browser, navigate to www.pearsonhighered.com/skills, locate the name of your textbook, and then follow the instructions on the website.

More Skills Find Duplicate Records

The purpose of a relational database is to avoid duplicate data. When tables contain many records, it is often difficult to discover when duplicate data exists. The Find Duplicates Query Wizard is used to find duplicate data quickly.

In More Skills 12, you will use the Find Duplicates Query Wizard to locate duplicate data and then correct the records with duplicate values. You will then run the query again to test your changes.

To begin, open your web browser, navigate to www.pearsonhighered.com/skills, locate the name of your textbook, and then follow the instructions on the website.

More Skills Find Unmatched Records

When two tables are related, each record in the table on the *many* side of the relationship must have a corresponding value in the table on the *one* side of the relationship. The Find Unmatched Query Wizard compares the values from two tables and then lists the records that do not have corresponding values.

In More Skills 13, you will use the Find Unmatched Query Wizard to find records that are missing a value in a related table. You will then correct the data and create a one-to-many relationship between the two tables.

To begin, open your web browser, navigate to www.pearsonhighered.com/skills, locate the name of your textbook, and then follow the instructions on the website.

More Skills Create Crosstab Queries

The Crosstab Query Wizard creates a special query that calculates the results of two groupings. One group displays down the left column and the other group displays across the top. Each remaining cell in the query displays a total, average, or other summary statistic for each pair of groupings.

In More Skills 14, you will create a crosstab query.

To begin, open your web browser, navigate to www.pearsonhighered.com/skills, locate the name of your textbook, and then follow the instructions on the website.

Key Terms

Online Help Skills

1. **Start** 🔵 Access. In the upper-right corner of the Access window, click the **Help** button 🔲. In the **Help** window, click the **Maximize** 🔳 button.

2. Click in the search box, type query criteria and then click the **Search** button. In the search results, click **Examples of query criteria**.

3. Read the article's introduction, and then, below **In this topic**, click **Overview**. Compare your screen with **Figure 1**.

Figure 1

4. Read the Overview section and watch the video to see if you can answer the following: What expression would you use to find all students who are over 30 years old? How would you change this expression to find students who are 18 or over?

Matching

Match each term in the second column with its correct definition in the first column by writing the letter of the term on the blank line in front of the correct definition.

_____ **1.** A wizard that quickly adds fields to a new query.

_____ **2.** A technology that displays Quick Info, ToolTips, and AutoComplete as you type expressions.

_____ **3.** Equal to (=) and greater than (>) are examples of this type of operator.

_____ **4.** This dialog box is used to add tables to an existing query.

_____ **5.** In the query design grid, two criteria placed in the same row use this logical operator.

_____ **6.** When two criteria are placed in different rows in the query design grid, this logical operator will be applied.

_____ **7.** This wildcard character can represent any combination of characters.

_____ **8.** This wildcard character can represent any single character.

_____ **9.** When using a field name in a calculated field, the field's name must start and end with this character.

_____ **10.** To add summary statistics to a query, this row must be added to the query.

A And

B Asterisk (*)

C Comparison

D IntelliSense

E Or

F Question mark (?)

G Show Table

H Simple Query

I Square bracket

J Total

Multiple Choice

Choose the correct answer.

1. In a query, criteria is added in this view.
   A. Datasheet
   B. Design
   C. Workspace

2. In a query, results are displayed in this view.
   A. Datasheet
   B. Design
   C. Design grid

3. An IntelliSense menu of commands that match the characters you are typing.
   A. AutoComplete
   B. Quick Info
   C. ToolTips

4. An IntelliSense box that explains the purpose of the selected AutoComplete.
   A. AutoComplete
   B. Quick Info
   C. ToolTips

5. In query criteria, dates are surrounded by this character.
   A. >
   B. !
   C. #

6. An operator that finds all numbers or dates between and including two values.
   A. And...Between
   B. Between...And
   C. In...Between

7. A combination of fields, mathematical operators, and pre-built functions that calculates values.
   A. Comparison operator
   B. Expression
   C. Quick Info

8. A data type used to store values that can have one of two possible values.
   A. Byte
   B. Switch
   C. Yes/No

9. The operator that is placed at the beginning of criteria that use wildcards.
   A. Like
   B. Similar
   C. Wildcard

10. A calculation for a group of data such as a total, an average, or a count.
    A. Calculated column
    B. Group formula
    C. Summary statistic

Topics for Discussion

1. You have created queries using the Simple Query Wizard and using Design view. Which method do you prefer, and why? What situations may be better suited to using the Simple Query Wizard? What situations may be better suited to using Design view?

2. Data that can be calculated from existing fields can be entered manually into its own field, or it can be included as a calculated field in a query. Which method would produce the most accurate results, and why?

Skill Check

To complete this database, you will need the following file:

- a02_Outings

You will save your database as:

- Lastname_Firstname_a02_Outings

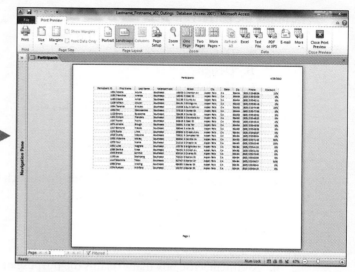

1. **Start** Access, and then open the student data file **a02_Outings**. Save the database in your **Access Chapter 2** folder with the name Lastname_Firstname_a02_Outings If necessary, enable the content.

2. Open the **Participants** table. Click the **Last Name** column. In the **Find group**, click the **Find** button. In the **Find What** box, type Binder and then click the **Find Next** button. **Close** the dialog box, and then change *Freddie Binder* to your own first and last name.

3. With the **Last Name** column active, in the **Sort & Filter group**, click the **Ascending** button.

4. Select the **Neighborhood** column, and then, in the **Sort & Filter** group, click the **Filter** button. In the **Filter** pane, clear the (**Select All**) check box, and then select the **Southeast** check box. Click **OK** to apply the filter.

Figure 1

5. **Close** the **Navigation Pane**. In the **Text Formatting group**, click the **Font Size arrow**, and then click **9**.

6. Select all the columns, and then double-click to resize their widths automatically.

7. On the **File tab**, click **Print**, and then click **Print Preview**. In the **Page Layout group**, click the **Landscape** button. Compare your screen with **Figure 1**. If you are printing this project, print the datasheet.

8. **Save**, and then **Close** the table. On the **Create tab**, in the **Queries group**, click **Query Wizard**. In the **New Query** dialog box, click **OK**.

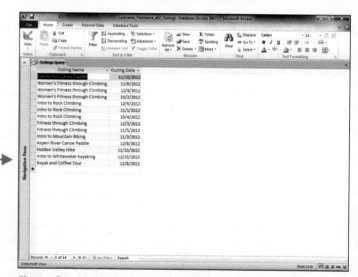

9. In the **Simple Query Wizard**, click the **Tables/Queries arrow**, and then click **Table: Outings**.

10. Click **Outing Name** and then click the **Move** button. Repeat the procedure to move **Outing Date** into **Selected Fields**, and then click **Finish**.

11. On the **Home tab**, click the **View** button, and then, in the **Outing Date** column **Criteria** box, type >10/1/2012

Figure 2

12. **Run** the query, double-click to resize the **Outing Name** column automatically, and then compare your screen with **Figure 2**.

■ **Continue to the next page to complete this Skill Check**

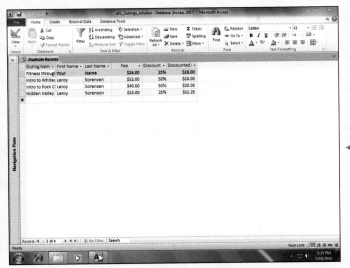

Figure 3

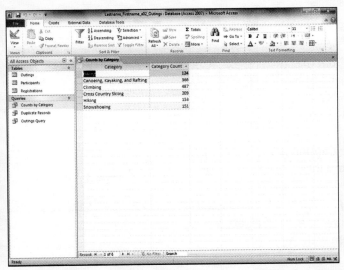

Figure 4

13. If you are printing your work, print the Outings Query datasheet. **Save**, and then **Close** the query.

14. On the **Create tab**, in the **Queries group**, click **Query Design**. Use the displayed **Show Table** dialog box to add the following tables in this order: **Outings, Registrations**, and **Participants**. **Close** the dialog box.

15. Double-click to add the following fields in this order: **Outing Name, First Name, Last Name, Fee**, and, from the bottom of the **Participants** table, **Discount**.

16. In the **Last Name** column **Criteria** box, type Sorens?n to show records for Sorensen or Sorenson. In the **Last Name** column **or** box, type your own last name.

17. In the first blank column, type the following label and expression: Discounted Fee:[Fee]-[Fee]*[Discount] If necessary, widen the column for the calculated field.

18. In the **Last Name** column, click the **Sort** box. Click the displayed **Sort arrow**, and then click **Ascending**.

19. Click **Save**. In the **Save As** dialog box, type Duplicate Records and then press [Enter].

20. **Run** the query, and then compare your screen with **Figure 3**. If the Enter Parameter Value dialog box displays, return to Design view and then repeat step 17, taking care to spell field names correctly and to include the square brackets.

21. If you are printing your work, print the datasheet. **Close** the **Duplicate Records** query.

22. **Open** the **Navigation Pane**. In the **Navigation Pane**, under **Queries**, right-click **Counts by Category**, and then click **Design View**.

23. On the **Design tab**, in the **Show/Hide group**, click the **Totals** button. Click in the **Registration ID** column **Total** box, click the displayed **Total arrow**, and then click **Count**.

24. With the **Registration ID** column still active, in the **Show/Hide group**, click the **Property Sheet** button. Click in the property sheet **Caption** box, type Category Count and then **Close** the property sheet.

25. Click **Save**, and then **Run** the query. Widen the **Category Count** column so that the entire label displays, and then compare your screen with **Figure 4**.

26. If you are printing your work, print the datasheet. **Save**, and then **Close** the **Counts by Category** query.

27. **Exit** Access. Submit your printouts or database file as directed by your instructor.

Done! You have completed the Skill Check

Assess Your Skills 1

To complete this database, you will need the following file:

- a02_Reviews

You will save your database as:

- Lastname_Firstname_a02_Reviews

1. **Start** Access, and then open **a02_Reviews**. Save the database in your **Access Chapter 2** folder as Lastname_Firstname_a02_Reviews If necessary, enable the content.

2. Open the **Employees** table. **Find** the record for *Cyril Calta* and replace his name with your own first and last name.

3. Filter the **Department** column so only the nine **Art Center** employees display, and then sort the datasheet in alphabetical order by **Last Name**. Change the datasheet's font size to **10**.

4. In **Print Preview**, change orientation to **Landscape**, and then **Save** the table. If you are printing your work, print the datasheet. **Close** the table.

5. Start the **Simple Query Wizard**. From the **Employees** table, add **First Name** and **Last Name**. From the **Reviews** table, add **Review Date, Attendance**, and **Customer Relations**. Use the wizard to name the query Employee Reviews and accept all other wizard defaults.

6. Switch to Design view. In the **Last Name** column **Criteria** box, add a criterion with a wildcard that accepts all last names starting with B and ending with thin Use a wildcard character that accepts any number of characters.

7. In the **Last Name** column **or** box, type your own last name.

8. Set the query to sort in alphabetical order by **Last Name**. Add a criterion to the **Review Date** column so that reviews after 12/31/2009 display.

9. In the first blank column, add a calculated field with the label Review Total Have the calculated field add the Attendance field to the Customer Relations field.

10. In the **Review Total** column just created, add a criterion so that only totals that are greater than or equal to 7 display. **Save**, and then **Run** the query. Verify that four records result as shown in **Figure 1**.

11. If asked, print the datasheet. **Close** the query.

12. Create a new query in Design view. From the **Employees** table, add **Departments**, and from the **Reviews** table add **Employee ID**. Add the **Total** row, group by **Department**, and **Count Employee ID**.

13. For the **Employee ID** column, set the **Caption** property to Number of Employees **Save** the query with the name Department Counts

14. **Run** the query, widen the **Number of Employees** column to display the entire caption, and then compare your screen with **Figure 2**.

15. If you are printing your work, print the datasheet. **Save**, and then **Close** the query.

16. **Exit** Access, and then submit your printouts or database file as directed by your instructor.

Done! You have completed Assess Your Skills 1

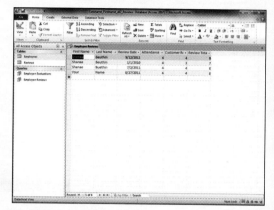

Figure 1

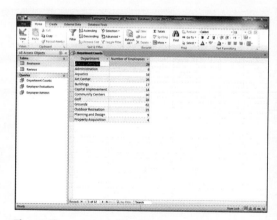

Figure 2

Assess Your Skills 3 and 4 can be found at www.pearsonhighered.com/skills.

Assess Your Skills 2

To complete this database, you will need the following file:

- a02_Camps

You will save your database as:

- Lastname_Firstname_a02_Camps

Figure 1

Figure 2

1. **Start** Access, and then open **a02_Camps**. Save the database in your **Access Chapter 2** folder as Lastname_Firstname_a02_Camps

2. Open the **Campers** table. **Find** the record for *Kurt Davion* and replace his name with your own first and last name.

3. **Filter** the **Parent/Guardian** column so that only **(Blanks)** display, and then sort the datasheet in alphabetical order by **Last Name**. Change the datasheet's font size to **10**.

4. In **Print Preview**, change orientation to **Landscape**, and then **Save** the table. If you are printing your work, print the datasheet. **Close** the table.

5. Start the **Simple Query Wizard**. From the **Camps** table, add **Camp Name** and **Start Date**. From the **Campers** table, add **First Name** and **Last Name**. Use the wizard to name the query July Campers and accept all other wizard defaults.

6. Switch to Design view. In the **Start Date** column **Criteria** box, enter an expression that will result in dates between 7/1/2012 and 7/31/2012.

7. In the **First Name** column **Criteria** box, add a criterion with a wildcard that accepts all first names starting with Carl

8. In the **Last Name** column **or** box, type your own last name.

9. Set the query to sort in alphabetical order by **Last Name**.

10. In the first blank column, add a calculated field with the label Discount Amount Calculate the amount by multiplying the Discount field by 75.

11. Click in the **Discount Amount** column **or** box, and then open the property sheet. On the property sheet **General** tab, click the **Format** box, click the displayed **Format arrow**, and, from the list, click **Currency**. **Close** the property sheet.

12. **Save**, and then **Run** the query. Widen the **Discount Amount** column to display the entire caption. Verify that three records result, as shown in **Figure 1**.

13. If asked, print the datasheet. **Save**, and then **Close** the query.

14. Create a new query in Design view. From the **Camps** table, add **Camp Name**, and from the **Registrations** table, add **Registration Number**. Add the **Total** row, and group by **Camp Name** and **Count** by **Registration Number**.

15. **Save** the query with the name Camp Counts **Run** the query, and then compare your screen with **Figure 2**.

16. If you are printing your work, print the datasheet. **Close** the query.

17. **Exit** Access, and then submit your printouts or database file as directed by your instructor.

Done! You have completed Assess Your Skills 2

Assess Your Skills Visually

To complete this database, you will need the following file:

- a02_Instructors

You will save your database as:

- Lastname_Firstname_a02_Instructors

Open the database **a02_Instructors**, and then using your own name, **Save** the database as Lastname_Firstname_a02_Instructors

Format the **Art Instructors** table as shown in **Figure 1**. Change the datasheet's font size to **10**, and then resize the columns to fit their data. Apply the **Raised** cell effect with each row color alternating between **White, Background 1** and the standard color **Green 2**. Format the grid line color to the standard color **Green 5**.

Sort the datasheet by **Last Name**. In the first record of the **Art Instructors** table, replace *Kacey Alkbsh* with your own name.

Save the datasheet changes. Print the datasheet or submit the database file as directed by your instructor.

Done! You have completed Assess Your Skills Visually

Instructor ID	First Name	Last Name	Street	City	State	Zip	Phone	Click to Add
A106	Your	Name	82522 E Madison St	Aspen Falls	CA	93463	(805) 555-7170	
A121	Bradford	Andrzejczyk	63734 W Meadow St	Aspen Falls	CA	93464	(805) 555-7316	
A107	Carrol	Chicharello	63471 S High St	Aspen Falls	CA	93463	(805) 555-6131	
A113	Faustino	Cummisky	44705 S Earle St	Aspen Falls	CA	93463	(805) 555-7475	
A105	Hazel	Ekwall	82075 N Mahoney St	Aspen Falls	CA	93463	(805) 555-5713	
A116	Brant	Floerke	23812 E Eastview Ct	Aspen Falls	CA	93463	(805) 555-4683	
A103	Beatriz	Handlin	23926 S Harrington Av	Aspen Falls	CA	93464	(805) 555-3580	
A117	Rey	Hasse	38789 E East St	Aspen Falls	CA	93464	(805) 555-4704	
A111	Cortez	Herke	58065 N Templewood Ct	Aspen Falls	CA	93464	(805) 555-8010	
A112	Anton	Hoffelt	19199 W Field Av	Aspen Falls	CA	93463	(805) 555-4937	
A102	Carlie	Litzenberg	75732 S Porter Pl	Aspen Falls	CA	93463	(805) 555-3997	
A114	Mohamed	Lonzo	83721 N Mayfield Rd	Aspen Falls	CA	93463	(805) 555-9831	
A119	Ron	Morey	70416 S Nelson Pl	Aspen Falls	CA	93464	(805) 555-2287	
A109	Larry	Moyerman	62877 N Strongs Av	Aspen Falls	CA	93463	(805) 555-9205	
A108	Macie	Ryhal	60034 W Meadow Brook Rd	Aspen Falls	CA	93464	(805) 555-5281	
A104	Mitchell	Screen	76117 W Second St	Aspen Falls	CA	93463	(805) 555-3976	
A101	Lana	Shane	5396 S West St	Aspen Falls	CA	93463	(805) 555-3817	
A118	Sherman	Stobb	8121 S Plain St	Aspen Falls	CA	93463	(805) 555-4462	
A100	Carolyne	Teeple	42018 N Horton St	Aspen Falls	CA	93464	(805) 555-6684	
A115	Dustin	Termilus	33533 S Lafayette St	Aspen Falls	CA	93463	(805) 555-4134	
A120	Boyce	Torgeson	38431 S Mayfield Rd	Aspen Falls	CA	93463	(805) 555-2202	
A110	Chasidy	Trowery	81976 W E Washington St	Aspen Falls	CA	93463	(805) 555-8726	

Figure 1

Skills in Context

To complete this database, you will need the following file:

- a02_Neighborhoods

You will save your database as:

- Lastname_Firstname_a02_Neighborhoods

Open **a02_Neighborhoods** and save the database in your **Access Chapter 2** folder as Lastname_Firstname_a02_Neighborhoods Create a summary query named Neighborhood Counts that counts the number of registrations from each neighborhood. The Neighborhood field is in the Students table, and the Registration ID field is in the Registrations table. The query will have five rows, one for each neighborhood. In the first column, display the neighborhood name, and in the second column, display the number of registered students. For the second column, change the caption to Number of Students In the datasheet, widen the Number of Students column to display the entire caption.

Print the datasheet or submit the database file as directed by your instructor.

Done! You have completed Skills in Context

Skills and You

To complete this database, you will need the following file:

- a02_Contacts

You will save your database as:

- Lastname_Firstname_a02_Contacts

Open a02_Contacts, and then save the database as Lastname_Firstname_a02_Contacts Open the Contacts table, and then add at least 12 personal contacts to the table. In the Contact Type field, enter either *Family, Friend,* or *Business* for each contact. Create a query that displays all the fields from the Contacts table. Add criteria to display only the contacts that you assigned as *Family*. Format the query datasheet as desired and assign the Landscape orientation. Print or submit the file as directed by your instructor.

Done! You have completed Skills and You

CHAPTER 3

Create Forms

▶ Forms are typically used to edit, delete, and add the records stored in database tables.

▶ Most forms show one record at a time so that you can work with just that data.

Your starting screen will look similar to this:

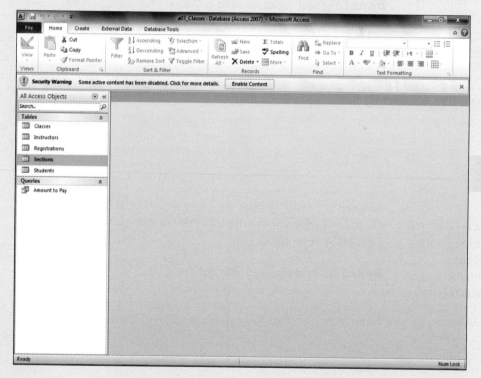

SKILLS
Skills 1-10 Training

At the end of this chapter, you will be able to:

Skill 1   Use the Form Wizard

Skill 2   Format Forms in Layout View

Skill 3   Use Forms to Modify Data

Skill 4   Use the Blank Form Tool

Skill 5   Customize Form Layouts

Skill 6   Add Input Masks

Skill 7   Apply Conditional Formatting

Skill 8   Create One-to-Many Forms

Skill 9   Enter Data Using One-to-Many Forms

Skill 10   Create Forms from Queries

MORE SKILLS

More Skills 11 Validate Fields

More Skills 12 Add Combo Boxes to Forms

More Skills 13 Create Multiple Item Forms

More Skills 14 Create Macros

Outcome

Using the skills listed to the left will enable you to create forms like these:

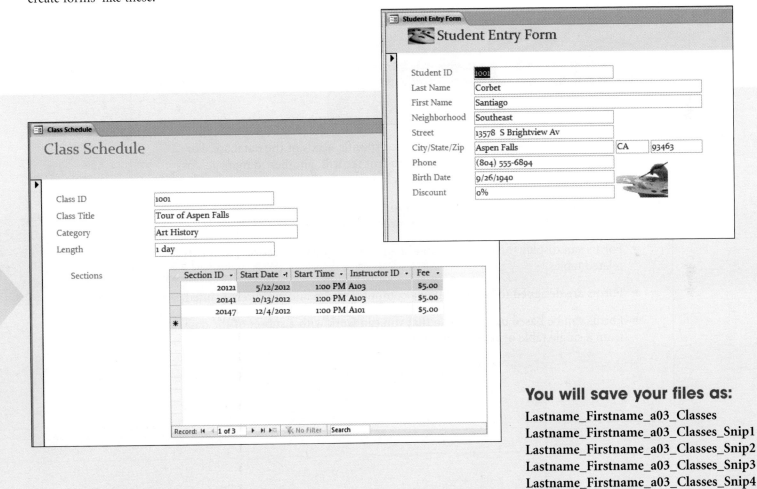

In this chapter, you will create documents for the Aspen Falls City Hall, which provides essential services for the citizens and visitors of Aspen Falls, California.

Introduction

- ▶ Forms are often designed to enter data for specific needs of the database. For example, one form is used to manage student records, another to manage class records, and another to register students into classes.

- ▶ Access has many methods for building forms so that you can choose the method that best creates the form you need.

- ▶ Forms can display the records from a single table or display records from two related tables.

- ▶ Forms are designed to be viewed on a computer screen and are rarely printed.

- ▶ Forms can be based on queries so that you can work with a subset of the data from a single table or several related tables.

Time to complete all
10 skills – 60 to 90 minutes

Find your student data files here:

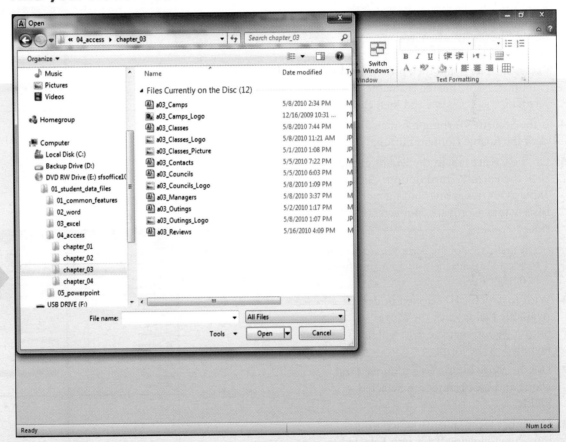

Student data files needed for this chapter:

- a03_Classes
- a03_Classes_Logo
- a03_Classes_Picture

► Access has several tools for creating forms. The Form Wizard is used to select multiple tables and specific fields for your form.

1. **Start** ⚫ Access. If necessary, Maximize ⬜ the window.

2. From the student files that came with this book, open **a03_Classes**.

3. Click the **File tab**, and then click **Save Database As**. In the **Save As** dialog box, display the file list where you are saving your files. Click **New folder**, type Access Chapter 3 and then press Enter two times. Name the file Lastname_Firstname_a03_Classes and then click **Save**.

4. If the Security Warning message displays, click the Enable Content button.

5. On the **Create tab**, in the **Forms group**, click the **Form Wizard** button. Click the **Tables/Queries arrow**, and then click **Instructors**. Compare your screen with Figure 1.

The first screen of the Form Wizard is used to select the fields that you want your form to display.

6. With **Instructor ID** selected under **Available Fields**, click the **Move** button ▷ so that the field will be included in the form.

7. Use the **Move** button ▷ to move **First Name** and **Last Name** into **Selected Fields**.

8. Use either technique just practiced to move the following fields into **Selected Fields** in this order: **Street**, **City**, **State**, **Zip**, and **Phone**. Do not move the Current W-4 field. Compare your screen with Figure 2.

■ **Continue to the next page to complete the skill** ▶

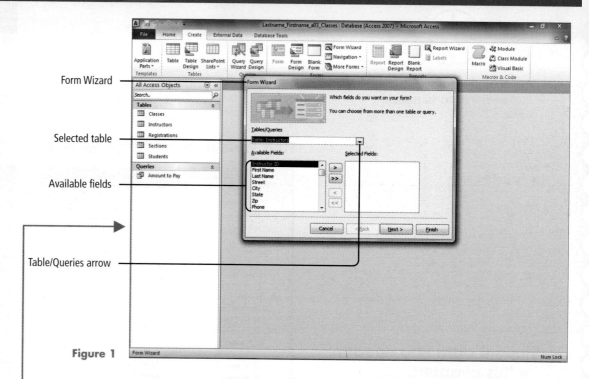

Form Wizard
Selected table
Available fields
Table/Queries arrow

Figure 1

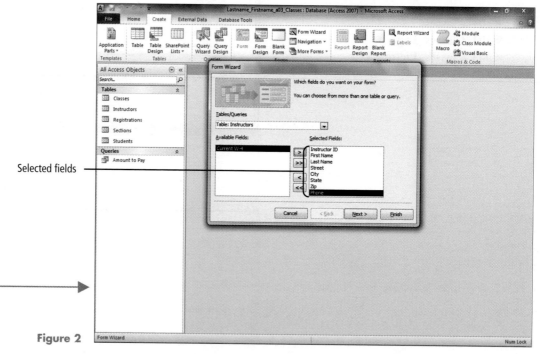

Selected fields

Figure 2

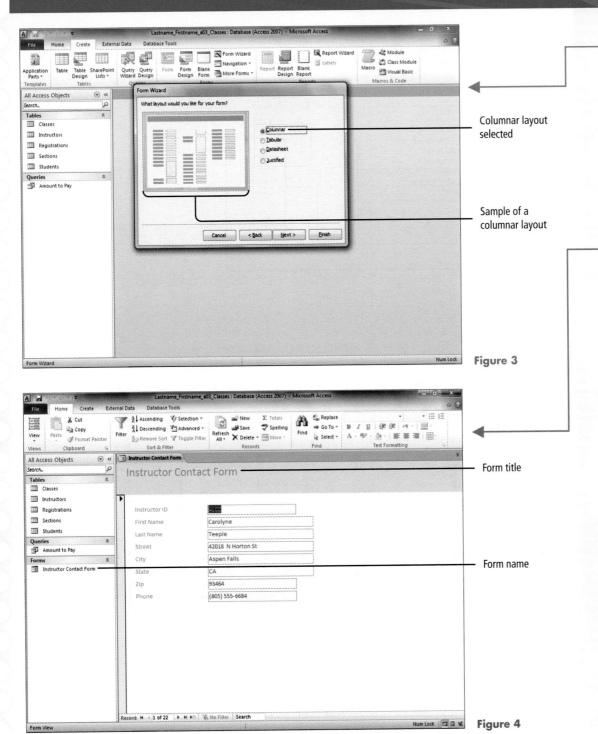

Columnar layout selected

Sample of a columnar layout

Figure 3

Form title

Form name

Figure 4

9. In the **Form Wizard**, click **Next**, and then compare your screen with **Figure 3**.

> You can use the Form Wizard to pick different layouts for your form. A *layout* determines how data and labels are arranged in a form or report. For example, the *columnar layout* places labels in the first column and data in the second column.

10. With **Columnar layout** selected, click **Next**. Under **What title do you want for your form**, replace *Instructors* with Instructor Contact Form

11. In the **Form Wizard**, click **Finish**, and then compare your screen with **Figure 4**.

> The title that you type in the last screen of the Form Wizard becomes the name of the form in the Navigation Pane and the theme last used in the database is applied. Here, the Adjacency theme has been applied.

12. Leave the form open for the next skill.

■ **You have completed Skill 1 of 10**

▶ *Layout view* is used to format a form or report while viewing a sample of the data.

1. With the **Instructor Contact Form** still open, on the **Home tab**, in the **Views group**, click the **View** button to switch to Layout view. Compare your screen with **Figure 1**.

   In Layout view, you can select individual labels and text boxes. A *label* is an object on a form or report that describes other objects on the report or form. Here, the Instructor ID text box is selected. A *text box* is an object on a form or report that displays the data from a field in a table or query.

2. On the **Design tab**, in the **Themes group**, click the **Themes** button. Scroll to the bottom of the **Themes** gallery, and then, in the third to last row, click the second theme—**Paper**.

3. In the **Header/Footer group**, click the **Date and Time** button. Compare your screen with **Figure 2**.

4. In the **Date and Time** dialog box, accept the default settings by clicking **OK** to insert the date and time into the form's header.

■ **Continue to the next page to complete the skill**

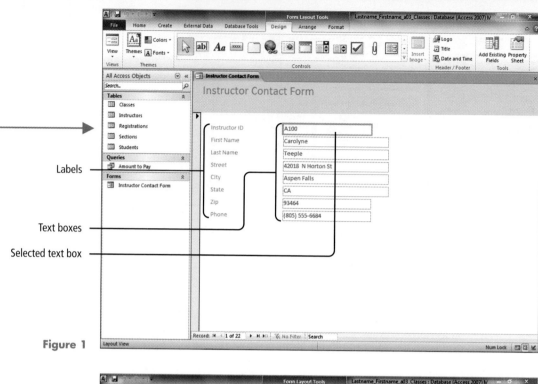

Labels

Text boxes

Selected text box

Figure 1

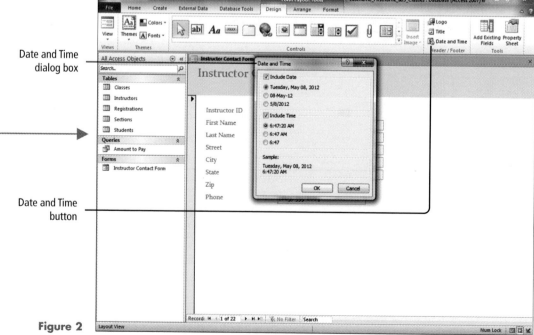

Date and Time dialog box

Date and Time button

Figure 2

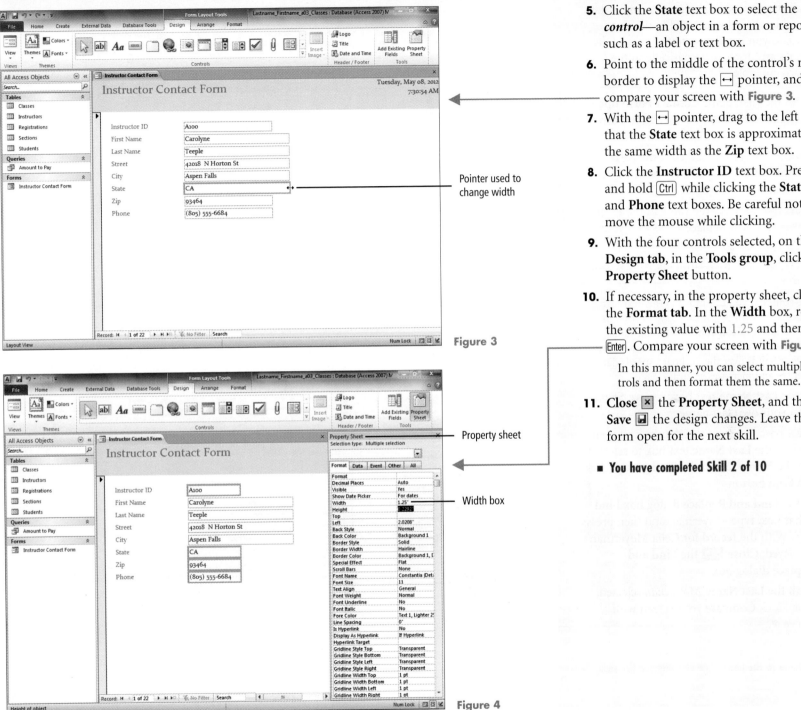

Pointer used to change width

Figure 3

Property sheet

Width box

Figure 4

5. Click the **State** text box to select the *control*—an object in a form or report such as a label or text box.

6. Point to the middle of the control's right border to display the ↔ pointer, and then compare your screen with **Figure 3**.

7. With the ↔ pointer, drag to the left so that the **State** text box is approximately the same width as the **Zip** text box.

8. Click the **Instructor ID** text box. Press and hold Ctrl while clicking the **State**, **Zip**, and **Phone** text boxes. Be careful not to move the mouse while clicking.

9. With the four controls selected, on the **Design tab**, in the **Tools group**, click the **Property Sheet** button.

10. If necessary, in the property sheet, click the **Format tab**. In the **Width** box, replace the existing value with 1.25 and then press Enter. Compare your screen with **Figure 4**.

   In this manner, you can select multiple controls and then format them the same.

11. **Close** ☒ the **Property Sheet**, and then **Save** 🖫 the design changes. Leave the form open for the next skill.

   ■ **You have completed Skill 2 of 10**

▶ Recall that forms are designed to input data into tables. You do not need to use the mouse as you key data into forms, and the changes are stored automatically in the underlying table.

1. With the **Instructor Contact Form** open, click the **View** button to switch to Form view.

2. On the Navigation bar, click the **Next record** button ▶ to display record 2 of 22—Lana Shane.

3. Press Enter to select the value in the **First Name** text box. Replace *Lana* with your own first name.

4. Press Enter, and then compare your screen with **Figure 1**. ——————

> Recall that you can move to the next text box in a form by pressing Enter or Tab. In this way, you can continue typing values without having to use the mouse. Keeping your hands over the keyboard speeds data entry and increases accuracy.

5. In the **Last Name** text box, replace *Shane* with your own last name.

6. Press Enter, to accept the change, and then click in the **Last Name** text box to select it. On the **Home** tab, in the **Find group**, click the **Find** button.

7. In the **Find and Replace** dialog box **Find What** box, type Moyerman and then press Enter. With the record for Celia Moyerman displayed, **Close** [×] the **Find and Replace** dialog box.

8. With the **Last Name** *Moyerman* selected, type Stock Compare your screen with **Figure 2**. ——————

■ **Continue to the next page to complete the skill**

Value in next field selected

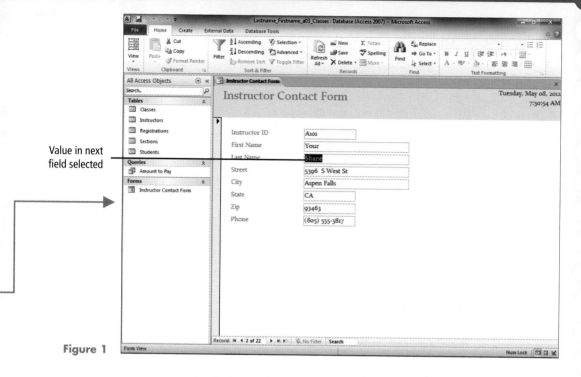

Figure 1

Last Name value changed

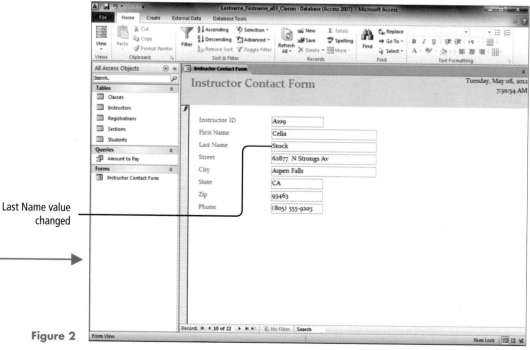

Figure 2

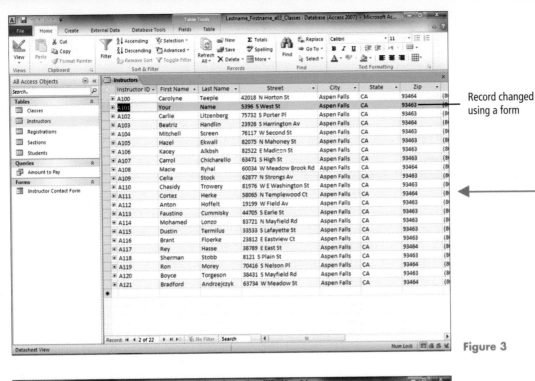

Record changed using a form

Figure 3

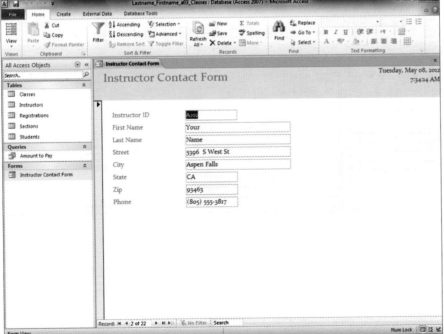

Figure 4

9. Close ☒ the form. In the **Navigation Pane**, double-click **Instructors** to open the table. In the Navigation bar, click the **Next record** button ▸ to select the second row, and then compare your screen with **Figure 3**.

As you enter data in a form, it is stored automatically in the table that the form is based on. Here, records 2 and 10 reflect the changes you made using the form.

10. Close ☒ the table. In the **Navigation Pane**, double-click **Instructor Contact Form** to open the form. Navigate to the second record—the record with your name. Compare your screen with **Figure 4**.

11. Start ◉ the **Snipping Tool**. In the **Snipping Tool** dialog box, click the **New button arrow**, and then click **Full-screen Snip**.

12. Click the **Save Snip** button 🖫. In the **Save As** dialog box, navigate to your **Access Chapter 3** folder, **Save** the file as Lastname_Firstname_a03_Classes_Snip1 and then **Close** ☒ the **Snipping Tool** window.

13. Close ☒ the form.

- **You have completed Skill 3 of 10**

▶ The Blank Form tool is used when you want to build a form by adding fields one at a time or arrange them in a different layout.

1. On the **Create tab**, in the **Forms group**, click the **Blank Form** button.

2. In the **Field List**, click **Show all tables**. In the **Field List**, to the left of **Students**, click the **Expand** button ⊞. Compare your screen with **Figure 1**.

3. In the **Field List**, double-click **Student ID** to add the field to the form. Double-click **First Name** to add the field to the form.

4. Continue to double-click to add the nine remaining fields starting with **Last Name** and ending with **Discount**. Compare your screen with **Figure 2**.

   When you add a field to the form, the other tables move to the lower sections of the Field List pane. Here, Registrations is a related table, and the other three tables are available, but they are not related to the Students table.

■ **Continue to the next page to complete the skill**

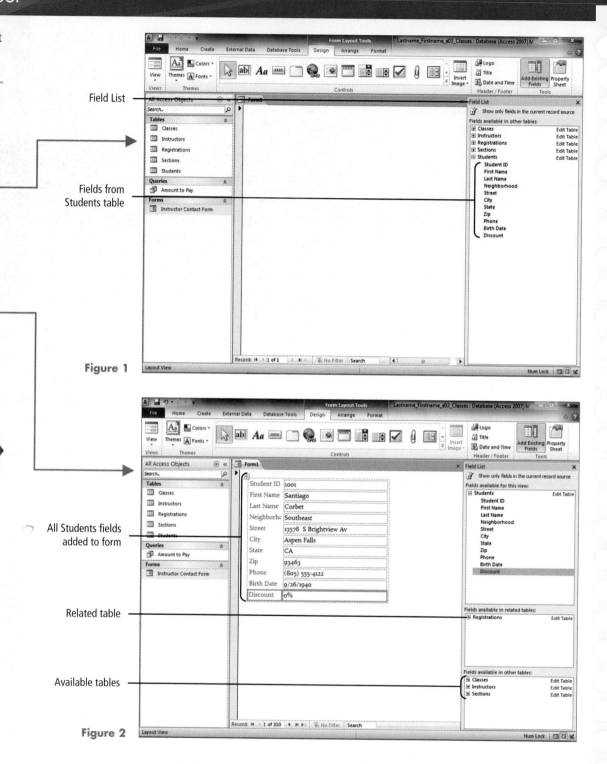

Field List

Fields from Students table

Figure 1

All Students fields added to form

Related table

Available tables

Figure 2

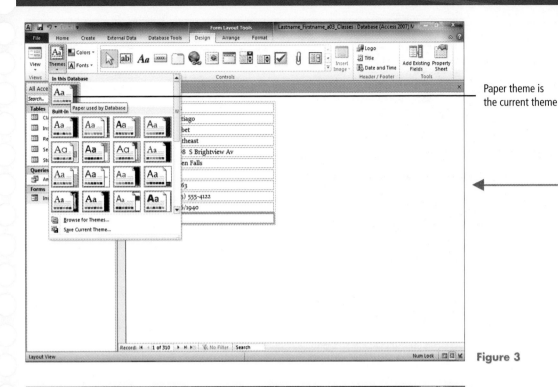

Paper theme is the current theme

Figure 3

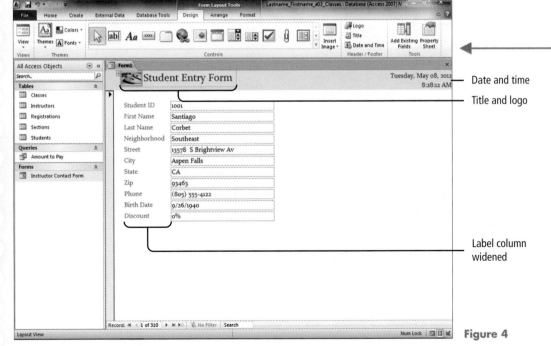

Date and time

Title and logo

Label column widened

Figure 4

5. **Close** ☒ the **Field List**. In the **Themes group**, click the **Themes** button. In the **Themes** gallery, under **In this Database**, point to the thumbnail, and then compare your screen with **Figure 3**.

> The ScreenTip should display *Paper used by Database*—the theme applied to the previous form.

6. Press [Esc] to close the gallery.

7. Click the **Neighborhood** label, and then with the ↔ pointer, drag to increase the column's width so that the entire label text displays.

8. On the **Design tab**, in the **Header/Footer group**, click the **Title** button, and then type Student Entry Form

9. In the **Header/Footer group**, click the **Logo** button. In the **Insert Picture** dialog box, navigate to the student files, select **a03_Classes_Logo**, and then click **OK**.

10. In the **Header/Footer group**, click the **Date and Time** button. In the **Date and Time** dialog box, click **OK**. Compare your screen with **Figure 4**.

11. Click **Save** 🖫. In the **Save As** dialog box, type Student Entry Form and then press [Enter]. Leave the form open for the next skill.

■ **You have completed Skill 4 of 10**

▶ Form and report layouts use *control grids*—cells arranged in rows and columns into which controls are placed.

▶ Control grids work much like tables. You can arrange several fields in a single row and merge multiple cells across rows and columns.

1. **Close** 〈〈 the **Navigation Pane**. With the **Student Entry Form** open, click the **State** text box to select the control.

2. Point to the **State** text box, and then with the 🖑 pointer, drag the control up and to the right. When the orange line displays to the right of the **City** text box, as shown in **Figure 1**, release the mouse button. ────

3. Point to the **Zip** text box, and then with the 🖑 pointer, drag the control to the right of the **State** text box, and then release the mouse button to move the text box and create a new column.

4. Select the **State** text box, point to the right border, and then with the ↔ pointer, drag to resize the column approximately as shown in **Figure 2**. Repeat to resize the **Zip** text box as shown in the figure.

5. Double-click in the **City** label, select the text *City*, and then type City/State/Zip

6. In the **First Name** row, click the **First Name** text box, press and hold [Shift] while clicking the last empty cell in the row. With the three cells selected, on the **Arrange tab**, in the **Merge/Split group**, click the **Merge** button.

▪ **Continue to the next page to complete the skill**

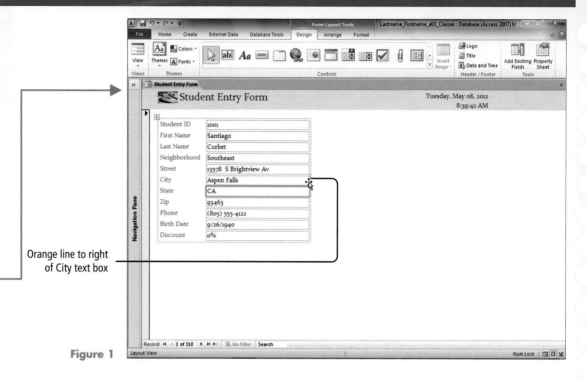

Orange line to right of City text box

Figure 1

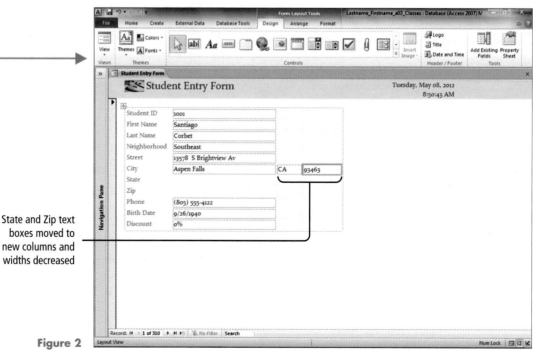

State and Zip text boxes moved to new columns and widths decreased

Figure 2

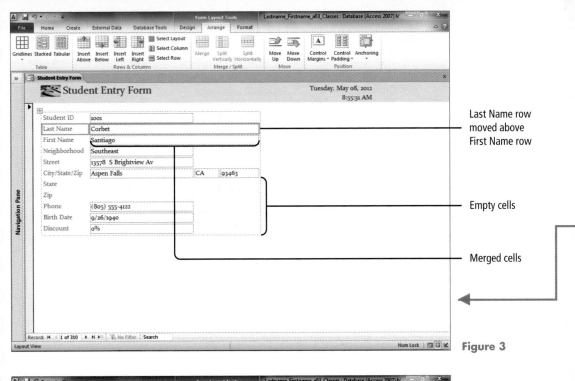

Last Name row
moved above
First Name row

Empty cells

Merged cells

Figure 3

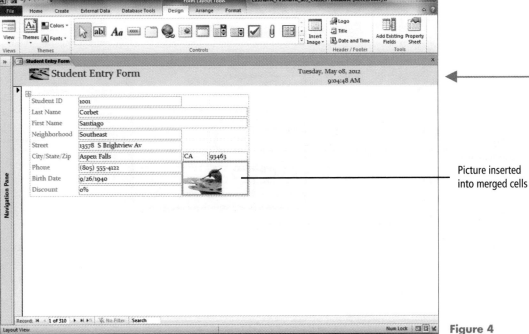

Picture inserted
into merged cells

Figure 4

7. In the **Last Name** row, repeat the technique just practiced to merge the last three cells in the row, and then merge the last three cells in the **Neighborhood** and **Street** rows.

8. Click the **Last Name** label to select it. Press and hold (Shift) while clicking the **Last Name** text box.

9. On the **Arrange tab**, in the **Move group**, click the **Move Up** button one time to move the **Last Name** row above the **First Name** row. Compare your screen with **Figure 3**.

10. Click the **State** label. Press and hold (Shift), while clicking the last empty cell in the **Zip** row. With the eight cells selected, press (Delete) to remove the two empty rows from the layout.

11. In the **Phone** row, click the first empty cell. Press and hold (Shift), and then click the last cell in the **Discount** row. With the six cells selected, in the **Merge/Split group**, click the **Merge** button.

12. On the **Design tab**, in the **Controls group**, click the **Insert Image** button, and then click **Browse**. In the **Insert Picture** dialog box, navigate to your student files. Click **a03_Classes_Picture**, and then click **OK**. Point �\ to the cell in the lower-right corner of the layout, and then click to insert the picture. Compare your screen with **Figure 4**.

13. Save 🖫 the form. Leave the form open for the next skill.

■ **You have completed Skill 5 of 10**

▶ An **Input mask** is a set of special characters that control what can and cannot be entered in a field.

1. With **Student Entry Form** open in Layout view, click the **Phone** text box. On the **Design tab**, in the **Tools group**, click **Property Sheet** button.

2. In the **Property Sheet**, click the **Data tab**. On the **Property Sheet Data tab**, click the **Input Mask** box, and then click the displayed **Build** button [⋯] to start the **Input Mask Wizard**. Compare your screen with **Figure 1**.

3. With **Phone Number** selected in the **Input Mask Wizard**, click **Next**. Click the **Placeholder character arrow**, and then click the number sign (#). Click in the **Try It** box, and then compare your screen with **Figure 2**.

   The Try It box displays a sample of the input mask in which you can try entering sample data. **Placeholder characters** are the symbols in an input mask that are replaced as you type data into the field. Here, the parentheses, space, and hyphen are in place, and number signs display where each number can be typed.

4. In the **Try It** box, click the first number sign, and then watch the box as you type 10 digits.

■ **Continue to the next page to complete the skill**

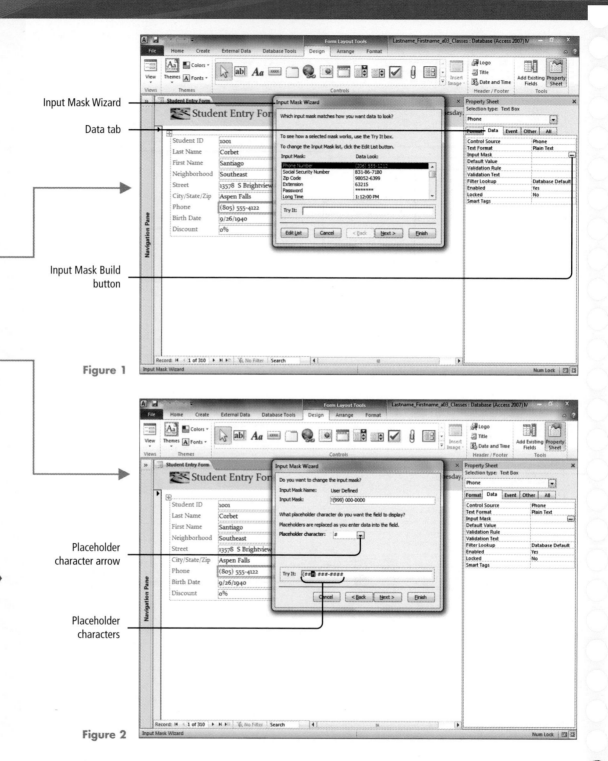

Input Mask Wizard

Data tab

Input Mask Build button

Figure 1

Placeholder character arrow

Placeholder characters

Figure 2

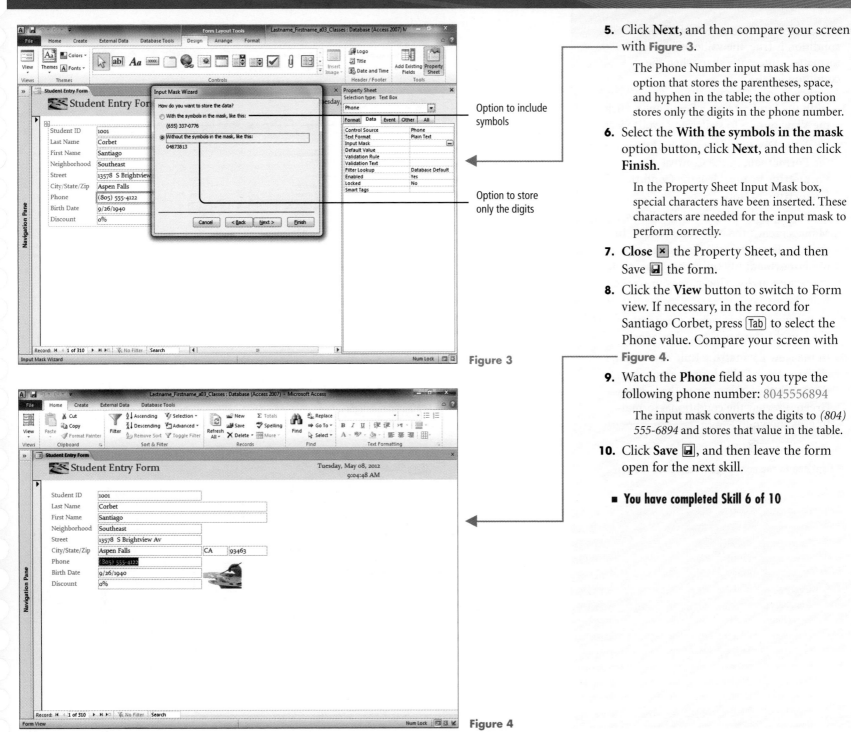

5. Click **Next**, and then compare your screen with **Figure 3**.

The Phone Number input mask has one option that stores the parentheses, space, and hyphen in the table; the other option stores only the digits in the phone number.

6. Select the **With the symbols in the mask** option button, click **Next**, and then click **Finish**.

In the Property Sheet Input Mask box, special characters have been inserted. These characters are needed for the input mask to perform correctly.

7. Close ✕ the Property Sheet, and then Save 🖫 the form.

8. Click the **View** button to switch to Form view. If necessary, in the record for Santiago Corbet, press Tab to select the Phone value. Compare your screen with **Figure 4**.

9. Watch the **Phone** field as you type the following phone number: 8045556894

The input mask converts the digits to *(804) 555-6894* and stores that value in the table.

10. Click **Save** 🖫, and then leave the form open for the next skill.

■ **You have completed Skill 6 of 10**

Figure 3

Figure 4

► You can format values so that when a condition is true, the value will be formatted differently than when the condition is false.

1. With the **Student Entry Form** open, click the **View** button to switch to Layout view.

2. Click the **Discount** text box, and then, on the **Format tab**, in the **Control Formatting group**, click the **Conditional Formatting** button.

3. In the **Conditional Formatting Rules Manager**, click the **New Rule** button. In the **New Formatting Rule** dialog box, under **Format only cells where the**, click the second **arrow**. Compare your screen with **Figure 1**.

4. In the conditions list, click **greater than**. Click in the third box, and then type 0

5. In the **New Formatting Rule** dialog box, click the **Font Color button arrow**, and then click the sixth color in the last row— **Green**. Preview the conditional formatting, as shown in **Figure 2**.

■ **Continue to the next page to complete the skill**

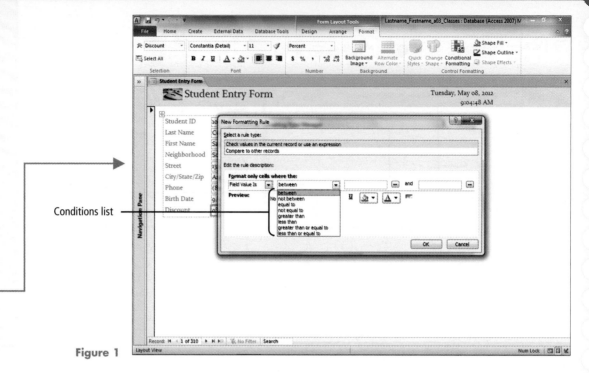

Conditions list

Figure 1

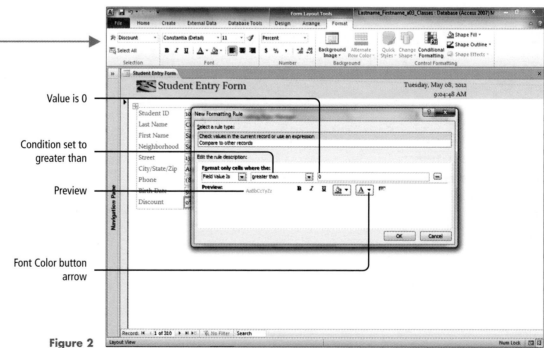

Value is 0

Condition set to greater than

Preview

Font Color button arrow

Figure 2

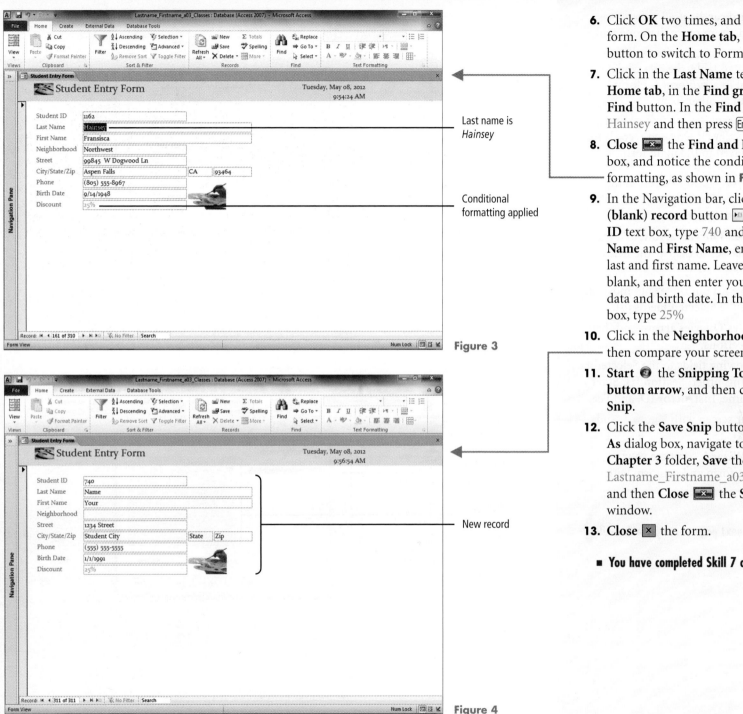

Last name is
Hainsey

Conditional
formatting applied

Figure 3

New record

Figure 4

6. Click **OK** two times, and then **Save** 🖫 the form. On the **Home tab**, click the **View** button to switch to Form view.

7. Click in the **Last Name** text box. On the **Home tab**, in the **Find group**, click the **Find** button. In the **Find What** box, type Hainsey and then press Enter.

8. **Close** the **Find and Replace** dialog box, and notice the conditional formatting, as shown in **Figure 3**.

9. In the Navigation bar, click the **New (blank) record** button. In the **Student ID** text box, type 740 and then, in **Last Name** and **First Name**, enter your own last and first name. Leave **Neighborhood** blank, and then enter your own contact data and birth date. In the **Discount** text box, type 25%

10. Click in the **Neighborhood** text box, and then compare your screen with **Figure 4**.

11. **Start** ⊕ the **Snipping Tool**, click the **New button arrow**, and then click **Full-screen Snip**.

12. Click the **Save Snip** button 🖫. In the **Save As** dialog box, navigate to your **Access Chapter 3** folder, **Save** the snip as Lastname_Firstname_a03_Classes_Snip2 and then **Close** the **Snipping Tool** window.

13. **Close** ✕ the form.

■ **You have completed Skill 7 of 10**

- ► The Form Wizard can be used to create forms with fields from more than one table.
- ► When the data in a form has records that are also in a related table, the related data can be displayed in a *subform*—a form contained within another form.
- ► A *one-to-many form* is a main form and a subform that displays the related records for the record displayed in the main form.

1. **Open** ⟫ the **Navigation Pane**. On the **Create tab**, in the **Forms group**, click the **Form Wizard** button.
2. Click the **Tables/Queries arrow**, and then click **Table: Classes** to display the fields from that table.
3. Click the **Move All** button ⟩⟩ to move all the fields into the **Selected Fields** list.
4. Click the **Tables/Queries arrow**, and then click **Table: Sections**.
5. Move the following fields to the **Selected Fields** list in this order: **Section ID**, **Start Date**, **Start Time**, **Instructor ID**, and **Fee**.
6. Compare your screen with **Figure 1**, and then click **Next**.
7. In the **Form Wizard**, compare your preview of the form and subform with **Figure 2**.

■ **Continue to the next page to complete the skill** ►

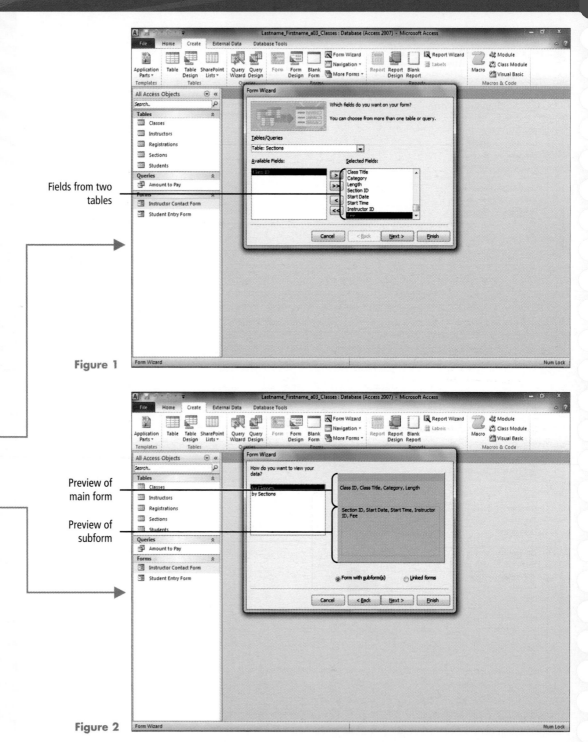

Fields from two tables

Figure 1

Preview of main form

Preview of subform

Figure 2

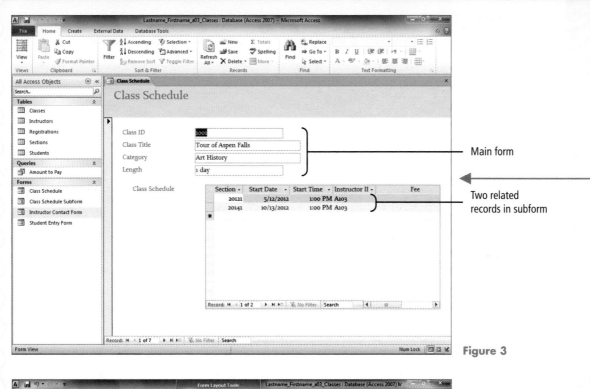

Main form

Two related
records in subform

Figure 3

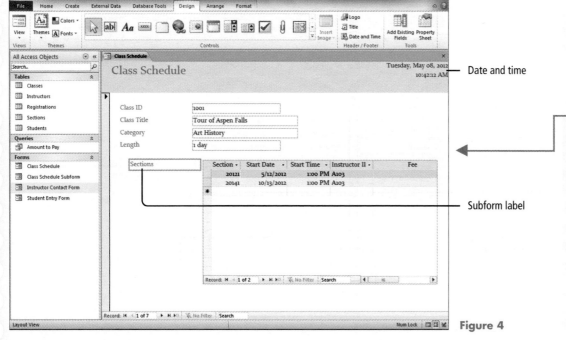

Date and time

Subform label

Figure 4

8. Click **Next**. Under **What layout would you like for your subform**, be sure that **Datasheet** is selected, and then click **Next**.

9. Under **What titles do you want for your forms**, replace the value in the **Form** box with Class Schedule Press Tab, and then replace the value in the **Subform** box, with Class Schedule Subform

10. Click **Finish**, and then compare your screen with **Figure 3**.

> The main form displays the data for one record at a time, and all the related records display in the subform datasheet. Here, the Tour of Aspen Falls record has two sections scheduled.
>
> A form and subform are saved as two separate forms. Here, both the main form—Class Schedule—and the subform—Class Schedule Subform—are listed in the Navigation Pane.

11. In the **Views group**, click the **View** button to switch to Layout view.

12. On the **Design tab**, in the **Header/Footer group**, click the **Date and Time** button, and click **OK**.

13. Click the subform label, and then replace the label text *Class Schedule* with Sections

14. **Save** 🖫 the design changes, and then compare your screen with **Figure 4**.

■ **You have completed Skill 8 of 10**

► In a one-to-many form, you can work with the data from two tables on a single screen.

1. With the **Class Schedule** form open, click the **View** button to switch to Form view.

2. In the **Sections** subform datasheet, click the **Select All** button ▭. In the datasheet header row, point to a line between two columns, and then with the ⊞ pointer, double-click to resize the column widths automatically.

3. Click in the **Start Date** column, and then, on the **Home tab**, in the **Sort & Filter group**, click the **Ascending** button. **Save** 🖫 the changes to the datasheet, and then compare your screen with **Figure 1**.

4. With the Tour of Aspen Falls class displayed in the main form, click the subform's **New (blank) record** button ▸⊛ to move to the subform's append row.

5. Type 20147 Press [Enter], and then type 12/4/2012 Assign a **Time** of 1:00 PM an **Instructor ID** of A101 and a **Fee** of $5.00 Press [Enter], and then compare your screen with **Figure 2**.

■ **Continue to the next page to complete the skill** ➤

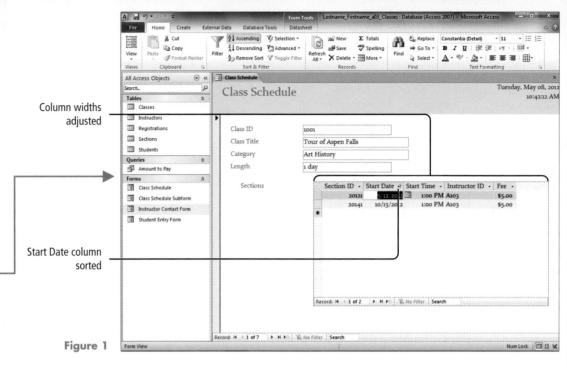

Column widths adjusted

Start Date column sorted

Figure 1

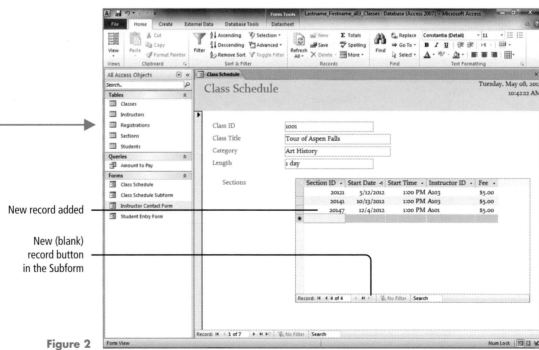

New record added

New (blank) record button in the Subform

Figure 2

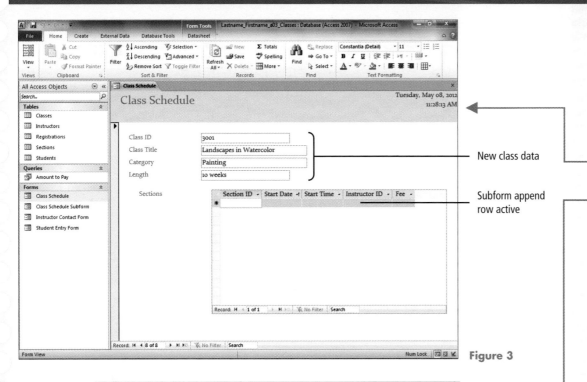

New class data

Subform append
row active

Figure 3

Section ID	Start Date	Start Time	Instructor ID	Fee
20148	2/1/2012	1:00 PM	A101	25
20149	3/7/2012	7:00 PM	A114	25
20150	4/4/2012	1:00 PM	A120	25

Figure 4

6. In the main form's Navigation bar, click the **New (blank) record** button ▸ to create a new class.

7. Use the form to add the following class data: **Class ID** is 3001 **Class Title** is Landscapes in Watercolor **Category** is Painting and **Length** is 10 weeks Press Enter to move to the subform append row. Compare your screen with **Figure 3**.

8. In the subform, enter the sections shown in **Figure 4**.

9. **Start** ◉ the **Snipping Tool**, click the **New button arrow**, and then click **Full-screen Snip**.

10. Click the **Save Snip** button 🖫. In the **Save As** dialog box, navigate to your **Access Chapter 3** folder, **Save** the snip as Lastname_Firstname_a03_Classes_Snip3 and then **Close** ✕ the **Snipping Tool** window.

11. **Close** ✕ the form.

■ **You have completed Skill 9 of 10**

▶ When you need to edit data for a specific subset of data, you can base the form on a query.

▶ A form based on a query displays only the records returned by the query's criteria.

1. In the **Navigation Pane**, under **Queries**, right-click **Amount to Pay**, and then, from the shortcut menu, click **Design View**.

2. In the **Discount** column **Criteria** box, type >0 **Close** ⎸«⎸ the **Navigation Pane**, and then compare your screen with **Figure 1**.

   The query displays records from four related tables and calculates the fee charged to students who have a discount.

3. Click **Save** ⎕. **Run** the query to display 18 records, and then **Close** ⎸×⎸ the query.

4. **Open** ⎸»⎸ the **Navigation Pane**. If necessary, under **Queries**, click one time to select **Amount to Pay**.

5. On the **Create tab**, in the **Forms group**, click the **Form** button. **Close** ⎸«⎸ the **Navigation Pane**, and then decrease the width of the text box columns approximately, as shown in **Figure 2**.

■ **Continue to the next page to complete the skill**

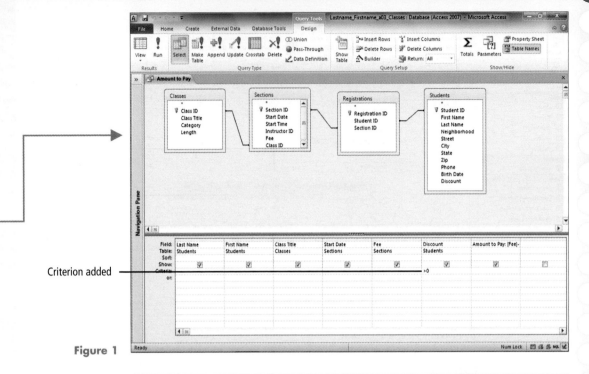

Criterion added

Figure 1

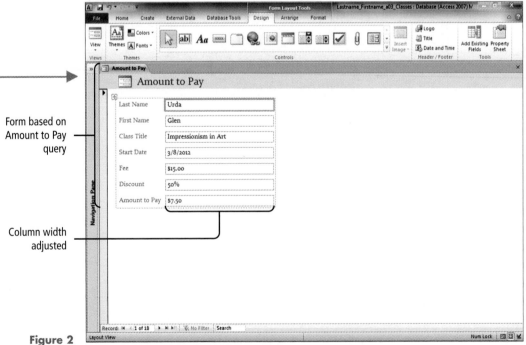

Form based on Amount to Pay query

Column width adjusted

Figure 2

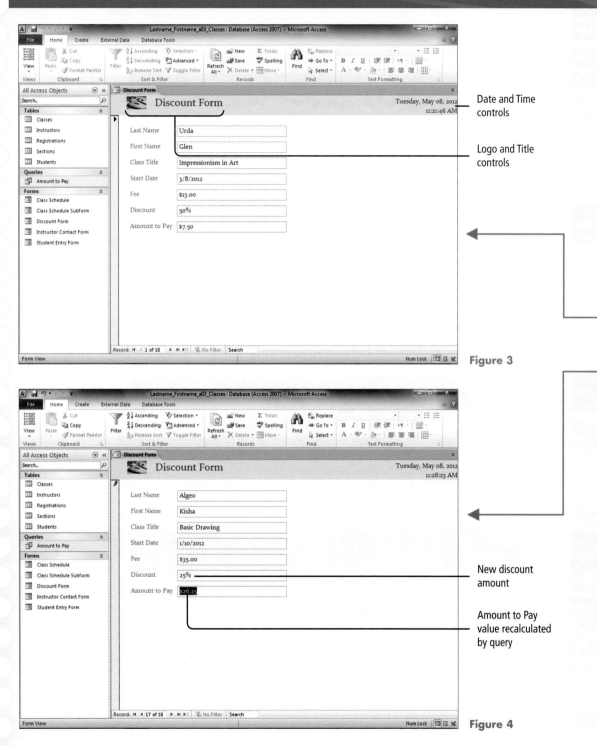

Date and Time controls

Logo and Title controls

Figure 3

New discount amount

Amount to Pay value recalculated by query

Figure 4

6. **Open** ≫ the **Navigation Pane**. On the **Design tab**, in the **Header/Footer group**, click the **Date and Time** button, and then click **OK**.

7. Double-click the form's **Title** control, select the text *Amount to Pay*, and then type Discount Form

8. In the **Header/Footer group**, click the **Logo** button. In the **Insert Picture** dialog box, navigate to the student files for this chapter, click **a03_Classes_Logo**, and then click **OK**.

9. Click **Save** 🖫. In the **Save As** box, type Discount Form and then press Enter.

10. Click the **View** button to switch to Form view, and then compare your screen with **Figure 3**.

11. **Find** the record for Kisha Algeo, select the **Discount** 75%, type 25 and then press Enter. Compare your screen with **Figure 4**.

12. **Start** ⊙ the **Snipping Tool**, click the **New button arrow**, and then click **Full-screen Snip**.

13. Click the **Save Snip** button 🖫. In the **Save As** dialog box, navigate to your **Access Chapter 3** folder, **Save** the snip as Lastname_Firstname_a03_Classes_Snip4 and then **Close** ✕ the **Snipping Tool** window.

14. **Close** ✕ the form, and then **Exit** Access. Print the snips or submit the database and snip files as directed by your instructor.

Done! You have completed Skill 10 of 10 and your database is complete!

More Skills

The following More Skills are located at **www.pearsonhighered.com/skills**

More Skills ⑪ Validate Fields

Designing databases involves setting field properties so that those who use the database enter data correctly. For example, the data type, field size, and input mask properties all limit the types of data that can be entered into a field. Validation rules are also written so that the desired values are entered into fields.

In More Skills 11, you will set the Field Size and Format field properties to validate data. You will then add a validation rule that limits what can be typed into the field.

To begin, open your web browser, navigate to www.pearsonhighered.com/skills, locate the name of your textbook, and then follow the instructions on the website.

More Skills ⑫ Add Combo Boxes to Forms

When you need to enter ID fields in forms, you can change the ID text box to a combo box that displays more information than just an ID number. For example, when you need to enter a Student ID, you can use a combo box to show the numbers and the student names.

In More Skills 12, you will view a form with a Student ID text box, and then replace that text box with a combo box that displays the student's name. You will then use the combo box to add a student to a class.

To begin, open your web browser, navigate to www.pearsonhighered.com/skills, locate the name of your textbook, and then follow the instructions on the website.

More Skills ⑬ Create Multiple Item Forms

A multiple items form displays records in rows so that several records may be viewed on a single screen. Multiple item forms appear similar to a datasheet, but offer the formatting and layout options of forms.

In More Skills 13, you will create a multiple item form and then format the form in Layout view. You will use the property sheet to change control width and height of the controls.

To begin, open your web browser, navigate to www.pearsonhighered.com/skills, locate the name of your textbook, and then follow the instructions on the website.

More Skills ⑭ Create Macros

Macros are used to perform a sequence of steps with a single click of the mouse. Using macros in forms and reports saves time and automates common tasks.

In More Skills 14, you will create two macros using two different methods, and then use the macros to update a report that is based on a query.

To begin, open your web browser, navigate to www.pearsonhighered.com/skills, locate the name of your textbook, and then follow the instructions on the website.

Key Terms

Online Help Skills

1. **Start** 🌐 Access. In the upper-right corner of the Access window, click the **Help** button 🔵. In the **Help** window, click the **Maximize** button 🔲.

2. Click in the search box, type Introduction to Forms and then click the **Search** button. In the search results, click **Introduction to Forms**.

3. Read the article's introduction, and then below **In this article**, click **Understand Layout view and Design view**. Compare your screen with **Figure 1**.

Figure 1

4. Read the Understand Layout view and Design view section to see if you can answer the following: What is the main advantage of using Layout view? What are the reasons for using Design view instead of Layout view?

Matching

Match each term in the second column with its correct definition in the first column by writing the letter of the term on the blank line in front of the correct definition.

____ **1.** The arrangement of data and labels in a form or report.

____ **2.** A tool used to create a form where the desired fields are selected before they are added to the form.

____ **3.** An Access feature that adds fields to the form when you double-click them in the Field List.

____ **4.** A small picture that can be added to a form header, typically to the left of the title.

____ **5.** A form control that displays the name of a form by default; the actual text can be edited later.

____ **6.** Cells arranged in rows and columns into which controls are placed.

____ **7.** A set of special characters that control what can and cannot be entered in a field.

____ **8.** A type of form that has a subform that displays related records from another table.

____ **9.** This name is often applied to the form that has a subform.

____ **10.** By default, subforms display in this view.

A Blank Form tool

B Control grid

C Datasheet

D Form Wizard

E Input mask

F Layout

G Logo

H Main form

I One-to-many form

J Title

Multiple Choice

Choose the correct answer.

1. An Access view used to format a form or report while viewing a sample of the data.
   - A. Design view
   - B. Form view
   - C. Layout view

2. A layout that places labels in the first column and data in the second column.
   - A. Columnar
   - B. Datasheet
   - C. Tabular

3. An Access view used to enter data in a form.
   - A. Data view
   - B. Form view
   - C. Layout view

4. Objects on a form or report that describe each field.
   - A. IntelliSense Quick Info boxes
   - B. Labels
   - C. Text boxes

5. Objects on a form or report that display the data from fields.
   - A. Labels
   - B. Text boxes
   - C. Titles

6. This property sheet tab contains the Input Mask property.
   - A. Data
   - B. Format
   - C. Other

7. The symbol in an input mask that is replaced as you type data into the field.
   - A. Data character
   - B. Input character
   - C. Placeholder character

8. Formatting that evaluates the values in a field and formats that data according to the rules you specify; for example, only values over 1000 will have bold applied.
   - A. Conditional formatting
   - B. Logical formatting
   - C. Rules-based formatting

9. A form contained within another form that displays records related to the other form.
   - A. Parent form
   - B. Relationship form
   - C. Subform

10. When you want to build a form for a subset of data, you can base the form on this.
    - A. Blank Form tool
    - B. Filtered table Query
    - C. Query

Topics for Discussion

1. You have created forms using three different methods: the Form tool, the Form Wizard, and the Blank Form tool. Which method do you prefer and why? What are the primary advantages of each method?

2. Recall that forms are used to enter data into a database. Consider the types of data businesses might store in a database. For example, a school needs a class registration form to enter students into classes. What type of forms might other businesses need to enter data?

Skill Check

To complete this database, you will need the following files:

- a03_Outings
- a03_Outings_Logo

You will save your files as:

- Lastname_Firstname_a03_Outings
- Lastname_Firstname_a03_Outings_Snip1
- Lastname_Firstname_a03_Outings_Snip2
- Lastname_Firstname_a03_Outings_Snip3

1. **Start** Access, and then open the student data file **a03_Outings**. Save the database in your **Access Chapter 3** folder with the name Lastname_Firstname_a03_Outings If necessary, enable the content.

2. On the **Create tab**, in the **Forms group**, click the **Form Wizard** button. In the **Form Wizard**, select the **Participants** table, and then move **Participant ID**, **First Name**, and **Last Name** into **Selected Fields**.

3. In the **Form Wizard**, select the **Registrations** table, and then move the **Registration ID** and **Outing ID** fields into **Selected Fields**. Click **Next** three times. Name the **Form** Registrants Accept the **Subform** name by clicking **Finish**.

4. In the subform, double-click to adjust the width of both columns automatically, and then click **Save**.

5. In the main form Navigation bar, click the **Last record** button. In the subform for Julia Saxton, enter a **Registration ID** of 1501 and an **Outing ID** of 100 Enter another record with a **Registration ID** of 1502 and an **Outing ID** of 101 Compare your screen with **Figure 1**. ⎯⎯⎯⎯

6. Create a **Full-screen Snip**, and then save it in your **Access Chapter 3** folder as Lastname_Firstname_a03_Outings_Snip1 **Close** the **Snipping Tool** window.

7. **Close** the form. In the **Navigation Pane**, right-click **Outings Query**, and then click **Design View**. In the **Outing Date** column **Criteria** box, type >9/1/2012 **Save**, **Run**, and then **Close** the query.

8. With the query selected in the **Navigation Pane**, on the **Create tab**, in the **Forms group**, click the **Form** button.

9. **Close** the **Navigation Pane**, and then decrease the width of the right column approximately, as shown in **Figure 2**. ⎯⎯⎯⎯

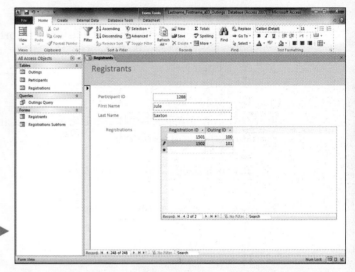

Figure 1

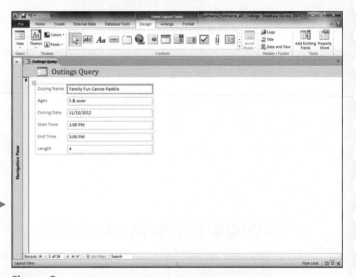

Figure 2

■ **Continue to the next page to complete this Skill Check** ▶

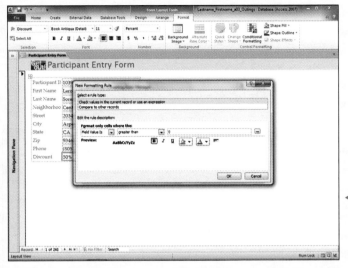

Figure 3

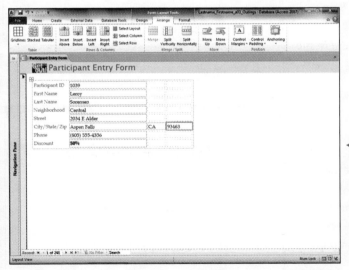

Figure 4

10. Create a **Full-screen Snip**, and then save it in your **Access Chapter 3** folder as Lastname_Firstname_a03_Outings_Snip2 **Close** the **Snipping Tool** window.

11. Click **Save**, type Fall Outings and then click **OK**. **Close** the form.

12. On the **Create tab**, in the **Forms group**, click the **Blank Form** button. In the **Field List**, show all tables, and then expand the **Participants** table.

13. In the **Field List**, double-click to add the 10 fields from the **Participants** table, starting with **Participant ID** and ending with **Discount**. Close the **Field List** pane.

14. Click **Save**, type Participant Entry Form and then click **OK**.

15. On the **Design tab**, click the **Themes** button, and then click the fourth thumbnail—**Apex**.

16. In the **Header/Footer group**, click the **Logo** button. In the **Insert Picture** dialog box, navigate to the student files for this chapter and then double-click **a03_Outings_Logo**. In the **Header/Footer group**, click the **Title** button.

17. Click the **Phone** text box, and then, in the **Tools group**, click the **Property Sheet** button. On the Property Sheet **Data tab**, click the **Input Mask** box, and click the displayed **Build** button. In the **Input Mask Wizard**, be sure that **Phone Number** is selected, and then click **Finish**. **Close** the **Property Sheet**.

18. Click the **Discount** text box, and then, on the **Format tab**, in the **Control Formatting group**, click **Conditional Formatting**. In the dialog box, click the **New Rule** button. Change the condition to **greater than** and then type 0 Click the **Bold** button and then compare your screen with **Figure 3**.

19. Click **OK** two times. Click the **State** text box, and then drag it to the right of the **City** text box to create a new column. Drag the **Zip** text box to the right of the **State** text box to create a new column.

20. Click the **State** label. Press and hold Shift, and then click the last empty cell in the **Zip** row. Press Delete to delete the two empty rows.

21. Double-click the **City** label, and then change the text to City/State/Zip

22. Drag to decrease the width of the **State** text box, and then decrease the width of the **Zip** text box approximately, as shown in **Figure 4**.

23. Switch to Form view. Create a **Full-screen Snip**, and then save it in your **Access Chapter 3** folder as Lastname_Firstname_a03_Outings_Snip3 **Close** the **Snipping Tool** window.

24. Click **Save**, and then **Exit** Access. Print the snips or submit the files as directed by your instructor.

Done! You have completed the Skill Check

Assess Your Skills 1

To complete this database, you will need the following files:

- a03_Camps
- a03_Camps_Logo

You will save your files as:

- Lastname_Firstname_a03_Camps
- Lastname_Firstname_a03_Camps_Snip1
- Lastname_Firstname_a03_Camps_Snip2
- Lastname_Firstname_a03_Camps_Snip3

1. **Start** Access, and then open **a03_Camps**. **Save** the database in your **Access Chapter 3** folder as Lastname_Firstname_a03_Camps If necessary, enable the content.

2. Start the **Blank Form** tool, and then add the eight fields from the **Directors** table in the order that they are listed in the **Field List** pane. **Save** the form as Director Entry Form

3. Apply the **Aspect** theme, add a logo using **a03_Camps_Logo**, and then add a **Title** with the name of the form.

4. Add a **Phone Number** input mask to the **Phone** text box using the default wizard settings.

5. Move the **State** text box in a new column to the right of the **City** text box, and then move the **Zip** text box into a new column to the right of the **State** text box. Delete the two empty rows, and then change the **City** label to City/State/Zip

6. Decrease the width of the **State** and **Zip** text boxes approximately, as shown in **Figure 1**.

7. Switch to Form view, and then add yourself as a new camp director.

8. Create a **Full-screen snip**, and then save it in your **Access Chapter 3** folder as Lastname_Firstname_a03_Camps_Snip1

9. **Save**, and then **Close** the form. Start the **Form Wizard**. From the **Directors** table, add the **First Name** and **Last Name** fields, and then,

from the **Camps** table, add all but the **Director ID** field. Accept all other **Form Wizard** defaults.

10. In Form view, navigate to the last record. Use the subform to add the following camps:

Camp ID	Camp Name	Start Date
8	Hoopa	8/13/2012
9	Paiute	8/20/2012

11. Create a **Full-screen snip**, and then save it in your **Access Chapter 3** folder as Lastname_Firstname_a03_Outings_Snip2

12. **Close** the form, and then open the **Discounted Fees** query in Design view. In the **Discount** column **Criteria** box, type >0 **Save**, **Run**, and then **Close** the query.

13. Use the **Form** tool to create a form based on the **Discounted Fees** query.

14. Apply conditional formatting to the **Discounted Fee** text box so that the text will be **Red** when the field value is **greater than** 100

15. Decrease the width of the text box column to approximately 3 inches. Switch to Form view, and then compare your screen with **Figure 2**.

16. Create a **Full-screen snip**. **Save** the snip in your **Access Chapter 3** folder as Lastname_Firstname_a03_Camps_Snip3

17. **Save** the form as Discounted Fees **Close** the form, and then **Exit** Access. Print the snips or submit the files as directed by your instructor.

Done! You have completed Assess Your Skills 1

Figure 1

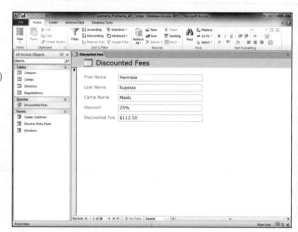

Figure 2

Assessment

Assess Your Skills 3 and 4 can be found at
www.pearsonhighered.com/skills.

Assess Your Skills 2

To complete this database, you will need the following file:

- a03_Reviews

You will save your files as:

- Lastname_Firstname_a03_Reviews
- Lastname_Firstname_a03_Reviews_Snip1
- Lastname_Firstname_a03_Reviews_Snip2
- Lastname_Firstname_a03_Reviews_Snip3

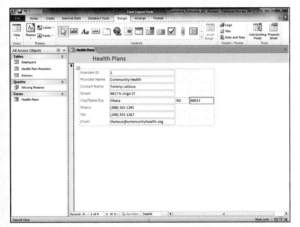

Figure 1

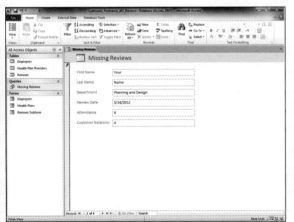

Figure 2

1. **Start** Access, and then open **a03_Reviews**. Save the database in your **Access Chapter 3** folder as Lastname_Firstname_a03_Reviews If necessary, enable the content.

2. Start the **Blank Form** tool, and then add the 10 fields from the **Health Plan Providers** table in the order that they are listed in the **Field List** pane. **Save** the form as Health Plans

3. Apply the **Composite** theme, and then add a **Title** with the name of the form. Increase the width of the label column so **Provider Name** displays in its label control.

4. Add **Phone Number** input masks to the **Phone** and **Fax** text boxes using the default wizard settings.

5. Move the **State** text box in a new column to the right of the **City** text box, and then move the **Zip** text box into a new column to the right of the **State** text box. Delete the two empty rows, and then change the **City** label to City/State/Zip

6. Decrease the width of the **State** and **Zip** text boxes approximately, as shown in **Figure 1**.

7. Switch to Form view, and then change the Community Health **Contact Name** to your name.

8. Create a **Full-screen snip**, and then save it in your **Access Chapter 3** folder as Lastname_Firstname_a03_Reviews_Snip1

9. **Save**, and then **Close** the form. Start the **Form Wizard**. From the **Employees** table, add the **First Name**, **Last Name**, and **Department** fields. From the **Reviews** table, add all but the **Employee ID** field. Accept all other Form Wizard defaults.

10. In the first record, change the name fields to your own first and last name. In the subform, automatically resize the column widths.

11. Create a **Full-screen Snip**, and then save it in your **Access Chapter 3** folder as Lastname_Firstname_a03_Reviews_Snip2

12. **Save**, and then **Close** the form. Open the **Missing Reviews** query in Design view. In the **Attendance** column **Or** box, below the existing Is Null criterion, type Is Null **Save**, **Run**, and then **Close** the query.

13. Use the **Form** tool to create a form based on the **Missing Reviews** query.

14. Decrease the width of the text box column to approximately 3 inches. In Form view, change the first record's **Attendance** value to 4 and the **Customer Relations** value to 4 Compare your screen with **Figure 2**.

15. Create a **Full-screen Snip**. **Save** the snip in your **Access Chapter 3** folder as Lastname_Firstname_a03_Reviews_Snip3

16. **Save** the form as Missing Reviews **Close** the form, and then **Exit** Access. Print the snips or submit the files as directed by your instructor.

Done! You have completed Assess Your Skills 2

Assess Your Skills Visually

To complete this database, you will need the following files:

- a03_Councils
- a03_Councils_Logo

You will save your database as:

- Lastname_Firstname_a03_Councils
- Lastname_Firstname_a03_Councils_Snip

Open the database **a03_Councils**, and then using your own name, save the database in your **Access Chapter 3** folder as Lastname_Firstname_a03_Councils

Use the Form Wizard to create the form shown in **Figure 1**. Include the **Council Name** field, and from the **Members** table, include the **First Name** and **Last Name** fields. The form uses the **Metro** theme. The title provided by the Form Wizard has been deleted and a new title inserted with the text Council Members The logo is from the student file **a03_Councils_Logo**. Arrange the subform and controls approximately as shown in the figure.

Use the form to enter the following members to the Planning Council:

Cyril Shore
Richie Bona
Hisako Lavoy
Octavio Coogan
Barton Bierschbach
Jung Ortolano
Jerrold Calhaun
Gwyneth Rondeau
Tammi Markewich

Save the form and subform. Create a **Full-Screen Snip** named a03_Councils_Snip Print the snip or submit the files as directed by your instructor.

Done! You have completed Assess Your Skills Visually

Figure 1

Skills in Context

To complete this database, you will need the following file:

- a03_Managers

You will save your files as:

- Lastname_Firstname_a03_Managers
- Lastname_Firstname_a03_Managers_Snip

Open **a03_Managers** and save the database in your **Access Chapter 3** folder as Lastname_Firstname_a03_Managers Create a form that displays all the records from the Managers table, but only those managers from the Parks and Recreation Department. Base the form on a query, and in the query criterion, type "Parks and Recreation" Be sure to include the quotation marks in the criterion. Apply an appropriate theme and a title with the text Parks and Recreation Managers Use the form to add yourself as a manager with the position of Health and Wellness Coordinator and an office number of 424 and a phone number of (805) 555-8492

Create a full-screen snip of the record with your name. Save the snip in your **Access Chapter 3** folder as a03_Managers_Snip Print the snip or submit the database file as directed by your instructor.

Done! You have completed Skills in Context

Skills and You

To complete this database, you will need the following file:

- a03_Contacts

You will save your files as:

- Lastname_Firstname_a03_Contacts
- Lastname_Firstname_a03_Contacts_Snip

Open **a03_Contacts**, and then save the database as Lastname_Firstname_a03_Contacts Create a form to enter contacts into the Contacts table. Format the form as appropriate, and then use the form to enter at least 10 personal contacts. Create a full-screen snip of the form. Save the snip in your **Access Chapter 3** folder as a03_Contacts_Snip Print or submit the file as directed by your instructor.

Done! You have completed Skills and You

CHAPTER 4

Create Reports

▶ Access reports are designed to present information on the screen or to be printed on paper.

▶ There are several methods that you can use to add fields to reports. You can then format and arrange the fields to make the information more meaningful.

Your starting screen will look similar to this:

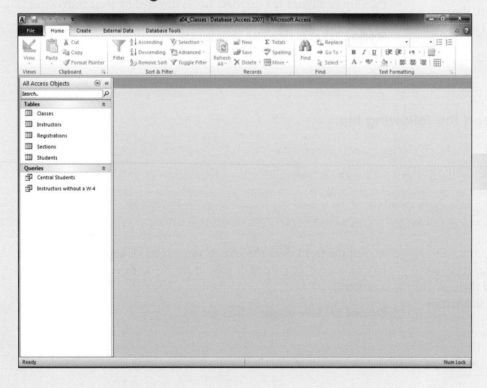

SKILLS

Skills 1–10 Training

At the end of this chapter, you will be able to:

Skill 1 Create Reports and Apply Themes
Skill 2 Modify Report Layouts
Skill 3 Prepare Reports for Printing
Skill 4 Use the Blank Report Tool
Skill 5 Group and Sort Reports
Skill 6 Format and Filter Reports
Skill 7 Create Label Reports
Skill 8 Use the Report Wizard
Skill 9 Modify Layouts in Design View
Skill 10 Add Totals and Labels to Reports

MORE SKILLS

More Skills 11 Export Reports to Word
More Skills 12 Export Reports as HTML Documents
More Skills 13 Create Parameter Queries
More Skills 14 Create Reports for Parameter Queries

Outcome

Using the skills listed to the left will enable you to create reports like these:

Impressionism in Art

1/12/2012   7:00 PM

Romona	Springate	(805) 555-6101
Mary	Dimmitt	(805) 555-9694
Wendolyn	Vandenburg	(805) 555-6211
Lupe	Fertal	(805) 555-5945
Erwin	Breach	(805) 555-7159
	Vane	(805) 555-7753
	Allegra	(805) 555-7388
	Delair	(805) 555-5849
	Tichi	(805) 555-2130
	Games	(805) 555-6972

10

3:00 PM

	Jeter	(805) 555-4837
	Fodness	(805) 555-4787
	Urda	(805) 555-8302
	Driskill	(805) 555-3718
	Favia	(805) 555-7194
	Luckow	(805) 555-4243
	Mulnix	(805) 555-3758
	Harland	(805) 555-5965
	Rhinehardt	(805) 555-8581
	Barlip	(805) 555-2761
	Ziv	(805) 555-7333
	Harland	(805) 555-5965

12

May 16, 2012   Page 3 of 7

astname_a04_Classes

Fritz Dagel
18857 E Butterfly Av
Aspen Falls, CA 93464

Pat Dietsche
97563 N Charles St
Aspen Falls, CA 93463

Ella Driskill
72809 N Church St
Aspen Falls, CA 93464

Beau Nakaoka
1421 S Dorr Dr
Aspen Falls, CA 93464

Your Name
14824 W Dogwood Ln
Aspen Falls, CA 93463

Bessie Pascorell
81580 E Carmen Dr
Aspen Falls, CA 93463

Tia Pearl
9636 E Dartmouth St
Aspen Falls, CA 93463

Instructor Assignments

Wednesday, May 16, 2012
9:02:06 AM

Instructor

A101	Lana	Shane			
Portrait Drawing		20127	1/9/2012	3:00 PM
Basic Drawing		20123	1/10/2012	7:00 PM

A103	Beatriz	Handlin			
Tour of Aspen Falls		20121	5/12/2012	1:00 PM

A105	Hazel	Ekwall			
Impressionism in Art		20125	1/12/2012	7:00 PM
Impressionism in Art		20131	3/8/2012	3:00 PM

A109	Celia	Moyerman			
Portrait Drawing		20133	3/13/2012	1:00 PM

A110	Chasidy	Trowery			
Beginning Watercolors		20124	1/11/2012	7:00 PM
Beginning Watercolors		20130	3/7/2012	7:00 PM

A112	Anton	Hoffelt			
Perspective Drawing		20126	1/14/2012	3:00 PM

A114	Mohamed	Lonzo			
Art History		20122	1/9/2012	7:00 PM
Art History		20128	3/5/2012	3:00 PM
Perspective Drawing		20132	3/9/2012	7:00 PM

A117	Rey	Hasse			
Basic Drawing		20129	3/6/2012	7:00 PM

You will save your database as:

Lastname_Firstname_a04_Classes

In this chapter, you will create documents for the Aspen Falls City Hall, which provides essential services for the citizens and visitors of Aspen Falls, California.

Introduction

▶ Reports present the results of a query or the data from a table. The fields can be formatted and arranged in a variety of ways.

▶ The records in reports can be grouped, sorted, and filtered to make the information more meaningful.

▶ You can build a report with fields from an entire table or query using the Report tool.

▶ When you want to select certain fields from one or more tables, you can create the report using the Report Wizard or Blank Report tool.

▶ When you need to print addresses on self-adhesive labels, you can create a labels report.

▶ Reports are modified in Layout or Design view. Report view shows the screen version reports, and Print Preview is used to view reports before printing.

Time to complete all
10 skills – 60 to 90 minutes

Find your student data files here:

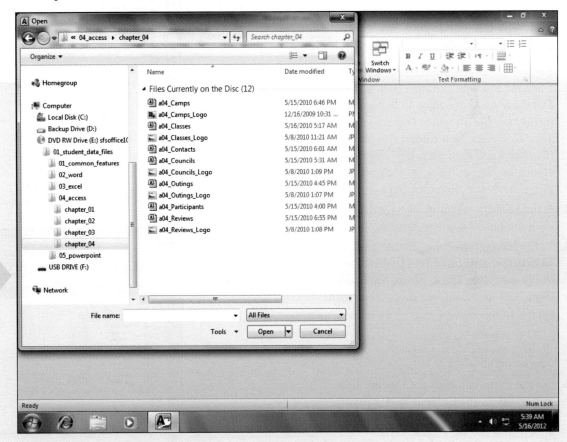

**Student data files needed
for this chapter:**

- a04_Classes
- a04_Classes_Logo

▶ Reports are often based on queries. You can add the fields that you need to the query, add criteria, and then use the Report tool to create a report to display the results of the query.

▶ After selecting a theme for your database, you can apply fonts or colors from a different theme.

1. **Start** 🕓 Access. If necessary, **Maximize** 🔲 the window.

2. From the student files that came with this book, open **a04_Classes**.

3. Click the **File tab**, and then click **Save Database As**. In the **Save As** dialog box, display the file list where you are saving your files. Click **New folder**, type Access Chapter 4 and then press [Enter] two times. Name the file Lastname_Firstname_ a04_Classes and then click **Save**.

4. If the Security Warning message displays, click the Enable Content button.

5. In the **Navigation Pane**, double-click **Instructors without a W-4** to view the query datasheet. **Close** 🔲 the **Navigation Pane**, and then compare your screen with **Figure 1**. ────────

> When you are working with an Access object, the status bar contains buttons for switching views.

6. On the status bar, click the **Design View** button 🔲. In the **Current W-4** column **Criteria** box, type No Compare your screen with **Figure 2**. ────────

7. **Save** 🔲, **Run**, and then **Close** ☒ the query.

■ **Continue to the next page to complete the skill**

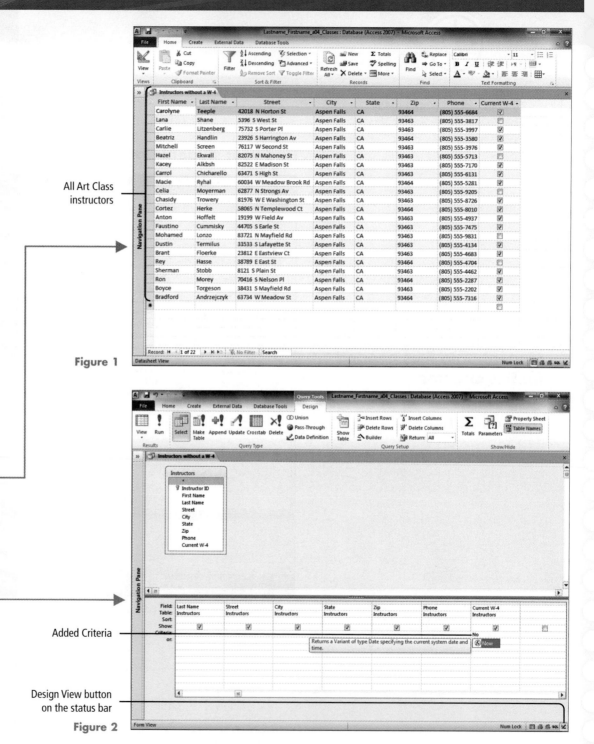

All Art Class instructors

Figure 1

Added Criteria

Design View button on the status bar

Figure 2

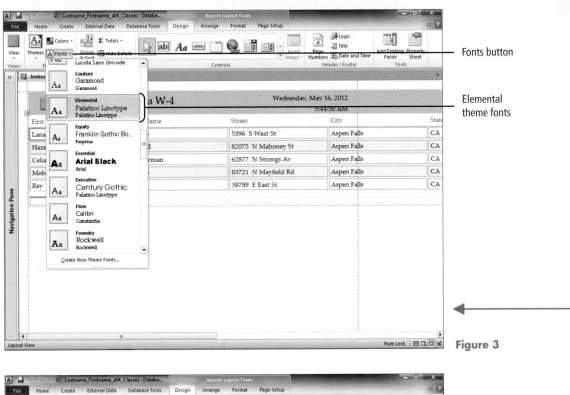

Fonts button

Elemental theme fonts

Figure 3

8. **Open** » the **Navigation Pane**. In the **Navigation Pane**, be sure the **Instructors without a W-4** is selected. On the **Create tab**, in the **Reports group**, click the **Report** button.

When a report is based on a query, the query criteria are applied to the report. Here, only the five instructors without a W-4 form on file are listed.

9. **Close** « the **Navigation Pane**. On the **Design tab**, in the **Themes group**, click the **Themes** button, and then click the second thumbnail in the fourth row— **Elemental**.

10. In the **Themes group**, click the **Fonts** button. Scroll down the list to display the **Elemental** font set, and then compare your screen with **Figure 3**.

When you select a theme, you are applying a set of fonts and a set of colors. Here, the Elemental font set includes Palatino Linotype for both labels and text boxes.

11. In the list of font sets, scroll down to locate and then click **Origin**. Compare your screen with **Figure 4**.

In this manner, you can combine your current theme with a color or font set from a different theme. Here, the report's fonts have changed to Bookman Old Style for the report header controls and Gill Sans MT for the values in the text boxes. The colors from the Elemental theme are still applied.

12. Click **Save** 🖫. In the **Save As** dialog box, click **OK** to save the report as Instructors without a W-4. Leave the report open for the next skill.

■ **You have completed Skill 1 of 10**

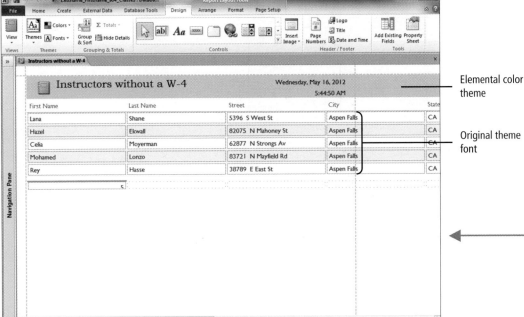

Elemental color theme

Original theme font

Figure 4

▶ Recall that forms and reports use layouts—cells arranged in rows and columns into which controls are placed. You can resize, delete, and merge these rows and columns so the report can be viewed on a screen without scrolling.

First Name column width decreased

1. With the **Instructors without a W-4** report still open in Layout view, click the **First Name** label. With the ↤ pointer over the right border of the label, drag to the left to resize the column, approximately as shown in **Figure 1**.

    When you resize one text box or label in a report's layout, all the label text boxes in that column are also resized. In this report, the First Name text box repeats five times—one row for each record in the query.

2. Click the **Last Name** label. On the **Design tab**, in the **Tools group**, click the **Property Sheet** button. On the property sheet **Format tab**, replace the **Width** value with 1.5"

3. Click the **Street** column to display its properties, and then change the column's **Width** to 2" Continue in this manner to set the remaining column widths using the values in **Figure 2**. Scroll as needed to select each column.

4. Click the **Current W-4 label**. On the **Arrange tab**, in the **Rows & Columns group**, click **Select Column**. Press ⌐Delete⌐ to remove the column from the report.

■ Continue to the next page to complete the skill ▶

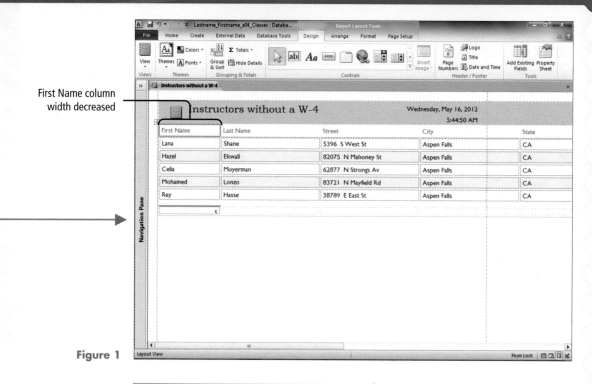

Figure 1

Column	Width
City	1.5"
State	0.5"
Zip	0.75"
Phone	1.5"

Figure 2

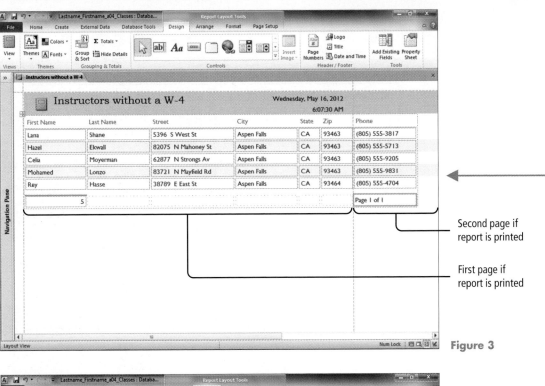

Figure 3

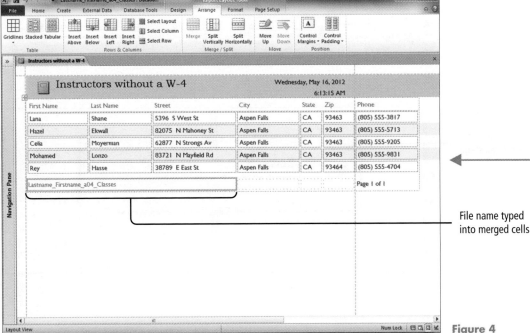

Figure 4

5. Scroll to the right as needed to display the text box with the value *Page 1 of 1*. With the ☒ pointer, drag the control into the empty cell below the **Phone** column.

6. With the *Page 1 of 1* text box still selected, on the property sheet **Format tab**, change the Height value to *.25"*

7. **Close** ☒ the property sheet, scroll the report all the way to the left, and then compare your screen with **Figure 3**.

   The entire report now displays within the width of a typical computer screen. The report is wider than a single sheet of paper, as indicated by the dashed vertical line.

8. On the layout's bottom row—the **Totals** row—click the text box that displays the value *5*. On the **Design tab**, in the **Grouping & Totals group**, click the **Totals** button, and then click **Count Records** to remove the Count Records control from the report.

9. In the **Totals** row, click the first empty cell. Press and hold ⟨Shift⟩ while clicking the third empty cell in the row.

10. With the three cells selected, on the **Arrange tab**, in the **Merge/Split group**, click the **Merge** button.

11. Click the cell just merged, and then using your own name, type Lastname_ Firstname_a04_Classes Press ⟨Enter⟩, and then compare your screen with **Figure 4**.

12. Click **Save** 🖫. Leave the report open for the next skill.

■ **You have completed Skill 2 of 10**

► When you need to print a report, you can adjust its margins and orientation to fit the size of a sheet of paper. You may also need to remove extra space from the report to prevent printing blank pages.

1. With the **Instructors without a W-4** report still open in Layout view, double-click the report title to enter Edit mode. To the right of *W-4*, add a space and then type Form

2. Click a blank area below the layout to leave Edit mode. On the **Design tab**, in the **Header / Footer group**, click the **Logo** button. In the **Insert Picture** dialog box, navigate to the student files, select **a04_Classes_Logo**, and then click **OK**.

3. On the status bar, click the **Print Preview** button ▣. In the **Zoom group**, click the **Two Pages** button, and then compare your screen with **Figure 1**. ───

   The first column is very close to the edge of the paper and the Phone column is on another sheet of paper.

4. In the **Page Size group**, click the **Margins** button, and then click **Normal**.

5. In the **Page Layout group**, click the **Landscape** button, and then compare your screen with **Figure 2**. ───

   When you modify a report so that all the controls fit within a single sheet of paper, some report elements may still extend to a second sheet of paper. When this happens, a warning displays that the second sheet will be empty.

■ **Continue to the next page to complete the skill**

Narrow margin ───

Phone column on second sheet of paper ───

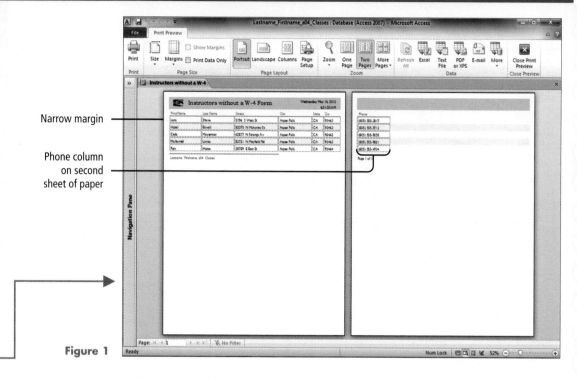

Figure 1

Microsoft Access message ───

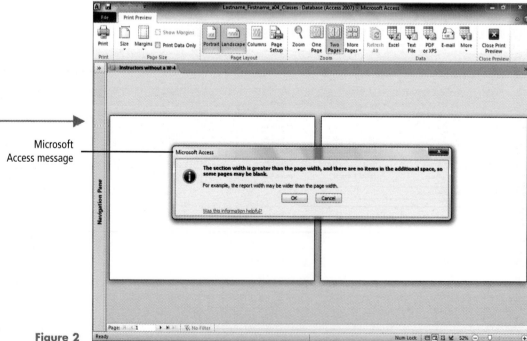

Figure 2

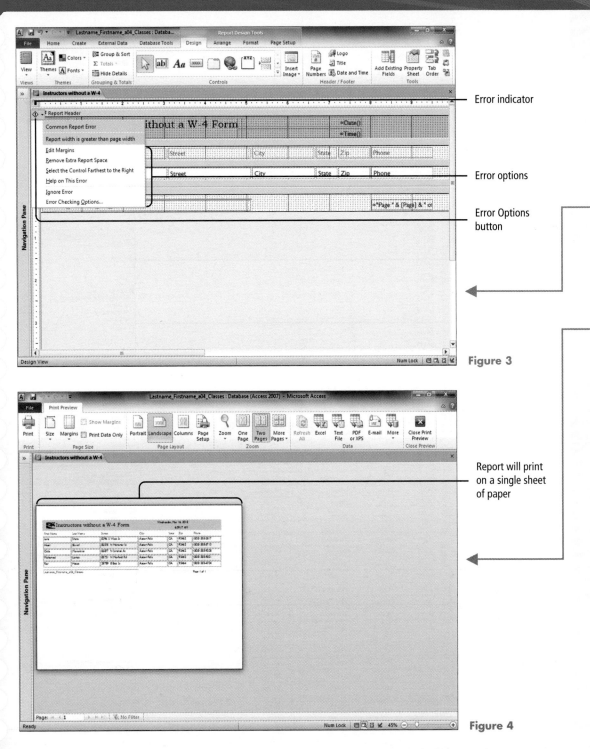

Error indicator

Error options

Error Options button

Figure 3

Report will print on a single sheet of paper

Figure 4

6. Read the message, and then click **OK**. Notice that all the controls are on the first page, but that the report still extends to a second sheet of paper.

7. On the status bar, click the **Design View** button. In the upper-left corner of the report, a green error indicator displays.

8. Click the error indicator, and then click the displayed **Error Options** button. Compare your screen with **Figure 3**.

   The Error Message describes the problem and lists commands with possible solutions to the problem.

9. In the **Error Message** list, click **Remove Extra Report Space**. On the status bar, click the **Print Preview** button, and then compare your screen with **Figure 4**.

   When extra space is removed, blank pages will not be printed. Here, the entire report displays on a single page.

10. If you are printing this project, click the Print button, click OK, and then retrieve the printout from the printer.

11. Click **Save**, and then **Close** the report.

   ■ **You have completed Skill 3 of 10**

► The Blank Report tool is used when you want to build a report by adding fields one at a time or to arrange the fields in a different layout.

1. On the **Create tab**, in the **Reports group**, click the **Blank Report** button.

2. In the **Field List pane**, click **Show all tables**. In the **Field List**, to the left of **Instructors**, click the **Expand** button ⊞.

3. In the **Field List**, double-click **Instructor ID** to add the field to the report. Compare your screen with **Figure 1**. ────────

   As you add fields with the Blank Report tool, the other tables move to the lower sections of the Field List pane. Here, the Sections table is a related table—it contains Instructor ID as a foreign key.

4. In the **Field List**, double-click **First Name** and **Last Name** to add them to the report.

5. In the **Field List**, under **Fields available in related tables**, **Expand** ⊞ the **Sections** table.

6. Double-click **Section ID**, and then compare your screen with **Figure 2**. ────────

   When you add a field from another table, that table moves to the upper pane of the Field List and any tables related to this table become available. Here, Classes and Registrations become available as related tables.

■ **Continue to the next page to complete the skill**

Tables currently used

Related tables

Other tables

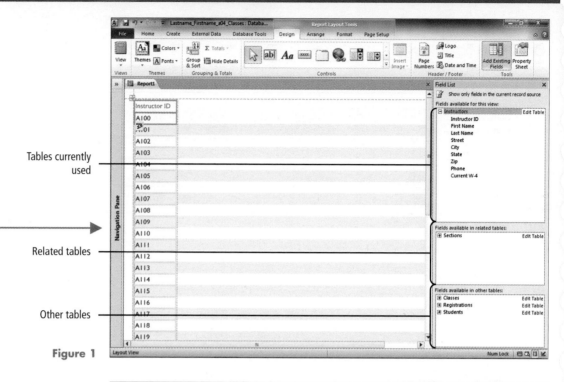

Figure 1

Sections table

Two tables related to Sections table

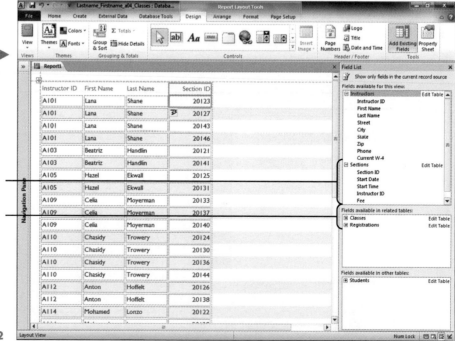

Figure 2

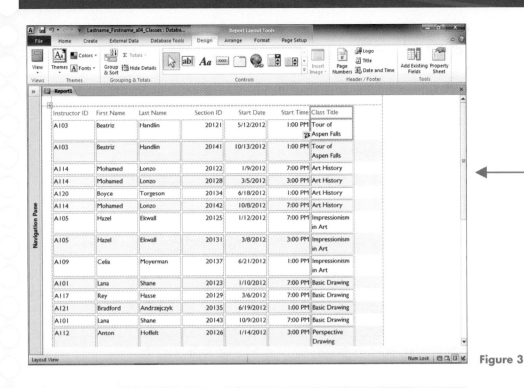

Figure 3

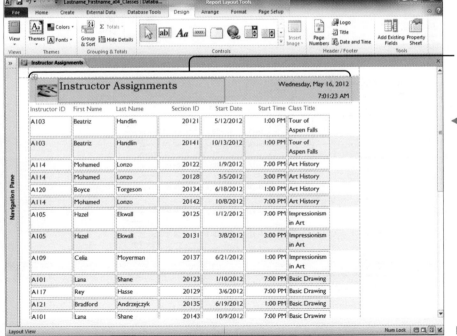

Controls added to report header

Figure 4

7. In the **Field List**, under **Sections**, double-click **Start Date** and **Start Time** to add the two fields to the report.

8. In the **Field List**, under **Fields available in related tables**, Expand ⊞ the **Classes** table. Double-click **Class Title** to add it to the report.

9. **Close** ⊠ the **Field List**, and then compare your screen with **Figure 3**.

10. In the **Header/Footer group**, click the **Logo** button. In the **Insert Picture** dialog box, navigate to the student files, select **a04_Classes_Logo**, and then click **OK**.

11. On the **Design tab**, in the **Header / Footer group**, click the **Title** button, type Instructor Assignments and then press Enter.

12. In the **Header/Footer group**, click the **Date and Time** button. In the **Date and Time** dialog box, click **OK**.

13. Click **Save** 🖫. In the **Save As** dialog box, type Instructor Assignments and then press Enter. Compare your screen with **Figure 4**.

14. Leave the report open for the next skill.

■ **You have completed Skill 4 of 10**

▶ Report data can be grouped and sorted to add meaning to it.

1. If necessary, open the Instructor Assignments report in Layout view. In the **Grouping & Totals group**, click the **Group & Sort** button to display the **Group, Sort, and Total** pane.

2. In the **Group, Sort, and Total** pane, click the **Add a group** button. In the list of fields, click the **Instructor ID** field to group the classes by instructor.

3. Click one of the **First Name** text boxes, and then, with the 🔏 pointer, drag the control up to the empty cell to the right of the **Instructor ID** text box.

4. Repeat the technique just practiced to move the **Last Name** text box to the empty cell to the right of the **First Name** text box. Compare your screen with **Figure 1**.

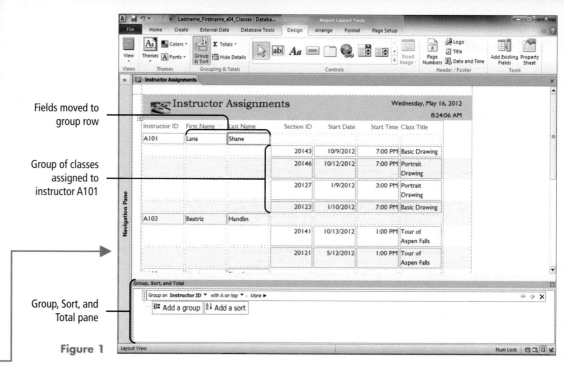

Fields moved to group row

Group of classes assigned to instructor A101

Group, Sort, and Total pane

Figure 1

Because the instructor names do not change within each group of Instructor IDs, they can be in the same row as the Instructor ID. In this way, the instructor name is not repeated in each section row.

5. At the top of the **Instructor ID** column, double-click the **Instructor ID** label to enter Edit mode. Change the label text to Instructor and then press [Enter].

6. Click the **First Name** label, and then press [Delete] to remove the label from the report. Repeat this technique to delete the **Last Name** and **Section ID** labels. Compare your screen with **Figure 2**.

■ **Continue to the next page to complete the skill**

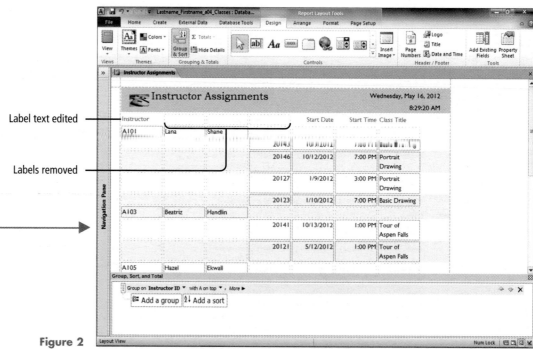

Label text edited

Labels removed

Figure 2

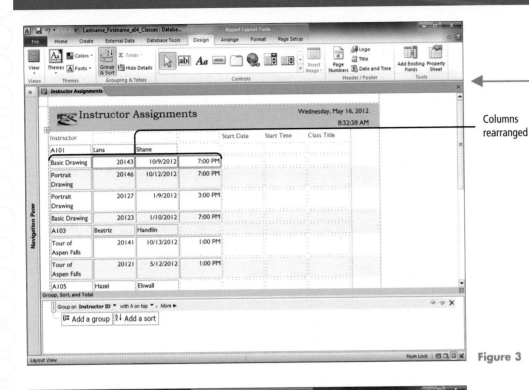

Columns rearranged

Figure 3

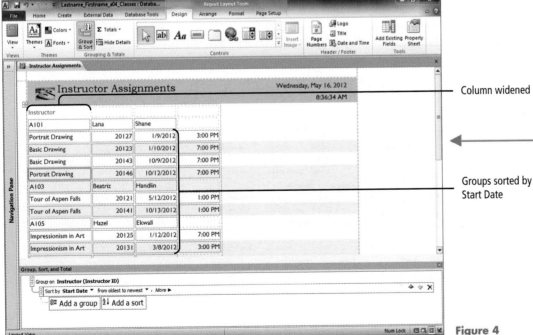

Column widened

Groups sorted by Start Date

Figure 4

7. Click one of the **Class Title** text boxes. With the pointer, drag the text box into the left-most empty cell in that row.

8. Click one of the **Section ID** text boxes, press and hold Shift, and then click one of the **Start Time** text boxes. With the three columns selected, drag the selected **Section ID** text box into the left-most empty cell in that row. Compare your screen with **Figure 3**.

9. Click an empty cell below the **Start Date** label. On the **Arrange tab**, in the **Rows & Columns group**, click the **Select Column** button. Press Delete to remove the column from the report.

10. Repeat the technique just practiced to delete the two empty columns on the right side of the layout.

11. Select one of the **Class Title** text boxes, and then, on the **Design tab**, in the **Tools group**, click the **Property Sheet** button. Set the control's **Width** property to 1.5"

12. **Close** ✕ the property sheet. In the **Group, Sort, and Total** pane, click the **Add a sort** button. In the list of fields, click **Start Date**. Compare your screen with **Figure 4**.

13. On the **Design tab**, in the **Grouping & Totals group**, click the **Group & Sort** button to close the pane.

14. **Save** 🖫 the report. Leave the report open for the next skill.

■ **You have completed Skill 5 of 10**

▶ Reports can be formatted to clarify the information that they contain. For example, group headings should be formatted to stand out from the details within each group.

▶ You can filter a report to show a subset of the data.

1. With the **Instructor Assignments** report open in Layout view, click the **Instructor ID** text box with the value *A101*. On the **Format tab**, in the **Font group**, click the **Bold** button 🅱.

2. With the **Instructor ID** text box still selected, in the **Font group**, click the **Font Size arrow**, and then click **12**.

3. With the **Instructor ID** text box still selected, in the **Font group**, double-click the **Format Painter** button ✒. With the 🔩 pointer, click the **First Name** text box with the value *Lana*. With the 🔩 pointer, click the **Last Name** text box with the value *Shane*. Compare your screen with **Figure 1**. ─────

   In this manner, the Format Painter can be used to copy all the formatting of one control to other controls. When the Format Painter is on, its button displays in gold on the Ribbon.

4. In the **Font group**, click the **Format Painter** button ✒ one time to turn it off.

5. On the **Format tab**, in the **Selection group**, click the **Object arrow**, and then click **Group Header0**. Compare your screen with **Figure 2**. ─────

   You can use the Selection group to select different objects in your report. Here, the entire header row for each group of instructors is selected.

▪ **Continue to the next page to complete the skill**

Format Painter button ───

Format Painter pointer ───

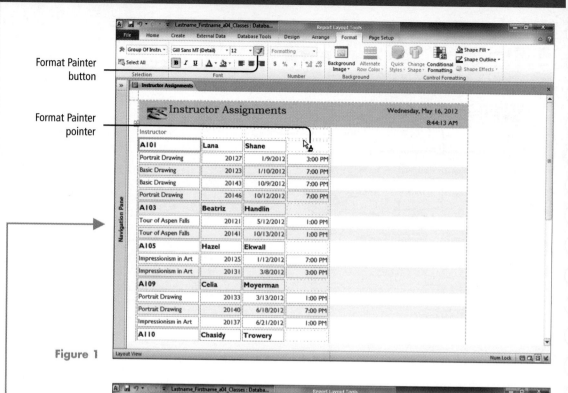

Figure 1

Object arrow ───

GroupHeader0 selected ───

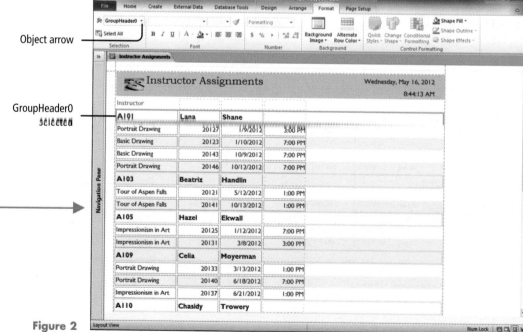

Figure 2

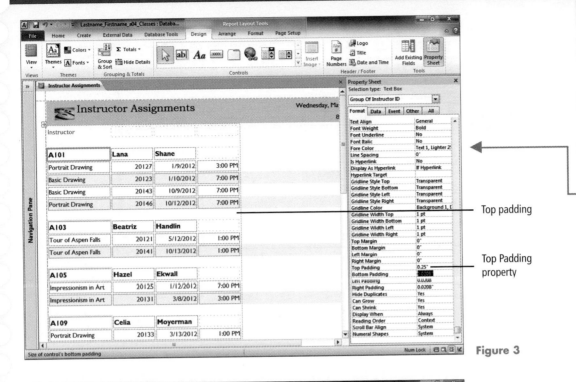

Top padding

Top Padding
property

Figure 3

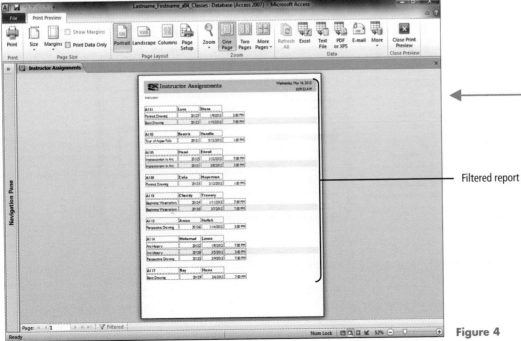

Filtered report

Figure 4

6. On the **Format tab**, in the **Background group**, click the **Alternate Row Color button arrow**, and then click **No Color**.

7. Click the **Instructor ID** text box with the value *A101*. On the **Design tab**, in the **Tools group**, click the **Property Sheet** button.

8. Scroll to the bottom of the property sheet **Format tab**. Change the **Top Padding** property to .25" Press Enter, and then compare your screen with **Figure 3**.

> *Padding* is the amount of space between a control's border and other controls on the form or report.

9. **Close** ☒ the property sheet. On the status bar, click the **Report View** button ▤. Scroll down to view the list of instructors and their assigned classes.

10. Scroll to the top of the report. In the classes for Beatriz Handlin, click the text box with the value *5/12/2012*.

11. In the **Sort & Filter group**, click the **Selection** button, and then click **On or Before 5/12/2012** to filter the report.

12. On the status bar, click the **Print Preview** button ▤. Compare your screen with **Figure 4**. If necessary, click the One Page button.

13. If you are printing your work, print the report.

14. Click **Save** ▤, and then **Close** ☒ the report. **Open** ≫ the **Navigation Pane**.

■ **You have completed Skill 6 of 10**

▶ A *label report* is a report formatted so that the data can be printed on a sheet of labels.

1. In the **Navigation Pane**, under **Queries**, double-click **Central Students** to display the records for students from the Central neighborhood.

2. In the first record, change *Eliseo* and *Brennan* to your own first and last names.

3. **Close** ☒ the query, and then on the **Create tab**, in the **Reports group**, click the **Labels** button.

4. In the **Label Wizard**, be sure that the **Filter by manufacturer** box displays the text **Avery**. Under **What label size would you like**, select the label size where **Product number** is **C2160**, as shown in **Figure 1**. ────────────►

   Each manufacturer identifies its label sheets using a product number. Access formats the report to match the dimensions of the selected sheet.

5. Click **Next**. If necessary, change the Font name to Arial and the Font weight to Light. Change the **Font size** to **10**.

6. Click **Next**. Under **Available fields**, click **First Name**, and then click the **Move** ☐ button to add the field to the Prototype label.

7. With the insertion point in the **Prototype label** and to the right of *{First Name}*, add a space, and then **Move** ☐ the **Last Name** field into the first line of the **Prototype label**.

8. Press **Enter**, and then **Move** ☐ the **Street** field into the second line of the **Prototype label**. Compare your screen with **Figure 2**. ────────────►

■ **Continue to the next page to complete the skill** ▶

Label Wizard

Product number is C2160

Manufacturer is Avery

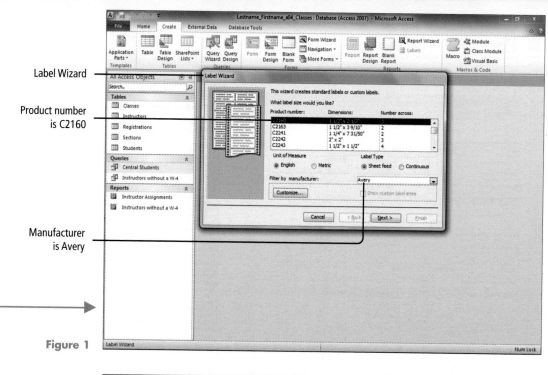

Figure 1

Fields added to Prototype label

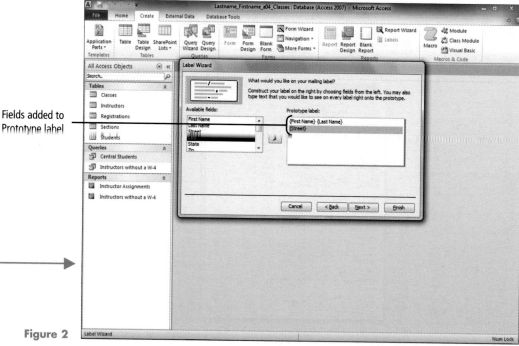

Figure 2

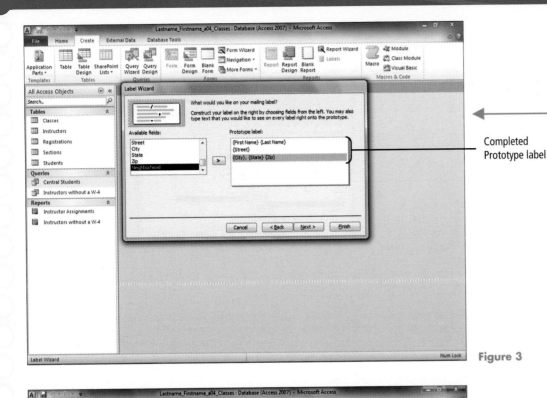

Completed
Prototype label

Figure 3

Completed labels
report

Figure 4

9. Press Enter, and then **Move** > the **City** field into the third line of the label. Add a comma followed by a space, and then add the **State** field. Add a space, and then add the **Zip** field. Compare your screen with **Figure 3**.

10. Click **Next** two times. Under **What name would you like for your report**, replace the existing name with Central Mailing Labels

11. Click **Finish** to open the report in Print Preview. In the **Zoom group**, click **One Page**. **Close** « the **Navigation Pane**, and then compare your screen with **Figure 4**.

12. If you are printing your work for this project, print the labels.

When printing a label report, your printer may require additional steps. Most printers will not print until a sheet of labels or sheet of paper is placed in the manual feed tray. Many printers, however, can print the report on plain paper. If you are working in a computer lab, check with your lab technician or instructor for what is required in your situation.

13. **Close** × the report.

■ **You have completed Skill 7 of 10**

▶ The Report Wizard can be used when you need fields from multiple tables. In the wizard, you can preview different groupings.

▶ After you create a report using the Report Wizard, it displays in Print Preview. When you close Print Preview, the report displays in Design view.

1. On the **Create tab**, in the **Reports group**, click the **Report Wizard** button.

2. Click the **Tables/Queries arrow**, and then click **Table: Classes** to display the fields from that table.

3. Click **Class Title**, and then click the **Move** button [>] to move the field into the **Selected Fields** list.

4. Click the **Tables/Queries arrow**, and then click **Table: Sections**. Move the **Start Date**, and then the **Start Time** fields into **Selected Fields**.

5. Click the **Tables/Queries arrow**, and then click **Table: Students**. Move the following fields in this order: **First Name**, **Last Name**, and **Phone**. Compare your screen with **Figure 1**.

6. In the **Report Wizard**, click **Next**, and then compare your screen with **Figure 2**.

The Report Wizard has screens in which you can change how the report will be viewed and grouped. Here, the report is grouped by Class Title—each section of a class will be listed under its Class Title. Within each section, the students in that section will be listed.

■ **Continue to the next page to complete the skill**

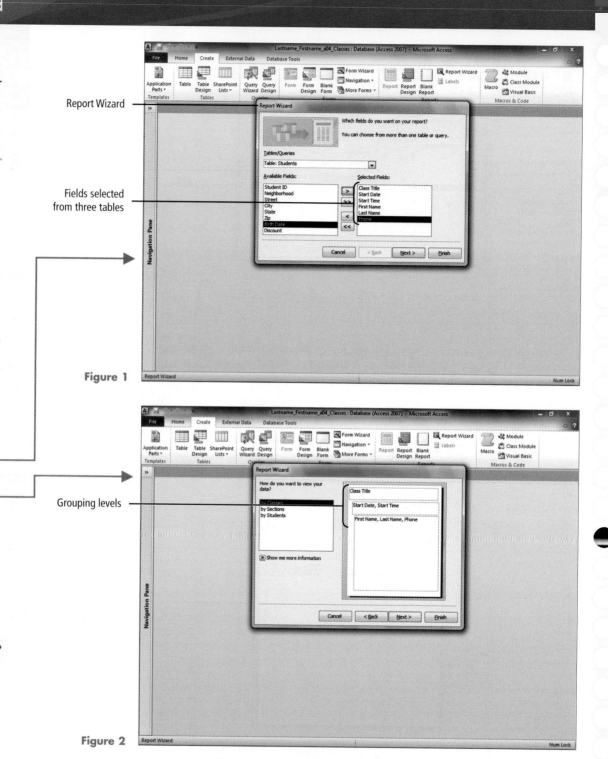

Report Wizard

Fields selected from three tables

Figure 1

Grouping levels

Figure 2

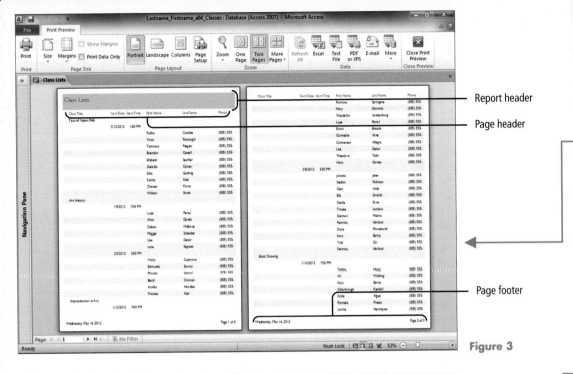

Figure 3

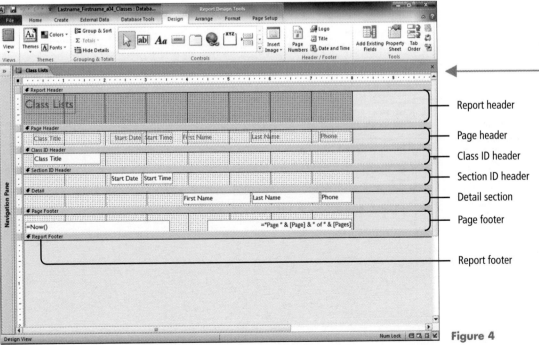

Figure 4

7. Click **Next** four times to accept the default Report Wizard settings for grouping, sorting, and layout.

8. Under **What title do you want for your report**, replace the value with Class Lists

9. Click **Finish**. In the **Zoom group**, click the **Two Pages** button. Compare your screen with **Figure 3**.

> A *report header* is an area at the beginning of a report that contains labels, text boxes, and other controls. Here, the report title, *Class Lists*, is in the report header.

> *Page headers* are areas at the top of each page that contain labels, text boxes, and other controls. Here, the labels for each column are in the page header.

> *Page footers* are areas at the bottom of each page that contain labels, text boxes, and other controls. Here, the date and page number text boxes are in the page footer.

10. Click the **Close Print Preview** button, and then compare your screen with **Figure 4**.

> In Design view, each report section has a bar above it with that section's name, and each group has its own header.

> In the Detail section, text boxes display in one row, and a sample of the data is not displayed or repeated for each record.

> A *report footer* is an area at the end of a report that contains labels, text boxes, and other controls. Here, the report has no report footer and the area below its bar is collapsed.

11. Leave the report open for the next skill.

■ **You have completed Skill 8 of 10**

► Design view can be used when you want more control over your layout.

1. If necessary, open the Class Lists report in Design view. In the **Report Header**, click the **Title** control one time, and then press Delete.

2. Just above the **Page Header** bar, point to the lower edge of the **Report Header**. When the ⊞ pointer displays, drag up, as shown in **Figure 1**.

   You can remove report headers and footers by deleting their controls and decreasing the section's height to zero.

3. In the **Page Header**, click the **Class Title** label. Press and hold Shift and then, in the **Page Header**, click each of the remaining labels. With the six labels selected, press Delete to remove the labels.

4. Point to the lower edge of the **Page Header**, and then with the ⊞ pointer, drag up to set the **Page Header** height to zero.

5. In the **Class ID Header**, click the **Class Title** text box. Press ← approximately five times to move the control one grid dot from the left edge of the report.

6. With the **Class Title** text box still selected, on the **Format tab, in the Font group,** click the **Bold** button. In the **Font group**, click the **Font Size arrow**, and then click **14**.

7. With the ↔ pointer, increase the width of the **Class Title** text box so that the control's right edge is on the **4 inch** vertical grid line. Compare your screen with **Figure 2**.

■ **Continue to the next page to complete the skill**

Report Header height set to zero

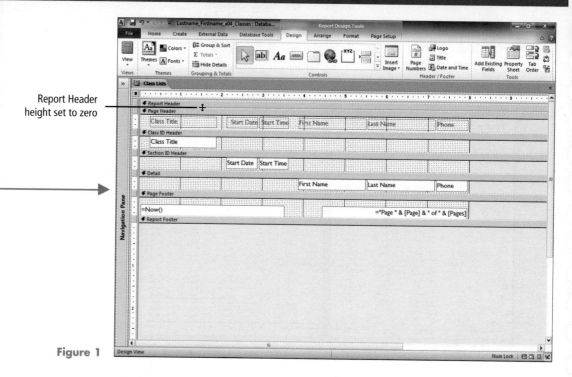

Figure 1

Page Header height set to zero

Class Title text box moved, formatted, and resized

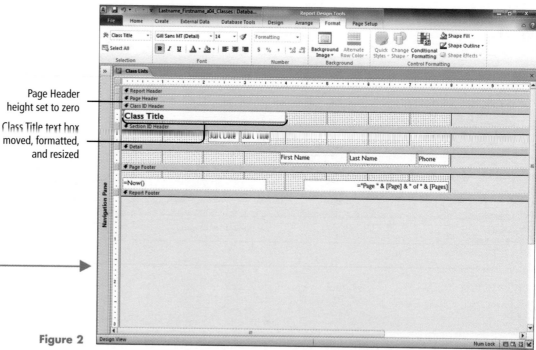

Figure 2

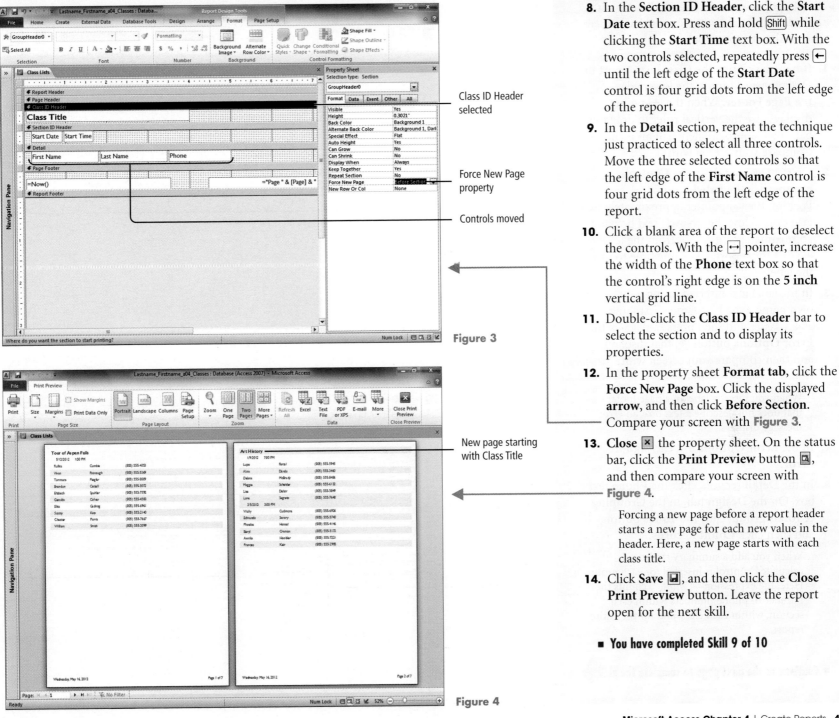

Class ID Header selected

Force New Page property

Controls moved

Figure 3

New page starting with Class Title

Figure 4

8. In the **Section ID Header**, click the **Start Date** text box. Press and hold (Shift) while clicking the **Start Time** text box. With the two controls selected, repeatedly press ⬅ until the left edge of the **Start Date** control is four grid dots from the left edge of the report.

9. In the **Detail** section, repeat the technique just practiced to select all three controls. Move the three selected controls so that the left edge of the **First Name** control is four grid dots from the left edge of the report.

10. Click a blank area of the report to deselect the controls. With the ↔ pointer, increase the width of the **Phone** text box so that the control's right edge is on the **5 inch** vertical grid line.

11. Double-click the **Class ID Header** bar to select the section and to display its properties.

12. In the property sheet **Format tab**, click the **Force New Page** box. Click the displayed **arrow**, and then click **Before Section**. Compare your screen with **Figure 3**.

13. **Close** ☒ the property sheet. On the status bar, click the **Print Preview** button 🔍, and then compare your screen with **Figure 4**.

    Forcing a new page before a report header starts a new page for each new value in the header. Here, a new page starts with each class title.

14. Click **Save** 💾, and then click the **Close Print Preview** button. Leave the report open for the next skill.

■ **You have completed Skill 9 of 10**

► In Design view, you can work directly with *calculated controls*—text boxes that display the results of expressions.

1. If necessary, open the Class Lists report in Design view. Point to the lower edge of the **Page Footer**. When the ⊞ pointer displays, use the vertical ruler to drag the bar down approximately half an inch. Compare your screen with **Figure 1**.

2. On the **Design tab**, in the **Controls group**, click the **Label** button ⟦Aa⟧. Position the ⟦ᴬ⟧ pointer approximately two grid dots below the =**Now()** text box and approximately 1 grid dot from the left edge of the report. Click one time to insert the label.

3. In the label just inserted, using your own name, type Lastname_Firstname_ a04_Classes and then press ⟦Enter⟧. Click the **Error Options** button ⟦◈⟧ that displays, and then compare your screen with **Figure 2**.

    When you insert a label in a page footer that does not describe a text box, an error message displays.

4. In the **Error Options** list, click **Ignore Error**.

5. In the **Detail** section, click the **Phone** text box. On the **Design tab**, in the **Grouping & Totals group**, click the **Totals** button, and then click **Count Records**.

    When you add a summary statistic, a calculated control is inserted for each group. Here, the expression =*Count(*)* counts the number of phone numbers within each section, within each class, and for the entire report.

■ **Continue to the next page to complete the skill** ▶

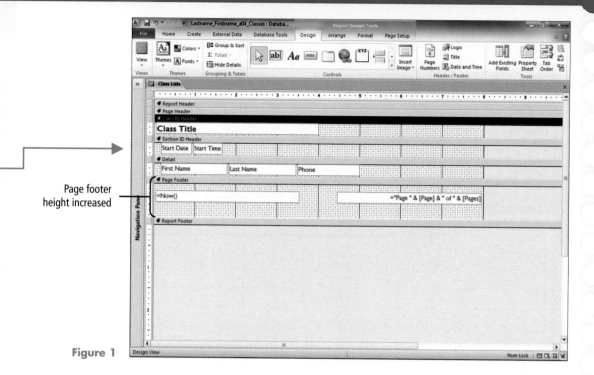

Page footer height increased

Figure 1

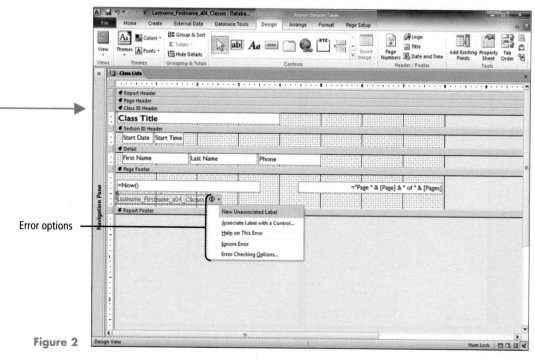

Error options

Figure 2

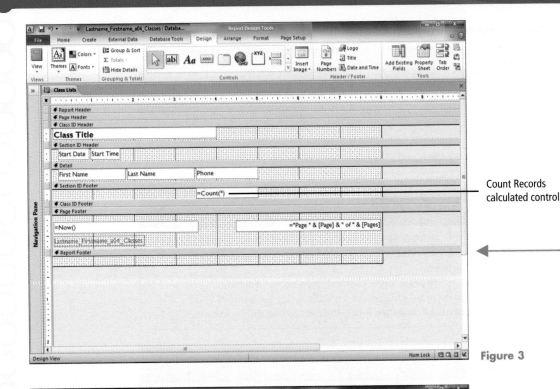

Count Records
calculated control

Figure 3

Students in two
sections of Basic
Drawing class

Class count

Figure 4

6. In the **Class ID Footer**, click the =**Count**(*) text box, and then press Delete. Drag to set the **Class ID Footer** height to zero. In the **Report Footer**, delete the =**Count**(*) text box. Compare your screen with **Figure 3**.

7. Click the **Class ID Header** bar to select the header. On the **Format tab**, in the **Background group**, click the **Alternate Row Color button arrow**, and then click **No Color**.

8. Click the **Section ID Header** bar, and then repeat the technique just practiced to set the **Alternate Row Color** to **No Color**. Repeat to remove the alternating row color from the **Section ID Footer**.

9. On the status bar, click the **Print Preview** button. On the Navigation bar, click the **Next Page** button to display page three and four. Compare your screen with **Figure 4**.

10. Click the **Print** button. In the **Print** dialog box, under **Print Range**, click in the **From** box, and then type 3 Click in the **To** box, and then type 3 If you are printing this project, click OK. Otherwise, click Cancel.

11. Click **Save**, and then **Close** the report.

12. **Open** the **Navigation Pane**, and then **Exit** Access. Submit your printouts or the database file as directed by your instructor.

Done! You have completed Skill 10 of 10 and your database is complete.

More Skills

The following More Skills are located at **www.pearsonhighered.com/skills**

More Skills (11) Export Reports to Word

You can export reports to other file formats so that you can work with the data in other applications. For example, you can export a report so that it can be opened in Word or sent as an email attachment.

In More Skills 11, you will export a report to another file format and then open that file in Word.

To begin, open your web browser, navigate to www.pearsonhighered.com/skills, locate the name of your textbook, and then follow the instructions on the website.

More Skills (12) Export Reports as HTML Documents

You can export reports so that they can be opened in a web browser. In this manner, reports can be published and shared on the World Wide Web.

In More Skills 12, you export a report as a Hypertext Markup Language (HTML) document and view the report in your web browser.

To begin, open your web browser, navigate to www.pearsonhighered.com/skills, locate the name of your textbook, and then follow the instructions on the website.

More Skills (13) Create Parameter Queries

You can build a query that asks you to type the criterion that should be applied. In this way, a single query can return several different data subsets depending on the values you type when the query is run.

In More Skills 13, you will create a parameter query that asks for a criterion. You will then run the query several times and type a different criterion each time. Each time, the query will display only the records that match the criterion that you type.

To begin, open your web browser, navigate to www.pearsonhighered.com/skills, locate the name of your textbook, and then follow the instructions on the website.

More Skills (14) Create Reports for Parameter Queries

You can use reports based on parameter queries. When the report is opened, it asks for a criterion and the report will display a subset of the data based on the value you type. In this manner, you can use a single report to display a variety of results without having to create multiple queries and reports.

In More Skills 14, create a report based on a parameter query. You will then run the report to display two different sets of data.

To begin, open your web browser, navigate to www.pearsonhighered.com/skills, locate the name of your textbook, and then follow the instructions on the website.

Key Terms

Online Help Skills

1. **Start**  Access. In the upper-right corner of the Access window, click the **Help** button. In the **Help** window, click the **Maximize** button.

2. Click in the search box, type Introduction to Controls and then click the **Search** button. In the search results, click **Introduction to controls**.

3. Read the article's introduction, and then below **In this article**, click **Understand layouts**. Compare your screen with **Figure 1**.

Figure 1

4. Read the **Understand layouts** section to see if you can answer the following: How are tabular control layouts different than stacked control layouts? How are they the same?

Matching

Match each term in the second column with its correct definition in the first column by writing the letter of the term on the blank line in front of the correct definition.

_____ **1.** Cells arranged in rows and columns into which controls are placed.

_____ **2.** To combine two or more cells in a tabular layout.

_____ **3.** This is used when you want to build a report by adding fields one at a time or arrange them in a different layout.

_____ **4.** A small picture that can be added to a report header, typically to the left of the title.

_____ **5.** To display a subset of records on a report that match a given criterion.

_____ **6.** The amount of space between a control's border and other controls on the form or report.

_____ **7.** An area at the beginning of a report that contains labels, text boxes, and other controls.

_____ **8.** An area at the top of each page that contains labels, text boxes, and other controls.

_____ **9.** An area at the bottom of each page that contains labels, text boxes, and other controls.

_____ **10.** An area at the end of a report that contains labels, text boxes, and other controls.

A Blank Report tool

B Filter

C Layout

D Logo

E Merge

F Padding

G Page Footer

H Page Header

I Report Footer

J Report Header

Multiple Choice

Choose the correct answer.

1. A tool that can create a report with a single click.
   A. Blank Report tool
   B. Report tool
   C. Report Wizard

2. A page orientation where the page is wider than it is tall.
   A. Landscape
   B. Portrait
   C. Wide

3. This can be removed from a report to prevent printing blank pages.
   A. Alternating row colors
   B. Extra space
   C. White space

4. This pane is used to add fields to a report in Layout view.
   A. Add Fields
   B. Blank Report
   C. Field List

5. This pane is used to group and sort reports.
   A. Group pane
   B. Group and Sort pane
   C. Group, Sort, and Total pane

6. A report formatted so that the data can be printed on a sheet of labels.
   A. Label report
   B. Mail report
   C. Merge report

7. This view is used when you want the most control over your report layout.
   A. Design view
   B. Layout view
   C. Print Preview

8. This property is changed when you need to add page breaks before report headers.
   A. Force New Page
   B. Padding
   C. Page Break

9. A text box that displays the result of an expression.
   A. Calculated control
   B. Expression box
   C. Label

10. When no alternating row color is desired, select this value.
    A. Blank
    B. None
    C. No Color

Topics for Discussion

1. You have created reports using three different methods: the Report tool, the Report Wizard, and the Blank Report tool. Which method do you prefer and why? What are the primary advantages of each method?

2. Consider the types of data that businesses might store in a database. For example, each instructor at a school needs a class roster listing each student in the class. What type of reports might other businesses need?

Skill Check

To complete this database, you will need the following files:

- a04_Outings
- a04_Outings_Logo

You will save your database as:

- Lastname_Firstname_a04_Outings

1. **Start** Access, and then open the student data file **a04_Outings**. Save the database in your **Access Chapter 4** folder with the name Lastname_Firstname_a04_Outings If necessary, enable the content.

2. On the **Create tab**, in the **Reports group**, click the **Blank Report** button. In the **Field List pane**, click **Show all tables**, and then expand the **Participants** table. Double-click to add the following fields: **First Name**, **Last Name**, and **Neighborhood**. Compare your screen with **Figure 1**. ⎯⎯⎯

3. **Close** the **Field List** pane. In the **Themes group**, click the **Fonts** button, and then click the first theme font—**Office**.

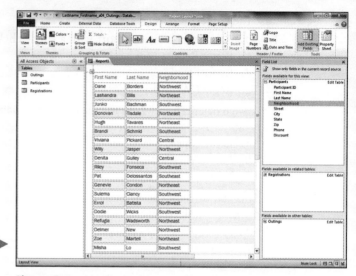

Figure 1

4. In the **Header / Footer group**, click the **Logo** button. In the **Insert Picture** dialog box, navigate to the student files for this chapter, click **a04_Outings_Logo**, and then click **OK**.

5. In the **Header / Footer group**, click the **Title** button, type Central Neighborhood Participants and then press [Enter].

6. In the **Grouping & Totals group**, click the **Group & Sort** button. In the **Group, Sort, and Total** pane, click **Add a group**, and then click **Neighborhood**.

7. Click the **Report View** button. In the **Sort & Filter group**, click the **Selection** button, and then click **Equals "Central"**.

8. Click **Save**, type Central Report and then click **OK**. Click the **Print Preview** button, and then compare your screen with **Figure 2**. If necessary, click the ⎯⎯⎯ One Page button.

9. If you are printing this project, print the report. **Close** the report.

10. On the **Create tab**, in the **Reports group**, click the **Report Wizard** button. If necessary, in the Report Wizard, click the Tables/Queries button, and click Table: Outings. Move the **Outing Name** and **Outing Date** fields into **Selected Fields**. Select the **Participants** table, move **First Name** and **Last Name**, and then click **Finish**.

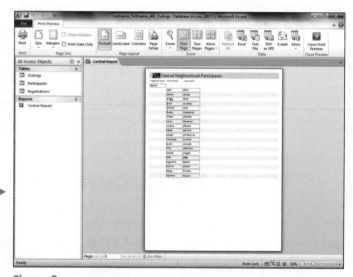

Figure 2

➤ ■ **Continue to the next page to complete this Skill Check**

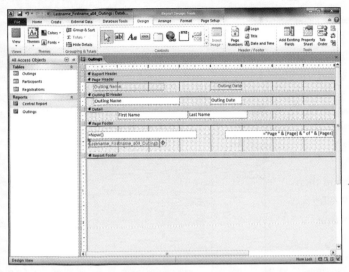

Figure 3

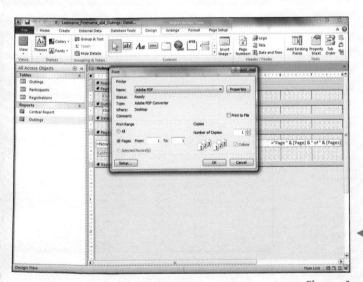

Figure 4

11. Click the **Close Print Preview** button. In the **Report Header**, click the **Title** control, and then press (Delete). Drag the lower edge of the **Report Header** to set the section's height to zero.

12. In the **Page Header**, click the **First Name** label. Press and hold (Shift), while clicking the **Last Name** label, and then press (Delete).

13. In the **Page Header**, click the **Outing Date** label. In the **Outing ID Header**, press (Shift) while clicking the **Outing Date** text box. Press (→) repeatedly to place the right edge of the two controls on the **5 inch** vertical grid line.

14. In the **Outing ID Header**, click the **Outing Name** text box. Drag to increase the width of the text box so that its right edge is on the **3 inch** vertical grid line.

15. Click the **Outing ID Header**. On the **Format tab**, in the **Background group**, click the **Alternate Row Color button arrow**, and then click **No Color**.

16. Double-click the **Outing ID Header**, and then, in the property sheet **Format tab**, change the **Force New Page** property to **Before Section**. **Close** the property sheet.

17. Click the **Outing Name** text box, and then, on the **Format tab**, in the **Font group**, click the **Bold** button. In the **Font group**, click the **Font Color button arrow**, and then click the last color in the first row—**Blue-Gray, Accent 6**.

18. In the **Font group**, click the **Format Painter** button one time, and then, in the **Outing ID Header**, click the **Outing Date** text box to apply the formatting.

19. In the **Detail** section, click the **First Name** text box. Press (Shift) while clicking the **Last Name** text box. Press (←) to place the left edge of the **First Name** field on the **1 inch** vertical grid line.

20. Point to the lower edge of the **Page Footer**, and then drag down to increase its height by approximately half an inch.

21. On the **Design tab**, in the **Controls group**, click the **Label** button. In the **Page Footer**, click approximately 1 grid dot below the =**Now**() calculated control and 1 grid dot from the left edge of the report. Using your own name, type Lastname_Firstname_a04_Outings Click **Save**, and then compare your screen with **Figure 3**.

22. On the **File tab**, click **Print**, and then click the **Print** button. Under **Print Range**, in the **From** box, type 1 In the **To** box, type 1 Compare your screen with **Figure 4**. If you are printing this project, click OK. Otherwise, click Cancel.

23. Click **Save, Close** the report, and then **Exit** Access. Submit as directed.

Done! You have completed the Skill Check

Assess Your Skills 1

To complete this database, you will need the following files:

- a04_Camps
- a04_Camps_Logo

You will save your file as:

- Lastname_Firstname_a04_Camps

1. **Start** Access, and then open the student data file **a04_Camps**. Save the database in your **Access Chapter 4** folder with the name Lastname_Firstname_a04_Camps

2. Use the **Blank Report** button to add these fields from the **Directors** table: **Director ID**, **First Name**, and **Last Name**. From the **Camps** table, add **Camp Name** and then **Start Date**.

3. Apply the **Equity** theme, and then apply the **Angles** theme font.

4. Add a logo using the file **a04_Camps_Logo**, and then add a title with the text Camp Directors

5. Group the report by **Director ID**, and then sort by **Start Date**.

6. Move the **First Name** text box up one row in the layout, and then move the **Last Name** text box up one row. Move the **Camp Name** text box to the row's first cell and the **Start Date** text box to the row's second cell.

7. Use the **Ribbon** to select **GroupHeader0**, and then remove the header's alternate row color.

8. Delete the two empty columns on the right of the report. Select the Director ID label, and then change its Top Padding property to 0.25" **Close** the property sheet, and then compare your screen with **Figure 1**.

9. **Save** the report as Camp Directors and then **Close** the report.

10. Use the **Report Wizard** button to add these fields from the **Camps** table: **Camp Name** and

Start Date. From the **Campers** table, add the **First Name**, **Last Name**, and **Parent/Guardian** fields. Accept all other wizard defaults.

11. In Design view, delete the report title, and then set the height of the **Report Header** to zero.

12. In the **Page Header**, delete the **First Name**, **Last Name**, and **Parent/Guardian** labels.

13. Increase the width of the **Start Date** text box so that its right edge is on the **3 inch** vertical grid line.

14. In the **Detail** section, select the three text boxes, and then move the **First Name** text box approximately six grid dots from the left edge of the report.

15. Select the **Camp ID Header**, remove the alternate row color, and then change its property to start a new page before each section.

16. Increase the height of the **Page Footer** by approximately half an inch. Below the =**Now()** calculated control, add a label with the file name as its text.

17. Filter the report to display only the campers registered in the **Yurok** camp. Click **Save**, and then compare your screen with **Figure 2**.

18. **Close** the report. If you are printing this project, print the two reports.

19. Click **Save**, and then **Exit** Access. Submit as directed by your instructor.

Done! You have completed Assess Your Skills 1

Figure 1

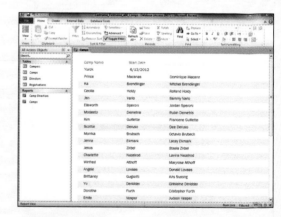

Figure 2

Assess Your Skills 2

To complete this database, you will need the following files:

- a04_Reviews
- a04_Reviews_Logo

You will save your file as:

- Lastname_Firstname_a04_Reviews

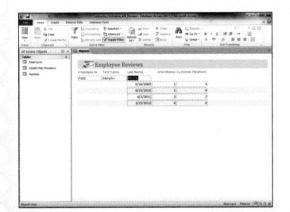

Figure 1

Figure 2

1. **Start** Access, and then open the student data file **a04_Reviews**. Save the database in your **Access Chapter 4** folder with the name Lastname_Firstname_a04_Reviews

2. Use the **Blank Report** button to add these fields from the **Employees** table: **Employee ID**, **First Name**, and **Last Name**. From the **Reviews** table, add **Review Date**, **Attendance**, and **Customer Relations**.

3. Apply the **Apex** theme, and then apply the **Office** theme font.

4. Add a logo using the file **a04_Reviews_Logo**, and then add a title with the text Employee Reviews

5. Group the report by **Employee ID**, and then sort by **Review Date**.

6. Move the **First Name** text box up one row in the layout, and then move the **Last Name** text box up one row. Move the **Review Date** text box one cell to the left, and then delete the empty column.

7. Filter the report so that only the records for *Marylin Mintor* display. Compare your screen with **Figure 1**.

8. **Save** the report as Employee Reviews If you are printing this project, print the report. **Close** the report.

9. Use the **Report Wizard** button to add the **Provider Name** field from the **Health Plan Providers** table: From the **Employees** table,

add the **First Name**, **Last Name**, and **Department** fields. Accept all other wizard defaults.

10. In the **Page Header**, delete all four labels, and then decrease the section height to zero.

11. In the **Detail** section, select the three text boxes, and then move the **First Name** text box approximately six grid dots from the left edge of the report.

12. Increase the width of the **Department** text box so that the right border is on the **6 inch** vertical grid line.

13. For the **Provider ID Header**, remove the alternate row color. Select the **Provider Name** text box, apply **Bold**, and then set the **Font Size** to 14.

14. Increase the height of the **Page Footer** by approximately half an inch. Below the =**Now()** calculated control, add a label with the file name as its text.

15. Filter the report to show only the employees enrolled in *Southwest Health*.

16. **Save**, and then switch to Print Preview, and then compare your screen with **Figure 2**. If you are printing this project, print the report.

17. **Close** the report. Click **Save**, and then **Exit** Access. Submit as directed by your instructor.

Done! You have completed Assess Your Skills 2

Assess Your Skills Visually

To complete this database, you will need the following files:

- a04_Councils
- a04_Councils_Logo

You will save your database as:

- Lastname_Firstname_a04_Councils

Open the database **a04_Councils**, and then, using your own name, save the database in your **Access Chapter 4** folder as Lastname_Firstname_a04_Councils

Use the Blank Report tool to create the report shown in **Figure 1**. Include three fields: **Council Name**, **First Name**, and **Last Name**, and group by **Council Name**. Arrange the fields as shown. The **Page Header** has been removed. The three cells in the **Council Name** row have been merged and the top padding has been set to 0.25" The **Council Name** has been formatted bold and size 14. The logo uses the file **a04_Councils_Logo** and the title has the text City Councils The report has the **Clarity** theme and the **Apex** theme font.

Save the report as City Council List Print the report or submit the database file as directed by your instructor.

Done! You have completed Assess Your Skills Visually

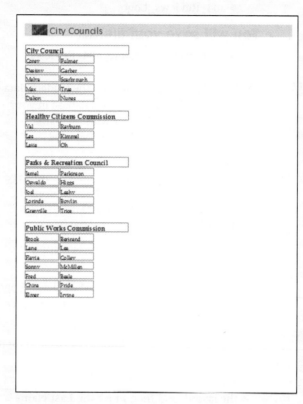

Figure 1

Skills in Context

To complete this database, you will need the following file:

- a04_Participants

You will save your database as:

- Lastname_Firstname_a04_Participants

Open **a04_Participants** and save the database in your **Access Chapter 4** folder as Lastname_Firstname_a04_Participants Create a query that can be used to create a mailing labels report. In the query, include the necessary name and address fields from the **Participants** table, and then filter the query so that only participants from the Central neighborhood display. Use the **Label Wizard** to create a label report. Arrange the fields in the standard mailing address format. Include space and punctuation where appropriate. Do not include the Neighborhood field.

Print the report or submit the database file as directed by your instructor.

Done! You have completed Skills in Context

Skills and You

To complete this database, you will need the following file:

- a04_Contacts

You will save your database as:

- Lastname_Firstname_a04_Contacts

Open **Lastname_Firstname_a03_Contacts** that you created in a previous chapter. If you do not have this database, open **a04_Contacts**, and then add at least 10 personal contacts to the **Contacts** table. Save the database as Lastname_Fistname_a04_Contacts Create a report for the **Contacts** table. Format and arrange the report as appropriate. Print the report or submit the database file as directed by your instructor.

Done! You have completed Skills and You

CHAPTER 1

Getting Started with PowerPoint 2010

▶ Microsoft Office PowerPoint is a presentation graphics software program that you can use to present information effectively to your audience.

▶ You can use PowerPoint to create electronic slide presentations and handouts.

Your starting screen will look similar to this:

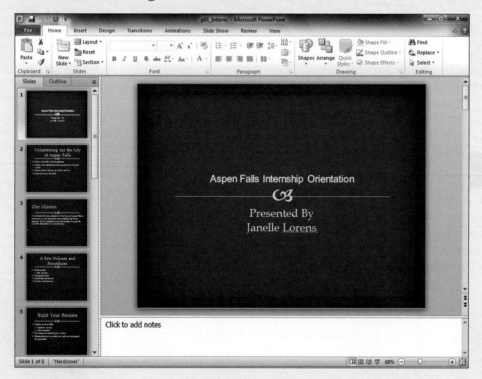

SKILLS

Skills 1-10 Training

At the end of this chapter, you will be able to:

Skill 1   Open, View, and Save Presentations

Skill 2   Edit and Replace Text in Normal View

Skill 3   Format Slide Text

Skill 4   Check Spelling and Use the Thesaurus

Skill 5   Insert Slides and Modify Slide Layouts

Skill 6   Insert and Format Pictures

Skill 7   Organize Slides Using Slide Sorter View

Skill 8   Apply Slide Transitions and View Slide Shows

Skill 9   Insert Headers and Footers and Print Presentation Handouts

Skill 10   Add Notes Pages and Print Notes

MORE SKILLS

More Skills 11   Type Text in the Outline Tab

More Skills 12   Use Keyboard Shortcuts

More Skills 13   Move and Delete Slides in Normal View

More Skills 14   Design Presentations for Audience and Location

Outcome

Using the skills listed to the left will enable you
to create a presentation like this:

You will save this presentation as:

Lastname_Firstname_p01_Interns

In this chapter, you will create documents for the Aspen Falls City Hall, which provides essential services for the citizens and visitors of Aspen Falls, California.

Introduction

- ► There are four views in PowerPoint—Normal, Slide Sorter, Slide Show, and Reading.

- ► Normal view is used to edit and format your presentation.

- ► In Slide Sorter view, you can organize your presentation by moving and deleting slides.

- ► In Slide Show view, your presentation displays as an electronic slide show.

- ► Reading view is optimized for viewing presentations on a computer screen— for example, during an online conference.

Time to complete all
10 skills – 60 minutes

Student data files needed
for this chapter:

- p01_Interns
- p01_Interns_Logo
- p01_Interns_City_Hall

Find your student data files here:

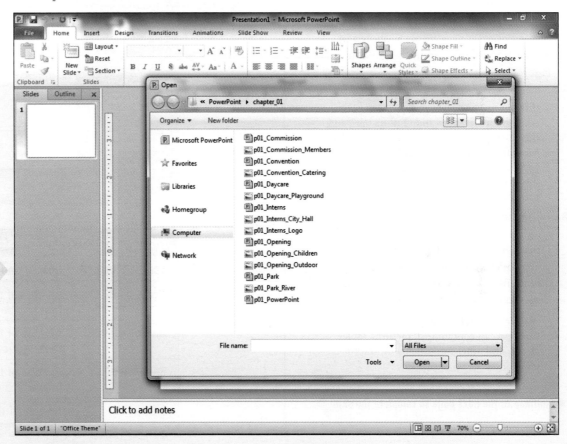

▶ When you start PowerPoint 2010, a new blank presentation displays.

▶ Save your changes frequently so that you do not lose any of your editing or formatting changes.

1. Click the **Start** button ⊙. From the **Start** menu, locate, and then start **Microsoft PowerPoint 2010**.

2. Take a moment to identify the main parts of the PowerPoint window as shown in **Figure 1** and described in the table in **Figure 2**.

   The PowerPoint window is divided into three parts—the Slide pane, the left pane containing the Slides and Outline tabs, and the Notes pane. The status bar displays the View and Zoom buttons and indicates the presentation design, the displayed slide number, and the number of slides in the presentation.

3. In the upper left corner of the PowerPoint window, click the **File tab**, and then click **Open**. In the **Open** dialog box, navigate to your student data files. Select **p01_Interns** and then click the **Open** button—or press Enter—to display **Slide 1** in the Slide pane.

   A *slide* is an individual page in a presentation and can contain text, pictures, tables, charts, and other multimedia or graphic objects.

▪ **Continue to the next page to complete the skill**

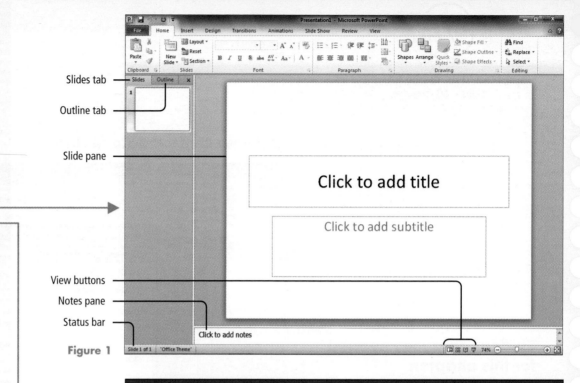

Figure 1

Microsoft PowerPoint Screen Elements

Screen Element	Description
Notes pane	An area of the Normal View window used to type notes that can be printed below a picture of each slide.
Outline tab	An area of the Normal View window that displays the presentation outline.
Slide pane	An area of the Normal View window that displays a large image of the active slide.
Slides tab	An area of the Normal View window that displays all of the slides in the presentation in the form of miniature images.
Status bar	A horizontal bar at the bottom of the presentation window that displays the current slide number, number of slides in a presentation, View buttons, Theme, and Zoom slider. The status bar can be customized to include other information.
View buttons	Buttons that change the presentation window view.

Figure 2

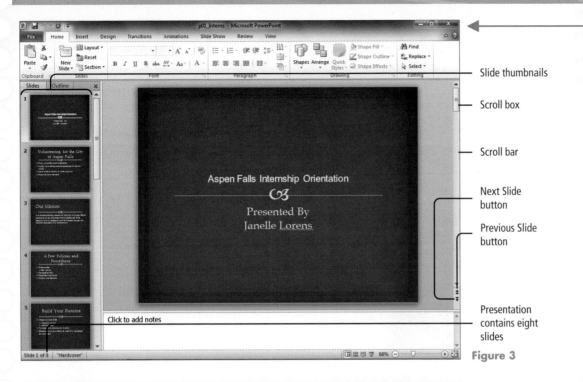

Slide thumbnails

Scroll box

Scroll bar

Next Slide button

Previous Slide button

Presentation contains eight slides

Figure 3

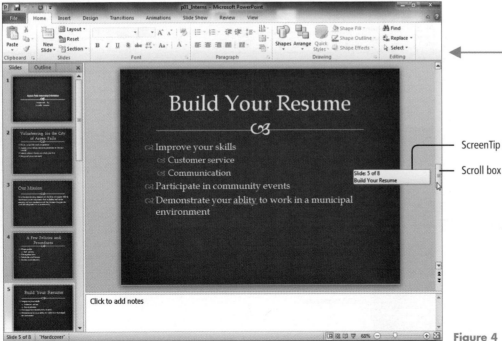

ScreenTip

Scroll box

Figure 4

4. Compare your screen with **Figure 3**.

At the left side of the PowerPoint window, on the Slides tab, the slide *thumbnails*—miniature images of presentation slides—and slide numbers display. A scroll bar to the right of the slide thumbnails is used to view additional slides. You can click a slide thumbnail to display it in the Slide pane. At the right side of the window, another scroll bar displays a scroll box and the Next Slide and Previous Slide buttons used to navigate in your presentation.

5. At the left of the PowerPoint window, on the **Slides tab**, click **Slide 2** to display it in the Slide pane. Click the slide thumbnails for **Slides 3** through **5** to view each slide. As you view each slide, notice that the vertical scroll bar at the right side of the PowerPoint window moves, indicating the relative location in the presentation of the slide that you are viewing.

6. At the right side of the PowerPoint window, point to the vertical scroll box, and then hold down the mouse button. A ScreenTip displays the slide number and slide title, as shown in **Figure 4**. Drag down to display **Slide 8**.

7. Drag the scroll box up to display **Slide 1**.

8. On the **File tab**, click **Save As**. Navigate to the location where you are saving your files, create a folder named PowerPoint Chapter 1 and then using your own name, save the presentation as Lastname_ Firstname_p01_Interns

■ **You have completed Skill 1 of 10**

► In **Normal view**, the PowerPoint window is divided into three areas—the Slide pane, the left pane containing the Slides and Outline tabs, and the Notes pane.

► Individual lines of bulleted text on a slide are referred to as **bullet points**.

► Bullet points are organized in list levels similar to an outline. A **list level** is identified by the indentation, size of text, and bullet assigned to that level.

► You can use the Replace command to change multiple occurrences of the same text in a presentation.

1. Display **Slide 3**, which contains two **placeholders**—boxes with dotted borders that are part of most slide layouts and that hold text or objects such as charts, tables, and pictures.

2. Near the end of the paragraph, click to the left of the letter *c* in the word *community* so that the insertion point displays before the word *community*, as shown in **Figure 1**.

3. Type family-oriented and then press Spacebar to insert the text to the left of the word *community*.

4. Display **Slide 2**, click at the end of the last bullet point—*Expand your network*—and then press Enter.

5. Press Tab to create a second-level, indented bullet point. Type Professional contacts and then press Enter. Type Mentors and friends and then compare your slide with **Figure 2**.

> Pressing Enter at the end of a bullet point results in a new bullet point at the same list level.

■ **Continue to the next page to complete the skill**

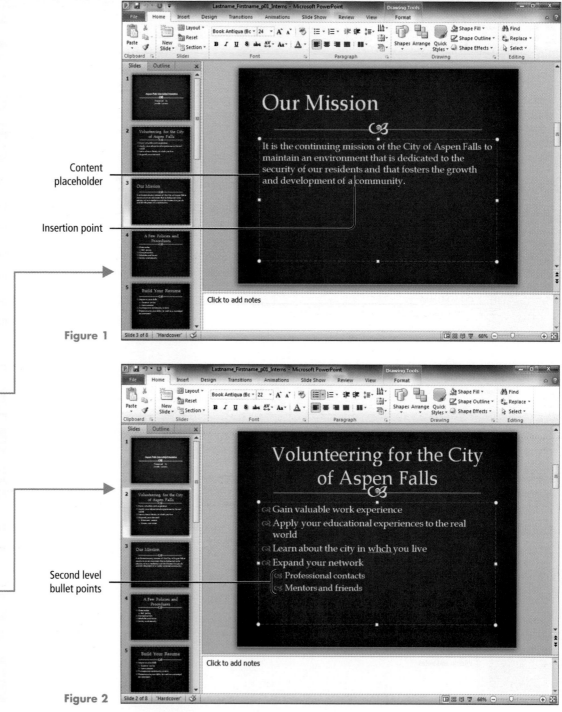

Content placeholder

Insertion point

Figure 1

Second level bullet points

Figure 2

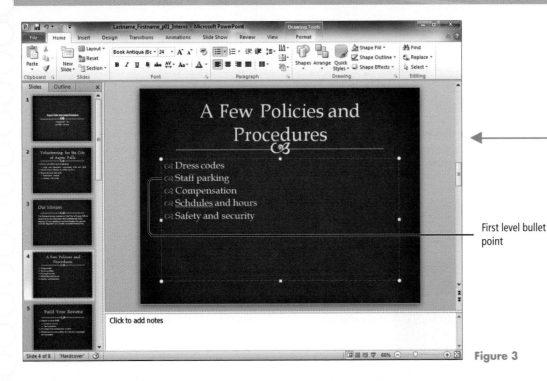

First level bullet point

Figure 3

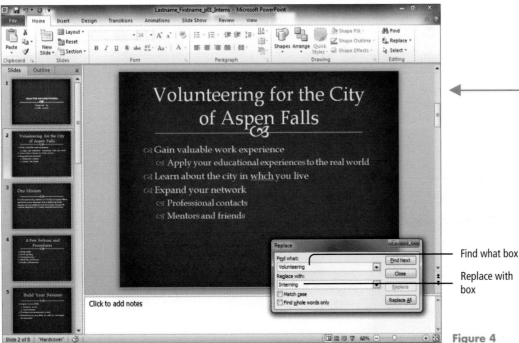

Find what box

Replace with box

Figure 4

6. Click anywhere in the second bullet point—*Apply your educational experiences to the real world.* On the **Home tab**, in the **Paragraph group**, click the **Increase List Level** button ▤.

   The selection is formatted as a second-level bullet point, indicated by the indent, smaller font size, and new bullet symbol.

7. Display **Slide 4**. Click anywhere in the second bullet point—*Staff parking*. On the **Home tab**, in the **Paragraph group**, click the **Decrease List Level** button ▤. Compare your screen with **Figure 3**.

   A first-level bullet point is applied to *Staff parking* at the same level as the other bullet points on this slide, as indicated by the bullet symbol and the increased font size.

8. Display **Slide 2** and notice the word *Volunteering* in the title placeholder.

   There is more than one instance in the presentation in which the word *Volunteering* is used instead of the word *Interning*.

9. On the **Home tab**, in the **Editing group**, click the **Replace** button. In the **Find what** box, type Volunteering and then click in the **Replace with** box. Type Interning and then compare your screen with **Figure 4**.

10. In the **Replace** dialog box, click the **Replace All** button to display a message box indicating that two replacements were made. Click **OK** to close the message box, and then in the **Replace** dialog box click the **Close** button. **Save** ▤ the presentation.

■ **You have completed Skill 2 of 10**

► A *font*, which is measured in *points*, is a set of characters with the same design and shape.

► Font styles and effects emphasize text and include bold, italic, underline, shadow, small caps, and outline.

► The horizontal placement of text within a placeholder is referred to as *text alignment*. Text can be aligned left, centered, aligned right, or justified.

1. Display **Slide 1** and drag to select the title text—*Aspen Falls Internship Orientation*

2. On the Mini toolbar, click the **Font Size** arrow [44 ·], and then click **32**.

3. With the title text still selected, on the **Home tab**, in the **Font group**, click the **Font** arrow [Calibri (Headings) ·]. Scroll the **Font** gallery, and then point to **Consolas** to display the Live Preview of the selected text in the font to which you are pointing, as shown in **Figure 1**.

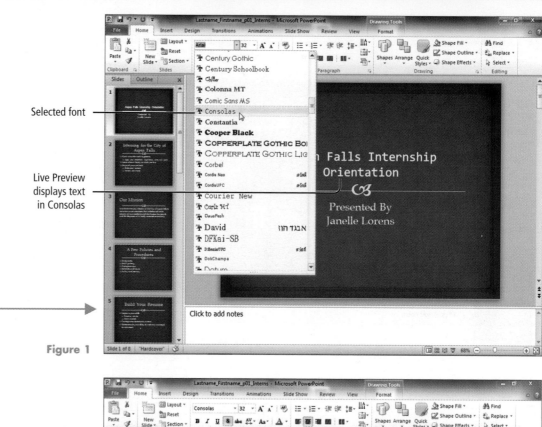

Selected font

Live Preview displays text in Consolas

Figure 1

4. In the **Font** gallery, click **Consolas**.

5. With the title text still selected, in the **Font group**, click the **Dialog Box Launcher** [⬚] to display the Font dialog box, as shown in **Figure 2**.

The Font dialog box provides additional font style and effect formatting options.

6. Under **Effects**, select **Small Caps**, and then click **OK**.

With small caps, lowercase characters are capitalized but are smaller than characters that were typed as capital letters.

■ **Continue to the next page to complete the skill**

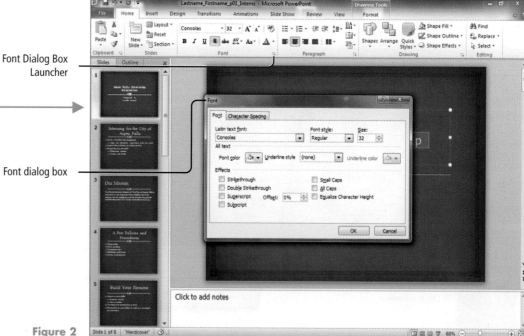

Font Dialog Box Launcher

Font dialog box

Figure 2

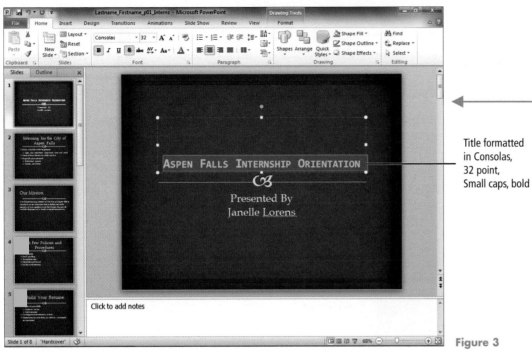

Title formatted
in Consolas,
32 point,
Small caps, bold

Figure 3

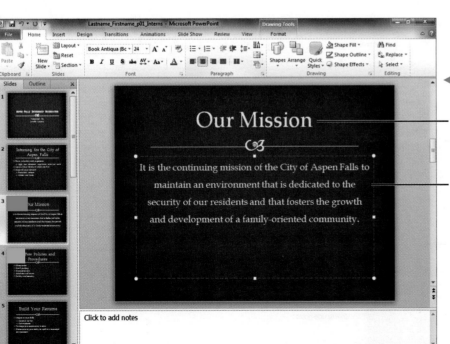

Title center
aligned

Paragraph
centered with
line spacing
of 1.5

Figure 4

7. With the title still selected, in the **Font group**, click the **Bold** button ⓑ, and then click the **Italic** button ⓘ.

8. If necessary, select the title. On the **Home tab**, in the **Font group**, click the **Italic** button ⓘ to turn off the italic formatting. Compare your slide with **Figure 3**.

> You can use the Mini toolbar, the Ribbon, or the Font dialog box to apply font styles and effects.

9. Display **Slide 3** and click the title text to select the title placeholder.

10. On the **Home tab**, in the **Paragraph group**, click the **Center** button ☰ to center align the title text.

11. Click anywhere in the content placeholder that contains the paragraph. In the **Paragraph group**, click the **Center** button ☰ to center align the paragraph within the content placeholder.

12. In the **Paragraph group**, click the **Line Spacing** button ☰. In the displayed list, click **1.5** to increase the space between lines in the paragraph. Compare your slide with **Figure 4**.

13. **Save** ⓗ the presentation.

■ **You have completed Skill 3 of 10**

▶ PowerPoint compares slide text with the words in the Office 2010 main dictionary. Words that are not in the main dictionary are marked with a red wavy underline.

▶ You can correct spelling errors using the shortcut menu or the spell check feature.

▶ The *thesaurus* is a research tool that provides a list of *synonyms*—words with the same meaning—for text that you select.

1. Display **Slide 5**. Notice that the word *ablity* is flagged with a red wavy underline, indicating that it is misspelled.

2. Point to *ablity* and click the right mouse button to display the shortcut menu with suggested solutions for correcting the misspelled word, as shown in **Figure 1**.

3. From the shortcut menu, click **ability** to correct the spelling of the word.

4. Display **Slide 1**. In the subtitle, notice that the name *Lorens* is flagged as misspelled, although it is a proper name and is spelled correctly.

    Proper names are sometimes flagged as misspelled even though they are correctly spelled.

5. Right-click **Lorens**, and from the shortcut menu, click **Ignore All**. Compare your slide with **Figure 2**.

    The Ignore All option instructs PowerPoint to ignore all occurrences of a word that is not in the main dictionary but that is spelled correctly. Thus, the red wavy underline is removed.

■ **Continue to the next page to complete the skill**

Misspelled word

Suggested spelling correction

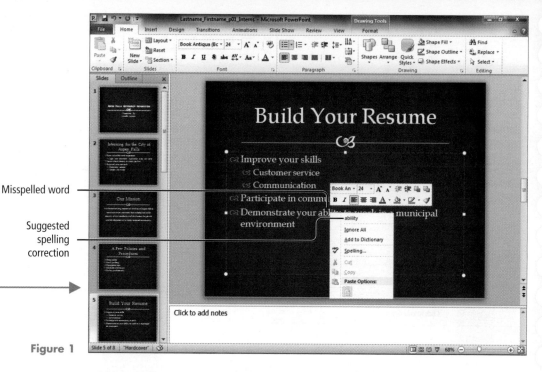

Figure 1

Lorens no longer flagged

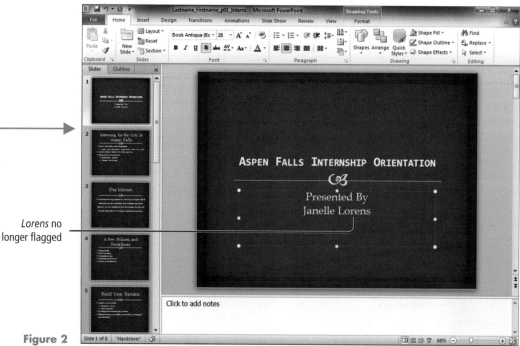

Figure 2

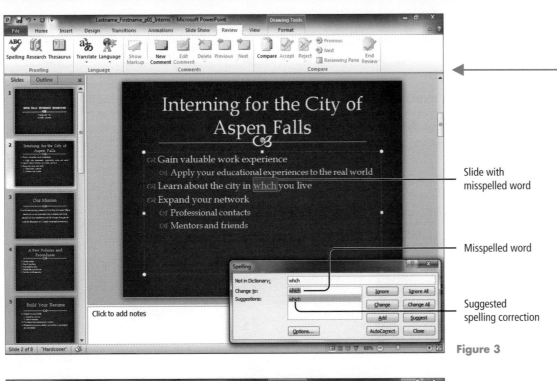

Slide with
misspelled word

Misspelled word

Suggested
spelling correction

Figure 3

6. On the **Review tab**, in the **Proofing group,** click the **Spelling** button to display the Spelling dialog box as shown in **Figure 3**.

The Spelling dialog box checks the spelling of an entire presentation. Here, the first spelling error—*whch*—is highlighted on Slide 2 and is also displayed in the Spelling dialog box. The Spelling dialog box provides options for correcting spelling, ignoring spelling, and adding words to the custom dictionary.

7. Under **Suggestions**, be sure that **which** is selected, and then click the **Change** button.

8. Continue using the Spelling dialog box in this manner to correct the spelling of two more words. When a message box indicates that the spell check is complete, click **OK**.

9. Scroll the presentation as necessary, and then display **Slide 3**. In the third line of the paragraph, point to the word *security*, and then click the right mouse button to display the shortcut menu.

10. Near the bottom of the shortcut menu, point to **Synonyms** to display the thesaurus list of suggested words to replace *security*. Click **safety**, as shown in **Figure 4**, to replace *security* with *safety*.

11. Save 💾 the presentation.

■ **You have completed Skill 4 of 10**

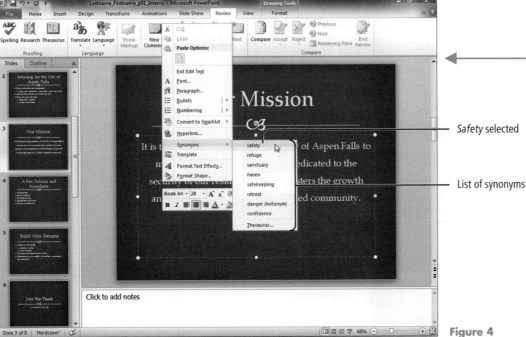

Safety selected

List of synonyms

Figure 4

▶ The arrangement of the text and graphic elements or placeholders on a slide is referred to as its *layout*.

▶ PowerPoint includes several predefined layouts used to arrange slide elements.

▶ To insert a new slide, display the slide that will come before the slide that you want to insert.

1. With **Slide 3** displayed, on the **Home tab**, in the **Slides group**, click the **New Slide** button to add a new slide with the same layout as the previous slide. If several slide layouts display, click Title and Content.

2. Click in the title placeholder, and then type Your Role as a City Intern

3. Select the title text, and then change the **Font Size** 〔" ·〕 to **48**.

4. Click in the content placeholder. Type Job descriptions and then press 〔Enter〕. Type Performance standards and then press 〔Enter〕. Type Evaluations and then press 〔Enter〕. Type Full-time opportunities and then compare your slide with **Figure 1**.

5. With **Slide 4** still active, on the **Home tab**, in the **Slides group**, click the **Layout** button to display the *Layout gallery*—a visual representation of several content layouts that you can apply to a slide.

6. Click **Two Content** as shown in **Figure 2**.

   The slide layout is changed to one that includes a title and two content placeholders. The existing text is arranged in the placeholder on the left side of the slide. For now, the placeholder on the right will remain blank.

■ **Continue to the next page to complete the skill** ➤

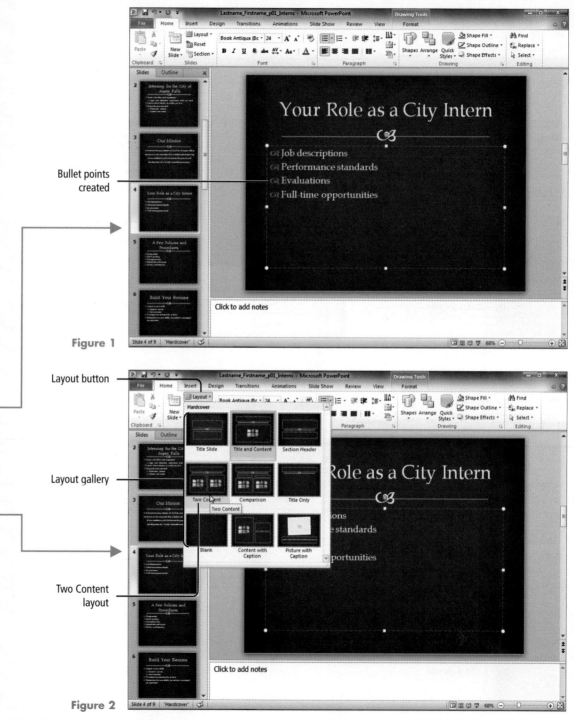

Figure 1

Figure 2

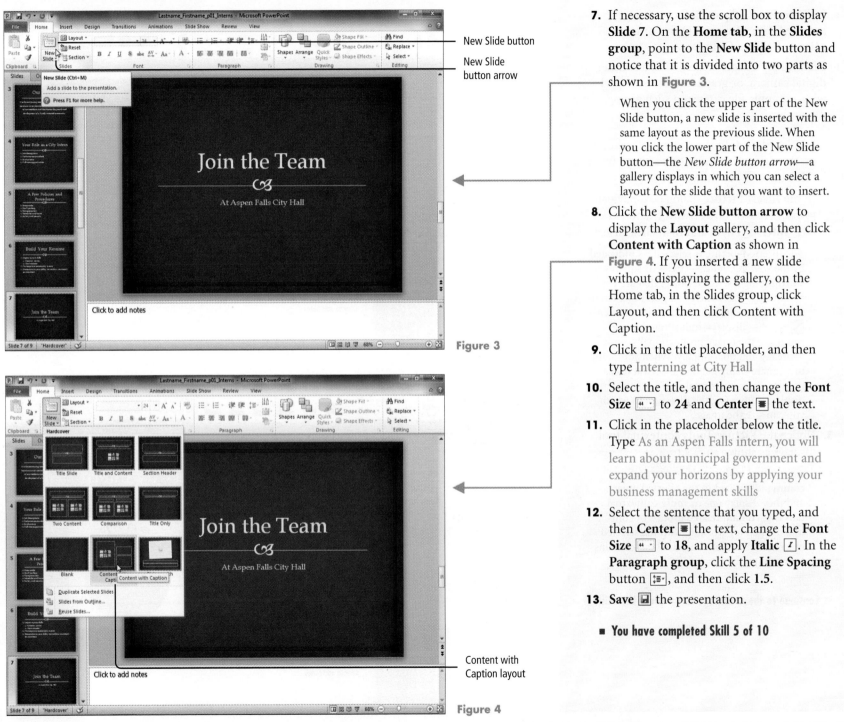

New Slide button

New Slide button arrow

Figure 3

Content with Caption layout

Figure 4

7. If necessary, use the scroll box to display **Slide 7**. On the **Home tab**, in the **Slides group**, point to the **New Slide** button and notice that it is divided into two parts as shown in **Figure 3**.

   When you click the upper part of the New Slide button, a new slide is inserted with the same layout as the previous slide. When you click the lower part of the New Slide button—the *New Slide button arrow*—a gallery displays in which you can select a layout for the slide that you want to insert.

8. Click the **New Slide button arrow** to display the **Layout** gallery, and then click **Content with Caption** as shown in **Figure 4**. If you inserted a new slide without displaying the gallery, on the Home tab, in the Slides group, click Layout, and then click Content with Caption.

9. Click in the title placeholder, and then type Interning at City Hall

10. Select the title, and then change the **Font Size** ⁴⁴ ⁻ to **24** and **Center** ≣ the text.

11. Click in the placeholder below the title. Type As an Aspen Falls intern, you will learn about municipal government and expand your horizons by applying your business management skills

12. Select the sentence that you typed, and then **Center** ≣ the text, change the **Font Size** ⁴⁴ ⁻ to **18**, and apply **Italic** *I*. In the **Paragraph group**, click the **Line Spacing** button ≣⁻, and then click **1.5**.

13. **Save** 🖫 the presentation.

- **You have completed Skill 5 of 10**

▶ In PowerPoint, *clip art* refers to images included with Microsoft Office or from Microsoft Office Online.

▶ *Pictures* are images created with a scanner, digital camera, or graphics software saved with a graphic file extension such as .jpg, .tif, or .bmp.

1. Display **Slide 4**. In the content placeholder on the right, click the **Insert Picture from File** button 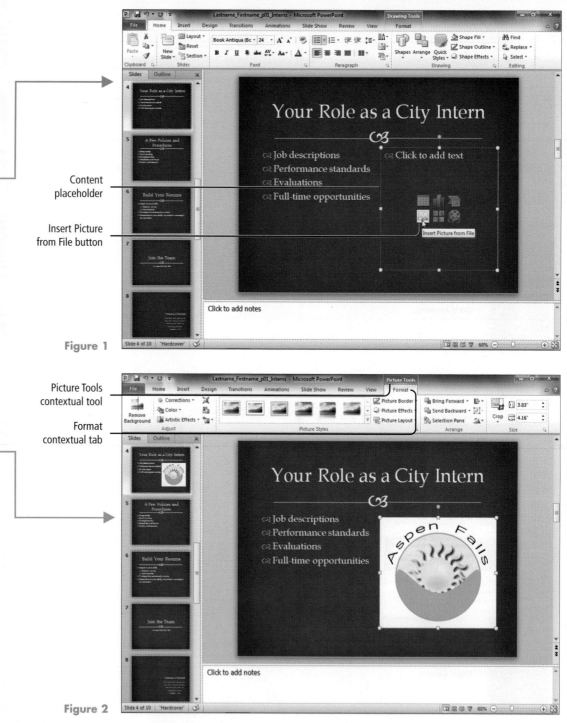 as shown in **Figure 1**.

2. In the **Insert Picture** dialog box, navigate to your student files for this chapter, click **p01_Interns_Logo**, and then click **Insert**.

   The inserted picture is selected, as indicated by the *sizing handles*—circles or squares surrounding a selected object that are used to adjust its size. When you point to a circular sizing handle, a diagonal resize pointer— or —displays, indicating that you can resize the image proportionally, both vertically and horizontally. When you point to a square sizing handle, a vertical resize pointer or horizontal resize pointer displays, indicating the direction in which you can size the image.

3. Notice the **Picture Tools** contextual tool displays as shown in **Figure 2**.

   Contextual tools enable you to perform commands related to the selected object, and they display one or more contextual tabs that contain related groups of commands used for working with the selected object. The Format contextual tab contains four groups.

■ **Continue to the next page to complete the skill**

Content placeholder

Insert Picture from File button

Figure 1

Picture Tools contextual tool

Format contextual tab

Figure 2

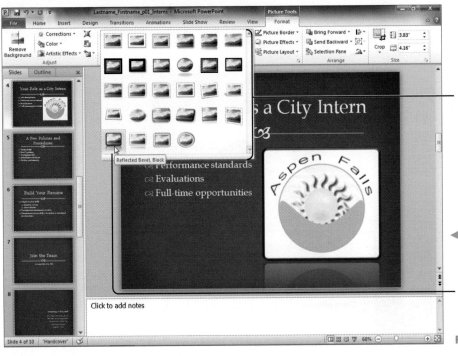

Picture Styles gallery

Reflected Bevel, Black picture style selected

Figure 3

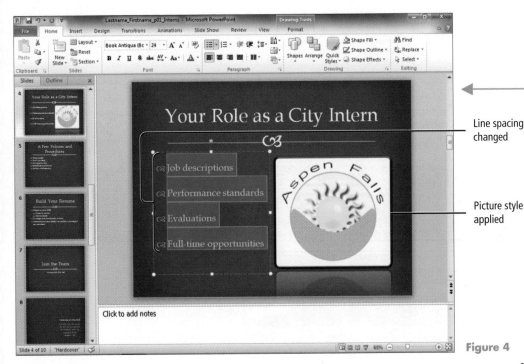

Line spacing changed

Picture style applied

Figure 4

4. On the **Format tab**, in the **Picture Styles group**, click the **More** button to display the **Picture Styles** gallery.

A *picture style* is a prebuilt set of formatting borders, effects, and layouts applied to a picture.

5. In the **Picture Styles** gallery, move your pointer over several of the picture styles and use Live Preview to see the effect of the style on your picture and to display the ScreenTip identifying the style.

6. Using the ScreenTips to verify your selection, point to the picture style—**Reflected Bevel, Black**—as shown in Figure 3.

7. Click **Reflected Bevel, Black** to apply the style to the picture.

8. In the left placeholder, select the four bullet points. On the **Home tab**, in the **Paragraph group**, click the **Line Spacing** button , and then click **2.0**. Compare your slide with Figure 4.

The additional line spacing balances the text with the picture.

9. Display **Slide 8**. In the content placeholder on the left, click the **Insert Picture from File** button . In the **Insert Picture** dialog box, navigate to your student files for this chapter, click **p01_Interns_City_Hall**, and then click **Insert**.

10. On the **Format tab**, in the **Picture Styles group**, click the third style—**Metal Frame**.

11. Save the presentation.

■ **You have completed Skill 6 of 10**

▶ *Slide Sorter view* displays all of the slides in your presentation as thumbnails.

▶ Slide Sorter view is used to rearrange and delete slides, to apply formatting to multiple slides, and to get an overall impression of your presentation.

▶ In Slide Sorter view, you can select multiple slides by holding down Shift or Ctrl.

1. In the lower right corner of the PowerPoint window, locate the **View** buttons as shown in **Figure 1**, and then click the **Slide Sorter** button to display all of the slide thumbnails.

2. If necessary, scroll the presentation so that Slides 7 through 10 are visible. Click **Slide 7** and notice that a thick outline surrounds the slide, indicating that it is selected. Hold down Shift and click **Slide 10** so that Slides 7 through 10 are selected.

   Using Shift enables you to select a group of sequential slides.

3. With the four slides selected, hold down Ctrl and then click **Slides 7** and **8**. Notice that only Slides 9 and 10 are selected, as shown in **Figure 2**.

   Using Ctrl enables you to select or deselect individual slides.

■ **Continue to the next page to complete the skill** ▶

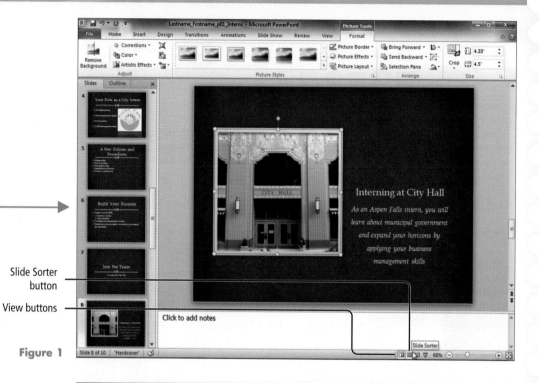

Slide Sorter button

View buttons

Figure 1

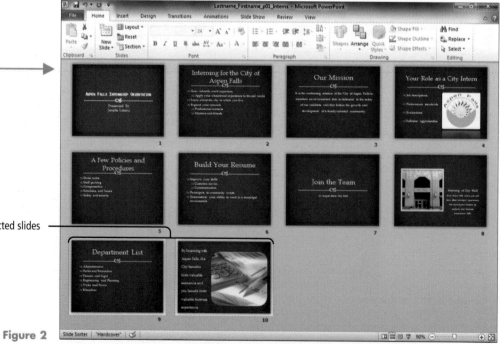

Selected slides

Figure 2

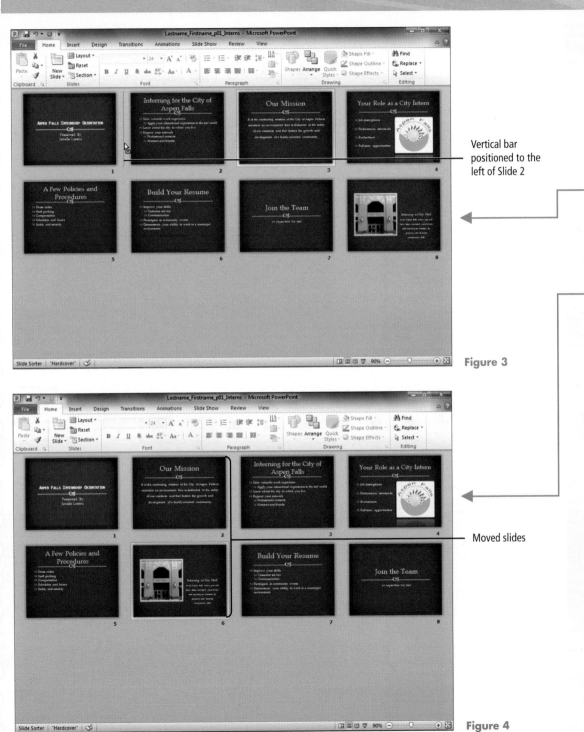

Vertical bar positioned to the left of Slide 2

Figure 3

Moved slides

Figure 4

4. Press Delete to delete Slides 9 and 10 and notice that your presentation contains eight slides.

5. If necessary, use the scroll bar so that **Slide 3** is visible. Click **Slide 3** to select it.

6. Point to **Slide 3**, hold down the left mouse button, and then drag the slide to the left until the displayed vertical bar is positioned to the left of **Slide 2**, as shown in **Figure 3**. Release the mouse button to move the slide.

7. Point to **Slide 8**, and then drag so that the vertical bar is displayed to the left of **Slide 6**. Release the mouse button to move the slide, and then compare your screen with **Figure 4**.

8. Double-click **Slide 1** to return the presentation to Normal view with Slide 1 displayed.

9. Save 🖫 the presentation.

■ **You have completed Skill 7 of 10**

► When a presentation is viewed as an electronic slide show, the entire slide fills the computer screen, and when your computer is connected to a projection system, an audience can view your presentation on a large screen.

► *Slide transitions* are motion effects that occur in Slide Show view when you move from one slide to the next during a presentation.

► You can choose from a variety of transitions, and you can control the speed and method with which the slides advance during a presentation.

---

1. With **Slide 1** displayed, click the **Transitions tab**. In the **Transition to This Slide group**, click the **More** button ⌐ to display the **Transitions** gallery as shown in **Figure 1**.

   The slide transitions are organized in three groups—Subtle, Exciting, and Dynamic Content.

2. Click several of the transitions to view the transition effects, using the **More** button ⌐ as necessary to display the gallery.

3. In the **Transition to This Slide group**, click the **More** button ⌐, and then under **Exciting**, click **Zoom**.

4. In the **Transition to This Slide group**, click the **Effect Options** button, and then compare your screen with **Figure 2**.

   The Effect Options menu lists the directions from which a slide transition displays.

5. Click **Out** to change the direction from which the slide transitions.

■ **Continue to the next page to complete the skill**

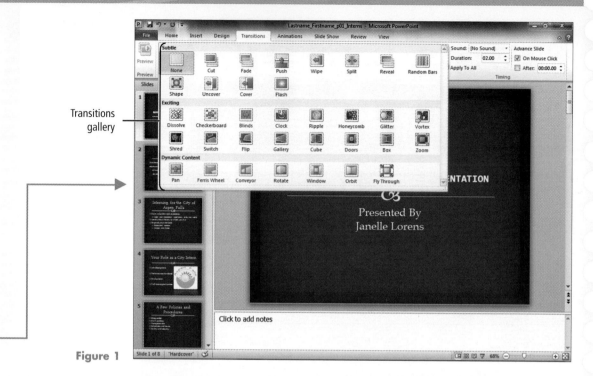

Transitions gallery

Figure 1

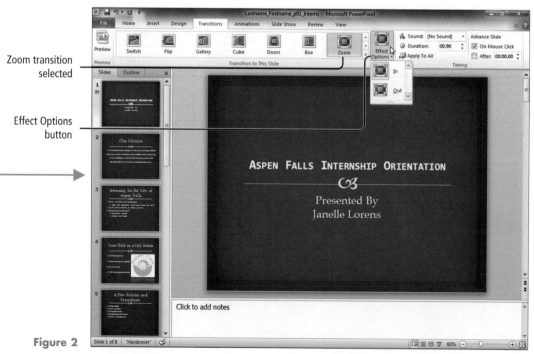

Zoom transition selected

Effect Options button

Figure 2

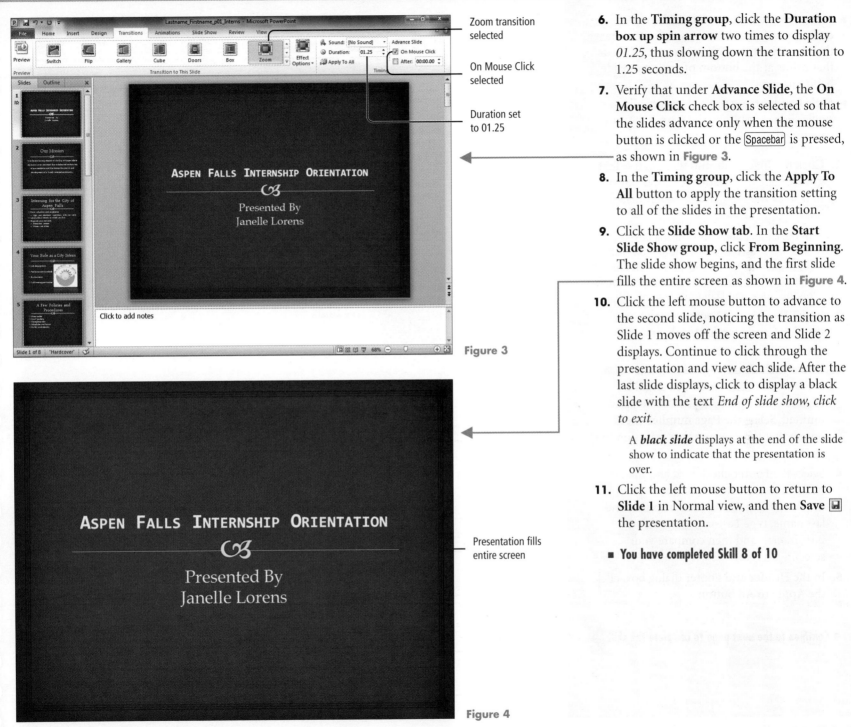

Zoom transition
selected

On Mouse Click
selected

Duration set
to 01.25

Figure 3

Presentation fills
entire screen

Figure 4

6. In the **Timing group**, click the **Duration box up spin arrow** two times to display *01.25*, thus slowing down the transition to 1.25 seconds.

7. Verify that under **Advance Slide**, the **On Mouse Click** check box is selected so that the slides advance only when the mouse button is clicked or the Spacebar is pressed, as shown in **Figure 3**.

8. In the **Timing group**, click the **Apply To All** button to apply the transition setting to all of the slides in the presentation.

9. Click the **Slide Show tab**. In the **Start Slide Show group**, click **From Beginning**. The slide show begins, and the first slide fills the entire screen as shown in **Figure 4**.

10. Click the left mouse button to advance to the second slide, noticing the transition as Slide 1 moves off the screen and Slide 2 displays. Continue to click through the presentation and view each slide. After the last slide displays, click to display a black slide with the text *End of slide show, click to exit.*

    A **black slide** displays at the end of the slide show to indicate that the presentation is over.

11. Click the left mouse button to return to **Slide 1** in Normal view, and then **Save** 🖫 the presentation.

■ **You have completed Skill 8 of 10**

► A *header* is text that prints at the top of each sheet of slide handouts. A *footer* is text that displays at the bottom of every slide or that prints at the bottom of a sheet of slide handouts.

► *Slide handouts* are printed images of a single slide or multiple slides on a sheet of paper.

1. Click the **Insert tab**, and then, in the **Text group**, click the **Header & Footer** button to display the Header and Footer dialog box.

   In the Header and Footer dialog box, the Slide tab is used to insert a footer on each individual slide. For most projects in this textbook, you will insert headers and footers on the Notes and Handouts tab.

2. In the **Header and Footer** dialog box, click the **Notes and Handouts tab**, and then compare your screen with **Figure 1**.

3. Under **Include on page**, if necessary, *clear* the Date and time check box and the Header check box so that these items are omitted. Select the **Page number** check box so that the page number prints on the slide handouts.

4. Select the **Footer** check box, and then notice that the insertion point displays in the Footer box. Using your own first and last name, type Lastname_Firstname_ p01_Interns and then compare your screen with **Figure 2**.

5. In the **Header and Footer** dialog box, click the **Apply to All** button.

■ **Continue to the next page to complete the skill**

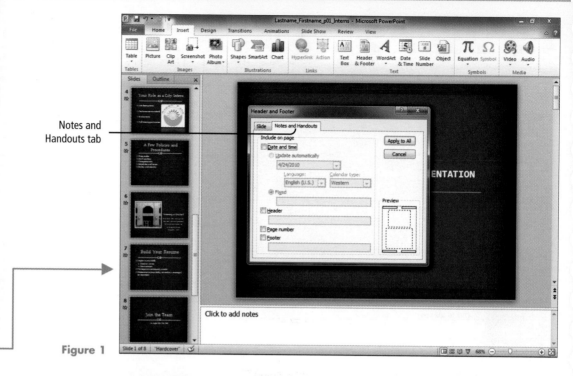

Notes and Handouts tab

Figure 1

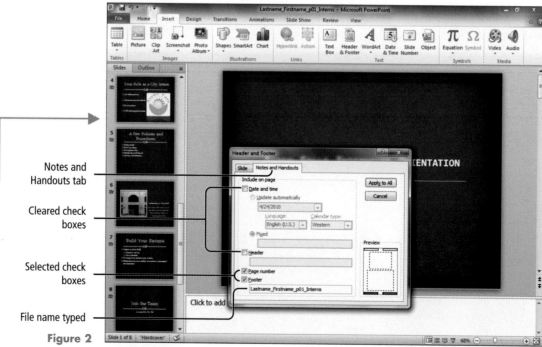

Notes and Handouts tab

Cleared check boxes

Selected check boxes

File name typed

Figure 2

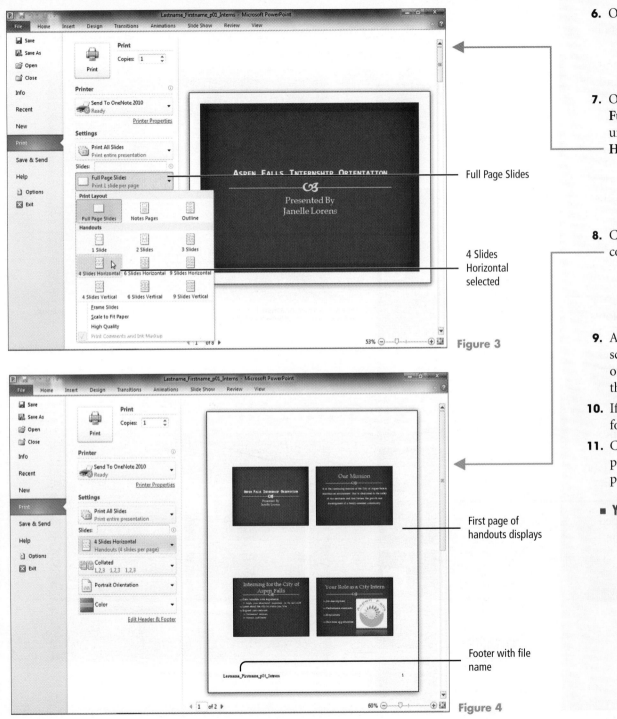

Full Page Slides

4 Slides Horizontal selected

Figure 3

First page of handouts displays

Footer with file name

Figure 4

6. On the **File tab**, click **Print**.

The Print page has tools you can use to select your desired print settings and displays a preview of your presentation exactly as it will print.

7. On the **Print page**, under **Settings**, click **Full Page Slides**, and then in the gallery, under **Handouts**, point to **4 Slides Horizontal** as shown in Figure 3.

Depending upon the type of printer connected to your computer, your slides may display in color, grayscale, or black and white.

8. Click **4 Slides Horizontal**, and then compare your screen with Figure 4.

Your presentation includes eight slides, and the first handout displays the first four slides. The footer displays on the handouts, not on the slides.

9. At the right side of the window, drag the scroll box down to display the second page of slide handouts, containing Slides 5 though 8.

10. If you are instructed to print your work for this project, click the Print button.

11. Click the **Home tab** to return to the presentation, and then **Save** the presentation.

■ **You have completed Skill 9 of 10**

▶ The ***Notes pane*** is an area of the Normal View window used to type notes that can be printed below a picture of each slide.

▶ ***Notes pages*** are printouts that contain the slide image in the top half of the page and speaker notes typed in the Notes pane in the lower half of the page.

▶ During a presentation, refer to your notes to review important points that you want to make while running a slide show.

1. Display **Slide 3**. Below the slide, click in the **Notes** pane and type There are numerous advantages to completing an internship with the Aspen Falls City Hall. Browse the city website to view comments made by interns from previous years. Compare your screen with **Figure 1**.

2. Select the text that you typed in the **Notes** pane, and then change the **Font Size** to **18**.

   In the Notes pane, the size of the text does not change. When you print the notes, the increased font size displays so that you can easily view the printed notes during the presentation.

3. Display **Slide 6**. Click in the **Notes** pane and type Ask your advisor for additional information on opportunities in other city departments. Compare your screen with **Figure 2**.

4. On **Slide 6**, select the text that you typed in the **Notes** pane, and then change the **Font Size** to **18**.

■ **Continue to the next page to complete the skill**

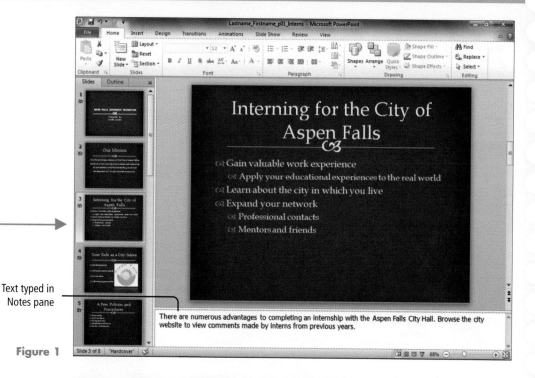

Text typed in Notes pane

Figure 1

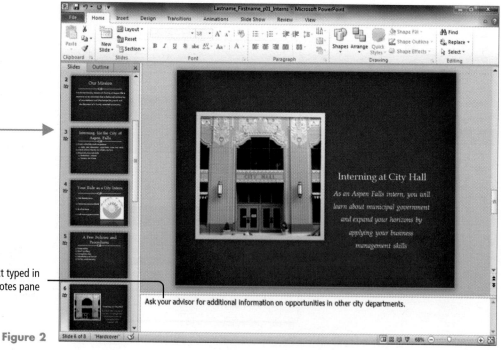

Text typed in Notes pane

Figure 2

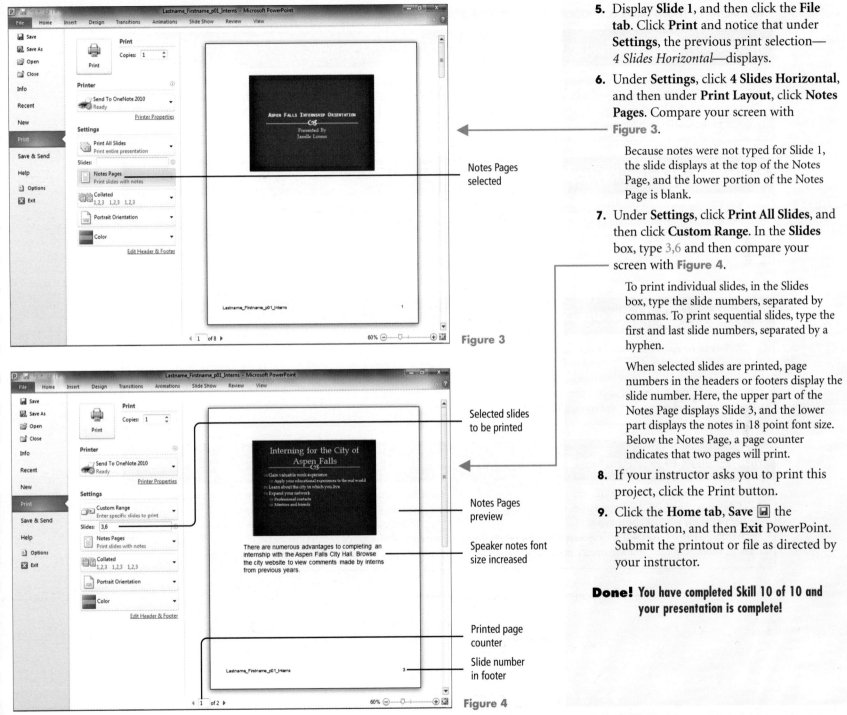

Figure 3

Figure 4

5. Display **Slide 1**, and then click the **File tab**. Click **Print** and notice that under **Settings**, the previous print selection—*4 Slides Horizontal*—displays.

6. Under **Settings**, click **4 Slides Horizontal**, and then under **Print Layout**, click **Notes Pages**. Compare your screen with **Figure 3**.

Because notes were not typed for Slide 1, the slide displays at the top of the Notes Page, and the lower portion of the Notes Page is blank.

7. Under **Settings**, click **Print All Slides**, and then click **Custom Range**. In the **Slides** box, type 3,6 and then compare your screen with **Figure 4**.

To print individual slides, in the Slides box, type the slide numbers, separated by commas. To print sequential slides, type the first and last slide numbers, separated by a hyphen.

When selected slides are printed, page numbers in the headers or footers display the slide number. Here, the upper part of the Notes Page displays Slide 3, and the lower part displays the notes in 18 point font size. Below the Notes Page, a page counter indicates that two pages will print.

8. If your instructor asks you to print this project, click the Print button.

9. Click the **Home tab**, **Save** 🔲 the presentation, and then **Exit** PowerPoint. Submit the printout or file as directed by your instructor.

Done! You have completed Skill 10 of 10 and your presentation is complete!

Notes Pages selected

Selected slides to be printed

Notes Pages preview

Speaker notes font size increased

Printed page counter

Slide number in footer

More Skills

The following More Skills are located at **www.pearsonhighered.com/skills**

More Skills ⑪ Type Text in the Outline Tab

The Outline tab is used when you want to create several slides that are composed primarily of text.

In More Skills 11, you will open a presentation and then type text in the Outline tab for two slides.

To begin, open your web browser, navigate to www.pearsonhighered.com/skills, locate the name of your textbook, and follow the instructions on the website.

More Skills ⑫ Use Keyboard Shortcuts

You can use keyboard shortcuts to apply commands instead of clicking buttons on the Ribbon or shortcut menu.

In More Skills 12, you will open a presentation and use keyboard shortcuts to apply font styles, change text alignment, and save a presentation.

To begin, open your web browser, navigate to www.pearsonhighered.com/skills, locate the name of your textbook, and follow the instructions on the website.

More Skills ⑬ Move and Delete Slides in Normal View

Slides can be moved in Normal view using the Slides tab. You can select multiple slides using Ctrl and Shift, and then delete or drag the selected slides to a new location in the presentation.

In More Skills 13, you will open a presentation, select and delete one slide, and then select and move a slide.

To begin, open your web browser, navigate to www.pearsonhighered.com/skills, locate the name of your textbook, and follow the instructions on the website.

More Skills ⑭ Design Presentations for Audience and Location

When you design a presentation, you should consider the size of the room in which the presentation will be viewed and the number of people who will be present.

In More Skills 14, you will review design tips for presenting in a large room, and then you will open a presentation and review

formatting changes that will improve the readability of the presentation when viewed by a large audience.

To begin, open your web browser, navigate to www.pearsonhighered.com/skills, locate the name of your textbook, and follow the instructions on the website.

Key Terms

Online Help Skills

1. Start 🔵 PowerPoint. In the upper right corner of the PowerPoint window, click the **Help** button 🔘. In the **Help** window, click the **Maximize** 🔳 button.

2. Click in the search box, type sections and then click the **Search** button 🔎. In the search results, click **Organize your slides into sections**.

3. Read the article's introduction, *Overview of sections*, and then below **In this article**, click **Add and name a section**. Compare your screen with **Figure 1**.

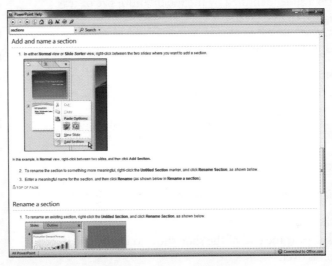

Figure 1

4. Scroll down to read the entire article and then see if you can answer the following: What is the purpose of dividing a presentation into sections?

Matching

Match each term in the second column with its correct definition in the first column. Write the letter of the term on the blank line in front of the correct definition.

____ **1.** The PowerPoint view in which the window is divided into three panes—the Slide pane, the left pane containing the Slides and Outline tabs, and the Notes pane.

____ **2.** Levels of text on a slide identified by the indentation, size of text, and bullet assigned to that level.

____ **3.** An individual line of bulleted text on a slide.

____ **4.** A box with dotted borders that is part of most slide layouts and that holds text or objects such as charts, tables, and pictures.

____ **5.** A feature that changes the horizontal placement of text within a placeholder.

____ **6.** A set of characters with the same design and shape.

____ **7.** A circle or square surrounding a selected object that is used to adjust its size.

____ **8.** A slide that displays at the end of the slide show to indicate that the presentation is over.

____ **9.** An area of the Normal View window used to type notes that can be printed below a picture of each slide.

____ **10.** A printout that contains the slide image in the top half of the page and speaker notes typed in the Notes pane in the lower half of the page.

A Black slide

B Bullet point

C Font

D List level

E Normal

F Notes page

G Notes pane

H Placeholder

I Sizing handle

J Text alignment

Multiple Choice

Choose the correct answer.

1. A research tool that provides a list of synonyms.
   - A. Reviewer
   - B. Spell check
   - C. Thesaurus

2. Words with the same meaning.
   - A. Synonyms
   - B. Antonyms
   - C. Prepositions

3. The arrangement of the text and graphic elements or placeholders on a slide.
   - A. Layout
   - B. Gallery
   - C. Design

4. Images included with Microsoft Office or from Microsoft Office Online.
   - A. Pictures
   - B. Vector graphics
   - C. Clip art

5. Tools used to perform specific commands related to a selected object.
   - A. Contextual tools
   - B. ScreenTips
   - C. Tool galleries

6. A prebuilt set of formatting borders, effects, and layouts applied to a picture.
   - A. Artistic effects
   - B. Picture styles
   - C. Picture designs

7. A motion effect that occurs in Slide Show view when you move from one slide to the next during a presentation.
   - A. Animation
   - B. Slide transition
   - C. Custom effect

8. Text that prints at the top of a sheet of slide handouts or notes pages.
   - A. Page numbers
   - B. Header
   - C. Footer

9. Text that displays at the bottom of every slide or that prints at the bottom of a sheet of slide handouts.
   - A. Page numbers
   - B. Header
   - C. Footer

10. Printed images of a single slide or multiple slides on a sheet of paper.
    - A. Notes
    - B. Slide handout
    - C. Footer

Topics for Discussion

1. PowerPoint 2010 provides a number of slide transitions that you can apply to your presentation. Do you think that it is important to apply one consistent transition to the entire presentation instead of applying a different transition to each slide? Why or why not?

2. When you applied the transition to the slides in the project in this chapter, you verified that the slides should advance when the mouse is clicked instead of advancing automatically after a few seconds. Why do you think that presentation slides should be advanced when the speaker clicks the mouse button instead of automatically?

Skill Check

To complete this presentation, you will need the following files:

- p01_Park
- p01_Park_River

You will save your presentation as:

- Lastname_Firstname_p01_Park

1. **Start** PowerPoint. From your student files, open **p01_Park**. Save the file in your **PowerPoint Chapter 1** folder as Lastname_Firstname_p01_Park

2. On **Slide 1**, select the title text—*Community Park Proposal*. In the **Font group**, click the **Font** arrow, and then click **Garamond**. Click the **Font Size** arrow, and then click **48**. Click the **Font Dialog Box Launcher**. In the **Font** dialog box, select **Small Caps**, and then click **OK**.

3. In the subtitle, click to the right of the word *Aspen*, and then, adding spaces as necessary, type Falls

4. In the **Editing group**, click **Replace**. In the **Find what** box, type north and then in the **Replace with** box type south Click **Replace All**. Click **OK**, and then **Close** the **Replace** dialog box.

5. Display **Slide 2**. Click in the title, and then in the **Paragraph group**, click **Center**. Select all of the bullet points. In the **Paragraph group**, click the **Line Spacing** button, and then click **1.5**.

6. Click anywhere in the third bullet point. In the **Paragraph group**, click the **Decrease List Level** button. Click in the last bullet point. In the **Paragraph group**, click the **Increase List Level** button, and then compare your slide with **Figure 1**.

7. Display **Slide 3**. On the **Home tab**, in the **Slides group**, click the *lower* part of the **New Slide** button. In the gallery, click **Title Slide**. In the title placeholder, type What will we do with the land at the current park location?

8. In the subtitle placeholder, type Develop or Remodel and then change the subtitle text **Font Size** to **36**. Compare your slide with **Figure 2**.

9. On the **Review tab**, in the **Proofing group**, click the **Spelling** button. Click **Change** to accept the spelling for *Municipal*, and then ignore the spelling for *Ramsburg*. **Close** the message box.

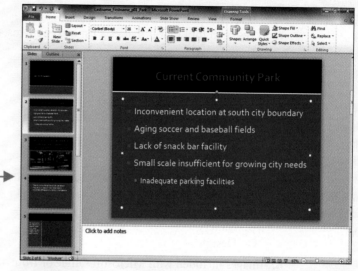

Figure 1

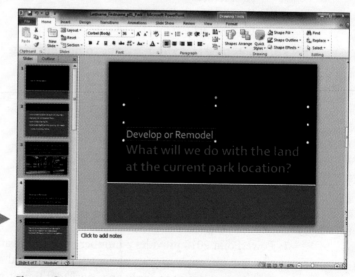

Figure 2

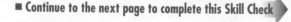 Continue to the next page to complete this Skill Check ▶

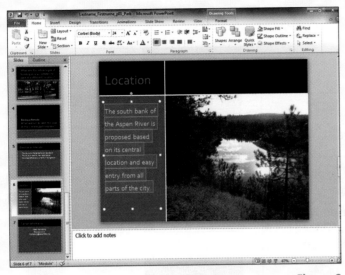

Figure 3

Figure 4

10. Display **Slide 6**. Right-click the word *entrance*. From the shortcut menu, point to **Synonyms**, and then click **entry**.

11. On the right side of **Slide 6**, click the **Insert Picture from File** button. From your student files, insert **p01_Park_River**. On the left side of the slide, select the text in the content placeholder. On the **Home tab**, in the **Paragraph group**, click the **Line Spacing** button, and then click **1.5**. Compare your slide with **Figure 3**.

12. Display **Slide 3**, and then select the picture. On the **Format tab**, in the **Picture Styles group**, click the **More** button, and then click the eleventh thumbnail—**Compound Frame, Black**.

13. Display **Slide 5**. On the **Home tab**, in the **Slides group**, click the **Layout** button, and then click **Two Content**. In the placeholder on the right, type Remodeling the park will increase the number of recreational facilities and then press Enter. Type Less expensive to remodel than develop

14. In the lower right corner of the PowerPoint window, click the **Slide Sorter** button. Select **Slide 7**, and then press Delete. Point to **Slide 6**, and then drag to position the vertical bar before **Slide 4** to move the slide. On the status bar, locate the View buttons, and then click the **Normal** button.

15. On the **Transitions tab**, in the **Transition to This Slide group**, click the **More** button, and then under **Subtle**, click **Wipe**. In the **Timing group**, click the **Durations box up spin arrow** one time to increase the **Duration** to *01.25*. Click **Apply to All**.

16. On the **Slide Show tab**, in the **Start Slide Show group**, click **From Beginning**, and then press the mouse button to advance through the slide show. When the black slide displays, click the mouse button or press Esc.

17. Display **Slide 2**. In the **Notes pane**, type The growing population in Aspen Falls warrants additional recreation facilities. Select the text and then change the **Font Size** to **18**.

18. On the **Insert tab**, in the **Text group**, click the **Header & Footer** button. Click the **Notes and Handouts tab**. Select the **Page number** check box, and then select the **Footer** check box. In the **Footer** box, type Lastname_Firstname_p01_Park and then click **Apply to All**.

19. **Save** the presentation, and then compare your completed presentation with **Figure 4**.

20. Print the presentation or submit the file as directed by your instructor, and then **Exit** PowerPoint.

Done! You have completed the Skill Check

Assess Your Skills 1

To complete this project, you will need the following files:

- p01_Commission
- p01_Commission_Members

You will save your presentation as:

- Lastname_Firstname_p01_Commission

1. **Start** PowerPoint. From the student files that accompany this textbook, open **p01_Commission**. **Save** the presentation in your **PowerPoint Chapter 1** folder as Lastname_Firstname_p01_Commission

2. On **Slide 1**, center the subtitle, change the font to **Arial** and the font size to **32**, and then apply **Small Caps**.

3. Display **Slide 2**, and then change the layout to **Two Content**. In the placeholder on the right, from your student files, insert the picture **p01_Commission_Members**, and then apply the **Compound Frame, Black** picture style.

4. With **Slide 2** still active, insert a new slide with the **Title and Content** layout. In the slide title, type Commission Responsibilities and then in the content placeholder, type the following four bullet points:

   Review new expansion plans
   Residential and commercial
   Recommend amendments to
      Planning Codes
   Design and development standards

5. Increase the list level of the second and fourth bullet points, and then select all of the bullet points and change the line spacing to **1.5**.

6. Use the thesaurus to change the word *expansion* to *development*.

7. Display **Slide 5**, and then change the layout to **Section Header**.

8. Display the presentation in **Slide Sorter** view, and then move **Slide 5** between **Slides 3 and 4**. Return the presentation to **Normal** view.

9. Apply the **Push** transition with the **From Top** effect option. Change the **Duration** to *01.50*. Apply the transition to all slides, and then view the slide show from the beginning.

10. Display **Slide 5**, and then in the **Notes** pane, type The Planning Commission is actively developing a plan for new construction in the city based on demographic projections through the year 2015. Change the speaker notes font size to **18**.

11. Correct all spelling errors in the presentation.

12. In the **Notes and Handouts** footer, insert the page number and the file name Lastname_Firstname_p01_Commission

13. Display the **Print** page, and then display **6 Slides Horizontal**. Compare your completed presentation with **Figure 1**. **Save** the presentation, and then print or submit the file as directed by your instructor.

   Done! You have completed Assess Your Skills 1

Figure 1

Assessment

Assess Your Skills 3 and 4 can be found at **www.pearsonhighered.com/skills**.

Assess Your Skills 2

To complete this presentation, you will need the following files:

- p01_Convention
- p01_Convention_Catering

You will save your presentation as:

- Lastname_Firstname_p01_Convention

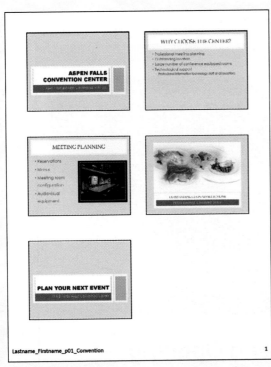

Figure 1

1. **Start** PowerPoint. From your student files, open **p01_Convention**. **Save** the presentation in your **PowerPoint Chapter 1** folder as Lastname_Firstname_p01_Convention

2. Display **Slide 3**. In the first bullet point, after the word *Professional*, type meeting and adjust spacing as necessary. Decrease the list level for the fourth bullet point, and then increase the list level for the fifth bullet point. Replace all instances of Hall with Center and then correct the spelling throughout the presentation.

3. Display **Slide 1**. Change the title font to **Arial Black** and the font size to **36**. Change the title alignment to **Align Text Right**. Select the subtitle, apply **Italic** and **Small Caps**, and then **Align Text Right**.

4. Display **Slide 4**, and then apply the same formatting to the title and subtitle as you did to the title and subtitle on Slide 1.

5. Display **Slide 2**. Select all four bullet points, and then change the line spacing to **1.5**. Apply the **Double Frame, Black** picture style to the picture.

6. With **Slide 2** still selected, insert a new slide with the **Picture with Caption** layout. In the title placeholder, type Outstanding Culinary Selections

7. In the caption placeholder, located below the title, type Professional catering staff Change the caption font size to **18**. In the picture placeholder, from your student files, insert the picture **p01_Convention_Catering**.

8. Display the presentation in **Slide Sorter** view. Delete **Slide 6**, and then move **Slide 4** between Slides 1 and 2. For all slides, apply the **Split** transition with the **Vertical In** effect option. View the slide show from the beginning.

9. Display **Slide 2** in **Normal** view, and then in the **Notes** pane, type The convention center is conveniently located in central Aspen Falls. Change the speaker notes font size to **18**.

10. In the **Notes and Handouts** footer, insert the page number and the file name Lastname_Firstname_p01_Convention

11. Compare your completed presentation with **Figure 1**. **Save** your presentation, and then print or submit the file as directed by your instructor.

Done! You have completed Assess Your Skills 2

Assess Your Skills Visually

To complete this presentation, you will need the following files:

- p01_Daycare
- p01_Daycare_Playground

You will save your presentation as:

- Lastname_Firstname_p01_Daycare

Open the file **p01_Daycare**. Save the file in your **PowerPoint Chapter 1** folder as Lastname_Firstname_p01_Daycare and then format the single slide presentation as a flyer as shown in **Figure 1**. To complete this presentation flyer, change the title font to **Corbel** size **36**. Change the font size for all other text to **18**. In the placeholder on the right, insert the picture **p01_Daycare_Playground** and apply the **Soft Edge Rectangle** picture style. In the Notes and Handouts footer, insert the page number and the file name Lastname_Firstname_p01_Daycare and then print or submit the file as directed by your instructor.

Done! You have completed Assess Your Skills Visually

Figure 1

Skills in Context

To complete this presentation, you will need the following files:

- p01_Opening
- p01_Opening_Outdoor
- p01_Opening_Children

You will save your presentation as:

- Lastname_Firstname_p01_ Opening

From your student files, open the **p01_Opening** presentation. Change the layout of Slide 2 to **Picture with Caption** and insert the **p01_Opening_Outdoor** picture in the picture placeholder. Apply an appropriate picture style. In the caption placeholder, change the font, font size, font effects, and line spacing so that the slide is formatted attractively. Insert a new Slide 3 using a layout of your choice. In the title placeholder, type Grand Opening Events and then for the slide content, provide a list of events that will take place at the grand opening ceremony, such as continental breakfast, arts and crafts, children's events, and teacher introductions.

At the end of the presentation, insert a slide using either the Content with Caption or the Picture with Caption layout. Use this slide to remind people of the date and time of the grand opening. Insert the picture **p01_Opening_Children** on this slide and apply an appropriate picture style. Apply slide transitions to all of the slides in the presentation and correct the spelling. Insert the file name and page number in the Notes and Handouts footer. Save your presentation as Lastname_Firstname_p01_Opening and then print or submit electronically.

Done! You have completed Skills in Context

Skills and You

To complete this presentation, you will need the following file:

- p01_PowerPoint

You will save your presentation as:

- Lastname_Firstname_p01_PowerPoint

From your student files, open **p01_PowerPoint**, and then on the first slide, add your name to the subtitle placeholder. Add a slide that describes your reasons for wanting to learn PowerPoint. Add a slide with the Content with Caption layout, and on it, describe how you plan to use PowerPoint personally or professionally. If you have a picture of yourself, add it to this slide, and then change font size and line spacing as necessary. If you do not have a picture of yourself, use a picture that depicts how you plan to use PowerPoint.

Insert a final slide with the Section Header layout and enter text that briefly summarizes in two lines—the title line and the subtitle line—your presentation. Add a footer to the presentation with the file name and page number, and then check spelling in the presentation. Save the presentation as Lastname_Firstname_p01_PowerPoint and then print or submit the file as directed by your instructor.

Done! You have completed Skills and You

CHAPTER 2

Format a Presentation

► Formatting is the process of changing the appearance of the text, layout, or design of a slide.

► Apply formatting to text and images to enhance your slides in a manner that conveys your message to your audience.

Your starting screen will look similar to this:

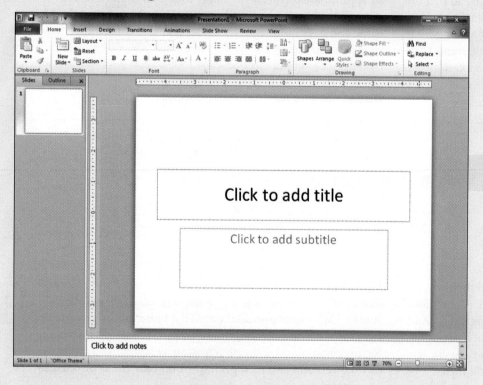

SKILLS
Skills 1-10 Training

At the end of this chapter, you will be able to:

Skill 1 Create New Presentations
Skill 2 Change Presentation Themes
Skill 3 Apply Font and Color Themes
Skill 4 Format Slide Backgrounds with Styles
Skill 5 Format Slide Backgrounds with Pictures and Textures
Skill 6 Format Text with WordArt
Skill 7 Change Character Spacing and Font Color
Skill 8 Modify Bulleted and Numbered Lists
Skill 9 Move and Copy Text and Objects
Skill 10 Use Format Painter and Clear All Formatting

MORE SKILLS

More Skills 11 Edit Slide Masters
More Skills 12 Save and Apply Presentation Templates
More Skills 13 Create Slides from Microsoft Word Outline
More Skills 14 Design Presentations with Contrast

Outcome

Using the skills listed to the left will enable you
to create a presentation like this:

You will save this presentation as:

Lastname_Firstname_p02_CS

In this chapter, you will create presentations for the Aspen Falls City Hall, which provides essential services for the citizens and visitors of Aspen Falls, California.

Introduction

- ▶ Apply PowerPoint themes to your presentations to create dynamic and professional-looking slides.

- ▶ Customize your presentation design by changing font colors, bullet symbols, and slide backgrounds.

- ▶ Before applying formatting, use the Live Preview feature to view the effect of different formatting on your slides.

Time to complete all
10 skills – 60 minutes

Find your student data files here:

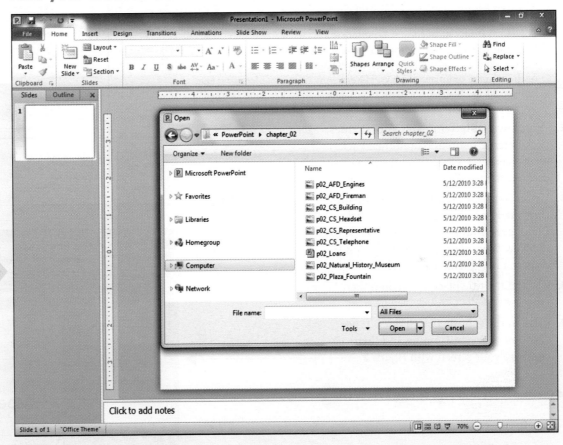

Student data files needed for this chapter:

- p02_CS_Building
- p02_CS_Headset
- p02_CS_Representative
- p02_CS_Telephone

► When you start PowerPoint, a new, blank presentation displays.

► In a new, blank presentation, black or grey text displays on a white background.

1. **Start** PowerPoint. On the **File tab**, click the **New tab** to display the **New** page as shown in **Figure 1**.

   The New page displays available templates, themes, and templates that you can download from Office.com. A *template* is a file upon which a presentation can be based. On the right side of the New page, a preview of the selected template displays. Here, a preview of the Blank presentation template displays.

2. Under **Available Templates and Themes**, click **Sample templates**, and then click several templates to display the preview of each on the right side of the **New** page.

3. Under **Available Templates and Themes**, click the **Home** button, and then click **Blank presentation**. On the right side of the **New** page, click the **Create** button to display a new blank presentation.

4. Click in the title placeholder, and then type Aspen Falls Utilities Department

5. Click in the subtitle placeholder. Type Customer Service Training and then compare your screen with **Figure 2**.

■ **Continue to the next page to complete the skill**

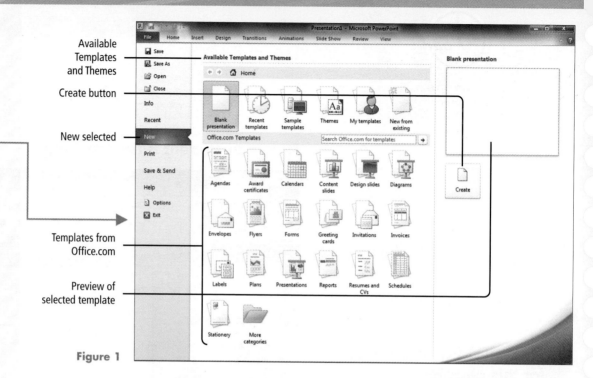

Available Templates and Themes

Create button

New selected

Templates from Office.com

Preview of selected template

Figure 1

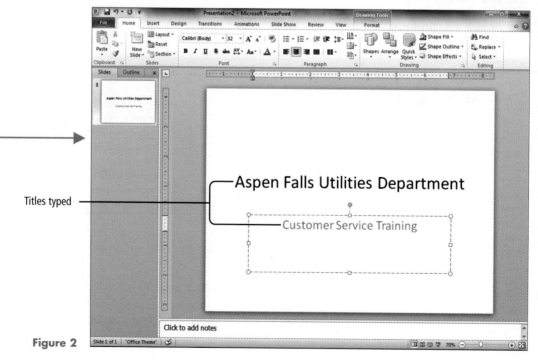

Titles typed

Figure 2

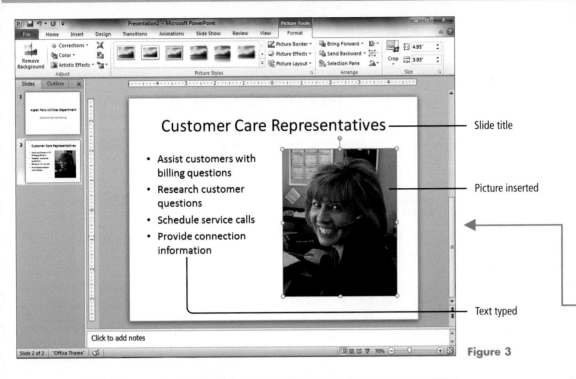

Slide title

Picture inserted

Text typed

Figure 3

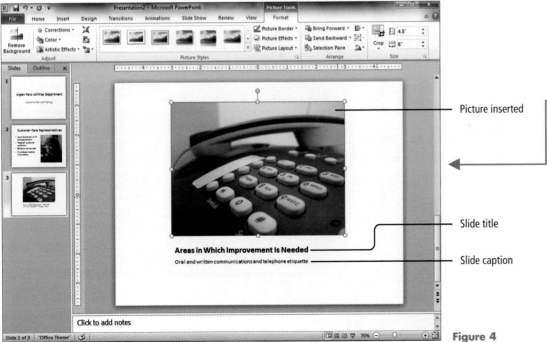

Picture inserted

Slide title

Slide caption

Figure 4

6. On the **Home tab**, in the **Slides group**, click the **New Slide button arrow**. In the gallery, click the **Two Content** thumbnail to insert a slide with the **Two Content** layout. In the title placeholder, type Customer Care Representatives

7. Click in the placeholder on the left, and then type the following four bullet points:

   Assist customers with billing questions
   Research customer questions
   Schedule service calls
   Provide connection information

8. In the placeholder on the right, click the **Insert Picture from File** button 📷, and then from your student files, insert the picture **p02_CS_Representative**. Compare your slide with **Figure 3**.

9. On the **Home tab**, in the **Slides group**, click the **New Slide button arrow**. In the gallery, click **Picture with Caption**. In the title placeholder, type Areas in Which Improvement Is Needed In the text placeholder, type Oral and written communications and telephone etiquette

10. In the picture placeholder, from your student files, insert **p02_CS_Telephone**, and then compare your slide with **Figure 4**.

11. On the Quick Access Toolbar, click **Save**. Navigate to the location where you are saving your files, create a folder named PowerPoint Chapter 2 and then using your own name, save the document as Lastname_Firstname_p02_CS

- **You have completed Skill 1 of 10**

► The presentation *theme* is a set of unified design elements—colors, fonts, and graphics—that provides a unique look for your presentation.

► The status bar displays the name of the theme applied to the presentation. The Office theme is the default theme applied to new presentations.

► To give the presentation a consistent design, choose one theme for all of the slides in the presentation.

1. Display **Slide 1**. On the **Design tab**, in the **Themes group**, click the **More** button ▼ to display the **Themes** gallery.

2. Under **Built-In**, point to the second theme—*Adjacency*—and notice that Live Preview displays the current slide with the selected theme as shown in **Figure 1**.

   Under Built-In, the default theme—Office— displays first. After the Office theme, the themes are arranged alphabetically and are identified by their ScreenTips.

3. Under **Built-In**, point to several themes and view the changes to the first slide.

   Each theme includes background colors, font styles, colors, sizes, and slide layouts specific to the theme.

4. Under **Built-In**, locate and click **Median** to apply the theme to all of the slides in the presentation. Compare your screen with **Figure 2**.

■ **Continue to the next page to complete the skill**

Adjacency theme

Themes gallery

Slide displays in Adjacency theme

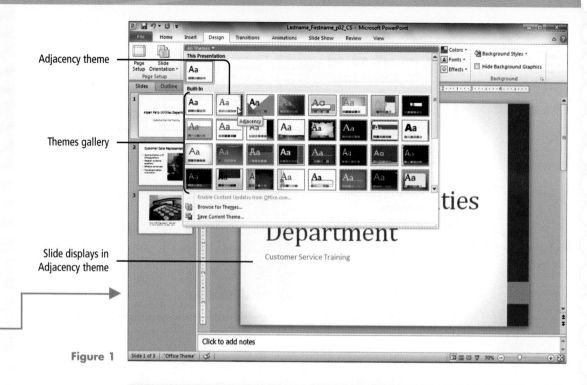

Figure 1

Median theme applied to all slides

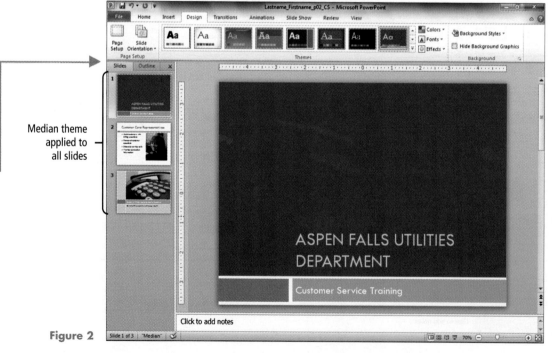

Figure 2

Title and caption text formatted

Figure 3

New slide created

Figure 4

5. Display **Slide 3**, and then select the title *Areas in Which Improvement Is Needed*. On the Mini toolbar, click the **Center** button 🖬.

6. Select the caption text *Oral and written communications and telephone etiquette.*

7. On the Mini toolbar, click the **Increase Font Size** button Ａ two times to change the font size to **20**. On the Mini toolbar, click the **Center** button 🖬, and then click the **Italic** button 𝐼. Compare your slide with **Figure 3**.

   After applying a new theme to a presentation, you should review each slide and make formatting changes as necessary. The fonts, layouts, and spacing associated with one theme may require that existing text and objects be resized or moved to display in a manner that is consistent and attractive in the newly applied theme.

8. Insert a **New Slide** with the **Title and Content** layout. In the title placeholder, type Make a Lasting Impression and then in the content placeholder, type the following three bullet points:

   Outstanding customer service is our first priority
   Excellent communication improves customer satisfaction
   Exceptional attention to detail results in improved accuracy

9. Compare your slide with **Figure 4**, and then **Save** 🖫 the presentation.

■ **You have completed Skill 2 of 10**

► Customize the presentation theme by changing the colors, fonts, effects, and background styles applied to a presentation.

► When you are using several pictures in a presentation, choose theme colors that complement the pictures you selected.

1. Display **Slide 1**. On the **Design tab**, in the **Themes group**, click the **Colors** button to display a list of color themes as shown in **Figure 1**.

   Theme colors are composed of a set of coordinated colors that are applied to the backgrounds, objects, and text in a presentation. The Median theme color is selected because the Median theme is applied to the presentation.

2. Point to each of the theme colors, and as you do so, notice the colors applied to **Slide 1**.

3. Click **Foundry** to change the theme colors of the presentation, and then compare your screen with **Figure 2**.

   You can apply a design theme to the presentation—in this case Median—and then change the colors by applying a different theme color. Although the presentation colors change, the overall design of the presentation and the slide layouts continue to be formatted using the Median theme.

■ **Continue to the next page to complete the skill**

Colors button

Theme colors

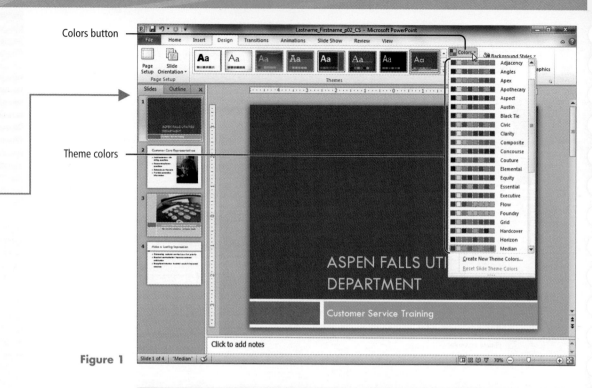

Figure 1

Foundry theme color applied to all slides

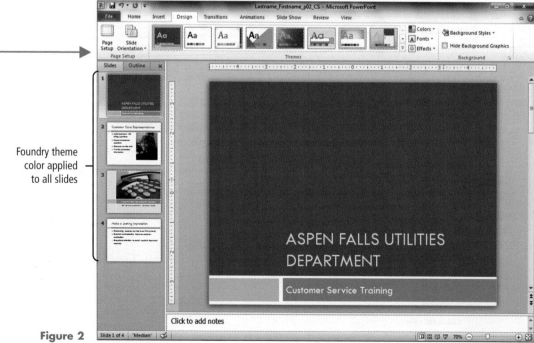

Figure 2

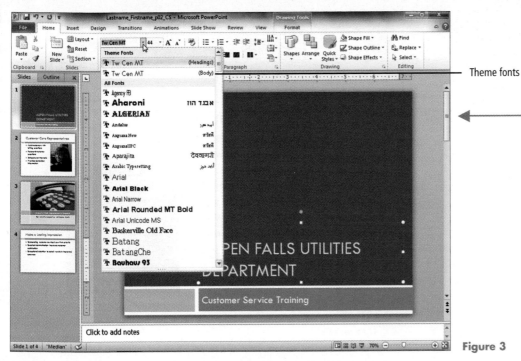

Theme fonts

Figure 3

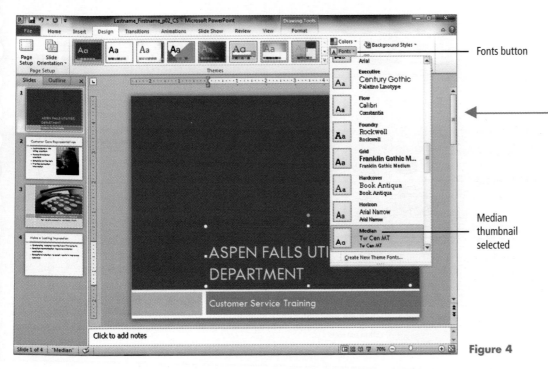

Fonts button

Median thumbnail selected

Figure 4

4. On **Slide 1**, click anywhere in the title placeholder. Click the **Home tab**, and then in the **Font group**, click the **Font button arrow** [Calibri (Headings)]. Notice that at the top of the Font list, under Theme Fonts, *Tw Cen MT (Headings)* and *Tw Cen MT (Body)* display, as shown in **Figure 3**.

> Every presentation theme includes *theme fonts* that determine the font applied to two types of slide text—headings and body. The *headings font* is applied to slide titles, and the *body font* is applied to all other text. Sometimes the heading and body fonts are the same, but they are different sizes. In other font themes, the heading and body fonts are different.

5. Click the **Design tab** to close the Font list, and then in the **Themes group**, click the **Fonts** button.

> The gallery displays fonts in pairs. The first font in each pair is the Headings font, and the second font is the Body font.

6. Scroll the **Theme Fonts** gallery, and notice that the *Median* theme font is selected as shown in **Figure 4**.

7. Point to several of the themes to view the changes to the slide text. Click the **Adjacency** theme, and then scroll through the presentation. Notice that the font changes have been applied to every slide.

> When you apply a new theme font to the presentation, the text on every slide is updated with the new heading and body fonts.

8. Save ■ the presentation.

■ **You have completed Skill 3 of 10**

▶ Customize the presentation design by applying a background style to your slides. A *background style* is a slide background fill variation that combines theme colors in different intensities or patterns.

▶ Background styles can be applied to a single slide or to all of the slides in the presentation.

▶ After you apply a background style, you can reset the background so that the original background associated with the presentation is applied to the slide.

1. Display **Slide 2**. On the **Design tab**, in the **Background group**, click the **Background Styles** button to display the **Background Styles** gallery as shown in **Figure 1**.

   The styles that display are designed to coordinate with the theme color applied to the presentation.

2. Point to each background and view the style applied to the slide, and then click **Style 10**.

   The Style 10 background style is applied to every slide in the presentation.

3. Display **Slide 1**. On the **Design tab**, in the **Background group**, click the **Background Styles** button. Point to the last style— **Style 12**—and then right-click to display the shortcut menu as shown in **Figure 2**.

■ **Continue to the next page to complete the skill**

Background Styles button

Background Styles gallery

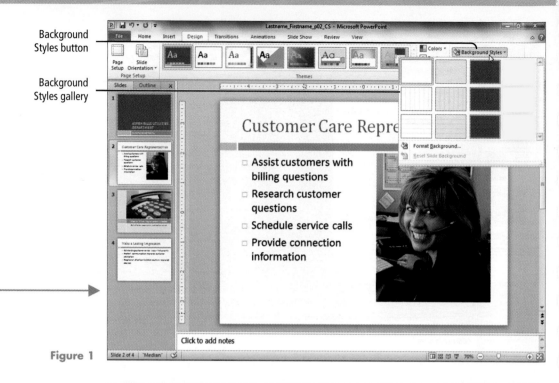

Figure 1

Shortcut menu

Style 12 selected

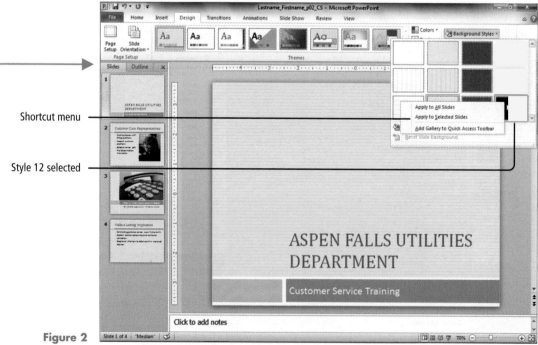

Figure 2

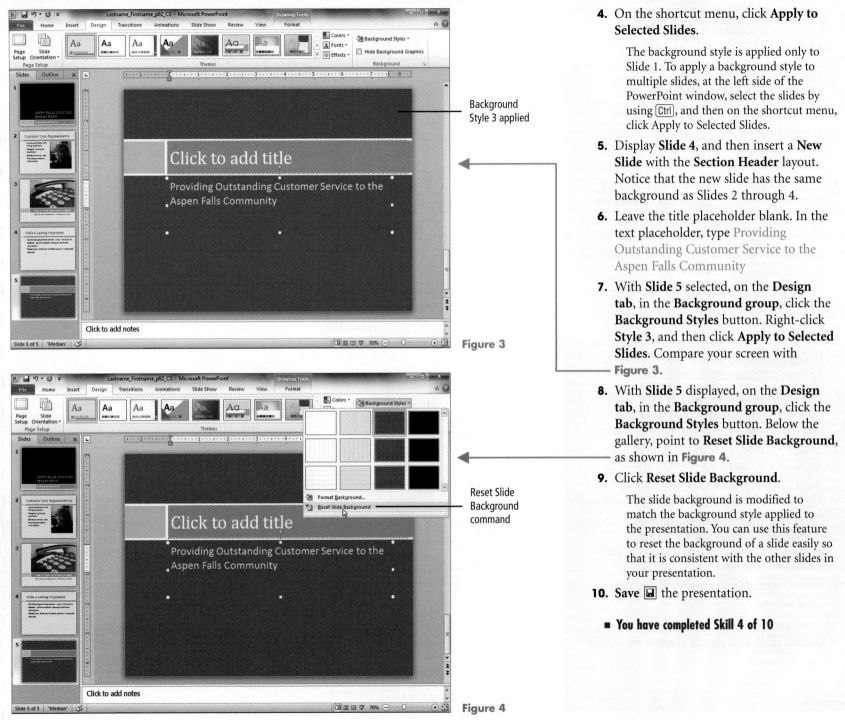

Background
Style 3 applied

Figure 3

Reset Slide
Background
command

Figure 4

4. On the shortcut menu, click **Apply to Selected Slides**.

   The background style is applied only to Slide 1. To apply a background style to multiple slides, at the left side of the PowerPoint window, select the slides by using Ctrl, and then on the shortcut menu, click Apply to Selected Slides.

5. Display **Slide 4**, and then insert a **New Slide** with the **Section Header** layout. Notice that the new slide has the same background as Slides 2 through 4.

6. Leave the title placeholder blank. In the text placeholder, type Providing Outstanding Customer Service to the Aspen Falls Community

7. With **Slide 5** selected, on the **Design tab**, in the **Background group**, click the **Background Styles** button. Right-click **Style 3**, and then click **Apply to Selected Slides**. Compare your screen with **Figure 3**.

8. With **Slide 5** displayed, on the **Design tab**, in the **Background group**, click the **Background Styles** button. Below the gallery, point to **Reset Slide Background**, as shown in **Figure 4**.

9. Click **Reset Slide Background**.

   The slide background is modified to match the background style applied to the presentation. You can use this feature to reset the background of a slide easily so that it is consistent with the other slides in your presentation.

10. Save ▣ the presentation.

■ **You have completed Skill 4 of 10**

► A slide can be formatted by inserting a picture or a texture on the slide background.

1. Display **Slide 4**, and then insert a **New Slide** with the **Title Only** layout.

2. On the **Design tab**, in the **Background group**, click the **Background Styles** button, and then click **Format Background**. Compare your screen with **Figure 1**.

3. In the **Format Background** dialog box, if necessary, select the **Picture or texture fill** option button, and then under **Insert from**, click the **File** button.

4. In the **Insert Picture** dialog box, navigate to your student files for this chapter, and then click **p02_CS_Building**. Click **Insert** to insert the picture on the slide background.

5. At the left side of the **Format Background** dialog box, click **Picture Color** to display options for changing picture color.

6. Under **Recolor**, click the **Presets button arrow**, and then click any of the color options. Notice the change to the picture.

7. Under **Recolor**, click the **Presets button arrow** again, and then point to the second color option—**Grayscale**—as shown in **Figure 2**. Click the **Grayscale** thumbnail.

    The background picture displays in *grayscale*—a black-and-white effect achieved through a series of shades of gray from white to black.

8. In the **Format Background** dialog box, click **Close**.

■ **Continue to the next page to complete the skill**

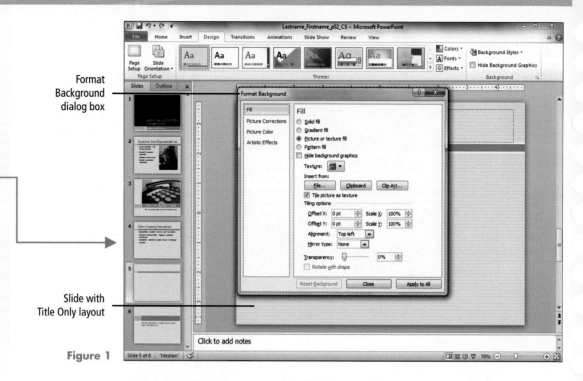

Format Background dialog box

Slide with Title Only layout

Figure 1

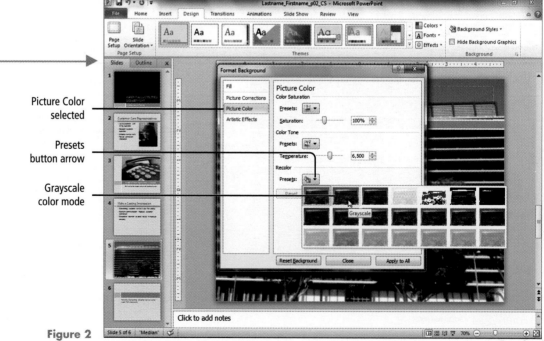

Picture Color selected

Presets button arrow

Grayscale color mode

Figure 2

Figure 3

Figure 4

9. On the **Design tab**, in the **Background group**, select the **Hide Background Graphics** check box, and then compare your screen with **Figure 3**.

Hide Background Graphics check box selected

   When graphics that are a part of the theme interfere with a background picture, hide the background graphics.

10. With **Slide 5** displayed, insert a **New Slide** with the **Picture with Caption** layout. In the picture placeholder, click the **Insert Picture from File** button. From your student files, insert the picture **p02_CS_Headset**. In the title placeholder, type Or By Phone and then change the **Font Size** to **36** and **Center** the text.

11. In the text placeholder, type Be Professional, Patient, and Courteous and then change the **Font Size** to **28**. **Center** the text.

12. On the **Design tab**, in the **Background group**, click the **Background Styles** button, and then click **Format Background**.

13. In the **Format Background** dialog box, if necessary, select the **Picture or texture fill** option button, and then click the **Texture** button to display the **Texture** gallery. Use the ScreenTips to locate the **Newsprint** texture as shown in **Figure 4**.

Texture button

Newsprint texture

   When applying a texture to the slide background, be sure to choose a texture that coordinates with the background colors on the rest of your slides.

14. Click **Newsprint**, and then in the **Format Background** dialog box, click **Close**.

15. Save the presentation.

■ **You have completed Skill 5 of 10**

► **WordArt** is a text style used to create decorative effects in your presentation.

► You can insert new WordArt, or you can convert existing text to WordArt.

1. Display **Slide 1**, and then select the title text. On the **Format tab**, in the **WordArt Styles group**, click the **More** button ⏷ to display the WordArt gallery.

2. Point to several WordArt styles and notice that Live Preview displays the title with the WordArt effect applied.

3. Under **Applies to Selected Text**, in the first row, point to the fourth WordArt style—**Fill - White, Outline - Accent 1**—as shown in **Figure 1**. Click the thumbnail and **Center** ▤ the title text.

4. Select the subtitle text. On the **Format tab**, in the **WordArt Styles group**, click the **More** button ⏷. In the **WordArt** gallery, under **Applies to All Text in the Shape**, click the second WordArt style—**Fill - Black, Background 1, Metal Bevel**—and then **Center** ▤ the text.

5. Display **Slide 5**. On the **Home tab**, in the **Slides group**, click the **Layout** button, and then click the **Blank** thumbnail to change the slide layout.

6. On the **Insert tab**, in the **Text group**, click the **WordArt** button. In the **WordArt** gallery, click the third WordArt style—**Fill - White, Drop Shadow**. Compare your screen with **Figure 2**.

   On the slide, a WordArt placeholder displays *Your text here*.

7. With the WordArt text selected, type Whether you assist customers on-site

   The placeholder expands to accommodate the text.

■ **Continue to the next page to complete the skill** ➤

Selected WordArt style

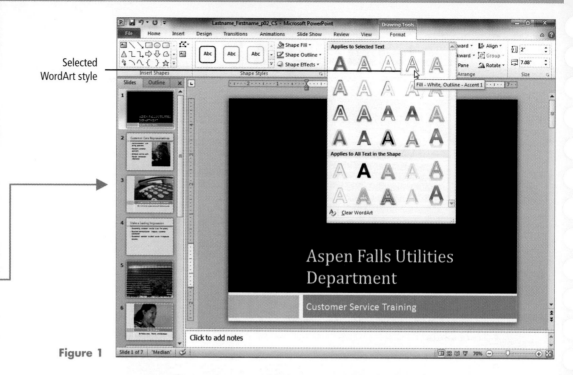

Figure 1

WordArt placeholder

Figure 2

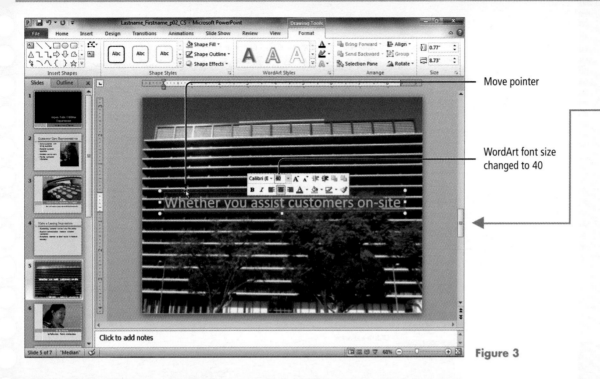

Move pointer

WordArt font size changed to 40

Figure 3

8. Select the **WordArt** text. On the Mini toolbar, click the **Font Size arrow** [44 ·], and then click **40** to resize the WordArt.

9. Point to the outer edge of the WordArt placeholder to display the [🔁] move pointer as shown in **Figure 3**.

10. While holding down the left mouse button, drag down and to the left so that the lower left corner of the WordArt placeholder aligns with the lower left corner of the slide, and then release the mouse button to move the WordArt.

11. With the WordArt still selected, point to its square, center-right sizing handle to display the [↔] pointer. Drag to the right so that the right edge of the WordArt placeholder aligns with the right edge of the slide.

12. On the **Format tab**, in the **Shape Styles group**, click the **Shape Fill** button to display the **Fill** gallery.

    The colors in the top row of the Fill gallery are the Foundry theme colors. The colors in the rows below the first row are light and dark variations of the theme colors and coordinate with the color theme. These colors can be used to change the *fill color*—the inside color of text or an object—so that the WordArt text displays prominently against the picture on the background.

13. Under **Theme Colors**, in the last row, click the sixth color—**Light Green, Accent 2, Darker 50%**—as shown in **Figure 4**.

    The WordArt text contrasts with the green fill color and the title is clearly visible on the slide.

14. Save [💾] the presentation.

■ **You have completed Skill 6 of 10**

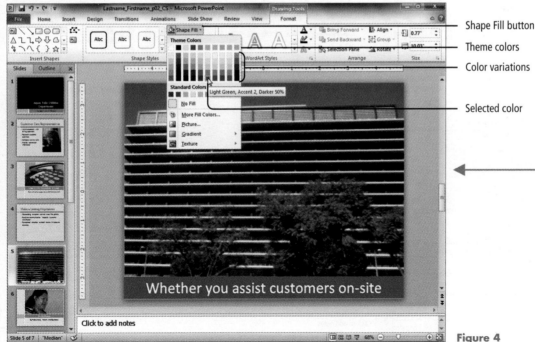

Shape Fill button

Theme colors

Color variations

Selected color

Figure 4

▶ When a selected font displays text that appears crowded in a placeholder, expand the horizontal spacing between characters.

▶ When a selected font displays text with excessive horizontal spacing, condense the spacing between characters.

▶ Change font colors to create contrast and emphasis on a slide.

1. If necessary, display **Slide 5**, and then select the WordArt text at the bottom of the slide. On the **Home tab**, in the **Font group**, click the **Bold** button ⬚.

    The bold text contrasts well with the dark background of the placeholder, but the characters are spaced tightly together.

2. With the text still selected, on the **Home tab**, in the **Font group**, click the **Character Spacing** button ⬚, and then in the list, click **More Spacing**. In the **Font** dialog box, click the **Spacing** arrow, and then click **Expanded**. In the **By** box, type 1.6 to expand the spacing between characters by 1.6 points. Compare your dialog box with **Figure 1**, and then click **OK** to apply the character spacing.

3. Display **Slide 3**, and then select the title. In the **Font group**, click the **Character Spacing** button ⬚, and then click **Tight** to reduce the amount of space between each character. Compare your slide with **Figure 2**.

■ **Continue to the next page to complete the skill**

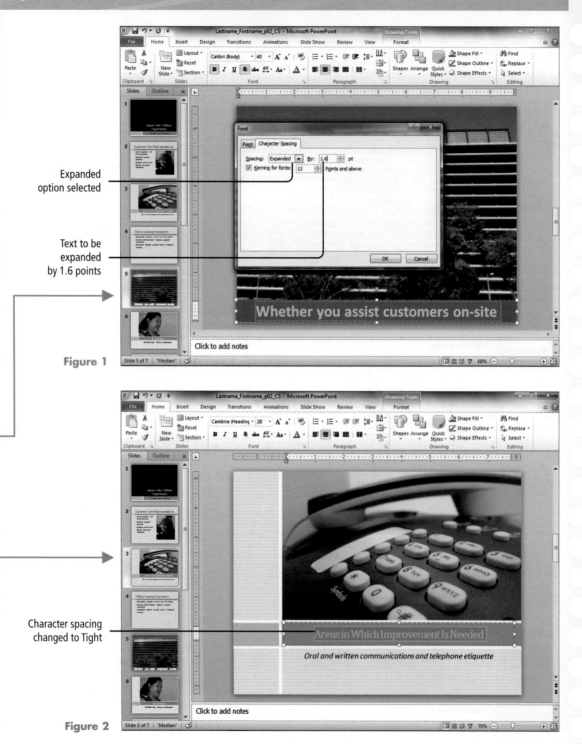

Expanded option selected

Text to be expanded by 1.6 points

Figure 1

Character spacing changed to Tight

Figure 2

Font Color button arrow

Black, Text 1 selected

Figure 3

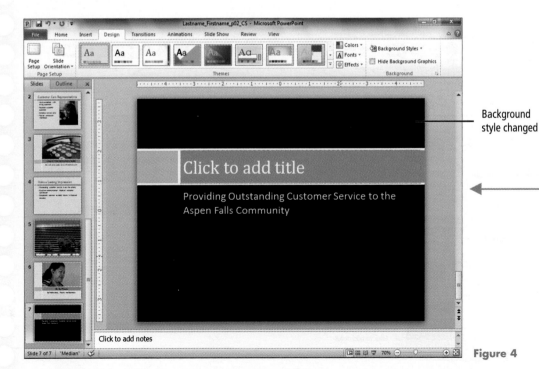

Background style changed

Figure 4

4. With the title still selected, on the **Home tab**, in the **Font group**, click the **Font Color button arrow** to display the **Font Color** gallery.

   The colors in the first row of the Font Color gallery are the colors associated with the presentation color theme.

5. In the first row, click the second color—**Black, Text 1**—to change the color of the selected text, as shown in **Figure 3**.

   In the Font group, the Font Color button displays the color that you just applied to the selection. If you want to apply the same color to another selection, you can click the Font Color button without displaying the color gallery.

6. Display **Slide 6**, and then select the title text. On the Mini toolbar, click the **Font Color** button to change the font color to black.

7. Display **Slide 7** and notice that the background does not provide sufficient contrast for the subtitle text. On the **Design tab**, in the **Background group**, click the **Background Styles** button. In the gallery, right-click **Style 4**, and then click **Apply to Selected Slides**. Compare your slide with **Figure 4**.

   To create contrast for the text on a slide, change either the font color or the slide background style.

8. **Save** the presentation.

   ▪ **You have completed Skill 7 of 10**

► The presentation theme includes default bullet styles for the bullet points in content placeholders. You can customize a bullet symbol by changing its style, color, and size.

► A numbered list can be applied to bullet points in place of bullet symbols.

1. Display **Slide 4**, and then in the content placeholder, select the three bullet points. On the **Home tab**, in the **Paragraph group**, click the **Numbering** button 三▾, and then compare your screen with **Figure 1**. If you clicked the Numbering button arrow and a gallery displays, in the first row, click the second Numbering option—1, 2, 3.

    The bullet symbols are replaced by numbers. The default color for the numbers—light green—is based on the Foundry color theme.

2. With the three numbered list items selected, click the **Numbering button arrow** 三▾, and then below the gallery, click **Bullets and Numbering**.

3. In the **Bullets and Numbering** dialog box, on the **Numbered tab**, click the **Color** button. Under **Theme Colors**, in the last row, point to the seventh color—**Sky Blue, Accent 3, Darker 50%**—as shown in **Figure 2**. Click to apply the new color.

4. In the **Size** box, replace the number with 100 so that the numbers will be the same size as the text. Click **OK** to apply the changes to the numbers in the list.

■ **Continue to the next page to complete the skill**

Numbering button

Numbering applied to list

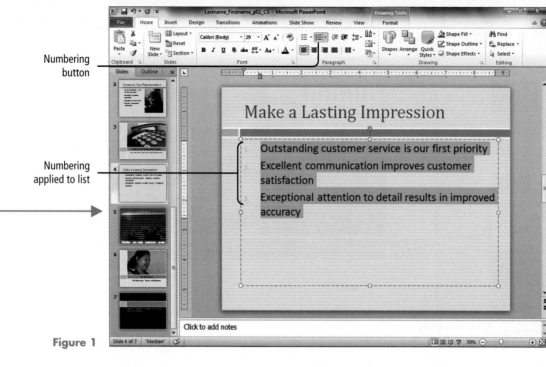

Figure 1

Numbering button arrow

Bullets and Numbering dialog box

Color button

Selected color

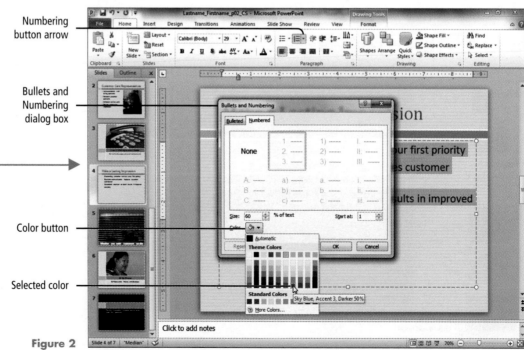

Figure 2

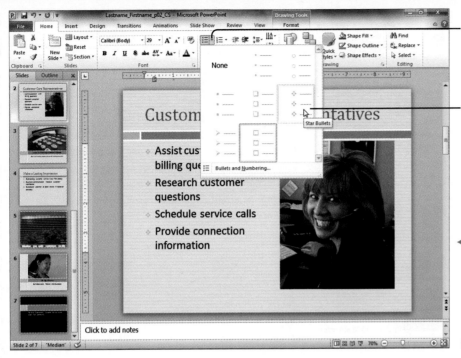

Bullets button arrow

Star Bullets thumbnail

Figure 3

Filled Square Bullets selected

Size changed to 90%

Bullet color changed

Figure 4

5. Display **Slide 2**. In the content placeholder, select the four bullet points.

6. With the four bullet points selected, on the **Home tab**, in the **Paragraph group**, click the **Bullets button arrow** to display the **Bullets** gallery. If your bullets disappeared, click the Bullets button again, and then repeat Step 6, making sure to click the Bullets *button arrow* instead of the Bullets *button*.

   The gallery displays several bullet characters that you can apply to the selection.

7. Point to the **Star Bullets** thumbnail as shown in **Figure 3**, and then click the thumbnail to change the bullet style for the selection.

8. With the four bullet points selected, click the **Bullets button arrow**, and then below the gallery, click **Bullets and Numbering**.

9. In the **Bullets and Numbering** dialog box, on the **Bulleted tab**, in the first row of the bullet gallery, click **Filled Square Bullets**. Click the **Color** button. Under **Theme Colors**, in the last row, click the seventh color—**Sky Blue, Accent 3, Darker 50%**.

10. In the **Size** box, replace the number with 90 and then compare your dialog box with **Figure 4**.

11. Click **OK** to apply the bullet style, color, and size, and then **Save** the presentation.

   ▪ **You have completed Skill 8 of 10**

► The Cut command removes selected text or graphics from your presentation and places the selection in the Clipboard.

► The Clipboard is a temporary storage area maintained by your operating system.

► The Copy command duplicates a selection and places it in the Clipboard.

1. Display **Slide 4**. In the content placeholder, position the pointer over the number **3**, and notice the pointer that displays as shown in **Figure 1**.

2. With the pointer positioned over the number **3**, click the mouse button, and notice that the number and the related text are selected.

    Clicking a list number or bullet symbol is an efficient way to select the entire point.

3. On the **Home tab**, in the **Clipboard group**, click the **Cut** button ✂ to remove the item from the slide and send it to the Clipboard.

4. In the second numbered list item, click in front of the *E* in the word *Excellent*. In the **Clipboard group**, click the **Paste** button to paste the selection to the new location. Notice that below the pasted text, the Paste Options button displays as shown in **Figure 2**, providing options for formatting pasted text. Also notice that the points are automatically renumbered when the order is changed.

■ **Continue to the next page to complete the skill**

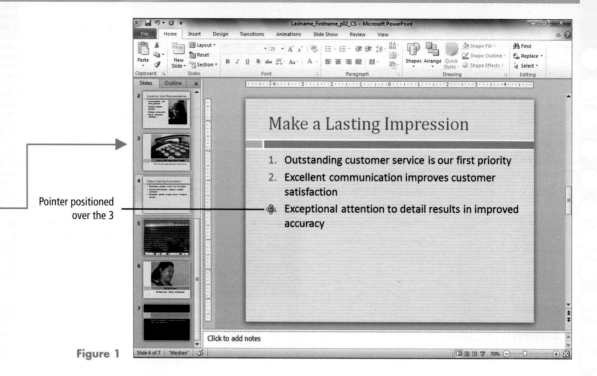

Pointer positioned over the 3

Figure 1

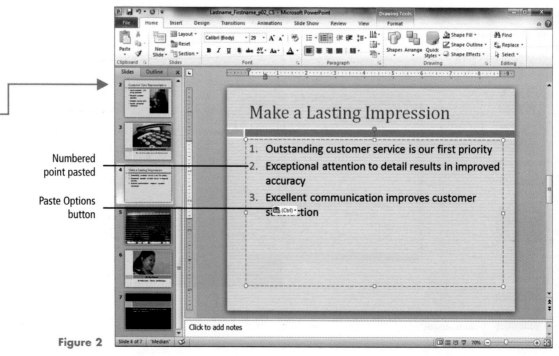

Numbered point pasted

Paste Options button

Figure 2

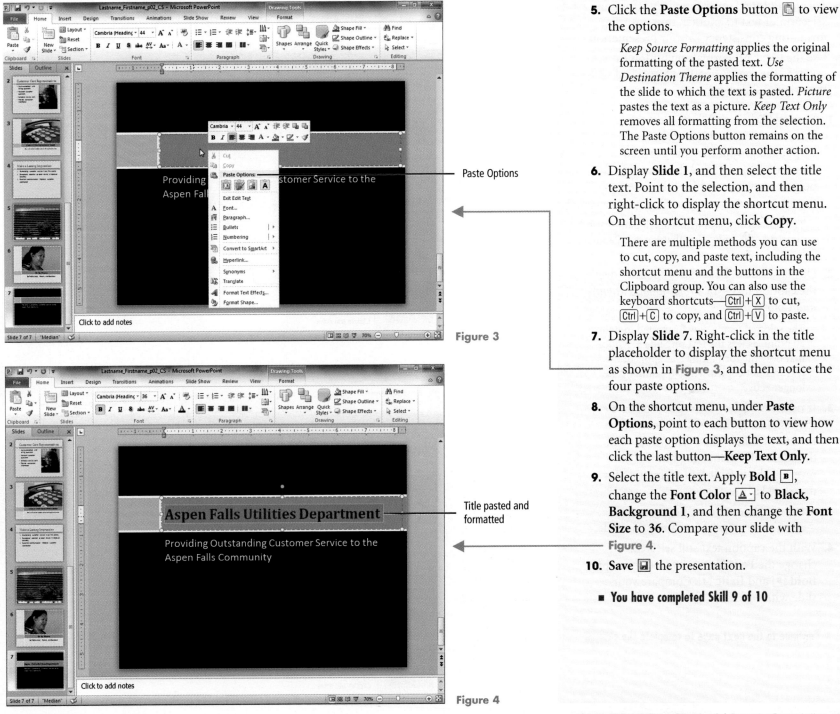

Figure 3

Figure 4

5. Click the **Paste Options** button to view the options.

   Keep Source Formatting applies the original formatting of the pasted text. *Use Destination Theme* applies the formatting of the slide to which the text is pasted. *Picture* pastes the text as a picture. *Keep Text Only* removes all formatting from the selection. The Paste Options button remains on the screen until you perform another action.

6. Display **Slide 1**, and then select the title text. Point to the selection, and then right-click to display the shortcut menu. On the shortcut menu, click **Copy**.

   There are multiple methods you can use to cut, copy, and paste text, including the shortcut menu and the buttons in the Clipboard group. You can also use the keyboard shortcuts—Ctrl+X to cut, Ctrl+C to copy, and Ctrl+V to paste.

7. Display **Slide 7**. Right-click in the title placeholder to display the shortcut menu as shown in **Figure 3**, and then notice the four paste options.

8. On the shortcut menu, under **Paste Options**, point to each button to view how each paste option displays the text, and then click the last button—**Keep Text Only**.

9. Select the title text. Apply **Bold** [B], change the **Font Color** [A▾] to **Black, Background 1**, and then change the **Font Size** to 36. Compare your slide with **Figure 4**.

10. **Save** the presentation.

■ **You have completed Skill 9 of 10**

Paste Options

Title pasted and formatted

▶ ***Format Painter*** copies *formatting* from one selection of text to another, thus ensuring formatting consistency in your presentation.

▶ Use the Clear All Formatting button to revert to the font formatting associated with the original slide layout.

1. Display **Slide 3**, and then select the word *Oral*. On the **Home tab**, in the **Clipboard group**, click the **Format Painter** button, and then position the pointer anywhere in the Slide pane. Compare your screen with **Figure 1**.

   The pointer displays with a small paintbrush attached to it, indicating that Format Painter is active.

2. Display **Slide 6**. Drag the pointer over the caption text—*Be Professional, Patient, and Courteous.*

   The selected text is now formatted in italic, 20 point, as was the text on Slide 3. Notice that only the formatting was applied; the text was not copied. The pointer is no longer active.

3. If necessary, select the caption text—*Be Professional, Patient, and Courteous.* On the **Home tab**, in the **Font group**, click the **Clear All Formatting** button to revert to the default font formatting for this slide layout.

   Use the Clear All Formatting button to revert to the original formatting on a slide.

4. With the caption text still selected, change the **Font Size** to **28**, and then apply **Bold** and **Italic**. Compare your slide with **Figure 2**.

■ **Continue to the next page to complete the skill**

Format Painter button

Format Painter pointer

Selected text

Figure 1

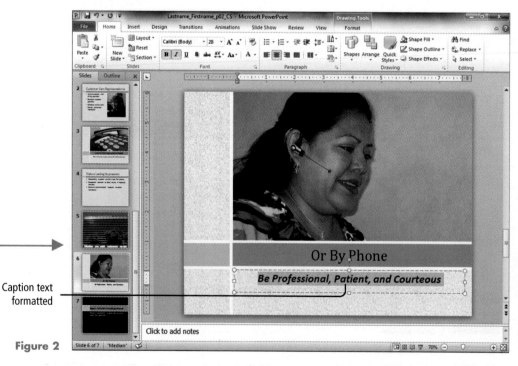

Caption text formatted

Figure 2

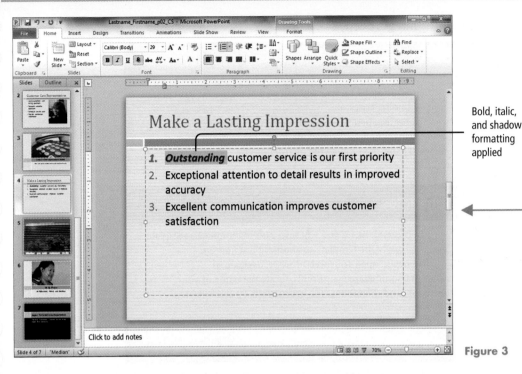

Bold, italic, and shadow formatting applied

Figure 3

Same formatting applied

Figure 4

5. Display **Slide 4**. In the first item, select the text *Outstanding*. On the **Home tab**, in the **Font group**, click the **Bold** button ⃞ᴮ, the **Italic** button ⃞ᴵ, and the **Shadow** button ⃞ˢ. Compare your slide with **Figure 3**.

6. With the text *Outstanding* still selected, on the **Home tab**, in the **Clipboard group**, *double-click* the **Format Painter** button ⃞.

   To apply formatting to multiple selections, double-click the Format Painter button.

7. In the second numbered item, click the word *Exceptional* to apply the selected formatting to the text. Notice that the ⃞ pointer is still active.

8. In the third numbered item, click the word *Excellent*. If you were unable to apply the formatting to the word *Excellent*, repeat Step 6, and then try again.

9. To turn off Format Painter, on the **Home tab**, in the **Clipboard group**, click the **Format Painter** button ⃞. Alternately, press ⃞Esc. Compare your slide with **Figure 4**.

10. Apply the **Wipe** transition with the **Effect Options** changed to **From Top** to all of the slides, and then view the slide show from the beginning.

11. Insert a **Header & Footer** on the **Notes and Handouts** that includes the **Date and time** updated automatically, a **Page number**, and the **Footer** Lastname_Firstname_p02_CS

12. **Save** ⃞ the presentation. Print your presentation or submit electronically, as directed by your instructor. **Exit** PowerPoint.

Done! You have completed Skill 10 of 10 and your presentation is complete!

More Skills

The following More Skills are located at **www.pearsonhighered.com/skills**

More Skills Edit Slide Masters

When you are formatting a presentation and want to change the format for every slide in the presentation, modify the slide master. The slide master holds information about the colors, fonts, and other objects that display on your slides.

In More Skills 11, you will edit a slide master by changing its font and bullet styles.

To begin, open your web browser, navigate to www.pearsonhighered.com/skills, locate the name of your textbook, and then follow the instructions on the website.

More Skills Save and Apply Presentation Templates

You can design your own custom presentation and save it as a template so that you can easily apply the template to another presentation.

In More Skills 12, you will save a presentation as a template and then apply the template to another presentation.

To begin, open your web browser, navigate to www.pearsonhighered.com/skills, locate the name of your textbook, and then follow the instructions on the website.

More Skills Create Slides from Microsoft Word Outline

The bullet points in a PowerPoint presentation are based on an outline in which the list levels are assigned to varying outline levels. An outline based on paragraph styles in Microsoft Word can be imported into PowerPoint to create slides.

In More Skills 13, you will import a Microsoft Word outline to create slides in a PowerPoint presentation.

To begin, open your web browser, navigate to www.pearsonhighered.com/skills, locate the name of your textbook, and then follow the instructions on the website.

More Skills Design Presentations with Contrast

Contrast is an important element of slide design because it enables the audience to clearly view presentation text, images, and objects.

In More Skills 14, you will review design principles that will assist you in creating contrast on your slides. You will view two slides and compare the difference in contrast created by using color and images.

To begin, open your web browser, navigate to www.pearsonhighered.com/skills, locate the name of your textbook, and then follow the instructions on the website.

Key Terms

Online Help Skills

1. **Start** 🔵 PowerPoint. In the upper right corner of the PowerPoint window, click the **Help** button 📄. In the **Help** window, click the **Maximize** 🔲 button.

2. Click in the search box, type Overview of themes and then click the **Search** button 🔍. In the search results, click **What is a theme?**

3. Below **In this article**, click **Overview of Office themes**. Compare your screen with **Figure 1**.

Figure 1

4. Scroll down to read the entire article and then see if you can answer the following: How does modifying a presentation theme color result in a dramatic change in a presentation?

Matching

Match each term in the second column with its correct definition in the first column by writing the letter of the term on the blank line in front of the correct definition.

____ **1.** A file upon which a presentation can be based.

____ **2.** A set of unified design elements that provides a look for your presentation, using colors, fonts, and graphics.

____ **3.** A theme that determines the font applied to two types of slide text—headings and body.

____ **4.** A font applied to slide titles.

____ **5.** A font applied to all slide text except titles.

____ **6.** A slide background fill variation that combines theme colors in different intensities or patterns.

____ **7.** A text style used to create decorative effects in a presentation.

____ **8.** The inside color of text or an object.

____ **9.** A command that removes selected text or graphics from a presentation and then moves the selection to the Clipboard.

____ **10.** A temporary storage area maintained by the operating system.

A Background style

B Body font

C Clipboard

D Cut

E Fill color

F Headings font

G Template

H Theme

I Theme font

J WordArt

Multiple Choice

Choose the correct answer.

1. The process of changing the appearance of the text, layout, or design of a slide.
   A. Editing
   B. Designing
   C. Formatting

2. The area of the PowerPoint window in which the name of the applied theme displays.
   A. Status bar
   B. Task pane
   C. Slide pane

3. The default theme in PowerPoint.
   A. Apex
   B. Office
   C. Urban

4. The coordinating set of colors applied to presentation backgrounds, objects, and text.
   A. Theme color
   B. Color palette
   C. Color gallery

5. A black-and-white effect achieved through a series of shades of gray from white to black.
   A. Sepia
   B. Gradient fill
   C. Grayscale

6. A format that you can change to create contrast and emphasis on a slide.
   A. Alignment
   B. Font color
   C. Layout

7. The command used to duplicate a selection.
   A. Format Painter
   B. Cut
   C. Copy

8. The command used to copy formatting from one selection to another.
   A. Format Painter
   B. Cut
   C. Copy

9. A command used to revert to font formatting associated with the original slide layout.
   A. Clear All Formatting
   B. Reset Format
   C. Reset Slide Layout

10. The mouse action necessary when Format Painter is used on multiple selections.
    A. Single-click
    B. Double-click
    C. Triple-click

Topics for Discussion

1. PowerPoint 2010 includes several themes that you can apply to your presentations. What should you consider when choosing a design theme for the presentations that you create?

2. Format Painter is an important tool used to maintain consistent formatting in a presentation. Why is consistency important when you format the slides in your presentations?

Assessment

Skill Check

To complete this presentation, you will need the following files:

- New blank presentation
- p02_Plaza_Fountain

You will save your presentation as:

- Lastname_Firstname_p02_Plaza

1. **Start** PowerPoint. In the new presentation, type the slide title The Plaza at Aspen Falls and the subtitle Opening Ceremony **Save** the file in your **PowerPoint Chapter 2** folder as Lastname_Firstname_p02_Plaza

2. Insert a **New Slide** with the **Title and Content** layout. In the title placeholder, type Event Activities In the text placeholder, type four bullet points: Ribbon cutting and Welcome address and Continental breakfast and Grand prize raffle

3. On the **Design tab**, in the **Themes group**, click the **More** button. Under **Built-In**, click **Urban**. In the **Themes group**, click the **Fonts** button, and then click **Metro**. Click the **Colors** button, and then click **Equity**. In the **Background group**, click the **Background Styles** button, and then click **Style 10**. Compare your screen with **Figure 1**.

4. Insert a **New Slide** with the **Blank** layout. On the **Design tab**, in the **Background group**, click the **Background Styles** button, and then click **Format Background**. In the **Format Background** dialog box, select **Picture or texture fill**, then under **Insert from**, click the **File** button. From your student files, insert **p02_Plaza_Fountain**. Click **Close**.

5. Insert a **New Slide** with the **Content with Caption** layout. Type the slide title Join the Celebration! In the left placeholder, type four bullet points: July 25 at 10 a.m. and Free events and Retail locations and park will be open and Raffle at 6 p.m.

6. Select the bullet points and change the **Line Spacing** to **1.5**. In the **Paragraph group**, click the **Bullets button arrow**, and then click **Bullets and Numbering**. Click **Arrow Bullets**, and then click the **Color button**. In the last row, click the fifth color—**Orange, Accent 1, Darker 50%**. In the **Size** box, type 80 and then click **OK**. Compare your screen with **Figure 2**.

■ Continue to the next page to complete this Skill Check

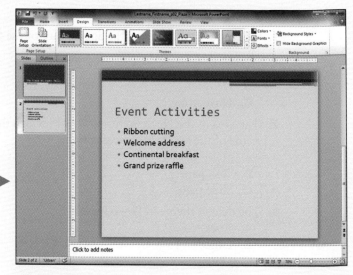

Figure 1

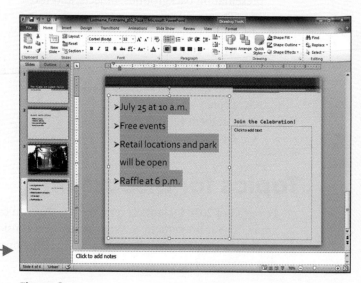

Figure 2

Figure 2

500 Format a Presentation | **Microsoft PowerPoint Chapter 2**

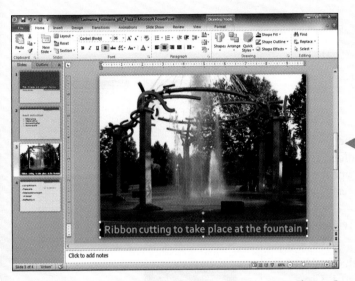

Figure 3

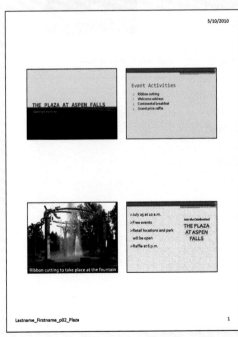

Figure 4

7. On the **Design tab**, in the **Background group**, click the **Background Styles** button, and then click **Format Background**. Select **Picture or texture fill**, and then click the **Texture** button. Click **Newsprint**, and then click **Close**.

8. Display **Slide 2**, and then select the four bullet points. On the **Home tab**, in the **Paragraph group**, click the **Numbering** button.

9. Display **Slide 3**. On the **Design tab**, in the **Background group**, select the **Hide Background Graphics** check box. On the **Insert tab**, in the **Text group**, click **WordArt**. Click the third WordArt style—**Fill - White, Drop Shadow**—and then replace the WordArt text with Ribbon cutting to take place at the fountain

10. Change the **Font Size** to **36**, and then point to the outer edge of the WordArt placeholder. Drag to align the placeholder with the lower left corner of the slide. Size the WordArt so that it extends from the left to the right edge of the slide.

11. On the **Format tab**, in the **Shape Styles group**, click the **Shape Fill** button. Under **Theme Colors**, in the last row, click the sixth color—**Dark Red, Accent 2, Darker 50%**.

12. Select the WordArt text. On the **Home tab**, in the **Font group**, click the **Character Spacing** button, and then click **More Spacing**. Click the **Spacing** arrow, click **Expanded**, and then click **OK**. Compare your screen with **Figure 3**.

13. Display **Slide 1**. On the **Design tab**, in the **Background group**, click the **Background Styles** button, right-click **Style 4**, and then click **Apply to Selected Slides**. Select the title. On the **Format tab**, in the **WordArt Styles group**, click the **More** button, and then under **Applies to Selected Text**, click the last style—**Gradient Fill - Brown, Accent 4, Reflection**.

14. On the **Home tab**, in the **Clipboard group**, click the **Copy** button. Display **Slide 4**, and then click in the text placeholder below the title. In the **Clipboard group**, click the **Paste** button. Change the **Font Size** to **40**, and then **Center** the text.

15. Display **Slide 1**. Select the subtitle. Apply **Bold** and **Italic**, and then on the **Home tab**, in the **Clipboard group**, click the **Format Painter** button.

16. Display **Slide 4**, and then drag the **Format Painter** pointer over the title—*Join the Celebration!*—**Center** the title and change the **Font Color** to **Black, Text 1**.

17. Insert a **Header & Footer** on the **Notes and Handouts** with the **Date and time**, the **Page number**, and the **Footer** Lastname_Firstname_p02_Plaza

18. **Save** the presentation, and then compare your presentation with **Figure 4**. Print or submit electronically.

Done! You have completed the Skill Check

Assess Your Skills 1

To complete this presentation, you will need the following files:

- New blank presentation
- p02_AFD_Engines
- p02_AFD_Fireman

You will save your presentation as:

- Lastname_Firstname_p02_Station

1. **Start** PowerPoint and display a blank presentation. Apply the **Verve** theme. Change the theme color to **Aspect**, and the theme font to **Origin**. **Save** the file in your **PowerPoint Chapter 2** folder as Lastname_Firstname_p02_Station

2. In the title placeholder, type Aspen Falls Fire District and then in the subtitle placeholder, type New Station Proposal Change the subtitle **Font Size** to **36**, and the **Font Color** to **Orange, Accent 1, Darker 25%**.

3. Insert a **New Slide** with the **Title and Content** layout. In the content placeholder, type the following bullet points: Add 3 engines and 15 firefighters and Locate in southern area of city and Fund by municipal bonds

4. Display **Slide 1**. **Copy** the subtitle and **Paste** the selection to the title placeholder on **Slide 2**. Delete any extra blank lines.

5. Insert a **New Slide** with the **Blank** layout. On the slide background insert from your student files the picture **p02_AFD_Engines**. Hide background graphics.

6. Insert the third WordArt style—**Fill - White, Drop Shadow**—with the text Proposed Engine Additions Drag the WordArt to the upper left corner of the slide. Size the WordArt so that it extends from the left to the right edge of the slide. Change the shape fill color to **Black, Background 1**.

7. Insert a **New Slide** with the **Title and Content** layout. In the title placeholder, type Rationale In the text placeholder, type four bullet points: Reduced emergency response time and Increased population growth and Expanded city boundaries and Increased commercial density

8. To the **Slide 4** title, apply the fourth WordArt style—**Fill - White, Outline - Accent 1**. Use **Format Painter** to apply the same style to the **Slide 1** subtitle. Change the subtitle text **Font Size** to **36**. If necessary, Align Right the subtitle.

9. Display **Slide 4**, and then insert a **New Slide** with the **Picture with Caption** layout. Display **Slide 1**, and then **Copy** the title and **Paste** it in the **Slide 5** title. In the text placeholder, type Dedicated to serving our community **Center** the text, and change the **Font Size** to **32**. In the picture placeholder, from your student files, insert **p02_AFD_Fireman**. Apply the **Soft Edge Rectangle** picture style.

10. Insert a **Header & Footer** on the **Notes and Handouts**. Include the date, page number, and the footer Lastname_Firstname_p02_Station

11. Compare your presentation with **Figure 1**. **Save** and then submit the file as directed.

Done! You have completed Assess Your Skills 1

Figure 1

Assess Your Skills 3 and 4 can be found at **www.pearsonhighered.com/skills**.

Assess Your Skills 2

To complete this presentation, you will need the following file:

- p02_Loans

You will save your presentation as:

- Lastname_Firstname_p02_Loans

Figure 1

1. **Start** PowerPoint. From your student files, open **p02_Loans**. Change the theme color to **Trek**, and change the theme font to **Verve**. Apply background **Style 12** to the entire presentation, and then **Save** the file in your **PowerPoint Chapter 2** folder as Lastname_Firstname_p02_Loans

2. On **Slide 1**, select the title, and then apply the last WordArt style—**Fill - Orange, Accent 1, Metal Bevel, Reflection**. Change the font size to **40**. Use **Format Painter** to apply the same formatting to the title on **Slide 4**.

3. Display **Slide 1**, and then select the subtitle. Apply **Bold**, and then expand the character spacing by 1 point. Use **Format Painter** to apply the same formatting to the subtitle on **Slide 4**.

4. Display **Slide 2**. Change the bullet style to **Star Bullets**, and then change the **Size** to 90 % of text. Move the last bullet point so that it is the first bullet point. Apply the **Rotated, White** picture style to the picture.

5. Display **Slide 3**, and then in the first bullet point, select the first word—*Apply*. Change the **Font Color** to the fifth color in the first row—**Orange, Accent 1**. Apply **Bold** and **Italic**, and then use **Format Painter** to apply the same formatting to the first word of each of the remaining bullet points. Convert the bullets to a numbered list, and change the **Color** of the numbers to **White, Text 1**.

6. Display **Slide 1**, and then format the slide background by applying the **Granite** texture. Apply the same background style to **Slide 4**.

7. With **Slide 4** displayed, apply the **Double Frame, Black** picture style to the picture.

8. Apply the **Wipe** transition to all of the slides in the presentation. View the slide show from the beginning.

9. Insert a **Header & Footer** on the **Notes and Handouts** that includes the page number and a footer with the text Lastname_Firstname_p02_Loans

10. Compare your completed presentation with **Figure 1**. **Save** your presentation, and then print or submit the file as directed by your instructor.

Done! You have completed Assess Your Skills 2

Assess Your Skills Visually

To complete this presentation, you will need the following files:

- New blank presentation
- p02_Natural_History_Museum

You will save your presentation as:

- Lastname_Firstname_p02_Museum

Start a new, blank presentation, and create the first two slides of a presentation as shown in **Figure 1**. To complete these two slides, apply the **Pushpin** theme. On **Slide 1**, change the title font size to **54**, and change the subtitle font size to **32**. On **Slide 2**, format the slide background by using the picture found in your student files—**p02_Natural_History_Museum**. Insert the appropriate WordArt style, type the text, and change the WordArt font size to **48**. Move and format the **Shape Fill** color as indicated in the figure. **Save** your presentation as Lastname_Firstname_p02_Museum and then insert the date, file name, and page number in the **Notes and Handouts** footer. **Save** the presentation, and then print or submit the file as directed by your instructor.

Done! You have completed Assess Your Skills Visually

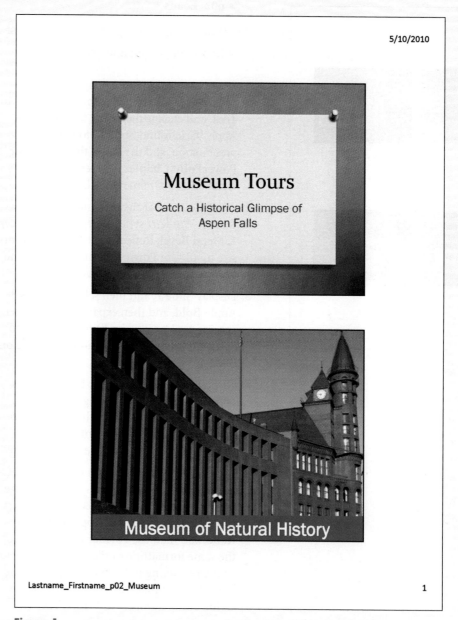

Figure 1

Skills in Context

To complete this presentation, you will need the following file:

- New blank presentation

You will save your presentation as:

- Lastname_Firstname_p02_Celebration

Each year the City of Aspen Falls hosts a Fourth of July celebration at the Aspen Falls Community Park. Using the skills you practiced in this chapter, create a presentation with five slides that describes the city's Fourth of July events, which include a parade, barbecue, games, arts and crafts fair, and fireworks. Create an appropriate title slide, and then on the second and third slides, provide a description of the event location and the celebration schedule. On the fourth slide, format the background with a picture that depicts the event, and include WordArt text that briefly describes the picture. On the fifth slide, provide a summary using the Section Header layout.

Apply an appropriate theme, and change fonts and colors as necessary. Save the presentation as Lastname_Firstname_p02_Celebration and then insert the file name and page number in the Notes and Handouts footer. Save the presentation, and then print or submit the file as directed by your instructor.

Done! You have completed Skills in Context

Skills and You

To complete this presentation, you will need the following file:

- New blank presentation

You will save your presentation as:

- Lastname_Firstname_p02_City

Using the skills you have practiced in this chapter, create a presentation with six slides describing a city that you would like to visit. Apply an appropriate theme, and change the fonts and colors themes. On at least one slide, format the slide background with a picture that depicts the city that you choose. On the first slide, format the slide title by using a WordArt style. Include in your presentation a numbered list that indicates at least four things that you would like to do or see in the city that you choose. The remaining slides may include information about the people, culture, and activities of the city.

Format the last slide with the Section Header layout, and enter text that briefly summarizes your presentation. Add a footer to the notes and handouts with the file name and page number, and then check spelling in the presentation. Save the presentation as Lastname_Firstname_p02_City and then print or submit electronically as directed by your instructor.

Done! You have completed Skills and You

CHAPTER 3

Enhance Presentations with Graphics

▶ Appropriate presentation graphics visually communicate your message and help your audience understand the points you want to convey.

▶ Review the graphics that you use, the text on your slides, and your spoken words to ensure that your presentation is coherent, precise, and accurate.

Your starting screen will look similar to this:

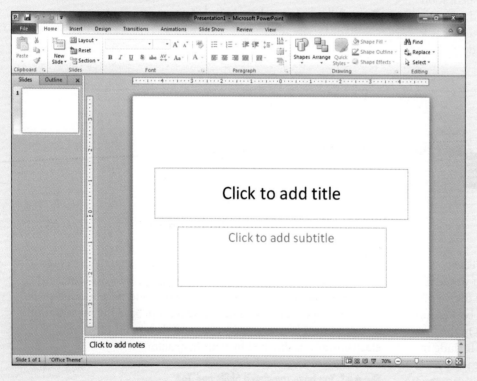

SKILLS
Skills 1-10 Training

At the end of this chapter, you will be able to:

Skill 1 Insert Slides from Other Presentations
Skill 2 Insert, Size, and Move Clip Art
Skill 3 Modify Picture Shapes, Borders, and Effects
Skill 4 Insert, Size, and Move Shapes
Skill 5 Add Text to Shapes and Insert Text Boxes
Skill 6 Apply Gradient Fills and Group and Align Graphics
Skill 7 Convert Text to SmartArt Graphics and Add Shapes
Skill 8 Modify SmartArt Layouts, Colors, and Styles
Skill 9 Insert Video Files
Skill 10 Apply Video Styles and Adjust Videos

MORE SKILLS

More Skills 11 Compress Pictures
More Skills 12 Save Groups as Picture Files
More Skills 13 Change Object Order
More Skills 14 Design Presentations Using Appropriate Graphics

Outcome

Using the skills listed to the left will enable you to create a presentation like this:

You will save this presentation as:

Lastname_Firstname_p03_Alliance

In this chapter, you will create presentations for the Aspen Falls City Hall, which provides essential services for the citizens and visitors of Aspen Falls, California.

Introduction

- ▶ In many organizations, team members commonly share presentations using slide libraries and file sharing procedures.

- ▶ When effective and illustrative diagrams are needed, you can use SmartArt graphics to list information and show process and relationships.

- ▶ When you have slides with many bullet points, consider inserting slides with SmartArt graphics to add interest and variety.

**Time to complete all
10 skills – 60 minutes**

Find your student data files here:

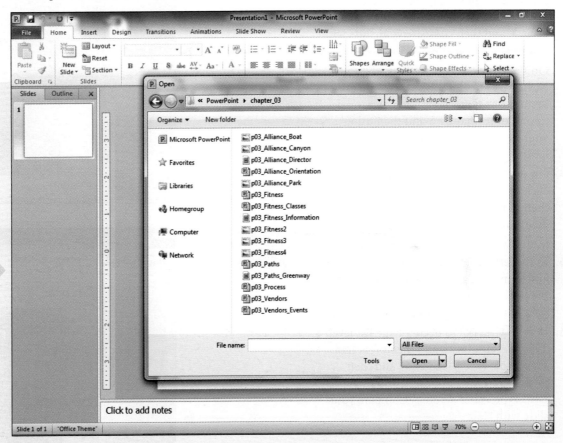

Student data files needed for this chapter:

- New blank presentation
- p03_Alliance_Orientation
- p03_Alliance_Canyon
- p03_Alliance_Director
- p03_Alliance_Boat
- p03_Alliance_Park

▶ Presentation slides can be shared using the Reuse Slides command so that frequently used content does not need to be recreated.

1. **Start** PowerPoint to display a new presentation. In the title placeholder, type Aspen Falls Employee Alliance and then in the subtitle placeholder, type Join the Club!

2. On the **Design tab**, in the **Background group**, click **Background Styles**. Click **Style 3**, and then compare your slide with **Figure 1**.

3. On the **Quick Access Toolbar**, click **Save**. Navigate to the location where you are saving your files, create a folder named PowerPoint Chapter 3 and then using your own name, save the document as Lastname_Firstname_p03_Alliance

4. On the **Home tab**, in the **Slides group**, click the **New Slide button arrow**, and then in the **Office Theme** gallery, click **Two Content**. In the title placeholder, type Employee Fitness Events

5. In the left placeholder, type Team sports and then press [Enter]. Press [Tab] to increase the list level. Type Soccer and then press [Enter]. Type Basketball and then press [Enter].

6. Press [Shift] + [Tab] to decrease the list level. Type Weekly classes and then press [Enter]. Press [Tab]. Type Kickboxing and then press [Enter]. Type Boot camp and then press [Enter]. Type Water aerobics Compare your slide with **Figure 2**.

■ **Continue to the next page to complete the skill**

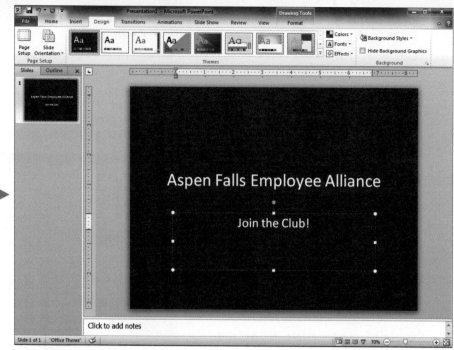

Figure 1

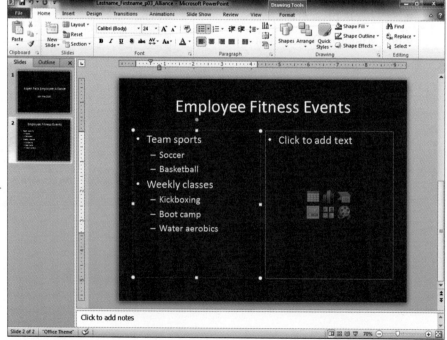

Figure 2

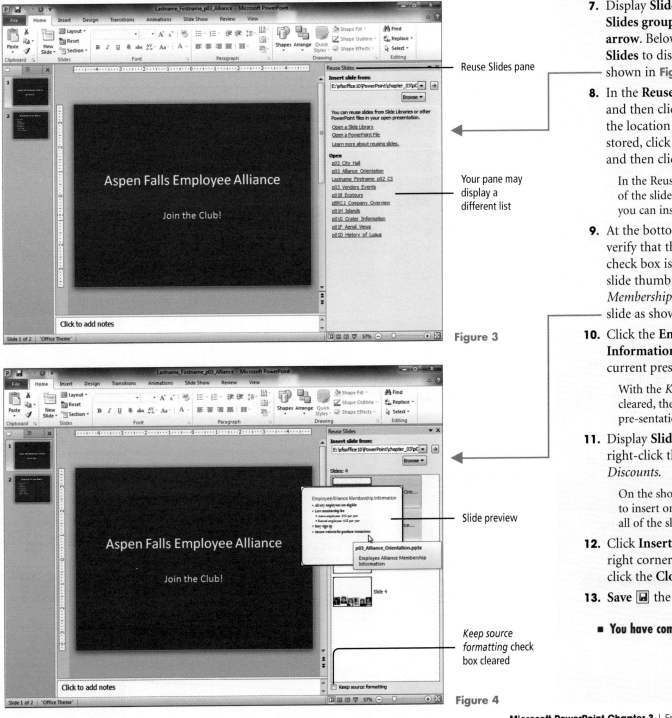

Reuse Slides pane

Your pane may display a different list

Figure 3

Slide preview

Keep source formatting check box cleared

Figure 4

7. Display **Slide 1**. On the **Home tab**, in the **Slides group**, click the **New Slide button arrow**. Below the gallery, click **Reuse Slides** to display the Reuse Slides pane as shown in **Figure 3**.

8. In the **Reuse Slides** pane, click **Browse**, and then click **Browse File**. Navigate to the location where your student files are stored, click **p03_Alliance_Orientation**, and then click **Open**.

   In the Reuse Slides pane, you can insert all of the slides from another presentation, or you can insert only the slides that you need.

9. At the bottom of the **Reuse Slides** pane, verify that the **Keep source formatting** check box is cleared. Point to the second slide thumbnail—*Employee Alliance Membership Information*—to preview the slide as shown in **Figure 4**.

10. Click the **Employee Alliance Membership Information** slide to insert it in the current presentation.

    With the *Keep source formatting* option cleared, the formatting of the current pre-sentation is applied to the inserted slide.

11. Display **Slide 3**. In the **Reuse Slides** pane, right-click the third slide—*Vacation Discounts*.

    On the shortcut menu, you have the option to insert only the selected slide or to insert all of the slides in the current presentation.

12. Click **Insert Slide**, and then in the upper right corner of the **Reuse Slides** pane, click the **Close** button ☒.

13. Save ☐ the presentation.

   ■ **You have completed Skill 1 of 10**

▶ Recall that clip art refers to images included with Microsoft Office, whereas pictures are images that are saved as a file with an extension such as .jpg, .bmp, or .tif.

1. Display **Slide 3**. In the placeholder on the right, click the **Clip Art** button 🖼 to display the Clip Art pane.

2. In the **Clip Art** pane, in the **Search for** box, replace any existing text with soccer sports equipment to search for images that contain the keywords *soccer*, *sports*, and *equipment*.

3. Click the **Results should be** arrow, and then clear or select the check boxes so that only **Photographs** is selected, as shown in **Figure 1**.

> When the Photographs check box is selected, only images that were created with a digital camera or a scanner will be searched.

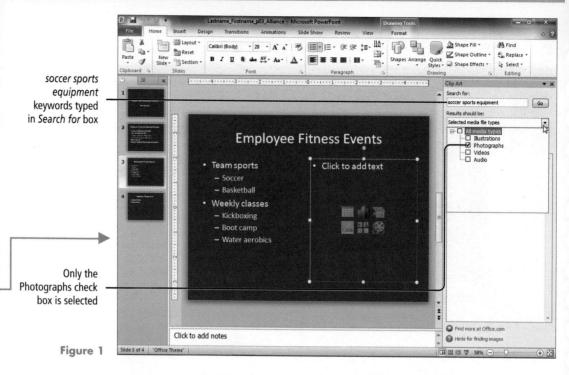

soccer sports equipment keywords typed in *Search for* box

Only the Photographs check box is selected

Figure 1

4. Click the **Results should be arrow** to close the list, and then select the **Include Office.com content** check box.

5. In the **Clip Art** pane, click **Go** to display the pictures that match the search criteria.

6. In the **Clip Art** pane, scroll as necessary to locate and then click the picture of the soccer ball in the net with the blue sky background, shown in **Figure 2**. If you are unable to locate the picture, insert a similar picture.

■ **Continue to the next page to complete the skill**

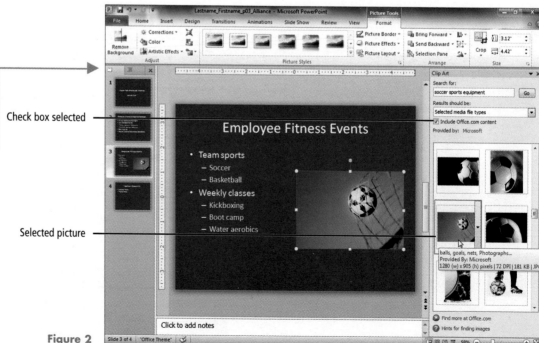

Check box selected

Selected picture

Figure 2

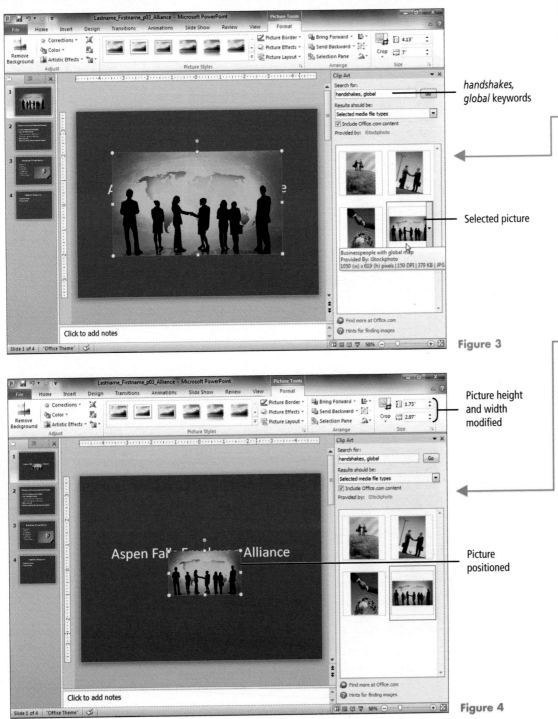

handshakes,
global keywords

Selected picture

Figure 3

Picture height
and width
modified

Picture
positioned

Figure 4

7. Display **Slide 1**. In the **Clip Art** pane, in the **Search for** box, replace the existing text with handshakes, global

8. Click the **Results should be** arrow, and if necessary, select only the **Photographs** check box. Click **Go**, and then locate and click the picture shown in **Figure 3**. If you are unable to locate the same picture, choose a similar picture.

9. On the **Format tab**, in the **Size group**, click in the **Shape Height** box 🔲 to select its displayed number. Type 1.75 and then press Enter.

   When you change the height of a picture in this manner, the width is adjusted proportionately.

10. Point to the picture to display the 🔀 pointer. Drag the picture to the center of the slide so that the subtitle and part of the title are covered as shown in **Figure 4**.

11. **Close** ☒ the **Clip Art** pane, and then **Save** 🔲 the presentation.

   ■ **You have completed Skill 2 of 10**

▶ Inserted pictures are usually rectangular, but they can be changed to a number of different shapes available in PowerPoint.

▶ *Picture effects* are picture styles that include shadows, reflections, glows, soft edges, bevels, and 3-D rotations.

1. On **Slide 1**, if necessary, select the picture.

2. On the **Format tab**, in the **Size group**, click the *lower* part of the Crop button— the **Crop button arrow**. Point to **Crop to Shape** to display the **Shape** gallery, and then compare your screen with **Figure 1**.

3. Under **Basic Shapes**, click the first shape—**Oval**—to change the shape of the picture from a rectangle to an oval.

4. In the **Picture Styles group**, click the **Picture Effects** button. Point to **Soft Edges**, and then point to each option and notice that the edges of the picture are blurred and softened.

5. Click **50 Point**, and then compare your screen with **Figure 2**. If necessary, point to the picture to display the pointer, and drag to position the picture as shown in **Figure 2**.

6. Display **Slide 3**, and then select the picture. On the **Format tab**, in the **Picture Styles group**, click the **Picture Effects** button. Point to **Shadow**, and then point to, but do not click, several of the options to view the shadow effects on the picture.

■ **Continue to the next page to complete the skill**

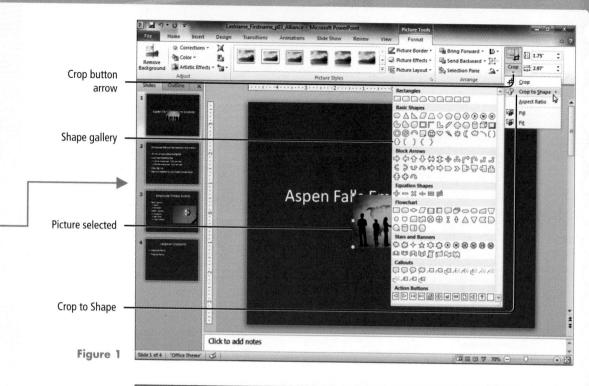

Crop button arrow

Shape gallery

Picture selected

Crop to Shape

Figure 1

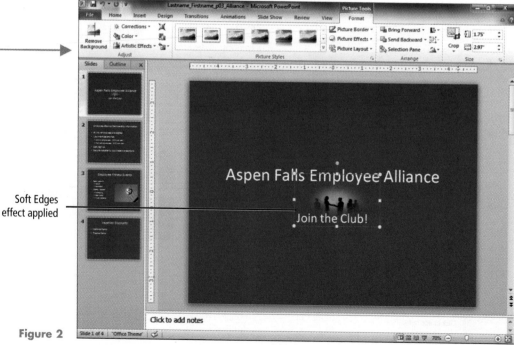

Soft Edges effect applied

Figure 2

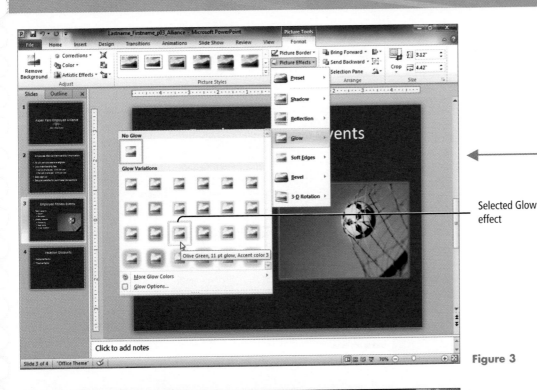

Selected Glow effect

Figure 3

7. Point to **Reflection**, and then point to, but do not click, several of the options to view the reflection effects on the picture.

8. Point to **Glow** to display the gallery.

   The Glow effect applies a diffused outline to the picture in varying intensities, using colors from the presentation theme.

9. In the third row, click the third glow variation—**Olive Green, 11 pt glow, Accent color 3**—as shown in **Figure 3**.

10. With the picture still selected, on the **Format tab**, in the **Picture Styles group**, click the **Picture Effects** button. Point to **Bevel**, and then under **Bevel**, click the first option—**Circle**.

    When you apply multiple effects to a picture in this manner, choose effects that complement the picture and the presentation theme.

11. With the picture still selected, on the **Format tab**, in the **Picture Styles group**, click the **Picture Border** button. Under **Theme Colors**, click the first color— **Black, Background 1**.

    A narrow border surrounds the picture between the bevel effect and the glow effect.

12. Click the **Picture Border** button again, and then point to **Weight**. Click **3 pt** to apply a thicker border.

13. Click a blank area on the slide so that nothing is selected, and then compare your slide with **Figure 4**.

14. Save 🖫 the presentation.

■ **You have completed Skill 3 of 10**

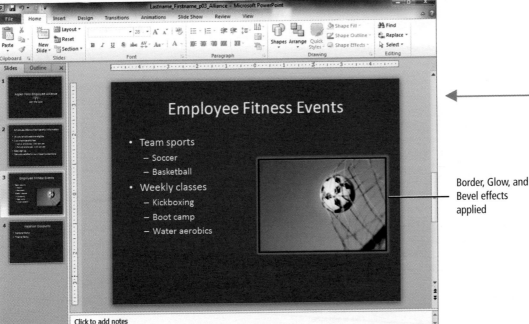

Border, Glow, and Bevel effects applied

Figure 4

▶ You can use shapes as design elements, particularly on slides with a simple background design.

1. Display **Slide 2**. On the **View tab**, in the **Show group**, if necessary, select the Ruler check box so that the rulers display in the Slide pane.

2. On the **Insert tab**, in the **Illustrations group**, click the **Shapes** button, and then under **Lines**, click the first shape—**Line**.

3. Align the ⊞ pointer with **4.5 inches** before zero on the horizontal ruler and **2.5 inches** above zero on the vertical ruler, as shown in **Figure 1**. ────

   As you position the pointer, the ruler displays *guides*—lines that display in the rulers to give you a visual indication of where the pointer is positioned.

4. Hold down Shift, and then drag to the right to **4.5 inches** after zero on the horizontal ruler. Release the mouse button.

   To draw a straight line, press Shift while dragging.

5. In the **Illustrations group**, click the **Shapes** button. Under **Basic Shapes**, in the first row, click **Diamond**. In the lower right corner of the slide, click one time to insert a one-inch-high diamond.

6. With the diamond selected, on the **Format tab**, in the **Size group**, click in the **Shape Height** box 🔟 to select the text *1"*. Type 0.25 and then click in the **Shape Width** box 🔲. Type 0.4 and then press Enter to resize the diamond. Compare your slide with **Figure 2**. ────

■ **Continue to the next page to complete the skill** ➤

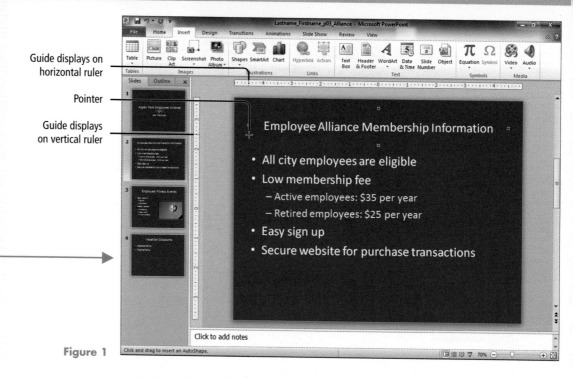

Guide displays on horizontal ruler

Pointer

Guide displays on vertical ruler

Figure 1

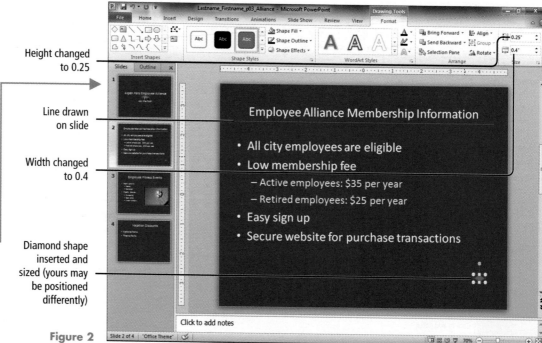

Height changed to 0.25

Line drawn on slide

Width changed to 0.4

Diamond shape inserted and sized (yours may be positioned differently)

Figure 2

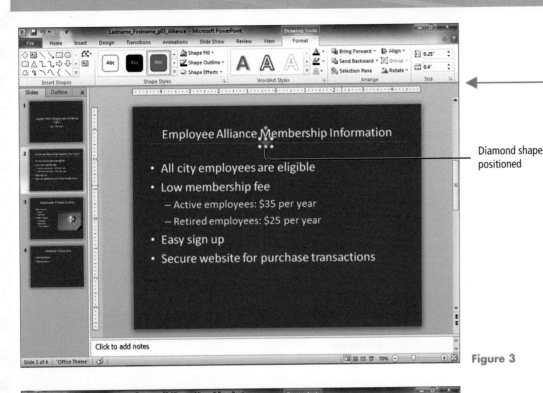

Diamond shape positioned

Figure 3

Height changed to 5.5

Width changed to 10

Rectangle positioned

Figure 4

7. Point to the diamond to display the pointer, and then drag the diamond so that it is positioned on the line below the *M* in *Membership* as shown in **Figure 3**.

8. Display **Slide 4**. On the **Home tab**, in the **Slides group**, click the **New Slide button arrow**, and then click **Reuse Slides** to display the **p03_Alliance_Orientation** slides in the Reuse Slides pane. If the slides from p03_Alliance_Orientation do not display in the Reuse Slides pane, click the Browse button, click Browse File, navigate to your student files, and then open p03_Alliance_Orientation.

9. In the **Reuse Slides** pane, click **Slide 4** to insert it in the presentation, and then **Close** ⊠ the pane.

10. On the **Insert tab**, in the **Illustrations group**, click the **Shapes** button. Under **Rectangles**, click the first shape—**Rectangle**. With the ⊞ pointer, drag from the upper left corner of the slide to the right edge of the slide and down to **2 inches** below zero on the vertical ruler.

11. With the rectangle selected, on the **Format tab**, in the **Size group**, change the **Shape Height** ⬚ value to 5.5 and then in the **Shape Width** box ⬚, type 10 Press Enter to resize the rectangle.

12. Compare your slide with **Figure 4**, and if necessary, drag the rectangle so that it is positioned as shown in the figure.

    The rectangle will overlap some of the pictures.

13. **Save** ⬚ the presentation.

■ **You have completed Skill 4 of 10**

► A **text box** is an object used to position text anywhere on a slide.

► In addition to being used as design elements, shapes can be used as containers for text.

1. On **Slide 5**, if necessary, select the rectangle.

   To insert text in a shape, select the shape, and then begin to type.

2. Type Questions? Press Enter, and then type Contact an Employee Alliance Associate Press Enter, type (805) 555-1087 and then compare your slide with **Figure 1**.

   When you type text in a shape, it is centered both horizontally and vertically within the shape.

3. Select the three lines of text, and then change the **Font Size** to **40**.

4. With the three lines of text still selected, on the **Format tab**, in the **WordArt Styles group**, click the **More** button ⧩. Under **Applies to All Text in the Shape**, click the third thumbnail in the first row—**Fill - Red, Accent 2, Warm Matte Bevel**.

5. In the **WordArt Styles group**, click the **Text Fill button arrow** ⧩ to display the gallery. Under **Theme Colors**, in the second column, click the first color—**White, Text 1**. Click in the gray area outside the slide so that nothing is selected, and then compare your slide with **Figure 2**.

   WordArt styles can be applied to the text in a shape.

■ **Continue to the next page to complete the skill**

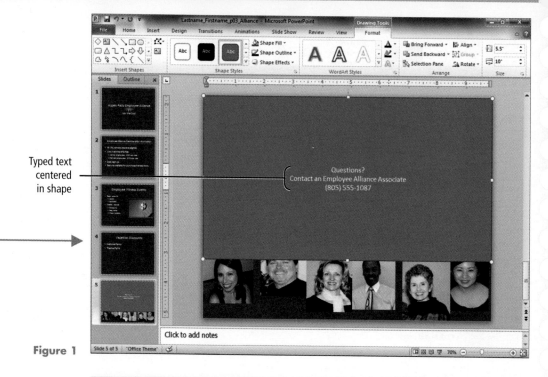

Typed text centered in shape

Figure 1

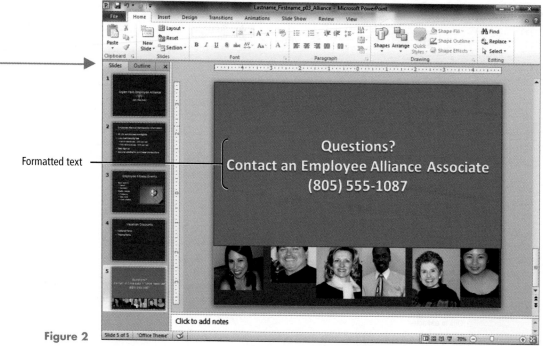

Formatted text

Figure 2

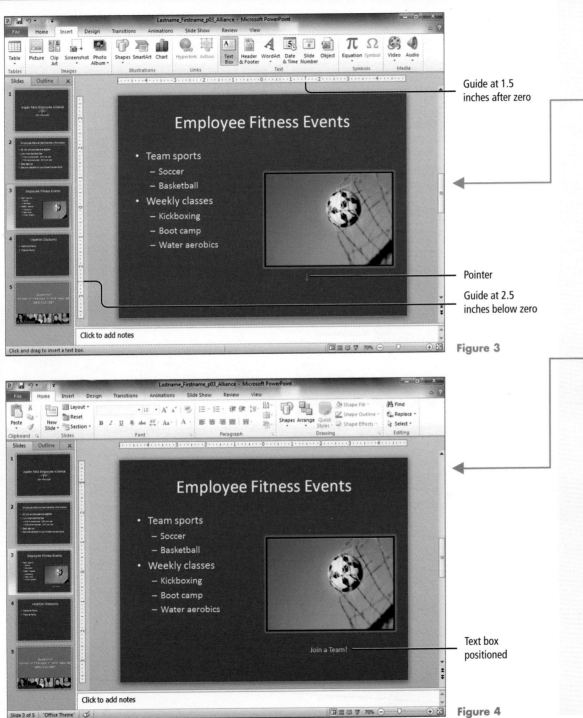

Guide at 1.5
inches after zero

Pointer

Guide at 2.5
inches below zero

Figure 3

Text box
positioned

Figure 4

6. Display **Slide 3**. On the **Insert tab**, in the **Text group**, click the **Text Box** button. Position the pointer on the slide aligned at **1.5 inches** after zero on the horizontal ruler and at **2.5 inches** below zero on the vertical ruler as shown in **Figure 3**.

7. Without moving the pointer, click one time to insert a text box. Type Join a Team! If the text box displays one character at a time in a vertical line, on the Quick Access Toolbar, click Undo, and then repeat Steps 6 and 7.

8. Click anywhere on the slide so that the text box is not selected.

   Unlike shapes, when a text box is inserted, it does not include borders or fill colors. Text inserted in a text box appears to be floating on the slide and is formatted in the same font as the body font used in content placeholders.

9. Compare your slide with **Figure 4**. If your text box is not positioned as shown in the figure, select the text box and then use the ⬆, ⬇, ⬅, or ➡ keys on your keyboard to *nudge*—move an object in small increments using the directional arrow keys—the text box so that it is positioned as shown.

10. **Save** 🖫 the presentation.

▪ **You have completed Skill 5 of 10**

▶ A *group* is a collection of multiple objects treated as one unit that can be copied, moved, or formatted.

1. Display **Slide 5**, and then select the rectangle. On the **Format tab**, in the **Shape Styles group**, click the **Shape Effects** button. Point to **Bevel**, and then click the second-to-last bevel— **Hard Edge**.

2. In the **Shape Styles group**, click the **Shape Fill** button. Point to **Gradient**, and then under **Dark Variations**, in the second row, click the second thumbnail—**From Center**—as shown in **Figure 1** to apply a gradient fill to the shape.

   A *gradient fill* is a gradual progression of colors and shades, usually from one color to another, or from one shade to another shade of the same color, to add a fill to a shape.

3. Display **Slide 2**. Select the diamond. Hold down Shift, and then click the line so that both objects are selected as shown in **Figure 2**. If you selected one of the place-holders, click anywhere on the slide to deselect the objects, and then try again.

4. On the **Format tab**, in the **Arrange group**, click the **Align** button, and then click **Align Center**. In the **Arrange group**, click the **Align** button, and then click **Align Middle** to align the shapes.

   The line and the diamond move so that their center points are aligned.

5. With the objects selected, on the **Format tab**, in the **Arrange group**, click the **Group** button, and then click **Group**. Sizing handles enclose the objects as one unit.

■ **Continue to the next page to complete the skill** ▶

From Center gradient fill

Figure 1

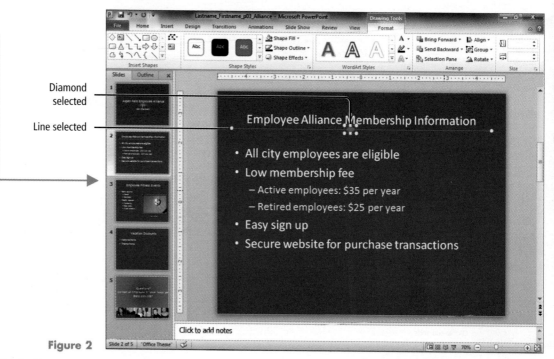

Diamond selected

Line selected

Figure 2

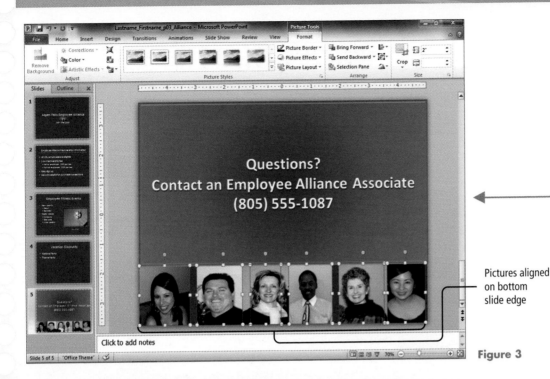

Pictures aligned on bottom slide edge

Figure 3

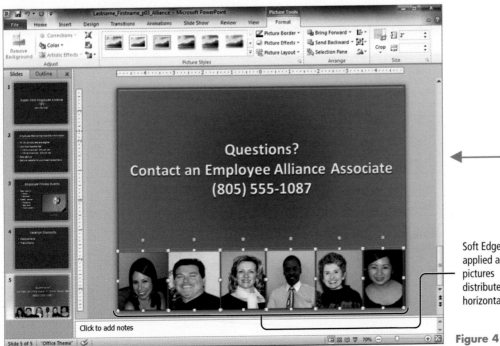

Soft Edges applied and pictures distributed horizontally

Figure 4

6. Display **Slide 5**. Hold down Shift, and then click each picture at the bottom of the slide so that all six of the pictures are selected. If you selected the rectangle, hold down Shift, and then click the rectangle so that it is not selected.

7. On the **Format tab**, in the **Arrange group**, click the **Align** button, and then click **Align to Slide**. Click the **Align** button, and then click **Align Bottom**. Compare your slide with **Figure 3**.

    The combination of the Align to Slide and Align Bottom options aligns the selected objects along the bottom of the slide.

8. With the pictures selected, on the **Format tab**, in the **Picture Styles group**, click the **Picture Effects** button. Point to **Soft Edges**, and then click **2.5 Point**.

9. With the pictures selected, on the **Format tab**, in the **Arrange group**, click the **Align** button. Click **Align Selected Objects**. Click the **Align** button, and then click **Distribute Horizontally**. Compare your slide with **Figure 4**.

    With Align Selected Objects selected, the pictures distribute evenly between the left edge of the left picture and the right edge of the right picture.

10. With the pictures selected, in the **Arrange group**, click the **Group** button, and then click **Group**. In the **Arrange group**, click the **Align** button. Click **Align Center** to center the group on the slide.

11. **Save** the presentation.

■ **You have completed Skill 6 of 10**

► A *SmartArt graphic* is a designer-quality visual representation of information that you can use to communicate your message or ideas effectively.

► You can include text and pictures in a SmartArt graphic, and you can apply colors, effects, and styles that coordinate with the presentation theme.

► You can convert text that you have already typed—such as a list—into a SmartArt graphic.

1. Display **Slide 4**, and then click anywhere in the bulleted list. On the **Home tab**, in the **Paragraph group**, click the **Convert to SmartArt Graphic** button 📊. Below the gallery, click **More SmartArt Graphics** to display the **Choose a SmartArt Graphic** dialog box. Compare your screen with **Figure 1.**

   The Choose a SmartArt Graphic dialog box is divided into three sections. The left section lists the SmartArt graphic types. The center section displays the layouts for the selected type. The third section displays a preview of the selected layout, along with a description of the layout.

2. On the left section of the dialog box, click each of the SmartArt graphic types to view the layouts in each category, and then in the center section of the dialog box, click several layouts to view their descriptions.

   The eight types of SmartArt graphics are summarized in **Figure 2.**

■ **Continue to the next page to complete the skill**

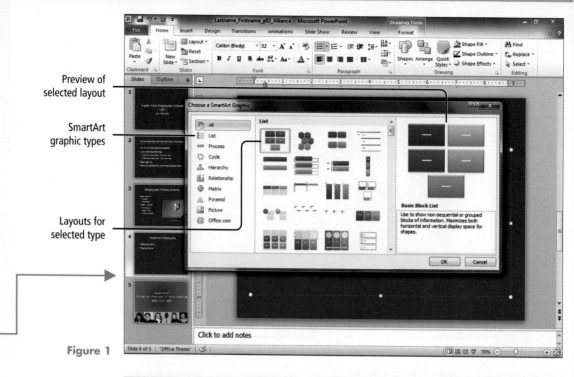

Preview of selected layout

SmartArt graphic types

Layouts for selected type

Figure 1

Figure 2

Microsoft PowerPoint SmartArt Layout Types	
Type	**Purpose**
List	Illustrates nonsequential information.
Process	Illustrates steps in a process or timeline.
Cycle	Illustrates a continual process.
Hierarchy	Illustrates a decision tree or creates an organization chart.
Relationship	Illustrates connections.
Matrix	Illustrates how parts relate to a whole.
Pyramid	Illustrates proportional relationships, with the largest component on the top or bottom.
Picture	Communicates messages and ideas using pictures in each layout.

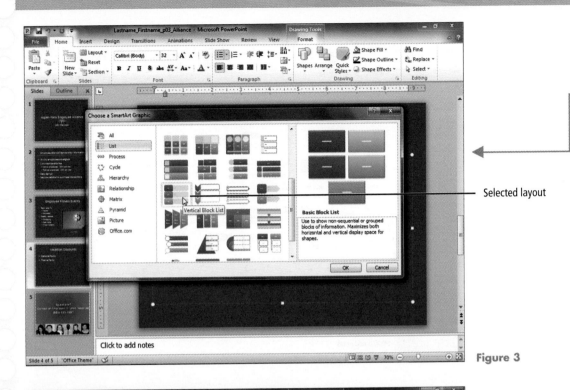

Selected layout

Figure 3

3. In the left section of the dialog box, click **List**, and then scroll the center section of the dialog box and use the ScreenTips to locate **Vertical Block List**. Compare your screen with **Figure 3**.

4. Click **Vertical Block List**, and then click **OK** to convert the bulleted list to a SmartArt graphic.

   The Text Pane button may be selected on the Ribbon, and the Text Pane may display to the left of the SmartArt graphic.

5. If the Text Pane displays, on the SmartArt Tools Design tab, in the Create Graphic group, click the Text Pane button so that the pane does not display.

6. Click anywhere in the text *National Parks*. On the **SmartArt Tools Design tab**, in the **Create Graphic group**, click the **Add Bullet** button to insert a shape to the right of *National Parks*. Type Grand Canyon, Yellowstone, Yosemite

7. Click in the *Theme Parks* shape, and then in the **Create Graphic group**, click the **Add Bullet** button. Type Nationwide

8. Click in the *Theme Parks* shape, and then in the **Create Graphic group**, click the **Add Shape** button to add a shape below *Theme Parks*. If you clicked the Add Shape button arrow and a menu displays, click Add Shape After.

9. Type Houseboats and then add a bullet. Type Lake Powell and Lake Mead

10. Compare your screen with **Figure 4**, and then **Save** 🖫 the presentation.

   ■ **You have completed Skill 7 of 10**

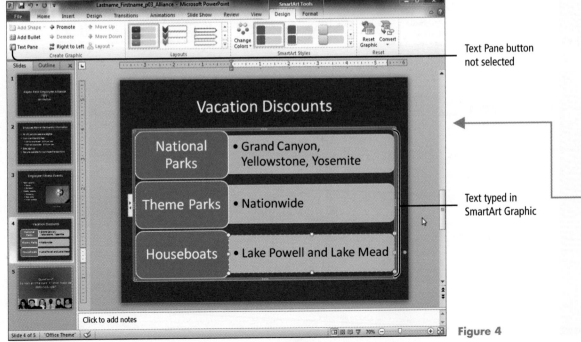

Text Pane button not selected

Text typed in SmartArt Graphic

Figure 4

▶ When you create a SmartArt graphic, choose a layout that provides the best visual representation of your information.

▶ The colors that you apply to a SmartArt graphic are coordinated with the presentation color theme.

▶ SmartArt styles include gradient fills and 3-D effects.

1. On **Slide 4**, if necessary, select the SmartArt graphic. Under **SmartArt Tools**, click the **Design tab**. In the **Layouts group**, click the **More** button ⬇, and then click **More Layouts** to display the **Choose a SmartArt Graphic** dialog box. Click **Picture** scroll up or down as necessary, and then click **Captioned Pictures** as shown in **Figure 1**.

2. Click **OK** to convert the SmartArt to the Captioned Pictures layout.

3. In the SmartArt, in the first rectangle, click the **Insert Picture from File** button 🖼. Navigate to the location where your student files are stored, click **p03_Alliance_Canyon**, and then click **Insert**.

4. In the middle rectangle, use the technique just practiced to insert **p03_Alliance_Park**, and then in the last rectangle, insert **p03_Alliance_Boat**. Compare your slide with **Figure 2**. If you moved the mouse when you clicked the Insert Picture from File button, the shape may have moved. If this happened, click Undo to reposition the shape, and then try again.

■ **Continue to the next page to complete the skill** ▶

Selected SmartArt

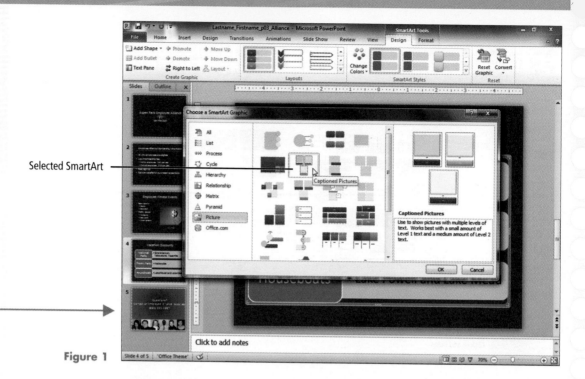

Figure 1

Three pictures inserted

Figure 2

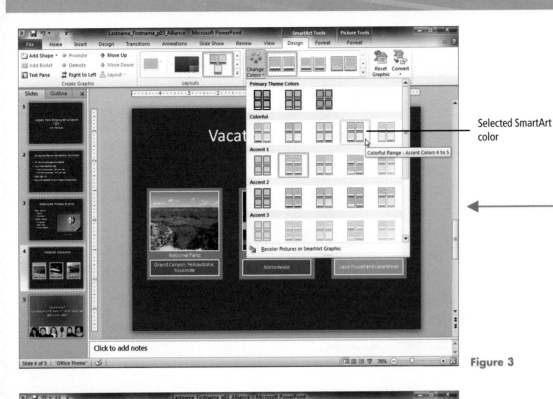

Figure 3

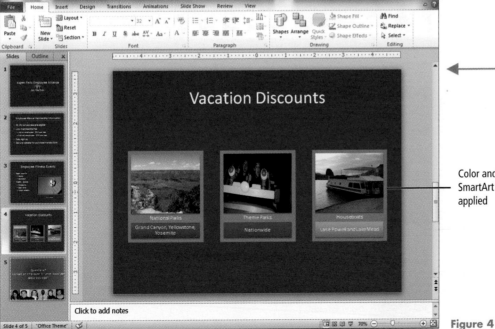

Figure 4

5. On the Ribbon, under **SmartArt Tools**, click the **Design tab**. In the **SmartArt Styles group**, click the **Change Colors** button to display the **Color** gallery.

   The colors that display in the gallery coordinate with the color theme.

6. Point to several of the color options to view the effect on the diagram. Then, under **Colorful**, point to the fourth style—**Colorful Range - Accent Colors 4 to 5**—as shown in **Figure 3**.

7. Click **Colorful Range - Accent Colors 4 to 5** to apply the color change to the SmartArt graphic.

8. On the **Design tab**, in the **SmartArt Styles group**, click the **More** button ⟱ to display the **SmartArt Styles** gallery. Point to several of the styles to view their effects on the diagram. Then, under **Best Match for Document**, click the fourth style—**Moderate Effect**. Click in a blank area of the slide, and then compare your screen with **Figure 4**.

9. **Save** 🖫 the presentation.

■ **You have completed Skill 8 of 10**

Selected SmartArt color

Color and SmartArt style applied

► You can insert, size, and move video files in a presentation, and you can control when the video will begin to play during a slide show.

1. Display **Slide 1**, and then insert a **New Slide** with the **Title and Content** layout. In the title placeholder, type Justin Tamari, AFEA Director

2. In the content placeholder, click the **Insert Media Clip** button 🖼️, and then navigate to the location where your student files are stored. Click **p03_Alliance_Director**, and then click **Insert**. Alternately, on the Insert tab, in the Media group, click the Video button. Compare your screen with **Figure 1**.

   The video displays in the center of the slide, and playback and volume controls display in the control panel below the video. Video formatting and editing tools display on the Ribbon.

3. If speakers are available, be sure that they are on, or insert headphones into the computer. On the control panel below the video, point to the **Play/Pause** button ▶ so that it is highlighted as shown in **Figure 2**.

4. Click the **Play/Pause** button ▶ to view the video. Alternately, press [Alt] + [P]. If necessary, on the control panel, click the Mute/Unmute button to adjust the volume on your system.

   As the video plays, the control panel displays the time that has elapsed since the start of the video.

■ **Continue to the next page to complete the skill** ▶

Video Tools

Mute/Unmute button

Video inserted

Move Forward 0.25 Seconds button

Move Back 0.25 Seconds button

Control panel

Play/Pause button

Figure 1

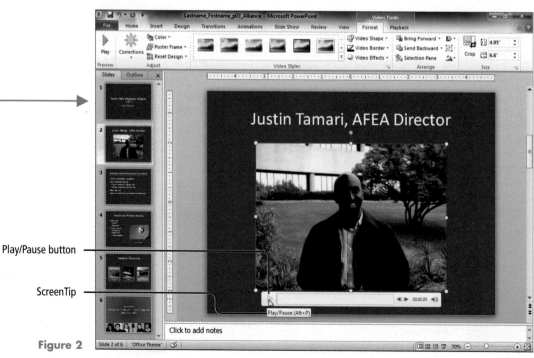

Play/Pause button

ScreenTip

Figure 2

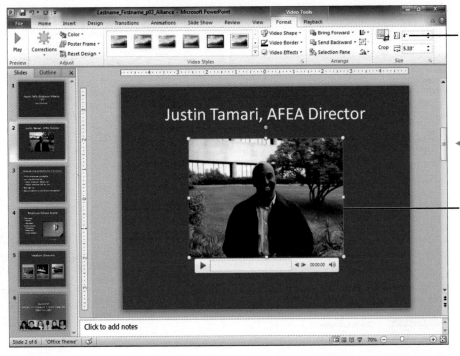

Video height changed to 4

Video centered horizontally on the slide

Figure 3

Justin Tamari, AFEA Director

Link select pointer displays

Control panel displays

Figure 4

5. On the **Format tab**, in the **Size group**, click in the **Video Height** box. Type 4 and then press Enter. Notice that the video width adjusts proportionately. On the **Format tab**, in the **Arrange group**, click the **Align** button, and then click **Align Center** to center the video horizontally on the slide. Compare your screen with **Figure 3**.

6. On the right side of the status bar, in the **View** buttons, click the **Slide Show** button to display **Slide 2** in the slide show. Point to the video to display the pointer, and then compare your screen with **Figure 4**.

When you point to the video during the slide show, the control panel displays.

7. With the pointer displayed, click the mouse button to view the video. When the video is finished, press Esc to exit the slide show.

8. If necessary, select the video. On the **Playback tab**, in the **Video Options group**, click the **Start** arrow, and then click **Automatically**. In the **View** buttons, click the **Slide Show** button to display **Slide 2** in the slide show. When the video is finished, press Esc to exit the slide show.

The Start Automatically option begins the video when the slide displays in the slide show. You can use this option if you want the video to begin playing without clicking the mouse button.

9. **Save** the presentation.

■ **You have completed Skill 9 of 10**

▶ You can apply styles and effects to a video and change the video shape and border.

▶ You can recolor a video so that it coordinates with the presentation theme.

1. On **Slide 2**, if necessary, select the video. On the **Format tab**, in the **Video Styles group**, click the **More** button ⊡. In the **Video Styles** gallery, under **Moderate**, click the seventh style—**Snip Diagonal Corner, Gradient**. Click on a blank area of the slide, and then compare your screen with **Figure 1**. ————

2. Select the video. On the **Format tab**, in the **Video Styles group**, click the **Video Effects** button. Point to **Shadow**, and then if necessary, scroll down to display the **Perspective** options.

3. Under **Perspective**, click the second thumbnail—**Perspective Diagonal Upper Right**.

4. With the video selected, on the **Format tab**, in the **Adjust group**, click the **Color** button.

   The Recolor gallery displays colors from the presentation theme that you can apply to the video.

5. Point to several of the thumbnails to view the color change, and then click the second thumbnail—**Grayscale**—to change the color of the video. Compare your screen with **Figure 2**. ————

6. On the **Format tab**, in the **Adjust group**, click the **Color** button, and then click the first thumbnail—**No Recolor**—to change the video color back to the original.

■ **Continue to the next page to complete the skill** ▷

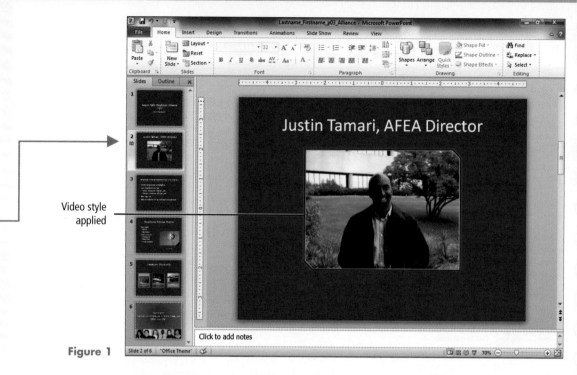

Video style applied

Figure 1

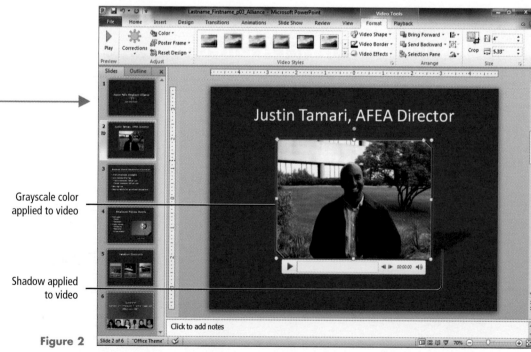

Grayscale color applied to video

Shadow applied to video

Figure 2

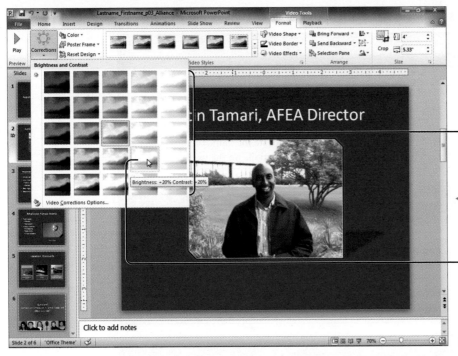

Brightness and
Contrast gallery

Brightness and
Contrast option
selected

Figure 3

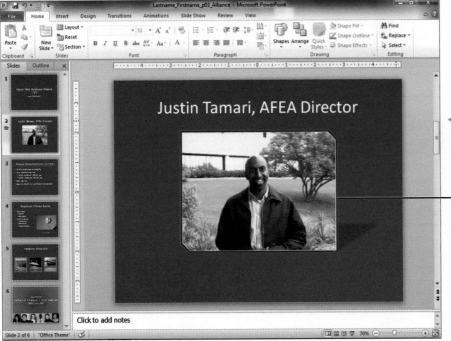

Brightness and
Contrast applied
to video

Figure 4

7. With the video selected, on the **Format tab**, in the **Adjust group**, click the **Corrections** button to display the **Brightness and Contrast** gallery.

   The Brightness and Contrast gallery displays combinations of brightness and contrast adjustments that you can apply to a video to improve color and visibility.

8. In the fourth column, point to the fourth thumbnail to display the ScreenTip **Brightness: +20% Contrast: +20%** as shown in **Figure 3**.

9. Click **Brightness: +20% Contrast: +20%** to apply the correction to the video, and then click anywhere on the slide so that the video is not selected. Compare your screen with **Figure 4**.

10. On the **Transitions tab**, in the **Transition to This Slide group**, click the **More** button. Under **Exciting**, click **Switch**. In the **Timing group**, click **Apply To All**. On the **Slide Show tab**, in the **Start Slide Show group**, click **From Beginning**, and then click the mouse button to advance the presentation. When the black slide displays, click one more time to return to your slides.

11. Insert a **Header & Footer** on the **Notes and Handouts** that includes the **Date and time**, a **Page number**, and the **Footer** Lastname_Firstname_p03_Alliance

12. **Save** the presentation. Print your pre-sentation or submit the file, as directed by your instructor. **Exit** PowerPoint.

Done! You have completed Skill 10 of 10 and your presentation is complete!

The following More Skills are located at **www.pearsonhighered.com/skills**

More Skills ⑪ Compress Pictures

The large file sizes of pictures from digital cameras or scanners can slow the delivery of a presentation and make your presentation files large. You can compress the presentation pictures so that the file size is smaller.

In More Skills 11, you will open a presentation, view the file size, compress the pictures in the presentation, and then view the changes to the file size.

To begin, open your web browser, navigate to www.pearsonhighered.com/skills, locate the name of your textbook, and then follow the instructions on the website.

More Skills ⑫ Save Groups as Picture Files

A group can be saved as a picture file so that you can insert it on another slide, insert it in another presentation, or use it in other programs. In this way, saving a group as a picture facilitates easy sharing among presentations and applications.

In More Skills 12, you will open a presentation, create a group, and then save the group as a picture. You will then insert the picture into other slides in the presentation.

To begin, open your web browser, navigate to www.pearsonhighered.com/skills, locate the name of your textbook, and then follow the instructions on the website.

More Skills ⑬ Change Object Order

When objects such as shapes and pictures are inserted on a slide, they often overlap. The first object inserted is positioned at the bottom of the stack, and the next object inserted is above the first object. You can change the order in which objects overlap by moving them backward and forward in the stack.

In More Skills 13, you will open a presentation and change the order of inserted objects.

To begin, open your web browser, navigate to www.pearsonhighered.com/skills, locate the name of your textbook, and then follow the instructions on the website.

More Skills ⑭ Design Presentations Using Appropriate Graphics

When you are creating a presentation, the graphics that you choose affect how your message is perceived by your audience. Thus, it is important to choose appropriate graphics for every presentation that you create.

In More Skills 14, you will review design principles that will assist you in choosing appropriate graphics for your slides. You will view two slides and compare the different messages conveyed when different graphics are used.

To begin, open your web browser, navigate to www.pearsonhighered.com/skills, locate the name of your textbook, and then follow the instructions on the website.

Key Terms

Online Help Skills

1. **Start** 🔵 PowerPoint. In the upper right corner of the PowerPoint window, click the **Help** button ⊙. In the **Help** window, click the **Maximize** 🔲 button.

2. Click in the search box, type video play options and then click the **Search** button 🔎. In the search results, click **Turn your presentation into a video**.

3. Below **In this article**, click **Why turn your presentation into a video?** Compare your screen with **Figure 1**.

Figure 1

4. Read the entire article and then see if you can answer the following: What are some of the advantages of turning your presentation into a video?

Matching

Match each term in the second column with its correct definition in the first column by writing the letter of the term on the blank line in front of the correct definition.

____ **1.** A command used to insert slides from another presentation into an existing presentation so that content does not need to be recreated.

____ **2.** Formatting options applied to pictures that include shadows, reflections, glows, soft edges, bevels, and 3-D rotations.

____ **3.** Lines that display in the rulers to give you a visual indication of where the pointer is positioned.

____ **4.** Objects such as lines and circles that can be used as design elements on a slide.

____ **5.** An object used to position text anywhere on a slide.

____ **6.** The action of moving an object in small increments by using the directional arrow keys.

____ **7.** Multiple objects treated as one unit that can be copied, moved, or formatted.

____ **8.** A fill effect in which one color fades into another.

____ **9.** A designer-quality visual representation of information that you can use to communicate your message or ideas effectively by choosing from among many different layouts.

____ **10.** A command used to change a list into a SmartArt graphic.

A Convert to SmartArt Graphic

B Gradient fill

C Group

D Guides

E Nudge

F Picture effects

G Reuse Slides

H Shapes

I SmartArt graphic

J Text box

Multiple Choice

Choose the correct answer.

1. The task pane that is used to insert slides from another presentation.
   - A. Insert Slides
   - B. Browse Slides
   - C. Reuse Slides

2. The name of the box in which the height of a picture can be changed.
   - A. Height Size
   - B. Shape Height
   - C. Crop Height

3. The default alignment applied to text typed in a shape.
   - A. Left
   - B. Center
   - C. Right

4. A SmartArt layout type that illustrates nonsequential information.
   - A. Process
   - B. Cycle
   - C. List

5. A SmartArt layout type that illustrates a continual process.
   - A. Hierarchy
   - B. Cycle
   - C. Process

6. A SmartArt layout type that illustrates a decision tree or creates an organization chart.
   - A. Relationship
   - B. Hierarchy
   - C. Pyramid

7. A SmartArt layout type that illustrates connections.
   - A. Relationship
   - B. Hierarchy
   - C. Pyramid

8. The tab in which video Start options are found.
   - A. Format
   - B. Playback
   - C. Design

9. The button that displays video Brightness and Contrast options.
   - A. Color
   - B. Design
   - C. Corrections

10. The button that displays the video Recolor gallery.
    - A. Color
    - B. Design
    - C. Corrections

Topics for Discussion

1. Some PowerPoint presenters advocate using only slides that consist of a single statement and a graphic so that the presentation reads like a story. Other presenters advocate using slides that combine the "single statement and graphics" approach with slides that include detail in the form of bullet points, diagrams, and pictures. What is the advantage of each of these approaches? Which approach would you prefer to use?

2. Sharing presentation slides among employees in an organization is a common practice. What types of information and objects do you think should be included on slides that are shared within an organization?

Skill Check

To complete this presentation, you will need the following files:

- p03_Fitness
- p03_Fitness_Classes
- p03_Fitness_Information
- p03_Fitness2
- p03_Fitness3
- p03_Fitness4

You will save your presentation as:

- Lastname_Firstname_p03_Fitness

1. **Start** PowerPoint, open **p03_Fitness**, and then display **Slide 3**. On the **Home tab**, in the **Slides group**, click the **New Slide button arrow**. Click **Reuse Slides**.

2. In the **Reuse Slides** pane, click the **Browse** button, and then click **Browse File**. From your student files, click **p03_Fitness_Classes**, and then click **Open**. In the **Reuse Slides** pane, click **Slide 2** to insert it, and then **Close** the pane. **Save** your presentation in your **PowerPoint Chapter 3** folder as Lastname_Firstname_p03_Fitness

3. Display **Slide 2**. In the content placeholder, click the **Clip Art** button. In the **Clip Art** task pane, in the **Search for** box, type exercise bicycle Click the **Results should be arrow**, and then select only the **Photographs** check box. Click **Go**. Click the picture of several exercise bicycles in a row, and then **Close** the task pane. Compare your screen with **Figure 1**.

4. With the picture selected, on the **Format tab**, in the **Size group**, change the **Shape Height** to 3.75 and then press Enter. Drag the picture to center it within the blue rectangle on the right side of the slide.

5. On the **Format tab**, in the **Size group**, click the **Crop button arrow**, and then click **Crop to Shape**. Under **Rectangles**, click **Rounded Rectangle**. In the **Picture Styles group**, click the **Picture Effects button**, point to **Bevel**, and then under **Bevel**, click the first effect—**Circle**.

6. On the **Insert tab**, in the **Text group**, click **Text Box**. Align the pointer at **0.5 inches** after zero on the horizontal ruler and at **2 inches** below zero on the vertical ruler, and then click. Type Join a Class! Click in a blank area of the slide, and then compare your slide with **Figure 2**.

7. On **Slide 3**, in the content placeholder, click the **Insert Media Clip** button. From your student files, insert **p03_Fitness_Information**. On the **Format tab**, in the **Size group**, change the **Video Height** to 3.5 and then drag the video so that it is centered in the dark blue rectangle.

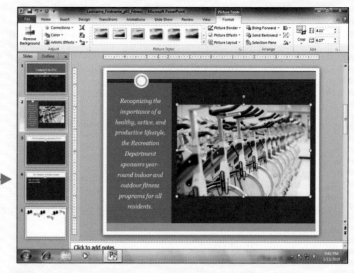

Figure 1

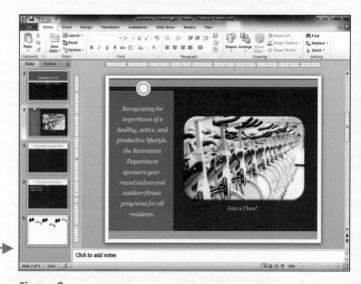

Figure 2

■ Continue to the next page to complete this Skill Check ▶

8. On the **Playback tab**, in the **Video Options group**, click the **Start arrow**, and then click **Automatically**. On the **Format tab**, in the **Video Styles group**, click the **More** button, and then under **Subtle**, select **Glow Rectangle**.

9. On **Slide 4**, click the bulleted list. On the **Home tab**, in the **Paragraph group**, click the **Convert to SmartArt Graphic** button. Click **More SmartArt Graphics**, and then click **Picture**. Scroll the gallery, and then locate and click **Vertical Picture List**. Click **OK**.

10. On the **Design tab**, in the **Create Graphic group**, click the **Add Shape** button, and then type Water Wonders

11. In the first shape, click the **Insert Picture from File** button. From your student files, insert **p03_Fitness2**. In the second shape, insert **p03_Fitness3**. In the last shape, insert **p03_Fitness4**.

12. Change the SmartArt colors to **Colorful - Accent Colors**, and then apply the first 3-D SmartArt style—**Polished**. Compare your slide with **Figure 3**.

13. Display **Slide 5**. Hold down Shift, and then click each picture. On the **Format tab**, in the **Arrange group**, click the **Align** button, and then click **Align to Slide**. Click the **Align** button, and then click **Align Top**.

14. With the pictures selected, click the **Align** button, and then click **Align Selected Objects**. Click the **Align** button, and then click **Distribute Horizontally**.

15. In the **Picture Styles group**, click the **Picture Effects** button. Point to **Soft Edges**, and then click **25 Point**. In the **Arrange group**, click the **Group** button, and then click **Group**.

16. On the **Insert tab**, in the **Illustrations group**, click **Shapes**. Under **Rectangles**, click **Rounded Rectangle**. Align the pointer with **4 inches** before zero on the horizontal ruler and with **2 inches** above zero on the vertical ruler. Drag to draw a rectangle that extends to **4 inches** after zero on the horizontal ruler and to **2 inches** below zero on the vertical ruler.

17. In the shape, type Contact the Aspen Falls Recreation Department and then press Enter. Type (805) 555-7895 and then change the **Font Size** to **40** for all of the text in the shape. Apply the **Flip** transition to all of the slides.

18. View the slide show. Insert a **Header & Footer** on the **Notes and Handouts** with a **Page number** and the **Footer** Lastname_Firstname_p03_Fitness Compare your presentation with **Figure 4**, and then **Save**. Print or submit the file as directed.

Done! You have completed the Skill Check

Figure 3

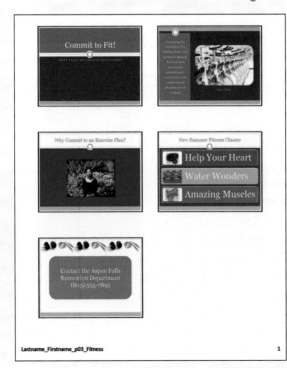

Figure 4

Assess Your Skills 1

To complete this presentation, you will need the following files:

- p03_Vendors
- p03_Vendors_Events

You will save your presentation as:

- Lastname_Firstname_p03_Vendors

1. **Start** PowerPoint, and then from your student files, open **p03_Vendors**. With **Slide 1** displayed, display the **Reuse Slides** pane, and then insert **Slide 3—Summer Events**—from the student data file **p03_Vendors_Events**. **Save** your presentation in your **PowerPoint Chapter 3** folder as Lastname_Firstname_p03_Vendors

2. On **Slide 2**, convert the text to a **Horizontal Bullet List** SmartArt. Change the SmartArt color to **Colorful Range - Accent Colors 4 to 5**, and then apply the **3-D Cartoon** SmartArt style.

3. On **Slide 4**, insert a **Bevel** basic shape. Draw the shape so that it extends from **4.5 inches** before zero on the horizontal ruler and **0 inches** on the vertical ruler to **4.5 inches** after zero on the horizontal ruler and **2.5 inches** below zero on the vertical ruler.

4. In the shape, type Summer events in Aspen Falls garner large tourist numbers. During the past five years, overall attendance has increased by 19 percent, and tourist spending has increased by 23 percent.

5. Increase the **Font Size** to **24**, and then change the **Font Color** to **Black, Text 1**. Apply a **Glow** shape effect—**Orange, 18 pt glow, Accent color 5**.

6. On **Slide 1**, insert a **Clip Art** by searching for a **Photograph** using keywords summer sun background Insert the picture of the yellow sun background. If you cannot locate the picture, choose another appropriate picture.

7. Change the **Height** of the picture to 3.5 and then change the shape to a **32-Point Star**—the last shape in the first row under **Stars and Banners**. Apply the **25 Point** Soft Edges picture effect. Using the **Align to Slide** option, change the alignment to **Align Center** and **Align Bottom**.

8. Insert a **Header & Footer** on the **Notes and Handouts**. Include a **Page number** and the **Footer** Lastname_Firstname_p03_Vendors **Save** the presentation, and print or submit as directed. Compare your completed presentation with **Figure 1**.

   Done! You have completed Assess Your Skills 1

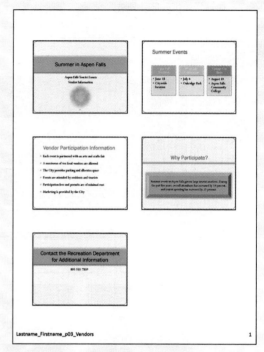

Figure 1

Assess Your Skills 2

Assess Your Skills 3 and 4 can be found at www.pearsonhighered.com/skills.

To complete this presentation, you will need the following files:

- p03_Paths
- p03_Paths_Greenway

You will save your presentation as:

- Lastname_Firstname_p03_Paths

Lastname_Firstname_p03_Paths   1

Figure 1

1. **Start** PowerPoint, and then from your student files, open **p03_Paths**. Save your presentation in your **PowerPoint Chapter 3** folder as Lastname_Firstname_p03_Paths

2. Display **Slide 2**, and then change the picture shape to the last shape under **Rectangles—Rounded Diagonal Corner Rectangle**. Apply the first **Bevel** effect—**Circle**—and then apply an **Orange, 8 pt glow, Accent color 2** picture effect.

3. Insert a **Text Box** positioned just below the lower left corner of the picture. Type View from Hacienda Point and then change the **Font Size** to **24** and the **Font Color** to **Light Yellow, Text 2**. Select the slide title, the picture, and the text box, and then align the selected objects using the **Align Center** option.

4. Display **Slide 3**, and then in the content placeholder, from your student files, insert the video **p03_Paths_Greenway**. Apply the **Intense, Reflected Perspective Right** video style, and then change the **Video Options** so that the video starts **Automatically** during the slide show.

5. **Adjust** the video by changing the **Corrections** option to **Brightness: 0% (Normal) Contrast: +20%**.

6. Display **Slide 4**, and then convert the bulleted list to a SmartArt Graphic with the

Alternating Flow layout located in the **Process** types. Change the SmartArt color to **Colored Outline - Accent 3**, and then apply the 3-D **Inset** SmartArt style.

7. On **Slide 5**, insert a **Wave** Stars and Banners shape that extends from **4 inches** before zero on the horizontal ruler and **2 inches** above zero on the vertical ruler to **4 inches** after zero on the horizontal ruler and **0** on the vertical ruler. Type Grand Opening on March 20 and then change the **Font Size** to **40**.

8. Apply a **Preset** shape effect—**Preset 8**—and then apply a **Bevel** shape effect—**Angle**.

9. Display **Slide 6**, and then align the four pictures by using the **Align Bottom** option. With the **Align to Slide** option selected, distribute the pictures horizontally. Apply a **50 Point Soft Edges** effect, and then **Group** the pictures. View the slide show from the beginning.

10. Insert a **Header & Footer** on the **Notes and Handouts**. Include a **Page number** and the **Footer** Lastname_Firstname_p03_Paths

11. Compare your completed presentation with **Figure 1**. **Save** the presentation, and then print or submit electronically.

Done! You have completed Assess Your Skills 2

Assess Your Skills Visually

To complete this presentation, you will need the following file:

- p03_Process

You will save your presentation as:

- Lastname_Firstname_p03_Process

Start PowerPoint, and then from your student files, open **p03_Process**. Format and edit the slide as shown in **Figure 1**. **Save** the file as Lastname_Firstname_p03_Process in your **PowerPoint Chapter 3** folder.

To complete this slide, apply the **Office** theme and apply the **Urban** theme colors. The content placeholder text is sized at **22** points. For the SmartArt graphic, use the **Repeating Bending Process** layout. After you create the SmartArt, drag the *Improve* shape so that it is centered as shown in **Figure 1**. Add a footer to the Notes and Handouts with the file name and page number, and then print or submit electronically, as directed by your instructor.

Done! You have completed Assess Your Skills Visually

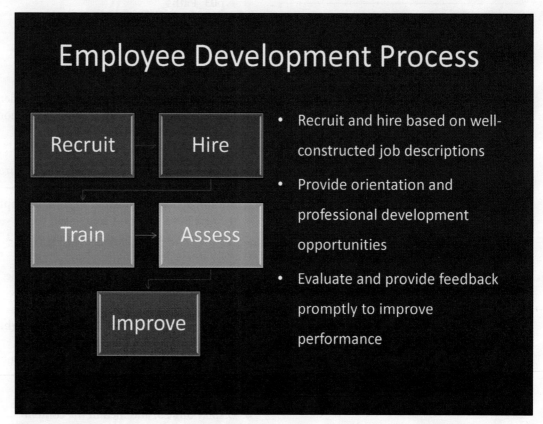

Figure 1

Skills in Context

To complete this presentation, you will need the following file:

- New blank PowerPoint presentation

You will save your presentation as:

- Lastname_Firstname_p03_Programs

Using the following information, create a presentation with an appropriate theme, and then create four slides that describe new programs offered to City employees. The presentation will be part of a larger presentation on employee benefits. On one slide, convert the text to a SmartArt graphic describing the programs, and then format the SmartArt appropriately. Insert and format at least one Clip Art image illustrating the programs.

To improve employee health and productivity, the City of Aspen Falls is offering several voluntary programs to City employees. The first program—*A City in Motion*—offers a free pedometer so that employees can record the number of steps taken each day. Human Resources will provide maps of walking routes adjacent to various city offices for those who want to walk with colleagues

before or after work or during lunch. The second program is *Fit in Aspen Falls*. All city employees are eligible to receive discounts on individual and family memberships at local fitness centers. The third program—*Wellness through the Week*—is a series of classes held during lunch hours or immediately after work, including yoga, preventive health care, stress reduction, health and nutrition, and more.

Save the presentation as Lastname_Firstname_p03_Programs Add a footer to the Notes and Handouts with the file name and page number, and then print or submit electronically as directed by your instructor.

Done! You have completed Skills in Context

Skills and You

To complete this presentation, you will need the following file:

- New blank PowerPoint presentation

You will save your presentation as:

- Lastname_Firstname_p03_Careers

Using the skills you have practiced in this chapter, create a presentation with an appropriate theme that includes four to six slides describing a career in which you are interested. On one slide, convert the text to a SmartArt graphic that either lists the credentials that you need or demonstrates the process that you must follow to be successful in this career. Insert and format pictures on at least two slides that illustrate people who have chosen this career.

Save the presentation as Lastname_Firstname_p03_Careers Add a footer to the Notes and Handouts with the file name and page number, and then check spelling in the presentation. Print or submit electronically, as directed by your instructor.

Done! You have completed Skills and You

CHAPTER 4

Present Data Using Tables, Charts, and Animation

▶ Tables and charts are used to present information in an organized manner that enables the audience to understand important data with ease.

▶ Animation effects enhance a presentation by drawing attention to important slide elements, particularly when the timing of animation effects is precisely controlled during a slide show.

Your starting screen will look like this:

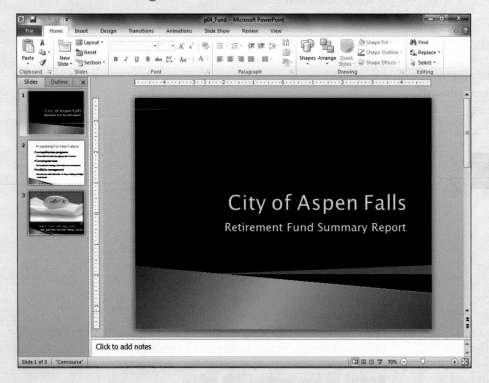

SKILLS myitlab
Skills 1-10 Training

At the end of this chapter, you will be able to:

Skill 1 Insert Tables
Skill 2 Modify Table Layouts
Skill 3 Apply Table Styles
Skill 4 Insert Column Charts
Skill 5 Edit and Format Charts
Skill 6 Insert Pie Charts
Skill 7 Apply Animation Entrance and Emphasis Effects
Skill 8 Modify Animation Timing and Use Animation Painter
Skill 9 Remove Animation and Modify Duration
Skill 10 Navigate Slide Shows

MORE SKILLS

More Skills 11 Prepare Presentations to Be Viewed Using Office PowerPoint Viewer
More Skills 12 Insert Hyperlinks in a Presentation
More Skills 13 Create Photo Albums
More Skills 14 Design Presentations with Appropriate Animation

Outcome

Using the skills listed to the left will enable you
to create a presentation like this:

You will save the presentation as:

Lastname_Firstname_p04_Fund

In this chapter, you will create presentations for the Aspen Falls City Hall, which provides essential services for the citizens and visitors of Aspen Falls, California.

Introduction

▶ Tables and charts can be used to present data in an organized manner. When possible, use charts to display numeric data, particularly when making comparisons between the data.

▶ Use chart and table styles to apply formatting in a manner that complements the presentation theme.

▶ Use animation in a manner that focuses audience attention on important slide information.

Find your student data files here:

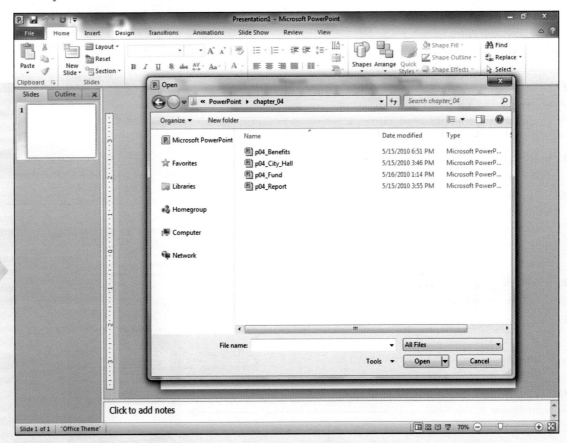

Student data files needed for this chapter:

- p04_Fund

► In a presentation, a *table* is used to organize and present information in columns and rows.

► In tables, text is typed into a *cell*—the intersection of a column and row.

1. **Start** PowerPoint. From your student files, **Open p04_Fund**. On the **File tab**, click **Save As**. Navigate to the location where you are saving your files, create a folder named PowerPoint Chapter 4 and then **Save** the presentation as Lastname_Firstname_p04_Fund

2. Display **Slide 2**, and then insert a **New Slide** with the **Title and Content** layout. In the title placeholder, type Active Membership and then **Center** ☰ the title.

3. In the content placeholder, click the **Insert Table** button ▦.

4. In the **Insert Table** dialog box, in the **Number of columns** box, type 3 and then press ⎯Tab⎯. In the **Number of rows** box, type 2 and then compare your screen with **Figure 1**. ────────

5. Click **OK** to create a table with three columns and two rows.

6. In the first row, click in the second cell. Type 2011 and then press ⎯Tab⎯.

   Pressing ⎯Tab⎯ moves the insertion point to the next cell in the same row.

7. Type 2012 and then compare your table with **Figure 2**. ────────

■ **Continue to the next page to complete the skill** ▶

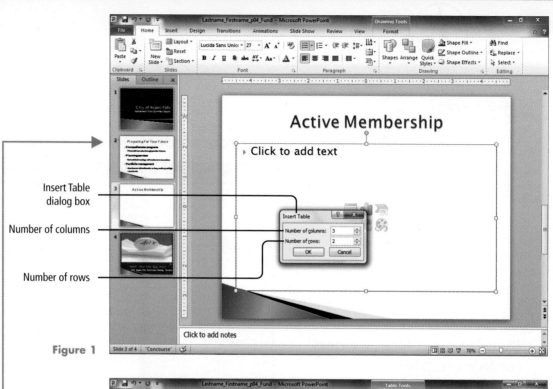

Insert Table dialog box

Number of columns

Number of rows

Figure 1

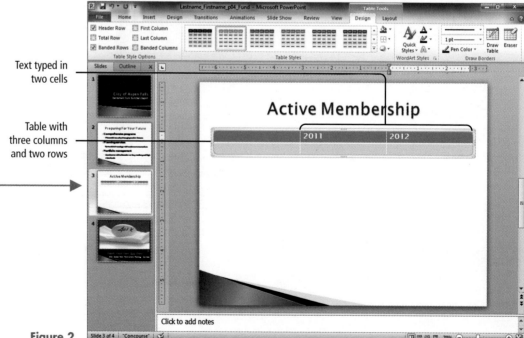

Text typed in two cells

Table with three columns and two rows

Figure 2

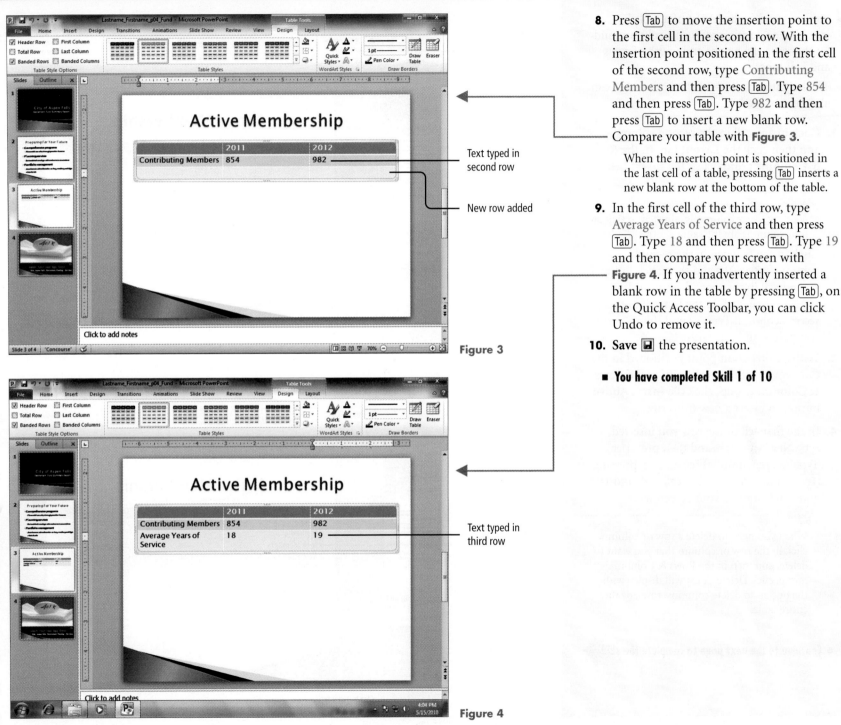

Figure 3

Figure 4

8. Press ⌨Tab to move the insertion point to the first cell in the second row. With the insertion point positioned in the first cell of the second row, type Contributing Members and then press ⌨Tab. Type 854 and then press ⌨Tab. Type 982 and then press ⌨Tab to insert a new blank row. Compare your table with **Figure 3**.

When the insertion point is positioned in the last cell of a table, pressing ⌨Tab inserts a new blank row at the bottom of the table.

9. In the first cell of the third row, type Average Years of Service and then press ⌨Tab. Type 18 and then press ⌨Tab. Type 19 and then compare your screen with **Figure 4**. If you inadvertently inserted a blank row in the table by pressing ⌨Tab, on the Quick Access Toolbar, you can click Undo to remove it.

10. Save 🖫 the presentation.

■ **You have completed Skill 1 of 10**

► You can modify the layout of a table by inserting or deleting rows and columns and by changing the height and width of rows and columns.

► The height and width of the entire table can also be modified.

1. Click in any cell in the second column, and then click the **Layout tab**. In the **Rows & Columns group**, click the **Insert Left** button.

> A new second column is inserted, and the width of every column is adjusted so that all four columns are the same width.

2. Click in the first cell in the second column. Type 2010 and then click in the second cell in the second column. Type 763 and then click in the last cell in the second column. Type 12 and then compare your table with **Figure 1**.

3. With the insertion point positioned in the third row, on the **Layout tab**, in the **Rows & Columns group**, click the **Insert Above** button to insert a new third row.

4. In the first cell of the row you inserted, type New Members and then press Tab. Type the remaining three entries, pressing Tab to move from cell to cell: 125 and 182 and 156 Compare your screen with **Figure 2**.

> When you need to delete a row or column, click in the row or column that you want to delete, and then in the Rows & Columns group, click Delete. A list will display with the option to delete columns, rows, or the entire table.

■ **Continue to the next page to complete the skill** ▸

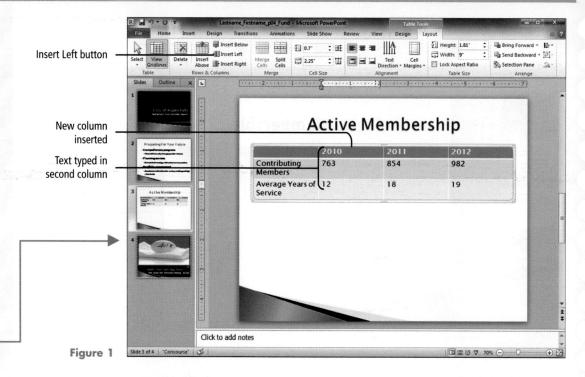

Insert Left button

New column inserted

Text typed in second column

Figure 1

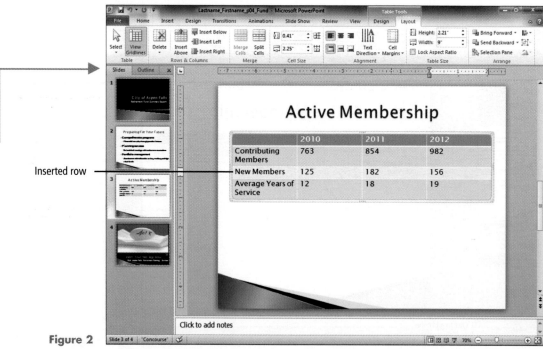

Inserted row

Figure 2

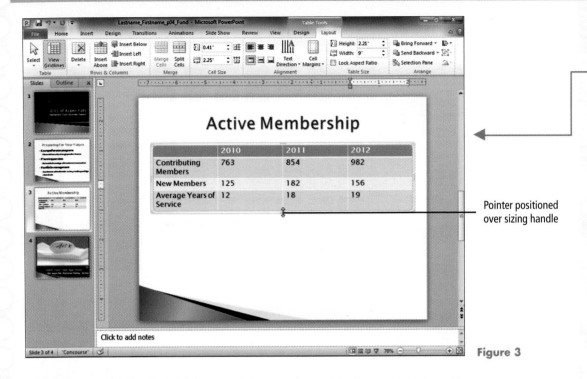

Pointer positioned over sizing handle

Figure 3

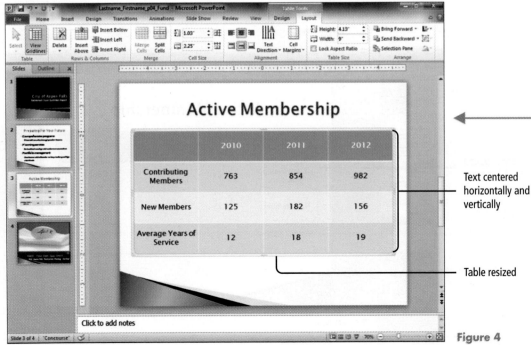

Text centered horizontally and vertically

Table resized

Figure 4

5. At the center of the lower border surrounding the table, point to the four dots—the sizing handle—to display the ⬍ pointer, as shown in **Figure 3**.

6. With the ⬍ pointer, drag down until the lower edge of the table extends to the **2 inch** mark below zero on the vertical ruler, and then release the mouse button to size the table.

7. Click in the first cell of the table. On the **Layout tab**, in the **Cell Size group**, click the **Distribute Rows** button ⊞.

> The Distribute Rows button adjusts the height of the rows in the table so that they are equal. If you do not select any rows, all of the table rows are adjusted. When you want to distribute certain table rows equally, select only the rows that you want to distribute. To distribute the width of columns equally, use the Distribute Columns button.

8. On the **Layout tab**, in the **Table group**, click the **Select** button, and then click **Select Table**. In the **Alignment group**, click the **Center** button ▤, and then click the **Center Vertically** button ▤.

> All of the text in the table is centered horizontally and vertically within the cells.

9. Compare your table with **Figure 4**, and then **Save** 🖫 your presentation.

■ **You have completed Skill 2 of 10**

▶ A *table style* applies borders and fill colors to the entire table in a manner consistent with the presentation theme.

▶ There are four color categories within the table styles—Best Match for Document, Light, Medium, and Dark.

1. Click in any cell in the table. Under the **Table Tools tab**, click the **Design tab**, and then in the **Table Styles group**, click the **More** button ▾. In the **Table Styles** gallery, point to several styles and watch as Live Preview displays the table with the selected style.

2. Under **Medium**, in the third row, point to the second style—**Medium Style 3 - Accent 1**—as shown in **Figure 1**.

3. Click **Medium Style 3 - Accent 1**.

   The cells in the first table row are filled with a blue color. In the remaining rows, the fill color alternates between white and light gray.

4. On the **Design tab**, in the **Table Style Options group**, clear the **Banded Rows** check box.

   The Table Style Options group controls where table style formatting is applied. For example, when the Banded Rows check box is cleared, the alternating fill colors are cleared from the table rows, and only the header row contains a fill color.

5. In the **Table Style Options group**, select the **Banded Rows** check box to reapply the light gray fill color to alternating rows. Compare your slide with **Figure 2**.

■ **Continue to the next page to complete the skill** ➤

Table Styles gallery

Selected style

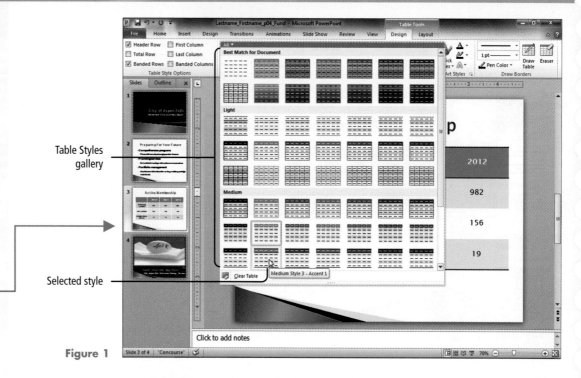

Figure 1

Style applied to table

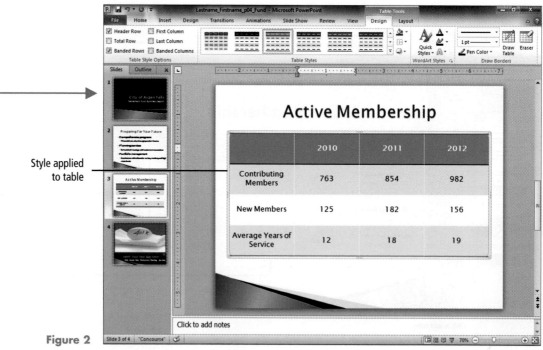

Figure 2

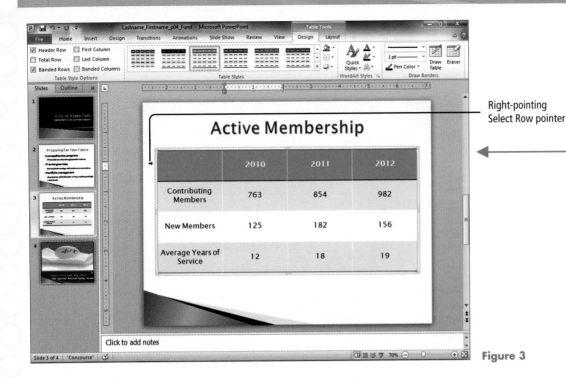

Right-pointing
Select Row pointer

Figure 3

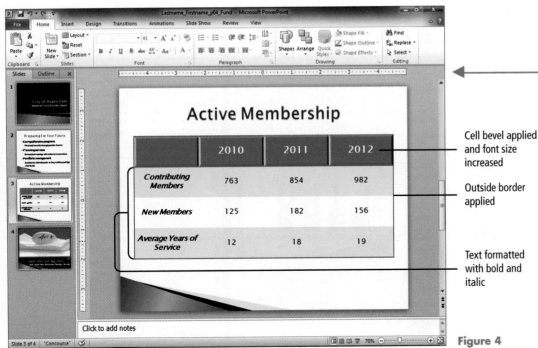

Cell bevel applied
and font size
increased

Outside border
applied

Text formatted
with bold and
italic

Figure 4

6. Move the pointer to the left of the first row in the table to display the Select Row ☞ pointer, as shown in **Figure 3**.

7. With the Select Row ☞ pointer pointing to the first row in the table, right-click to select the entire row and to display the Mini toolbar and shortcut menu. On the Mini toolbar, change the **Font Size** ⟨44 ·⟩ to **24**.

8. With the first row still selected, under the **Table Tools tab**, on the **Design tab**, in the **Table Styles group**, click the **Effects** button ⬜. Point to **Cell Bevel**, and then under **Bevel**, click the first bevel— **Circle**—to apply the effect to the first table row.

9. In the first column, drag to select the second, third, and fourth cells. On the **Home tab**, in the **Font group**, apply **Bold** ⟨B⟩, and then apply **Italic** ⟨I⟩.

10. On the **Layout tab**, in the **Table group**, click **Select**, and then click **Select Table**. On the **Table Tools Design tab**, in the **Table Styles group**, click the **Borders button arrow** ⟨⊞·⟩, and then click **Outside Borders**.

11. Click in a blank area of the slide, and then verify that a thin border displays on the outside edges of the table as shown in **Figure 4**. **Save** ⬚ the presentation.

■ **You have completed Skill 3 of 10**

▶ A ***chart*** is a graphic representation of numeric data.

▶ A ***column chart*** is useful for illustrating comparisons among related categories.

1. With **Slide 3** displayed, insert a **New Slide** with the **Title and Content** layout. In the title placeholder, type Fund Rate of Return by Risk Factor and then change the **Font Size** to **36**. **Center** the title.

2. In the content placeholder, click the **Insert Chart** button. On the left side of the **Insert Chart** dialog box, click several of the chart types to view the chart gallery. Then, click **Column**, as shown in **Figure 1**.

3. Click the first chart—**Clustered Column**—and then click **OK**. Compare your screen with **Figure 2**.

On the one side of your screen, the PowerPoint window displays a column chart. On the other side of your screen, an Excel worksheet displays columns and rows that intersect to form cells. A cell is identified by its column letter and row number.

The worksheet contains sample data in a data range outlined in blue, from which the chart in the PowerPoint window is generated. The column headings—*Series 1*, *Series 2*, and *Series 3*—display in the chart ***legend***, which identifies the patterns or colors that are assigned to the data in the chart. The row headings—*Category 1*, *Category 2*, *Category 3*, and *Category 4*—display along the bottom of the chart as ***category labels***—labels that identify the categories of data in a chart.

■ **Continue to the next page to complete the skill**

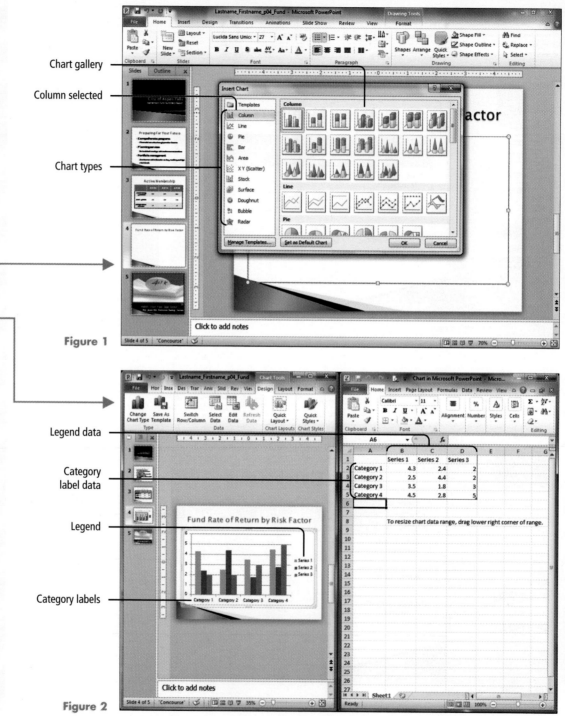

Chart gallery

Column selected

Chart types

Figure 1

Legend data

Category label data

Legend

Category labels

Figure 2

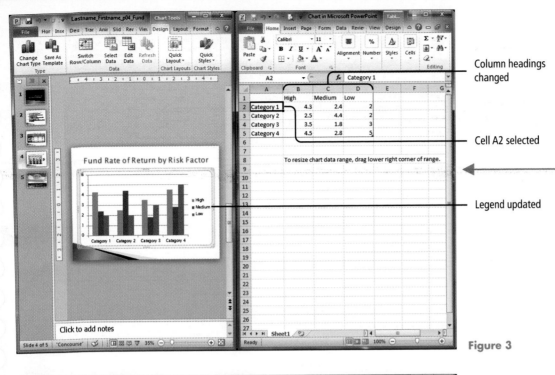

Column headings changed

Cell A2 selected

Legend updated

Figure 3

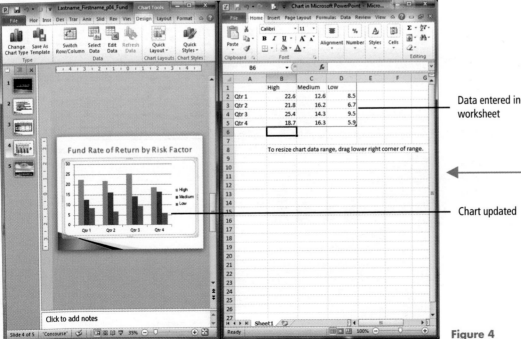

Data entered in worksheet

Chart updated

Figure 4

4. In the **Excel** window, click in cell **B1**, containing the text *Series 1*. Type High and then press Tab to move to cell **C1**. In the PowerPoint window, notice that the chart legend is updated to reflect the change in the Excel worksheet.

5. In cell **C1**, containing the text *Series 2*, type Medium Press Tab. In cell **D1**, type Low and then press Tab. Compare your screen with **Figure 3**, and verify that cell A2 is selected.

> When the rightmost cell in a blue, outlined range of data is selected, pressing Tab makes the first cell in the next row active.

6. Beginning in cell **A2**, type the following data, pressing Tab to move from cell to cell:

	High	Medium	Low
Qtr 1	22.6	12.6	8.5
Qtr 2	21.8	16.2	6.7
Qtr 3	25.4	14.3	9.5
Qtr 4	18.7	16.3	

7. In cell **D5**, which contains the number 5, type 5.9 and then press Enter. Compare your screen with **Figure 4**. If you have made any typing errors, click in the cell that you want to change, and then retype the data.

8. In the **Excel** window, click the **Close** button ⊠.

> You are not prompted to save the Excel worksheet because the worksheet data is part of the PowerPoint presentation. When you save the presentation, the Excel data is saved with it.

9. Save 🖫 the presentation.

■ **You have completed Skill 4 of 10**

► After a chart is created, you can edit the data values in the Excel worksheet. Changes made in the Excel worksheet immediately display in the PowerPoint chart.

► Charts are formatted by applying predefined styles and by modifying chart elements.

1. On **Slide 4**, if necessary, click the chart so that it is selected. On the **Chart Tools Design tab**, in the **Data group**, click **Edit Data** to display the Excel worksheet.

   Each of the twelve cells containing the numeric data that you entered are **data points**—individual data plotted in a chart. Each data point is represented in the chart by a **data marker**—a column, bar, or other symbol that represents a single data point. Related data points form a **data series** and are assigned a unique color or pattern represented in the chart legend. Here there is a data series for *High*, one for *Medium*, and one for *Low*.

2. In the **Excel** worksheet, click cell **B2**, which contains the value *22.6*. Type 18.5 and then watch the chart as you press Enter. Compare your screen with **Figure 1**.

   In the chart, the first data marker in Qtr 1 is decreased to reflect the change to the data.

3. In the **Excel** worksheet, click cell **D5**, which contains the value *5.9*. Type 7.2 and then press Enter. Compare your screen with **Figure 2**.

4. In the **Excel** window, click the **Close** button ▣.

■ **Continue to the next page to complete the skill** ▸

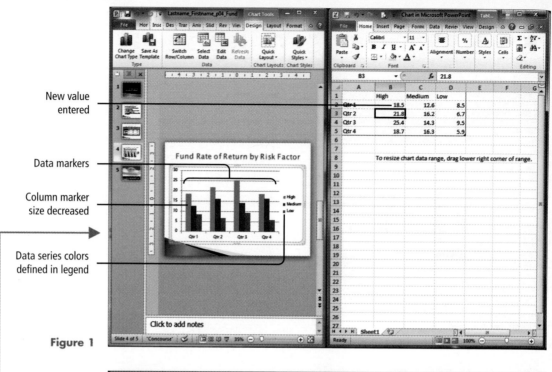

New value entered

Data markers

Column marker size decreased

Data series colors defined in legend

Figure 1

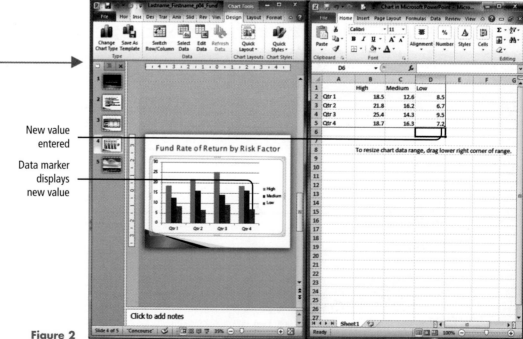

New value entered

Data marker displays new value

Figure 2

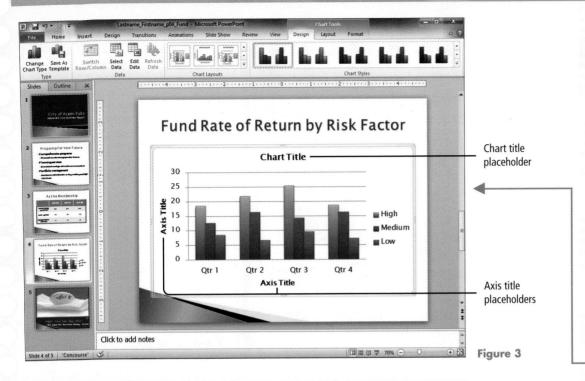

Chart title placeholder

Axis title placeholders

Figure 3

5. If necessary, click the chart so that it is selected. Under **Chart Tools**, on the **Design tab**, in the **Chart Styles group**, click the **More** button ⊟ to display the **Chart Styles** gallery.

A *chart style* is a prebuilt set of effects, colors, and backgrounds designed to work with the presentation theme. For example, you can have flat or beveled columns, colors that are solid or transparent, and backgrounds that are dark or light.

6. The thumbnails in the **Chart Style** gallery are numbered sequentially. In the second column, locate and click **Style 26**.

7. On the **Design tab**, in the **Chart Layouts group**, click the **More** button ⊟ to display the **Chart Layout** gallery, which provides options for adding and positioning chart elements such as titles. Click the ninth layout—**Layout 9**—and then compare your screen with **Figure 3**.

Placeholders for the chart title and axis titles display.

8. Click the **Chart Title** placeholder, and then type As of June 30, 2012 Below the chart, click the **Axis Title** placeholder, and the press Delete to remove the category axis title. To the left of the chart, click the **Axis Title** placeholder. Type Percent and then click on a blank area of the slide so that the chart is not selected. Compare your screen with **Figure 4**.

9. Save 🖫 the presentation.

■ **You have completed Skill 5 of 10**

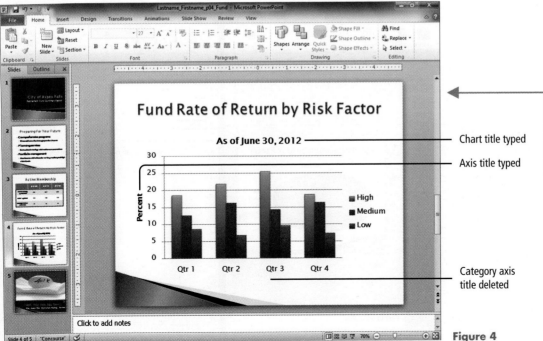

Chart title typed

Axis title typed

Category axis title deleted

Figure 4

► A *pie chart* is used to illustrate percentages or proportions and includes only one data series.

► When creating a chart, you may need to delete unwanted data from the Excel worksheet so that it does not display in the chart.

1. Display **Slide 3**, and then add a **New Slide** with the **Title and Content** layout. In the title placeholder, type Fund Allocation by Risk Factor and then **Center** ☰ the title.

2. In the content placeholder, click the **Insert Chart** button 📊. On the left side of the **Insert Chart** dialog box, click **Pie**. On the right side of the dialog box, under **Pie**, click the second chart—**Pie in 3-D**—and then click **OK**.

3. In the displayed **Excel** worksheet, click cell **B1**, which contains the word *Sales*. Type Amount and then press Tab. Type High and then press Tab. Type 293 and then press Tab. Type Medium and then press Tab. Type 562 and then press Tab. Type Low and then press Tab. Type 388 and then press Tab. Compare your screen with **Figure 1**.

   The sample data in the worksheet contains two columns and five rows as defined by the blue outline in the worksheet. In this chart, the 4th Qtr data in row 5 is unnecessary.

4. In the **Excel** worksheet, position the pointer over the row heading **5** so that the ➡ pointer displays as shown in **Figure 2**.

■ **Continue to the next page to complete the skill**

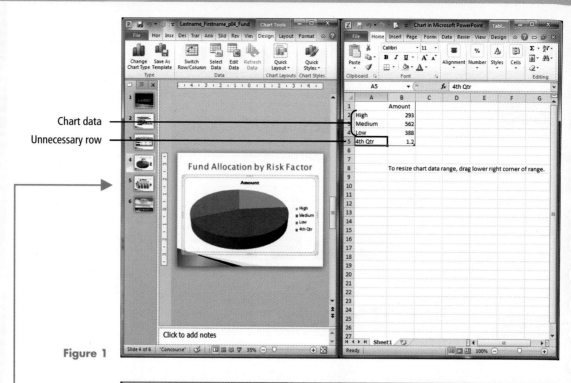

Chart data

Unnecessary row

Figure 1

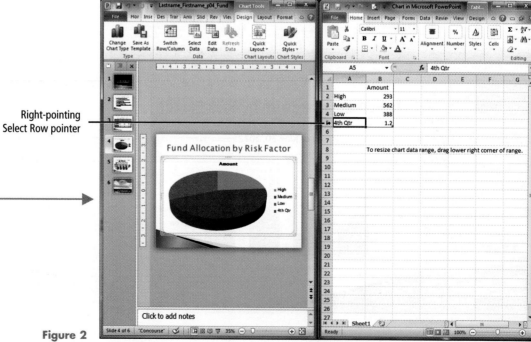

Right-pointing
Select Row pointer

Figure 2

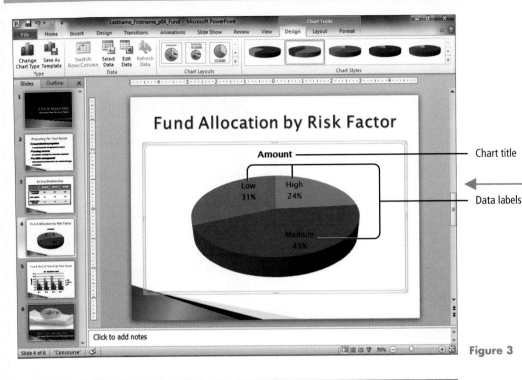

Figure 3

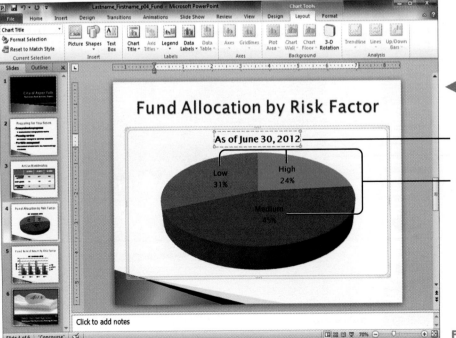

Figure 4

5. With the ➡ pointer displayed, click the right mouse button to select the row and to display the shortcut menu. In the shortcut menu, click **Delete** to delete the extra row from the worksheet.

6. **Close** the Excel window.

7. Under **Chart Tools**, click the **Design tab**, and then in the **Chart Layouts group**, click the first layout—**Layout 1**. Compare your screen with **Figure 3**.

   Recall that a pie chart includes one data series. Thus, the legend is usually omitted, and *data labels*—text that identifies data markers—are positioned on or outside of the pie slices. Layout 1 displays a title and the category names and the percentage that each slice represents of the total.

8. Click anywhere in the chart title— *Amount*—so that the title is selected. Type As of June 30, 2012 to replace the title.

9. On the **Layout tab**, in the **Labels group**, click **Data Labels**, and then click **Center**. Compare your screen with **Figure 4**.

   The data labels are centered within each pie slice.

10. On the **Chart Tools Design tab**, in the **Chart Styles group**, click the **More** button. In the second column, click **Style 10**, and then **Save** the presentation.

■ **You have completed Skill 6 of 10**

► *Animation* adds a special visual or sound effect to an object on a slide.

1. Display **Slide 1**. On the **Transitions tab**, in the **Transition to This Slide group**, click **Wipe**, and then in the **Timing group**, click the **Apply To All** button.

2. Click in the title. On the **Animations tab**, in the **Animation group**, click the **More** button ⏷ to display the **Animation** gallery. If necessary, scroll the Animation gallery to view the types of animation effects. Compare your screen with **Figure 1.**

   An *Entrance effect* is an animation that brings an object or text onto the screen. An *Emphasis effect* is an animation that emphasizes an object or text that is already displayed. An *Exit effect* is an animation that moves an object or text off the screen.

3. Under **Entrance**, point to several animations to view the effects, and then click **Split** to apply the effect. Compare your screen with **Figure 2.**

   The number 1 displays to the left of the title placeholder, indicating that the title is the first object in the slide animation sequence. The number will not display during the slide show.

4. On the **Animations tab**, in the **Animation group**, click the **Effect Options** button, and then click **Vertical Out**.

   The Effect Options control the direction and sequence in which the animation displays.

■ **Continue to the next page to complete the skill**

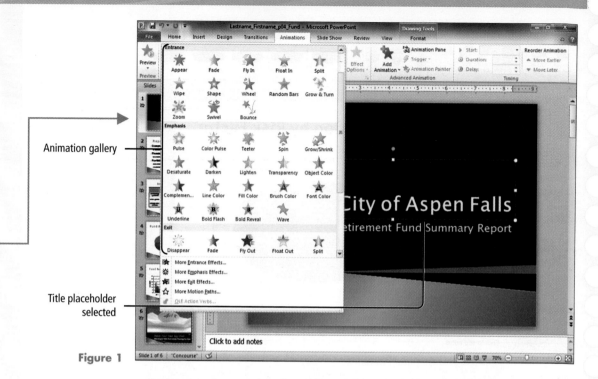

Animation gallery

Title placeholder selected

Figure 1

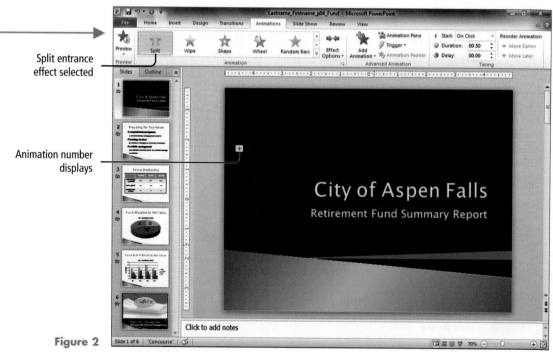

Split entrance effect selected

Animation number displays

Figure 2

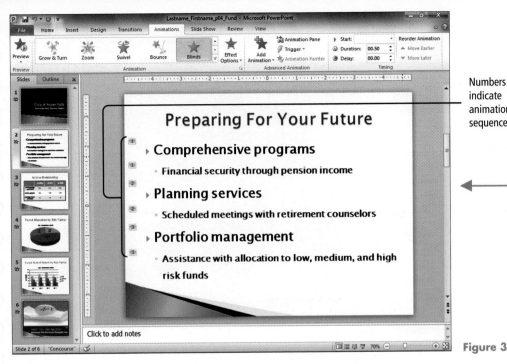

Numbers indicate animation sequence

Figure 3

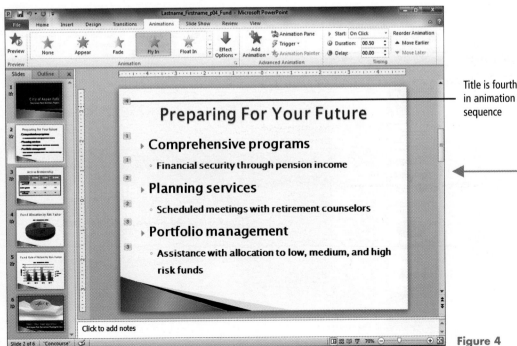

Title is fourth in animation sequence

Figure 4

5. Display **Slide 2**, and then click in the bulleted list. On the **Animations tab**, in the **Animation group**, click the **More** button ⊡. Below the gallery, click **More Entrance Effects**.

> The Change Entrance Effect dialog box displays additional entrance effects grouped in four categories: Basic, Subtle, Moderate, and Exciting.

6. Under **Basic**, click **Blinds**, and then click **OK**. Compare your screen with **Figure 3**.

> The numbers 1, 2, and 3 display to the left of the content placeholder, indicating the order in which the bullet points will display. For example, the first bullet point and its subordinate bullet are both numbered 1 and will display at the same time.

7. Click in the title. In the **Animation group**, click the **More** button ⊡, and then click **Fly In**. Click the **Effect Options** button, and then click **From Top**. Compare your screen with **Figure 4**.

> The number 4 displays next to the title text placeholder, indicating that the title is the fourth item in the animation sequence.

8. Display **Slide 6**, and then select the blue title. In the **Animation group**, click the **More** button ⊡. Under **Emphasis**, click **Grow/Shrink**.

9. On the status bar, on the **View** buttons, click the **Slide Show** button 🖵, and then click the mouse button to view the emphasis effect. Press (Esc) to exit the slide show.

10. **Save** 🖫 the presentation.

■ **You have completed Skill 7 of 10**

▶ Timing options control when animated items display in the animation sequence.

▶ *Animation Painter* is used to copy animation settings from one object to another.

1. Display **Slide 1**, and then select the title placeholder. Recall that the number 1 displayed to the left of the placeholder indicates that the title is first in the slide animation sequence.

2. On the **Animations tab**, in the **Timing group**, click the **Start** arrow to display three options—*On Click, With Previous,* and *After Previous.* Compare your screen with **Figure 1**.

   On Click begins the animation sequence when the mouse button is clicked or the [Spacebar] is pressed. *With Previous* begins the animation sequence at the same time as any animation preceding it or, if it is the first animation, with the slide transition. *After Previous* begins the animation sequence immediately after the completion of the previous animation.

3. Click **After Previous**.

   The number 1 is changed to 0, indicating that the animation will begin immediately after the slide transition; the presenter need not click the mouse button or press [Spacebar] to display the title.

4. With the title selected, on the **Animations tab**, in the **Advanced Animation group**, click the **Animation Painter** button. Point to the subtitle to display the 🔖 pointer as shown in **Figure 2**.

▪ **Continue to the next page to complete the skill**

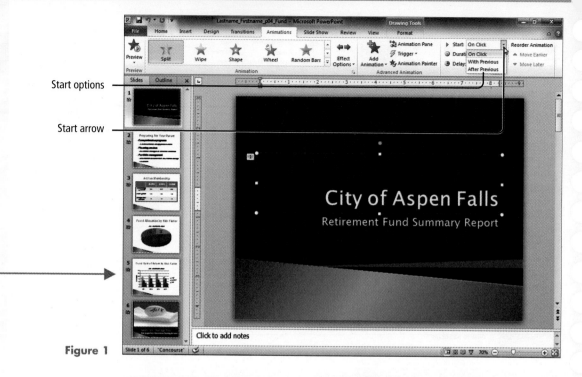

Start options
Start arrow

Figure 1

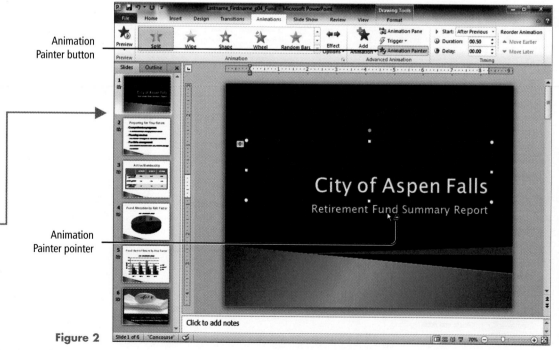

Animation Painter button

Animation Painter pointer

Figure 2

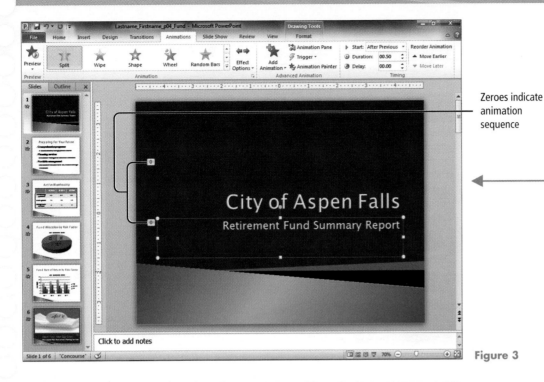

Zeroes indicate animation sequence

Figure 3

5. Click the subtitle to copy the animation from the title to the subtitle, and then compare your screen with **Figure 3**.

   The title and the subtitle display zeroes, indicating that each begins immediately upon completion of the previous animation.

6. On your keyboard, press [F5] to view the slide show. Notice that the title displays immediately after the slide transition, and the subtitle animations display immediately after the title animation is completed.

7. Click the mouse button to display **Slide 2**. Continue to click the mouse button to display each of the first-level points and their associated second-level points. Click the mouse button one more time and notice that the title displays after the list text. Press [Esc] to return to Normal view.

8. On **Slide 2**, select the title, and notice that the number 4 is highlighted. On the **Animations tab**, in the **Timing group**, click the **Move Earlier** button, and then compare your screen with **Figure 4**.

   The title animation number changes to 1, indicating that it is the first animated object on the slide. You can use the Move Earlier and Move Later buttons to change the animation order of selected objects.

9. With the title selected, in the **Timing group**, click the **Start** arrow, and then click **After Previous** so that the title displays immediately after the slide transition.

10. Save 🖫 the presentation.

   ■ **You have completed Skill 8 of 10**

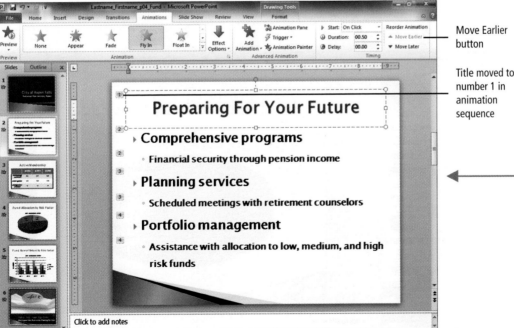

Move Earlier button

Title moved to number 1 in animation sequence

Figure 4

▶ You can change the duration of an animation effect by making it longer or shorter.

▶ When an animation effect interferes with the flow of the presentation, you can remove the effect.

1. Display **Slide 3**. Click anywhere in the table to select it. On the **Animations tab**, in the **Animation group**, click **Fade** to apply the animation to the table.

2. With the table selected, on the **Animations tab**, in the **Animation group**, click the first thumbnail—**None**. Compare your screen with **Figure 1**.

   It is not necessary to animate every object on every slide. In this slide, the slide transition provides sufficient animation to draw attention to the table.

3. Display **Slide 4**, and then select the pie chart. On the **Animations tab**, in the **Animation group**, click the **More** button ☐, and then under **Entrance**, click **Wipe** to apply the animation to the chart. In the **Animation group**, click the **Effect Options** button, and then under **Direction**, click **From Top**.

4. At the left of the **Animation tab**, click the **Preview** button, and notice that the Wipe effect is a rapid animation. In the **Timing group**, click the **Duration up spin arrow** two times to increase the **Duration** to **01.00**—1 second. Compare your screen with **Figure 2**.

   You can set the duration of an animation by typing a value in the Duration box, or you can use the up and down spin arrows to increase and decrease the duration in increments.

▪ **Continue to the next page to complete the skill**

None selected

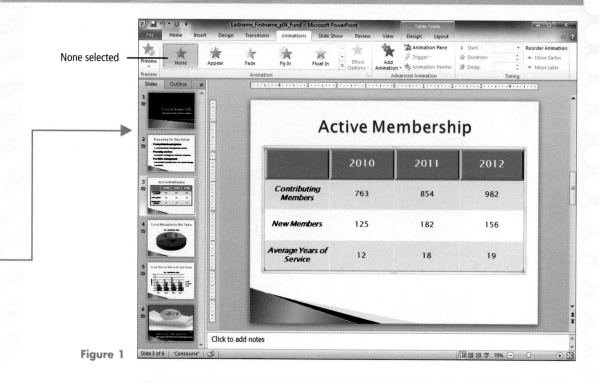

Figure 1

Duration up spin arrow

Duration set to 01.00

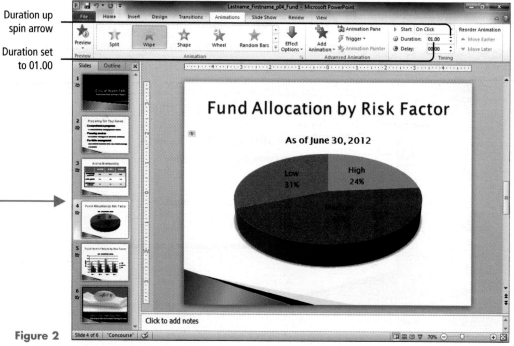

Figure 2

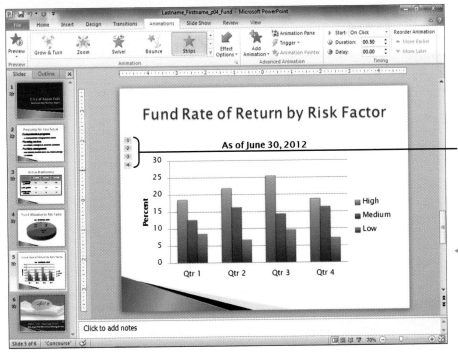

Numbers indicate that four parts of chart are animated

Figure 3

Start option set to After Previous

Delay up spin arrow

Delay set to 00.50

Figure 4

5. On the **Animations tab**, click the **Preview** button to view the longer duration of the Wipe effect.

6. Display **Slide 5**, and then select the chart. On the **Animations tab**, in the **Animation group**, click the **More** button ⬇, and then click **More Entrance Effects**. Under **Basic**, click **Strips**, and then click **OK**.

7. In the **Animation group**, click the **Effect Options** button, and then under **Sequence**, click **By Series**. Notice that the animation first displays the chart plot area, then the High series, then the Medium series, and last, the Low series. Compare your screen with **Figure 3**.

   The numbers 1 through 4 correspond to the four parts of the chart that are animated when the By Series option is selected.

8. Display **Slide 6**, and then select the slide title. Recall that the Grow/Shrink entrance effect has been applied to the slide title.

9. On the **Animations tab**, in the **Timing group**, click the **Start arrow**, and then click **After Previous**. In the **Timing group**, click the **Delay up spin arrow** two times to display **00.50**. Compare your screen with **Figure 4**.

   You can use Delay to begin a selected animation after a specified amount of time has elapsed.

10. View the slide show from the beginning, clicking the mouse button to advance through the slides.

11. **Save** 🖫 the presentation.

   ■ **You have completed Skill 9 of 10**

▶ During a slide show, a *navigation toolbar* displays in the lower left corner of the slide. You can use the navigation toolbar to go to any slide while the slide show is running.

1. On the **Slide Show tab**, in the **Start Slide Show group**, click the **From Beginning** button. Click the mouse button to display **Slide 2**.

2. Point to the lower left corner of the slide, and notice that a left-pointing arrow displays, as shown in **Figure 1**.

   The left-pointing arrow is a navigation tool that, when clicked, displays the previous slide.

3. Move the pointer slightly to the right, and notice that a pen displays.

   The pen can be used to *annotate*—write on the slide while the slide show is running.

4. Move the pointer to the right, and notice that a slide displays.

5. Click the **Slide** button to display a menu. Point to **Go to Slide**, and notice that the slide numbers and titles display as shown in **Figure 2**.

   You can navigate to any slide in the presentation by using the Go to Slide option. Thus, if an audience member has a question that is relevant to another slide, you can easily display the slide without exiting the presentation.

6. In the list of slides, click **4 Fund Allocation by Risk Factor** to display the fourth slide. Click the mouse button so that the pie chart displays.

■ **Continue to the next page to complete the skill**

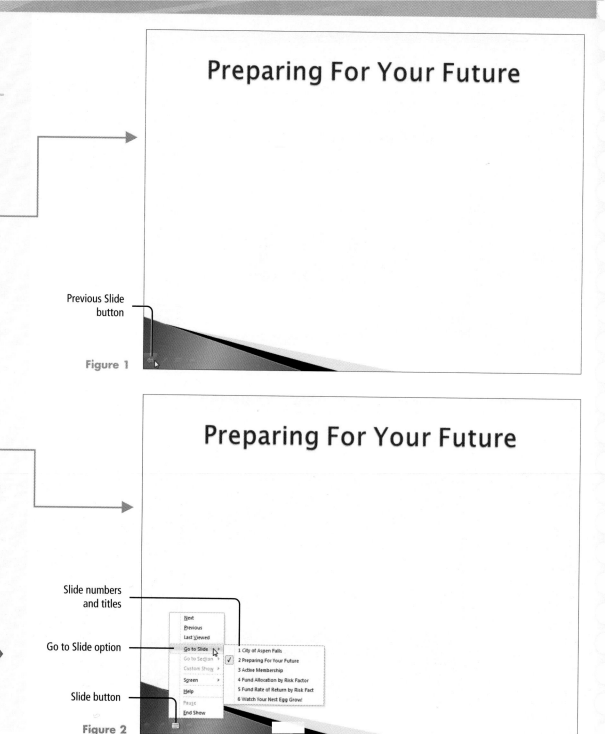

Previous Slide button

Figure 1

Slide numbers and titles

Go to Slide option

Slide button

Figure 2

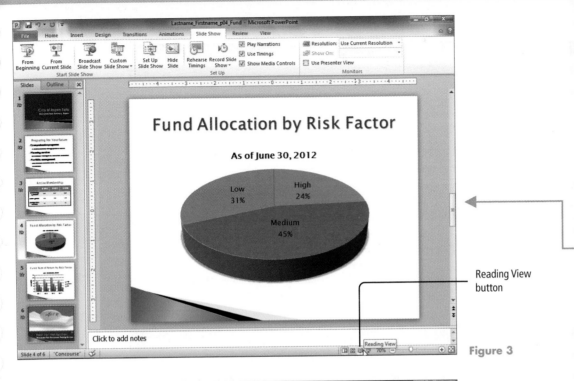

Reading View
button

Figure 3

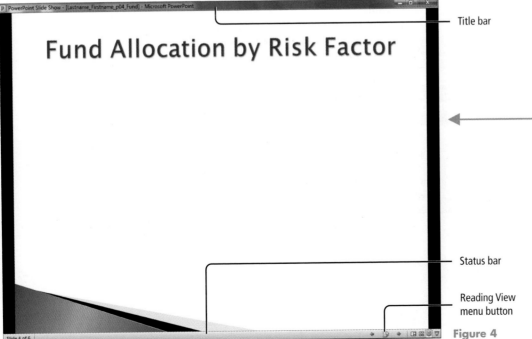

Title bar

Status bar

Reading View
menu button

Figure 4

7. On your keyboard, press B.

The B key is a toggle key that displays a black screen. During a slide show, it may be desirable to pause a presentation so that a discussion can be held without the distraction of the presentation visuals. Rather than turning off the projection system or ending the slide show, you can display the slide as a black screen and then redisplay the same slide when you are ready to resume the presentation.

8. On your keyboard, press B to redisplay **Slide 4**. Press Esc to end the slide show.

9. On the **View** buttons, locate the **Reading View** button, as shown in **Figure 3**.

Recall that you can use Reading View to display a presentation in a manner similar to a slide show, except that the taskbar, title bar, and status bar remain available in the presentation window. This view is useful when you are making a presentation during a web conference.

10. Click the **Reading View** button, and then compare your screen with **Figure 4**.

11. Press Esc to return to Normal view, and then insert a **Header & Footer** on the **Notes and Handouts**. Include the **Page number** and the **Footer** Lastname_Firstname_p04_Fund

12. **Save** the presentation. Print or submit the file, as directed by your instructor. **Exit** PowerPoint.

Done! You have completed Skill 10 of 10 and your presentation is complete!

The following More Skills are located at **www.pearsonhighered.com/skills**

More Skills Prepare Presentations to Be Viewed Using Office PowerPoint Viewer

When you are delivering a presentation, it is not always possible to use your own computer equipment and software. When PowerPoint 2010 is not available on the system that you will use for your presentation, you can prepare the presentation to be viewed using the Office PowerPoint Viewer.

In More Skills 11, you will prepare a presentation to be viewed on a system that does not have PowerPoint 2010 installed.

To begin, open your web browser, navigate to www.pearsonhighered.com/skills, locate the name of your textbook, and then follow the instructions on the website.

More Skills Insert Hyperlinks in a Presentation

Hyperlinks include text, buttons, and images that when clicked during a slide show, activate another slide or a website.

In More Skills 12, you will open a presentation and insert a hyperlink to a website.

To begin, open your web browser, navigate to www.pearsonhighered.com/skills, locate the name of your textbook, and then follow the instructions on the website.

More Skills Create Photo Albums

You can use PowerPoint 2010 to create a photo album presentation that is composed primarily of pictures.

In More Skills 13, you will create a photo album with several pictures.

To begin, open your web browser, navigate to www.pearsonhighered.com/skills, locate the name of your textbook, and then follow the instructions on the website.

More Skills Design Presentations with Appropriate Animation

Animation effects, when used properly, can emphasize important presentation information and provide a method for improving presentation pace and timing.

In More Skills 14, you will review design concepts for applying appropriate animation in a presentation.

To begin, open your web browser, navigate to www.pearsonhighered.com/skills, locate the name of your textbook, and then follow the instructions on the website.

Key Terms

Online Help Skills

1. **Start** 📊 PowerPoint. In the upper right corner of the PowerPoint window, click the **Help** button 📋. In the **Help** window, click the **Maximize** 🔲 button.

2. Click in the search box, type animate text or objects and then click the **Search** button 🔍. In the search results, click **Animate text or objects**.

3. Read the introductory text, and then below **In this article**, click **View a list of animations currently on the slide**. Compare your screen with Figure 1.

Figure 1

4. Read the entire article and then see if you can answer the following: What animation effect information can be viewed in the Animation task pane?

Matching

Match each term in the second column with its correct definition in the first column by writing the letter of the term on the blank line in front of the correct definition.

____ **1.** In a table or worksheet, the rectangular box formed by the intersection of a column and row.

____ **2.** A format used to organize and present information in columns and rows.

____ **3.** Predefined formatting that applies borders and fill colors to a table so that it is consistent with the presentation theme.

____ **4.** A graphic representation of numeric data.

____ **5.** A chart type useful for illustrating comparisons among related categories.

____ **6.** Text that identifies the categories of data in a chart.

____ **7.** Text that identifies a data marker in a chart.

____ **8.** A column, bar, area, dot, pie slice, or other symbol that represents a single data point.

____ **9.** Individual data plotted in a chart.

____ **10.** Visual or sound effects added to an object on a slide.

A Animation

B Cell

C Chart

D Column chart

E Category label

F Data label

G Data marker

H Data point

I Table

J Table style

Multiple Choice

Choose the correct answer.

1. A prebuilt set of effects, colors, and backgrounds applied to a chart that is designed to work with the presentation theme.
   A. Chart layout
   B. Chart style
   C. Chart effect

2. A group of related data points.
   A. Data series
   B. Data label
   C. Data marker

3. A chart element that identifies the patterns or colors that are assigned to the data in the chart.
   A. Data series
   B. Data label
   C. Legend

4. A type of chart used to illustrate percentages or proportions using only one series of data.
   A. Column chart
   B. Line chart
   C. Pie chart

5. A type of animation that brings a slide element onto the screen.
   A. Entrance effect
   B. Emphasis effect
   C. Exit effect

6. Animation that emphasizes an object or text that is already displayed.
   A. Entrance effect
   B. Emphasis effect
   C. Exit effect

7. Animation that moves an object or text off the screen.
   A. Entrance effect
   B. Emphasis effect
   C. Exit effect

8. A feature that copies animation settings from one object to another.
   A. Format Painter
   B. Animation Painter
   C. Copy and Paste

9. The action of writing on a slide while the slide show is running.
   A. Annotate
   B. Edit
   C. Navigation

10. A toolbar used to go to any slide while the slide show is running.
    A. Animation toolbar
    B. Slide Show toolbar
    C. Navigation toolbar

Topics for Discussion

1. When you apply animation to a slide, you can also apply sound effects. Do you think that using sound in a presentation is an effective technique for keeping the audience focused? Why or why not?

2. Recall that a column chart is used to compare data, and a pie chart is used to illustrate percentages or proportions. Give examples of the types of data that an organization such as the City of Aspen Falls might use in a column or a pie chart.

Skill Check

To complete this presentation, you will need the following file:

- p04_Report

You will save your presentation as:

- **Lastname_Firstname_p04_Report**

1. **Start** PowerPoint. From your student files, **Open p04_Report**. **Save** the presentation in your **PowerPoint Chapter 4** folder as Lastname_Firstname_p04_Report

2. Display **Slide 3**. In the content placeholder, click the **Insert Table** button. In the **Insert Table** dialog box, in the **Number of columns** box, type 2 and then click **OK**.

3. In the first table cell, type Month and then press Tab. Type Ending Cash Balance and then press Tab. Type January and then press Tab. Type 33,713,918 and then press Tab to create a new row. Type February and then press Tab. Type 28,688,318 and then press Tab. Type March and then press Tab. Type 35,987,156

4. With the insertion point positioned in the last column, on the **Layout tab**, in the **Rows & Columns group**, click the **Insert Right** button. In the new column, type the text shown in the table in **Figure 1**.

5. Point to the table's bottom center sizing handle—the four dots. Drag down until the lower edge of the table extends to the **3 inch** mark below zero on the vertical ruler.

6. Click in the table, and then on the **Layout tab**, in the **Table group**, click **Select**, and then click **Select Table**. In the **Cell Size group**, click the **Distribute Rows** button. In the **Alignment group**, click the **Center** button, and then click the **Center Vertically** button.

7. Under **Table Tools**, click the **Design tab**, and then in the **Table Styles group**, click the **More** button. Under **Medium**, in the third row, click **Medium Style 3 - Accent 2**. Select the first table row, and then change the **Font Size** to **24**. Select the remaining table text, and then change the **Font Size** to **20**. Click in a blank area of the slide, and then compare your slide with **Figure 2**.

Comments
Increased revenue from sales and property tax
Increased facilities capital expenditures
Increased revenue from bond issue

Figure 1

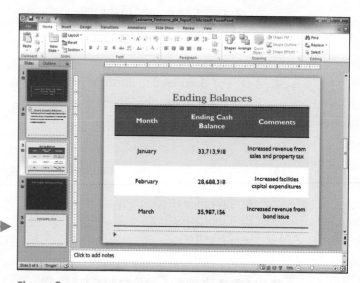

Figure 2

■ Continue to the next page to complete this Skill Check ▶

8. Display **Slide 4**. In the content placeholder, click the **Insert Chart** button. With the first chart—**Clustered Column**—selected, click **OK**. In the **Excel** window, click cell **B1**, containing the text *Series 1*. Type General and then type the remaining data shown in **Figure 3**, pressing Tab to move from cell to cell.

9. In the **Excel** worksheet, point to row heading **5**, and then right-click. In the shortcut menu, click **Delete**. **Close** Excel.

10. With the chart selected, on the **Chart Tools Design tab**, in the **Chart Styles group**, click the **More** button. Click **Style 26**.

11. Display **Slide 5**. In the content placeholder, click the **Insert Chart** button. Insert a **Pie in 3-D**. In the **Excel** worksheet, click cell **B1**. Type Expenditures and then press Tab. Type January and then press Tab. Type 2287769 and then press Tab. Type February and then press Tab. Type 4589760 and then press Tab. Type March and then press Tab. Type 3200336 and then press Tab. Position the pointer over row heading **5**, right-click, and then on the shortcut menu, click **Delete**. **Close** Excel.

12. On the **Chart Tools Design tab**, in the **Chart Layouts group**, click **Layout 1**. On the **Layout tab**, in the **Labels group**, click **Data Labels**, and then click **Center**.

13. Display **Slide 2**, and then click the bulleted list. On the **Animations tab**, in the **Animation group**, click **Fly In**. Click the **Effect Options** button, and then click **From Left**. In the **Timing group**, click the **Duration up arrow** to change the duration to **00.75**. Select the title. In the **Animation group**, click the **More** button, and then click **None**.

14. Display **Slide 4**, and then select the chart. On the **Animations tab**, in the **Animation group**, click the **More** button, and then under **Emphasis**, click **Transparency**. In the **Timing group**, click the **Duration up arrow** three times to display **00.50**. Click the **Start arrow**, and then click **With Previous**.

15. Display **Slide 1**, and then select the title. On the **Animations tab**, in the **Timing group**, click the **Start arrow**. Select **After Previous**. With the title selected, in the **Advanced Animation group**, click **Animation Painter**, and then click the subtitle. View the slide show from the beginning, and then display the presentation in **Reading View**. Return to **Normal** view.

16. Insert a **Header & Footer** on the **Notes and Handouts**. Include a **Page number** and the **Footer** Lastname_Firstname_p04_Report

17. **Save**, and then compare your presentation with **Figure 4**. Submit as directed, and then **Exit** PowerPoint.

Done! You have completed the Skill Check

	General	Utilities	Assessments
January	2568700	1698470	1875020
February	3258694	1833241	1221900
March	2794127	2057964	2384005

Figure 3

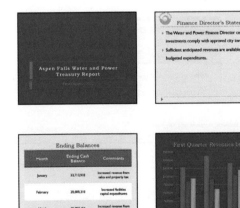
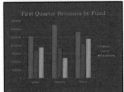
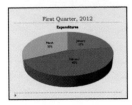

Lastname_Firstname_p04_Report   1

Figure 4

Assess Your Skills 1

To complete this presentation, you will need the following file:

- p04_City_Hall

You will save your presentation as:

- Lastname_Firstname_p04_City_Hall

1. **Start** PowerPoint. From your student files, open **p04_City_Hall**. Save the presentation in your **PowerPoint Chapter 4** folder as Lastname_Firstname_p04_City_Hall

2. Display **Slide 3**. In the content placeholder, insert a table with 2 columns and 5 rows. In the five cells of the first column, type the following headings: Project and Exterior and Interior and Parking and Landscape In the second column, type the following: Percent Complete and 85% and 45% and 20% and 0%

3. Insert a third column to the right of the *Percent Complete* column. Type the following: Completion Date and November 2013 and January 2014 and June 2014 and July 2014 Size the table so that its lower edge aligns at the **3 inch** mark below zero on the vertical ruler. If necessary, distribute the rows, and then apply the **Medium Style 3 - Accent 1** table style. Center the text horizontally and vertically within the cells. Animate the table by applying the **Wipe** entrance effect.

4. Display **Slide 4**. Insert a **Pie in 3-D** chart. In the **Excel** worksheet, in cell **B1**, type Cost Beginning in cell **A2**, enter the following data:

Exterior	1257500
Interior	1258650
Parking	750000

5. In the **Excel** window, delete row **5**, and then **Close** Excel. Change the chart layout to **Layout 1**, and then delete the chart title. Apply the **Style 10** chart style, and change the **Data Labels** placement to **Center**.

6. Display **Slide 2**, and then remove the animation effect from the title placeholder.

7. With **Slide 2** displayed, select the content placeholder, and then apply the **Split** entrance effect and change the **Effect Options** to **Vertical Out**.

8. Display **Slide 5**, and then apply the **Dissolve In** entrance effect to the picture. Change the **Duration** to **00.75** and the **Delay** to **00.25**. Apply the **Darken** emphasis effect to the caption. For both the caption and the picture, modify the **Start** option to **After Previous**.

9. View the slide show from the beginning, and use the navigation toolbar to display **Slide 4** after you display **Slide 1**. Return to **Slide 1**, and then view the presentation in the correct order.

10. Insert a **Header & Footer** on the **Notes and Handouts**. Include a **Page number** and the **Footer** Lastname_Firstname_p04_City_Hall

11. **Save**, and then compare your presentation with **Figure 1**. Print your presentation or submit the file, as directed by your instructor. **Exit** PowerPoint.

Done! You have completed Assess Your Skills 1

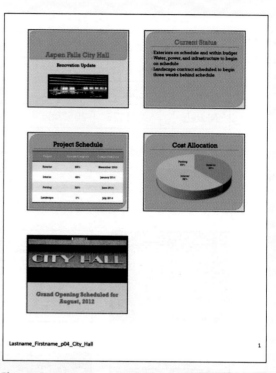

Figure 1

Assess Your Skills 2

Assess Your Skills 3 and 4 can be found at **www.pearsonhighered.com/skills**.

To complete this presentation, you will need the following file:

- p04_Benefits

You will save your presentation as:

- Lastname_Firstname_p04_Benefits

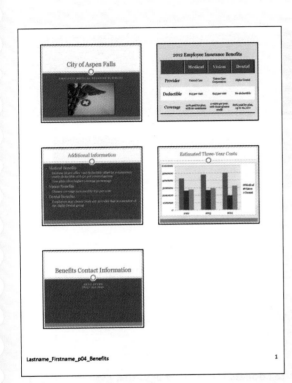

Lastname_Firstname_p04_Benefits   1

Figure 1

1. **Start** PowerPoint. From your student files, **Open p04_Benefits**. **Save** the presentation in your **PowerPoint Chapter 4** folder as Lastname_Firstname_p04_Benefits

2. Display **Slide 2**. In the content placeholder, insert a table with 3 columns and 4 rows. In the first row, type the following headings: Medical and Vision and Dental In the second row, type United Care and Vision Care Corporation and Alpha Dental In the third row type $15 per visit and $25 per visit and No deductible In the fourth row, type 90% paid by plan, with no maximum and 2 visits per year, with $250 glasses credit and 80% paid by plan, up to $2,000

3. Insert a column to the left of the first column. Beginning in the second row, type the following headings: Provider and Deductible and Coverage

4. Size the table so that its lower edge aligns at the **3 inch** mark below zero on the vertical ruler. Distribute the rows, and then apply the **Medium Style 3 - Accent 1** table style. Center the table text horizontally and vertically. Change the first row and first column **Font Size** to **28**, and then apply the **Circle** cell bevel effect to the first row. **Animate** the table by applying the **Wipe** effect.

5. Display **Slide 4**, and then insert a **Clustered Column** chart. In the **Excel** worksheet, in cell **B1**, type Medical In cell **C1** type Vision

and in cell **D1** type Dental Beginning in cell **A2** enter the following data:

2012	4228550	2586430	2758490
2013	4752280	2687500	2896430
2014	4967870	1889480	3198560

6. In the **Excel** worksheet, delete row **5**, and then **Close** Excel. Apply the **Style 34** chart style, and then use **Animation Painter** to copy the animation from the table on **Slide 2** to the chart on **Slide 4**.

7. Edit the chart data by changing the *2013 Vision* data in cell **C3** to 2622330

8. On **Slide 3**, apply the **Float In** entrance effect to the content placeholder.

9. On **Slide 5**, apply the **Fly In** entrance effect to the title. Change the **Effect Options** to **From Top**. Use the **Reorder Animation** options to move the title animation earlier so that it displays before the subtitle. Set the title and subtitle animations to start **After Previous**. View the slide show from the beginning.

10. Insert a **Header & Footer** on the **Notes and Handouts**. Include a **Page number** and the **Footer** Lastname_Firstname_p04_Benefits

11. **Save**, and then compare your presentation with Figure 1. Print your presentation or submit the file, as directed by your instructor. **Exit** PowerPoint.

Done! You have completed Assess Your Skills 2

Assess Your Skills Visually

To complete this presentation, you will need the following file:

- New blank PowerPoint presentation

You will save your presentation as:

- Lastname_Firstname_p04_Accounts

Start PowerPoint. Create the table as shown in **Figure 1**. **Save** the file as Lastname_Firstname_p04_Accounts in your **PowerPoint Chapter 4** folder. To complete this presentation, use the **Module** design theme. Type and align the text as shown in the figure, and apply the **Light Style 2 - Accent 1** table style. In the first table row, change the **Font Size** to **24**, and apply a **Circle** bevel effect. Add a footer to the **Notes and Handouts** with the file name and page number, and then print or submit the file, as directed by your instructor.

Done! You have completed Assess Your Skills Visually

Savings Account Comparison

Account Type	Description	Rate
Savings Account	Traditional account for short-term needs	1%
Savings Certificate	Competitive rates Guaranteed return	1.5% to 3.5%
Money Market Account	Minimum $2,500 balance Unlimited withdrawals	1.25% to 1.75%
Individual Retirement Account	Invest after-tax dollars	2.25% to 4.5%

Figure 1

Skills in Context

To complete this presentation, you will need the following file:

- New blank PowerPoint presentation

You will save your presentation as:

- Lastname_Firstname_p04_Power

Using the information provided, create a presentation in which the first slide title is Aspen Falls Utilities Division and the subtitle is Power Distribution and Usage Apply a design theme. Create two more slides, one with a table and one with a pie chart, that include information about the types of power that the city uses and its distribution to customers. The city's power supply is composed of 52% hydroelectric power, 28% natural gas, 15% renewable energy sources, and 5% coal. On a monthly basis, the average distribution of power in megawatt hours is 705,500 for residential customers, 1,322,600 for commercial customers, and 587,900 for industrial customers.

Format the chart and table with styles, and apply animation to each. Insert a footer with the file name on the **Notes and Handouts**. Print or submit electronically, as directed by your instructor.

Done! You have completed Skills in Context

Skills and You

To complete this presentation, you will need the following file:

- New blank PowerPoint presentation

You will save your presentation as:

- Lastname_Firstname_p04_Cars

Using the skills you have practiced in this chapter, create a presentation with four slides in which you compare three cars that you would be interested in purchasing. Apply an appropriate presentation theme. On one slide, insert a table with three columns that includes the vehicle name, price range, and description of important features. On another slide, insert a column chart that compares the prices of the three vehicles. On

the last slide, insert a picture of the car that you would like to purchase, and include at least three bullet points indicating why you chose the vehicle. Apply animation to the slides, and insert an appropriate footer. Print or submit electronically, as directed by your instructor.

Done! You have completed Skills and You

CHAPTER 1

Integrating Word, Excel, Access, and PowerPoint

▶ Microsoft Office is an integrated application suite—the data and objects in one application can be used in another application.

▶ Data and objects can be copied and pasted, moved, linked, or embedded among the applications.

Your starting screen will look similar to this:

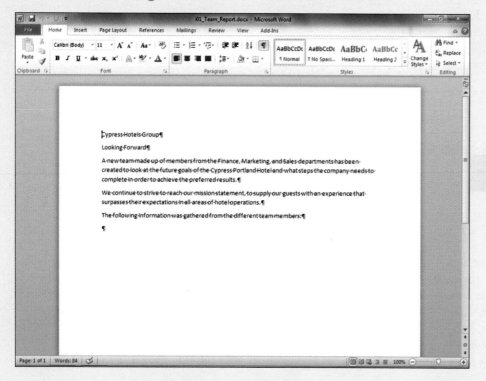

SKILLS

Skills 1-10 Training

At the end of this chapter, you will be able to:

Skill 1 Move Text Between Word Documents
Skill 2 Apply Heading Styles in Word
Skill 3 Create a PowerPoint Presentation from a Word Document
Skill 4 Insert and Modify a Shape in PowerPoint
Skill 5 Import a Word Table into an Excel Workbook
Skill 6 Insert a Shape from PowerPoint into Word and Excel
Skill 7 Create and Work with an Excel Table
Skill 8 Link Data Between Office Applications Using OLE
Skill 9 Create Envelopes Using Data from Access
Skill 10 Create Name Tags Using Data in Excel

MORE SKILLS

More Skills 11 Insert Subtotals in Excel and Link Data to a Word Document
More Skills 12 Insert Slides from Another Presentation
More Skills 13 Move and Copy Excel Worksheets and Consolidate Data
More Skills 14 Compare Shared Excel Workbooks

Outcome

Using the skills listed to the left will enable you to create documents like these:

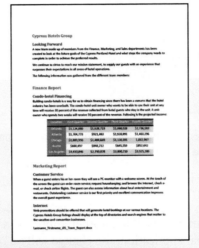

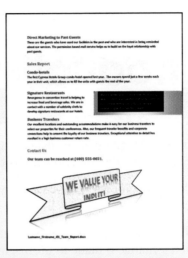

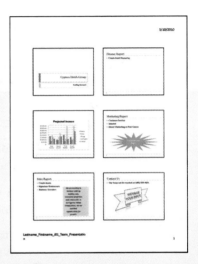

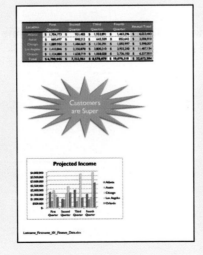

You will save these documents as:

Lastname_Firstname_i01_Accounting_Tags.docx
Lastname_Firstname_i01_Envelopes_Merged.docx
Lastname_Firstname_i01_Envelopes.docx
Lastname_Firstname_i01_Finance_Data.xlsx
Lastname_Firstname_i01_Name_Tags.docx
Lastname_Firstname_i01_Speakers.xlsx
Lastname_Firstname_i01_Team_Presentation.pptx
Lastname_Firstname_i01_Team_Report.docx

In this chapter, you will create files for the Cypress Hotels Group, which has large hotels located in major vacation and business destinations in North America.

Introduction

▶ You can copy an object or data created in one Office application and paste the object or data into another Office application.

▶ A Word document can be created by inserting text from other Word documents.

▶ Data or objects in one application can be linked to another application file. When a change is made in the original application, the change will be reflected in the destination file.

▶ The mail merge feature in Word allows you to create envelopes or name tags from a list of names and addresses in an Access or Excel file.

Time to complete all
10 skills – 50 to 90 minutes

Find your student data files here:

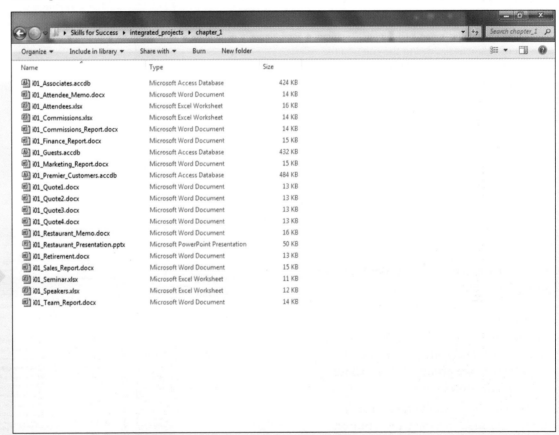

Student data files needed for this chapter:

- New blank PowerPoint presentation

- i01_Associates.accdb

- i01_Finance_Report.docx

- i01_Marketing_Report.docx

- i01_Sales_Report.docx

- i01_Speakers.xlsx

- i01_Team_Report.docx

► Text from one Word document can be inserted into another document.

1. Click **Start** . Click **Control Panel**, and then click **Appearance and Personalization**. Under **Folder Options**, click **Show hidden files and folders**. Under **Advanced settings**, clear the **Hide extensions for known file types** check box. Click **OK**, and then click **Close** .

    This setting will display a *file extension*— a set of characters added to the end of a file name that identifies each file type—in all folder windows and window title bars.

2. **Start** Word. Navigate to your student files, and then open **i01_Team_Report. docx**. Click the **File tab**, and then click **Save As**. Navigate to the location where you are saving your files, create a folder named Integrated Projects Chapter 1 and then using your first and last names, **Save** the document as Lastname_Firstname_ i01_Team_Report Compare your screen with **Figure 1**. ─────────

3. On the **Insert tab**, in the **Header & Footer group**, click the **Footer** button, and then click **Edit Footer**. On the **Design tab**, in the **Insert group**, click the **Quick Parts** button, and then click **Field**. Under **Field names**, click **FileName**, and then click **OK**. In the **Close group**, click the **Close Header and Footer** button.

4. Press Ctrl + End. On the **Insert tab**, in the **Text group**, click the **Object button arrow**, and then click **Text from File**. Compare your screen with **Figure 2**. ─────────

■ **Continue to the next page to complete the skill** ➤

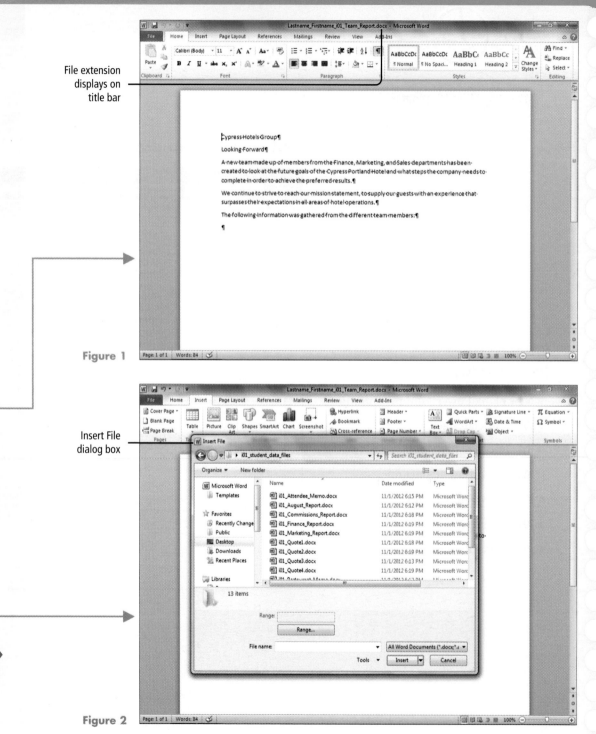

File extension displays on title bar

Figure 1

Insert File dialog box

Figure 2

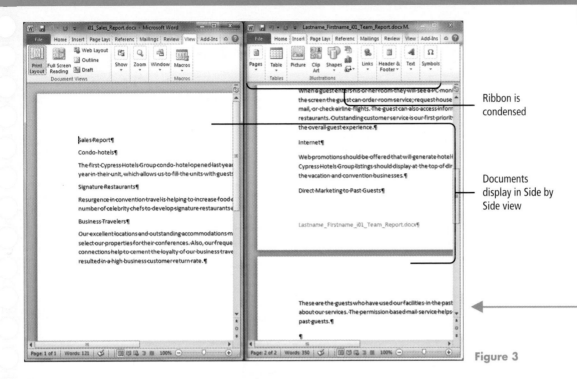

Ribbon is condensed

Documents display in Side by Side view

Figure 3

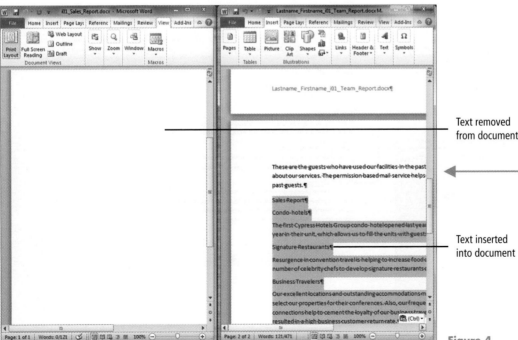

Text removed from document

Text inserted into document

Figure 4

5. In the **Insert File** dialog box, navigate to your student files. Select **i01_Finance_ Report.docx**, and then click **Insert**.

The text from the file *i01_Finance_Report* is inserted into the current document.

6. If necessary, on the Home tab, in the Paragraph group, click the Show/Hide button ¶ . Below the tabbed text just inserted, follow the technique from the previous steps to insert the text from **i01_Marketing_ Report.docx**.

7. Open the student data file **i01_Sales_ Report.docx**.

8. On the **View tab**, in the **Window group**, click the **View Side by Side** button. Notice that the ribbon does not fully display in this view, as shown in **Figure 3**.

9. Scroll down, and notice *synchronous scrolling*—both documents scroll together—is enabled.

10. With the **i01_Sales_Report.docx** window active, press Ctrl + A to select all of the text in the document. Move the mouse pointer on top of the blue selected text, and then press and hold down the left mouse button. Drag the text to the end of the document in the **Lastname_ Firstname_i01_Team_Report** window. Compare your screen with **Figure 4**.

The text is moved from the *i01_Sales_Report* document into the document *Lastname_Firstname_i01_Team_Report*.

11. Close i01_Sales_Report. When prompted, do not save the changes.

12. Save Lastname_Firstname_i01_ Team_Report.docx.

■ **You have completed Skill 1 of 10**

▶ Applying a heading style to text enables you to format all of the heading text at one time.

▶ A *shortcut menu* shows a list of commands relevant to a particular item and is displayed when you right-click an item.

1. Press Ctrl + End to move the insertion point to the end of the document.

2. Type Contact Us and then press Enter. Type Our team can be reached at (480) 555-0031. and then press Enter.

3. Press Ctrl + Home to move the insertion point to the beginning of the document.

4. Select the first paragraph, *Cypress Hotels Group*.

5. On the **Home tab**, in the **Styles group**, click the **Heading 1** button, and then compare your screen with **Figure 1**.

6. Select the text *Finance Report*. Press and hold Ctrl, and then select the paragraphs *Marketing Report*, *Sales Report*, and *Contact Us*.

7. Release Ctrl. With the four headings selected, click the **Heading 1** button.

8. Press Ctrl + Home to move the insertion point to the beginning of the document.

9. Using the same technique, select the paragraphs *Looking Forward, Condo-hotel Financing, Customer Service, Internet, Direct Marketing to Past Guests, Condo-hotels, Signature Restaurants, Business Travelers*, and the last paragraph, beginning *Our team can be reached*. In the **Styles group**, click the **Heading 2** button. Compare your screen with **Figure 2**.

■ **Continue to the next page to complete the skill**

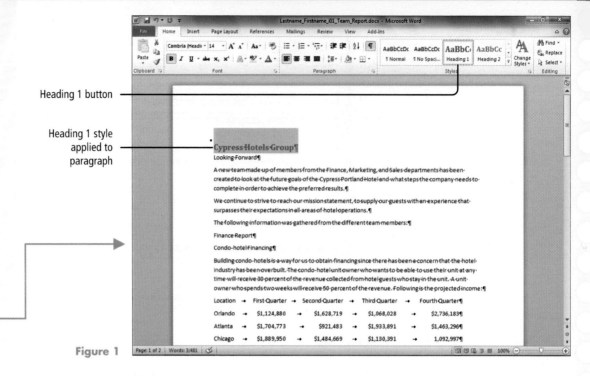

Heading 1 button

Heading 1 style applied to paragraph

Figure 1

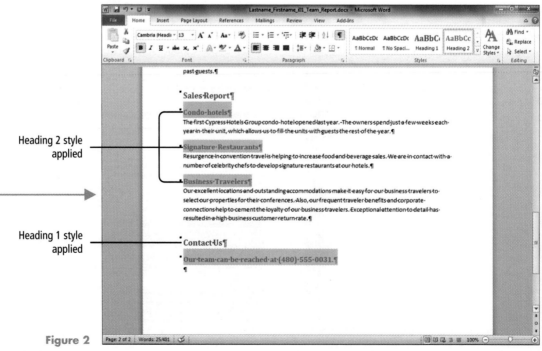

Heading 2 style applied

Heading 1 style applied

Figure 2

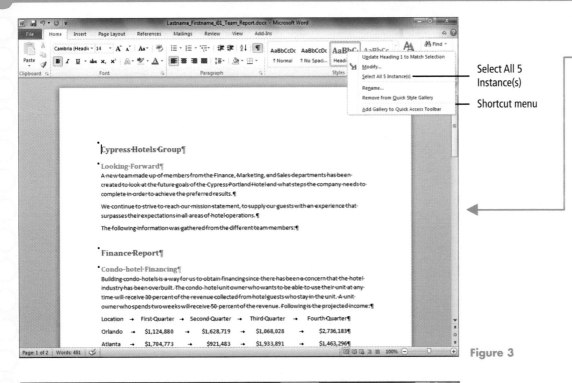

Select All 5
Instance(s)

Shortcut menu

Figure 3

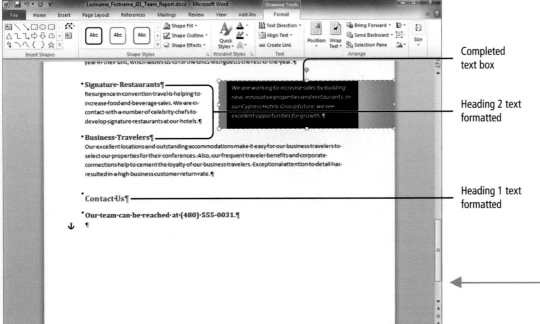

Completed
text box

Heading 2 text
formatted

Heading 1 text
formatted

Figure 4

10. Press Ctrl + Home. In the **Styles group**, right-click the **Heading 1** button, and then compare your screen with **Figure 3**.

11. From the **shortcut menu**, click **Select All 5 Instance(s)**.

> The five paragraphs with the Heading 1 style format are selected.

12. In the **Font group**, click the **Font Color button arrow** [A▾], and then click the last color in the sixth row—**Orange, Accent 6, Darker 50%**.

> The five paragraphs with the Heading 1 style are formatted simultaneously.

13. In the **Styles group**, right-click the **Heading 2** button. From the shortcut menu, click **Select All 9 Instance(s)**.

14. Change the **Font Color** to the fourth color in the fifth row—**Dark Blue, Text 2, Darker 25%**.

15. Press Ctrl + End to move the insertion point to the end of the document.

16. On the **Insert tab**, in the **Text group**, click the **Text Box** button. In the displayed gallery, scroll down, and then click **Contrast Quote**.

> A *text box*—a movable, resizable container for text or graphics—is inserted.

17. With the text box still selected, type We are working to increase sales by building new, innovative properties and restaurants. In our Cypress Hotels Group future, we see excellent opportunities for growth. Compare your screen with **Figure 4**.

18. Click **Save** [💾], and then **Exit** Word.

- **You have completed Skill 2 of 10**

▶ A Word document can be inserted into a PowerPoint presentation, which lets you avoid retyping the same data. You save time and ensure the accuracy of the data.

▶ A Word document must be closed before you can insert it into a PowerPoint presentation.

1. **Start** 🔘 PowerPoint. On the **Home tab**, in the **Slides group**, click the **New Slide button arrow**, as shown in **Figure 1.**

2. Click **Slides from Outline**. In the **Insert Outline** dialog box, navigate to your **Integrated Projects Chapter 1** folder. Select **Lastname_Firstname_i01_ Team_Report**, and then click **Insert**.

   A six-slide PowerPoint presentation is created from the paragraphs you styled as Heading 1 and Heading 2 in the Word document. Body text and objects, such as the text box, will not be inserted into the presentation.

3. Click the **File tab**, and then click **Save As**. Navigate to your **Integrated Projects Chapter 1** folder, and then using your own first and last names, **Save** the presentation as Lastname_Firstname_ i01_Team_ Presentation

4. On the **Insert tab**, in the **Text group**, click the **Header & Footer** button. In the **Header and Footer** dialog box, click the **Notes and Handouts tab**. Select the **Footer** check box, and then type Lastname_Firstname_i01_Team_ Presentation

5. If necessary, clear any other check boxes in the dialog box. Compare your screen with **Figure 2.**

6. Click **Apply to All**.

■ **Continue to the next page to complete the skill**

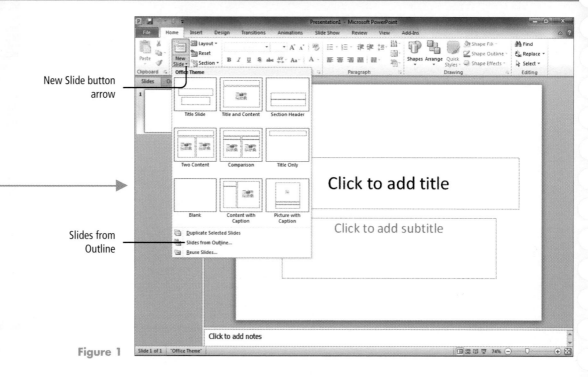

New Slide button arrow

Slides from Outline

Figure 1

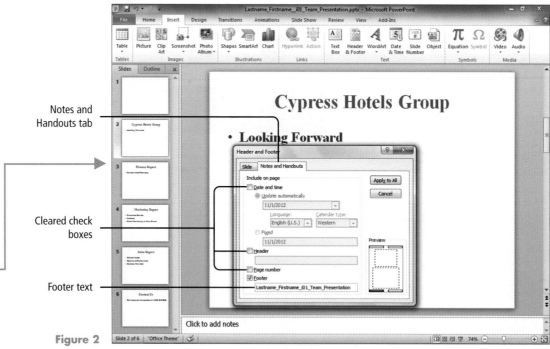

Notes and Handouts tab

Cleared check boxes

Footer text

Figure 2

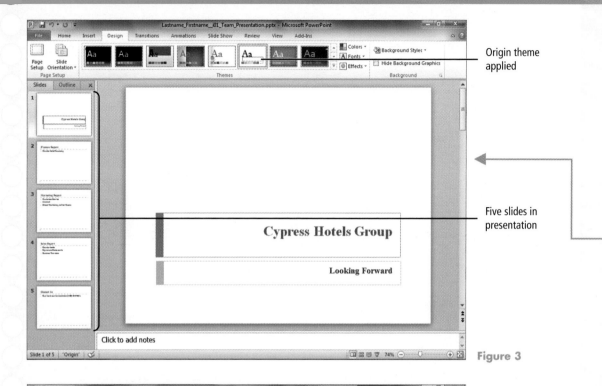

Origin theme applied

Five slides in presentation

Figure 3

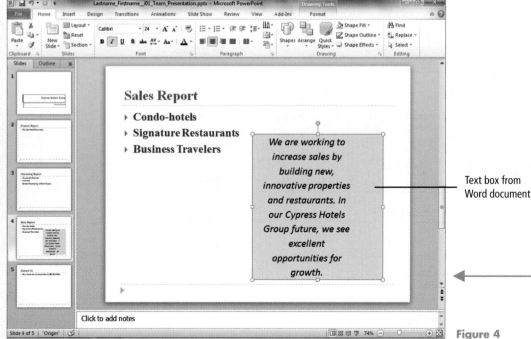

Text box from Word document

Figure 4

7. Right-click **Slide 1**. From the shortcut menu, click **Delete Slide**.

   Slide 1 is deleted. Slide 2 becomes Slide 1, and all other slides are renumbered. The presentation now contains five slides.

8. On the **Home tab**, in the **Slides group**, click the **Layout** button, and then click **Title Slide**.

   The layout of Slide 1 is changed to a title slide.

9. On the **Design tab**, in the **Themes group**, click the **More** button ⊡, and then click the **Origin** theme. Compare your screen with **Figure 3**.

10. **Start** 🔵 Word. From your **Integrated Projects Chapter 1** folder, **Open** the document **Lastname_Firstname_i01_Team_Report**.

11. Scroll to the second page of the document. Click the text box, and then click the border of the text box to select the entire text box. On the **Home tab**, in the **Clipboard group**, click the **Copy** button 🗎.

12. Make **Lastname_Firstname_i01_Team_Presentation** the active window, and then display **Slide 4**.

13. On the **Home tab**, in the **Clipboard group**, click the **Paste** button.

14. Select the text in the text box. On the Mini toolbar, click the **Font Size button arrow** ⟨" ·⟩, and then click **24**. Click the **Font Color button arrow** ⟨A ·⟩, and then click the second color in the first row— **Black, Text 1**. In the **Paragraph group**, click the **Center** button ▤.

15. Move the text box to approximately **1 inch** from the bottom right corner. Compare your screen with **Figure 4**.

16. **Save** 🖫 the presentation.

■ **You have completed Skill 3 of 10**

▶ **Shapes** are objects such as stars and banners that can be inserted to emphasize a point.

▶ Shapes may have a yellow **adjustment handle**—a diamond-shaped handle used to adjust the appearance but not the size of the shape.

▶ You can modify a shape with a **shape effect**—a predesigned format that makes the shape look more professional.

1. Display **Slide 5**. On the **Insert tab**, in the **Illustrations group**, click the **Shapes** button, and then under **Stars and Banners**, click the first shape in the second row—**Up Ribbon**.

2. Click the middle of the slide to insert the shape. On the **Format tab**, in the **Size group**, click the **Shape Height** box, type 2.5 and then press Enter. Click the **Shape Width** box, type 7.5 and then press Enter. In the **Arrange group**, click the **Align** button 🖻, and then click **Align Center**. Click the **Align** button 🖻 again, and then click **Align Middle**. Compare your screen with **Figure 1**.

3. In the **Shape Styles group**, click the **Shape Fill** button, point to **Texture**, and then click the first texture in the fourth row—**Newsprint**.

4. On the **Drawing Tools Format tab**, in the **WordArt Styles group**, click the **More** button ▾, and then under **Applies to All Text in the Shape**, click the last style in the first row—**Fill - Blue-Gray, Accent 1, Plastic Bevel, Reflection**. Type We value your input! and then compare your screen with **Figure 2**.

■ **Continue to the next page to complete the skill** ▶

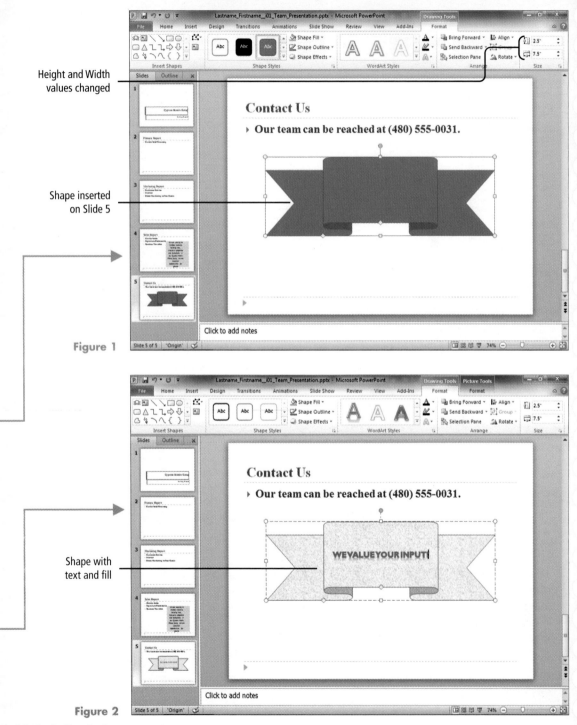

Height and Width values changed

Shape inserted on Slide 5

Figure 1

Shape with text and fill

Figure 2

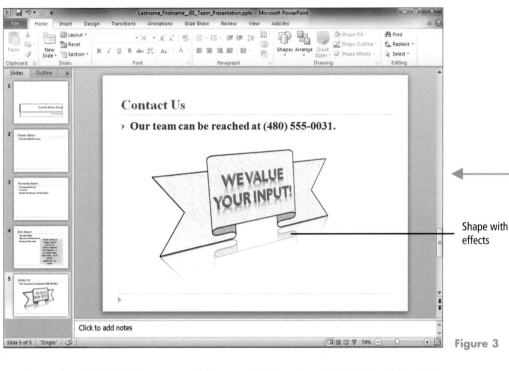

Figure 3

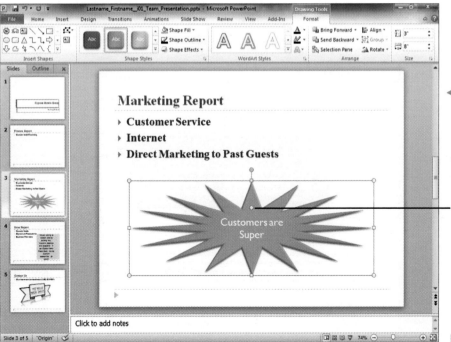

Shape with effects

Yellow adjustment handle

Figure 4

5. Select the text, and then from the Mini toolbar, change the **Font Size** to **36**. In the **Shape Styles group**, click the **Shape Outline** button, and then click **Black, Text 1**.

6. Click the **Shape Effects** button, and then point to **3-D Rotation**. Under **Perspective**, click the first effect in the third row—**Perspective Contrasting Right**.

7. Click the **Shape Effects** button again, and then point to **Reflection**. In the **Reflection** gallery, under **Reflection Variations**, click the first effect in the first row—**Tight Reflection, touching**. Click a blank area in the slide, and then compare your screen with **Figure 3**.

8. Display **Slide 3**. Using the same techniques, insert the shape **16-Point Star** in the middle of the slide. Increase the **Shape Height** to 3 and then increase the **Shape Width** to 8. Move the shape to the lower middle part of the slide.

9. Type Customers are Super select the text, and then change the **Font Size** to 24.

10. Point at the yellow adjustment handle and drag down approximately **1/2"**.

11. In the **Shapes Style group**, click the **More** button ⏷, and then click the third shape in the sixth row—**Intense Effect - Ice Blue, Accent 2**. Compare your screen with **Figure 4**.

12. **Save** 🖫 the presentation.

■ **You have completed Skill 4 of 10**

► If you have a table of numbers in Word, you can copy and paste the numbers into Excel and then generate formulas in the Excel workbook.

► Formulas are equations that perform calculations on values.

1. Make **Lastname_Firstname_i01_Team_ Report** the active window.

2. On the first page, beginning with the text *Location*, select the six lines of tabbed text.

3. On the **Insert tab**, in the **Tables group**, click the **Table** button, and then click **Convert Text to Table**. In the **Convert Text to Table** dialog box, click **OK**, and then notice that the tabbed text is converted to a table, as displayed in **Figure 1**.

4. On the **Design tab**, in the **Table Styles group**, click the **More** button. Click the second style in the fifth row—**Medium Shading 2 - Accent 1**.

5. On the **Layout tab**, in the **Alignment group**, click the **Align Center** button.

6. In the **Cell Size group**, click the **AutoFit** button, and then click **AutoFit Contents**.

7. In the **Table group**, click the **Properties** button. In the **Table Properties** dialog box, under **Alignment**, click **Center**, and then click **OK**. Compare your screen with **Figure 2**.

   The cell contents are centered vertically and horizontally, and the table is horizontally centered on the page.

8. With the table still selected, on the **Home tab**, in the **Clipboard group**, click the **Copy** button.

■ **Continue to the next page to complete the skill**

Tabbed text converted to a table

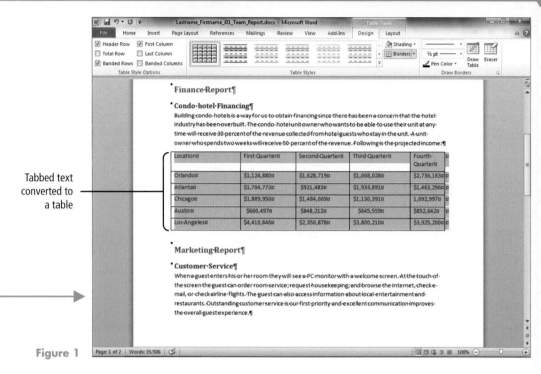

Figure 1

Table is centered horizontally on the page

Text is centered within each table cell

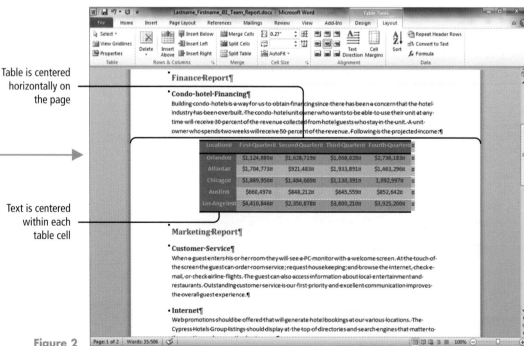

Figure 2

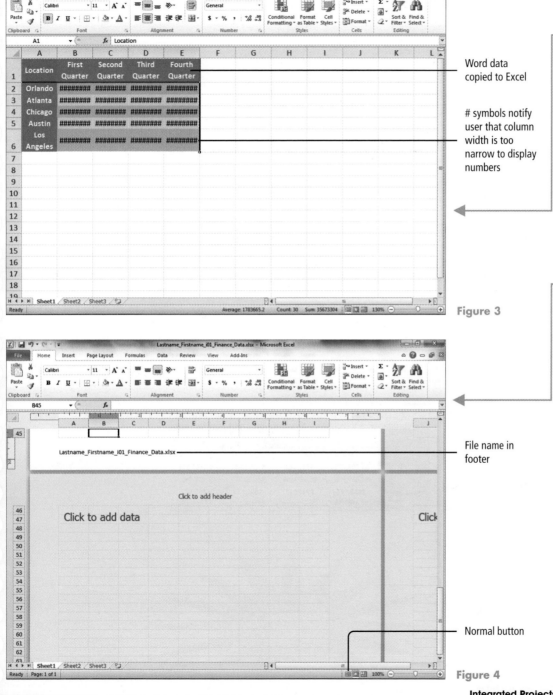

Word data copied to Excel

symbols notify user that column width is too narrow to display numbers

Figure 3

File name in footer

Normal button

Figure 4

9. **Start** Excel. With cell **A1** as the active cell, on the **Home tab**, in the **Clipboard group**, click the **Paste** button, and then compare your screen with **Figure 3**.

10. Click the **File tab**, and then click **Save As**. Navigate to your **Integrated Projects Chapter 1** folder, and then **Save** the workbook as Lastname_Firstname_i01_Finance_Data

11. On the **Insert tab**, in the **Text group**, click the **Header & Footer** button. In the **Navigation group**, click the **Go to Footer** button, click just above the word **Footer**, and then in the **Header & Footer Elements group**, click the **File Name** button.

12. Click a cell above the footer, and then compare your screen with **Figure 4**.

13. On the status bar, click the **Normal** button, and then press Ctrl + Home to move to cell **A1**.

14. Select columns **A:E**. On the **Home tab**, in the **Cells group**, click the **Format** button, and then click **Column Width**. In the **Column Width** dialog box, type 12 and then click **OK**. In the **Font group**, click the **Bold** button to remove the bold format.

15. Select row **1**. Click the **Format** button, and then click **Row Height**. In the **Row Height** dialog box, type 33 and then click **OK**.

16. On the **Page Layout tab**, in the **Themes group**, click the **Themes** button, and then click **Origin**. **Save** the document.

■ **You have completed Skill 5 of 10**

► Shapes created in PowerPoint can be copied and pasted into Word and Excel documents.

► You can collect objects from a number of documents on the Clipboard and then paste them into other documents.

1. Make the PowerPoint presentation **Lastname_Firstname_i01_Team_ Presentation** the active window.

2. On the **Home tab**, click the **Clipboard Dialog Box Launcher** 🔲.

3. If any items display in the **Clipboard** task pane, click the **Clear All** button.

4. Display **Slide 3**. Click the star shape, and then click the border of the shape to select the entire shape. In the **Clipboard group**, click the **Copy** button 🔲.

5. Display **Slide 5**. Click the shape, and then click the border of the shape. Click the **Copy** button 🔲.

> Both shapes display in the Clipboard task pane.

6. Make the Excel workbook **Lastname_ Firstname_i01_Finance_Data** the active window.

7. Click cell **A10**. On the **Home tab**, click the **Clipboard Dialog Box Launcher** 🔲.

8. In the **Clipboard** task pane, click the **Star** shape and then **Close** 🗙 the **Clipboard** task pane. Compare your screen with **Figure 1**.

9. With the shape selected, point to the middle right sizing handle so that the ↔ pointer displays. Hold down the mouse button, drag left to the grid line between **columns F** and **G**, and then release the mouse button. Compare your screen with **Figure 2**.

■ **Continue to the next page to complete the skill** ▶

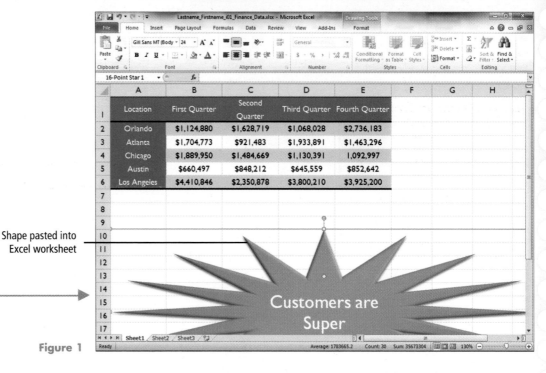

Shape pasted into Excel worksheet

Figure 1

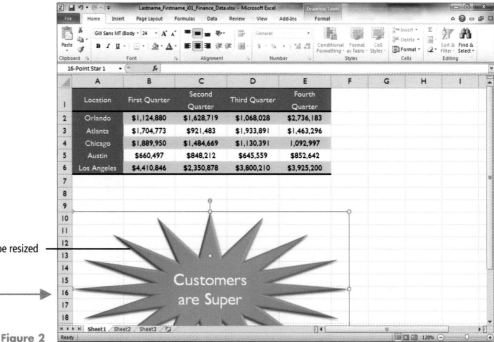

Shape resized

Figure 2

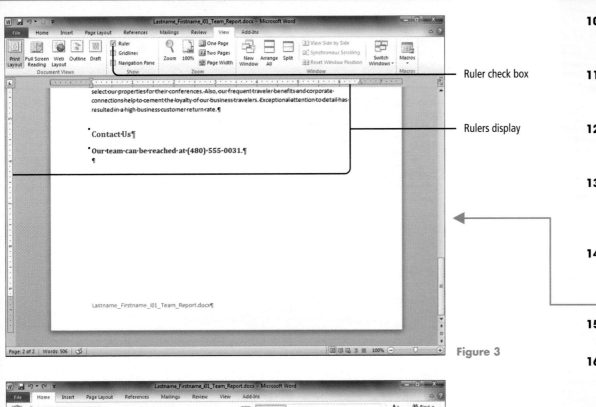

Ruler check box

Rulers display

Figure 3

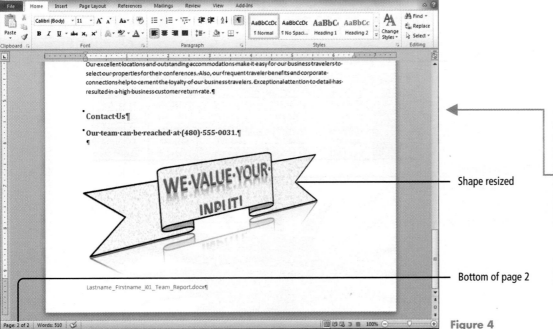

Shape resized

Bottom of page 2

Figure 4

10. Click the **Sheet2** sheet tab. Hold down Ctrl, and then click the **Sheet3** sheet tab. Release Ctrl.

11. On the **Home tab**, in the **Cells group**, click the **Delete button arrow**, and then click **Delete Sheet**.

12. Right-click the **Sheet1** sheet tab, and then click **Rename**. Type Quarterly Data and then press Enter.

13. Click **Save** 🖫, and then make **Lastname_Firstname_i01_Team_Report** the active window. Press Ctrl + End to move to the end of the document.

14. If the ruler does not display, on the **View tab**, in the **Show/Hide group**, select the **Ruler** check box. Compare your screen with **Figure 3**.

15. On the **Home tab**, click the **Clipboard Dialog Box Launcher** 🖫.

16. In the **Clipboard** task pane, click the **Up Ribbon** shape to paste the shape into the Word document. **Close** ☒ the **Clipboard** task pane.

17. On the **Picture Tools Format tab**, in the **Size group**, click the **Shape Height** box, type 1.5 and then press Enter. In the **Arrange group**, click the **Align** button 🖳, and then click **Align Bottom**. Click the **Align** button 🖳, and then click **Align Center**. Press Ctrl + End, to verify the position of the shape by the ruler. Compare your screen with **Figure 4**.

18. **Save** 🖫 the file, and then **Exit** Word. Make **Lastname_Firstname_i01_Team_Presentation** the active window, and then **Close** ☒ the **Clipboard** task pane.

■ **You have completed Skill 6 of 10**

- An Excel table enables you to format, sort, filter, and perform calculations on a group of related data.

- *Criteria* are conditions that you specify to limit choices. A *filter* hides rows that do not meet the criteria.

- A *filter drop-down list* is a control that displays a list of filter options for each column in the header row of an Excel table.

---

1. Make the Excel workbook **Lastname_Firstname_i01_Finance_Data** the active window. On the **Page Layout tab**, in the **Page Setup group**, click the **Margins** button, and then click **Narrow**.

2. Click cell **A1**. On the **Home tab**, in the **Styles group**, click the **Format as Table** button, and then click **Table Style Light 9**. In the **Format As Table** dialog box, click **OK**. Click cell **F1**, and then compare your screen with **Figure 1**.

   The range is converted into an *Excel table*— a series of rows and columns that contain related data that are managed independently from the data in other rows and columns on the worksheet.

3. In cell **F1**, type Annual Total and then press Enter.

   AutoExpansion automatically includes an adjoining column in an Excel table.

4. With cell **F2** active, in the **Editing group**, click the **Sum** button Σ, and then press Enter to create a calculated column. Increase the width of **column F** to **12**, and then compare your screen with **Figure 2**.

   In an Excel table, a *calculated column* uses a single formula that adjusts for each row.

■ **Continue to the next page to complete the skill**

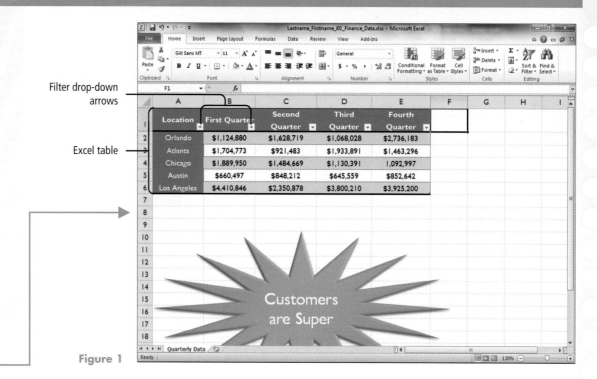

Filter drop-down arrows

Excel table

Figure 1

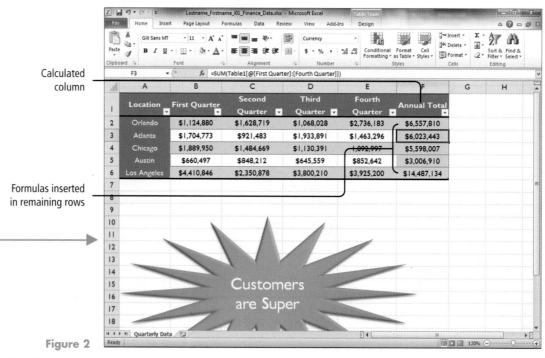

Calculated column

Formulas inserted in remaining rows

Figure 2

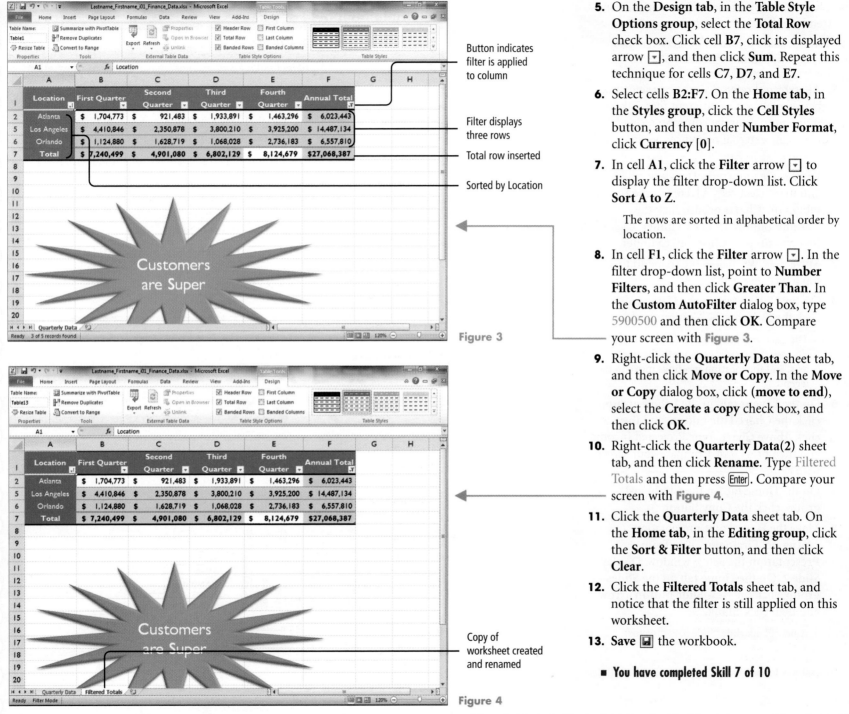

Button indicates filter is applied to column

Filter displays three rows

Total row inserted

Sorted by Location

Figure 3

Copy of worksheet created and renamed

Figure 4

5. On the **Design tab**, in the **Table Style Options group**, select the **Total Row** check box. Click cell **B7**, click its displayed arrow ▾, and then click **Sum**. Repeat this technique for cells **C7**, **D7**, and **E7**.

6. Select cells **B2:F7**. On the **Home tab**, in the **Styles group**, click the **Cell Styles** button, and then under **Number Format**, click **Currency [0]**.

7. In cell **A1**, click the **Filter** arrow ▾ to display the filter drop-down list. Click **Sort A to Z**.

> The rows are sorted in alphabetical order by location.

8. In cell **F1**, click the **Filter** arrow ▾. In the filter drop-down list, point to **Number Filters**, and then click **Greater Than**. In the **Custom AutoFilter** dialog box, type 5900500 and then click **OK**. Compare your screen with **Figure 3**.

9. Right-click the **Quarterly Data** sheet tab, and then click **Move or Copy**. In the **Move or Copy** dialog box, click (**move to end**), select the **Create a copy** check box, and then click **OK**.

10. Right-click the **Quarterly Data(2)** sheet tab, and then click **Rename**. Type Filtered Totals and then press Enter. Compare your screen with **Figure 4**.

11. Click the **Quarterly Data** sheet tab. On the **Home tab**, in the **Editing group**, click the **Sort & Filter** button, and then click **Clear**.

12. Click the **Filtered Totals** sheet tab, and notice that the filter is still applied on this worksheet.

13. Save 🖫 the workbook.

■ **You have completed Skill 7 of 10**

▶ Charts enable users to see comparisons and trends in data.

▶ You can share information between files through linked or embedded objects.

1. An *external reference* creates a reference between objects in different files. Take a moment to examine common terms regarding external references, as described in the table in **Figure 1**.

2. Display the **Quarterly Data** worksheet, and then select cells **A1:E6**. On the **Insert tab**, in the **Charts group**, click the **Column** button. Under **Cylinder**, click the first chart type—**Clustered Cylinder**.

3. Move the chart below the shape so that its top left corner is in cell **A27**.

4. On the **Design tab**, in the **Data group**, click the **Switch Row/Column** button.

> The data series in the chart is switched. The quarter headings move to the horizontal axis, and the location headings move to the legend.

5. On the **Layout tab**, in the **Labels group**, click the **Chart Title** button, and then click **Above Chart**. Type Projected Income and then press [Enter]. Compare your screen with **Figure 2**.

6. On the **Home tab**, in the **Clipboard group**, click the **Copy** button .

7. Make the PowerPoint presentation **Lastname_Firstname_i01_Team_ Presentation** the active window. Display **Slide 2**. On the **Home tab**, in the **Slides group**, click the **New Slide button arrow**, and then click **Blank**.

> A new blank slide, Slide 3, is inserted.

■ **Continue to the next page to complete the skill**

External References	
Type	**Description**
OLE	*Object linking and embedding* is a program-integration technology that shares information between programs through linked or embedded objects.
Source file	The file that contains the original information that is used to create a linked or an embedded object.
Destination file	The file into which a linked or an embedded object is inserted.
Linked object	An object that maintains a connection between the source and destination files. Linked data or objects are stored in the source file.
Embedded object	An object that becomes part of the destination file. If the source file is modified, the embedded object does not change.

Figure 1

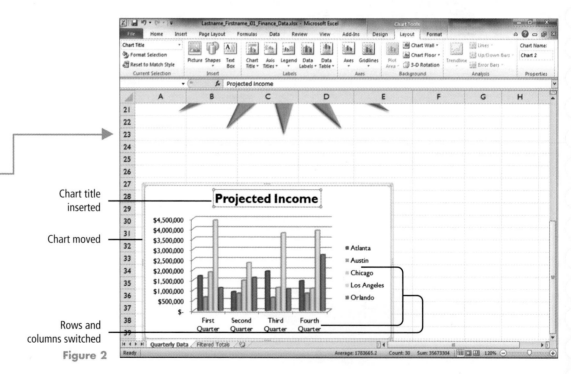

Chart title inserted

Chart moved

Rows and columns switched

Figure 2

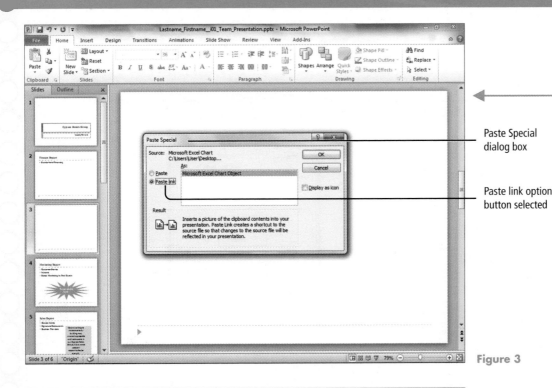

Paste Special
dialog box

Paste link option
button selected

Figure 3

8. In the **Clipboard group**, click the **Paste button arrow**, and then click **Paste Special**. In the **Paste Special** dialog box, select the **Paste link** option button, as shown in Figure 3.

   The chart will be pasted as a *Microsoft Office Excel Chart Object*. Here, the *Paste* option button creates an embedded object. The *Paste link* option button creates a linked object.

9. In the **Paste Special** dialog box, click **OK**. On the **Format tab**, increase the **Shape Height** to **5"**.

10. In the **Arrange group**, click the **Align** button, and then click **Align Middle**. Click the **Align** button again, and then click **Align Center**.

11. Make the Excel source file **Lastname_Firstname_i01_Finance_Data** the active window. Notice in the chart that *Los Angeles* had the highest projected income in the first quarter. Click cell **B5**, type 1410846 and then press Enter. Scroll down to verify that the Los Angeles first-quarter column reflects the new value.

12. Make the destination file **Lastname_Firstname_i01_Team_Presentation** the active window. Compare your Los Angeles first-quarter column with Figure 4. If necessary, right-click the chart, and then in the shortcut menu, click Update Link.

   The chart is a linked object. Changes made in the source file are reflected in the destination file.

13. **Save** the presentation, and then **Exit** PowerPoint. **Save** the workbook, and then **Exit** Excel.

   ■ **You have completed Skill 8 of 10**

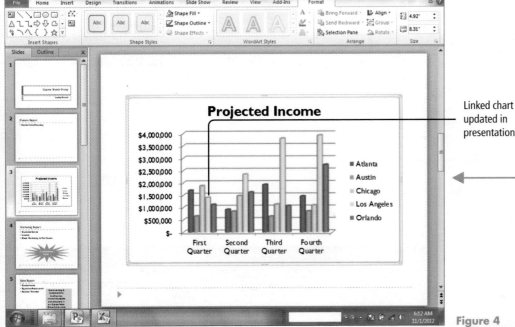

Linked chart updated in presentation

Figure 4

▶ The mail merge feature in Word lets you create customized letters, e-mail messages, envelopes, or labels.

▶ In mail merge, the *main document* contains the text that remains constant. The *data source* contains the information—such as names and addresses—that changes with each letter or envelope.

1. **Start** ⊙ Access. On the **File tab**, click **Open**, navigate to your student data files, and then open **i01_Associates**.

2. **Open** the **Associates** table, notice the number of records and some of the names and addresses. **Exit** Access.

3. **Start** ⊙ Word. **Save** the new document in your **Integrated Projects Chapter 1** folder as Lastname_Firstname_i01_Envelopes If necessary, display formatting marks.

4. On the **Mailings tab**, in the **Start Mail Merge group**, click the **Start Mail Merge** button, and then click **Envelopes**. In the **Envelope Options** dialog box, verify that the **Envelope size** is **Size 10**, as shown in **Figure 1**.

5. In the **Envelope Options** dialog box, click **OK**. Notice that an envelope displays on your screen.

6. At the top left corner of the displayed envelope, type your first and last names, and then press Enter. Type 6803 N River Ave and then press Enter. Type Tampa, FL 33605 and then compare your screen with **Figure 2**.

7. On the **Mailings tab**, in the **Start Mail Merge group**, click the **Select Recipients** button, and then click **Use Existing List**.

■ Continue to the next page to complete the skill ▶

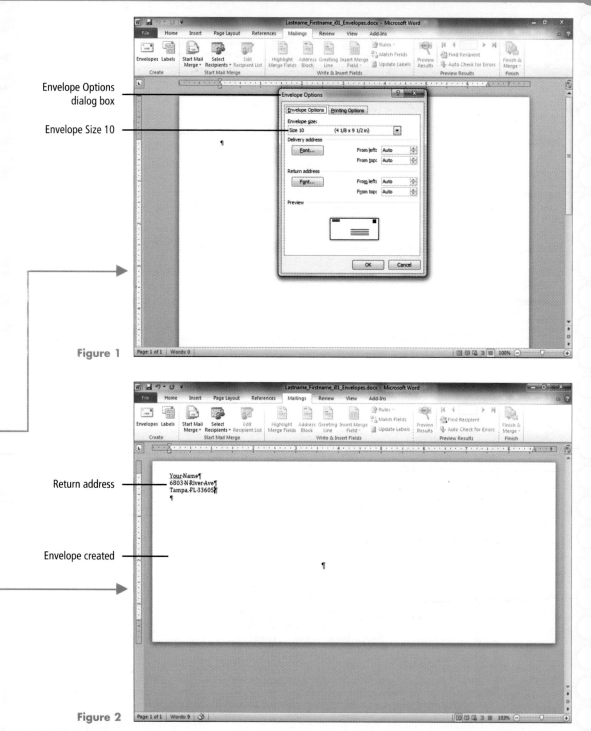

Envelope Options dialog box

Envelope Size 10

Figure 1

Return address

Envelope created

Figure 2

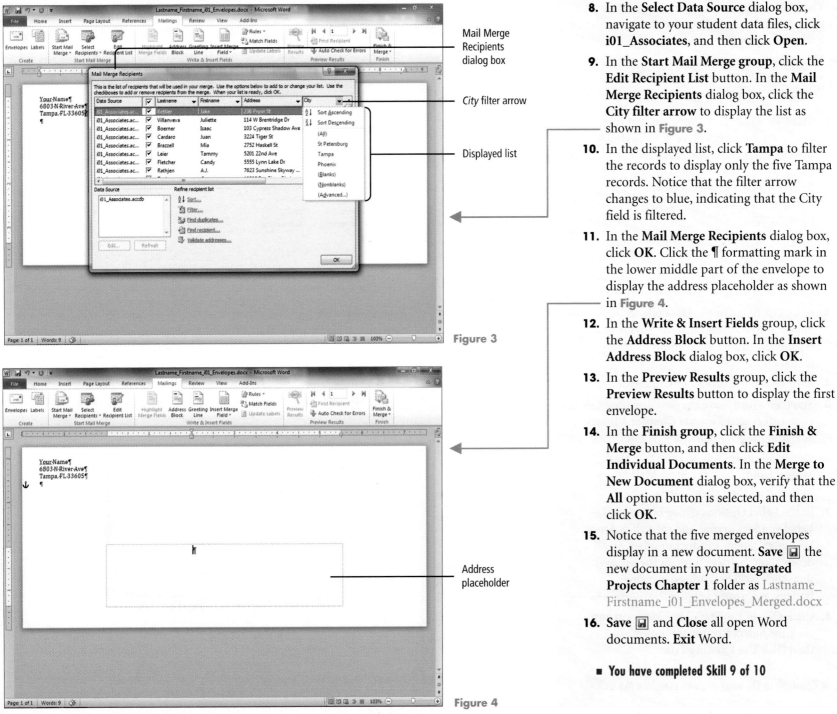

Mail Merge
Recipients
dialog box

City filter arrow

Displayed list

Figure 3

Address
placeholder

Figure 4

8. In the **Select Data Source** dialog box, navigate to your student data files, click **i01_Associates**, and then click **Open**.

9. In the **Start Mail Merge group**, click the **Edit Recipient List** button. In the **Mail Merge Recipients** dialog box, click the **City filter arrow** to display the list as shown in **Figure 3**.

10. In the displayed list, click **Tampa** to filter the records to display only the five Tampa records. Notice that the filter arrow changes to blue, indicating that the City field is filtered.

11. In the **Mail Merge Recipients** dialog box, click **OK**. Click the ¶ formatting mark in the lower middle part of the envelope to display the address placeholder as shown in **Figure 4**.

12. In the **Write & Insert Fields** group, click the **Address Block** button. In the **Insert Address Block** dialog box, click **OK**.

13. In the **Preview Results** group, click the **Preview Results** button to display the first envelope.

14. In the **Finish group**, click the **Finish & Merge** button, and then click **Edit Individual Documents**. In the **Merge to New Document** dialog box, verify that the **All** option button is selected, and then click **OK**.

15. Notice that the five merged envelopes display in a new document. **Save** 🖫 the new document in your **Integrated Projects Chapter 1** folder as Lastname_ Firstname_i01_Envelopes_Merged.docx

16. **Save** 🖫 and **Close** all open Word documents. **Exit** Word.

■ **You have completed Skill 9 of 10**

▶ The mail merge feature can sort or filter records before the records are merged with a Word document.

▶ Mail merge can use a variety of data sources, including Access, Excel, Outlook, Word, or an HTML file.

1. **Start** ⊕ Excel. From your student files, **Open i01_Speakers**. **Save** the workbook in your **Integrated Projects Chapter 1** folder as Lastname_Firstname_i01_ Speakers Add the file name in the worksheet's left footer, and then return to **Normal** view.

2. In cell **A50**, type your first name, and then press Tab. In cell **B50**, type your last name, and then press Enter. Compare your screen with **Figure 1.**

3. Click cell **B50**. On the **Data tab**, in the **Sort & Filter** group, click the **Sort A to Z** button ⏷ to sort the column in alphabetical order.

4. **Save** 🖫 the workbook, and then **Exit** Excel.

5. **Start** ⊕ Word. **Save** the new document in your **Integrated Projects Chapter 1** folder as Lastname_Firstname_i01_Name_Tags

6. On the **Mailings tab**, in the **Start Mail Merge group**, click the **Start Mail Merge** button, and then click **Labels**.

7. In the **Label Options** dialog box, click the **Label vendors arrow**, and then click **Avery US Letter**. Under **Product number**, scroll down about halfway through the list, and then click **5095 Self Adhesive Name Badges**, as shown in **Figure 2.**

8. Click **OK**. In the **Start Mail Merge group**, click the **Select Recipients** button, and then click **Use Existing List**.

■ **Continue to the next page to complete the skill** ▶

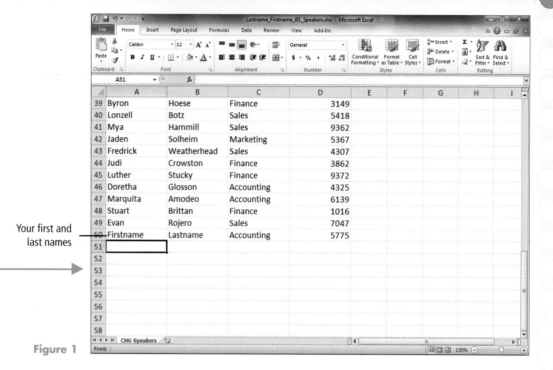

Your first and last names

Figure 1

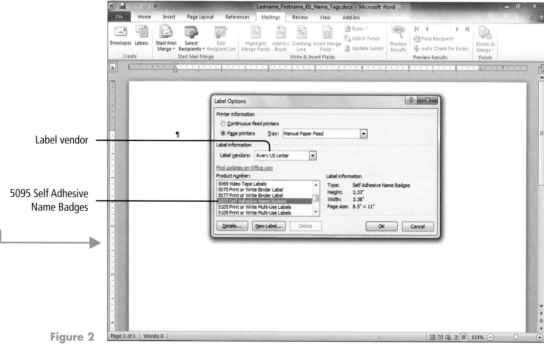

Label vendor

5095 Self Adhesive Name Badges

Figure 2

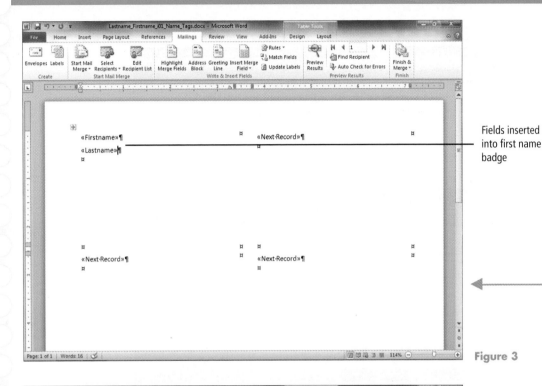

Fields inserted
into first name
badge

Figure 3

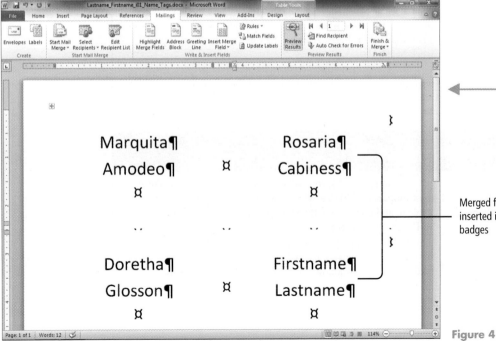

Merged fields
inserted in name
badges

Figure 4

9. In the **Select Data Source** dialog box, navigate to your **Integrated Projects Chapter 1** folder, and then open **Lastname_Firstname_i01_Speakers**. In the **Select Table** dialog box, click **OK**.

10. Click the **Edit Recipient List** button. In the **Mail Merge Recipients** dialog box, click the **Department filter arrow**, and then click **Accounting**. Verify that six records display, and then click **OK**.

11. In the **Write & Insert Fields group**, click the **Insert Merge Field button arrow**, and then click **Firstname**. Press Enter. Click the **Insert Merge Field button arrow**, and then click **Lastname**. Compare your screen with **Figure 3**.

12. Above the first label, click the **Layout Selector** ⊞. On the Mini toolbar, change the **Font Size** to **28**. On the **Layout tab**, in the **Alignment group**, click the **Align Center** button.

13. On the **Mailings tab**, in the **Write & Insert Fields group**, click the **Update Labels** button. In the **Preview Results group**, click the **Preview Results** button to display the six merged name tags as shown in **Figure 4**.

14. In the **Finish group**, click the **Finish & Merge** button, and then click **Edit Individual Documents**. In the **Merge to New Document** dialog box, click **OK**. **Save** the document in your **Integrated Projects Chapter 1** folder as Lastname_Firstname_i01_Accounting_Tags.

15. **Save** and **Close** all open Word documents, and then **Exit** Word.

16. Submit your files as directed by your instructor.

Done! You have completed Skill 10 of 10 and your document is complete!

The following More Skills are located at **www.pearsonhighered.com/skills**

More Skills Insert Subtotals in Excel and Link Data to a Word Document

Excel can calculate summary statistics, such as totals or averages, by using the SUBTOTAL function. You can link data in Excel to a Word document. When the data in Excel is updated, the subtotals in the linked Word document will update.

In More Skills 11, you will open an Excel workbook, insert subtotals, and then link the data to a Word document.

To begin, open your web browser, navigate to www.pearsonhighered.com/skills, locate the name of your textbook, and then follow the instructions on the website.

More Skills Insert Slides from Another Presentation

PowerPoint slides can be duplicated in the same presentation, or slides can be added from a different presentation. You can guarantee consistency between presentations by reusing slides from other presentations.

In More Skills 12, you will open a presentation and duplicate slides. You will then reuse slides from a different presentation.

To begin, open your web browser, navigate to www.pearsonhighered.com/skills, locate the name of your textbook, and then follow the instructions on the website.

More Skills Move and Copy Excel Worksheets and Consolidate Data

An Excel worksheet can be moved or copied in the same workbook or to a different Excel workbook. The Move or Copy tool is used to organize worksheets from different workbooks into a single workbook.

In More Skills 13, you will open three Excel workbooks and then copy the worksheets into one workbook. You will then create a summary worksheet to display the totals of the three copied worksheets.

To begin, open your web browser, navigate to www.pearsonhighered.com/skills, locate the name of your textbook, and then follow the instructions on the website.

More Skills Compare Shared Excel Workbooks

A shared workbook allows many users to view and make changes in the workbook at the same time. You can use the Compare and Merge Workbooks feature to compare the changes that have been made before you update the workbook.

In More Skills 14, you will open a shared workbook, add the Compare and Merge Workbooks icon to the Quick Access Toolbar, and then merge the workbooks. You will then accept and reject the changes.

To begin, open your web browser, navigate to www.pearsonhighered.com/skills, locate the name of your textbook, and then follow the instructions on the website.

Key Terms

Online Help Skills

1. Start 🔵 Word. In the upper right corner of the Word window, click the Help button 🔵. In the Help window, click the Maximize 🔲 button.

2. Click in the search box, type set password and then click the Search button 🔍. In the search results, click **Protect your document, workbook, or presentation with passwords, permission, and other restrictions**

3. Compare your screen with **Figure 1**.

Figure 1

4. Read the entire article to see if you can answer the following: Why would you password protect a file?

Matching

Match each term in the second column with its correct definition in the first column by writing the letter of the term on the blank line in front of the correct definition.

____ **1.** A set of characters added to the end of a file name that identify the file type or format.

____ **2.** A list of commands relevant to a particular item that displays when the item is right-clicked.

____ **3.** A yellow diamond-shaped handle used to adjust the appearance but not the size of objects.

____ **4.** An object that can be inserted to emphasize a point.

____ **5.** The conditions specified to limit which records are included in the result of a filter.

____ **6.** A range of rows and columns that contain related data that is managed independently from the data in other rows and columns on the worksheet.

____ **7.** A control that displays a list of filter and sort options for a column in an Excel table or Access datasheet.

____ **8.** An object that becomes part of the destination file.

____ **9.** An object that maintains a connection between the source and destination files.

____ **10.** An application-integration technology used to share information between programs.

A Adjustment handle

B Criteria

C Embedded object

D Excel table

E File extension

F Filter drop-down list

G Linked object

H OLE

I Shape

J Shortcut menu

Multiple Choice

Choose the correct answer.

1. This is a movable, resizable container for text or graphics.
   - **A.** Shape box
   - **B.** Text box
   - **C.** Content box

2. This feature hides Excel rows or Access records that do not meet certain criteria.
   - **A.** Filter
   - **B.** Sort
   - **C.** Arrange

3. This Excel feature automatically includes an adjoining column in an Excel table.
   - **A.** Add column
   - **B.** Insert
   - **C.** AutoExpansion

4. This Excel table feature uses a single formula that automatically adjusts for each row.
   - **A.** Planned column
   - **B.** Calculated column
   - **C.** Insert column

5. This creates a reference between objects in different files.
   - **A.** Internal reference
   - **B.** External reference
   - **C.** Location reference

6. Object linking and embedding is a program-integration technology that shares information between these objects.
   - **A.** Programs
   - **B.** Characters
   - **C.** Paragraphs

7. This file contains the original information that is used to create a linked or embedded object.
   - **A.** Source file
   - **B.** Destination file
   - **C.** Secondary file

8. This is the file into which a linked or embedded object is inserted.
   - **A.** Source file
   - **B.** Destination file
   - **C.** Secondary file

9. This part of the mail merge feature contains the text that remains constant.
   - **A.** Data souce
   - **B.** Secondary file
   - **C.** Main document

10. This part of the mail merge feature contains the information that changes with each document.
    - **A.** Data souce
    - **B.** Secondary file
    - **C.** Main document

Topics for Discussion

1. In this chapter, you practiced inserting text and objects from one Office application into another. When might this capability be helpful to a team member?

2. In this chapter, you created a calculated column in an Excel table. Explain why it is faster and more accurate to use a calculated column rather then typing a formula in each Excel row.

Skill Check 1

To complete this project, you will need the following files:

- New blank Word document
- i01_Restaurant_Memo.docx
- i01_Restaurant_Presentation.pptx

You will save your files as:

- Lastname_Firstname_i01_Restaurant_Income.xlsx
- Lastname_Firstname_i01_Restaurant_Memo.docx
- Lastname_Firstname_i01_Restaurant_Presentation.pptx

1. **Open** the Word document **i01_Restaurant_Memo**. **Save** the document in your **Integrated Projects Chapter 1** folder as Lastname_Firstname_i01_Restaurant_Memo and then add the file name to the footer.

2. Select the eight lines of tabbed text. On the **Insert tab**, in the **Tables group**, click the **Table** button. Click **Convert Text to Table**, and then click **OK**.

3. On the **Design tab**, in the **Table Styles group**, click the **More** button, and then click the fifth style in the fifth row—**Medium Shading 2 - Accent 4**.

4. On the **Layout tab**, in the **Cell Size group**, click the **AutoFit** button, and then click **AutoFit Contents**. In the **Table group**, click the **Properties** button. Under **Alignment**, click **Center**, and then click **OK**. Select the cells containing numbers. In the **Alignment group**, click the **Align Center Right** button. Compare your screen with **Figure 1**.

5. **Save** the Word document. Select the table, and then on the **Home tab**, in the **Clipboard group**, click the **Copy** button.

6. **Start** Excel. **Save** the new workbook in your **Integrated Projects Chapter 1** folder as Lastname_Firstname_i01_Restaurant_Income and then add the file name to the left side of the footer. Return to **Normal** view, and then press Ctrl + Home. On the **Home tab**, in the **Clipboard group**, click the **Paste** button.

7. In the **Styles group**, click the **Format As Table** button, and then click **Table Style Light 12**. In the **Format As Table** dialog box, click **OK**.

8. On the **Home tab**, in the **Cells group**, click the **Format** button, and then click **Row Height**. In the **Row Height** dialog box, type 30, and then click **OK**. Compare your screen with **Figure 2**.

9. Make cell **E1** the active cell. Type Totals and then press Enter.

■ Continue to the next page to complete this Skill Check ▶

Figure 1

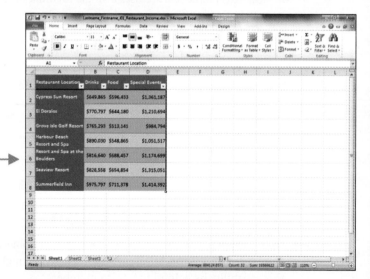

Figure 2

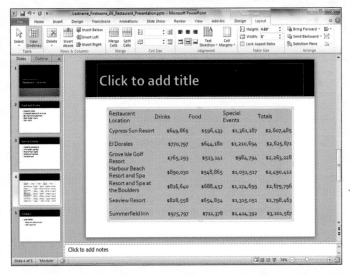

Figure 3

Figure 4

10. Verify that cell **E2** is the active cell. In the **Editing group**, click the **Sum** button, and then press Enter.

11. Select **columns B:E**. In the **Cells group**, click the **Format** button, and then click **Column Width**. In the **Column Width** dialog box, type 14, and then click **OK**. Click **A1**, and then **Save** the workbook.

12. **Open** the PowerPoint presentation **i01_Restaurant_Presentation**. **Save** the presentation in your **Integrated Projects Chapter 1** folder as Lastname_ Firstname_i01_Restaurant_Presentation and then add the file name to all the Notes and Handouts footers.

13. On the **Design tab**, in the **Themes group**, click the **Module** theme. Display **Slide 3**. On the **Home tab**, in the **Slides group**, click the **New Slide button arrow**, and then click **Title Only**.

14. Make the Excel workbook **Lastname_Firstname_i01_Restaurant_Income** the active window. Select cells **A1:E8**, and then **Copy** the range of cells.

15. Make the presentation **Lastname_Firstname_i01_Restaurant_Presentation** the active window. If necessary, display Slide 4. On the **Home tab**, in the **Clipboard group**, click the **Paste** button.

16. On the **Layout tab**, in the **Table Size group**, increase the **Height** to **4.5"**, and then increase the **Width** to **8"**. In the **Arrange group**, click the **Align** button, and then click **Align Center**.

17. Select all the table cells, and then change the **Font Size** to **18**. Compare your screen with **Figure 3**.

18. On **Slide 4**, click the **Title** placeholder, and then type Restaurant Income by Location

19. Display **Slide 3**. On the **Insert tab**, in the **Illustrations group**, click the **Shapes** button, and then under **Stars and Banners**, click the fifth shape in the second row—**Vertical Scroll**. Click the right side of **Slide 3** to insert the shape.

20. On the **Format tab**, in the **Size group**, increase the **Height** to **4"**, and then increase the **Width** to **3"**. In the **Shape Styles group**, click the **Shape Effects** button. Point to **Shadow**, and then under **Perspective**, click **Perspective Diagonal Upper Left**.

21. Type Our special events depend on our customer loyalty and then select the text. On the Mini toolbar, change the **Font Size** to **28**. Move the shape to the right side of the slide. Compare your screen with **Figure 4**.

22. **Save** and then **Close** the files. Submit your files as directed by your instructor.

Done! You have completed Skill Check 1

Skill Check 2

To complete this project, you will need the following files:

- New blank Word document
- i01_Seminar.xlsx
- i01_Guests.accdb

You will save your files as:

- Lastname_Firstname_i01_Seminar_Tags.docx
- Lastname_Firstname_i01_Sales_Tags.docx
- Lastname_Firstname_i01_Guest_Envelopes.docx
- Lastname_Firstname_i01_85017_Envelopes.docx

1. **Start** Word. **Save** the new document in your **Integrated Projects Chapter 1** folder as Lastname_Firstname_i01_Seminar_Tags

2. On the **Mailings tab**, in the **Start Mail Merge group**, click the **Start Mail Merge** button, and then click **Labels**. In the **Labels Options** dialog box, click the **Label vendors arrow**, and then click **Avery US Letter**. Under **Product number**, click **5095 Self Adhesive Name Badges**, and then click **OK**.

3. In the **Start Mail Merge group**, click the **Select Recipients** button, and then click **Use Existing List**. In the **Select Data Source** dialog box, locate and **Open** the Excel workbook **i01_Seminar**, and then click **OK**. In the **Select Table** dialog box, click **OK**.

4. In the **Start Mail Merge group**, click the **Edit Recipient List** button. In the **Mail Merge Recipients** dialog box, click the **Department** filter arrow, and then click **Sales**. Compare your screen with **Figure 1**.

5. In the **Mail Merge Recipients** dialog box, click **OK**.

6. On the **Mailings tab**, in the **Write & Insert Fields group**, click the **Insert Merge Field button arrow**, and then click **Firstname**. Press Enter. Click the **Insert Merge Field button arrow**, and then click **Lastname**. Above the first label, click the **Layout Selector**. On the Mini toolbar, change the **Font Size** to **26**. Compare your screen with **Figure 2**.

7. In the **Write & Insert Fields group**, click the **Update Labels** button. In the **Preview Results group**, click the **Preview Results** button.

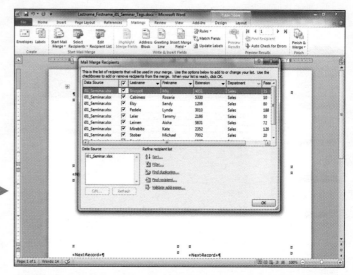

Figure 1

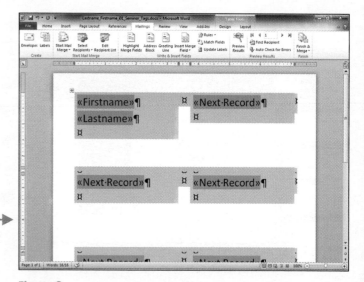

Figure 2

- Continue to the next page to complete this Skill Check

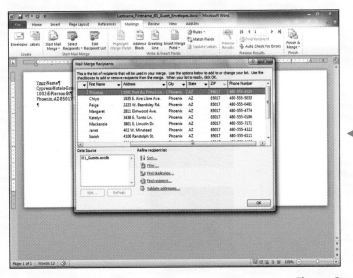

Figure 3

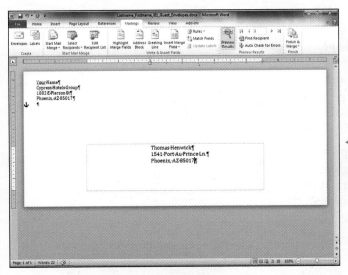

Figure 4

8. In the **Finish group**, click the **Finish & Merge** button, and then click **Edit Individual Documents**. In the **Merge to New Document** dialog box, click **OK**.

9. In the first name tag, delete the name, and then type your first and last names. **Save** the merged document in your **Integrated Projects Chapter 1** folder as Lastname_Firstname_i01_Sales_Tags and then **Close** the document.

10. Make **Lastname_Firstname_i01_Seminar_Tags** the active window. Insert the file name as a footer, and then **Save** and **Close** the document.

11. Create a new blank Word document. **Save** the new document in your **Integrated Projects Chapter 1** folder as Lastname_Firstname_i01_Guest_Envelopes

12. On the **Mailings tab**, in the **Start Mail Merge group**, click the **Start Mail Merge** button. Click **Envelopes**. In the **Envelope Options** dialog box, verify the *Envelope size* is **Size 10**, and then click **OK**.

13. At the top left corner of the envelope, type Your Name and then press Enter. Type Cypress Hotels Group and then press Enter. Type 1002 E Pierson St and then press Enter. Type Phoenix, AZ 85017

14. Using the techniques from the previous steps, select recipients from an existing list using the Access database **i01_Guests**.

15. In the **Start Mail Merge group**, click the **Edit Recipient List** button. In the **Mail Merge Recipients** dialog box, scroll to the right, click the **ZIP** filter arrow, and then click **85017**. Scroll to the right to view the **ZIP** column, and compare your screen with **Figure 3**.

16. In the **Mail Merge Recipients** dialog box, click **OK**.

17. Click the lower middle part of the envelope to display an address placeholder. In the **Write & Insert Fields group**, click the **Address Block** button, and then click **OK**. In the **Preview Results group**, click the **Preview Results** button. Compare your screen with **Figure 4**.

18. In the **Finish group**, click the **Finish & Merge** button. Click **Edit Individual Documents**, and then click **OK**. **Save** the new merged document in your **Integrated Projects Chapter 1** folder as Lastname_Firstname_i01_85017_Envelopes and then **Close** the document.

19. **Save** and then **Close** the document **Lastname_Firstname_i01_Guest_Envelopes**. Submit your files as directed by your instructor.

Done! You have completed Skill Check 2

Assess Your Skills 1

To complete this project, you will need the following files:

- New blank PowerPoint presentation
- i01_Retirement.docx
- i01_Quote1.docx
- i01_Quote2.docx
- i01_Quote3.docx
- i01_Quote4.docx

You will save your files as:

- Lastname_Firstname_i01_Retirement.docx
- Lastname_Firstname_i01_Retirement_Presentation.pptx

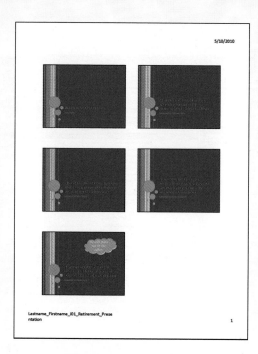

1. **Open** the Word document **i01_Retirement**. **Save** the file in your **Integrated Projects Chapter 1** folder as Lastname_Firstname_i01_Retirement Insert the file name in the footer.

2. In the second paragraph, replace the text *Your Name* with your own first and last names.

3. At the end of the document, insert the file **i01_Quote1**, and then insert the file **i01_Quote2**.

4. **Open i01_Quote3. Copy** and **Paste** the text to the end of **Lastname_Firstname_i01_Retirement. Close i01_Quote3**.

5. **Open i01_Quote4**. Move the text to the end of the **Lastname_Firstname_i01_Retirement** document. **Close i01_Quote4**. If prompted, do not save the changes.

6. Apply the **Oriel** theme. Select *Your Name* and the four paragraphs beginning *Submitted by*, and then apply the **Heading 2** style.

7. Select the paragraph *Retirement Celebration* and the four quotations, and then apply the **Heading 1** style.

8. Select all five instances of the **Heading 2** format, and then change the font color to the sixth color in the first row—**Blue, Accent 2**. **Save** the document, and then **Exit** Word.

9. **Start** PowerPoint. Insert the Word document **Lastname_Firstname_i01_Retirement**. **Save** the presentation in your **Integrated Projects Chapter 1** folder as Lastname_Firstname_i01_Retirement_Presentation Add the file name to all Notes and Handouts footers.

10. Apply the **Oriel** theme, and then delete **Slide 1**. Change the layout of all five slides to **Section Header**.

11. On **Slide 5**, insert the shape **Cloud**—found under **Basic Shapes**. Increase the **Shape Height** to 2" and the **Shape Width** to 4". Add the **Bevel** shape effect, **Soft Round**. Type We will miss you in the office Change the **Font Size** to **28**, and then apply **Italic**. Move the shape to the top right corner of the slide.

12. **Save** the presentation, and then **Copy** the shape. **Open Lastname_Firstname_i01_Retirement**, and then **Paste** the shape at the end of the document. Resize the shape to display all the text. **Save** the document.

13. Compare your completed documents with **Figure 1**. Submit your files as directed by your instructor.

Done! You have completed Assess Your Skills 1

Figure 1

Assess Your Skills 2

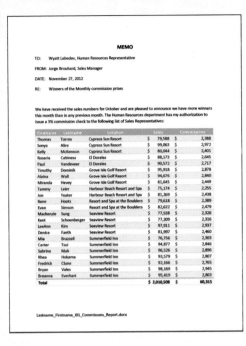

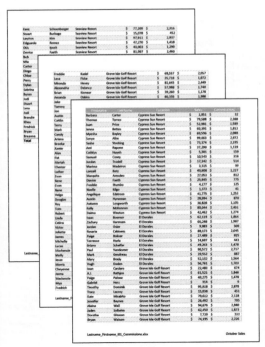

Figure 1

To complete this project, you will need the following files:

- i01_Commissions.xlsx
- i01_Commissions_Report.docx

You will save your files as:

- Lastname_Firstname_i01_Commissions.xlsx
- Lastname_Firstname_i01_Commissions_Report.docx

1. **Start** Excel, and **Open i01_Commissions**. Save the workbook in your **Integrated Projects Chapter 1** folder as Lastname_Firstname_i01_Commissions Add the file name to the worksheet's left footer, and then add the sheet name to the right footer. Return to **Normal** view.

2. Click cell **A2**. Format the range as an Excel table using the table style **Table Style Medium 7**.

3. In cell **E1**, type Commissions **AutoFit** the column widths of **columns A:E**.

4. In cell **E2**, enter the formula =D2*3% and then format the values in **column E** with the Cell Style **Currency [0]**.

5. Sort the **Location column** in ascending order. Filter the **Sales column** to display numbers greater than **75000**.

6. In the Excel table, insert a **Total Row**. In column **D**—the Sales column—on the **Total row**, insert the **SUM** function. If necessary, widen column D to display the total.

7. Create a copy of the **October Sales** worksheet. Rename the new worksheet **October Sales(2)** to October Prize Winners

8. On the **October Sales** worksheet, remove the filter, and then **Save** the workbook.

9. **Start** Word, and then open **i01_Commissions_ Report**. Save the document in your **Integrated Projects Chapter 1** folder as Lastname_Firstname_i01_Commissions_Report and then add the file name to the footer.

10. Make the Excel workbook **Lastname_Firstname_i01_Commissions** the active window. Make the **October Prize Winners** worksheet the active sheet, and then copy the filtered data in the range **A1:E118**.

11. Make the Word document **Lastname_Firstname_i01_Commissions_Report** the active window. Move to the end of the document, and then **Paste** the copied Excel data.

12. In Word, select the table, and then apply the **AutoFit Contents** command. **Save** the document.

13. Compare your completed documents with **Figure 1**. **Exit** Word, and then **Exit** Excel. Submit your files as directed by your instructor.

Done! You have completed Assess Your Skills 2

Assess Your Skills 3

To complete this project, you will need the following files:

- New blank Word document
- i01_Premier_Customers.accdb

You will save your files as:

- Lastname_Firstname_i01_Premier_Envelopes.docx
- Lastname_Firstname_i01_MA_Envelopes.docx
- Lastname_Firstname_i01_MA_Premier_Tags
- Lastname_Firstname_i01_MA_Tampa_Tags

1. **Start** Word. **Save** the new document in your **Integrated Projects Chapter 1** folder as Lastname_Firstname_i01_Premier_Envelopes

2. Start a Mail Merge document for **Envelopes**. Use the **Size 10** envelope. In the top left corner of the envelope, using your first and last names, type Your Name and then press Enter. Type Cypress Hotels Group and then press Enter. Type 33 Herman Ave and then press Enter. Type Concord, MA 01742

3. **Select Recipients** using the existing list in the Access student data file **i01_Premier_Customers**.

4. **Filter** the recipients to display the three people from the **State** of **MA**.

5. In the address placeholder, insert the **Address Block**, and then **Preview Results**.

6. **Finish & Merge** the document, and then **Save** the new document in your **Integrated Projects Chapter 1** folder as Lastname_Firstname_i01_MA_Envelopes

7. Compare your merged envelopes with **Figure 1**. **Save** and **Close** your document.

8. **Start** Word. **Save** the new document in your **Integrated Projects Chapter 1** folder as Lastname_Firstname_i01_Premier_Tags

9. Start a Mail Merge document for **Labels**. Use the *Label vendor* **Avery US Letter** and the *Product number* 5095 **Self Adhesive Name Badges**.

10. **Select Recipients** using the existing list in the Access student data file **i01_Premier_Customers**.

11. **Filter** the recipients to display the five people from the **City** of **Tampa**.

12. Insert the merge field **First_Name**, and then press Enter. Insert the merge field **Last_Name**. Select all the labels, and then change the **Font Size** to **24**.

13. Update the labels, and then preview the results. **Finish & Merge** the document.

14. In the first name tag, change the name to your first and last names. **Save** the new document in your **Integrated Projects Chapter 1** folder as Lastname_Firstname_i01_Tampa_Tags

15. Compare your merged labels with **Figure 1**. **Exit** Word, and then submit your files as directed by your instructor.

Done! You have completed Assess Your Skills 3

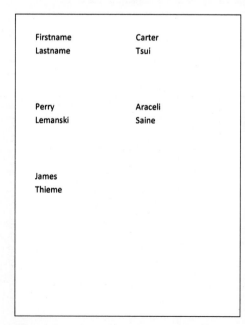

Figure 1

Assess Your Skills 4

To complete this project, you will need the following files:

- i01_Attendee_Memo.docx
- i01_Attendees.xlsx

You will save your files as:

- Lastname_Firstname_i01_Attendee_Memo.docx
- Lastname_Firstname_i01_Attendees.xlsx

1. **Start** Excel, and then open **i01_Attendees**. **Save** the workbook in your **Integrated Projects Chapter 1** folder as Lastname_Firstname_i01_Attendees On both worksheets, add the file name to the worksheet's left footer, and add the sheet name to the right footer. Return to **Normal** view.

2. On the **Conference Attendees** worksheet, type the following data in row **17**:

Firstname	Your first name
Lastname	Your last name
Location	Seaview Resort
Department	Marketing

3. Format the data as a table using the **Table Style Light 11**. AutoFit the column width of columns **A:D**. In the Excel table, filter the **Department** column to display **Marketing**, and then **Sort** the **Location** column in **Ascending** order. **Save** the workbook.

4. **Start** Word, and then from the student data files, open the document **i01_Attendee_Memo**. **Save** the document in your **Integrated Projects Chapter 1** folder as Lastname_Firstname_i01_Attendee_Memo Insert the file name in the footer.

5. Make the Excel workbook **Lastname_Firstname_i01_Attendees** the active window. On the **Conference Attendees** sheet, **Copy** the filtered range **A1:D17**. Make the Word document

   Lastname_Firstname_i01_Attendee_Memo the active window. Click in the blank line below the paragraph beginning *The list of,* and then **Paste** the Excel data.

6. Make the Excel workbook **Lastname_Firstname_i01_Attendees** the active window, and then press (Esc). On the **Marketing Expenses** worksheet, **Copy** the chart. Make the Word document **Lastname_Firstname_i01_Attendee_Memo** the active window. Click in the blank line below the paragraph beginning *We also have,* and then use **Paste Special** to link the Excel data as a **Microsoft Excel Chart Object**. Adjust the size of the chart to fit the chart at the bottom of page 1. **Save** the Word document.

7. Make the Excel workbook **Lastname_Firstname_i01_Attendees** the active window. On the **Marketing Expenses** worksheet, click cell **B4**, and then enter 12447 Verify that the change is reflected in the chart.

8. Make the Word document **Lastname_Firstname_i01_Attendee_Memo** the active window. Right-click the chart, and then click **Update Link**.

9. Compare your completed documents with **Figure 1**. **Save** your documents, and then **Exit** Word and **Exit** Excel. Submit your files as directed by your instructor.

Done! You have completed Assess Your Skills 4

Figure 1

CHAPTER 2

More Integrated Projects for Word, Excel, Access, and PowerPoint

▶ Each Microsoft Office application has different strengths. Exporting data from one application to another enables you to use the strengths of each application without having to retype the data.

▶ Shared data can be linked or embedded, depending on the final use for the data.

Your starting screen will look similar to this:

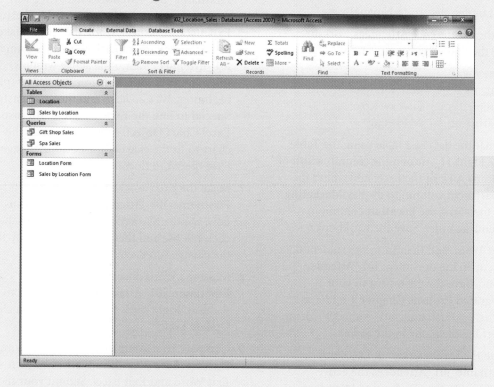

SKILLS

Skills 1–10 Training

At the end of this chapter, you will be able to:

Skill 1 Create an Access Append Query
Skill 2 Export Data from Access into Excel
Skill 3 Create an Excel PivotTable Report
Skill 4 Create External References Between Excel Workbooks
Skill 5 Insert a SmartArt Organization Chart into PowerPoint
Skill 6 Insert an Excel PivotTable into PowerPoint
Skill 7 Insert a PowerPoint Outline in Word and Create a Cover Page and Table of Contents
Skill 8 Link and Embed Data from Excel into Word
Skill 9 Export Data from Access to an RTF File and Insert the File into Word
Skill 10 Insert Objects from PowerPoint into Word

MORE SKILLS

More Skills 11 Create an Excel PivotChart and Link the PivotChart to Word
More Skills 12 Create a Hyperlink Between PowerPoint, Word, and Excel Files
More Skills 13 Insert a Total Row in an Excel Table and Link the Table to PowerPoint
More Skills 14 Compare Word Documents

Outcome

Using the skills listed to the left will enable you to create documents like these:

You will save your files as:

Lastname_Firstname_i02_Convention_Sales.docx
Lastname_Firstname_i02_Convention_Sales.rtf
Lastname_Firstname_i02_Golf_Isle_Sales.accdb
Lastname_Firstname_i02_Inventory.xlsx
Lastname_Firstname_i02_Location_Categories.xlsx

Lastname_Firstname_i02_Location_Sales.accdb
Lastname_Firstname_i02_Meeting_Notes.docx
Lastname_Firstname_i02_Meeting.rtf
Lastname_Firstname_i02_Sales_Meeting.pptx

In this chapter, you will create files for the Cypress Hotels Group, which has large hotels located in major vacation and business destinations in North America.

Introduction

▶ When data is stored in several Access databases, an append query enables you to combine all the data into one database.

▶ Excel provides a PivotTable report tool. Exporting data from Access into Excel enables you to create PivotTable reports from Access data.

▶ External references in Excel are useful when keeping worksheets together in the same workbook is not practical.

▶ Once created, data and objects can be linked or embedded in other files.

**Time to complete all
10 skills – 50 to 90 minutes**

Find your student data files here:

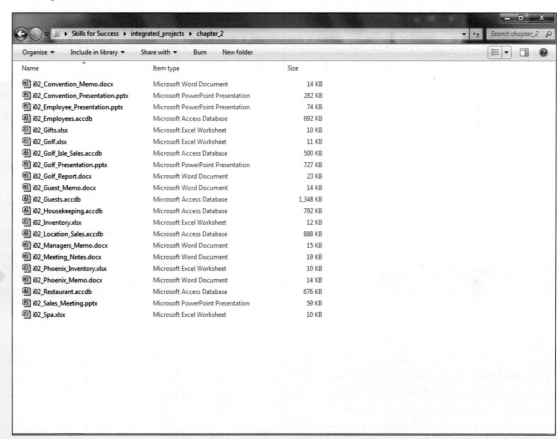

Student data files needed for this chapter:

- i02_Golf_Isle_Sales.accdb
- i02_Inventory.xlsx
- i02_Location_Sales.accdb
- i02_Meeting_Notes.docx
- i02_Sales_Meeting.pptx

► An ***append query*** is a query that adds records to a destination table.

► In an append query, the data types in the source table must be compatible with the data types in the destination table. The Undo button will not remove records added by an append query.

1. On your computer, be sure that your file extensions display. **Start** Access. Open **i02_Location_Sales**. On the **File tab**, click **Save Database As**. Navigate to the location where you are saving your files, create a folder named Integrated Projects Chapter 2 and then **Save** the database as Lastname_Firstname_i02_Location_Sales and enable the content. **Open** the **Sales by Location** table, view the records, and notice there are no records from the L7000 location. **Close** the table. **Close** the database.

2. **Open i02_Golf_Isle_Sales.accdb**. Using the techniques from the previous step, **Save** the database in the **Integrated Projects Chapter 2** folder as Lastname_Firstname_i02_Golf_Isle_Sales

3. Enable the content. On the **Create tab**, in the **Queries group**, click the **Query Design** button. In the **Show Table** dialog box, verify that the Sales table is selected, click **Add**, and then **Close** the dialog box. Double-click the four field names to add the fields to the design grid, and then compare your screen with **Figure 1**.

4. **Save** the query as Sales Query On the **Design tab**, in the **Results group**, click the **Run** button, and then compare your screen with **Figure 2**.

■ **Continue to the next page to complete the skill**

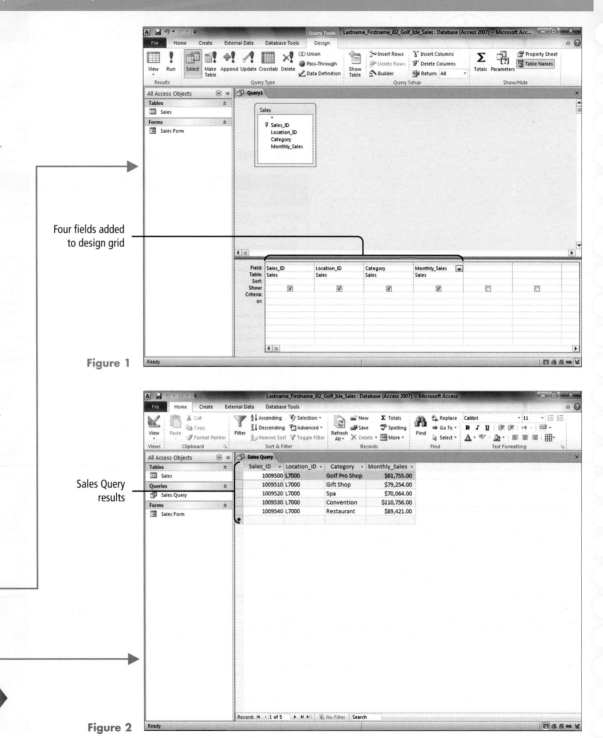

Four fields added to design grid

Figure 1

Sales Query results

Figure 2

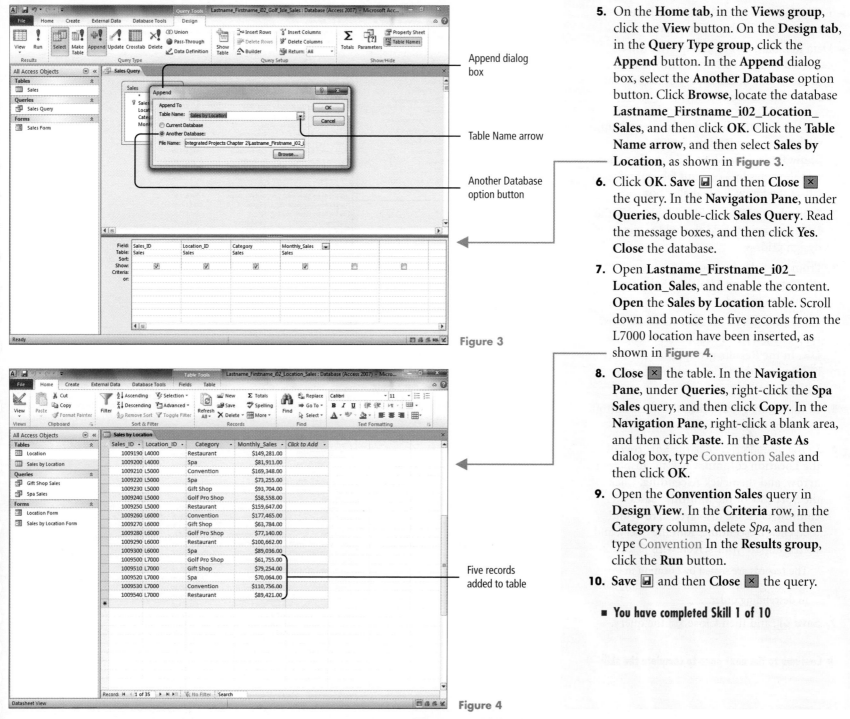

5. On the **Home tab**, in the **Views group**, click the **View** button. On the **Design tab**, in the **Query Type group**, click the **Append** button. In the **Append** dialog box, select the **Another Database** option button. Click **Browse**, locate the database **Lastname_Firstname_i02_Location_ Sales**, and then click **OK**. Click the **Table Name arrow**, and then select **Sales by Location**, as shown in **Figure 3**.

6. Click **OK**. **Save** 🖫 and then **Close** ✕ the query. In the **Navigation Pane**, under **Queries**, double-click **Sales Query**. Read the message boxes, and then click **Yes**. **Close** the database.

7. Open **Lastname_Firstname_i02_ Location_Sales**, and enable the content. **Open** the **Sales by Location** table. Scroll down and notice the five records from the L7000 location have been inserted, as shown in **Figure 4**.

8. **Close** ✕ the table. In the **Navigation Pane**, under **Queries**, right-click the **Spa Sales** query, and then click **Copy**. In the **Navigation Pane**, right-click a blank area, and then click **Paste**. In the **Paste As** dialog box, type Convention Sales and then click **OK**.

9. Open the **Convention Sales** query in **Design View**. In the **Criteria** row, in the **Category** column, delete *Spa*, and then type Convention In the **Results group**, click the **Run** button.

10. **Save** 🖫 and then **Close** ✕ the query.

■ **You have completed Skill 1 of 10**

Append dialog box

Table Name arrow

Another Database option button

Figure 3

Five records added to table

Figure 4

▶ Exporting data from Access into Excel creates a copy of the selected data.

▶ Data in tables, forms, and queries can be exported with or without its formatting, and the details of the export operation can be saved for future use.

1. On the **Create tab**, in the **Queries group**, click the **Query Design** button. In the **Show Table** dialog box, **Add** the **Location** and the **Sales by Location** tables, and then **Close** the **Show Table** dialog box.

2. From the **Location** table, double-click the **Location** field to add the field to the design grid.

3. From the **Sales by Location** table, add the **Category** and **Monthly_Sales** fields to the design grid.

4. Click **Save** 🖫. In the **Save As** dialog box, type Category by Location and then click **OK**. In the **Results group**, click the **Run** button, and then compare your screen with **Figure 1**.

5. In the **Views group**, click the **View** button to return to Design view.

6. In the design grid, click the **Sort row** of the **Location column**. Click the displayed **arrow**, and then click **Ascending**. Click the **Sort row** of the **Monthly_Sales column**, click the displayed **arrow**, and then click **Descending**. **Run** the query, and then compare your screen with **Figure 2**.

   The records are sorted by Location in ascending order and then by Monthly_Sales in descending order.

7. **Save** 🖫, and then **Close** ✕ the query.

■ **Continue to the next page to complete the skill**

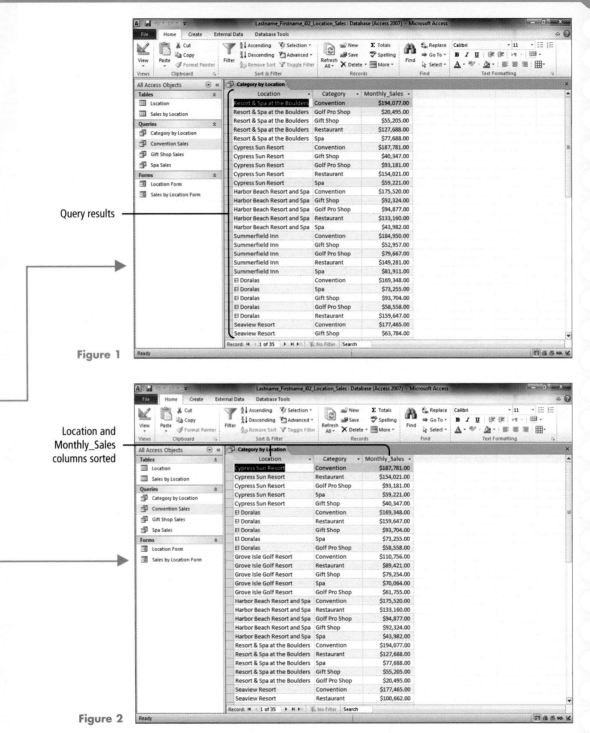

Query results

Figure 1

Location and Monthly_Sales columns sorted

Figure 2

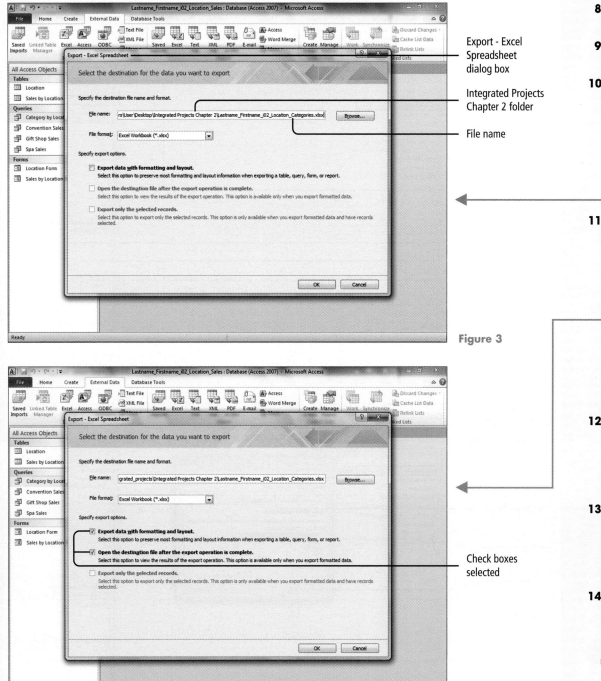

Figure 3

Figure 4

8. In the **Navigation Pane**, under **Queries**, select the **Category by Location** query.

9. On the **External Data tab**, in the **Export group**, click the **Excel** button.

10. In the **Export - Excel Spreadsheet** dialog box, click the **Browse** button. In the **File Save** dialog box, navigate to your **Integrated Projects Chapter 2** folder. In the **File name** box, type Lastname_ Firstname_i02_Location_Categories and then click **Save**. Compare your screen with **Figure 3**.

11. In the **Export - Excel Spreadsheet** dialog box, under **Specify export options**, select the **Export data with formatting and layout** check box, and the **Open the destination file after the export operation is complete** check box. Compare your screen with **Figure 4**.

   Selecting these export options will preserve most formatting and layout information in the Excel file and will open the Excel file for you to view the results of the export operation.

12. In the **Export - Excel Spreadsheet** dialog box, click **OK**.

   The Excel workbook displays. The records from the Access query Category by Location have been copied to the Excel workbook.

13. Make **Lastname_Firstname_i02_ Location_Sales** the active window. In the **Export - Excel Spreadsheet** dialog box, notice that the export settings can be saved, and then click **Close**.

14. Make **Lastname_Firstname_i02_ Locations_Categories** the active window. If necessary, Maximize the window.

■ **You have completed Skill 2 of 10**

▶ A *PivotTable report* is an interactive, cross-tabulated Excel report that summarizes and analyzes data—such as database records—from various sources, including ones that are external to Excel.

▶ In a PivotTable report, each Excel column becomes a PivotTable field that summarizes multiple rows of information.

1. Click cell **A1**. On the **Insert tab**, in the **Tables group**, click the **PivotTable** button. In the **Create PivotTable** dialog box, click **OK**. If the PivotTable Field List pane does not display, on the Options tab, in the Show group, click the Field List button. In the **PivotTable Field List** pane, select the **Location** check box. Compare your screen with **Figure 1**.

2. In the **PivotTable Field List** pane, drag the **Category** field to the **Report Filter** area. Drag the **Monthly_Sales** field to the **Values** area. In the **Values** area, click the **Sum of Monthly_Sales arrow**, and then click **Value Field Settings**. In the **Value Field Settings** dialog box, in the **Custom Name** box, type Monthly Sales and then click the **Number Format** button. In the **Format Cells** dialog box, click **Currency**, and then change the **Decimal places** to **0**. Click **OK**, and then compare your screen with **Figure 2**.

3. In the **Value Field Settings** dialog box, click **OK**. Select the range **A6:B6**. On the **Home tab**, in the **Font group**, click the **Fill Color button arrow** ⬛▾, and then click the fourth color in the third row— **Dark Blue, Text 2, Lighter 60%**.

■ **Continue to the next page to complete the skill** ▶

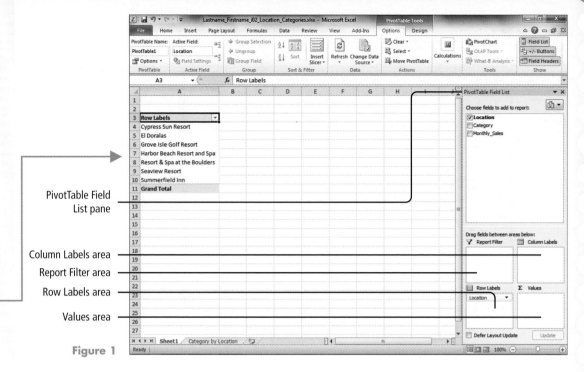

PivotTable Field List pane

Column Labels area
Report Filter area
Row Labels area
Values area

Figure 1

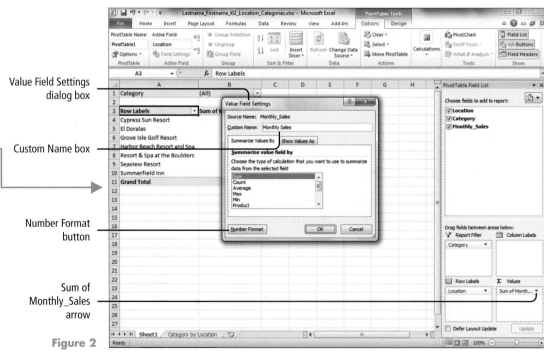

Value Field Settings dialog box

Custom Name box

Number Format button

Sum of Monthly_Sales arrow

Figure 2

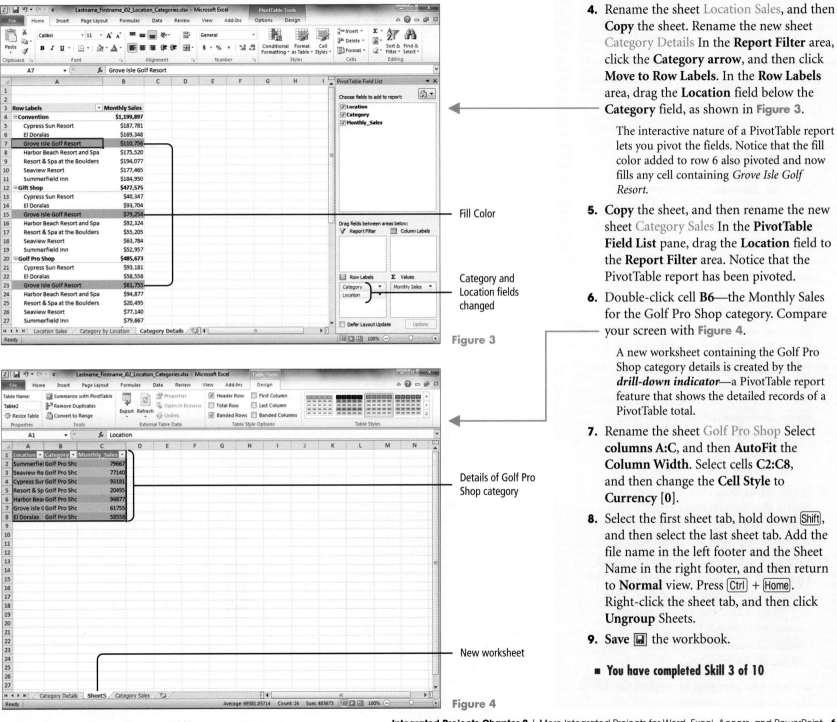

Fill Color

Category and
Location fields
changed

Figure 3

Details of Golf Pro
Shop category

New worksheet

Figure 4

4. Rename the sheet Location Sales, and then **Copy** the sheet. Rename the new sheet Category Details In the **Report Filter** area, click the **Category arrow**, and then click **Move to Row Labels**. In the **Row Labels** area, drag the **Location** field below the **Category** field, as shown in Figure 3.

> The interactive nature of a PivotTable report lets you pivot the fields. Notice that the fill color added to row 6 also pivoted and now fills any cell containing *Grove Isle Golf Resort*.

5. **Copy** the sheet, and then rename the new sheet Category Sales In the **PivotTable Field List** pane, drag the **Location** field to the **Report Filter** area. Notice that the PivotTable report has been pivoted.

6. Double-click cell **B6**—the Monthly Sales for the Golf Pro Shop category. Compare your screen with Figure 4.

> A new worksheet containing the Golf Pro Shop category details is created by the *drill-down indicator*—a PivotTable report feature that shows the detailed records of a PivotTable total.

7. Rename the sheet Golf Pro Shop Select **columns A:C**, and then **AutoFit** the **Column Width**. Select cells **C2:C8**, and then change the **Cell Style** to **Currency [0]**.

8. Select the first sheet tab, hold down ⇧Shift, and then select the last sheet tab. Add the file name in the left footer and the Sheet Name in the right footer, and then return to **Normal** view. Press Ctrl + Home. Right-click the sheet tab, and then click **Ungroup** Sheets.

9. **Save** 🔲 the workbook.

■ **You have completed Skill 3 of 10**

► Recall that an external reference in Excel is a reference to a cell or range in another Excel workbook.

► A *name*—a word or string of characters that represents a cell, range of cells, formula, or constant value—can be used in external references. External references that use names do not change when they are moved or copied.

1. On the **File tab**, click **Open**, and then open **i02_Inventory.xlsx**. **Save** the workbook in your **Integrated Projects Chapter 2** folder as Lastname_Firstname_i02_Inventory

2. On the **Golf Pro Shop** worksheet, click cell **B2**, and then compare your screen with **Figure 1**.

3. Click the **Name Box**, type Golf_Contact press Enter, and then press Tab. In the **Name Box**, type Golf_Phone and then press Enter.

4. On the **Spa** worksheet, use the same technique to name cell **B2** Spa_Contact and cell **C2** Spa_Phone Click the **Name Box arrow**, and then compare your screen with **Figure 2**.

   All names in the workbook are displayed. Names in Excel cannot contain spaces.

5. In the **Name Box**, click **Golf_Contact**. Notice that the cell represented by the name—cell **B2** on the Golf Pro Shop worksheet—is now the active cell.

6. **Save** 🖫 the workbook. Make **Lastname_Firstname_i02_Location_Categories** the active window. **Insert** a new worksheet, and then rename the new worksheet Contacts In cell **A1**, type Inventory Contacts In cell **A3**, type Golf Pro Shop and in cell **A4**, type Spa

■ **Continue to the next page to complete the skill** ▶

Name Box

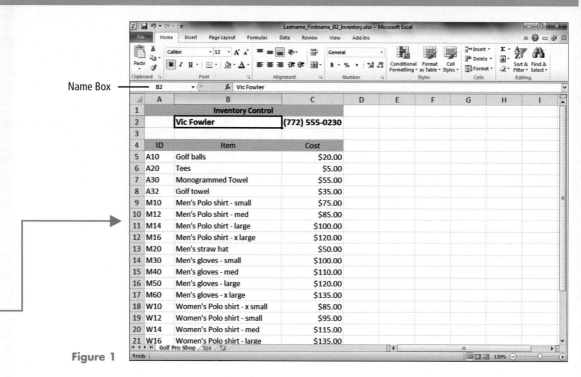

Figure 1

List of Names

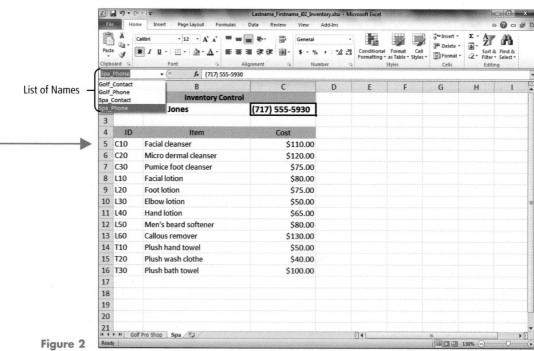

Figure 2

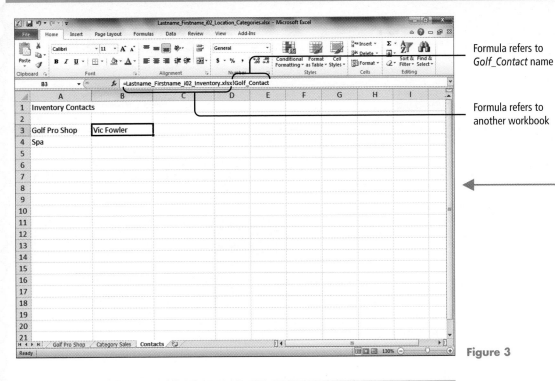

Formula refers to *Golf_Contact* name

Formula refers to another workbook

Figure 3

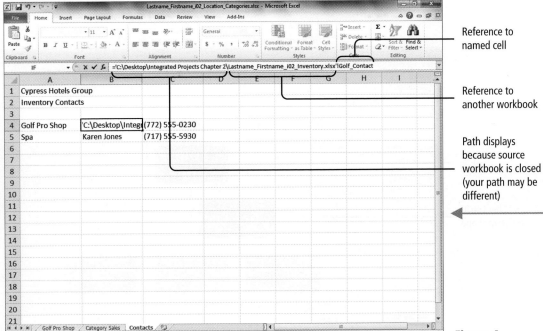

Reference to named cell

Reference to another workbook

Path displays because source workbook is closed (your path may be different)

Figure 4

7. Select **A3:C3**, and then change the **Column Width** to 15 In cell **B3**, type = and then make the **Lastname_Firstname_i02_Inventory** window active. On the **Golf Pro Shop** worksheet, click cell **B2**, and then on the **formula bar**, click the **Enter** button ☑. Compare your screen with **Figure 3**.

8. In cell **C3**, type = and then make the **Lastname_Firstname_i02_Inventory** window active. On the **Golf Pro Shop** worksheet, click cell **C2**, and then press [Enter]. Using the same technique, in cell **B4**, create an external reference to **Spa_Contact**, and then in cell **C4**, create an external reference to **Spa_Phone**.

9. In the **Contacts** worksheet, right-click the **row 1** header, and then click **Insert**. In cell **A1**, type Cypress Hotels Group

10. Make **Lastname_Firstname_i02_Inventory** the active window. **Group** the worksheets, **Insert** the file name in the left footer, and then return to **Normal** view. **Insert** a new row 1, and then in cell **A1**, type Cypress Hotels Group Select the range **A1:C1**. Add the **Accent4 Cell Style**, click **Merge & Center** ☷, and then change the **Font Size** to **14**. **Ungroup** the worksheets, and then **Save** and **Close** the workbook.

11. In **Lastname_Firstname_i02_Location_Categories**, click cell **B4**. Compare your screen with **Figure 4**.

    A row was inserted in both worksheets, and the named cells are still correct in the external references.

12. Select the range **A1:C1**. Click **Merge & Center** ☷, and apply the **Cell Style 40% - Accent4**. **Save** ☐ the workbook.

■ **You have completed Skill 4 of 10**

▶ An ***organization chart*** graphically represents the structure of an organization, such as department managers and nonmanagement employees.

▶ Effects and animation can be added to a SmartArt organization chart.

1. **Start** ⊙ PowerPoint, and open **i02_ Sales_Meeting**. **Save** the file in your **Integrated Projects Chapter 2** folder as Lastname_Firstname_i02_Sales_Meeting **Add** the file name to all Notes and Handouts footers.

2. Display **Slide 6**. In the lower placeholder, click the **Insert SmartArt Graphic** button ⊞. In the **Choose a SmartArt Graphic** dialog box, click **Hierarchy**. Click **Organization Chart**, and then click **OK**. On the **Design tab**, in the **Create Graphic group**, verify that the **Text Pane** button is selected. The ***Text pane*** is the pane to the left of a SmartArt graphic and is where the text that appears in the SmartArt graphic can be entered and edited. Compare your screen with **Figure 1**.

   Shapes can be identified by their location and connecting lines. A ***superior*** is placed above any other shape. An ***assistant*** is placed below the superior shape but above subordinates. A ***subordinate*** is placed below and connected to a superior shape. A ***coworker*** is next to another shape that is connected to the same superior.

3. In the **Text Pane**, with the first bullet point selected and using your own first and last names, type Your Name and then click in the second bullet point. Type Chet Lee as shown in **Figure 2**.

■ **Continue to the next page to complete the skill**

Text Pane button

Organization chart

Superior shape

Text pane

Assistant shape

Subordinate and coworker shapes

Figure 1

Your Name in superior shape

Chet Lee in assistant shape

Figure 2

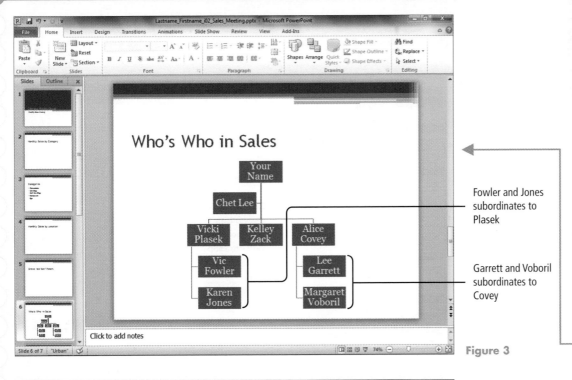

Fowler and Jones subordinates to Plasek

Garrett and Voboril subordinates to Covey

Figure 3

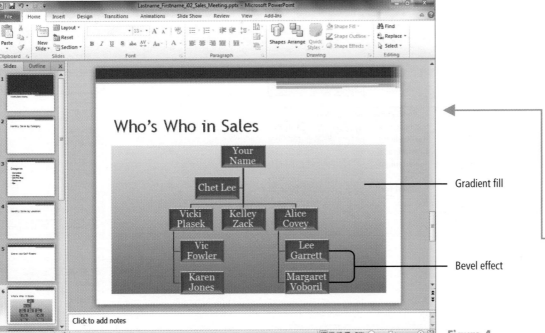

Gradient fill

Bevel effect

Figure 4

4. In the next three bullet points, type Vicki Plasek and Kelley Zack and then Alice Covey In the **Create Graphic group**, click the **Text Pane** button to close the Text pane.

5. Click the first coworker shape—Vicki Plasek. In the **Create Graphic group**, click the **Add Shape button arrow**, and then click **Add Shape Below**. In the new subordinate shape, type Vic Fowler With the Fowler shape selected, click the **Add Shape button arrow**, and then click **Add Shape After**. In the new subordinate shape, type Karen Jones

6. Using the same technique, select the shape for **Alice Covey**, and then add two subordinate shapes with the text Lee Garrett and Margaret Voboril Click a blank area of the slide, and then compare your screen with **Figure 3**.

7. Click the organization chart, and then click the border of the placeholder containing the organization chart. On the **Format tab**, in the **Shape Styles group**, click the **Shape Fill** button, and then click the third color in the first row—**Gray-25%, Background 2**. Click the **Shape Fill** button, point to **Gradient**, and then click **Linear Up**—the second variation in the third row.

8. In the **Shape Styles group**, click the **Shape Effects** button. Point to **Bevel**, and then under **Bevel**, click the second effect in the second row—**Soft Round**. Click a blank area of the slide, and then compare your screen with **Figure 4**.

9. **Save** 🖫 the presentation.

- **You have completed Skill 5 of 10**

▶ An Excel PivotTable report can be copied into another Microsoft Office application.

1. Make **Lastname_Firstname_i02_ Location_Categories** the active window. If necessary, make the Category Sales worksheet the active sheet. Click cell **A5**.

2. On the **Options tab**, in the **Actions group**, click the **Select** button, and then click **Entire PivotTable**. On the **Home tab**, in the **Clipboard group**, click the **Copy** button.

3. Make **Lastname_Firstname_i02_Sales_ Meeting** the active window, and then display **Slide 2**. Click the **Paste button arrow**, and then click **Paste Special**. In the **Paste Special** dialog box, click **Bitmap**, and then click **OK**. On the **Format tab**, in the **Size group**, increase the **Shape Height** to 4". In the **Arrange group**, click the **Align** button, and then click **Align Center**. Click a blank section of the slide, and then compare your screen with **Figure 1**.

4. Make **Lastname_Firstname_i02_ Location_Categories** the active window. Press (Esc) to cancel the Copy command. In cell **B1**, click the **arrow**. In the displayed filter box, click **Grove Isle Golf Resort**, and then click **OK**. Compare your screen with **Figure 2**.

   The PivotTable report has been filtered to display only the information from the Grove Isle Golf Resort location.

5. Using the technique from the previous steps, **Select** and then **Copy** the PivotTable.

■ Continue to the next page to complete the skill ►

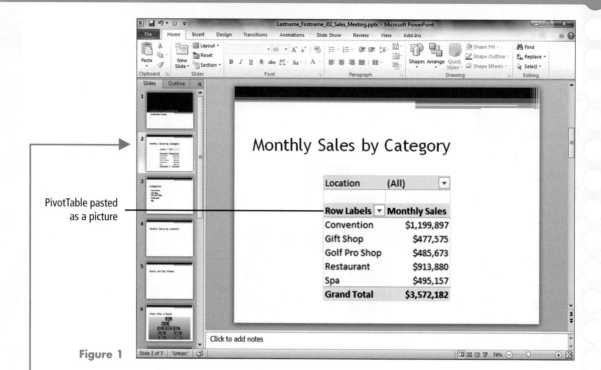

PivotTable pasted as a picture

Figure 1

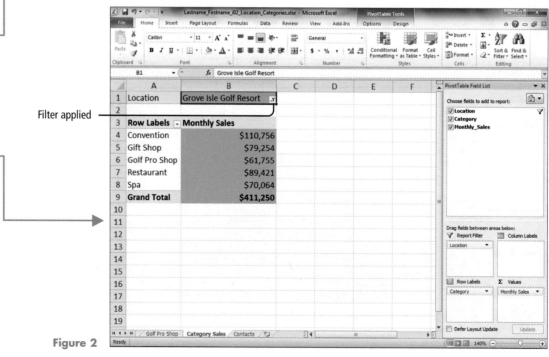

Filter applied

Figure 2

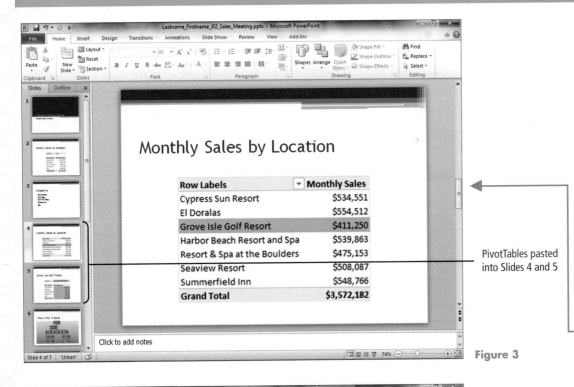

PivotTables pasted into Slides 4 and 5

Figure 3

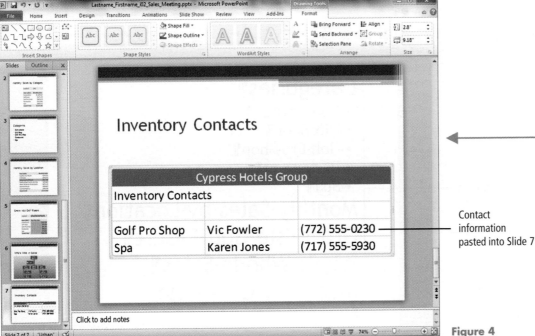

Contact information pasted into Slide 7

Figure 4

6. Make **Lastname_Firstname_i02_Sales_Meeting** the active window.

   The Excel object in Slide 2 did not change because the object was pasted as a picture, not linked to the Excel workbook.

7. Display **Slide 5**. **Paste** the PivotTable as a **Bitmap**, increase the **Shape Height** to 4", and then click **Align Center**.

8. Make **Lastname_Firstname_i02_Location_Categories** the active window, and then press Esc. Click the **Location Sales** sheet tab. Select and then **Copy** cells A3:B11. Make **Lastname_Firstname_i02_Sales_Meeting** the active window, and then display **Slide 4**. **Paste** the PivotTable as a **Bitmap**, increase the **Shape Height** to 4", and then click **Align Center**. Click a blank section of the slide, and then compare your screen with **Figure 3**.

9. Make **Lastname_Firstname_i02_Location_Categories** the active window. Press Esc, and then **Save** the workbook. Click the **Contacts** sheet tab, and then select and **Copy** the range A1:C5.

10. Make **Lastname_Firstname_i02_Sales_Meeting** the active window, and then display **Slide 7**. Click the **Paste button arrow**, and then click **Paste Special**. In the **Paste Special** dialog box, select the **Paste link** option button, verify that **Microsoft Excel Worksheet Object** is selected, and then click **OK**. Increase the **Shape Height** to 2.8", click **Align Center**, and then compare your screen with **Figure 4**.

11. **Save** the presentation.

■ **You have completed Skill 6 of 10**

► A PowerPoint presentation can be saved as an outline in the Outline/RTF file type. **_Rich Text Format (RTF)_** is a file format designed to move text between different applications while preserving the text's formatting. This text-only document provides smaller file sizes and the ability to share files with others who may not have the same version of the software.

► PowerPoint graphics are not included in an Outline/RTF file opened in Word.

1. In **Lastname_Firstname_i02_Sales_ Meeting**, click the **File tab**, and then click **Save As**. In the **Save As** dialog box, navigate to the folder **Integrated Projects Chapter 2**, and then change the file name to Lastname_Firstname_i02_Meeting Click the **Save as type arrow**, and then click **Outline/RTF (*.rtf)**. Compare your screen with **Figure 1**.

2. In the **Save As** dialog box, click **Save**.

3. **Start** 🪟 Word. Open **i02_Meeting_ Notes**, and then **Save** the document in your **Integrated Projects Chapter 2** folder as Lastname_Firstname_i02_Meeting_ Notes

4. Scroll to the next page, locate the paragraph beginning *We have been tracking sales,* and then click the first blank line after the paragraph. On the **Insert tab**, in the **Text group**, click the **Object button arrow**, and then click **Text from File**. In the **Insert File** dialog box, navigate to the **Integrated Projects Chapter 2** folder, select **Lastname_Firstname_i02_ Meeting.rtf**, and then click **Insert**. Compare your screen with **Figure 2**.

■ **Continue to the next page to complete the skill**

Save As dialog box

Save as type: Outline/RTF (*.rtf)

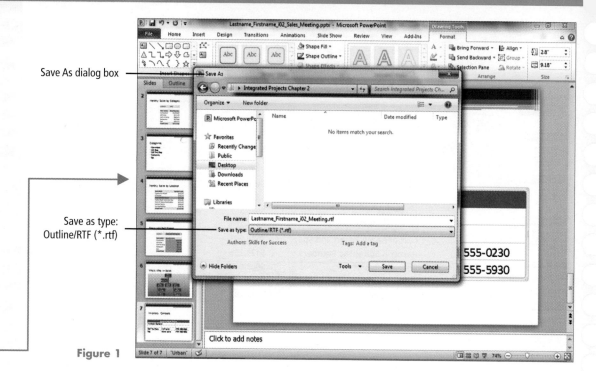

Figure 1

Inserted text

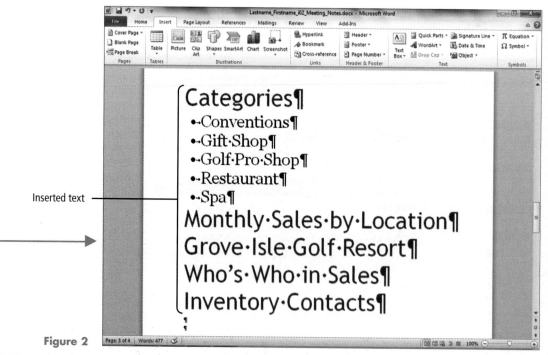

Figure 2

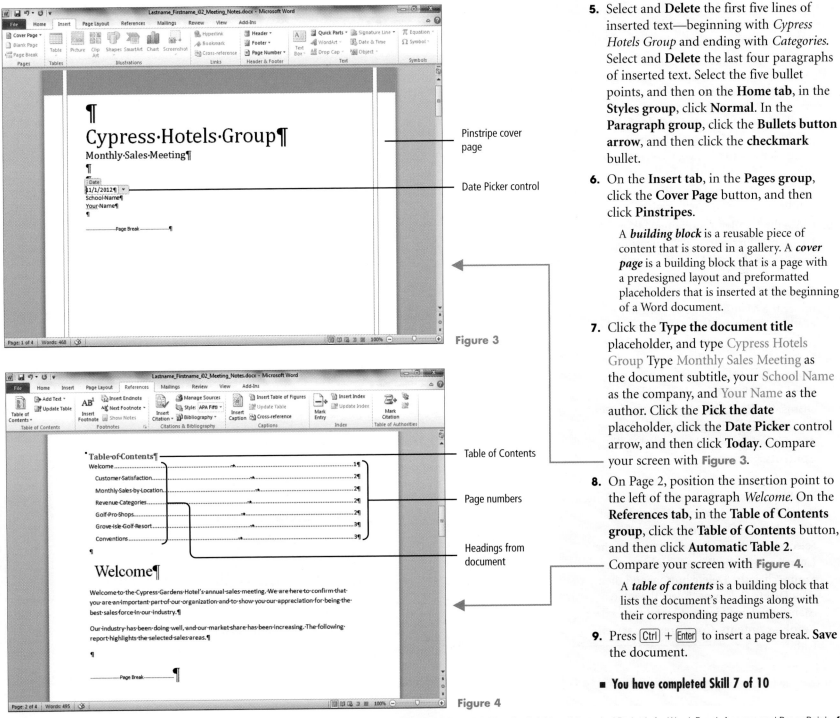

Pinstripe cover page

Date Picker control

Figure 3

Table of Contents

Page numbers

Headings from document

Figure 4

5. Select and **Delete** the first five lines of inserted text—beginning with *Cypress Hotels Group* and ending with *Categories*. Select and **Delete** the last four paragraphs of inserted text. Select the five bullet points, and then on the **Home tab**, in the **Styles group**, click **Normal**. In the **Paragraph group**, click the **Bullets button arrow**, and then click the **checkmark** bullet.

6. On the **Insert tab**, in the **Pages group**, click the **Cover Page** button, and then click **Pinstripes**.

> A ***building block*** is a reusable piece of content that is stored in a gallery. A ***cover page*** is a building block that is a page with a predesigned layout and preformatted placeholders that is inserted at the beginning of a Word document.

7. Click the **Type the document title** placeholder, and type Cypress Hotels Group Type Monthly Sales Meeting as the document subtitle, your School Name as the company, and Your Name as the author. Click the **Pick the date** placeholder, click the **Date Picker** control arrow, and then click **Today**. Compare your screen with **Figure 3**.

8. On Page 2, position the insertion point to the left of the paragraph *Welcome*. On the **References tab**, in the **Table of Contents group**, click the **Table of Contents** button, and then click **Automatic Table 2**. Compare your screen with **Figure 4**.

> A ***table of contents*** is a building block that lists the document's headings along with their corresponding page numbers.

9. Press [Ctrl] + [Enter] to insert a page break. **Save** the document.

■ **You have completed Skill 7 of 10**

▶ Data that will not change, such as end-of-month results, can be embedded into another application.

▶ Data that will change can be linked so that data changed in the source file will also change in the destination file.

1. On the **Insert tab**, in the **Header & Footer group**, click the **Page Number** button. Point to **Bottom of Page**, scroll down, and then click **Accent Bar 4**. On the left side of the footer, insert the file name, and then compare your screen with **Figure 1**.

2. **Close** the **Header and Footer**. Make **Lastname_Firstname_i02_Location_Categories** the active window. Click the **Location Sales** sheet tab, and then **Copy** the range **A3:B11**. In Word, under the *Monthly Sales by Location* heading, click the blank line at the end of the paragraph, and then click the **Paste** button. In the first cell of the table, delete the text *Row Labels*, and then type Locations Select the table, and then change the **Font Size** to **12**. On the **Layout tab**, in the **Cell Size group**, click the **AutoFit** button, and then click **AutoFit Contents**.

3. Using the same technique, from the **Golf Pro Shop** worksheet, **Copy** cells **A1:C8**. In Word, **Paste** the data in the blank line at the end of the **Golf Pro Shops** section. Select the table heading *Category*. On the **Layout tab**, in the **Rows & Columns group**, click the **Delete** button, and then click **Delete Columns**. Select the table, change the **Font Size** to **12**, and then select **AutoFit Contents**. Compare your screen with **Figure 2**.

■ **Continue to the next page to complete the skill**

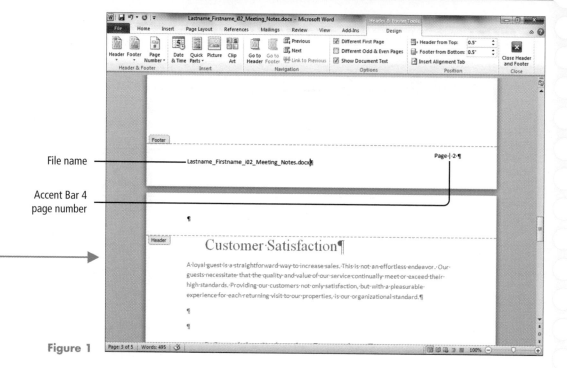

File name

Accent Bar 4
page number

Figure 1

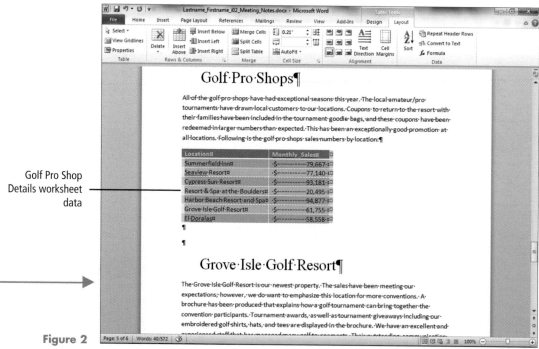

Golf Pro Shop
Details worksheet
data

Figure 2

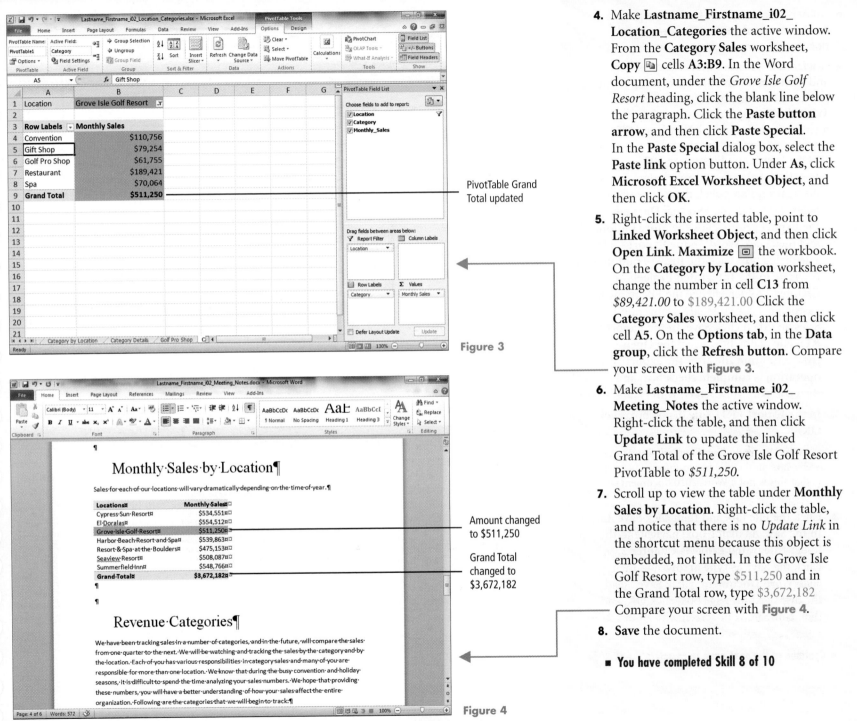

Figure 3

Figure 4

PivotTable Grand Total updated

Amount changed to $511,250

Grand Total changed to $3,672,182

4. Make **Lastname_Firstname_i02_ Location_Categories** the active window. From the **Category Sales** worksheet, **Copy** cells **A3:B9**. In the Word document, under the *Grove Isle Golf Resort* heading, click the blank line below the paragraph. Click the **Paste button arrow**, and then click **Paste Special**. In the **Paste Special** dialog box, select the **Paste link** option button. Under **As**, click **Microsoft Excel Worksheet Object**, and then click **OK**.

5. Right-click the inserted table, point to **Linked Worksheet Object**, and then click **Open Link**. Maximize the workbook. On the **Category by Location** worksheet, change the number in cell **C13** from *$89,421.00* to $189,421.00 Click the **Category Sales** worksheet, and then click cell **A5**. On the **Options tab**, in the **Data group**, click the **Refresh button**. Compare your screen with **Figure 3**.

6. Make **Lastname_Firstname_i02_ Meeting_Notes** the active window. Right-click the table, and then click **Update Link** to update the linked Grand Total of the Grove Isle Golf Resort PivotTable to *$511,250*.

7. Scroll up to view the table under **Monthly Sales by Location**. Right-click the table, and notice that there is no *Update Link* in the shortcut menu because this object is embedded, not linked. In the Grove Isle Golf Resort row, type $511,250 and in the Grand Total row, type $3,672,182 Compare your screen with **Figure 4**.

8. **Save** the document.

■ **You have completed Skill 8 of 10**

▶ An Access table, query, form, or report can be exported from Access to a Word document.

▶ A *wizard* is a feature that asks questions and then creates an object according to the provided answers. In Access, the **Export Wizard** will export data in a variety of formats, including Excel, Word, and RTF.

1. Make **Lastname_Firstname_i02_ Location_Sales** the active window. In the **Navigation Pane**, click the **Conventions Sales** query. On the **External Data tab**, in the **Export group**, click the **More** button, and then click **Word**. In the **Export - RTF File** dialog box, click the **Browse** button. Navigate to the **Integrated Projects Chapter 2** folder, change the **File name** to Lastname_Firstname_i02_Convention_ Sales and then click **Save**. In the **Export - RTF File** dialog box, select the **Open the destination file after the export operation is complete** check box, and then compare your screen with **Figure 1**.

2. In the **Export - RTF File** dialog box, click **OK**.

    In the Word window, *Compatibility Mode* displays on the title bar to inform the user that this is not a Word 2010 document—it is an RTF file.

3. Click the **File tab**, and then click **Save As**. In the **Save As** dialog box, navigate to the folder **Integrated Projects Chapter 2**. Click the **Save as type arrow**, and then click **Word Document**. Click **Save**. Read the displayed message box, click **OK**, and then compare your screen with **Figure 2**.

■ **Continue to the next page to complete the skill** ▶

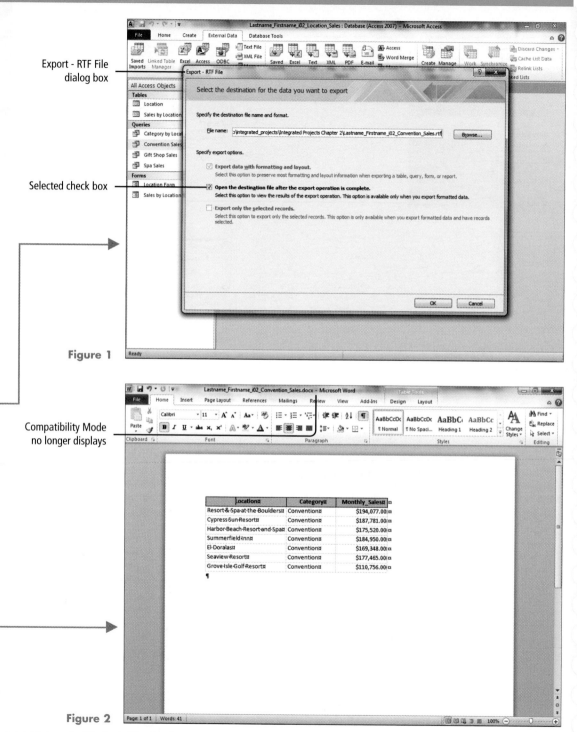

Export - RTF File dialog box

Selected check box

Figure 1

Compatibility Mode no longer displays

Figure 2

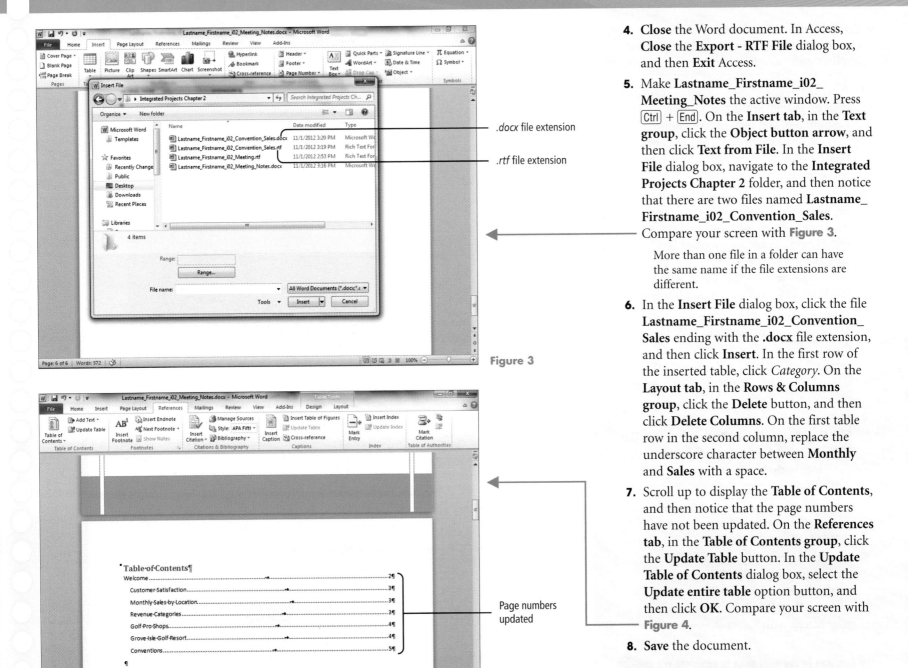

.docx file extension

.rtf file extension

Figure 3

Page numbers updated

Figure 4

4. **Close** the Word document. In Access, **Close** the **Export - RTF File** dialog box, and then **Exit** Access.

5. Make **Lastname_Firstname_i02_ Meeting_Notes** the active window. Press Ctrl + End. On the **Insert tab**, in the **Text group**, click the **Object button arrow**, and then click **Text from File**. In the **Insert File** dialog box, navigate to the **Integrated Projects Chapter 2** folder, and then notice that there are two files named **Lastname_ Firstname_i02_Convention_Sales**. Compare your screen with **Figure 3**.

   More than one file in a folder can have the same name if the file extensions are different.

6. In the **Insert File** dialog box, click the file **Lastname_Firstname_i02_Convention_ Sales** ending with the **.docx** file extension, and then click **Insert**. In the first row of the inserted table, click *Category*. On the **Layout tab**, in the **Rows & Columns group**, click the **Delete** button, and then click **Delete Columns**. On the first table row in the second column, replace the underscore character between **Monthly** and **Sales** with a space.

7. Scroll up to display the **Table of Contents**, and then notice that the page numbers have not been updated. On the **References tab**, in the **Table of Contents group**, click the **Update Table** button. In the **Update Table of Contents** dialog box, select the **Update entire table** option button, and then click **OK**. Compare your screen with **Figure 4**.

8. **Save** the document.

   ■ **You have completed Skill 9 of 10**

▶ Complex objects, such as a SmartArt organization chart, can be copied from one application to another.

1. Press [Ctrl] + [End], type Our Sales Team and then press [Enter]. Select the heading *Conventions*, and then on the **Home tab**, in the **Clipboard group**, click the **Format Painter** button ⚽. Select the text **Our Sales Team**.

2. Press [Ctrl] + [End], and then type We are fortunate to have a group of people that have quickly melded as a team. Their collaborative effort has resulted in an impressive increase in sales. The structure of our sales team is illustrated in the following organization chart: Press [Enter].

3. Make **Lastname_Firstname_i02_Sales_ Meeting** the active window, and then display **Slide 6**. Click the border of the placeholder containing the SmartArt organization chart, and then **Copy** 🖹 the organization chart.

4. Make **Lastname_Firstname_i02_ Meeting_Notes** the active window. On the **Home tab**, in the **Clipboard group**, click the **Paste** button. Compare your screen with **Figure 1**.

   The SmartArt organization chart, with all its shapes, formatting, and names, is pasted at the end of the document.

5. Place the insertion point to the left of the heading *Our Sales Team*, and then on the **Insert tab**, in the **Pages group**, click the **Page Break** button. Compare your screen with **Figure 2**.

■ **Continue to the next page to complete the skill** ▶

SmartArt organization chart in document

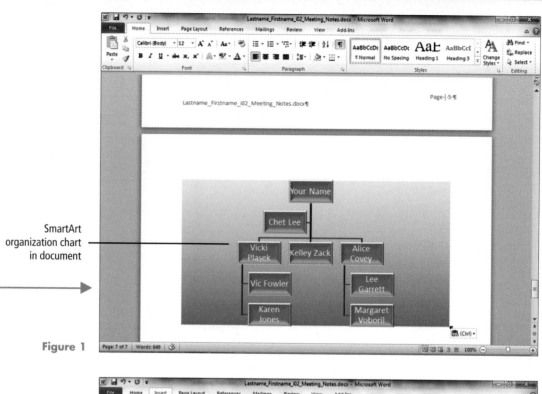

Figure 1

Heading at the top of a page

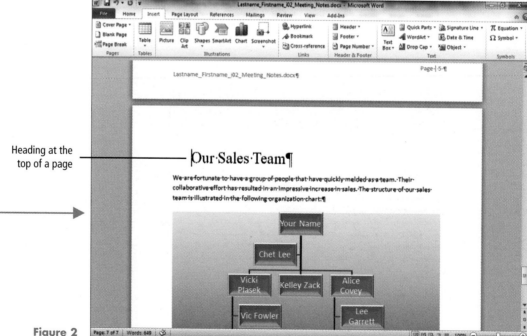

Figure 2

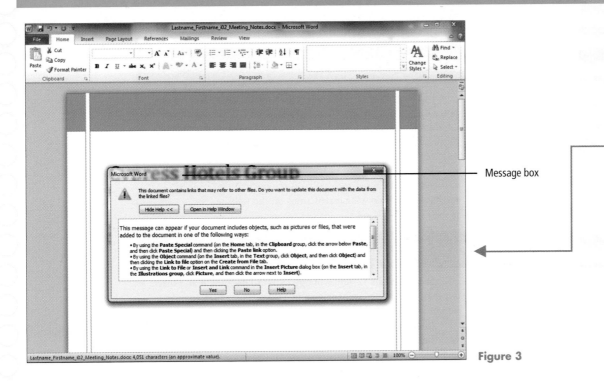

Message box

Figure 3

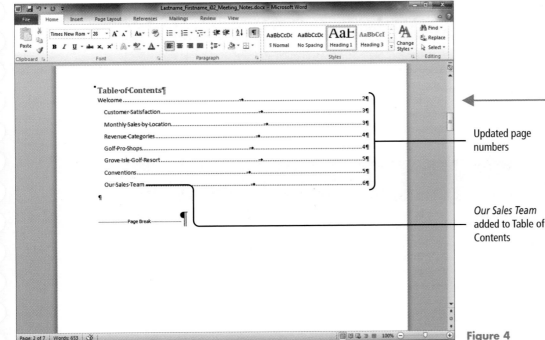

Updated page numbers

Our Sales Team added to Table of Contents

Figure 4

6. **Save** the document, and **Exit** Word. **Save** the presentation, and **Exit** PowerPoint. **Save** the workbook, and **Exit** Excel.

7. **Start** Word. Navigate to your student files, and open **Lastname_Firstname_i02_ Meeting_Notes**. In the displayed message box, click **Show Help**, and then compare your screen with **Figure 3**.

   The message box notifies you that there are links in the document.

8. In the message box, click **Yes**. View the *Table of Contents*, and notice the page numbers for *Revenue Categories* and all of the headings that follow it. Press and hold down Ctrl, and then in the **Table of Contents**, click the *Revenue Categories* heading.

   The Table of Contents is linked to each of the document's headings and can be used to navigate to each heading.

9. With the insertion point in front of the *Revenue Categories* heading, **Insert** a **Page Break**. Place the insertion point to the left of the *Grove Isle Golf Resort* heading, and then **Insert** a **Page Break**. View the *Table of Contents*, and notice that it did not automatically update. Right-click the **Table of Contents**, and then click **Update Field**. In the **Update Table of Contents** dialog box, select the **Update entire table** option button, and then click **OK**. Click outside of the Table of Contents, and then compare your screen with **Figure 4**.

10. **Save** the document, and then **Exit** Word. Submit your files as directed by your instructor.

Done! You have completed Skill 10 of 10 and your document is complete!

The following More Skills are located at **www.pearsonhighered.com/skills**

More Skills ⑪ Create an Excel PivotChart and Link the PivotChart to Word

In Excel, a PivotChart report is used to visualize the summary data in a PivotTable report, and to easily see comparisons, patterns, and trends. Both a PivotTable report and a PivotChart report enable you to make informed decisions about critical data in your business.

In More Skills 11, you will create an Excel PivotTable report and a PivotChart report. Then you will open a Word document and link the PivotChart to the document. You will make changes to the source data in Excel, and verify that the changes are reflected in the linked PivotChart in Word.

To begin, open your web browser, navigate to www.pearsonhighered.com/skills, locate the name of your textbook, and follow the instructions on the website.

More Skills ⑫ Create a Hyperlink Between PowerPoint, Word, and Excel Files

You can insert a hyperlink for quick access to related information in an existing file, on a web page, in a specific location of the same file, or to an e-mail address.

In More Skills 12, you will open a Word document and insert hyperlinks to related information in a PowerPoint presentation and in an Excel workbook.

To begin, open your web browser, navigate to www.pearsonhighered.com/skills, locate the name of your textbook, and follow the instructions on the website.

More Skills ⑬ Insert a Total Row in an Excel Table and Link the Table to PowerPoint

In an Excel table, you can display the total row that displays as the last row in the Excel table. Each cell of the total row contains a drop-down list, so you can select the function that you want to use to calculate the total.

In More Skills 13, you will open an Excel workbook. You will create an Excel table and insert a Total row. You will then link the Excel table to a PowerPoint presentation.

To begin, open your web browser, navigate to www.pearsonhighered.com/skills, locate the name of your textbook, and follow the instructions on the website.

More Skills ⑭ Compare Word Documents

If you send a document for review to several reviewers and each reviewer returns the document containing their changes, you can combine the documents two at a time until all the reviewer changes have been incorporated into a single document.

In More Skills 14, you will open a document and then compare it with documents containing comments from different reviewers.

To begin, open your web browser, navigate to www.pearsonhighered.com/skills, locate the name of your textbook, and follow the instructions on the website.

Key Terms

Online Help Skills

1. Start 🌐 Excel. In the upper right corner of the Excel window, click the Help button 📝. In the Help window, click the Maximize 🔲 button.

2. Click in the search box, type pivottable and then click the Search button 🔎. In the search results, click **Overview of PivotTable and PivotChart reports**.

3. Read the article's introduction, and then below In this article, click **Ways to work with a PivotTable report**. Compare your screen with **Figure 1**.

Figure 1

4. Read the section to see if you can answer the following: Explain the benefits of arranging fields in a PivotTable report.

Matching

Match each term in the second column with its correct definition in the first column by writing the letter of the term on the blank line in front of the correct definition.

____ **1.** An interactive, cross-tabulated Excel report that summarizes and analyzes data.

____ **2.** A PivotTable report feature that shows the detailed records of a PivotTable total.

____ **3.** A word or string of characters that represents a cell, range of cells, formula, or constant value.

____ **4.** A SmartArt object that represents the management structure of an organization.

____ **5.** In an organization chart, a shape that is placed below the superior shape but above subordinate shapes.

____ **6.** A portable document format that can be read by nearly all word processing programs and that retains most text and paragraph formatting.

____ **7.** A reusable piece of content or other document part that is stored in galleries.

____ **8.** A page with a predesigned layout that is always inserted at the beginning of a Word document, no matter where the cursor appears in the document.

____ **9.** A feature that asks questions and then creates an item according to the provided answers.

____ **10.** In Access, a feature that will export data in a variety of formats.

A Assistant

B Building block

C Cover page

D Drill-down indicator

E Export Wizard

F Name

G Organization chart

H PivotTable report

I Rich Text Format

J Wizard

Multiple Choice

Choose the correct answer.

1. This type of Access query adds a set of records from one or more source tables to one or more destination tables.
   A. Simple query
   B. Append query
   C. Join query

2. Selecting this option check box will preserve most formatting and layout information when exporting data from Access to Excel.
   A. Export data with formatting and layout
   B. Transfer data with formatting and layout
   C. Relocate data with formatting and layout

3. An Excel column becomes this in a PivotTable report, and will summarize multiple rows of information.
   A. Record
   B. Range
   C. Field

4. In Excel, this is a reference to a cell or range in another Excel workbook.
   A. Location reference
   B. Outside reference
   C. External reference

5. This pane is to the left of a SmartArt graphic and is where the text that appears in the graphic can be entered and edited.
   A. Navigation pane
   B. Text pane
   C. Editing pane

6. In an organization chart, this shape is placed above any other shape.
   A. Superior shape
   B. Coworker shape
   C. CEO shape

7. This list of the headings in a Word document will provide an overview of the topics discussed.
   A. Range of subjects
   B. Topics table
   C. Table of contents

8. This block is a reusable piece of content that is stored in a gallery.
   A. Building block
   B. Structure block
   C. Organization block

9. This PivotTable report feature shows the detailed records of a PivotTable total.
   A. Detailed total report
   B. Drill-down indicator
   C. Report generator

10. This Access feature will export data in a variety of formats, including Excel and Word.
    A. Export wizard
    B. Data exporter
    C. Transfer wizard

Topics for Discussion

1. Integration lets you move data between Microsoft Office applications. How does integration help when you are analyzing data?

2. How can integration help a team present their ideas and results to management?

Skill Check 1

To complete this project, you will need the following files:

- i02_Golf_Presentation.pptx
- i02_Golf_Report.docx

You will save your files as:

- Lastname_Firstname_i02_Golf_Outline.rtf
- Lastname_Firstname_i02_Golf_Presentation.pptx
- Lastname_Firstname_i02_Golf_Report.docx

1. **Start** PowerPoint. From your student files, open **i02_Golf_Presentation**. **Save** the presentation in the **Integrated Projects Chapter 2** folder as Lastname_Firstname_i02_Golf_Presentation Add the file name to all Notes and Handouts footers.

2. Display **Slide 5**. In the placeholder, click the **Insert SmartArt Graphic** button. In the **Choose a SmartArt Graphic** dialog box, click **List**. In the **Choose a SmartArt Graphic** dialog box, click **Basic Block List**—the first subtype—and then click **OK**. If necessary, on the Design tab, in the Create Graphic group, click the Text Pane button to display the Text pane.

3. In the **Text pane**, type the following locations: Cypress Sun Resort and Grove Isle Golf Resort and Resort & Spa at the Boulders and Harbor Beach Resort and Spa and El Doralas and Seaview Resort and then compare your screen with **Figure 1**.

4. In the **Create Graphic group**, click the **Text Pane** button. In the **SmartArt Styles group**, click the **More** button. Click **Cartoon**—under **3-D**, the third style in the first row. Click the **Change Colors** button, and then under **Accent 2**, click the last color in the row—**Transparent Gradient Range - Accent 2**. Compare your screen with **Figure 2**.

5. On the **Slide Show tab**, in the **Start Slide Show group**, click the **From Beginning** button, and then view the presentation. **Save** the presentation.

6. Click the **File tab**, and then click **Save As**. In the **Save As** dialog box, navigate to the **Integrated Projects Chapter 2** folder, and then change the file name to Lastname_Firstname_i02_Golf_Outline Click the **Save as type arrow**, and then click **Outline/RTF (*.rtf)**. Click **Save**.

- Continue to the next page to complete this Skill Check

Figure 1

Figure 2

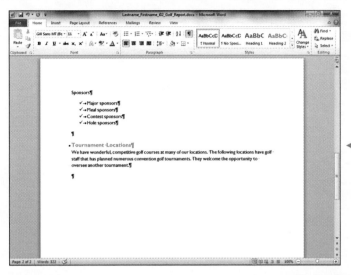

Figure 3

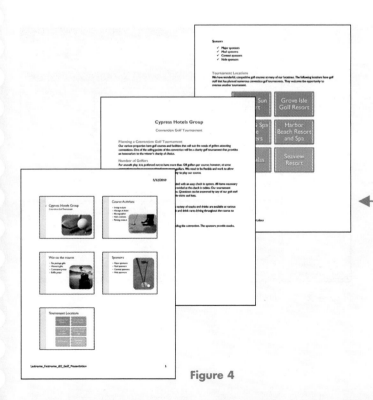

Figure 4

7. **Start** Word. From your student files, open **i02_Golf_Report**. **Save** the document in the **Integrated Projects Chapter 2** folder as Lastname_Firstname_i02_Golf_Report and then add the file name to the footer.

8. Move the insertion point to the end of the document. On the **Insert tab**, in the **Text group**, click the **Object button arrow**, and then click **Text from File**. In the **Insert File** dialog box, navigate to the **Integrated Projects Chapter 2** folder, select the RTF file **Lastname_Firstname_i02_Golf_Outline**, and then click **Insert**.

9. Scroll up, select the first two paragraphs of inserted text—*Cypress Hotels Group* and *Convention Golf Tournament*—and then **Delete** the paragraphs. Select the remaining inserted text. On the **Home tab**, in the **Styles group**, click the **Normal** style.

10. Select the five paragraphs beginning with *Swing analysis*. On the **Home tab**, in the **Paragraph group**, click the **Bullets button arrow**, and then click the **checkmark** bullet. Select the four paragraphs beginning with *Tee package gifts*, and then add the **checkmark** bullets. Select the four paragraphs beginning with *Major sponsors*, and then add the **checkmark** bullets.

11. Select the heading *Course Activities and Sponsors*, and then on the **Home tab**, in the **Clipboard group**, click the **Format Painter** button. At the end of the document, select the text *Tournament Locations*. Place the insertion point in the blank line after the *Tournament Locations* heading, and then type We have wonderful, competitive golf courses at many of our locations. The following locations have golf staff that has planned numerous convention golf tournaments. They welcome the opportunity to oversee another tournament. Press Enter, and then compare your screen with **Figure 3**.

12. Make **Lastname_Firstname_i02_Golf_Presentation** the active window, and then display **Slide 5**. Click the border of the placeholder containing the SmartArt graphic, and then **Copy** the SmartArt.

13. Make **Lastname_Firstname_i02_Golf_Report** the active window. Move the insertion point to the end of the document, and then on the **Home tab**, in the **Clipboard group**, click the **Paste** button.

14. Compare your screen with the completed documents in **Figure 4**. **Save** and then **Close** the files. Submit your files as directed by your instructor.

Done! You have completed Skill Check 1

Skill Check 2

To complete this project, you will need the following files:

- i02_Employees.accdb
- i02_Housekeeping.accdb
- i02_Restaurant.accdb

You will save your files as:

- Lastname_Firstname_i02_Employees.accdb
- Lastname_Firstname_i02_Employees.xlsx
- Lastname_Firstname_i02_Housekeeping.accdb
- Lastname_Firstname_i02_Restaurant.accdb

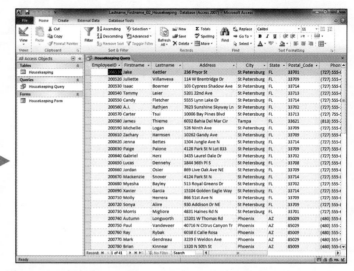

1. **Start** Access. From your student files, open **i02_Employees**. Click the **File tab**, and then click **Save Database As**. Navigate to the **Integrated Projects Chapter 2** folder. **Save** the database as Lastname_Firstname_i02_Employees and then **Close** the database.

2. From your student files, open the Access database **i02_Housekeeping**. **Save** the database in the **Integrated Projects Chapter 2** folder as Lastname_Firstname_i02_Housekeeping If the Security Warning message displays, enable the content. On the **Create tab**, in the **Queries group**, click the **Query Design** button. In the **Show Table** dialog box, verify that Housekeeping is selected, click **Add**, and then **Close** the dialog box. Double-click the nine field names to add the fields to the design grid. **Save** the query as Housekeeping Query On the **Design tab**, in the **Results group**, click the **Run** button, and then compare your screen with **Figure 1**.

Figure 1

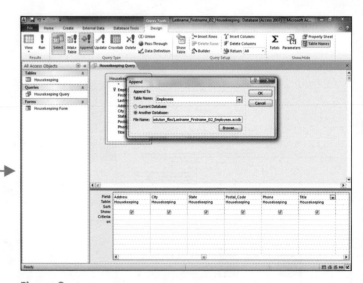

3. On the **Home tab**, in the **Views group**, click the **View** button. On the **Design tab**, in the **Query Type group**, click the **Append** button. In the **Append** dialog box, select the **Another Database** option button. Click **Browse**, locate **Lastname_Firstname_i02_Employees**, and then click **OK**. Click the **Table Name** arrow, and then select **Employees**. Compare your screen with **Figure 2**.

4. In the **Append** dialog box, click **OK**. **Save** and then **Close** the query. In the **Navigation** pane, double-click **Housekeeping Query**. In both the message boxes, click **Yes. Close** the database.

5. From your student files, open the Access database **i02_Restaurant**. **Save** the database in the **Integrated Projects Chapter 2** folder as Lastname_Firstname_i02_Restaurant If the Security Warning message displays, enable the content.

Figure 2

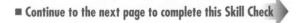
- Continue to the next page to complete this Skill Check

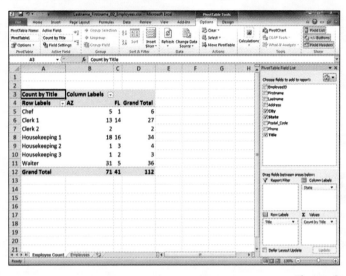

Figure 3

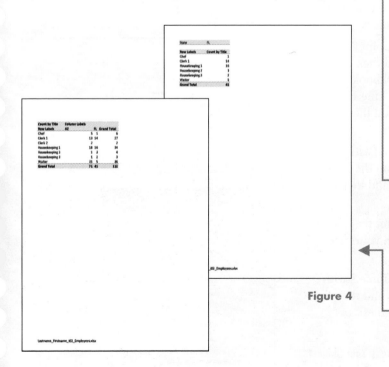

Figure 4

6. On the **Create tab**, in the **Queries group**, click the **Query Design** button. In the **Show Table** dialog box, verify that Restaurant Employees is selected, click **Add**, and then **Close** the dialog box. Add the nine field names to the design grid. **Save** the query as Restaurant Employees Query On the **Design tab**, in the **Results group**, click the **Run** button. On the **Home tab**, in the **Views group**, click the **View** button. On the **Design tab**, in the **Query Type group**, click the **Append** button. In the **Append** dialog box, select the **Another Database** option button. Click **Browse**, locate **Lastname_Firstname_i02_Employees**, and then click **OK**. Click the **Table Name arrow**, and then select **Employees**. In the **Append** dialog box, click **OK**. **Save** and then **Close** the query. In the **Navigation** pane, double-click **Restaurant Employees Query**. In both the message boxes, click **Yes**. **Close** the database.

7. Open **Lastname_Firstname_i02_Employees**. In the **Navigation Pane**, click the **Employees** table. On the **External Data tab**, in the **Export group**, click the **Excel** button. In the **Export - Excel spreadsheet** dialog box, click the **Browse** button. In the **File Save** dialog box, navigate to your **Integrated Projects Chapter 2** folder. Type the file name Lastname_Firstname_i02_Employees and then click **Save**. Under **Specify export options**, select the **Export data with formatting and layout** check box, and then click **OK**. **Close** the dialog box, and then **Exit** Access.

8. **Start** Excel, and then open **Lastname_Firstname_i02_Employees**. Click cell **A1**. On the **Insert tab**, in the **Tables group**, click the **PivotTable** button. In the **Create PivotTable** dialog box, click **OK**. If necessary, display the PivotTable Field List pane.

9. In the **PivotTable Field List** pane, drag the **Title** field to the **Row Labels** area, and then drag the **State** field to the **Column Labels** area. Drag the **City** field to the **Values** area. In the **Values** area, click the **Count of City arrow**, and then click **Value Field Settings**. In the **Value Field Settings** dialog box, in the **Custom Name** box, type Count by Title Under **Summarize value field by**, verify that Count is selected, and then click **OK**. Rename the sheet Employee Count and then compare your screen with **Figure 3**.

10. Create a copy of the **Employee Count** worksheet, and then rename the new sheet as FL Employee Count In the **PivotTable Field List** pane, drag the **State** field from the **Column Labels** area to the **Report Filter** area. In cell **B1**, click the **arrow**. From the displayed list, click **FL**, and then click **OK**.

11. Group the worksheets. Add the file name in the left footer, and then return to **Normal** view. Click cell **A1**, and then ungroup the worksheets.

12. Compare your screen with the completed document in **Figure 4**. **Save** and then **Close** the files. Submit your files as directed by your instructor.

Done! You have completed Skill Check 2

Assess Your Skills 1

To complete this project, you will need the following files:

- i02_Gifts.xlsx
- i02_Phoenix_Inventory.xlsx
- i02_Spa.xlsx
- i02_Golf.xlsx
- i02_Phoenix_Memo.docx

You will save your files as:

- Lastname_Firstname_i02_Phoenix_Inventory.xlsx
- Lastname_Firstname_i02_Phoenix_Memo.docx

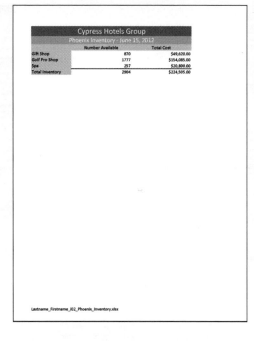

1. **Start** Excel, and then open **i02_Phoenix_Inventory**. **Save** the workbook in your **Integrated Projects Chapter 2** folder as Lastname_Firstname_i02_Phoenix_Inventory Add the file name in the worksheet's left footer, and then return to **Normal** view.

2. **Open** the Excel files **i02_Gifts**, **i02_Golf**, and **i02_Spa**. Make **Lastname_Firstname_i02_Phoenix_Inventory** the active window. In cell **B4**, create an external reference to cell **D17** in the workbook **i02_Gifts**, and then in cell **C4**, create an external reference to cell **E17** in **i02_Gifts**.

3. In cell **B5**, create an external reference to cell **D34** in the workbook **i02_Golf**, and then in cell **C5**, create an external reference to cell **E34** in **i02_Golf**. In cell **B6**, create an external reference to cell **D14** in the workbook **i02_Spa**, and then in cell **C6**, create an external reference to cell **E14** in **i02_Spa**.

4. In cells **B7:C7**, use the SUM function to total **columns B:C**. Format **C4:C7** with the **Currency Number** style. Select cells **B7:C7**, and apply a **Top Border**. **Save** the workbook. **Close** the Excel files **i02_Gifts**, **i02_Golf**, and **i02_Spa**.

5. **Start** Word, and then open **i02_Phoenix_Memo**. **Save** the document in your **Integrated Projects Chapter 2** folder as Lastname_Firstname_i02_Phoenix_Memo and then add the file name to the footer.

6. Make **Lastname_Firstname_i02_Phoenix_Inventory** the active window, and then **Copy** the cells **A1:C7**. Make **Lastname_Firstname_i02_Phoenix_Memo** the active window. Move the insertion point to the end of the document, and then use **Paste Special** to link the Excel data to the Word document as a **Microsoft Excel Worksheet Object**.

7. Right-click the inserted table, point at **Linked Worksheet Object**, and then click **Open Link**. **Maximize** the workbook. Edit cell **B2** to Phoenix Inventory - June 15, 2012 and edit cell **A4** to Gift Shop and then edit cell **A5** to Golf Pro Shop

8. **Save** the Excel workbook. Make **Lastname_Firstname_i02_Phoenix_Memo** the active window. Right-click the table, and then click **Update Link**.

9. At the top of the document, after the heading *FROM*, replace *Your Name* with your first and last names.

10. Compare your completed documents with **Figure 1**. **Save** your document, and then **Exit** Word. **Exit** Excel. Submit your files as directed by your instructor.

Done! You have completed Assess Your Skills 1

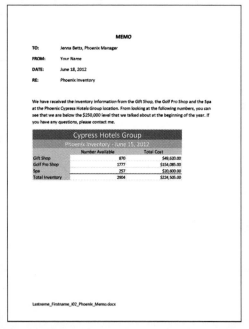

Figure 1

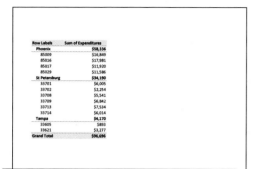

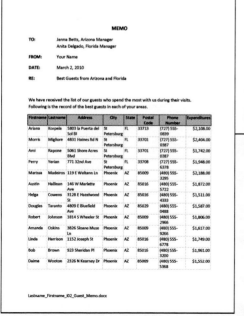

Figure 1

Assess Your Skills 2

To complete this project, you will need the following files:

- i02_Guests.accdb
- i02_Guest_Memo.docx

You will save your files as:

- Lastname_Firstname_i02_Guests.xlsx
- Lastname_Firstname_i02_Guest_Memo.docx

1. **Start** Access, and then open **i02_Guests**. In the **Navigation Pane**, click the **Guests** table. Export the table to an Excel workbook. **Save** the file in your **Integrated Projects Chapter 2** folder as Lastname_Firstname_i02_Guests Export the data with the formatting and layout.

2. **Run** the **Best Guests** query. Notice that the query lists the guests with expenditures over $1,500. Export the query results as an RTF file. **Save** the RTF file in your **Integrated Projects Chapter 2** folder as Lastname_Firstname_i02_Best_Guests **Close** the database, and then **Exit** Access.

3. **Start** Excel, and then open **Lastname_Firstname_i02_Guests**. On the **Page Layout tab**, change the **Width** to **1 page**. Using the data in cells **A1:H95**, insert a PivotTable on a new sheet. In the **PivotTable Field List** pane, drag the **City** field and then the **Postal Code** field to the **Row Labels** area. Drag the **Expenditures** field to the **Values** area. Open the **Value Field Settings** dialog box, and then change the **Number Format** to **Currency** with zero decimal places. Rename the worksheet Expenditures by Postal Code and then add the file name in the left footer of both worksheets. Return to **Normal** view, and make cell **A1** the active cell. **Save** the workbook.

4. **Start** Word, and then open **i02_Guest_Memo**. **Save** the file in your **Integrated Projects Chapter 2** folder as Lastname_Firstname_i02_Guest_Memo and then add the file name to the footer. At the top of the document, after *FROM*, replace *Your Name* with your first and last names.

5. Move the insertion point to the end of the document. Insert the RTF file **Lastname_Firstname_i02_Best_Guests**, and then resize the table cells to **AutoFit Window**.

6. Move to the end of the document, and then type We have provided the sales information organized by Postal Code so you can see the result of the new promotional materials. If you have any questions, please contact me. Press [Enter].

7. Make **Lastname_Firstname_i02_Guests** the active window. On the **Expenditures by Postal Code** worksheet, **Copy** the range **A4:B19**. Make **Lastname_Firstname_i02_Guest_Memo** the active window. At the end of the document, **Paste** the Excel data. Select the table, and then change the **Font Size** to **12**. Resize the table cells to **AutoFit Contents**.

8. Compare your completed files with **Figure 1**. **Save** your files, **Exit** Word, and then **Exit** Excel. Submit your files as directed by your instructor.

Done! You have completed Assess Your Skills 2

Assess Your Skills 3

To complete this project, you will need the following files:

- i02_Convention_Memo.docx
- i02_Convention_Presentation.pptx

You will save your files as:

- Lastname_Firstname_i02_Convention_List.rtf
- Lastname_Firstname_i02_Convention_Memo.docx

1. **Start** PowerPoint, and then open **i02_Convention_Presentation**. Display **Slide 4**. Under *Restaurants*, add three bullet points Coffee and Rolls and Lunch buffet and Served meals These three bullet points should be indented and should look the same as the bullet points under Golf Pro Shop.

2. **Save** the presentation as an Outline/RTF file in your **Integrated Projects Chapter 2** folder with the name Lastname_Firstname_i02_Convention_List **Close** the presentation. If asked, do not save the presentation. **Exit** PowerPoint.

3. **Start** Word, and then open **i02_Convention_ Memo**. **Save** the document in your **Integrated Projects Chapter 2** folder as Lastname_Firstname_i02_Convention_Memo and then add the file name to the footer. At the top of the document, after *FROM*, replace *Your Name* with your first and last names.

4. Place the insertion point at the end of the document. **Insert** the text from the RTF file **Lastname_Firstname_i02_Convention_List**.

5. Select the inserted text. Change the **Font** to **Calibri**, the **Font Size** to **12**, and the **Font Color** to **Automatic**.

6. Delete the first two paragraphs of inserted text, *Cypress Hotels Group* and *Conventions*.

7. Select the 10 paragraphs with the bulls-eye bullet—starting with *Quality* and ending with *Pool for the Children*. On the **Home tab**, click the **Bullets button arrow**, and then click the **solid round** bullet. Select the first four paragraphs with the solid round bullet points, and then click the **Decrease Indent** button. Select all the other bullet points, excluding the paragraphs *Customer Requirements*, *Facilities available*, and *Activities*. Click the **Bullets button arrow**, and then click the **checkmark**. Select the first four paragraphs with the checkmark bullet points, and then click the **Increase Indent** button.

8. Verify that the document is a one-page document. If not, move the insertion point to the end of the document and delete any blank lines.

9. Compare your completed document with **Figure 1**. **Save** your document, and then submit your files as directed by your instructor.

Done! You have completed Assess Your Skills 3

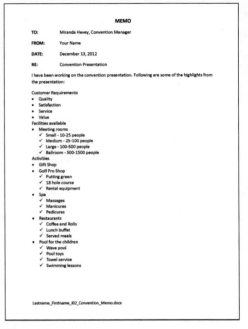

Figure 1

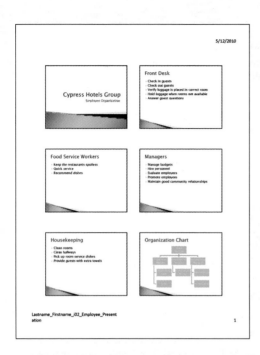

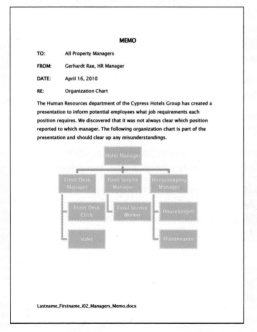

Figure 1

Assess Your Skills 4

To complete this project, you will need the following files:

- i02_Employee_Presentation.pptx
- i02_Managers_Memo.docx

You will save your files as:

- Lastname_Firstname_i02_Employee_Presentation.pptx
- Lastname_Firstname_i02_Managers_Memo.docx

1. **Start** PowerPoint, and then open **i02_Employee_Presentation**. **Save** the presentation in your **Integrated Projects Chapter 2** folder as Lastname_Firstname_i02_Employee_Presentation and then add the file name to all Notes and Handouts footers.

2. Display **Slide 6**, and then in the lower placeholder, click the **Insert SmartArt Graphic** button. Click **Hierarchy**, and then insert an **Organization Chart**. In the superior shape, type Hotel Manager and then delete the assistant shape. In the three subordinate shapes, type Front Desk Manager and Food Service Manager and Housekeeping Manager

3. Under the shape *Front Desk Manager*, add two subordinate shapes, and then in the shapes, type Front Desk Clerk and Valet

4. Under the shape *Food Service Manager*, add a subordinate shape, and then in the shape, type Food Service Worker

5. Under the shape *Housekeeping Manager*, add two subordinate shapes, and then in the shapes, type Housekeeper and Maintenance **Save** the presentation.

6. **Start** Word, and then open **i02_Managers_Memo**. **Save** the document in your **Integrated Projects Chapter 2** folder as Lastname_Firstname_i02_Managers_Memo and then add the file name to the footer.

7. Place the insertion point at the end of the paragraph beginning *The Human Resources department*, and then type The following organization chart is part of the presentation and should clear up any misunderstandings.

8. Make **Lastname_Firstname_i02_Employee_Presentation** the active window. On **Slide 6**, click the placeholder border to select the SmartArt organization chart, and then **Copy** the chart.

9. Make **Lastname_Firstname_i02_Managers_Memo** the active window, and then place the insertion point at the end of the document. **Paste** the organization chart. If necessary, resize the organization chart so that it displays at the bottom of the first page.

10. Compare your completed documents with **Figure 1**. **Save** your files, **Exit** Word, and then **Exit** PowerPoint. Submit your files as directed by your instructor.

Done! You have completed Assess Your Skills 4

Glossary

3-D Short for three-dimensional.

3-D reference A reference to the same cell or range on multiple worksheets.

Absolute cell reference A cell reference that remains the same when it is copied or filled to other cells. An absolute cell reference takes the form $A$1.

Accounting number format A number format that applies comma separators where appropriate, inserts a fixed U.S. dollar sign aligned at the left edge of the cell, applies two decimal places, and leaves a small amount of space at both the right and left edges of the cell to accommodate parentheses for negative numbers.

Action arguments Additional instructions that determine how a macro action should run.

Active cell The cell outlined in black in which data is entered when you begin typing.

Adjustment handle A diamond-shaped handle used to adjust the appearance but not the size of most objects.

After Previous An animation option that begins the animation sequence immediately after the completion of the previous animation.

Anchor A symbol to the left of a paragraph mark that indicates which paragraph the picture is associated with.

AND logical operator A logical comparison of two criteria that is true only when both criteria outcomes are true.

Animation Visual or sound effects added to an object on a slide.

Animation Painter A feature that copies animation settings from one object to another.

Annotate The action of writing on a slide while the slide show is running.

Append query An Access query that adds records to a destination table.

Append row A blank row in a datasheet in which a new record is entered.

Area chart A chart type that emphasizes the magnitude of change over time.

Argument The values that a function uses to perform operations or calculations. The type of argument a function uses is specific to the function. Common arguments include numbers, text, cell references, and names.

Arithmetic operator A symbol that specifies a mathematical operation such as addition or subtraction.

Assistant In an organization chart, a shape that is placed below the superior shape but above

Asterisk (*) wildcard A wildcard that matches any combination of characters.

Attachment data type An Access data type used to store files such as Word documents or digital photo files.

AutoComplete An IntelliSense menu of commands that match the characters you are typing.

AutoCorrect Corrects common spelling errors as you type; for example, if you type teh, Word will automatically correct it to the.

AutoExpansion An Excel feature that automatically includes an adjoining column into an Excel table.

AutoFit Automatically changes the column width to accommodate the longest entry.

AutoNumber A field that automatically enters a unique, numeric value when a record is created.

AVERAGE function A function that adds a group of values and then divides the result by the number of values in the group.

Axis A line bordering the chart plot area used as a frame of reference for measurement.

Background style A slide background fill variation that combines theme colors in different intensities or patterns.

Bar chart A chart type that illustrates comparisons among individual items.

Between...And operator An operator that finds all numbers or dates between and including two values.

Bibliography A list of sources referenced in a document and listed on a separate page at the end of the document.

Black slide A slide that displays at the end of the slide show to indicate that the presentation is over.

Body font A font applied to all slide text except titles.

Browser Software that is used to view websites and navigate the web.

Building block A reusable piece of content or another document part that is stored in a gallery.

Bullet point An individual line of bulleted text on a slide.

Bulleted list A list of items with each item introduced by a symbol such as a small circle or check mark.

Calculated column An Excel table feature that uses a single formula that adjusts for each row and automatically expands to include additional rows so that the formula is immediately extended to those rows.

Calculated control A text box that displays the result of an expression.

Calculated field A column added to a query that derives its value from other fields.

Caption An Access field property that sets the label that displays in datasheets, forms, and reports.

Cascading delete A referential integrity option where you can delete a record on the one side of the relationship, and all the related records on the many side will also be deleted.

Cascading update A referential integrity option where you can edit the primary key values in one table, and all the related records in the other table will update accordingly.

Category axis The axis that displays the category labels.

Category label A label that identifies the categories of data in a chart.

Cell The box formed by the intersection of a row and column.

Cell address The column letter and row number that identify a cell; also called the cell reference.

Cell reference The column letter and row number that identify a cell; also called a cell address.

Cell style A prebuilt set of formatting characteristics, such as font, font size, font color, cell borders, and cell shading.

Chart A graphic representation of numeric data.

Chart layout A prebuilt set of chart elements that can include a title, legend, and labels.

Chart sheet A workbook sheet that contains only a chart and is useful when you want to view a chart separately from the worksheet data.

Chart style A prebuilt chart format that applies an overall visual look to a chart by modifying its graphic effects, colors, and backgrounds.

Citation A note in the document that refers the reader to a source in the bibliography.

Clip art A set of images, drawings, photographs, videos, and sound included with Microsoft Office or accessed from Microsoft Office Online.

Clipboard A temporary storage area that holds text or an object that has been cut or copied.

Clustered bar chart A chart type useful for comparing values across categories; bar charts organize categories along the vertical axis and values along the horizontal axis.

Color scales Visual guides that help the user understand data distribution and variation.

Column break An applied column end that forces the text following the break to the top of the next column but does not automatically create a new page.

Column chart A chart type useful for illustrating comparisons among related categories.

Column heading The letter that displays at the top of a column.

Combo box A control that has a text box and a list that is hidden until you click its arrow.

Comma cell style A cell style that adds commas where appropriate and applies the same formatting as the Accounting number format but without a dollar sign.

Comment A note that is attached to a cell, separate from other cell content.

Compact and Repair A command that rebuilds database files so that data and database objects are stored more efficiently.

Comparison operator An operator used to compare two values; for example, = (equal to) and < (less than).

Conditional formatting A type of formatting that applies formatting only to values that meet the conditions that you specify.

Content control In a template, text or a field that is formatted as a placeholder and is designated by a border when you click the placeholder text.

Contents Underlying formulas and data in a cell.

Contextual tool Tools used to perform specific commands related to the selected object.

Contrast The difference in brightness between two elements on a slide, such as the background and the text or the background and a graphic. When a slide background and slide objects or text do not have enough contrast, the message may be lost.

Control An object in a form or report such as a label or text box.

Control grid Cells arranged in rows and columns into which controls are placed.

Copy A command that places a copy of the selected text or object in the Clipboard.

Cover page A page with a predesigned layout that is always inserted at the beginning of a Word

Coworker In an organization chart, a shape next to another shape that is connected to the same

Criteria (Access) The conditions used in a query to select the records you are looking for.

Criteria (Excel) Conditions specified to limit choices.

Crosstab query A type of select query that calculates a sum, average, or similar statistic and then groups the results by two sets of values.

Currency data type A number formatted to display the dollar sign and two decimals.

Cut A command that removes the selected text or object and stores it in the Clipboard.

Data bar Provides a visual cue to the reader about the value of a cell relative to other cells. The length of the data bar represents the value in the cell.

Data label Text that identifies a data marker on a chart.

Data marker A column, bar, area, dot, pie slice, or other symbol that represents a single data point.

Data point A chart value that originates in an Excel worksheet cell, a Word table cell, or an Access field.

Data series In a chart, data points that are related to one another.

Data source The part of the Word mail merge feature that contains the information, such as names and addresses, that changes with each letter or label.

Data type Specifies the type of information that a field will hold, for example, text, number, date, and currency.

Database A structured collection of related information about people, events, and things.

Database management system Software used to manage and interact with the database.

Database object A basic part of a database that allows you to work with the database; for example, tables, queries, forms, and reports.

Datasheet An Access view that displays records in rows and fields in columns similar to an Excel spreadsheet.

Date Picker A feature used to enter dates by clicking dates on a calendar.

Date/Time data type An Access data type that stores numbers in the date or time format.

DBMS See database management system.

Description An Access field property used to document a field's purpose; it displays in the status bar of the datasheet when field is active.

Design grid The lower half of the Query tab, which lists the fields that will display in the query results.

Design view A view in which the structure and behavior of database objects are modified.

Destination file A file into which a linked or an embedded object is inserted.

Detail sheet A worksheet with cells referred to by summary sheet formulas.

Dialog box A box where you can select multiple settings.

Displayed value Data displayed in a cell.

Document Information Panel A panel that displays above the worksheet window in which properties or property information is added, viewed, or updated.

Document properties Information about a document that can help you identify or organize your files, such as the name of the document author, the file name, and keywords.

Document theme A set of design elements that provides a unified look for colors, fonts, and graphics.

Dot leader A series of evenly spaced dots that precede a tab stop.

Double-spacing The equivalent of a blank line of text displayed between each line of text in a paragraph.

Drag To move the mouse while holding down the left mouse button and then to release it at the appropriate time.

Drag and drop A method of moving objects, in which a selection is pointed to and then dragged to a new location.

Drill-down indicator A PivotTable report feature that shows the detailed records of a PivotTable total.

Drop cap The first letter (or letters) of a paragraph, enlarged and either embedded in the text or placed in the left margin.

Edit To insert text, delete text, or replace text in an Office document, spreadsheet, or presentation.

Edit mode A form mode where you can add new records and change existing records.

Em dash Word processing name for a long dash in a sentence, which marks a break in thought, similar to a comma but stronger.

Embedded chart A chart that is placed on the worksheet containing the data. An embedded chart is beneficial when you want to view or print a chart with its source data.

Embedded object An object that becomes part of the destination file. If the source file is modified, the embedded object does not change.

Emphasis effect Animation that emphasizes an object or text that is already displayed.

Encrypt To hide data in a file by making it unreadable until the correct password is entered.

Endnote A reference placed at the end of a section or a document.

Entity relationship diagram A visual model used to design the database.

ERD Entity relationship diagram; a visual model used to design the database.

Error indicator A green triangle that indicates a possible error in a formula.

Error value A message that displays whenever a formula cannot perform the calculations in the formula.

Excel table A series of rows and columns that contain related data that is managed independently from the data in other rows and columns on the worksheet.

Exit effect Animation that moves an object or text off the screen.

Explode Pulling out one or more slices of a 3-D pie chart to emphasize a specific slice or slices.

Export Wizard In Access, a feature that will export data in a variety of formats, including Excel, Word, and RTF.

Expression A combination of fields, mathematical operators, and pre-built functions that calculates values in tables, forms, queries, and reports.

External reference A reference between objects in different files.

Field (Access) A set of common characteristics around which a table is organized.

Field (Excel) In a PivotTable, summarizes multiple rows of information from the source data.

Field (Word) A category of data—such as a file name, a page number, or the current date—that can be inserted into a document.

Field Size An Access field property that limits the number of characters that can be typed into a text or number field.

File extension A set of characters added to the end of a file name that identifies the file type.

Fill color The inside color of text or an object.

Fill handle The small black square in the lower right corner of the selection.

Filter A feature that hides Excel rows or Access records that do not meet certain criteria.

Filter drop-down list A control that displays a list of filter and sort options for a column in an Excel table or Access datasheet.

Find and Replace A command that enables you to find and then replace a character or string of characters in a worksheet or in a selected range.

Find duplicates query A query that searches a field and then displays any records that contain duplicate values. The query can then be used to remove the duplicate values.

First line indent The location of the beginning of the first line of a paragraph to the left edge of the remainder of the paragraph.

Floating object An object or graphic that can be moved independently of the surrounding text.

Font A set of characters with the same design and shape.

Font style Bold, italic, or underline emphasis added to text.

Footer (PowerPoint) Text that displays at the bottom of every slide or that prints at the bottom of a sheet of slide handouts.

Footer (Word) Reserved area for text, graphics, and fields that displays at the bottom of each page in a document.

Footnote A reference placed at the bottom of the page.

Foreign key A field in one table that is also the primary key of a second table; it is used to create a relationship with that table.

Form A database object used to enter new records, delete records, or update existing records.

Format To change the appearance of the text, such as changing the text color to red.

Format Painter A command that copies formatting from one selection of text to another.

Formatting mark A character that displays on the screen, but does not print, indicating where the Enter key, the Spacebar, and the Tab key were pressed; also called nonprinting characters.

Formula An equation that performs mathematical calculations on number values in the worksheet.

Formula AutoComplete A feature that assists in inserting functions.

Formula bar A bar below the Ribbon that displays the value contained in the active cell and is used to enter or edit values or formulas.

Freeze Panes A command used to keep rows or columns visible when scrolling in a worksheet. The frozen rows and columns become separate panes.

Function A prewritten Excel formula that takes a value or values, performs an operation, and returns a value or values.

Future value (Fv) In a loan, the value at the end of the time periods, or the cash balance you want to attain after the last loan payment is made. The future value for a loan is usually zero.

Gallery A visual display of choices from which you can choose.

General format The default number format that does not display commas or trailing zeros to the right of a decimal point.

Goal Seek A what-if analysis tool that finds a specific value for a cell by adjusting the value of another cell.

Gradient fill A gradual progression of colors and shades, usually from one color to another or from one shade to another shade of the same color, to add a fill to a shape.

Grayscale A black-and-white effect achieved through a series of shades of gray from white to black.

Grid line A line between the cells in a table or spreadsheet.

Group A collection of multiple objects treated as one unit that can be copied, moved, or formatted.

Guides Lines that display in the rulers to give you a visual indication of where the pointer is positioned.

Hanging indent The first line of a paragraph extends to the left of the rest of the paragraph.

Header (Word) Reserved area for text, graphics, and fields that displays at the top of each page in a document.

Header (PowerPoint) Text that prints at the top of each sheet of slide handouts.

Headings font A font applied to slide titles.

Horizontal alignment The orientation of the left or right edges of the paragraph—for example, flush with the left or right margins.

HTML document A text file with instructions for displaying the content in a web browser.

Hyperlink Text or other object that displays another document, a location within a document, or a web page on the Internet.

Hyperlink data type An Access data type that stores links to websites or files located on your computer.

IF function A function that checks whether criteria is met and then returns one value when the condition is TRUE and another value when the condition is FALSE.

Indent The position of paragraph lines in relation to the page margins.

Indeterminate relationship A relationship that does not enforce referential integrity.

Insertion point A vertical line that indicates where text will be inserted when you start typing.

IntelliSense A technology that displays Quick Info, ToolTips, and AutoComplete as you type expressions.

Interest The charge for borrowing money; generally a percentage of the amount borrowed.

Is Null This operator returns records when that field has no value.

Junction table The middle table in a many-to-many relationship.

Justified Paragraph text is aligned flush with both the left margin and the right margin.

Keyboard shortcut A combination of keys on the keyboard, usually using the Ctrl key, the Shift key, or the Alt key, that provides a quick way to activate a command.

KeyTip An icon that displays in the Ribbon to indicate the key that you can press to access Ribbon commands.

Label (Access) An object on a form or report that describes other objects on the report or form.

Label (Excel) Text data in a cell; also called a text value.

Label report A report formatted so that the data can be printed on a sheet of labels.

Landscape orientation A page orientation in which the printed page is wider than it is tall.

Layout (Access) The arrangement of data and labels in a form or report.

Layout (PowerPoint) The arrangement of the text and graphic elements or placeholders on a slide.

Layout gallery A visual representation of several content layouts that you can apply to a slide.

Layout view An Access view used to format a report or form while being able to view a sample of the data.

Leader A series of characters that form a solid, dashed, or dotted line that fills the space preceding a tab stop.

Leader character A character such as a dash or a dot that is repeated to fill the space preceding a tab stop.

Legend A box that identifies the patterns or colors that are assigned to the data series or categories in a chart.

Line chart A chart type that illustrates trends over time, with time displayed along the x-axis and the data point values connected by a line.

Line spacing The vertical distance between lines of text in a paragraph.

Linked object An object that maintains a connection between the source and destination files. Linked data or objects are stored in the source file. If the source file is modified, the linked object is also modified.

List level Levels of text on a slide identified by the indentation, size of text, and bullet assigned to that level.

Live Preview A feature that displays the result of a formatting change if you select it.

Logical function A function that applies a logical test to determine whether a specific condition is met.

Logical test Any value or expression that can be evaluated as TRUE or FALSE.

Macro A sequence of commands that can be performed as one task.

Macro actions Prebuilt sets of instructions that perform tasks when the macro is run.

Macro Builder An object tab with prebuilt commands that you can select and modify to build a macro.

Mail merge A Word feature that creates customized letters or labels by combining a main document with a data source.

Main document The part of the Word mail merge feature that contains the text that remains constant.

Manual line break Moves the remainder of the paragraph following the insertion point to a new line while keeping the text in the same paragraph.

Manual page break Forces a page to end, and places subsequent text at the top of the next page.

Many-to-many relationship A relationship where one record in either of the outer tables can have many associated records in the other outer table.

Margin The space between the text and the top, bottom, left, and right edges of the paper when you print the document.

MAX function A function that returns the largest value in a range of cells.

Memo data type An Access data type that stores up to 65,535 characters of text data and the formatting assigned to that text.

Metadata Information and personal data that is stored with a document.

MIN function A function that returns the smallest value in a range of cells.

Mini toolbar A toolbar with common formatting buttons that displays after you highlight text.

Multiple item form A form that displays records in rows and columns in the same manner that a datasheet does.

Name A word that represents a cell or a range of cells that can be used as a cell or range reference. Names used in formulas and functions clarify the meaning of the formula and assist in navigating large worksheets.

Name Box An area by the formula bar that displays the active cell reference.

Navigation toolbar A toolbar that is used to navigate to any slide while the slide show is running.

Nonprinting character A character that displays on the screen, but does not print, indicating where the Enter key, the Spacebar, and the Tab key were pressed; also called formatting marks.

Normal view (Excel) A view that maximizes the number of cells visible on the screen.

Normal view (PowerPoint) A view in which the window is divided into three areas—the Slide pane, the pane containing the Slides and Outline tabs, and the Notes pane.

Notes Page A printout that contains the slide image in the top half of the page and speaker notes typed in the Notes pane in the lower half of the page.

Notes pane An area of the Normal View window used to type notes that can be printed below a picture of each slide.

NOW function A function that returns the serial number of the current date and time.

Nudge The action of moving an object in small increments by using the directional arrow keys.

Null In queries and filters, this means that the field is empty and has no value.

Null Empty A field that has no value is null.

Number data type An Access data type that stores numeric values.

Number format A specific way that Excel displays numbers.

Number value Numeric data in a cell.

Numbered list A list of items with each item introduced by a consecutive number or letter to indicate definite steps, a sequence of actions, or chronological order.

Object (Access) A basic part of a database that allows you to work with the database; for example, tables, queries, forms, and reports.

Object (Word) Item such as graphics, charts, or spreadsheets created by Word or other programs—or text from a Word file.

Object linking and embedding A program-integration technology that shares information between programs through linked or embedded objects.

Office Clipboard A temporary storage area maintained by Office that can hold up to 24 items.

OLE See Object linking and embedding.

On Click An animation option that begins the animation sequence when the mouse button is clicked or the Spacebar is pressed.

One-to-many form A main form and a subform that displays all the related records for the record displayed in the main form.

One-to-many relationship A relationship where a record in the first table can have many associated records in the second table.

Operator precedence The mathematical rules for performing calculations within a formula.

OR logical operator A logical comparison of two criteria that is true if either of the criteria outcomes is true.

Organization chart A chart that graphically represents the hierarchy of relationships between individuals and groups in an organization.

Outline A Word feature that displays headings and body text, formatted so that headings and all

associated subheadings and body text move along with the heading.

Padding The amount of space between a control's border and other controls on the form or report.

Page footer An area at the bottom of each page that contain labels, text boxes, and other controls.

Page header An area at the top of each page that contains labels, text boxes, and other controls.

Page Layout view A view where you prepare your document or spreadsheet for printing.

Paragraph spacing The vertical distance above and below each paragraph.

Parameter query A query that displays an input box that asks for criteria each time the query is run.

Paste To insert a copy of the text or an object stored in the Clipboard.

Paste area The target destination for data that has been cut or copied.

Photo album A presentation composed of pictures.

Picture An image created with a scanner, digital camera, or graphics software that has been saved with a graphic file extension such as .jpg, .tif, or .bmp.

Picture effects Picture styles that include shadows, reflections, glows, soft edges, bevels, and 3-D rotations.

Picture Style A prebuilt set of formatting borders, effects, and layouts applied to a picture.

Pie chart A chart type that illustrates the relationship of parts to a whole.

PivotChart report A graphical representation of the data in a PivotTable report.

PivotTable report An interactive, cross-tabulated Excel report that summarizes and analyzes data—such as database records—from various sources, including ones that are external to Excel.

Placeholder A box with dotted borders that is part of most slide layouts and that holds text or objects such as charts, tables, and pictures.

Placeholder character The symbol in an input mask that is replaced as you type data into the field.

Placeholder text Reserved space in shapes into which personalized text is entered.

PMT function Calculates the payment for a loan based on constant payments and a constant interest rate.

Point Measurement of the size of a font; each point is 1/72 of an inch.

Portrait orientation A page orientation in which the printed page is taller than it is wide.

Present value (Pv) The initial amount of the loan; the total amount that a series of future payments is worth today.

Primary key The field that uniquely identifies each record in a table.

Principal The initial amount of the loan; the total amount that a series of future payments is worth today. Also called the present value (Pv) of a loan.

Print Preview An Access view used to work with a report that will be printed.

Protected View A view applied to documents downloaded from the Internet that allows you to decide if the content is safe before working with the document.

Query A database object that displays a subset of the data in response to a specific question.

Query design workspace The upper half of the Query tab, which displays the available tables and fields that the query can use.

Question mark (?) wildcard A wildcard character that matches any single character.

Quick Info An IntelliSense box that explains the purpose of the selected AutoComplete.

Quick Start data type A set of fields that can be added with a single click. For example, the Address data type inserts five fields for storing postal addresses.

Quick Style A style that can be accessed from a Ribbon gallery of thumbnails.

RAM The computer's temporary memory.

Range Two or more cells on a worksheet that are adjacent.

Range finder An Excel feature that outlines all of the cells referenced in a formula. It is useful for verifying which cells are used in a formula and for editing formulas.

Rate The percentage that is paid for the use of borrowed money.

Read-only mode A mode where you cannot save your changes.

Record The collection of related information that displays in a single row of a database table.

Referential integrity A rule that keeps related values synchronized. For example, the foreign key value must match one of the primary key values in the other table.

Relational database A database that joins two tables by placing common fields in related tables.

Relationship The joining of two tables using common fields.

Relative cell reference Refers to cells based on their position in relation to (relative to) the cell that contains the formula.

Report A database object designed to display table data or query results on the screen or in printed form.

Report footer An area at the end of a report that contains labels, text boxes, and other controls.

Report header An area at the beginning of a report that contains labels, text boxes, and other controls.

Rich Text Format A text format designed to work with many different types of programs.

Right-click Click the paragraph with the right mouse button.

Row heading The number that displays at the left of a row.

RTF An acronym for Rich Text Format

Screen shot A picture of your computer screen, a window, or a selected region saved as a file that can be printed or shared electronically.

ScreenTip Informational text that displays when you point to commands or thumbnails in the Ribbon.

Section A portion of a document that can be formatted differently from the rest of the document.

Section break Marks the end of one section and the beginning of another section.

Separator character In a list, a character such as a comma or a tab that separates elements of the paragraph.

Serial number A sequential number.

Series A group of numbers, text, dates, or time periods that come one after another in succession—for example, the months January, February, March.

Shape An object that can be inserted to emphasize a point. A shape can be any one of a variety of objects such as stars, banners, and callouts.

Shape effect A predesigned format that makes a shape look more professional.

Shared workbook An Excel workbook that allows different users to view and make changes in the workbook at the same time.

Sheet tab A label along the lower border of the workbook window that identifies each worksheet or chart sheet.

Shortcut menu A list of commands related to the type of object that you right-click.

Simple Query Wizard A Wizard used to quickly adds fields to a new query.

Single form layout A form that displays one record at a time.

Single-spacing No extra space is added between lines of text in a paragraph.

Sizing handle A small square or circle at the corner or side of a selected object that is dragged to increase or decrease the size of the object.

Slide An individual page in a presentation that can contain text, pictures, tables, charts, and other multimedia or graphic objects.

Slide handout Printed images of a single slide or multiple slides on a sheet of paper.

Slide master The top slide in a hierarchy of slides that stores information about the theme and slide layouts of a presentation, including the background, colors, fonts, effects, placeholder sizes, and positioning.

Slide Sorter view The PowerPoint view in which all of the slides in the presentation display as thumbnails.

Slide transition A motion effect that occurs in Slide Show view when you move from one slide to the next during a presentation.

SmartArt graphic A designer-quality visual representation of information used to communicate messages or ideas effectively by choosing from among many different layouts.

Snip A screen capture created with the Snipping Tool.

Source data The data used to create a PivotTable report.

Source file A file that contains the original information that is used to create a linked or an embedded object.

Sparkline A tiny chart used to show data trends.

Split bar A border that separates two different parts of a document that has been split into two sections.

Spreadsheet The primary document that you use in Excel to store and work with data; also called a worksheet.

Stacked layout A form or report layout in which labels display the field names in the left column, and text boxes display the corresponding field values in the right column.

Statistical function A predefined formula that describes a collection of data—for example, totals, counts, and averages.

Style A predefined set of formats that can be applied to text, a paragraph, a table cell, or a list.

Subdatasheet A datasheet that displays related records from a related table. The related table must be on the many side of the relationship.

Subform A form contained within another form that displays records related to the other form.

Subordinate In an organization chart, a shape that is placed below and connected to a superior shape.

SUM An Excel function that adds all the numbers in a range of cells.

Summary sheet A worksheet that displays and summarizes totals from other worksheets.

Summary statistic A calculation for a group of data such as a total, an average, or a count.

Superior In an organization chart, a shape that is placed above any other shape.

Synchronous scrolling When both Word documents scroll together.

Synonym A word with the same meaning.

Tab scrolling buttons The buttons to the left of the sheet tabs used to display Excel sheet tabs that are not in view.

Tab stop A specific location on a line of text, marked on the Word ruler, to which you can move the insertion point by pressing the Tab key; used to align and indent text.

Table Text or numbers displayed in a row and column format to make the information easier to read and understand.

Table (Access) The database object that stores the data in rows and columns.

Table of contents A list of the headings in a document that will provide an overview of the topics covered in the document.

Table style A prebuilt combination of borders and fill colors applied to the entire table in a manner consistent with the presentation theme.

Template (Excel) A prebuilt workbook used as a pattern for creating new workbooks. You use a template to build a workbook without having to start from a blank workbook.

Template (PowerPoint) A file upon which a presentation can be based.

Template (Word) A preformatted document structure that defines the basic document settings, such as font, margins, and available styles.

Text alignment The horizontal placement of text within a placeholder.

Text box (Access) An object on a form or report that displays the data from a field in a table or query.

Text box (PowerPoint) An object used to position text anywhere on a slide.

Text box (Word) A movable, resizable container for text or graphics.

Text data type An Access data type that stores up to 255 characters of text.

Text effect A set of decorative formats, such as outlines, shadows, text glow, and colors that make text stand out in a document.

Text pane The pane to the left of a SmartArt graphic, in which the text that displays in the SmartArt

Text value Character data in a cell; also called a label.

Text wrap A format that displays text on multiple lines within a cell.

Text wrapping The manner in which text displays around an object.

Theme A set of unified design elements that provides a unique look for your presentation, using colors, fonts, and graphics.

Theme color A set of coordinated colors that are applied to the backgrounds, objects, and text in a presentation.

Theme font A theme that determines the font applied to two types of slide text—headings and body.

Thesaurus A research tool that lists words that have the same or similar meaning to the word you are looking up.

Three-color scale A color scale that compares a range of cells by using a gradation of three colors; the shades represent higher, middle, or lower values.

Three-dimensional Refers to an image that appears to have all three spatial dimensions—length, width, and depth.

Thumbnail A miniature image of a presentation slide.

Toggle button A button used to turn a feature both on and off.

Top/Bottom Rules Enables the user to apply conditional formatting to the highest or lowest values in a range of cells.

Total cell style A cell style that applies a single top border, which indicates that calculations were performed on the numbers above, and a double bottom border, which indicates the calculations are complete.

Total row A row that displays as the last row in an Excel table and provides functions in drop-down lists for each column.

Triple-click Click three times fairly quickly without moving the mouse.

Truncated Cut off.

Two-color scale A color scale that compares a range of cells by using a gradation of two colors; the shade of the color represents higher or lower values.

Underlying formula The formula as displayed in the formula bar.

Underlying value Data displayed in the formula bar.

Unique An Access field property that requires that each record contain a unique value.

Unmatched data A condition where the data in one field does not have a corresponding value in a related table.

URL An acronym that stands for Uniform Resource Locator and that identifies a web address.

Validation message The text that displays in a message box when a validation rule is broken during data entry.

Validation rule A field property that requires specific values be entered into a field.

Value Data in a cell.

Value axis The axis that displays the worksheet's numeric data.

Volatile The result of a function will not remain as entered but will be updated each time the workbook is opened.

Wildcard A special character, such as an asterisk, used in query criteria to allow matches for any combination of letters or characters.

Windows Live A free online storage that can be used to save and open your files from any computer connected to the Internet.

Windows Live ID A unique name and password—a Hotmail or Windows Live e-mail user name and password, for example.

Windows Live network A group of people whom you have invited to share files or to chat using Instant Messenger.

With Previous An animation option that begins the animation sequence at the same time as the animation preceding it or, if it is the first animation, with the slide transition.

Wizard A feature that asks questions and then creates an object according to the provided answers.

Word wrap Automatically moves text from the right edge of a paragraph to the beginning of the next line as necessary to fit within the margins.

WordArt A text style used to create decorative effects in a presentation.

Workbook A file that you can use to organize various kinds of related information.

Worksheet The primary document you use in Excel to store and work with data; also called a spreadsheet.

x-axis Another name for the horizontal axis of a chart.

y-axis Another name for the vertical axis of a chart.

Yes/No data type An Access data type that stores values that can have one of two possible values for example, yes and no, or true and false.

Index

 The internet icon represents Index entries found within More Skills on the Companion Website: www.pearsonhighered.com/skills

654 Index | **Skills for Success with Microsoft® Office 2010**

SINGLE PC LICENSE AGREEMENT AND LIMITED WARRANTY

READ THIS LICENSE CAREFULLY BEFORE OPENING THIS PACKAGE. BY OPENING THIS PACKAGE, YOU ARE AGREEING TO THE TERMS AND CONDITIONS OF THIS LICENSE. IF YOU DO NOT AGREE, DO NOT OPEN THE PACKAGE. PROMPTLY RETURN THE UNOPENED PACKAGE AND ALL ACCOMPANYING ITEMS TO THE PLACE YOU OBTAINED THEM. *THESE TERMS APPLY TO ALL LICENSED SOFTWARE ON THE DISK EXCEPT THAT THE TERMS FOR USE OF ANY SHAREWARE OR FREEWARE ON THE DISKETTES ARE AS SET FORTH IN THE ELECTRONIC LICENSE LOCATED ON THE DISK:*

1. GRANT OF LICENSE and OWNERSHIP: The enclosed computer programs ("Software") are licensed, not sold, to you by Prentice-Hall, Inc. ("We" or the "Company") and in consideration of your purchase or adoption of the accompanying Company textbooks and/or other materials, and your agreement to these terms. We reserve any rights not granted to you. You own only the disk(s) but we and/or our licensors own the Software itself. This license allows you to use and display your copy of the Software on a single computer (i.e., with a single CPU) at a single location for academic use only, so long as you comply with the terms of this Agreement. You may make one copy for back up, or transfer your copy to another CPU, provided that the Software is usable on only one computer.

2. RESTRICTIONS: You may not transfer or distribute the Software or documentation to anyone else. Except for backup, you may not copy the documentation or the Software. You may not network the Software or otherwise use it on more than one computer or computer terminal at the same time. You may not reverse engineer, disassemble, decompile, modify, adapt, translate, or create derivative works based on the Software or the Documentation. You may be held legally responsible for any copying or copyright infringement which is caused by your failure to abide by the terms of these restrictions.

3. TERMINATION: This license is effective until terminated. This license will terminate automatically without notice from the Company if you fail to comply with any provisions or limitations of this license. Upon termination, you shall destroy the Documentation and all copies of the Software. All provisions of this Agreement as to limitation and disclaimer of warranties, limitation of liability, remedies or damages, and our ownership rights shall survive termination.

4. DISCLAIMER OF WARRANTY: THE COMPANY AND ITS LICENSORS MAKE NO WARRANTIES ABOUT THE SOFTWARE, WHICH IS PROVIDED "AS-IS." IF THE DISK IS DEFECTIVE IN MATERIALS OR WORKMANSHIP, YOUR ONLY REMEDY IS TO RETURN IT TO THE COMPANY WITHIN 30 DAYS FOR REPLACEMENT UNLESS THE COMPANY DETERMINES IN GOOD FAITH THAT THE DISK HAS BEEN MISUSED OR IMPROPERLY INSTALLED, REPAIRED, ALTERED OR DAMAGED. THE COMPANY DISCLAIMS ALL WARRANTIES, EXPRESS OR IMPLIED, INCLUDING WITHOUT LIMITATION, THE IMPLIED WARRANTIES OF MERCHANTABILITY AND FITNESS FOR A PARTICULAR PURPOSE. THE COMPANY DOES NOT WARRANT, GUARANTEE OR MAKE ANY REPRESENTATION REGARDING THE ACCURACY, RELIABILITY, CURRENTNESS, USE, OR RESULTS OF USE, OF THE SOFTWARE.

5. LIMITATION OF REMEDIES AND DAMAGES: IN NO EVENT, SHALL THE COMPANY OR ITS EMPLOYEES, AGENTS, LICENSORS OR CONTRACTORS BE LIABLE FOR ANY INCIDENTAL, INDIRECT, SPECIAL OR CONSEQUENTIAL DAMAGES ARISING OUT OF OR IN CONNECTION WITH THIS LICENSE OR THE SOFTWARE, INCLUDING, WITHOUT LIMITATION, LOSS OF USE, LOSS OF DATA, LOSS OF INCOME OR PROFIT, OR OTHER LOSSES SUSTAINED AS A RESULT OF INJURY TO ANY PERSON, OR LOSS OF OR DAMAGE TO PROPERTY, OR CLAIMS OF THIRD PARTIES, EVEN IF THE COMPANY OR AN AUTHORIZED REPRESENTATIVE OF THE COMPANY HAS BEEN ADVISED OF THE POSSIBILITY OF SUCH DAMAGES. SOME JURISDICTIONS DO NOT ALLOW THE LIMITATION OF DAMAGES IN CERTAIN CIRCUMSTANCES, SO THE ABOVE LIMITATIONS MAY NOT ALWAYS APPLY.

6. GENERAL: THIS AGREEMENT SHALL BE CONSTRUED IN ACCORDANCE WITH THE LAWS OF THE UNITED STATES OF AMERICA AND THE STATE OF NEW YORK, APPLICABLE TO CONTRACTS MADE IN NEW YORK, AND SHALL BENEFIT THE COMPANY, ITS AFFILIATES AND ASSIGNEES. This Agreement is the complete and exclusive statement of the agreement between you and the Company and supersedes all proposals, prior agreements, oral or written, and any other communications between you and the company or any of its representatives relating to the subject matter. If you are a U.S. Government user, this Software is licensed with "restricted rights" as set forth in subparagraphs (a)-(d) of the Commercial Computer-Restricted Rights clause at FAR 52.227-19 or in subparagraphs (c)(1)(ii) of the Rights in Technical Data and Computer Software clause at DFARS 252.227-7013, and similar clauses, as applicable.

Should you have any questions concerning this agreement or if you wish to contact the Company for any reason, please contact in writing:

Multimedia Production
Higher Education Division
Prentice-Hall, Inc.
1 Lake Street
Upper Saddle River NJ 07458